PEARSON CRIMINAL JUSTICE

SOC 3640- Sociology of Law Enforcemnt
Dr. Crawford
Western Michigan University

PEARSON

Senior Vice President, Editorial: Patrick F. Boles
Senior Acquisitions Editor: Debbie Coniglio
Editorial Assistant: Jeanne Martin
Development Editor: Christina Martin
Operations Manager: Eric M. Kenney
Production Manager: Jennifer Berry
Art Director: Renée Sartell
Cover Designers: Josh Read and Kristen Kiley

Cover Art: Police Car: Courtesy of Veer/Alloy Photography. Gavel: Courtesy of iStockphoto/Christine Balderas. Behind the Bars: Courtesy of iStockphoto/Simon Podgorsek.

Printed in the United States of America.

Please visit our website at *www.pearsonlearningsolutions.com.*

Attention bookstores: For permission to return any unsold stock, contact us at *pe-uscustomreturns@pearson.com*.

Pearson Learning Solutions, 501 Boylston Street, Suite 900, Boston, MA 02116
A Pearson Education Company
www.pearsoned.com

ISBN 10: 1-256-24666-2
ISBN 13: 978-1-256-24666-4

Contents

History

History

COMING TO AMERICA—STRUGGLE AND TRANSFORMATION

When we pull back the layers of government services, the most fundamental and indispensable virtues are public safety and social order.

—*Hon. David A. Hardy, Washoe County District Court, Reno, Nevada*

The police are the public and . . . the public are the police.

—*Sir Robert Peel, 1829*

International Association of Chiefs of Police

Learning Objectives

AS A RESULT OF READING THIS CHAPTER, THE STUDENT WILL:

- Understand the four major police-related offices and their functions during the early English and colonial periods
- Be aware of the major contributions of selected individuals to the development of policing (e.g., Peel's principles, Vollmer's professionalism)
- Know the legacies of colonial policing that remained intact after the American Revolution
- Comprehend the three primary eras of policing and the main characteristics of each
- Be able to list the three early issues of American policing and to describe their present status
- Understand the unique characteristics of law enforcement as it existed in the Wild West
- Be aware of the definitions and advantages of the political and professional eras of policing
- Know the fundamental nature of the civil rights movement, and how the police and minorities were often pitted against one another
- Understand what led to the development of the community-oriented policing and problem-solving (COPPS) era and some of its main features
- Be able to explain how policing has come full circle today, returning to its origins

Introduction

To understand contemporary policing in America, it is necessary to understand its antecedents; we will gain a better understanding of this history by looking at its three eras. The police, it has been said, are "to a great extent, the prisoners of the past. Day-to-day practices are influenced by deeply ingrained traditions."[1] Another reason for analyzing historical developments and trends is that several discrete legacies have been transmitted to modern police agencies. In view of the significant historical impact on modern policing, it is necessary to turn back the clock to about A.D. 900.

Therefore, we begin with a brief history of the evolution of four primary criminal justice officers—sheriff, constable, coroner, and justice of the peace—from early England to the twentieth century in America. We then examine policing from its early beginnings in England to the American colonial period, when volunteers watched over their "human flock." The concepts of patrol, crime prevention, authority, professionalism, and discretion can be traced to the colonial period. We move on to the adoption of full-time policing in American cities (in what is termed the political era, with its predominant issues, political influences, and other problems) and on the

Western frontier. Then we consider the reform, or professional era, the movement to professionalize the police by removing them from politics (and, at the same time, the citizenry) and casting them as crime fighters; included here is a look at the tumultuous 1960s and 1970s, which often saw the police pitted against minority groups who were seeking equal rights. Next, we discuss the movement away from the professional model into the community era, centering on the influence of the President's Crime Commission; this portion of the chapter also briefly considers community-oriented policing and problem solving (COPPS), including its three eras. Included at the chapter's end are a summary, key terms and concepts, review questions, and several scenarios and activities that provide opportunities for you to learn by doing.

English and Colonial Officers of the Law

All four of the primary criminal justice officials of early England—the sheriff, constable, coroner, and justice of the peace—either still exist or existed until recently in the United States. Accordingly, it is important to have a basic understanding of these offices, including their early functions in England and, later, in America. Following is a brief discussion of each.

Sheriff

The word **sheriff** is derived from the term *shire reeve—shire* meaning "county" and *reeve* meaning "agent of the king." The shire reeve appeared in England before the Norman conquest of 1066. His job was to maintain law and order in the tithings. (Tithings will be discussed further in the next section.) The office survived in England, although the sheriff was never a popular officer in England, and since the nineteenth century the sheriff has had no police powers. When the office began, the sheriff assisted the king in fiscal, military, and judicial affairs and was referred to as the "king's steward." As men could buy their appointment from the Crown, the office was often held by nonresidents of the county who seemed intent only upon fattening their purses and abusing the public. In addition, English sheriffs were often charged with being lazy in the pursuit of criminals. Indeed, by the late thirteenth century, sheriffs were forbidden to act as justices. The position of coroner was created to act as a monitor over the sheriff. Thereafter, the status and responsibility of the position began to diminish. In response, just before his death, King Edward I granted to the counties the right to select their sheriffs. With the subsequent appearance of the justice of the peace, the sheriff's office declined in power even further. At the present time in England, a sheriff's only duties are to act as officer of the court, summon juries, and enforce civil judgments.[2]

The first sheriffs in America appeared in the early colonial period, where control over sheriffs has rested with the county electorate since 1886. Today, the American sheriff remains the basic source of rural crime control. When the office appeared in the American colonies, it was little changed from the English model. However, the power of appointment was originally vested in the governor, and the sheriff's duties included apprehending criminals, caring for prisoners, executing civil process, conducting elections, and collecting taxes.[3]

In the late nineteenth century, the sheriff became a popular figure in the legendary Wild West (discussed later in this chapter). The frontier sheriffs often used the concept of *posse comitatus*, an important part of the criminal justice machine that allowed the sheriff to deputize common citizens to assist in the capture of outlaws, among other tasks. Overall, by the turn of the twentieth century the powers and duties of the sheriff in America had changed very little in status or function. In fact, the office has not changed much today.

Constable

Like the sheriff, the **constable** can be traced back to Anglo-Saxon times. The office began during the reign of Edward I, when every parish or township had a constable. As

A leatherhead and his sentry box. Called leatherheads because of their leather helmets, the constable watch patrolled the city from sentry boxes in the early decades of the 1800s. They wore helmets for protection against falling debris from fires, a constant danger in cities with many wooden buildings. *(Courtesy NYPD Photo Unit)*

the county militia turned more and more to matters of defense, the constable alone pursued felons—hence the ancient custom of citizens raising a loud "hue and cry" and joining in pursuit of criminals lapsed into disuse. During the Middle Ages, there was as yet no high degree of specialization. The constable had a variety of duties, including collecting taxes, supervising highways, and serving as magistrate. The office soon became subject to election and was conferred upon local men of prominence. However, the creation of the office of justice of the peace around 1200 quickly changed this trend forever; soon the constable was limited to making arrests only with warrants issued by a justice of the peace. As a result, the office, deprived of social and civic prestige, was no longer attractive. It carried no salary, and the duties were often dangerous. In addition, there was heavy attrition in the office, so the constable's term was limited to one year in an attempt to attract officeholders; in 1856 Parliament completely discarded the office.[4]

The office of constable experienced a similar process of disintegration in the colonies. However, the American constables, usually two in each town, were given control over the night watch. By the 1930s, state constitutions in twenty-one states provided for the office of constable, but constables still received no pay, and like their British colleagues they enjoyed little prestige or popularity after the early 1900s. The position fell into disfavor largely because most constables were untrained and were believed to be wholly inadequate as officials of the law.[5]

Coroner

The office of **coroner** is more difficult to describe. It has been used to fulfill many different roles throughout its history and has steadily changed over the centuries. There is no agreement concerning the date when the coroner first appeared in England, but there is general consensus that the office was functioning by the end of the twelfth century.

From the beginning, the coroner was elected; his duties included oversight of the interests of the Crown, not only in criminal matters but in fiscal matters as well. In felony cases, the coroner could conduct a preliminary hearing, and the sheriff often came to the coroner's court to preside over the coroner's jury. The coroner's inquest provided another means of power and prestige, determining the cause of death and the party responsible for it. Initially, coroners were elected for life. Soon becoming unhappy with the absence of compensation, however, eventually they were given the right to charge fees for their work.[6]

As was true of sheriffs and constables, at first the office of the coroner in America was only slightly different than what it had been in England. The office was slow in gaining recognition in America, as many of the coroners' duties were already being performed by the sheriffs and justices of the peace. By 1933, the coroner was recognized as a separate office in two-thirds of the states. Tenure was generally limited to two years. By then, however, the office had been stripped of many of its original functions, especially its fiscal roles. In many states, the coroner legally served as sheriff when the elected sheriff was disabled or disqualified. However, since the early part of the twentieth century, the coroner has basically performed a single function: determining the causes of all deaths by violence or under suspicious circumstances. The coroner or his or her assistant is expected to determine the causes and effects of wounds, lesions, contusions, fractures, poisons, and more. The coroner's inquest resembles a grand jury at which the coroner serves as a kind of presiding magistrate. If the inquest determines that the deceased came to his or her death through criminal means, the coroner may issue a warrant for the arrest of the accused party.[7]

The primary debate regarding the office of coroner has centered on the qualifications needed to hold the office. Many states have traditionally allowed laypeople, as opposed to physicians, to be coroners. Thus people of all backgrounds—ranging from butchers to musicians—have occupied this powerful office.[8]

Justice of the Peace

The **justice of the peace (JP)** can be traced back as far as 1195 in England. By 1264 the *custos pacis*, or conservator of the peace, nominated by the king for each county, presided over criminal trials. Early JPs were wealthy landholders. They allowed constables to make arrests by issuing them warrants. Over time, this practice removed power from constables and sheriffs. By the sixteenth century, the office came under criticism because of the caliber of the people holding it. Officeholders were often referred to as "boobies" and "scum of the earth."[9] The only qualification necessary was being a wealthy landowner who was able to buy his way into office.

By the early twentieth century, England had abolished the property-holding requirement, and many of the medieval functions of the JP's office were removed. Thereafter, the office possessed extensive but strictly criminal jurisdiction, with no jurisdiction whatsoever in civil cases. This contrasts with the American system, which gives JPs limited jurisdiction in both criminal and civil cases.

The JP's office in the colonies was a distinct change from the position as it existed in England. JPs were elected to office and given jurisdiction in both civil and criminal cases. By 1930, the office had constitutional status in all of the states. JPs have long been allowed to collect fees for their services. As in England, it is typically not necessary to hold a law degree or to have pursued legal studies in order to be a JP in the United States.[10]

Perhaps the most colorful justice of the peace was Roy Bean, popularized in film as the sole peace officer in a 35,000-square-mile area west of the Pecos River, near Langtry, Texas. Bean was known to hold court in his shack, where signs hung on the front porch proclaimed, "Justice Roy Bean, Notary Public," "Law West of the Pecos," and "Beer Saloon." Cold beer and the law undoubtedly shared many quarters on the Western Frontier.

JPs are today what they perhaps were intended to be—lay and inexpert upholders of the law. On the whole, the office has declined from dignity to obscurity and ridicule. As one observer noted, this loss of prestige can never be recovered.[11]

Justice of the Peace Roy Bean, Langtry, Texas, about 1900. *(Courtesy Library of Congress)*

The Old English System of Policing

Like much of the American criminal justice system, modern American policing can be traced directly to its English heritage. Ideas concerning community policing, crime prevention, the posse, constables, and sheriffs were developed from English policing. Beginning about A.D. 900, the role of law enforcement was placed in the hands of common citizens. Each citizen was responsible for aiding neighbors who might be victimized by outlaws.[12] No formal mechanism existed with which to police the villages, and the informal voluntary model that developed was referred to as "kin police."[13] Slowly this model developed into a more formalized community-based system.

After the Norman conquest of 1066, a community-based system called "frankpledge" was established. This system required that every male above the age of 12 form a group with nine of his neighbors. This group, called a tithing, was sworn to help protect fellow citizens and to apprehend and deliver to justice any of its members who committed a crime. Tithingmen were not paid salaries for their work, and they were required to perform certain duties under penalty of law.[14] Ten tithings were grouped into a hundred, directed by a constable who was appointed by a nobleman. The constable was the first police official with law enforcement responsibility greater than simply protecting his neighbors. As the tithings were grouped into hundreds, the hundreds were grouped into shires, which are similar to today's counties.

By the late sixteenth century, however, wealthier merchants and farmers became reluctant to take their turn in the rotating job of constable. The office was still unpaid, and the duties were numerous. Wealthier men paid the less fortunate to serve in their place until there came a point at which no one but the otherwise unemployable would serve as constable. Thus from about 1689 on, the demise of the once-powerful office was swift. All who could afford to pay their way out of service as constable to King George I did so.[15]

Meanwhile, the JP was rewarded in proportion to the number of people he convicted, so extortion was rampant. Ingenious criminals were able to exploit this state of affairs to great advantage. One such criminal was Jonathan Wild, who, in the early 1700s obtained single-handed control over most of London's criminals. Wild's system was simple: After ordering his men to commit a burglary, he would meet the victim and courteously offer to return the stolen goods for a commission. That he could have operated such a business for so long is a testimony to the corrupt nature of the magistrates of the "trading justice" period.[16]

This early English system, in large measure voluntary and informal, continued with some success well into the eighteenth century. By 1800, however, the collapse of its two primary offices and the growth of large cities, crime, and civil disobedience required that the system be changed. The British Parliament was soon forced to consider and adopt a more dependable system.

Policing in Colonial America

The first colonists transplanted the English policing system, with all of its virtues and faults, to seventeenth- and eighteenth-century America. Most of the time, the colonies were free of crime as the settlers busied themselves carving out a farm and a living. Occasionally colonists ran afoul of the law by violating or neglecting some moral obligation. They then found themselves in court for working on the Sabbath, cursing in public, failing to pen animals properly, or begetting children out of wedlock. Only two "crime waves" of note occurred during the seventeenth century, both in Massachusetts. In one case, between 1656 and 1665, Quakers who dared challenge the religion of the Puritan colony were whipped, banished, and, in three instances, hanged. The second "crime wave" involved witchcraft. Several alleged witches were hanged in 1692 in Salem; dozens more languished in prison before the hysteria abated.[17]

Review: *History and Professionalism of the Police.*

Once colonists settled into villages, including Boston (1630), Charleston (1680), and Philadelphia (1682), local ordinances provided for the appointment of constables, whose duties were much like those of their English predecessors. County governments, again drawing on English precedent, appointed sheriffs as well. The county sheriff, appointed by a governor, became the most important law enforcement official, particularly when the colonies were small and rural. The sheriff apprehended criminals, served subpoenas, appeared in court, and collected taxes. The sheriff was also paid a fixed amount for each task performed; the more taxes he collected, for example, the higher his pay.[18]

Criminal acts were so infrequent as to be largely ignored. Service as a constable or watchman was obligatory, and for a few years citizens did not seem to mind this duty. But as towns grew and the task of enforcing the laws became more difficult and time-consuming, the colonists, like their English counterparts, began to evade the duty when possible. The "watch-and-ward" responsibility of citizens became more of a comical "snooze-and-snore" system. New Amsterdam's Dutch officials introduced a paid watch in 1658, and Boston tried the concept in 1663, but the expense quickly forced both cities to discontinue the practice.[19]

Unfortunately for these eighteenth-century colonists, their refusal to provide a dependable voluntary policing system came at a time when economic, population, and crime growth required a reliable police force. The citizen-participation model of policing was breaking down, and something had to be done, especially in the larger colonies. Philadelphia devised a plan, enacted into law, restructuring the way the watch was performed. The law empowered officials, called wardens, to hire as many watchmen as needed; the powers of the watch were increased; and the legislature levied a tax to pay for it. Instead of requiring all males to participate, only male citizens interested in making money needed to join the watch. Philadelphia's plan was moderately successful, and other cities were soon inspired to follow its example and offer tax-supported wages for watches.[20]

From the middle to the late eighteenth century, massive social and political unrest caused police problems to increase even more. From 1754 to 1763, the French and Indian War disrupted colonial society. In 1783, after the American Revolution had ended, property and street crime continued to flourish, and the constabulary and the watches were unable to cope with it. Soon it became evident that, like the English, the American people needed a more dependable, formal system of policing.

Legacies of the Colonial Period

As uncomplicated and sedate as colonial law enforcement seems, especially when compared to contemporary police problems, the colonial period is very important to the history of policing because many of the basic ideas that influence modern policing were developed during that era. Specifically, the colonial period transmitted three legacies to contemporary policing.[21]

First, as just discussed, the colonists committed themselves to local (as opposed to centralized) policing. Second, the colonists reinforced that commitment by creating a theory of government called **republicanism**. Republicanism asserted that power can be divided, and it relied on local interests to promote the general welfare. Police chiefs and sheriffs might believe that they alone know how to address crime and disorder, but under republicanism, neighborhood groups and local interest blocs have input with respect to crime-control policy. Republicanism thus established the controversial political framework within which the police would develop during the next two hundred years.[22]

Finally, the colonial period witnessed the onset of the theory of crime prevention. This legacy would alter the shape of policing after 1800 and would eventually lead to the emergence of modern police agencies.

The population of England had doubled between 1700 and 1800. Parliament, however, had done nothing to solve the problems that arose from social change. Each municipality or county, therefore, was left to solve its problems in piecemeal fashion. After 1750, practically every English city increased the number of watchmen and constables, hoping to address the problem of crime and disorder but not giving any thought to whether this ancient system of policing still worked. However, the cities did adopt paid, rather than voluntary, watches.[23]

London probably suffered the most from this general inattention to social problems; awash in crime, whole districts had become criminal haunts that no watchmen visited and no honest citizens frequented. Thieves became very bold, robbing their victims in broad daylight on busy streets. In the face of this situation, English officials still continued to prefer the existing policing arrangements over any new ideas. However, three men—Henry Fielding, his half brother John Fielding, and Patrick Colquhoun—began to experiment with possible solutions and laid the foundation on which later reformers would build new ideas.

Henry Fielding's acute interest in, and knowledge of, policing led to his 1748 appointment as chief magistrate of Bow Street in London. He soon became one of England's most acclaimed theorists in the area of crime and punishment. Fielding's primary argument was that the severity of the English penal code, which provided for the death penalty for a large number of offenses, including the theft of a handkerchief, did not work in controlling criminals. He believed the country should reform the criminal code to deal more with the origins of crime. In 1750, Fielding made the pursuit of criminals more systematic by creating a small group of "thief takers." Victims of crime paid handsome rewards for the capture of their assailants, so these volunteers stood to profit nicely by pursuing criminals.[24]

When Henry Fielding died in 1754, John Fielding succeeded him as Bow Street magistrate. By 1785, his thief takers had evolved into the Bow Street Runners—some of the most famous policemen in English history. While the Fieldings were considering how to create a police force that could deal with changing English society, horrible punishments and incompetent policing continued throughout England.

Henry Fielding. *(Courtesy Library of Congress)*

Patrick Colquhoun was a wealthy man who was sincerely interested in improving social conditions in England. In 1792, Colquhoun was appointed London magistrate, and for the next quarter of a century he focused on police reform. Like the Fieldings, he wrote lengthy treatises on the police, and he soon established himself as an authority on police reform. Colquhoun believed that government could, and should, regulate people's behavior. This notion contradicted tradition and even constitutional ideals, undermining the old principle that the residents of local communities, through voluntary watchmen and constables, should police the conduct of their neighbors. Colquhoun also endorsed three ideas originally set forth by the Fieldings: (1) the police should have an intelligence service for gathering information about offenders; (2) a register of known criminals and unlawful groups should be maintained; and (3) a police gazette should be published to assist in the apprehension of criminals and to promote the moral education of the public by publicizing punishments such as whipping, the pillory, and public execution. To justify these reforms, Colquhoun estimated that London in 1800 had ten thousand thieves, prostitutes, and other criminals who stole goods valued at more than a half million pounds from the riverside docks alone.[25]

Colquhoun also believed that policing should maintain the public order, prevent and detect crime, and correct bad manners and morals. He did not agree with the centuries-old notion that watchmen—who, after all, were amateurs—could adequately police the communities. Thus Colquhoun favored a system of paid professional police officers who would be recruited and maintained by a centralized governmental authority. Colquhoun believed that potential criminals could be identified before they did their unlawful deeds.[26] Thus began the notion of proactive policing—that is, preventing the crime before it occurs. Colquhoun died before his proposals were adopted, and as the eighteenth century ended, the structure of policing in England and America was largely unchanged. However, both nations had experienced the inadequacies of the older form of policing. Although new ideas had emerged, loyalties to the old system of policing would remain for some time.

Police Reform in England and America, 1829–1860

Two powerful trends in England and America brought about changes in policing in both countries in the early and mid nineteenth century. The first was urbanization, and the second was industrialization. These developments generally increased the standard of living for both Americans and western Europeans. Suddenly, factories needed sober, dependable people who could be trusted with machines. To create a reliable workforce, factory owners began advocating temperance. Clearly a new age, a new way of thinking, had begun. Crime also increased during this period. Thus social change, crime, and unrest made the old system of policing obsolete. A new policing system was needed, one that could deal effectively with criminals, maintain order, and prevent crime.[27]

In England, workers protested against new machines, food riots, and an ongoing increase in crime. The British army, traditionally used to disperse rioters, was becoming less effective as people began resisting its commands. In 1822, England's ruling party, the Tories, moved to consider new alternatives. The prime minister appointed Sir Robert Peel to establish a police force to combat the problems. Peel, a wealthy member of Parliament who was familiar with the reforms suggested by the Fieldings and Colquhoun, found that many English people objected to the idea of a professional police force, thinking it a possible restraint on their liberty. They also feared a stronger police organization because the criminal law was already quite harsh, as it had been for many years. By the early nineteenth century, there were 223 crimes in England for which a person could be hanged. Because of these two obstacles, Peel's efforts to gain support for full-time, paid police officers failed for seven years.[28]

Peel finally succeeded in 1829. He had established a base of support in Parliament and had focused on reforming only the metropolitan police of London rather than trying to create policing for the entire country. Peel submitted a bill to Parliament. This bill, which was very vague about details, was called "An Act for

Sir Robert Peel. *(Courtesy Library of Congress)*

Improving the Police in and Near the Metropolis." Parliament passed the Metropolitan Police Act of 1829. The General Instructions of the new force stressed its preventive nature, specifying that "the principal object to be attained is 'the prevention of crime.' The security of person and property will thus be better effected, than by the detection and punishment of the offender after he has succeeded in committing the crime."[29] The act called on the home secretary to appoint two police commissioners to command the new organization. These two men were to recruit "a sufficient number of fit and able men" as constables.[30] Peel chose a former military colonel, Charles Rowan, as one commissioner, and a barrister (attorney), Richard Mayne, as the other. They divided London into seventeen divisions, using crime data as the primary basis for creating the boundaries. Each division had a commander called a superintendent; each superintendent had a force of four inspectors, sixteen sergeants, and 165 constables. Thus London's Metropolitan Police immediately consisted of nearly 3,000 officers. The commissioners decided to put their constables in a uniform (a blue coat, blue pants, and a black top hat) and to arm them with a short baton (known as a "truncheon") and a rattle for raising an alarm. Each constable was to wear his own identifying number on his collar, where it could be easily seen.[31]

Interestingly, the London police (nicknamed "bobbies" after Sir Robert Peel) quickly met with tremendous public hostility. Wealthy people resented their very existence and became particularly incensed at their attempts to control the movements of their horse-drawn coaches. Several aristocrats ordered their coachmen to whip the officers or simply drive over them. Juries and judges refused to punish those who assaulted the police. Defendants acquitted by a hostile judge would often sue the officer for false arrest. Policing London's streets in the early 1830s proved to be a very dangerous and lonely business. The two commissioners, Rowan and Mayne, fearing that public hostility might kill off the police force, moved to counter it. The bobbies were continually told to be respectful yet firm when dealing with the public. Citizens were invited to lodge complaints if their officers were truly unprofessional. This policy of creating public support gradually worked; as the police became more moderate in their conduct, public hostility also declined.[32]

Peel, too, proved to be very farsighted and keenly aware of the needs of both a professional police force and the public that would be asked to maintain it. Indeed, Peel saw that the poor quality of policing contributed to social disorder. Accordingly, he drafted several guidelines for the force, many of which focused on community relations. He wrote that the power of the police to fulfill their duties depended on public approval of their actions; that as public cooperation increased, the need for physical force by the police would decrease; that officers needed to display absolutely impartial service to law; and that force should be employed by the police only when attempts at persuasion and warning had failed, and then they should use only the minimal degree of force possible. Peel's remark that "the police are the public, and the public are the police" emphasized his belief that the police are first and foremost members of the larger society.[33]

A "Peeler" (circa 1829). "Peeler," "Robert," and "Bobby" were all early names for a police officer, the latter remaining as a nickname today. *(Courtesy NYPD Photo Unit)*

During this initial five-year period, Peel endured the largest police turnover rate in history. Estimates vary widely, but the following is thought to be fairly accurate: 1,341 constables resigned from London's Metropolitan Police from 1829 to 1834; that's roughly half of the constables on the force. The pay of three shillings a day was meager, and probably few of the officers ever considered the position as a career.[34]

Peel drafted nine **principles of policing**. Most, if not all, are relevant to today's police community:

1. To prevent crime and disorder, as an alternative to their repression by military force and by severity of legal punishment.

2. To recognize always that the power of the police to fulfill their functions and duties is dependent on public approval of their existence, actions and behaviour, and on their ability to secure and maintain public respect.
3. To recognize always that to secure and maintain the respect and approval of the public means also the securing of willing cooperation of the public in the task of securing observance of laws.
4. To recognize always that the extent to which the cooperation of the public can be secured diminishes, proportionately, the necessity of the use of physical force and compulsion for achieving police objectives.
5. To seek and to preserve public favour, not by pandering to public opinion, but by constantly demonstrating absolutely impartial service to law, in complete independence of policy, and without regard to the justice or injustices of the substance of individual laws; by ready offering of individual service and friendship to all members of the public without regard to their wealth or social standing; by ready exercise of courtesy and friendly good humour; and by ready offering of individual sacrifice in protecting and preserving life.
6. To use physical force only when the exercise of persuasion, advice and warning is found to be insufficient to obtain public cooperation to an extent necessary to secure observance of law or to restore order; and to use only the minimum degree of physical force which is necessary on any particular occasion for achieving a police objective.
7. To maintain at all times a relationship with the public that gives reality to the historic tradition that the police are the public and that the public are the police; the police being only members of the public who are paid to give full-time attention to duties which are incumbent on every citizen, in the interests of community welfare and existence.
8. To recognize always the need for strict adherence to police-executive functions, and to refrain from even seeming to usurp the powers of the judiciary of avenging individuals or the state, and of authoritatively judging guilt and punishing the guilty.
9. To recognize always that the test of police efficiency is the absence of crime and disorder, and not the visible evidence of police action in dealing with them.[35]

Note that Peel's emphasis is on the *prevention* of crime. Peel felt that all efforts of the police were to be directed toward that end, and all other work of the police flowed from attempting to prevent crimes from occurring: the security of person and property, the preservation of the public tranquility, and ultimately the arrest, conviction, and punishment of those who in fact commit crimes. By the same token, Peel is implying that when many offenses are committed in a given area, police leaders and planners must recognize that their efforts are lacking in that locus and must govern their actions accordingly.

Also note that Peel's principles of 1829 relate very closely to the tenets of community policing—the current era of policing. Peel observed that the police are situated to proactively curb criminal activity and to provide order in the community, are no different from the people they are to serve, and should be visible in the community and interact with its citizens.

If Peel could speak today, however, he would likely indicate great displeasure with both the political and the reform (professional) eras of policing that came to pass in the United States (discussed below) because their motives and practices served to move the police away from his views of policing and into directions that were in opposition to his nine principles.

Policing Comes to the United States: The Political Era—1840s to 1930s

The English experiment with policing was not going unnoticed in the United States. Americans had been observing Peel's successful experiment with the bobbies on the patrol beat. However, industrialization and social upheaval had not reached the proportions here that they had in England, so there was not the same urgent need for full-time policing. Yet by the 1840s, when industrialization began in earnest in America, U.S. officials began to watch the police reform movement in England more closely.

Eventually, of course, policing would become entrenched in America and evolve through three full eras: political, reform, and community. To gain a better understanding of these three eras, an overview of each is provided in Table 1.

Review: *American Policing Eras.*

Table 1
The Three Eras of Policing

	Political Era (1840s to 1930s)	**Reform Era (1930s to 1980s)**	**Community Era (1980s to Present)**
Authorization	Politics and law	Law and professionalism	Community support (political), law, and professionalism
Function	Broad social services	Crime control	Broad provision of services
Organizational design	Decentralized	Centralized and classical	Decentralized using task forces and matrices
Relationship to community	Intimate	Professional and remote	Intimate
Tactics and technology	Foot patrol	Preventive patrol and rapid response to calls	Foot patrol, problem solving, and public relations
Outcome	Citizen and political satisfaction	Crime control	Quality of life and citizen satisfaction

Source: Adapted from George L. Kelling and Mark H. Moore, *The Evolving Strategies of Policing* (Washington, DC: U.S. Department of Justice, National Institute of Justice Perspectives on Policing, November 1988).

Imitating Peel

When the movement to improve policing did begin in America in the 1840s, it occurred in New York City. (Philadelphia, with a private bequest of $33,000, actually began a paid daytime police force in 1833; however, it was disbanded three years later.) The police reform movement had actually begun in New York in 1836, when the mayor advocated a new police organization that could deal with civil disorder. The city council denied the mayor's request, saying that, instead, citizens should simply aid one another in combating crime.

Efforts at police reform thus stayed dormant until 1841, when a highly publicized murder case resurrected the issue, showing again the incompetence of the officers under the old system of policing. Mary Cecilia Rogers left her New York home one day and disappeared; three days later, her body was discovered in the Hudson River. The public and newspapers clamored for the police to solve the crime. The police appeared unwilling to investigate until an adequate reward was offered.[36] Edgar Allan Poe's 1850 short story "The Mystery of Marie Roget" was based on this case. The Rogers case and the police response did more to encourage police reorganization than all of the previous cries for change. Thus began the **political era of policing**.

In 1844, the New York State legislature passed a law establishing a full-time preventive police force for New York City. However, this new body came into being in a very different form than in Europe. The American version, as begun in New York City, was deliberately placed under the control of the city government and city politicians. The American plan required that each ward in the city be a separate patrol district, unlike the European model, which divided the districts along the lines of criminal activity. The process for selecting officers was also different. The mayor chose the recruits from a list of names submitted by the aldermen and tax assessors of each ward; the mayor then submitted his choices to the city council for approval. This system adhered to the principles of republicanism and resulted in most of the power over the police going to the ward aldermen, who were seldom concerned about selecting the best people for the job. Instead, the system allowed and even encouraged political patronage and rewards for friends.[37]

The law also provided for the hiring of eight hundred officers—not nearly enough to cover the city—and for the hiring of a chief of police, who had no power to hire officers, assign them to duties, or fire them. Furthermore, the law did not require the officers to wear uniforms; instead, they were to carry a badge or other emblem for identification. Citizens would be hard-pressed to recognize an officer when they needed one. As a result of the law, New York's officers would be patrolling a beat around the clock, and pay scales were high enough to attract good applicants. At the same time, the position of constable was dissolved. Overall, these were important reforms over the old system and provided the basis for continued improvements that the public supported.[38]

It did not take long for other cities to adopt the general model of the New York City police force. New Orleans and Cincinnati adopted plans for a new police force in 1852, Boston and Philadelphia followed in 1854, Chicago in 1855, and Baltimore and Newark in 1857.[39] By 1880, virtually every major American city had a police force based on Peel's model.

Early Issues and New Traditions

Three important issues confronted these early American police officers as they took to the streets between 1845 and 1869: whether the police should be in uniform, whether they should be armed, and whether they should use force.

The issue of a police uniform was important for several reasons. First, the lack of a uniform negated one of the basic principles of crime prevention—that police officers be visible. Crime victims wanted to find a police officer in a hurry. Further, uniforms would make it difficult for officers to avoid their duties since it would strip them of their anonymity. Interestingly, police officers themselves tended to prefer not to wear a uniform. They contended that the uniform would hinder their work because criminals would recognize them and flee and that the uniform was demeaning and would destroy their sense of manliness and democracy. One officer went so far as to argue that the sun reflecting off his badge would warn criminals of his approach; another officer hired an attorney and threatened to sue if he were compelled to don a uniform. To remedy the problem, New York City officials took advantage of the fact that their officers served four-year terms of office; when those terms expired in 1853, the city's police commissioners announced they would not rehire any officer who refused to wear a uniform. Thus New York became the first American city with a uniformed police force. It was followed in 1860 by Philadelphia, where there was also strong police objection to the policy. In Boston (1858) and Chicago (1861), police accepted the adoption of uniforms more easily.[40]

A more serious issue confronting politicians and the new police officers was the carrying of arms. At stake was the personal safety of the officers and the citizens they served. Nearly everyone viewed an armed police force with considerable suspicion. However, after some surprisingly calm objections by members of the public, who noted that the London police had no need to bear arms, it was agreed that an armed police force was unavoidable. Of course, America had a long tradition that citizens had the right—sometimes even the duty—to own firearms. And armed only with nightsticks, the new police could hardly withstand attacks by armed assailants. The public allowed officers to carry arms simply because there was no alternative, which was a significant change in American policing and a major point of departure from the English model. Practically from the first day, then, the American police have been much more open to the idea of carrying weapons.[41]

Eventually the use of force, the third issue, would become necessary and commonplace for American officers. Indeed, the uncertainty about whether an offender was armed perpetuated the need for an officer to rely on physical prowess for survival on the streets.

Attempts at Reform in Difficult Times

By 1850, American police officers still faced a difficult task. In addition to maintaining order and coping with vice and crime, they would, soon after putting on the uniform, be separated from their old associates and viewed with suspicion by most citizens.

With few exceptions, the work was steady, and layoffs were uncommon. The nature of the work and the possibility of a retirement pension tied officers closely to their jobs and their colleagues. By 1850, there was a surplus of unskilled labor, particularly in the major eastern cities. The desire for economic security was reason enough for many able-bodied men to try to enter police service. New York City, for example, paid its police officers about twice as much as unskilled laborers could earn. Police departments had about twice as many applicants as positions. The system of political patronage prevailed in most cities, even after civil service laws attempted to introduce merit systems for hiring police.[42]

In New York, the police reform board was headed by Theodore Roosevelt, who sought applications for the department from residents in upstate areas. When these officers, later called bushwhackers, were appointed, they were criticized by disgruntled Tammanyites (corrupt New York City politicians) who favored the political patronage system. The Tammanyites complained that the bushwhackers "could not find their way to a single station house."[43] Roosevelt's approach violated the American tradition of hiring local boys for local jobs.[44] Citizens saw these new uniformed anomalies as people who wanted to spoil their fun or close their saloons on Sunday.

Tradition became the most important determinant of police behavior: A major teaching tool was the endless string of war stories the recruit heard, and the emphasis in most departments was on doing things as they had always been done. Innovation was frowned upon, and the veterans impressed on the rookies the reasons why things had to remain the same.[45]

The police officers of the late nineteenth century were kept busy with riots, strikes, parades, and fires. These events often made for hostile interaction between citizens and the police. Labor disputes often meant long hours of extra duty for the officers, for which no extra pay was received. This, coupled with the fact that the police did not engage in collective bargaining, resulted in the police having little empathy or identification with strikers or strikebreakers. Therefore the use of the baton to put down riots, known as the "baton charge," was not uncommon.[46]

During the late nineteenth century, large cities gradually became more orderly places. The number of riots dropped. In the post–Civil War period, however, ethnic group conflict sometimes resulted in individual and group acts of violence and disorder. Hatred of Catholics and Irish Protestants led to the killing and wounding of over one hundred people in large eastern cities. Still, American cities were more orderly in 1900 than they had been in 1850. The possibility of violence involving labor disputes remained, and race riots increased in number and intensity after 1900, but daily urban life became more predictable and controlled. And then American cities absorbed millions of newcomers after 1900.[47]

Increased Politics and Corruption

A more developed urban life also promoted order. Work groups and social clusters provided a sense of integration and belonging. Immigrants established benefit societies, churches, synagogues, and social clubs. Irish-Americans constituted a heavy proportion of the police departments by the 1890s; they made up more than one-fourth of the New York City police force as early as the 1850s. Huge proportions of Irish officers were also found in Boston, Chicago, Cleveland, and San Francisco.[48]

Ethnic and religious disputes were found in many police departments. In Cleveland, for example, Catholics and Masons distrusted one another, while in New York, the Irish officers controlled many hirings and promotions. And there were still strong political influences at work. Politics were played to such an extent that even nonranking patrol officers used political backers to obtain promotions, desired assignments, and transfers.

Police corruption also surfaced at this time. Corrupt officers wanted beats close to the gamblers, saloonkeepers, madams, and pimps—people who could not operate if the officers were "untouchable" or "100 percent coppers."[49] Political pull for corrupt officers could work for or against them; the officer who incurred the wrath of his superiors could be transferred to the outposts, where he would have no chance for financial advancement.

In New York, officers routinely committed perjury to protect one another against civilian complaints. An early form of "internal affairs" thus developed in the 1890s: the "shoofly," a plainclothes officer who checked on the performance of the patrol officers. When Theodore Roosevelt served as police commissioner in New York, he frequently made clandestine trips to the beats to check on his officers; any malingerers found in the saloons were summoned to headquarters in the morning.[50]

CAREER PROFILE

Name: Francis O'Neill, Chicago

Position: Chief of Police, Chicago, Illinois, 1903

The watchman of a century ago with his lantern and staff who called out the passing hours in stentorian tones during the night is now but a tradition. He has been succeeded by a uniformed constabulary and police who carry arms and operate under semi-military discipline. The introduction of electricity as a means of communication between stations was the first notable advance in the improvement of police methods. I remember the time when the manipulation of the dial telegraph by the station keeper while sending messages excited the greatest wonder and admiration. The adoption of the Morse system of telegraphy was a long step forward and proved of great advantage. In 1876, all desk sergeants were required to take up the immediate study of the Morse system of telegraphy. Scarcely one-fourth of them became proficient before modern science, advancing in leaps and bounds, brought forth that still more modern miracle—the telephone. Less than one-quarter century ago the policeman on post had no aid from science in communicating with his station or in securing assistance in case of need. When required by duty to care for the sick and injured or to remove a dead body, an appeal to the owner of some suitable vehicle was his only resource. These were desperate times for policemen in a hostile country with unpaved streets. The patrol wagon and signal service have effected a revolution in police methods. The forward stride from the lanterned night watch, with staff, to the uniformed and disciplined police officer of the present, equipped with telegraph, telephone, signal service, and the Bertillon system of identification, is indeed an interesting one to contemplate.

Source: Proceedings of the International Chiefs of Police, Tenth Annual Convention, May 12–14, 1903, p. 67.

Meanwhile, on the American Frontier . . .

While large cities in the East were struggling to overcome social problems and establish preventive police forces, the western half of America was anything but passive. Many historians believe that the true character of Americans developed on the frontier. Rugged individualism, independence, and simplicity of manners and behavior lent dignity to American life.

Most Americans are fascinated by this period of police history, a time when heroic marshals engaged in gunfights in Dodge City and other wild cowboy towns. But this period is also riddled with exaggerated legends and half-truths. During the second half of the nineteenth century, the absence of government created a confusing variety of forms of policing in the West. Large parts of the West were under federal control, some had been organized into states, and still others were under Native American control, at least on paper. Law enforcement was performed largely by federal marshals and their deputies. Once a state was created within a territory, its state legislature had the power to attempt to deal with crime by appointing county sheriffs. Otherwise, there was no uniform method for attempting to control the problems of the West.

When the people left the wagon trains and their relatively law-abiding ways, they attempted to live together in communities. Many different ethnic groups—Anglo-Americans, Mexicans, Chinese, Native Americans, freed blacks, Australians, Scandinavians, and others—competed for often scarce resources and fought one another violently, often with mob attacks. Economic conflicts were frequent between cattlemen and sheepherders, and they often led to major range wars. There was constant labor strife in the mines. The bitterness of slavery remained, and many men with firearms skills learned during the Civil War turned to outlawry after leaving the service. (Jesse James was one such person.) In spite of these difficulties, westerners did manage to establish peace by relying on a combination of four groups who assumed responsibility for law enforcement: private citizens, U.S. marshals, businessmen, and town police officers.[51]

Private citizens usually helped to enforce the law by joining a posse or making individual efforts. An example of citizen policing was the formation of vigilante committees. Between 1849 and 1902, there were 210 vigilante movements in the United States, most of them in California.[52] While throughout history many vigilante groups have practiced "informal justice" by illegally taking the law into their own hands, breaking the law with violence and force, they also performed valuable work by ridding their communities of dangerous criminals. The Career Profile on the previous page is an essay written at the dawn of the twentieth century and reflects the changes in technologies and methods of that era.

Federal marshals were created by congressional legislation in 1789. As marshals began to appear on the frontier, the vigilantes tended to disappear. The marshals enforced federal laws, so they had no jurisdiction over matters not involving a federal offense. They could act only in cases involving theft of mail, crimes against railroad property, murder on federal lands (much of the West was federal property for many decades), and a few other crimes. Their primary responsibility was in civil matters arising from federal court decisions. Federal marshals obtained their office through political appointment; therefore they did not need any prior experience and were politically indebted. Initially, they received no salary but were instead compensated with fees and rewards. Because chasing outlaws did not pay as much as serving civil process papers, the marshals tended to prefer the more lucrative, less dangerous task of serving court paperwork. Congress saw the folly in this system and, in 1896, enacted legislation providing regular salaries for marshals.[53]

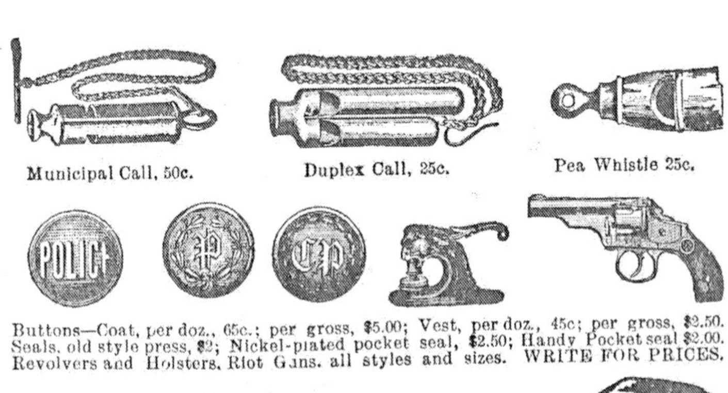

Municipal Call, 50c.
Duplex Call, 25c.
Pea Whistle 25c.
POLICE
Buttons—Coat, per doz., 65c.; per gross, $5.00; Vest, per doz., 45c; per gross, $2.50. Seals, old style press, $2; Nickel-plated pocket seal, $2.50; Handy Pocket seal $2.00. Revolvers and Holsters, Riot Guns, all styles and sizes. WRITE FOR PRICES.

66
Cell Pails, Cedar, Porcelain lined, $2.50; Bulls-Eye Oil Lamps, regulation, solid brass nickeled, $3.50; brass, $3; Japanned, $2; Metal Wreaths, gilt or German Silver, 15c; numbers 5c. each; wired on wreaths, 5c. extra each wreath; Bean's Hard Glove, $2, made of Sole Leather, neatly covered, easily carried in place of Club or Billet.
TOWER'S PATENT DOUBLE LOCK HANDCUFFS AND LEG IRONS

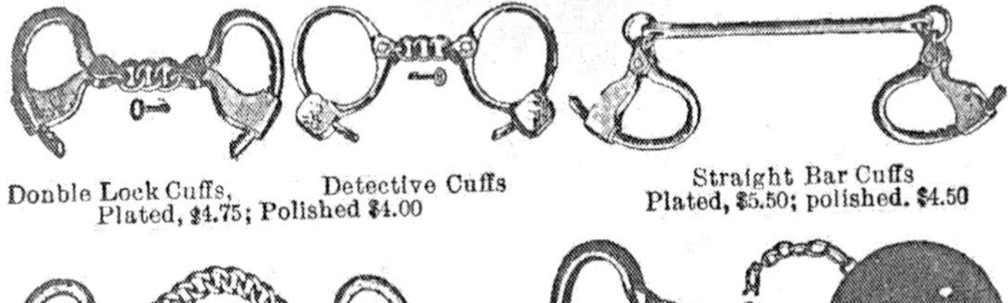

Donble Lock Cuffs,
Detective Cuffs
Plated, $4.75; Polished $4.00
Straight Bar Cuffs
Plated, $5.50; polished. $4.50

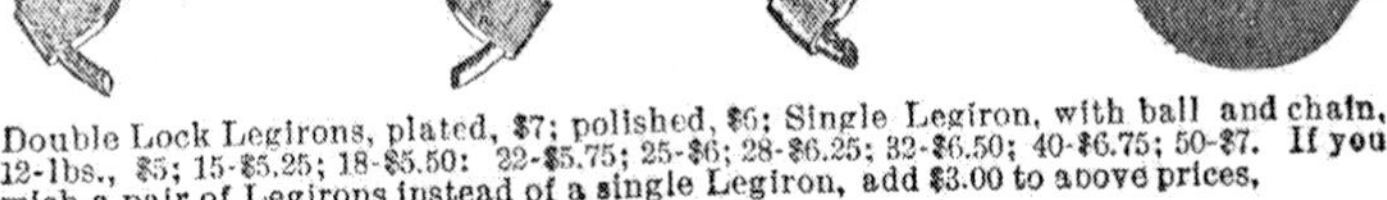

Double Lock Legirons, plated, $7; polished, $6; Single Legiron, with ball and chain, 12-lbs., $5; 15-$5.25; 18-$5.50; 22-$5.75; 25-$6; 28-$6.25; 32-$6.50; 40-$6.75; 50-$7. If you wish a pair of Legirons instead of a single Legiron, add $3.00 to above prices.

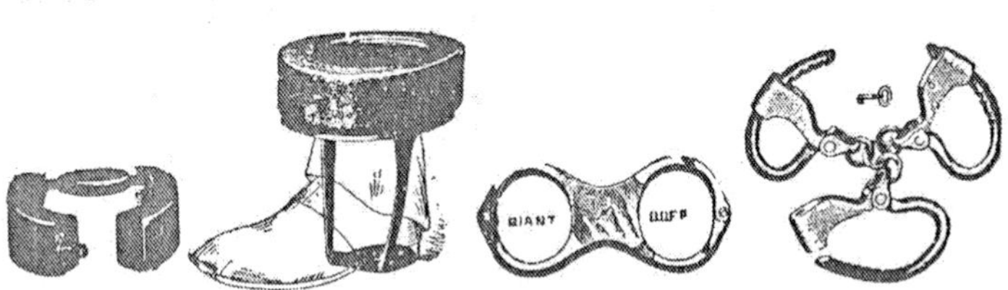

GIANT
CUFF
Leininger's Shackle (Oregon Boot.)
11-lbs. $9.00; 15-lbs. $9.50.
Giant Cuffs,
$6.00
Cuffs for three hands,
Plated, $7; polished, $6
Extra Handcuff and Legiron Keys, 25 cents each.

Turn-of-the-century police equipment.

When a territory became a state, the primary law enforcement functions usually fell to local sheriffs and marshals. Train robbers such as Jesse James and the Dalton Gang were among the most famous outlaws to violate federal laws. Many train robbers became legendary for having the courage to steal from the despised railroad owners. What is often overlooked in the tales of these legendary outlaws is their often total disregard for the safety and lives of their victims. To combat these criminals, federal marshals found their hideouts, and railroad companies and other businesses often offered rewards for information leading to their capture. Occasionally, as in the case of Jesse James and the Daltons, the marshals' work was done for them—outlaws were often killed by friends (usually for a reward) or by private citizens.[54]

Gunfights in the West actually occurred very rarely; few individuals on either side of the law actually welcomed stand-up gunfights. It was infinitely more sensible to find cover from which to have a shootout. Further, handguns were not the preferred weapon—a double-barreled shotgun could do far more damage than a handgun at close range.

Local law enforcement came about as people settled into communities. Town meetings were held during which a government was established and local officials were elected. Sheriffs quickly became important officials, but they spent more time collecting taxes, inspecting cattle brands, maintaining jails, and serving civil papers than they did actually dealing with outlaws. In addition, with the growing use of U.S. marshals to uphold the law (some of the more storied ones being Wyatt Earp, "Wild Bill" Hickok, and William "Bat" Masterson), most people were inclined to be law abiding.[55]

Only forty-five violent deaths from all causes can be found in western cow towns from 1870 to 1885, when they were thriving. This low figure reflects the real nature of the cow towns. Businessmen had a vested interest in preventing crime from occurring and in not hiring a trigger-happy sheriff or marshal. They tended to avoid hiring individuals like John Slaughter, sheriff of Cochise County, Arizona, who never brought a prisoner back alive for eight years. Too much violence ruined a town's reputation and harmed the local economy.[56]

The Entrenchment of Political Influence

Partly because of their closeness to politicians, police during the early twentieth century began providing a wide array of services to citizens. In some cities, they operated soup lines, helped find lost children, and found jobs and temporary lodging in station houses for newly arrived immigrants.[57] Police organizations were typically quite decentralized, with cities divided into precincts and run like small-scale departments, hiring, firing, managing, and assigning personnel as necessary. Officers were often recruited from the same ethnic stock as the dominant groups in the neighborhoods and lived in the beats they patrolled, and they were allowed considerable discretion in handling their individual beats. Detectives operated from a caseload of "persons" rather than offenses, relying on their charges to inform on other criminals.[58]

Officers were integrated into neighborhoods. This strategy proved useful; it helped contain riots, and the police helped immigrants establish themselves in communities and find jobs. There were weaknesses as well: The intimacy with the community, closeness to politicians, and decentralized organizational structure (and its inability to provide supervision of officers) also led to police corruption. The close identification of police with neighborhoods also resulted in discrimination against strangers, especially ethnic and racial minorities. Police officers often ruled their beats with the "end of their nightsticks" and practiced "curbside justice."[59] The lack of organizational control over officers also caused some inefficiencies and disorganization; thus the image of the bungling Keystone Kops was widespread.

The Reform Era: 1930s to 1980s

Attempts to Thwart Political Patronage

During the early nineteenth century, reformers sought to reject political involvement by the police, and civil service systems were created to eliminate patronage and ward influences in hiring and firing police officers. In some cities, officers were not permitted to live in the same beat they patrolled in order to isolate them as completely as possible from political influences. Police departments became one of the most autonomous agencies in urban government.[60] However, policing also became a matter viewed as best left to the discretion of police executives. Police organizations became law enforcement agencies with the sole goal of controlling crime. Any noncrime activities they were required to do were considered "social work." The **reform era of policing** (also termed the **professional era of policing**) would soon be in full bloom.

The scientific theory of administration was adopted, as advocated by Frederick Taylor during the early twentieth century. Taylor first studied the work process, breaking down jobs into their basic steps and emphasizing time and motion studies, all with the goal of maximizing production. From this emphasis on production and unity of control flowed the notion that police officers were best managed by a hierarchical pyramid of control. Police leaders routinized and standardized police work; officers were to enforce laws and make arrests whenever they could. Discretion was limited as much as possible. When special problems arose, special units (e.g., vice, juvenile, drugs, tactical) were created rather than problems being assigned to patrol officers.

The Era of August Vollmer

The policing career of **August Vollmer** has been established as one of the most important periods in the development of police professionalism (see Exhibit 1). In April 1905 at age twenty-nine, Vollmer became the town marshal in Berkeley, California. At that time, policing had become a major issue all across America. Big-city police departments had become notorious for their corruption, and politics rather than professional principles dominated most police departments.[61]

EXHIBIT 1.1

The Crib of Modern Law Enforcement

A Chronology of August Vollmer and the Berkeley Police Department

1905 Vollmer is elected Berkeley town marshal. Town trustees appoint six police officers at a salary of $70 per month.

1906 Trustees create detective rank. Vollmer initiates a red light signal system to reach beat officers from headquarters; telephones are installed in boxes. A police records system is created.

1908 Two motorcycles are added to the department. Vollmer begins a police school.

1909 Vollmer is appointed Berkeley chief of police under a new charter form of government. Trustees approve the appointment of a Bertillon expert and the purchase of fingerprinting equipment. A modus operandi file is created, modeled on the British system.

1911 All patrol officers are using bicycles.

1914 Three privately owned autos are authorized for patrol use.

1915 A central office is established for police reports.

1916 Vollmer urges Congress to establish a national fingerprint bureau (later created by the FBI in Washington, D.C.), begins annual lectures on police procedures, and persuades biochemist Albert Schneider to install and direct a crime laboratory at headquarters.

1917 Vollmer has the first completely motorized force; officers furnish their own automobiles. Vollmer recruits college students for part-time police jobs. He begins consulting with police and reorganizing departments around the country.

1918 Entrance examinations are initiated to measure the mental, physical, and emotional fitness of recruits; a part-time police psychiatrist is employed.

1919 Vollmer begins testing delinquents and using psychology to anticipate criminal behavior. He implements a juvenile program to reduce child delinquency.

1921 Vollmer guides the development of the first lie detector and begins developing radio communications between patrol cars, handwriting analysis, and use of business machine equipment (a Hollerith tabulator).

Following his retirement from active law enforcement in 1932, Vollmer traveled around the world to study police methods. He continued serving as professor of police administration at the University of California, Berkeley, until 1938, and authored or co-authored four books on police and crime from 1935 to 1949. He died in Berkeley in 1955.

Vollmer commanded a force of only three deputies; his first act as town marshal was to request an increase in his force from three to twelve deputies in order to form day and night patrols. Obtaining that, he soon won national publicity for being the first chief to order his men to patrol on bicycles. Time checks he had run demonstrated that officers on bicycles would be able to respond three times more quickly to calls than men on foot possibly could. His confidence growing, Vollmer next persuaded the Berkeley City Council to purchase a system of red lights. The lights, hung at each street intersection, served as an emergency notification system for police officers—the first such signal system in the country.[62]

In 1906, Vollmer, curious about the methods criminals used to commit their crimes, began to question the suspects he arrested. He found that nearly all criminals used their own peculiar method of operation, or **modus operandi**. In 1907, following an apparent suicide case that Vollmer suspected of being murder, Vollmer sought the advice of a professor of biology at the University of California. He then became convinced of the value of scientific knowledge in criminal investigation.[63]

Vollmer's most daring innovation came in 1908: the idea of a police school. The first formal training program for police officers in the country drew on the expertise

August Vollmer as town marshal, police chief, and criminalist. *(Courtesy Samuel G. Chapman)*

of university professors as well as police officers. The school included courses on police methods and procedures, fingerprinting, first aid, criminal law, anthropometry, photography, public health, and sanitation. In 1917, the curriculum was expanded from one to three years.[64]

In 1916, Vollmer persuaded a professor of pharmacology and bacteriology to become a full-time criminalist in charge of the department's criminal investigation laboratory. By 1917, Vollmer had his entire patrol force operating out of automobiles; it was the first completely mobile patrol force in the country. And in 1918, to improve the quality of police recruits in his department, he began to hire college students as part-time officers and to administer a set of intelligence, psychiatric, and neurological tests to all applicants. Out of this group of "college cops" came several outstanding and influential police leaders, including O. W. Wilson, who served as police chief in Wichita and Chicago and as the first dean of the school of criminology at the University of California. Then, in 1921, in addition to experimenting with the lie detector, two of Vollmer's officers installed a crystal set and earphones in a Model T touring car, thus creating the first radio car.

These and other innovations at Berkeley had begun to attract attention from municipal police departments across the nation, including Los Angeles, which persuaded Vollmer to serve a short term there as chief of police beginning in August 1923. Gambling, the illicit sale of liquor (Prohibition was then in effect), and police corruption were major problems in Los Angeles. Vollmer hired ex-criminals to gather intelligence information on the criminal network. He also promoted honest officers, required three thousand patrol officers to take an intelligence test, and, using those tests, reassigned personnel.[65] He was already unpopular with crooks and corrupt politicians, and these personnel actions made Vollmer very unpopular within the department as well. When he returned to Berkeley in 1924, he had made many enemies, and his attempts at reform had met with too much opposition to have any lasting effect. It would not be until the 1950s, under Chief William Parker, that the Los Angeles Police Department (LAPD) would become a leader in this reform era of policing.[66]

Vollmer, although a leading proponent of police professionalism, also advocated the idea that the police should function as social workers. He believed the police should do more than merely arrest offenders, that they should also seek to prevent crime by "saving" offenders.[67] He suggested that police work closely with existing social welfare agencies, inform voters about overcrowded schools, and support the expansion of recreational facilities, community social centers, and antidelinquency agencies. Basically, he was suggesting that the police play an active part in the life of the community. These views were very prescient; today, his ideas are being implemented in the contemporary movement toward community policing and problem-oriented policing. Yet the major thrust of police professionalization had been to insulate the police from politics. This contradiction illustrated one of the fundamental ambiguities of the whole notion of professionalism.[68]

In the late 1920s, Vollmer was appointed the first professor of police administration in the country at the University of Chicago. Upon returning to Berkeley in 1931, he received a similar appointment at the University of California, a position he held concurrently with the office of chief of police until his retirement from the force in 1932. He continued to serve as a university professor until 1938.[69]

The Crime Fighter Image

The 1930s marked an important turning point in the history of police reform. O. W. Wilson emerged as the leading authority on police administration, the police role was redefined, and the crime fighter image gained popularity.

Wilson, who learned from J. Edgar Hoover's transformation of the Federal Bureau of Investigation (FBI) into a highly prestigious agency, became the principal architect of the police reform strategy.[70] Hoover, appointed FBI director in 1924, had raised the eligibility and training standards of recruits and had developed an incorruptible crime-fighting organization. Municipal police found Hoover's path a compelling one.

Professionalism came to mean a combination of managerial efficiency and technological sophistication and an emphasis on crime fighting. The social work aspects of the policing movement fell into almost total eclipse. In sum, under the professional model of policing, officers were to remain in their "rolling fortresses," going from one call to the next with all due haste. As Mark Moore and George Kelling observed, "In professionalizing crime fighting . . . citizens on whom so much used to depend [were] removed from the fight."[71]

The Wickersham Commission

Another important development in policing, one that was strongly influenced by August Vollmer, was the creation of the Wickersham Commission. President Calvin

Coolidge had appointed the first National Crime Commission in 1925, in an admission that crime control had become a national problem. This commission was criticized for working neither through the states nor with professionals in criminal justice, psychiatry, social work, or the like. Nevertheless, coming on the heels of World War I, the crime commission took advantage of FBI Director J. Edgar Hoover's popular "war on crime" slogan to enlist public support. Political leaders and police officials also loudly proclaimed the "war on crime" concept; it continued the push for police professionalism.

Coolidge's successor, President Herbert Hoover, became concerned about the lax enforcement of Prohibition, which had taken effect in 1920. It was common knowledge that an alarming number of American police chiefs and sheriffs were accepting bribes in exchange for overlooking moonshiners; other types of police corruption were occurring as well.

Hoover replaced the National Crime Commission with the National Commission on Law Observance and Enforcement—popularly known as the **Wickersham Commission** after its chairman, former U.S. Attorney General George W. Wickersham. This presidential commission completed the first national study of crime and criminal justice, issued in fourteen reports. Two of those reports, the "Report on Police" and the "Report on Lawlessness in Law Enforcement," represented a call by the federal government for increased police professionalism.

The "Report on Police" was written in part by August Vollmer, and his imprint on this and other reports is evident. The "Report on Lawlessness in Law Enforcement" concerned itself with police misconduct and has received the greatest public attention, both then and now. The report indicated that the use by the police of third-degree suspect interrogation methods (including the infliction of physical or mental pain to extract confessions) was widespread in America. This report, through its recommendations, mapped out a path of professionalism in policing for the next two generations. The Wickersham Commission recommended, for example, that the corrupting influence of politics should be removed from policing. Police chief executives should be selected on merit, and patrol officers should be tested and should meet minimal physical standards. Police salaries, working conditions, and benefits should be decent, the commission stated, and there should be adequate training for both preservice and in-service officers. The commission also called for the use of policewomen (in cases involving juveniles and females), crime-prevention units, and bureaus of criminal investigation.

Many of these recommendations represented what progressive police reformers had been wanting for the previous forty years; unfortunately, President Hoover and his administration could do little more than report the Wickersham Commission's recommendations before leaving office.

Police as the "Thin Blue Line": William H. Parker

The movement to transform the police into professional crime fighters found perhaps its staunchest champion in **William H. Parker**, who began as a patrol officer with the

LAPD in 1927. Parker used his law degree to advance his career, and by 1934 he was the LAPD's trial prosecutor and an assistant to the chief.[72]

Parker became police chief in 1950. Following an uproar over charges of police brutality in 1951, he conducted an extensive investigation that resulted in the dismissal or punishment of over forty officers. Following this incident, he launched a campaign to transform the LAPD. His greatest success, typical of the new professionalism, came in administrative reorganization. The command structure was simplified as Parker aggressively sought ways to free every possible officer for duty on the streets, including forcing the county sheriff's office to guard prisoners and adopting one-person patrol cars. Parker also made the rigorous selection and training of personnel a major characteristic of the LAPD. Higher standards of physical fitness, intelligence, and scholastic achievement weeded out many applicants, while others failed the psychiatric examinations.

Once accepted, recruits attended a thirteen-week academy that included a rigorous physical program, rigid discipline, and intensive study. Parker thus molded an image of a tough, competent, polite, and effective crime fighter by controlling recruitment. During the 1950s, this image made the LAPD the model for reform across the nation; thus the 1950s marked a turning point in the history of professionalism.[73]

Parker conceived of the police as a "thin blue line," protecting society from barbarism and Communist subversion. He viewed urban society as a jungle, needing the restraining hand of the police; only the law and law enforcement saved society from the horrors of anarchy. The police had to enforce the law without fear or favor. Parker opposed any restrictions on police methods. The law, he believed, should give the police wide latitude to use wiretaps and to conduct search and seizure. For him, the Bill of Rights was not absolute but relative. Any conflict between effective police operation and individual rights should be resolved in favor of the police, he believed, and the rights of society took precedence over the rights of the individual. He thought that evidence obtained illegally should still be admitted in court and that the police could not do their jobs if the courts and other civilians were continually second-guessing them.

Basically, Parker believed that some "wicked men with evil hearts" preyed on society and that the police must protect society from attack by them. But Parker's brand of professional police performance lacked total public support. Voters often supported political machines that controlled and manipulated the police in anything but a professional manner; the public demanded a police department that was subject to political influence and manipulation and then condemned the force for its crookedness. The professional police officer was in the uncomfortable position of offering a service that society required for its very survival but that many people did not want at all.[74]

1960s and 1970s: Police Vis-à-vis Youth and Minorities—and the Struggle for Civil Rights

Certainly any review of the history of policing would be lacking if it did not discuss the **civil rights movement** that predominated the late 1960s and 1970s and pitted the nation's police against many of its college-age youths and minority groups (with many members of both groups viewing the police as "pigs" and representing the "establishment"). National groups (e.g., Students for a Democratic Society, Black Panthers, Student Nonviolent Coordinating Committee) represented both sides, some violent, others nonviolent. As Benjamin Disraeli once said, "No man will treat with indifference the principle of race. It is the key to history."[75]

The 1960s were a time of great tumult, civil disobedience, social turbulence, and tremendous progress in civil rights. Inner-city residents rioted in several major cities, protestors denounced military involvement in Vietnam, and assassins' bullets ended the life of President John F. Kennedy (1963) as well as those of his brother U.S. Senator Robert F. Kennedy (1968) and Dr. Martin Luther King, Jr. (1968). The country was witnessing tremendous upheaval, and incidents such as the **Democratic National Convention (1968)** in Chicago raised many questions about the police and their function and role; each night Americans witnessed scenes on national television of Chicago police officers gassing and clubbing protesters, news photographers and reporters, and other citizens in what was subsequently termed in the investigative Walker Report and in many other accounts as the Chicago "police riot."[76]

The reform (or professional) era of policing was in bloom, however, so the police were firmly ensconced in their patrol vehicles, being reactive to crime and quite removed from personal contact with the public while on random patrol and focusing on quantitative measures of their effectiveness: numbers of arrests, response time, calls for service, numbers of officers in patrol cars, numbers of miles officers drove per shift, and so on. Police training and university police science programs were booming, the latter making campuses rich with these "cash cow" programs taught largely by practitioners, with federal grants and GI benefits paying for officers' tuition, books, and often their living expenses. But the failure of the professional era became most apparent during the aforementioned urban riots, sit-ins, sniper attacks against police, gang violence, and other forms of unrest and upheaval of the time.

Specifically, Harlem, Watts, Newark, and Detroit all were scenes of major race riots during the 1960s. There were seventy-five civil disorders involving African Americans and the police in 1967 alone, with at least eighty-three people killed, mostly African Americans. In addition, many police officers and firefighters were killed or injured. Property damage in these riots totaled hundreds of millions of dollars. The 1970s busing programs that were introduced to integrate schools resulted in white "backlash" and more interracial conflict.

In the late 1980s police–community relations appeared to worsen, with a major riot in Miami, Florida, in 1989. Also in the 1980s, affirmative action programs led to charges of reverse discrimination and more dominant-group backlash. More recent decades have witnessed burning and looting in Miami; Los Angeles; Atlanta; Las Vegas; Washington, D.C.; St. Petersburg, Florida; and other cities. These incidents have demonstrated that the same tensions that found temporary release on the streets of African American communities in the past still remain with us.

The police, viewed by many during the professional era as the "thin blue line" per William Parker, were involved in all of the social changes described above.

Although at times police were used to prevent minority group members from demonstrating on behalf of civil rights, at other times the police were required to protect those same protesting minorities from the wrath of the dominant group and others who opposed peaceful demonstrations. Over time, alienation developed from these contacts. Thus, members of both groups had an uneasy coexistence with a good deal of emotional "baggage" based on what they had seen, heard, or been told of their interactions throughout history.

History has shown that problems in police–community relations are actually part of a larger problem of racism in American society. The highly respected National Academy of Sciences concluded nearly two decades ago that "black crime and the position of blacks within the nation's system of criminal justice administration are related to past and present social opportunities and disadvantages and can be best understood through consideration of blacks' overall social status."[77] More recent mass gatherings in Washington, D.C., engendered by such groups as the Southern Christian Leadership Conference and the Rainbow Coalition, have involved protests against racial profiling (discussed later), police brutality, and other perceived prejudices toward people of color; such assemblies would indicate that the Academy's statement is still valid today. Minority group members remain frustrated because the pace of gains in our society has not kept pace with their expectations.

A Retreat from the Professional Model

Coming Full Circle to Peel: President's Crime Commission

Until the period described above, the 1960s and 1970s, there had been few inquiries concerning police functions and methods for two reasons.[78] First was a tendency on the part of the police to resist outside scrutiny. Functioning in a bureaucratic environment, the police, like other bureaucrats, were sensitive to outside research. Many police administrators perceived a threat to their career and to the image of the organization, and they were also concerned about the legitimacy of the research itself. There was a natural reluctance to invite trouble. Second, few people in policing perceived a need to challenge traditional methods of operation. The "If it ain't broke, don't fix it" attitude prevailed, particularly among old-school administrators. Some ideas were etched in stone, such as the belief that more police personnel and vehicles equaled more patrolling and, therefore, less crime, a quicker response rate, and a happier citizenry. A corollary belief is that the more officers riding in the patrol car, the better. The methods and effectiveness of detectives and their investigative techniques were not even open to debate.

As Herman Goldstein stated, however, "Crises stimulate progress. The police came under enormous pressure in the late 1960s and early 1970s, confronted with concern about crime, civil rights demonstrations, racial conflicts, riots and political protests."[79]

Concurrent with, and because of, the aforementioned turmoil, five national commissions attempted to examine police methods and practices during the 1960s and 1970s, each viewing them from different perspectives. Of particular note is a commission whose findings are still widely cited today and that provided the impetus to return the police to the community: the President's Commission on Law Enforcement and the Administration of Justice. Termed the **President's Crime Commission**, this body was charged by President Lyndon Johnson to find solutions to America's internal crime problems, including the root causes of crime, the workings of the justice system, and the hostile, antagonistic relations between the police and civilians. Among the commission's recommendations for the police were hiring more minority members as officers to improve police–community relations, upgrading the quality of police officers through better-educated officers, promoting to supervisory positions college-educated individuals, screening applicants more rigorously, and providing intensive preservice training for new recruits. It was proposed that a higher caliber of recruits would raise police service delivery, promote tranquility within the community, and relegate police corruption to a thing of the past.[80]

The President's Crime Commission brought policing full circle, restating several of the same principles that were laid out by Sir Robert Peel in 1829: that the police should be close to the public, that poor quality of policing contributed to social disorder, and that the police should focus on community relations. Thus, by 1970 there had been what was termed a systematic demolition of the assumptions underlying the professional era of policing.[81] Few authorities on policing today could endorse the basic approaches to police management that were propounded by O. W. Wilson or William Parker. We now know much that was still unknown by the staff of the President's Crime Commission in 1967. For example, we have learned that adding more police or intensifying patrol coverage does not reduce crime and that neither faster response time nor additional detectives will improve clearance rates.

The Community Era: 1980s to Present

In the early 1970s, it was suggested that the performance of patrol officers would improve by redesigning their job based on motivators.[82] This suggestion later evolved into a concept known as **team policing**, which sought to restructure police departments, improve police–community relations, enhance police officer morale, and facilitate change within the police organization. Its primary element was a decentralized neighborhood focus for the delivery of police services. Officers were to be generalists, trained to investigate crimes and basically attend to all of the problems in their area; a team of officers would be assigned to a particular neighborhood and would be responsible for all police services in that area.

In the end, however, team policing failed for several reasons. Most of the experiments were poorly planned and hastily implemented, resulting in street officers who did not understand what they were supposed to do. Many mid-management personnel felt threatened by team policing and did not support the experiment.

There were other developments for the police during the late 1970s and early 1980s. Foot patrol became more popular, and many jurisdictions (such as Newark, New Jersey; Boston, Massachusetts; and Flint, Michigan) even demanded it. In Newark, an evaluation led to the conclusions that officers on foot patrol were easily seen by residents, produced a significant increase in the level of satisfaction with police service, led to a significant reduction of perceived crime problems, and resulted in a significant increase in the perceived level of neighborhood safety.[83]

These findings shattered several long-held myths about measures of police effectiveness. In addition, research conducted during the 1970s suggested that information could help police improve their ability to deal with crime. These studies, along with studies of foot patrol and fear reduction, created new opportunities for police to work with citizens to do something about crime problems. Police discovered that when they asked citizens about their priorities, citizens appreciated their asking and often provided useful information.

Simultaneously, the problem-oriented approach to policing was being tested in Madison, Wisconsin; Baltimore County, Maryland; and Newport News, Virginia. Studies there found that police officers have the capacity to do problem solving successfully and can work well with citizens and other agencies. Also, citizens seemed to appreciate working with police. Moreover, this approach gave officers more autonomy to analyze the underlying causes of problems and to find creative solutions. Crime control remained an important function, but equal emphasis was given to prevention.

In sum, following are some of the factors that set the stage for the demise of the professional era and the emergence of the **community era of policing:**

- Narrowing of the police mission to crime fighting
- Increased cultural diversity in our society
- Detachment of patrol officers in patrol vehicles
- Increased violence in our society
- Scientific view of management, stressing efficiency more than effectiveness, quantitative policing more than qualitative policing
- Increased dependence on high-technology equipment rather than contact with the public
- Isolation of police administration from community and officer input
- Concern about police violation of the civil rights of minorities
- Burgeoning attempts by the police to adequately reach the community through crime prevention, team policing, and police–community relations

Today, community oriented policing and problem solving (COPPS) is recognized as being on the cutting edge of what is new in policing.[84]

SUMMARY

This chapter has presented the evolution of policing through its three eras, and some of the individuals, events, and national commissions that were instrumental in taking policing through those eras. It has also shown how the history of policing may be said to have come full circle to its roots, wherein it was intended to operate with the consent and assistance of the public. Policing is now attempting to throw off the shackles of tradition and become more community oriented.

This historical overview also reveals that many of today's policing issues and problems actually began surfacing many centuries ago: graft and corruption, negative community relations, police use of force, public unrest and rioting, general police accountability, the struggle to establish the proper roles and functions of the police, the police subculture, and the tendency to withdraw from the public, cling to tradition, and be inbred. All in all, however, it would seem the police learned well their lessons from history, as these problems do not pervade the nation's 17,000 agencies or their 800,000 officers. The community era is spreading and thriving in today's police world.

KEY TERMS

August Vollmer
civil rights movement
community era of policing
constable
coroner
Democratic National Convention (1968)
justice of the peace (JP)
modus operandi
political era of policing
President's Crime Commission
principles of policing
professional era of policing
reform era of policing
republicanism
sheriff
team policing
Wickersham Commission
William H. Parker

REVIEW QUESTIONS

1. What were the major police-related offices and their functions during the early English and colonial periods?
2. What legacies of colonial policing remained intact after the American Revolution?
3. List the three early issues of American policing, and describe their present status.
4. What unique characteristics of law enforcement existed in the Wild West? What myths concerning early western law enforcement continue today?
5. What were some of the major characteristics of the political and reform eras of policing? How did they square with the earlier principles of policing as set forth by Sir Robert Peel?
6. What led to the development of the contemporary community-oriented policing and problem-solving era, and what are some of its main features?
7. How can it be said that policing has come full circle, returning to its origins?

LEARN BY DOING

As indicated in the Preface, this section comports with the early-1900s teaching of famed educator John Dewey, who advocated the "learning by doing" approach to education, or problem-based learning. It also comports with the popular learning method espoused by Benjamin Bloom in 1956, known as Bloom's Taxonomy, in which he called for "higher-order thinking skills"—critical and creative thinking that involves analysis, synthesis, and evaluation.[85] The following scenarios and activities will shift your attention from textbook-centered instruction and move the emphasis to student-centered projects. By being placed in these hypothetical situations, you can thus learn—and apply—some of the concepts covered in this chapter, develop skills in communication and self-management, solve problems, and understand and address current community issues.

1. You have been tasked by the police chief to develop—and present—a one-hour History of Policing class as part of the curriculum at the Regional Police Academy. Prepare an outline, timeline of police history, and presentation that will satisfy this request. Be sure to include the major developments for each policing era.
2. Your criminal justice professor assigns you to examine your local police organizations and then, if they exist, to compare the duties of the four early English policing offices (e.g., sheriff, constable, justice of the peace, coroner) with their present status and function (or, if more appropriate, at the time of their demise) in your particular area.
3. Assume that, as part of an assigned research paper on the history of policing, you seek to interview a retired police officer(s) concerning the changes in police methods and philosophy over the past several decades (as well as areas in which policing has remained unchanged); hopefully you would be particularly determined to locate and interview a woman who entered the field as a sworn officer in the 1970s or 1980s, and learn of the unique challenges that were faced.

mycrimekit™

Go to MyCrimeKit.com and discover additional study tools and resources related to this chapter.

- Key Terms
- Review Questions
  - Multiple Choice Questions
  - True/False
  - Fill in the Blank
  - Essay
- MEDIA REVIEW: where you will once again review the *history and professionalism of the police*. You also will have an opportunity to visit the different *policing eras* covered in this chapter.

- FLASHCARDS: to test your knowledge of this chapter.
- NEW YORK TIMES: where you can read the latest articles related to criminology and criminal law.
- THE CAREER CENTER: where you can explore career opportunities in criminal justice and criminology.
- THE ONLINE RESEARCH LIBRARY: where you can explore the Cybrary and Research Navigator.

NOTES

1. Samuel Walker, *The Police in America: An Introduction* (New York: McGraw-Hill, 1983), p. 2.
2. Bruce Smith, *Rural Crime Control* (New York: Columbia University, 1933), p. 40.
3. Ibid., pp. 42–44.
4. Ibid.
5. Ibid.
6. Ibid., pp. 182–84.
7. Ibid., pp. 188–89.
8. Ibid., p. 192.
9. Ibid., pp. 218–22.
10. Ibid., pp. 245–46.
11. Ibid.
12. Craig Uchida, "The Development of American Police: An Historical Overview," in *Critical Issues in Policing: Contemporary Readings*, eds. Roger G. Dunham and Geoffrey P. Alpert (Prospect Heights, IL: Waveland Press, 1989), p. 14.
13. Charles Reith, *A New Study of Police History* (London: Oliver and Boyd, 1956).
14. Carl Klockars, *The Idea of Police* (Beverly Hills, CA: Sage, 1985).
15. Ibid., pp. 45–46.
16. Ibid., p. 46.
17. David R. Johnson, *American Law Enforcement History* (St. Louis: Forum Press, 1981), p. 4.
18. Ibid., p. 5.
19. Ibid.
20. Ibid., p. 6.
21. Ibid., p. 1.
22. Ibid., pp. 8–10.
23. Ibid., p. 11.
24. Ibid., p. 13.
25. David A. Jones, *History of Criminology: A Philosophical Perspective* (Westport, CT: Greenwood Press, 1986), p. 64.
26. Johnson, *American Law Enforcement History*, pp. 14–15.
27. Ibid., pp. 17–18.
28. Ibid., pp. 18–19.

29. Leon Radzinowicz, *A History of English Criminal Law and Its Administration from 1750,* vol. IV, *Grappling for Control* (London: Stevens and Son, 1968), p. 163.
30. Johnson, *American Law Enforcement History,* p. 19.
31. Ibid., pp. 19–20.
32. Ibid., pp. 20–21.
33. A. C. Germann, Frank D. Day, and Robert R. J. Gallati, *Introduction to Law Enforcement and Criminal Justice* (Springfield, IL: Charles C Thomas, 1962), p. 63.
34. Clive Emsley, *Policing and Its Context, 1750–1870* (New York: Schocken, 1983), p. 37.
35. Charles Reith, *A Short History of the British Police* (London: Oxford University Press, 1948).
36. Johnson, *American Law Enforcement History,* p. 26.
37. Ibid., pp. 26–27.
38. Ibid., p. 27.
39. Ibid.
40. Ibid., pp. 28–29.
41. Ibid., pp. 30–31.
42. James F. Richardson, *Urban Policing in the United States* (London: Kennikat Press, 1974), pp. 47–48.
43. James F. Richardson, *The New York Police: Colonial Times to 1901* (New York: Oxford Press, 1970), p. 259.
44. Richardson, *Urban Policing in the United States,* p. 48.
45. Richardson, *The New York Police,* pp. 195–201.
46. Richardson, *Urban Policing in the United States,* p. 51.
47. Ibid.
48. Ibid., pp. 53–54.
49. Ibid., pp. 55–56.
50. Ibid., pp. 59–60.
51. Johnson, *American Law Enforcement History,* p. 92.
52. Ibid.
53. Ibid., pp. 96–97.
54. Ibid., p. 98.
55. U.S. Department of Justice, United States Marshals Service, “The Marshals Service Turns 215,” www.usmarshals.gov/monitor/215-0402.pdf (accessed July 6, 2010).
56. Johnson, *American Law Enforcement History,* pp. 100–101.
57. Eric H. Monkkonen, *Police in Urban America, 1860–1920* (New York: Cambridge University Press, 1981), p. 158.
58. John E. Eck, *The Investigation of Burglary and Robbery* (Washington, DC: Police Executive Research Forum, 1984).
59. George L. Kelling, “Juveniles and Police: The End of the Nightstick,” in *From Children to Citizens,* vol. II, *The Role of the Juvenile Court,* ed. Francis X. Hartmann (New York: Springer-Verlag, 1987).
60. Herman Goldstein, *Policing a Free Society* (Cambridge, MA: Ballinger, 1977).
61. August Vollmer, “Police Progress in the Past Twenty-Five Years,” *Journal of Criminal Law and Criminology* 24 (1933): 161–75.

62. Alfred E. Parker, *Crime Fighter: August Vollmer* (New York: Macmillan, 1961).
63. Nathan Douthit, "August Vollmer," in *Thinking About Police: Contemporary Readings,* ed. Carl B. Klockars (New York: McGraw-Hill, 1983), p. 102.
64. Ibid.
65. Paul Jacobs, *Prelude to Riot: A View of Urban America from the Bottom* (New York: Random House, 1966), pp. 13–60.
66. Ibid.
67. Samuel Walker, *A Critical History of Police Reform: The Emergence of Professionalism* (Lexington, MA: Lexington Books, 1977), p. 81.
68. Ibid., pp. 80–83.
69. For a chronology of Vollmer's career and a listing of his publications, see Gene E. Carte and Elaine H. Carte, *Police Reform in the United States: The Era of August Vollmer, 1905–1932* (Berkeley: University of California Press, 1975).
70. Orlando Wilson, *Police Administration* (New York: McGraw-Hill, 1950).
71. Mark H. Moore and George L. Kelling, "'To Serve and Protect': Learning from Police History," *The Public Interest* 70 (Winter 1983): 49–65.
72. Johnson, *American Law Enforcement History,* pp. 119–20.
73. Ibid., pp. 120–21.
74. Richardson, *Urban Policing in the United States,* pp. 139–43.
75. Benjamin Disraeli, *Endymion* (New York: D. Appleton & Co., 1880), pp. 249–50.
76. Daniel Walker, *Rights in Conflict: The Violent Confrontation of Demonstrators and Police in the Parks and Streets of Chicago During the Week of the Democratic National Convention of 1968—A Report Submitted to the National Commission on the Causes and Prevention of Violence* (Steubenville, OH: Braceland Brothers, 1968), p. 233; also see "Chicago Examined: Anatomy of a Police Riot," *Time,* December 6, 1968, www.time.com/time/magazine/article/0,9171,844633-5,00.html (accessed July 6, 2010).
77. National Academy of Sciences, *A Common Destiny: Blacks and American Society* (Washington, DC: National Academy Press, 1989), p. 453.
78. Peter K. Manning, "The Researcher: An Alien in the Police World," in *The Ambivalent Force: Perspectives on the Police,* 2nd ed. (Hinsdale, IL: Dryden Press, 1976), pp. 103–21.
79. Herman Goldstein, *Problem-Oriented Policing* (New York: McGraw-Hill, 1990), p. 9.
80. William G. Doerner, *Introduction to Law Enforcement: An Insider's View* (Englewood Cliffs, NJ: Prentice Hall, 1992), pp. 21–23.
81. Samuel Walker, "'Broken Windows' and Fractured History: The Use and Misuse of History in Recent Police Patrol Analysis," in *Classics in Policing,* ed. Steven G. Brandl and David E. Barlow (Cincinnati, OH: Anderson, 1996), pp. 97–110.
82. Thomas J. Baker, "Designing the Job to Motivate," *FBI Law Enforcement Bulletin* 45 (1976): 3–7.
83. Police Foundation, *The Newark Foot Patrol Experiment* (Washington, DC: Author, 1981).
84. Ibid., p. 71.
85. Benjamin S. Bloom, *Taxonomy of Educational Objectives, Handbook I: The Cognitive Domain* (New York: David McKay, 1956).

Federal and State Agencies

Federal and State Agencies

PROTECTING OUR BORDERS

Islamic governments have never and will never be established through peaceful solutions and cooperative councils. They are established as they always have been . . . by pen and gun . . . by word and bullet . . . by tongue and teeth.

—*Terrorist manual*

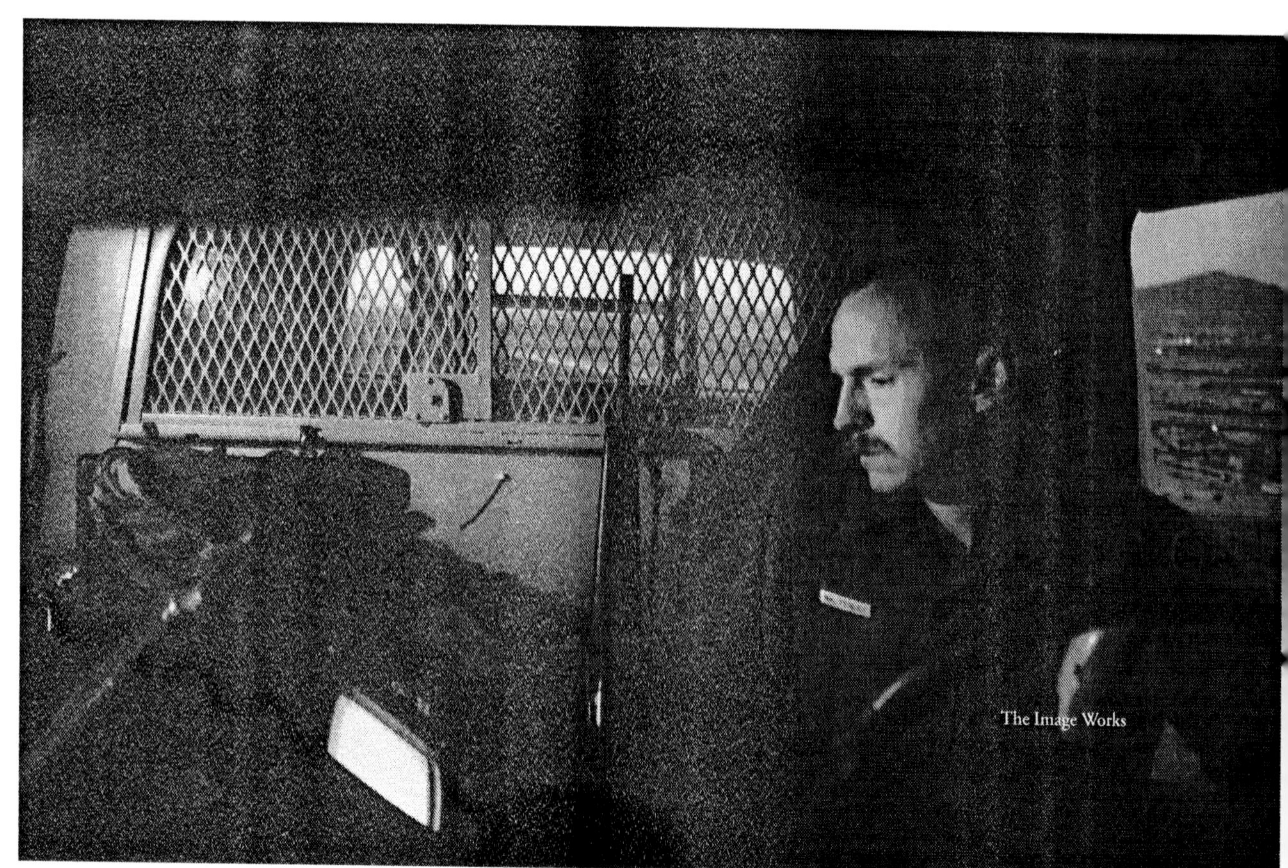

The Image Works

Learning Objectives

AS A RESULT OF READING THIS CHAPTER, THE STUDENT WILL:

- Be aware of the major organizations that compose the Department of Homeland Security and their primary functions
- Know the functions of the primary law enforcement agencies within the Department of Justice as well as other major federal and state organizations
- Know where and how federal agents are trained
- Understand the purposes of the Uniform Crime Reports and the National Crime Information Center
- Know the types of state-level police and law enforcement agencies as well as their various functions

Introduction

This chapter reflects the impact of the events of September 11, 2001, when foreign terrorists attacked the United States on its own soil. No segment of U.S. society was altered more than the nation's police organizations, particularly the **federal law enforcement agencies**. Therefore, this chapter examines how our federal and state law enforcement agencies are now structured and function, particularly during this time when our nation's very existence depends on the ability to be proactive to prevent more terrorist attacks.

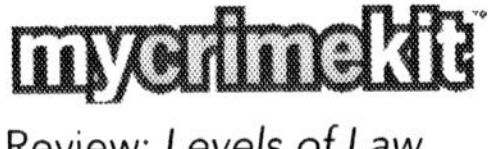

Review: *Levels of Law Enforcement.*

This chapter begins with a broad view of federal law enforcement agencies that possess arrest and firearms authority, and then it focuses on the major agencies and offices that comprise the Department of Homeland Security (DHS). Next is a discussion of the retooled U.S. Department of Justice and its four primary law enforcement organizations: the Federal Bureau of Investigation (FBI); the Bureau of Alcohol, Tobacco, Firearms, and Explosives (ATF); the Drug Enforcement Administration (DEA); and the U.S. Marshals Service (USMS); (included in this chapter section is an exhibit describing the role and functions of the International Criminal Police Organization, or INTERPOL). Then the chapter reviews the functions of three related organizations: the Central Intelligence Agency (CIA); the Criminal Investigation Division of the Internal Revenue Service (IRS); and the Federal Law Enforcement Training Center (FLETC). Next is an overview of state agencies. Included at the chapter's end are a discussion of some career requirements and considerations, a summary, key terms and concepts, review questions, and several scenarios and activities providing opportunities for you to learn by doing.

Federal Law Enforcement Agencies with Arrest and Firearms Authority

This section describes the major law enforcement arms of the federal government, most of which are found within DHS and the Department of Justice. Bear in mind that a number of other federal agencies—such as the U.S. Postal Service, the Veterans Administration, National Park Service, U.S. Capitol Police, Bureau of Indian Affairs, U.S. Fish and Wildlife Service, and U.S. Forest Service—also employ full-time officers with authority to carry firearms and make arrests.

Agencies Within the Department of Homeland Security

To combat terrorism in the aftermath of September 11, the **Department of Homeland Security (DHS)** was formed by H.R. 5005, the Homeland Security Act of 2002. DHS was activated in January 2003 and immediately put 80,000 new federal employees to work and committed $32 billion toward safeguarding the nation, developing vaccines to protect against biological or chemical threats, training and equipping first responders (local police, firefighters, and medical personnel), and funding science and technology projects to counter the use of biological weapons and assess vulnerabilities. Since 2003, more than $100 billion has been appropriated by the federal government to support homeland security. Figure 1 shows the current organizational structure of DHS.[1]

An overhead view of Ground Zero on 9/11. *(Courtesy U.S. Customs and Border Protection, photographer James Tourtellotte)*

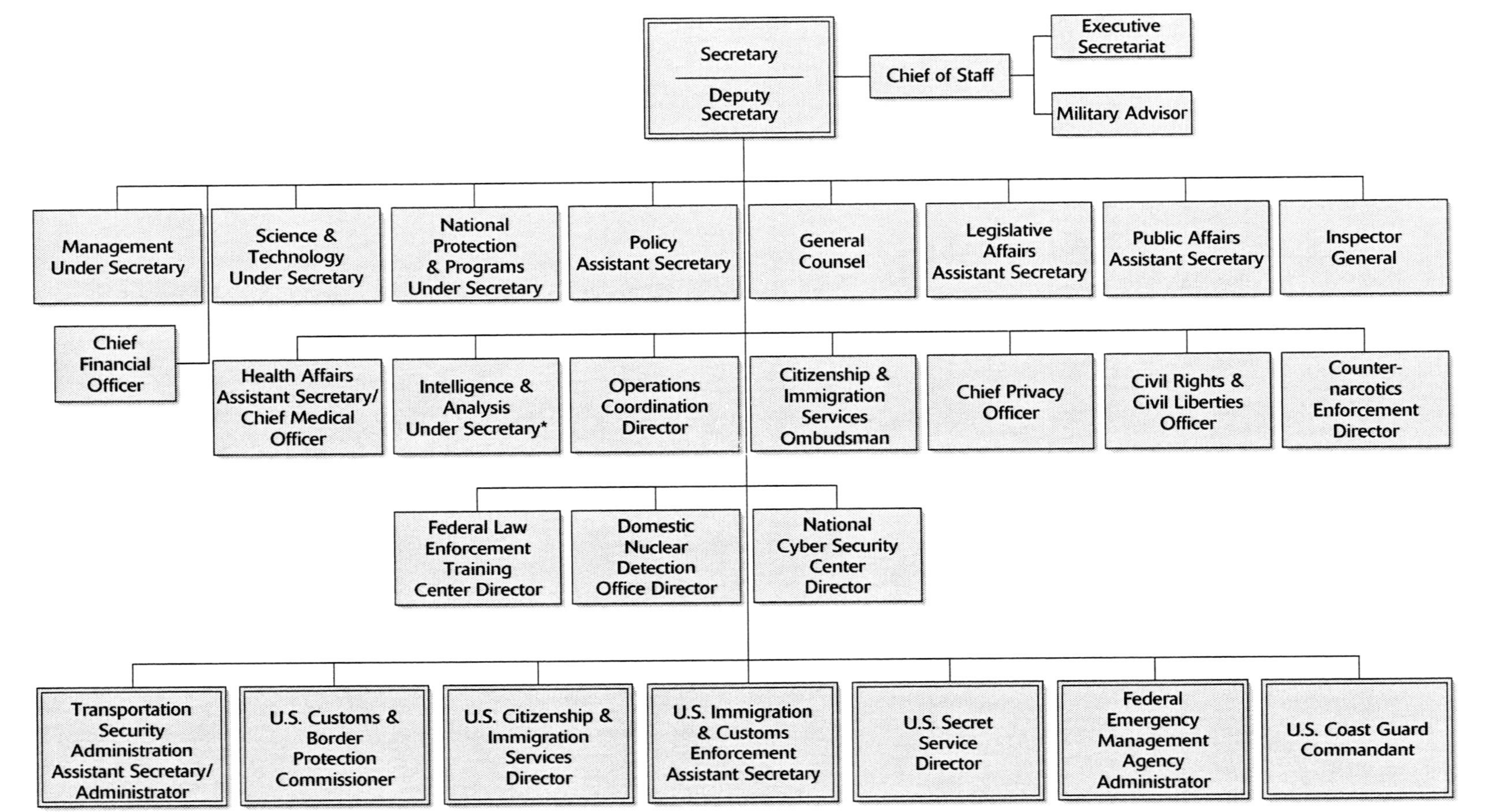

Figure 1
U.S. Department of Homeland Security Organizational Chart

Source: U.S. Department of Homeland Security, www.dhs.gov/xlibrary/assets/DHS_OrgChart.pdf (accessed July 26, 2010).

Following are brief descriptions of the major agencies that compose the DHS:

- The *Directorate for National Protection and Programs* consists of five divisions and works to advance DHS's risk-reduction mission. Reducing risk requires an integrated approach that encompasses both physical and virtual threats and their associated human elements.
- The *Science and Technology Directorate* is the primary research and development arm of the department. It provides federal, state, and local officials with the technology and capabilities to protect the homeland.
- The *Office of Health Affairs* coordinates all DHS medical activities to ensure appropriate preparation for and response to incidents having medical significance.
- The *Federal Emergency Management Agency (FEMA) Directorate* prepares the nation for hazards, manages federal response and recovery efforts following any national incident, and administers the National Flood Insurance Program.
- *U.S. Customs and Border Protection (CBP)* is one of the largest federal law enforcement agencies, with more than 17,000 Border Patrol agents, 1,000 CBP

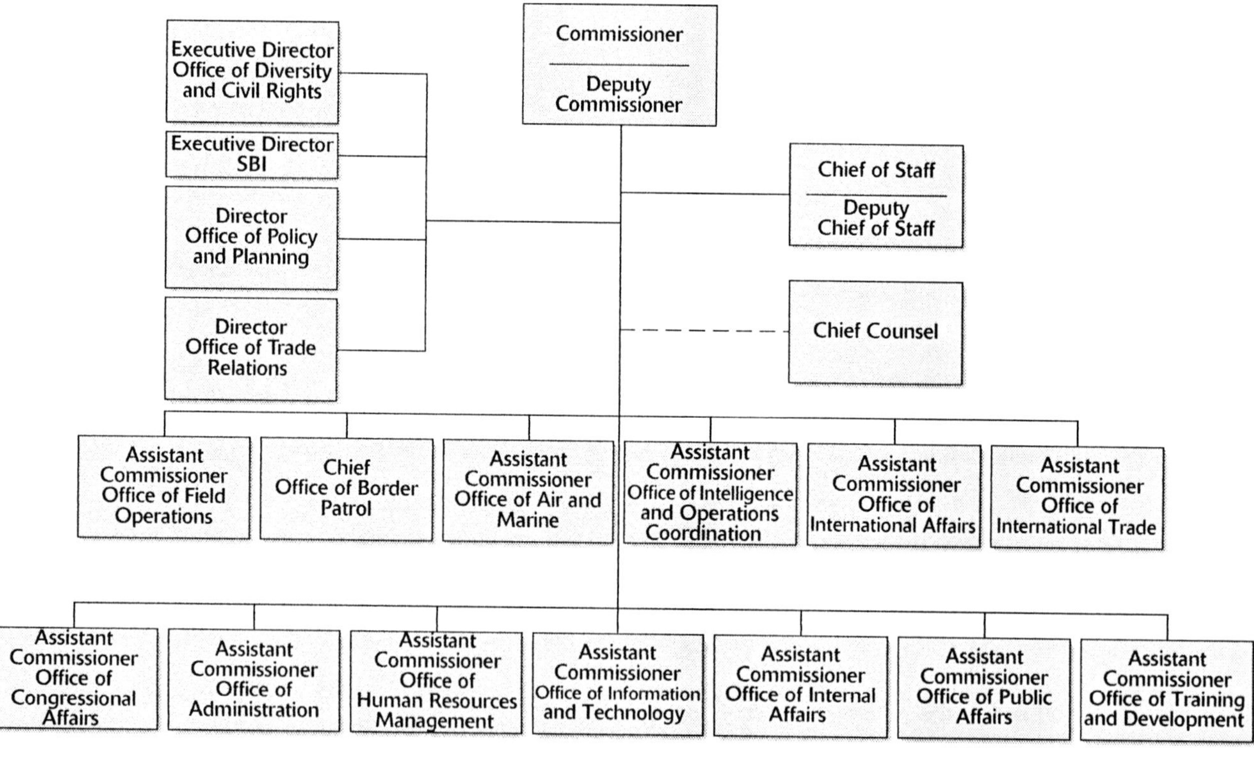

Figure 2

U.S. Customs and Border Protection Organizational Chart

Source: U.S. Customs and Border Protection, www.cbp.gov/linkhandler/cgov/about/organization/orgcha1.ctt/orgcha1.pdf (accessed July 26, 2010).

air and marine agents, and almost 22,000 CBP officers and agriculture specialists, together with the nation's largest law enforcement canine program. To prevent terrorists and terrorist weapons from entering the United States, CBP is responsible for protecting U.S. borders, while simultaneously facilitating the flow of legitimate trade and travel. On a typical day the CBP will process more than a million passengers and pedestrians, execute more than 70 arrests at ports of entry, and seize 7,600 pounds of narcotics in 70 seizures at its 317 ports of entry. The CBP protects nearly 7,000 miles of border with Canada and Mexico and 95,000 miles of shoreline.[2]

Figure 2 shows the organizational structure of CBP, and the Career Profile briefly describes the work of a Border Patrol agent.

- *Immigration and Customs Enforcement (ICE)* is the largest investigative arm of DHS with more than 20,000 employees worldwide. ICE is responsible for identifying and shutting down vulnerabilities both in the nation's borders and in economic, transportation, and infrastructure security. ICE employees work in offices nationally and around the world. The following

mycrimekit™
Video: *Career Profile: ICE Special Agent.*

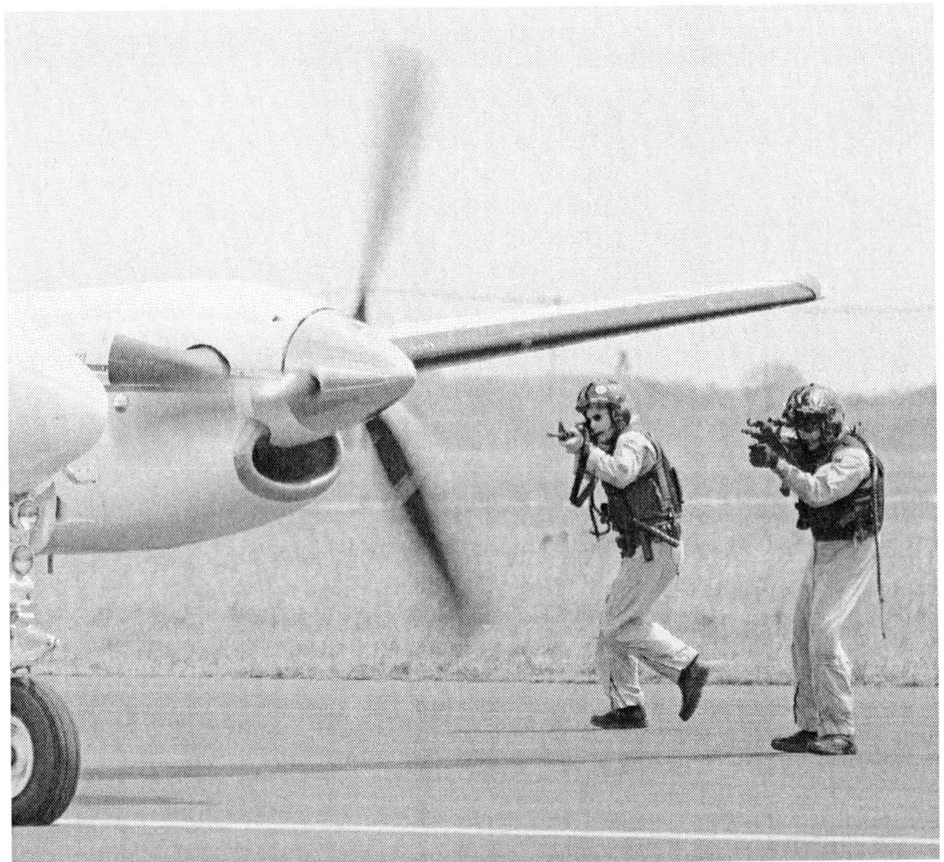

CBP agents make an enforcement stop of an airplane. *(Courtesy U.S. Customs and Border Protection, photographer James Tourtellotte)*

CAREER PROFILE

Name: Spencer Oswald

Position: Customs and Border Patrol Agent

City, State: El Paso, TX

College attended: University of South Alabama

Majors: Criminal Justice and Spanish

Year hired: 2008

Please give a brief description of your job:

Apprehending terrorists and terrorist weapons illegally entering the United States. Detect, apprehend, and deter smugglers of humans, drugs, and contraband.

What appealed to you most about the position, when you applied for it?

The adventure and excitement. This position allows me to use my education in criminal justice and Spanish. I also wanted to serve my country and help make it a safer place to live.

How would you describe the interview process?

The interview was intense and focused mainly upon my ability to make decisions quickly. This included determining the most appropriate course of action in difficult, stressful, and life-threatening situations. These decisions must always be made with a concern for personal and public safety.

What is a typical day like?

No two days are the same, but typically I work a ten-hour shift. The work setting varies depending on the geographic area assigned. Sometimes I am in the desert looking for signs of illegal entry. At other times I may be in a city questioning suspicious individuals at a bus stop. Agents usually work alone, but sometimes an agent can be part of a large operation involving numerous federal and local police agencies.

What qualities/characteristics are most helpful for this job?

The ability to speak Spanish is an absolute requirement. An agent must communicate in a clear, concise manner whenever engaging the public. It also helps to have a commanding self-presence. When agents appear prepared, well-trained, and professional, they are less likely to have their authority challenged. This increases the level of safety for both agents and the public.

What is a typical starting salary?

New agents are usually assigned at the GS-5 (about $37,000) or GS-7 (about $42,000) levels.

(**Author's note:** New CBP agents are hired at the GL-5, GL-7, or GL-9 grade level, depending on education and experience; the base starting salaries as of mid-2010 are GL-5—$36,658; GL-7—$41,729, and GL-9—$46,542.)

What is the salary potential as you move up into higher-level jobs?

The Border Patrol has noncompetitive pay grades, meaning that an agent will be promoted every year until he or she reaches the GS-12 level, which usually takes about three and a half years. However, if an agent demonstrates extraordinary ability, a supervisor can recommend him or her for an early promotion. Currently, a GS-12's salary is $75,000 and can increase to about $96,000.

What career advice would you give someone in college beginning to study criminal justice?

Take your classes seriously, and take plenty of writing-intensive classes to develop effective writing skills. These are crucial for writing reports and documents on the job. Supervisors and other members of the criminal justice system review these documents.

As mentioned, it is also crucial to be able to converse in Spanish. The Border Patrol will provide you with language training, but it is fast paced and tends to focus on giving commands rather than conversing. Take as many Spanish classes as possible. I would also recommend enrolling in a study-abroad program for immersion in a Spanish-speaking culture.

Be familiar with the U.S. Constitution. Actually sit down and read it from start to finish. To do so is often an eye-opening experience. Familiarity with immigration and nationality law is also useful, so take plenty of legal and pre-law classes.

four main branches of ICE work with other law enforcement and intelligence entities:

- *The Office of Investigations* investigates a wide range of domestic and international activities that violate immigration and customs laws and threaten national security.

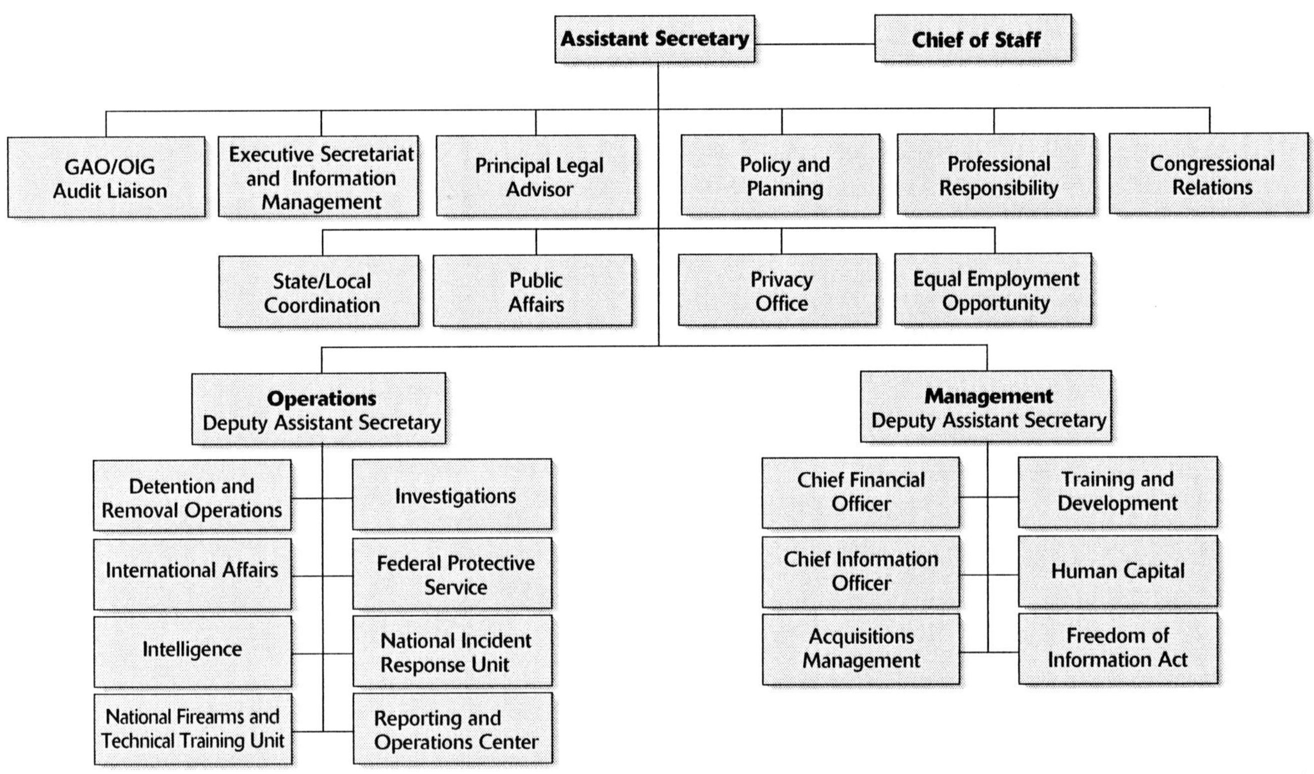

Figure 3
U.S. Immigration and Customs Enforcement Organizational Chart
Source: U.S. Immigration and Customs Enforcement, www.ice.gov/about/leadership/index.htm (accessed July 26, 2010).

- The *Office of Detention and Removal Operations* ensures the departure from the United States of all illegal aliens through the fair enforcement of the nation's immigration laws.
- The *Federal Protective Service* is responsible for policing, securing, and ensuring a safe environment in which federal agencies can conduct their business at more than 8,800 federal facilities nationwide.
- The *Office of Intelligence* collects, analyzes, and disseminates strategic and tactical intelligence data.[3]

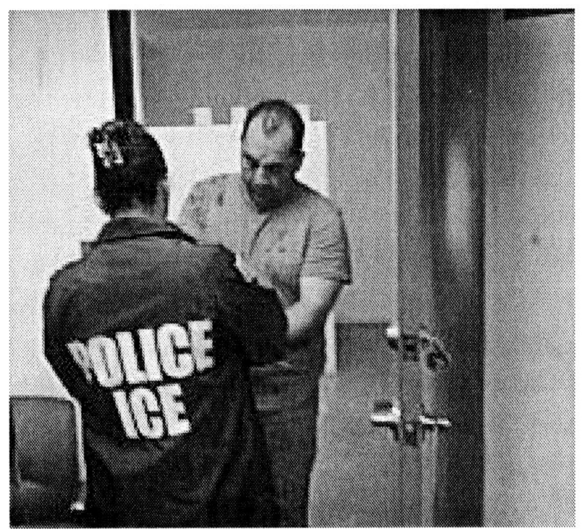

An ICE agent takes a suspect into custody. *(Courtesy Immigration and Customs Enforcement)*

- The *Office of Intelligence and Analysis* is responsible for using information and intelligence from multiple sources to identify and assess current and future threats to the United States.
- The *Office of Operations Coordination* is responsible for monitoring the security of the United States on a daily basis and coordinating activities within the department and with governors, DHS advisors, law enforcement partners, and

critical infrastructure operators in all fifty states and more than fifty major urban areas nationwide.

- The *Domestic Nuclear Detection Office* works to enhance the nuclear detection efforts of federal, state, territorial, tribal, and local governments and the private sector and to ensure a coordinated response to such threats.
- The *Transportation Security Administration (TSA)* protects the nation's transportation systems. TSA employs 48,000 personnel at 457 airports who screen approximately two million people per day to ensure travel safety. Agents also inspect air carrier operations to the United States, assess security of airports overseas, fly air marshal missions, and train overseas security personnel.[4]
- The *Federal Law Enforcement Training Center (FLETC)* provides career-long training to law enforcement professionals to help them fulfill their responsibilities safely and proficiently. FLETC serves as an interagency law enforcement training organization for more than 85 federal agencies; provides services to state, local, and international law enforcement agencies; and graduates approximately 25,000 students per year. The center is headquartered at Glynco, Georgia.[5]
- The *Citizenship and Immigration Services* is responsible for the administration of immigration and naturalization adjudication functions and the establishment of immigration services policies and priorities.
- The *Coast Guard* protects the public, the environment, and U.S. economic interests in the nation's ports, on its waterways, along the coast, on international waters, or in any maritime region as required to support national security.
- The *Secret Service* protects the president and other high-level officials and investigates counterfeiting and other financial crimes, including financial institution fraud, identity theft, computer fraud, and computer-based attacks on our nation's financial, banking, and telecommunications infrastructure. The Secret Service's Uniformed Division protects the White House complex and the vice president's residence as well as foreign embassies and missions in the Washington, D.C., area. The Secret Service has agents assigned to approximately 125 offices located in cities throughout the United States and in select foreign cities.[6]

See Exhibit 1 for information on INTERPOL.

The Department of Justice

The **Department of Justice** is headed by the attorney general, who is appointed by the U.S. president and approved by the Senate. The president also appoints the attorney general's assistants and the U.S. attorneys for each of the judicial districts. The U.S. attorneys in each judicial district control and supervise all federal criminal prosecutions and represent the government in legal suits in which it is a party. These attorneys may appoint committees to investigate other governmental agencies or offices when questions of wrongdoing are raised or when possible violations of federal law are suspected or detected.

EXHIBIT 1

Interpol

The official seal of INTERPOL.
(Courtesy INTERPOL)

INTERPOL is the oldest, the best-known, and probably the only truly international crime-fighting organization for crimes committed on an international scale, such as drug trafficking, bank fraud, money laundering, and counterfeiting. INTERPOL agents do not patrol the globe, nor do they make arrests or engage in shootouts. They are basically intelligence gatherers who have helped many nations work together in attacking international crime since 1923.[1]

Lyon, France, serves as the headquarters for INTERPOL's crime-fighting tasks and its 188 member countries.[2] Today INTERPOL has six priority crime areas: corruption, drugs and organized crime, financial and high-tech crime, fugitives, public safety and terrorism, and trafficking in human beings. It also manages a range of databases with information on names and photographs of known criminals, wanted persons, fingerprints, DNA profiles, stolen or lost travel documents, stolen motor vehicles, child sex abuse images, and stolen works of art. INTERPOL also disseminates critical crime-related data through its system of international notices. There are seven kinds of notices, of which the most well-known is the Red Notice, an international request for an individual's arrest.[3]

INTERPOL has one cardinal rule: It deals only with common criminals; it does not become involved with political, racial, or religious matters. It has a basic three-step formula for offenses that all nations must follow for success: pass laws specifying the offense is a crime; prosecute offenders and cooperate in other countries' prosecutions; and furnish INTERPOL with and exchange information about crime and its perpetrators. This formula could reverse the trend that is forecast for the world at present: an increasing capability by criminals for violence and destruction. The following crimes, because they are recognized as crimes by other countries, are covered by almost all U.S. treaties of extradition: murder, rape, bigamy, arson, robbery, burglary, forgery, counterfeiting, embezzlement, larceny, fraud, perjury, and kidnapping.[4]

INTERPOL's annual report may be viewed at: www.interpol.int/Public/ICPO/InterpolAtWork/iaw2008.pdf

1. "INTERPOL: An Overview," www.interpol.int/Public/ICPO/FactSheets/GI01.pdf (accessed July 10, 2010).
2. Ibid.
3. Ibid.
4. Michael Fooner, *INTERPOL: Issues in World Crime and International Criminal Justice* (New York: Plenum Press, 1989), p. 179.

The Department of Justice is the official legal arm of the government of the United States. Within the Justice Department are several law enforcement organizations that investigate violations of federal laws; we will discuss the Federal Bureau of Investigation; Bureau of Alcohol, Tobacco, Firearms, and Explosives; Drug Enforcement Administration; and U.S. Marshals Service.

Figure 4 shows the organizational chart for the Department of Justice.

Federal Bureau of Investigation (FBI)

Beginnings

The FBI was created and funded through the Department of Justice Appropriation Act of 1908. The FBI was first known as the Bureau of Investigation. With thirty-five agents,

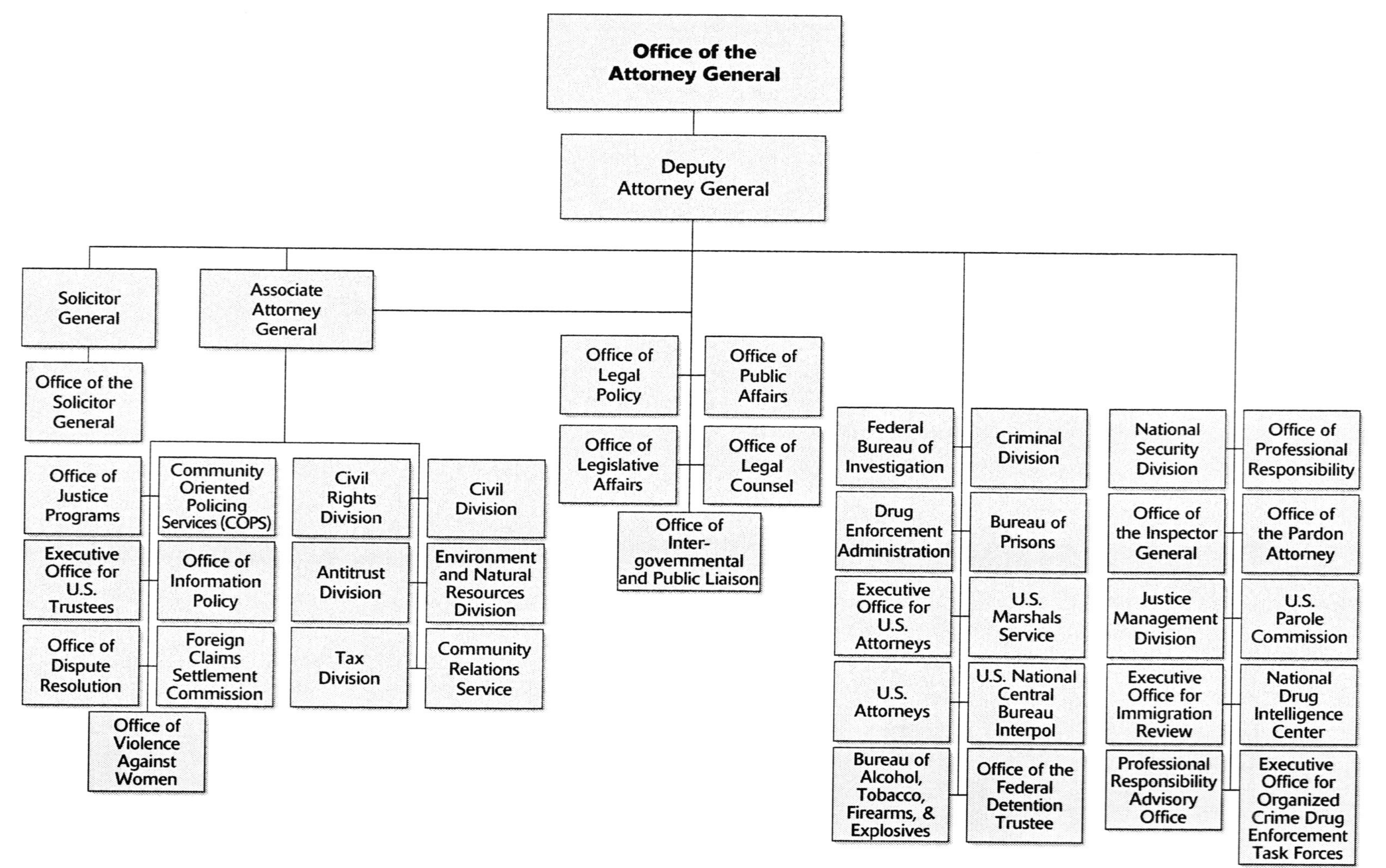

Figure 4

Department of Justice, Office of the Attorney General, Organizational Chart

Source: Department of Justice, www.justice.gov/agencies/index-org.html (accessed July 26, 2010).

it originally had no specific duties other than the "prosecution of crimes," focusing on bankruptcy fraud, antitrust crimes, neutrality violations, and crimes on Native American reservations. Espionage and sabotage incidents during World War I, coupled with charges of political corruption reaching into the Department of Justice and the bureau itself, prompted angry demands for drastic changes.[7]

J. Edgar Hoover. *(Courtesy FBI)*

A new era was begun for the FBI in 1924 with the appointment of J. Edgar Hoover as director; he served in that capacity until his death in 1972. Hoover was determined that the organization would become a career service in which appointments would be made strictly on personal qualifications and abilities, and promotions would be based on merit. Special agents were college graduates, preferably with degrees in law or accounting. A rigorous course of training had to be completed, and agents had to be available for assignment wherever their services might be needed. Hoover coordinated the development of the Uniform Crime Reporting system, and during his tenure in office many notorious criminals, such as Bonnie Parker, Clyde Barrow, and John Dillinger, were tracked and captured or killed. The building housing the FBI Headquarters in Washington, D.C., bears his name.[8]

The bureau's Identification Division was created on July 1, 1924, and its laboratory opened in 1932. Then, in 1933, all of the bureau's functions were consolidated and transferred to a Division of Investigation, which became the Federal Bureau of Investigation on March 22, 1935.

Contemporary Priorities and Roles

Today the FBI has fifty-six field offices, approximately four hundred resident agencies, and more than fifty foreign liaison posts called legal attachés. About 19,500 nonsworn employees perform professional, administrative, technical, or other functions in support of the FBI's 13,000 sworn special agents.[9]

The national priorities of the FBI have been modified in major fashion since September 11, 2001; today the following are its top three priority areas:[10]

1. Counterterrorism: to neutralize terrorist cells and operatives in the United States and to help dismantle terrorist networks worldwide.
2. Counterintelligence: exposing, preventing, and investigating intelligence activities on U.S. soil; foreign espionage strikes at the heart of national security, impacting political, military, and economic strengths.
3. Cybercrime: to stop serious computer intrusions and the spread of malicious codes; to identify and thwart online sexual predators who meet and exploit children and deal in child pornography; and to dismantle criminal enterprises engaging in Internet fraud.

Other priorities include combating public corruption, civil rights violations (e.g., hate crimes, human trafficking), organized crime, white-collar crime, and major thefts/violent crimes.

Figure 5
Federal Bureau of Investigation Organizational Chart
Source: Federal Bureau of Investigation, www.fbi.gov/aboutus/todaysfbi/org_chart.jpg (accessed July 26, 2010).

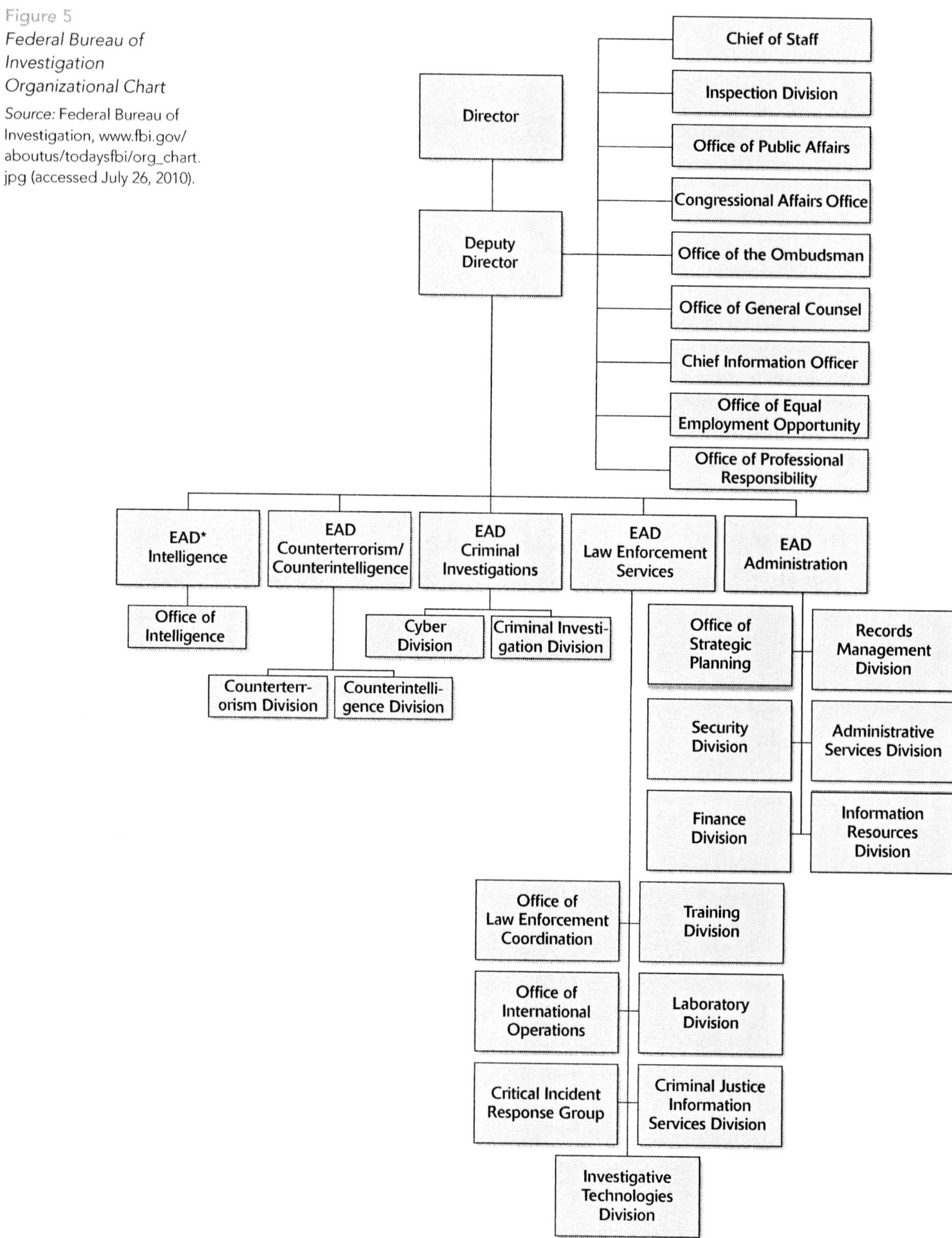

Recently, the FBI was given new powers to aid its reform efforts to battle terrorism. The bureau can now monitor Internet sites, libraries, churches, and political organizations. In addition, under revamped guidelines, agents can attend public meetings for the purpose of preventing terrorism.[11] The bureau also participates with local police in dozens of task forces that target fugitives and violent gangs nationwide.

But counterterrorism still constitutes only a fraction of the bureau's workload; the FBI also continues to investigate bank robberies, white-collar crimes, and organized crime and drug syndicates—staples of the agency's workload for a long time—while it combats radical Islamic fundamentalism and global terrorism with a workforce in which just 1 percent of the FBI's 12,200 agents have any familiarity with the Arabic language.[12]

Ancillary Investigative, Training, and Reporting Services

Today the FBI's laboratory examines blood, hair, firearms, paint, handwriting, typewriters, and other types of evidence. Highly specialized techniques are now utilized—at no charge to state police and local police agencies—for analysis of DNA, explosives, hairs and fibers, tool marks, drugs, plastics, and bloodstains.

Another feature of the bureau is its National Academy, which graduated its first class in 1935. Today thousands of local police managers from across the country have received training at the National Academy in Quantico, Virginia, which has twenty-one buildings on 385 acres. The FBI also provides extensive professional training to national supervisory-level police officers at the National Academy.

A very successful function of the FBI, inaugurated in 1950, is its "Ten Most Wanted Fugitives" list, which over the years has contained many notable fugitives. As of 2000, the bureau had caught about 460 top ten fugitives; the Internet has helped to invigorate the program, with the "Ten Most Wanted" Web page receiving about 25 million hits per month.[13]

The FBI also operates the **National Crime Information Center (NCIC)**, through which millions of records relating to stolen property and missing persons and fugitives are instantaneously available to local, state, and federal authorities across the United States and Canada. Following are some of the categories of individuals and items that are included in the NCIC files.[14]

1. Categories of individuals covered by the system:
   - Wanted persons (for whom warrants are outstanding, who have committed or have been identified with a felony or serious misdemeanor offense); an escaped or wanted juvenile; missing persons (e.g., those with proven physical/mental disability or who are senile, or who are possibly kidnapped, are missing after a catastrophe, are members of violent criminal gangs or terrorist organizations), and unidentified deceased persons.
2. Categories of records in the system:
   - Stolen vehicles, vehicle parts or plates, boats, guns, articles, securities, and vehicles wanted in conjunction with felonies or serious misdemeanors.

In a related vein, one of the FBI's several annual publications is the **Uniform Crime Reports (UCR)**, which includes crime data reported from more than fifteen thousand state and local police agencies concerning twenty-nine types of offenses: eight Part I (or index) offenses (criminal homicide, forcible rape, robbery, aggravated assault, burglary, larceny–theft, motor vehicle theft, and arson) and twenty-one Part II offenses. The UCR also includes a so-called crime clock, shown in Figure 6.

Several shortcomings characterize the UCR data, however. First, the data are dependent on crimes being reported to, and by, the police; many crime victims do not report their victimization to the police, so there is the so-called shadow of crime—those crimes that are hidden and unknown. Furthermore, the reporting system is not uniform, so crimes may be reported incorrectly or inaccurately. In addition, the UCR operates under the hierarchy rule, which means that when a number of separate crimes are committed as part of a single act (e.g., a burglar enters a home and then, at gunpoint, robs the residents living there, and then murders one of them when a struggle ensues), only the most serious crime—the murder—will be reported to the FBI. At best, UCR has several limitations and must be used cautiously.

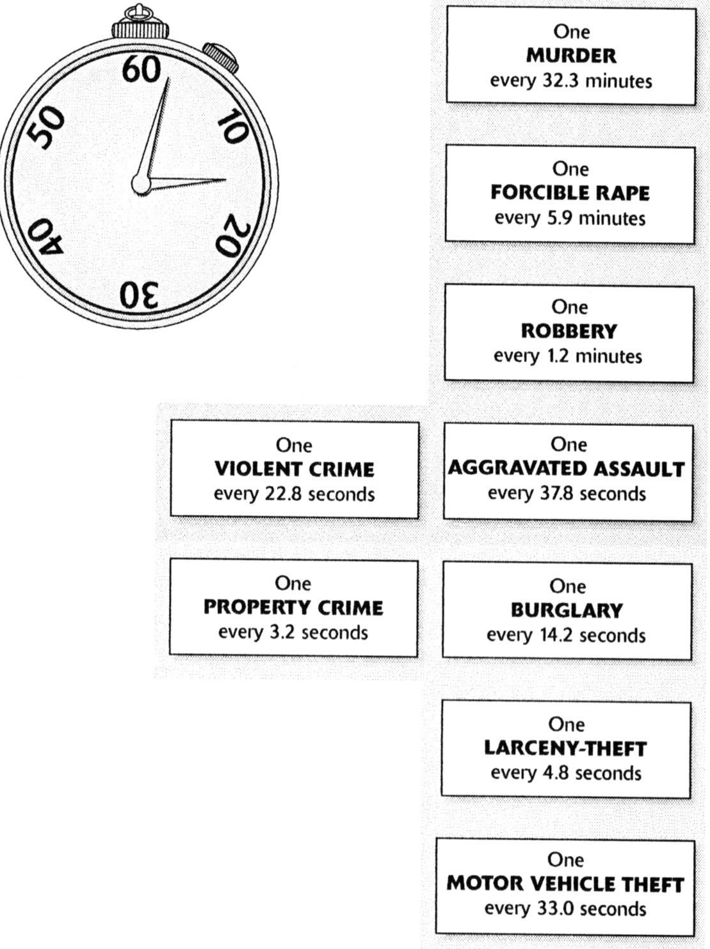

60
10
20
30
40
50
One
MURDER
every 32.3 minutes
One
FORCIBLE RAPE
every 5.9 minutes
One
ROBBERY
every 1.2 minutes
One
VIOLENT CRIME
every 22.8 seconds
One
AGGRAVATED ASSAULT
every 37.8 seconds
One
PROPERTY CRIME
every 3.2 seconds
One
BURGLARY
every 14.2 seconds
One
LARCENY-THEFT
every 4.8 seconds
One
MOTOR VEHICLE THEFT
every 33.0 seconds

Figure 6
Crime Clock Statistics
Source: Federal Bureau of Investigation, fbi.gov/ucr/cius2008/about/crime_clock.html (accessed July 26, 2010).

A large amount of information concerning the FBI's application and hiring process—including its minimum requirements and the kinds of knowledge, skills, and abilities it is now seeking for special agents and professional staff—is available on the agency's Web site at www.fbijobs.gov/1.asp.

Bureau of Alcohol, Tobacco, Firearms, and Explosives (ATF)

mycrimekit

Video: *Career Profile: ATF Agent.*

The ATF originated as a unit within the IRS in 1862, when certain alcohol and tobacco tax statutes were created. The next year, Congress authorized the hiring of three "detectives" to aid in the prevention, detection, and punishment of tax evaders. Originally called the Alcohol, Tobacco, Tax Unit, it eventually became the Alcohol, Tobacco, and Firearms Division within the IRS. In 1972, it became the Bureau of Alcohol, Tobacco, and Firearms, under the direct control of the Treasury Department; in January 2003, it was moved to the Justice Department and renamed the Bureau of Alcohol, Tobacco, Firearms, and Explosives.[15]

Like the FBI and several other federal agencies, the ATF has a rich and colorful history, much of which has involved capturing bootleggers and disposing of illegal whiskey stills during Prohibition.[16] From 1920 to 1933, congressional Prohibition legislation (the Volstead Act) made it illegal to manufacture, possess, or sell intoxicating liquors in the United States (with a few exceptions). Still, the country was awash with liquor. History is replete with accounts of violations of Prohibition laws; much has been written and portrayed in movies of that era, when the moonshiners tried to outsmart and outrun the law.[17] Speakeasies (secret bars) proliferated across America to satisfy the American yearning for liquor. This era bolstered the popularity of such G-men (short for "government man," meaning a federal agent) as Eliot Ness; the 1960s television program and later film *The Untouchables* were inspired by his career.

The ATF administers the U.S. Criminal Code provisions concerning alcohol and tobacco smuggling and diversion. The ATF is also responsible for enforcing all federal laws relating to firearms, explosives, and arson. ATF agents work with federal, state, and local law enforcement organizations and seek to battle terrorism, prevent crime, conduct fair and effective industry regulation, and provide training and expertise to federal, state, local, and international law enforcement partners. The Homeland Security Act of 2002 transferred these enforcement activities of the ATF, along with certain other functions, from the Department of the Treasury to the Department of Justice. ATF's sworn and nonsworn personnel work primarily in twenty-three field divisions across the fifty states, with offices as well in Guam, the Virgin Islands, Puerto Rico, Mexico, Canada, Colombia, and France.[18]

ATF also maintains a Bomb and Arson Tracking System, which allows local, state, and other federal agencies to share information about bomb and arson cases; four National Response Teams of highly trained agents that can be deployed to major explosion and fire scenes in the United States; an International Response Team that provides assistance in other countries; thirty-two explosives-detection canine teams; and three national laboratory facilities.[19]

mycrimekit

Video: *Career Profile: DEA Agent.*

Drug Enforcement Administration (DEA)

The DEA began with the passage of the Harrison Narcotic Act, signed into law on December 17, 1914, by President Woodrow Wilson. The act made it unlawful for any "nonregistered" person to possess heroin, cocaine, opium, morphine, or any of their by-products. Drug enforcement began in 1915, and during that first year, agents seized forty-four pounds of heroin and achieved 106 convictions (mostly the result of illicit activities of physicians).[20]

In the 1920s, federal narcotics agents focused on organized gangs of Chinese immigrants suspected of importing opium. In 1920, Prohibition was enacted; the Narcotics Division of the Prohibition Unit of the Revenue Bureau consisted of 170 agents working out of seventeen offices around the country. New authority was granted to agents by the Narcotic Drugs Import and Export Act of 1922.

Today's DEA is also an outgrowth of the former Bureau of Narcotics, which was established in 1930 under the direct control of the Treasury Department. In 1968, the Bureau of Narcotics was transferred from the Treasury to the Department of Justice and was renamed the Bureau of Narcotics and Dangerous Drugs. In 1973, the DEA was established under a plan that combined the functions of several agencies. In January 1982, the DEA was given primary responsibility for drug and narcotics enforcement, sharing this jurisdiction with the FBI.

The major responsibilities of the DEA's 5,200 agents, under the U.S. Code, include the following:[21]

- Full investigation and preparation for the prosecution of suspects connected with illicit drugs seized at U.S. ports of entry and international borders
- Conduct of all relations with drug-enforcement officials of foreign governments
- Full coordination and cooperation with state and local police officials on joint drug-enforcement efforts
- Regulation of the legal manufacture of drugs and other controlled substances

The DEA maintains 227 domestic offices in 21 divisions throughout the United States and 87 foreign offices in 63 countries.[22] Figure 7 depicts DEA's various programs and operations.

mycrimekit

Video: *Career Profile: US Marshal.*

U.S. Marshals Service (USMS)

The USMS is one of the oldest federal law enforcement agencies, established under the Judiciary Act of 1789; George Washington appointed thirteen marshals, one for each of the original thirteen states. The USMS formally assumed the responsibility for the apprehension of federal fugitives in 1979.[23]

Today the USMS has ninety-four U.S. marshals, one for each federal court district. Each district headquarters office is managed by a politically appointed U.S. marshal and a chief deputy U.S. marshal, who direct a staff of supervisors, investigators, deputy marshals, and administrative personnel. As in the so-called Wild West, the backbone of the USMS today is the deputy U.S. marshals—numbering about 3,300 deputy U.S. marshals and criminal investigators today—who pursue and arrest fugitives (about 36,000 per year) wanted for federal violations; pursue escaped federal

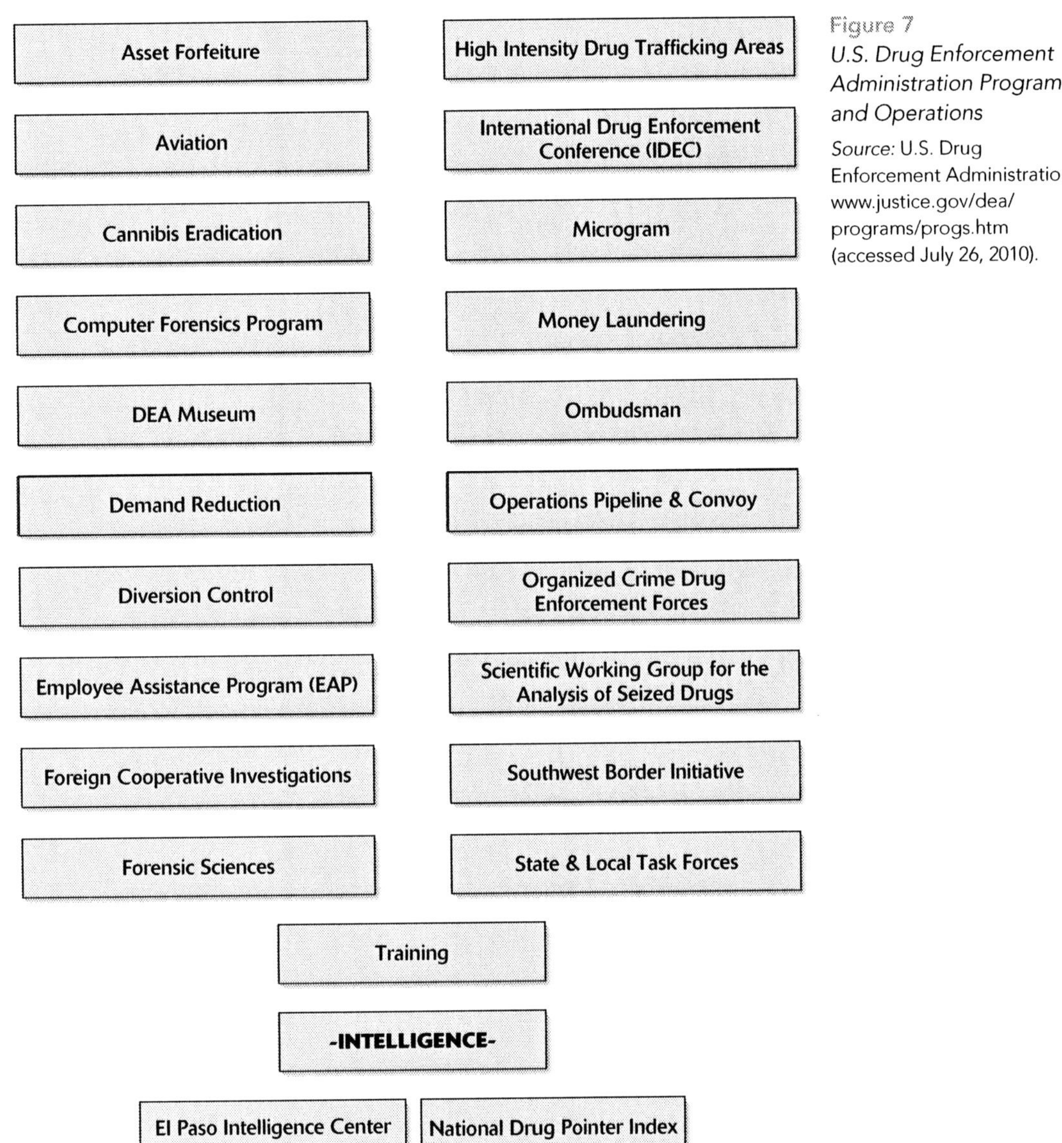

Figure 7
U.S. Drug Enforcement Administration Programs and Operations
Source: U.S. Drug Enforcement Administration, www.justice.gov/dea/programs/progs.htm (accessed July 26, 2010).

prisoners; transport federal prisoners (about 380,000 per year); and provide a secure environment for judges, attorneys, witnesses, and others in the federal courts.[24]

In 1971, the USMS created the Special Operations Group (SOG), consisting of a well-trained elite group of deputy marshals. The group provides support in priority or dangerous situations, such as the movement of a large group of high-risk prisoners, and at trials involving alleged drug traffickers or members of subversive groups. Another important function of the USMS is the operation of the Witness Protection Program. Federal witnesses are sometimes threatened by defendants or their associates (for example, they sometimes testify against organized crime figures). If certain criteria are met, the USMS will provide a complete change of identity for witnesses and their families, including new Social Security numbers, residences, and employment. This protection program was established in 1970.[25]

Other Federal Agencies

Central Intelligence Agency (CIA)

Although not a law enforcement agency, the CIA is of significance at the federal level to the nation's security and warrants a brief discussion. The National Security Act of 1947 established the National Security Council, which in 1949 created a subordinate organization, the CIA. Considered the most clandestine government service, the CIA participates in undercover and covert operations around the world for the purposes of managing crises and providing intelligence during the conduct of war.[26]

To accomplish its mission, the CIA engages in research and development and deploys high technology for intelligence purposes. After the 2001 terrorist attacks in the United States, the CIA created special centers to address such issues as counterterrorism, counterintelligence, international organized crime and narcotics trafficking, and arms control intelligence.[27]

The CIA is an independent agency responsible through its director to the U.S. president. Using weekly news magazines and its Web site, the agency has recruited applicants for employees in its National Clandestine Service, where employees can have "a career with unmatched opportunities and extraordinary experiences."[28] Applicants must have a bachelor's degree (with a preferred grade-point average of 3.0 or higher) and an interest in international affairs and national security, impeccable integrity, strong interpersonal skills, and excellent written and oral skills. Individuals who are hired with critical language skills can qualify for a hiring bonus of up to $35,000.[29]

Because relatively little is known about this federal agency, its organizational chart is provided at Figure 8.

Internal Revenue Service (IRS)

Video: *Career Profile: IRS Special Agent.*

The IRS has as its main function the monitoring and collection of federal income taxes from American individuals and businesses. Since 1919, the IRS has had a Criminal Investigation (CI) Division employing "accountants with a badge."

The CI branch of the IRS is comprised of approximately 4,400 employees worldwide, approximately 2,800 of whom are special agents whose investigative jurisdiction includes tax, money laundering, and Bank Secrecy Act laws. While other federal agencies also have investigative jurisdiction for money laundering and some bank secrecy act violations, IRS is the only federal agency that can investigate potential criminal violations of the Internal Revenue Code.[30]

The first chief of the Special Intelligence Unit, Inspector Elmer I. Irey, gained notoriety by participating in investigations that included income tax evasion charges against organized crime kingpin Alphonse ("Al") Capone and the kidnapping of Charles Lindbergh's baby in 1932.[31] Since then, the list of celebrated, prosecuted CI "clients" has been impressive and includes federal judges, prominent politicians, and athletes. Indeed, today there is a much greater appreciation for what a financial investigator can do for almost any type of criminal investigation.[32]

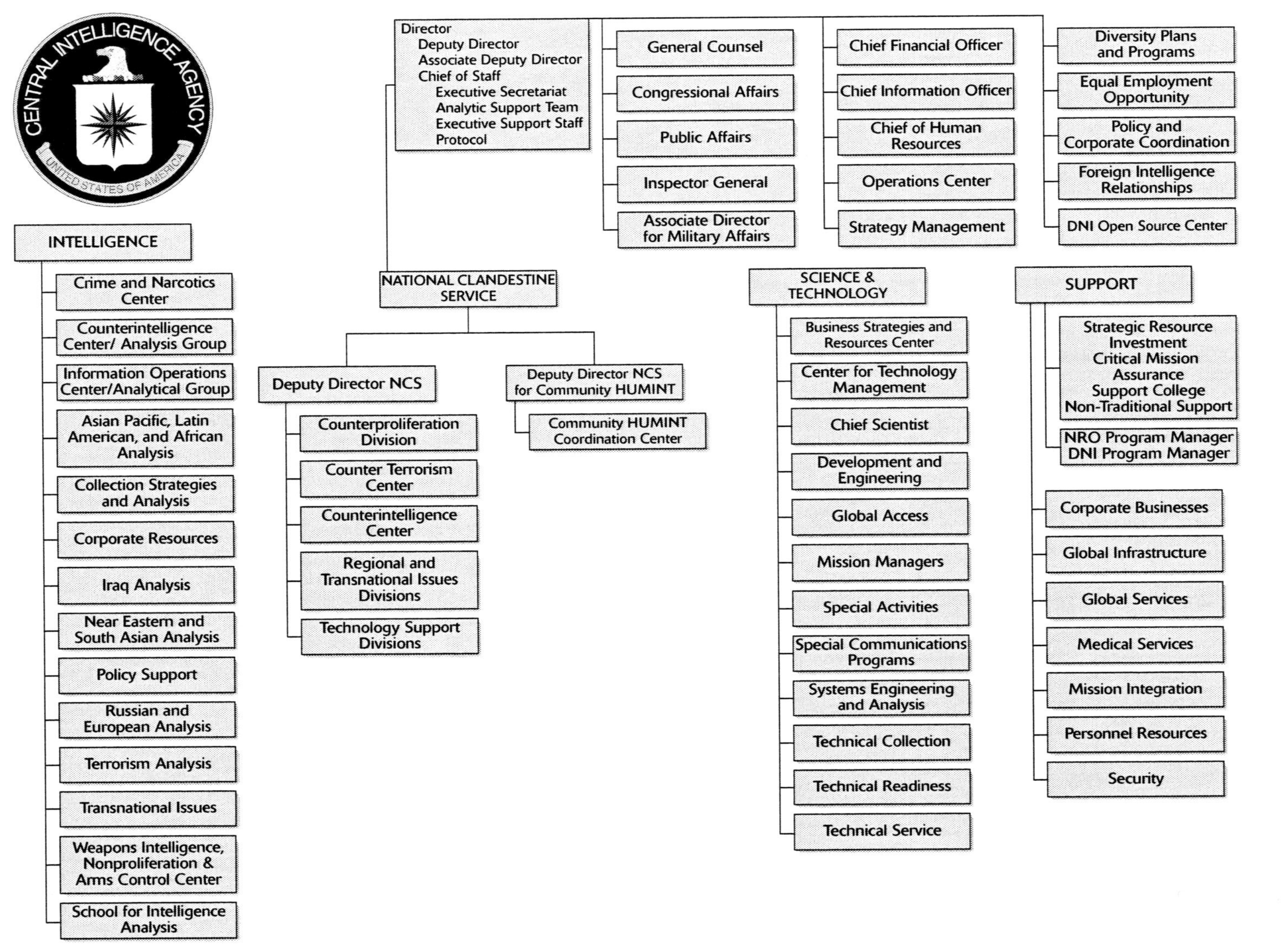

Figure 8
Central Intelligence Agency Organizational Chart
Source: Central Intelligence Agency, www.cia.gov/about-cia/leadership/cia-organization-chart.html (accessed July 26, 2010).

comparative CLOSEUP ▸▸ Police Role and Accountability in China

Drug traffickers are escorted by Chinese police during a trial at Guangzhou's Intermediate People's Court. China marked this anti-drug day by executing sixty-four people accused of drug crimes.
(Courtesy AP Wide World Photos)

China—a nation with 1.3 billion people and covering 3.7 million square miles—has traditionally had a police state. Unhindered by constitutional or judicial restraints, police have long operated with virtual impunity, earning a reputation with citizens as unprincipled thugs more concerned about hitting arrest quotas than protecting and serving. But after several highly publicized incidents of malfeasance and incompetence, China's police are undergoing a process of scrutiny and even reform.

In 2004, the Ministry of Public Security banned the use of torture during the interrogation of suspects, abolished "custody-and-repatriation" rules that enabled police to detain migrant workers with little cause, prohibited officers from drinking alcohol while carrying sidearms, and ordered officers out of their stations and into their neighborhoods. Much reform remains to be done, however. A recent study showed that officers in some provinces work an average of 11 hours a day, with only one day off every three weeks. They're often called upon for unlikely duties, such as collecting fines from delinquent taxpayers and from violators of the one-child policy. And they are woefully paid: salaries average $100–$150 per month.[1]

Still, the police keep tight control over the population through the household registration system and extensive surveillances. Every citizen must register his or her residence in a locality with the police; neighborhood committees are established in all neighborhoods. No strangers can enter a neighborhood without being noticed immediately and reported promptly to the police.[2]

1. Adapted from Matt Forney, "Police Under Fire," *Time*, September 29, 2003, www.time.com/time/magazine/article/0,9171,490739,00.html (accessed July 10, 2010).
2. Yue Ma, "The Police Law 1995, Organization, Function, Powers, and Accountability of the Chinese Police," *Policing: An International Journal of Police Strategy and Management* 20 (1997):130–131.

IRS agents are armed; the U.S. Code authorizes them to execute search warrants, make arrests without warrants for tax-related offenses, and seize property related to violations of the tax laws. Agents engage in money-laundering investigations under Title 18 of the U.S. Code and investigate for tax and currency violations any individuals who organize, direct, and finance high-level criminal enterprises.[33]

The CI Division enforces nearly all of the provisions of the Bank Secrecy Act, requiring financial institutions or individuals to report certain domestic and foreign currency transactions to the federal government. The CI Division also enforces the wagering tax laws and conducts investigations related to the pornography industry. Another important area of the division is the Questionable Refund Program, which attempts to detect and stop fictitious claims for tax refunds.

Federal Law Enforcement Training Center (FLETC)

The **Federal Law Enforcement Training Center (FLETC)**, which was established in 1970 and remains part of the U.S. Treasury Department, offers law enforcement training for personnel from many federal agencies. In 1975, the center was located in

Glynco, Georgia, where it occupies a 1,500-acre campus with state-of-the-art classrooms and provides training for about seventy-five U.S. federal law enforcement organizations.[34] Other domestic campuses are located in Artesia, New Mexico; Charleston, South Carolina; and Cheltenham, Maryland.

Like most of the federal agencies discussed in this chapter, FLETC has been struggling to meet new demands placed on it since the September 11 attacks. A significant surge in hiring by federal agencies (particularly in the new Federal Air Marshal Service and Transportation Security Administration) has resulted in an influx of a large number of law enforcement personnel at FLETC's campuses around the country.

In the fiscal year preceding the terrorist attacks, more than 21,000 students spent over 101,000 student weeks of training at FLETC's campuses; in the fiscal year following the attacks, more than 28,000 students spent about 157,000 weeks in training at these campuses. This latter figure represented a 72 percent increase in weeks of training since fiscal year 1999.[35]

To help address the demands placed on FLETC, its annual budget of about $146 million includes 754 full-time staff members.

State Agencies

State Police and Law Enforcement Agencies: General Types

As with federal law enforcement organizations, a variety of police and law enforcement agencies are found in 49 states (Hawaii does not have a state law enforcement organization). Perhaps the first distinction that might be made at the state level is between state police or highway patrol organizations and the **state bureaus of investigation (SBIs)**. State police organizations perform general law enforcement functions and are engaged in patrol, traffic control, crash investigation, and related functions. Although the public typically views state troopers while they are engaged in random patrol and enforcing traffic laws on state highways, troopers actually perform a surprising variety of nontraffic functions. As an example, although the Missouri State Highway Patrol (MSHP) states on its Web site that its troopers provide assistance to motorists and investigate "highway traffic crashes and other roadway emergencies," it also states that "other responsibilities include assisting local peace officers upon request, investigating crimes, and enforcing criminal laws."[36] Figure 9 shows the MSHP organizational structure.

SBIs, as their name implies, are investigative in nature and might be considered a state's equivalent to the FBI; they investigate all manner of cases assigned to them by their state's laws and usually report to the state's attorney general. SBI investigators are plainclothes agents who usually investigate both criminal and civil cases involving the state and/or multiple jurisdictions. They also provide technical support to local agencies in the form of laboratory or record services and may be asked by the city and county agencies to assist in investigating more serious crimes (e.g., homicide).[37]

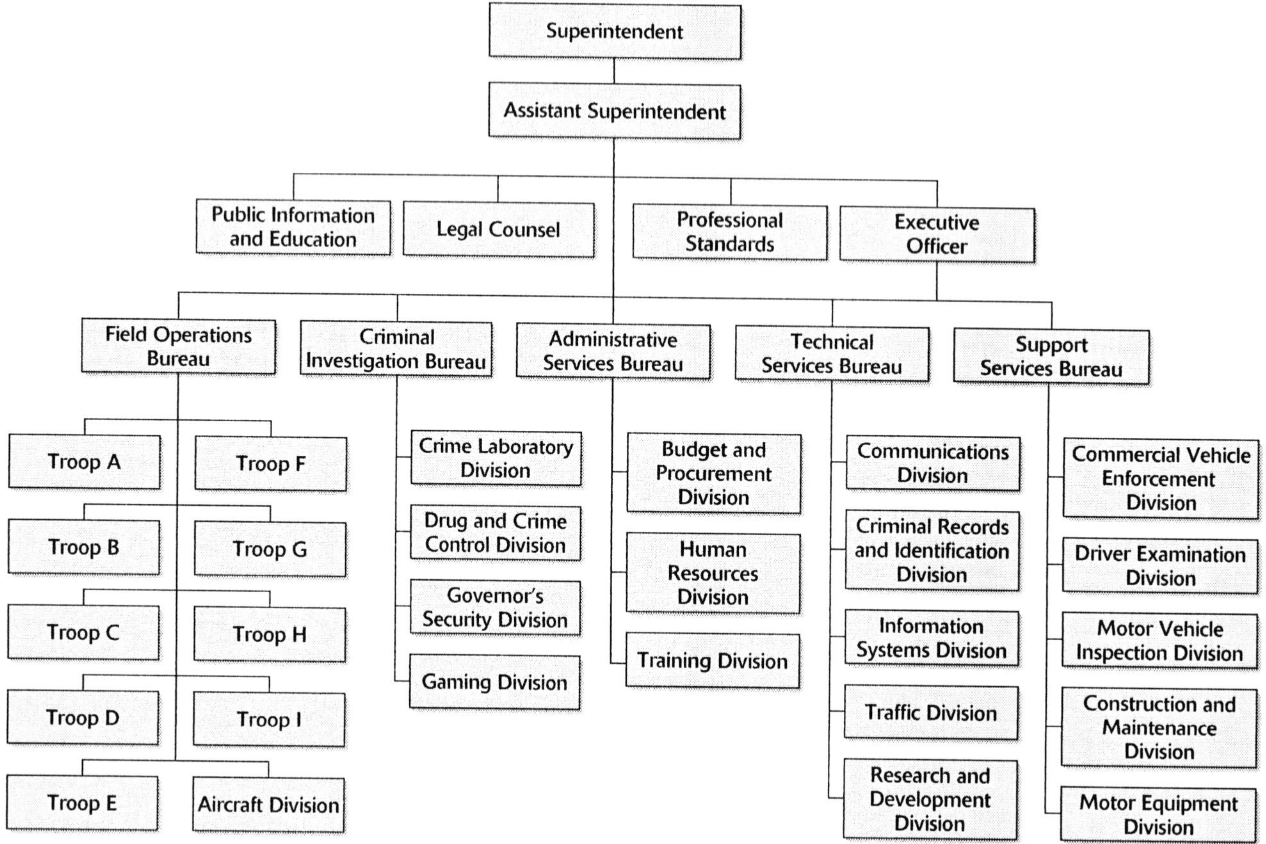

Figure 9

Missouri State Highway Patrol Organizational Structure

Source: Missouri State Highway Patrol, www.mshp.dps.mo.gov/MSHPWeb/Publications/OtherPublications/documents/2008AnnualReport.pdf (accessed July 26, 2010).

A Variety of State Police Duties

State-level police and law enforcement agencies perform a variety of functions aside from traffic and investigations, however, including special operations and special units, with 42 of the 49 state agencies (85.7 percent) having sworn personnel assigned to special weapons and tactics (SWAT) teams; 35 (71.4 percent) having personnel in search and rescue assignments; 36 (73.5 percent) having personnel assigned either full-time or part-time to special drug units; and 37 (75.5 percent) having personnel assigned either full-time or part-time to multi-agency drug task forces. Some state personnel are also assigned to court-related functions: 37 (75.5 percent) of the 49 state agencies use personnel for executing warrants, and 6 (12.2 percent) have personnel assigned to court security.[38]

mycrimekit

Video: *Career Profile: State Trooper.*

Also, given that state troopers are commonly seen in their patrol vehicles, the general public might be surprised to know that, of the 49 state law enforcement agencies, 14 (28.9 percent) deploy bicycle patrols, 9 (18.4 percent) maintain foot patrols, 9 (18.4 percent) have marine patrols, and 25 (51.0 percent) use motorcycle patrols.[39]

Other Special-Purpose State Agencies

In addition to the traffic, investigative, and other units mentioned above, several other **special-purpose state agencies,** including police and other law enforcement organizations, have developed over time to meet particular needs. For example, many state attorney general's offices have units and investigators that investigate white-collar crimes; fraud against or by consumers, Medicare providers, and food stamp recipients; and crimes against children and seniors.[40]

States may also have limited-purpose units devoted to enforcing the following:

- Alcoholic beverage laws (regarding the distribution and sale of such beverages, monitor bars and liquor stores, and so on)
- Fish and game laws (relating to hunting and fishing, to ensure that such persons have proper licenses, and do not poach, hunt, or fish out of season, exceed their limit, and so on)
- State statutes and local ordinances on college and university campuses
- Agricultural laws, to include cattle brand inspection and enforcement
- Commercial vehicle laws, such as those federal and state laws pertaining to interstate carriers' (i.e., tractor-trailer rigs) weights and permits, and ordinances applying to taxicabs

Most of these organizations have their own training academies, but some—campus police officers and fish and game agents, for example—may attend the regular police academies that train county deputies and local police officers.

Data Collection

An area that has become sensitive and thus important for the state police is data collection for the purpose of identifying, reducing, and preventing any bias-based policing. Of the nation's 49 state law enforcement agencies whose primary duties include highway patrol, 29 (59.2 percent) require their traffic patrol officers to record motorists' race or ethnicity during traffic stops. In addition, 12 of these 29 (41.4 percent) state agencies also require specialized units (such as investigative units) to collect race or ethnicity data. Also, 22 of the 50 (44.9 percent) states require officers to record race or ethnicity data for all officer-initiated stops, and seven in more limited circumstances.[41]

Career Considerations

Key elements—known as KSAs (for knowledge, skills, and abilities)—of employment in many federal as well as state law enforcement positions are as follows:

- U.S. citizenship
- Age requirement—applicants must be under 37 years of age
- Written test

- Structured oral interview—typically consisting of situational questions posed by an oral board that do not require technical questions
- Writing sample assessment—applicants might, for example, be provided with a photograph and then asked to prepare a narrative report describing the overall scene and details shown in the photograph.
- Medical exam—to test for any chronic disease or condition affecting the respiratory, cardiovascular, gastrointestinal, musculoskeletal, digestive, nervous, endocrine, or genitourinary systems that would impair full performance of the job duties; it might also include vision and hearing examinations
- Drug testing—satisfactory completion of a drug test is a condition of placement
- Background investigation[42]

Furthermore, the following minimum qualifications may also be in effect prior to an offer of employment, depending on the agency:

- Successful hirees will attend and successfully complete a mandatory basic training program of about six months' duration.
- Any person convicted of a crime of domestic violence cannot lawfully possess a firearm or ammunition (see 18 U.S.C. Section 1001).
- Persons required to carry a firearm while performing their duties must satisfactorily complete the firearms component.
- Positions may require mobility, not only as concerns some travel related to the duties of the job, but also in terms of assignment to a duty station; applicants must sign a mobility agreement.[43]

Several government and nongovernment Web sites offer information concerning federal state and local law enforcement careers, including the following:

- USAJOBS, jobsearch.usajobs.gov (search for "Corrections Officer")
- Federal Jobs Net, "Law Enforcement Jobs," federaljobs.net/law.htm
- Dennis V. Damp, *The Book of U.S. Government Jobs: Where They Are, What's Available, and How to Get One,* federaljobs.net/us7.htm
- Police Employment, The Police Job Board, "Federal Police Jobs," jobs.police-employment.com/federal-police
- Copcareer.com, www.copcareer.com/federal/federalpage.htm

More general information concerning federal employment may be obtained from the U.S. Office of Personnel Management, www.opm.gov. The federal hiring process normally takes eighteen to thirty months.

One's academic performance can enhance his or her pay scale in the federal system. For example, the U.S. Department of Homeland Security's recruitment memo currently states the following:

With a four-year degree and a grade-point average (GPA) **less than** 3.0

- First-year salary range is: $47,441 to $55,979
- After **five** years, it is: $100,502 to $118,589

With a four-year degree and GPA **above** 3.0:

- First-year salary range is: $54,000 to $63,718
- After **four** years, it is: $100,502 to $118,589

With a **master's** degree:

- First-year salary range is: $60,224 to $71,061
- After **three** years, it is: $100,502 to $118,589[44]

Clearly, it literally pays to have a higher GPA or a master's degree with this organization.

SUMMARY

Although modern policing in the United States is still based on the nineteenth-century British model of the Metropolitan Police of London, a tremendous amount of specialization has evolved in today's sphere of policing, especially among federal, state, and local agencies. Policing has developed into a highly organized discipline with many branches and narrow fields of jurisdiction and responsibility. This has happened not so much because of needs being demonstrated by formal research but because of the necessity of keeping abreast of activities of sophisticated criminals and would-be terrorists who would violate the peace and dignity of people in many different ways.

Specifically, this chapter described the major federal law enforcement agencies of the new Department of Homeland Security, the Department of Justice, and other federal agencies and provided an overview of state police agencies. Perhaps what was most evident is how the law enforcement agencies of the federal government have retooled to meet today's challenge of terrorism.

It is clear that now, more than any other time in the history of the United States, "business as usual" cannot be the order of the day. Federal and state law enforcement agencies must take a more farsighted approach to their work while learning new methods for preventing and responding to potential terrorist attacks. This chapter has demonstrated that law enforcement agencies must be—and are being—flexible as the need arises.

KEY TERMS

Bureau of Alcohol, Tobacco, Firearms, and Explosives (ATF)
Central Intelligence Agency (CIA)
Department of Homeland Security (DHS)
Department of Justice
Drug Enforcement Administration (DEA)

Federal Bureau of Investigation (FBI)
federal law enforcement agencies
Federal Law Enforcement Training Center (FLETC)
Internal Revenue Service (IRS)
National Crime Information Center (NCIC)
special-purpose state agencies
state bureaus of investigation (SBI)
Uniform Crime Reports (UCR)
U.S. Marshals Service (USMS)

REVIEW QUESTIONS

1. What are the major component agencies of DHS and their primary functions?
2. What are the major functions of the four agencies of the Department of Justice that are described in this chapter?
3. Where and how are federal agents trained?
4. What functions do the CIA and the IRS perform?
5. What are the primary differences between federal and state law enforcement agencies?

LEARN BY DOING

1. Your criminal justice professor requires you to prepare a research paper on the measures that have been adopted by federal law enforcement and state and local police for homeland security, to include the training that has been provided in the event of a terrorist attack or other critical incident, cooperative agreements with other agencies that are in place for such situations, and so on.
2. You have been requested to provide a two-hour block of instruction concerning federal and state law enforcement agencies for your police department's Citizens' Police Academy; prepare a lecture covering the major agencies—and their functions—that comprise both the Department of Justice and the Department of Homeland Security; include such ancillary functions as the FBI's Uniform Crime Reports and NCIC, as well as the complementary roles of INTERPOL.
3. As your department's public information officer, you have been invited by a local civic organization to appear at a noon luncheon to discuss your agency's roles and functions. During your presentation, someone in the audience raises her hand and asks how the duties of the local police department and sheriff's offices generally differ from those of your state-level police organization. How would you respond?
4. Assume that you and a fellow student of criminal justice are engaged in a conversation about law enforcement careers. Your friend is undecided about whether to seek employment in a federal, state, or local agency upon graduating; furthermore, he wonders about the possible pros and cons of working at each level, as well as working within a large-, medium-, or small-size agency. How would you respond?

mycrimekit

Go to MyCrimeKit.com and discover additional study tools and resources related to this chapter.

- Key Terms
- Review Questions
  - Multiple Choice Questions
  - True/False
  - Fill in the Blank
  - Essay
- MEDIA REVIEW: where you can review the *levels of law enforcement.*
- MEDIA VIDEO: where you can once again learn about *different careers within the criminal justice field.*
- FLASHCARDS: to test your knowledge of this chapter.
- *NEW YORK TIMES:* where you can read the latest articles related to criminology and criminal law.
- THE CAREER CENTER: where you can explore career opportunities in criminal justice and criminology.
- THE ONLINE RESEARCH LIBRARY: where you can explore the Cybrary and Research Navigator.

NOTES

1. "DHS Organization," www.dhs.gov/xabout/structure/editorial_0644.shtm (accessed July 9, 2010); and U.S. Department of Homeland Security, "Department Components and Subagencies," www.dhs.gov/xabout/structure (accessed July 9, 2010).
2. U.S. Department of Homeland Security, "Department Subcomponents and Agencies," www.dhs.gov/xabout/structure (accessed July 9, 2010); and "U.S. Customs and Border Protection, 'On a Typical Day,'" www.cbp.gov/xp/cgov/about/organization (accessed July 9, 2010).
3. U.S. Department of Homeland Security, Immigration and Customs Enforcement, "Overview," www.ice.gov/about/index.htm (accessed July 10, 2010).
4. U.S. Department of Homeland Security, Transportation Security Administration, "Workforce: Who We Are," www.tsa.gov/who_we_are/workforce/index.shtm (accessed July 10, 2010); also see U.S. Department of Homeland Security, Transportation Security Administration, "TSA: Global Strategies," www.tsa.gov/approach/harmonization.shtm (accessed July 10, 2010).
5. "Welcome to FLETC," www.fletc.gov (accessed July 28, 2009).

6. United States Secret Service, "Frequently Asked Questions About the United States Secret Service," www.secretservice.gov/faq.shtml#employees (accessed July 9, 2010).
7. David R. Johnson, *American Law Enforcement History* (St. Louis: Forum Press, 1981), pp. 166–170.
8. Ibid.
9. U.S. Department of Justice, Federal Bureau of Investigation, "About Us—Quick Facts," www.fbi.gov/quickfacts.htm (accessed July 10, 2010).
10. U.S. Department of Justice, Federal Bureau of Investigation, "What We Investigate," www.fbi.gov/hq.htm (accessed July 10, 2010).
11. "FBI Seeks Sweeping New Powers," *The Nation*, August 22, 2008, www.thenation.com/article/fbi-seeks-sweeping-new-powers (accessed July 10, 2010).
12. "FBI Agents Still Lacking Arabic Skills," www.washingtonpost.com/wp-yn/content/article/2006/10/10/AR2006101001388.html (accessed February 9, 2007).
13. Jeff Glasser, "In Demand for Fifty Years: The FBI's 'Most Wanted' List—Good Publicity, and a History of Success," *U.S. News and World Report*, March 20, 2000, p. 60.
14. U.S. Department of Justice, Federal Bureau of Investigation, "National Crime Information Center (NCIC)," www.fas.org/irp/agency/doj/fbi/is/ncic.htm (accessed July 10, 2010).
15. Bureau of Alcohol, Tobacco, Firearms, and Explosives, "Changes in ATF Resulting from the Signing of the Homeland Security Bill: Two Separate Bureaus Created" (press release), www.atf.gov/press/releases/2002/11/112702-atf-changes-from-homeland-security-bill.html (accessed July 10, 2010).
16. For an excellent overview of the duties of federal law enforcement agents as well as other state and local personnel, see, for example, Department of Labor, Bureau of Labor Statistics, "Occupational Outlook Handbook: Police and Detectives," www.bls.gov/oco/ocos160.htm (accessed July 10, 2010); and James Stinchcomb, *Opportunities in Law Enforcement and Criminal Justice Careers*, rev. ed. (New York: McGraw-Hill, 2003).
17. Bureau of Alcohol, Tobacco, Firearms, and Explosives, "ATF Snapshot 2004," www.atf.gov/publications/general/snapshots/atf-snapshot-2004.html (accessed July 10, 2010).
18. Ibid.
19. Ibid.
20. U.S. Department of Justice, Drug Enforcement Administration, "DEA Mission Statement," www.justice.gov/dea/agency/mission.htm (accessed July 10, 2010).
21. Ibid.
22. U.S. Department of Justice, Drug Enforcement Administration, "DEA Office Locations," www.usdoj.gov/dea/agency/domestic.htm (accessed July 10, 2010).
23. U.S. Department of Justice, U.S. Marshals Service, *The FY 1993 Report to the U.S. Marshals* (Washington, DC: Author, 1994), pp. 188–189.
24. U.S. Marshals Service, "Facts Sheets: Facts and Figures," www.usmarshals.gov/duties/factsheets/facts-1209.html (accessed July 10, 2010).
25. Ibid.

26. Central Intelligence Agency, "CIA Vision, Mission, & Values," https://www.cia.gov/about-cia/cia-vision-mission-values/index.html (accessed July 10, 2010).
27. Central Intelligence Agency, "About CIA," https://www.cia.gov/about-cia/index.html (accessed July 10, 2010).
28. "Central Intelligence Agency," *U.S. News and World Report*, October 30, 2006, p. 59; and Central Intelligence Agency, "Careers," https://www.cia.gov/careers/index.html (accessed July 10, 2010).
29. Ibid.
30. Internal Revenue Service, "Criminal Investigation (CI) At-a-Glance," www.irs.gov/irs/article/0,,id=98398,00.html (accessed July 10, 2010).
31. Ludovic Kennedy, "The Airman and the Carpenter: The Lindbergh Kidnapping and the Framing of Richard Hauptmann," *Seton Hall Law Review* 14, 574–98.
32. Don Vogel, quoted in Department of the Treasury, Internal Revenue Service, *CI Digest* 1827 (June 1994):12.
33. U.S. Department of Treasury, Internal Revenue Service, "Criminal Enforcement," www.irs.gov/compliance/enforcement/index.html (accessed July 10, 2010).
34. Department of the Treasury, Federal Law Enforcement Training Center, *Catalog of Training Programs* (Washington, DC: Author, 1995), p. 1.
35. General Accounting Office, *Federal Law Enforcement Training Center: Capacity Planning and Management Oversight Need Improvement*, Report to Congressional Requesters (Washington, DC: Author, July 2003), p. 7; for contemporary information concerning FLETC, see www.fletc.gov (accessed July 10, 2010).
36. Missouri State Highway Patrol, "A Career as a Trooper," www.mshp.dps.mo.gov/MSHPWeb/PatrolDivisions/HRD/Trooper/troopCareer.html (accessed July 10, 2010).
37. About.com, "State Bureau of Investigation: Encyclopedia," experts.about.com/e/s/st/State_Bureau_of_Investigation.htm (accessed July 10, 2010).
38. U.S. Department of Justice, Bureau of Justice Statistics, *Law Enforcement Management and Administrative Statistics, 2000: Data for Individual State and Local Agencies with 100 or More Officers* (Washington, DC: Author, April 2004), pp. 247–249.
39. Ibid.
40. See, for example, State of California, Department of Justice, Office of the Attorney General, ag.ca.gov/consumers.php (accessed July 10, 2010).
41. U.S. Department of Justice, Bureau of Justice Statistics, *Traffic Stop Data Collection Policies for State Police, 2004* (Washington, DC: Author, June 2005), p. 1.
42. Gregory M. White, Resident Agent in Charge, U.S. Department of Homeland Security, U.S. Immigration and Customs Enforcement, personal communication, October 29, 2009.
43. Ibid.
44. Ibid.

Preparing for the Street

Preparing for the Street

RECRUITING, TRAINING, AND SOCIALIZATION

I think the necessity of being ready increases. Look to it.

—*Abraham Lincoln*

Chance only favors the prepared mind.

—*Louis Pasteur*

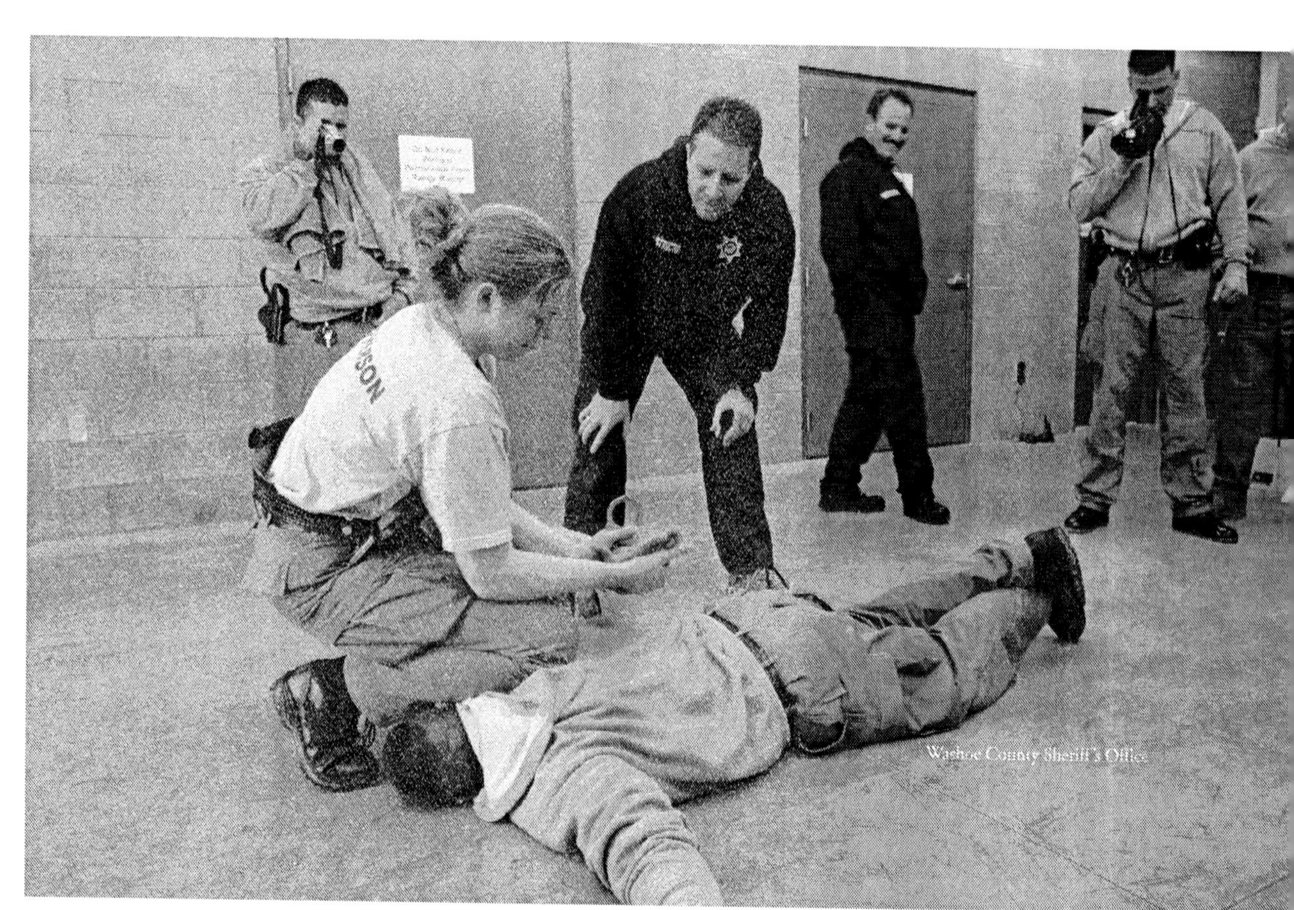

Washoe County Sheriff's Office

Learning Objectives

AS A RESULT OF READING THIS CHAPTER, THE STUDENT WILL:

- Understand some of the problems confronting today's police recruiters and some unique measures being tried to obtain a viable applicant pool
- Be able to explain the general hiring process and types of tests and examinations that are used to hire and train police officers
- Understand the assessment center concept and its functions for hiring and promoting the best personnel
- Know the kinds of skills and knowledge that are imparted to police trainees during their academy training and the typical subjects that are found in a police academy curriculum
- Understand the methods and purposes of both the FTO and PTO programs
- Be aware of what is meant by the term *working personality* and how it is developed and functions
- Be able to define police cynicism and explain how it operates
- Be able to delineate the ideal traits of police officers
- Know why the crime fighter image is the greatest obstacle in accepting a realistic view of the police role
- Be able to describe the primary functions and styles of policing
- Be able to explain the status and challenges of women and minorities in policing, as well as difficulties with recruiting and retaining them

Introduction

This chapter generally describes how an officer's career begins and, to a large extent, how his or her occupational personality is formed. Studying the subculture of the police helps us define the "cop's world" and the officer's role in it; this subculture shapes the officer's attitudes, values, and beliefs.

The idea of a police subculture was first proposed by William Westley in his 1950 study of the Gary, Indiana, Police Department, where he found, among many other things, a high degree of group cohesion, secrecy, and violence.[1] It is now widely accepted that the police develop traditions, skills, and attitudes that are unique to their occupation because of their duties and responsibilities.[2]

We begin at the threshold, looking at some of the methods, challenges, and problems connected with the recruitment of qualified individuals. Then we track the typical police applicant's progression through the various types of tests that may be employed—written, psychological, physical, oral, character, and medical screening—and discuss the assessment center.

Then we examine formal police training at the academy, where the initiation of the officer-to-be into the police subculture commences in earnest. The chapter discusses types of academies as well as their general curriculum and some of the informal learning that takes place there. We then look at postacademy training—the field training officer concept—and in-service training later in one's career. Following that we take a look at how officers adopt their working personality: formal and informal rules, customs, and beliefs of the occupation. This portion of the chapter includes an assessment of the traits that make a good officer. Then we examine the roles, functions, and styles of policing, and following that we consider women and minorities in policing. A summary, review questions, and several scenarios and activities that provide opportunities to learn by doing conclude the chapter.

mycrimekit

Review: *Traits of a Good Law Enforcement Officer.*

First Things First: Recruiting Qualified Applicants

Wanted: Those Who Walk on Water

Recruiting that results in an adequate pool of applicants is an extremely important facet of the police hiring process. August Vollmer stated:

> [Law enforcement candidates should] have the wisdom of Solomon, the courage of David, the patience of Job and leadership of Moses, the kindness of the Good Samaritan, the diplomacy of Lincoln, the tolerance of the Carpenter of Nazareth, and, finally, an intimate knowledge of every branch of the natural, biological and social sciences.[3]

Many people believe that the police officer has the most difficult job in America. Police officers are solitary workers, spending most of their time on the job unsupervised. Also, people who are hired today will become the supervisors of the future. For all these reasons, police agencies must attempt to attract the best individuals possible.

Police applicants typically come from lower-middle-class or working-class backgrounds;[4] they generally have a high school education and a history of employment. They also tend, at the application stage, to be enthusiastic, idealistic, uninformed about the reality of police work, and very different from the stereotype of the police officer as authoritarian, suspicious, and insensitive.[5]

Some studies indicate that police applicants are primarily motivated by the need for job security.[6] Other researchers have found that both males and females listed the same six factors—desire to help people, job security, crime fighting, job excitement, prestige, and a lifetime interest—as strong positive influences in their career choices.[7] Joel Lefkowitz concluded that police candidates were lower than average in their desire to do autonomous work,[8] and other studies have indicated that applicants tend to favor a more directive leadership style. Such findings are not unusual, given that most police agencies are highly structured and paramilitary in nature. Studies do not establish that police candidates fit the stereotypes of harsh, controlling people who wish to dominate others. Leadership, or the ability to take charge of situations, is a desirable attribute, however. Some researchers have found that the typical police applicant is very similar to the average college student.[9]

Bruce Carpenter and Susan Raza, using the Minnesota Multiphasic Personality Inventory (MMPI), found that police applicants differed from the general population in several important ways.[10] Police applicants, they learned, are somewhat more psychologically healthy, are generally less depressed and anxious, and are more assertive and interested in making and maintaining social contacts. Furthermore, few police aspirants have emotional difficulties, and they have a greater tendency to present a good impression of themselves than the general population does. They are a more homogeneous group.

Female police applicants tend to be more assertive and nonconforming and to have a higher energy level than male applicants; they are also less likely to identify with traditional sex roles than male applicants. Older police applicants tend to be less satisfied, have more physical complaints, and are more likely to develop physical symptoms under stress than younger applicants. Applicants to large city police forces are generally less likely to have physical complaints and have a higher energy level than applicants to small or medium-size agencies. (This is probably explained by the fact that applicants in large cities are significantly younger.[11]) Some departments are under a mandate to recruit special groups of people, such as women, African Americans, and Hispanics; several cities have also recruited homosexuals.

What psychological qualities should agencies seek? According to psychologist Lawrence Wrightsman,[12] it is important that police applicants be incorruptible and have high moral character. They should be well adjusted, able to carry out the hazardous and stressful tasks of policing without "cracking up," and thick-skinned enough to operate without defensiveness. They should have a genuine interest in people and a compassionate sense of the innate dignity of others. Applicants should also be free of emotional reactions, they should not be impulsive or overly aggressive, and they should be able to exercise restraint. This is especially important given their active role in crime detection.

Finally, they need logical skills to assist in their investigative work. An interesting example of some of the logical skills needed for police work is provided by Al Seedman, former chief of detectives in the New York City Police Department (NYPD):

> In the woods just outside of town they found the skeleton of a man who'd been dead for three months or so. I asked whether this skeleton showed signs of any dental work. But the local cops said no, although the skeleton had crummy teeth. No dental work at all. Now, if he'd been wealthy, he could have afforded to have his teeth fixed. If he'd been poor, welfare would have paid. If he was a union member, their medical plan would have covered it. So this fellow was probably working at a low-paying non-unionized job, but making enough to keep off public assistance. Also, since he didn't match up to any family's missing-person report, he was probably single, living alone in an apartment or hotel. His landlord never reported him missing, either, so

> most likely he was also behind on his rent and the landlord probably figured he had just skipped. But even if he had escaped his landlord, he would never have escaped the tax man. The rest was simple. I told these cops to wait until the year is up. Then they can go to the IRS and get a printout of all single males making less than $10,000 a year but more than the welfare ceiling who paid withholding tax in the first three quarters but not in the fourth. Chances are the name of their skeleton will be on that printout.[13]

Other desirable traits of entry-level officers are discussed later in this chapter.

Recruiting Problems and Successes

Certainly the recruitment of quality police officers is key to the values and culture of any police organization. Police recruitment issues are such a concern at present that a national meeting was recently convened by the U.S. Department of Justice, the National Institute of Justice, and the RAND Corporation to discuss these issues.

The current "cop crunch" is exacerbated in many cities by exploding growth, a competitive job market, natural catastrophes (e.g., Hurricane Katrina in New Orleans), and struggles to retain diversity.[14] Furthermore, this crunch comes at a time when today's police need a stronger focus on problem-solving skills, ability to collaborate with the community, and a greater capacity to use technology.[15] Adding to the problems are today's higher incidence of obesity, major debt, drug use, and criminal records that are found among potential recruits.[16]

The requirement that applicants possess college credits is believed to make recruitment problems more acute. Several agencies that now require two years of college credits believe that this standard has reduced their applicant pool significantly. At the same time, a Census Bureau report put the average salary of a nonsupervisory police officer at $34,700; this compares to the average $40,546 that a technical support worker can expect to make and the average $51,351 that managers or executives earn. According to NAPO, add to that the media attention given to corrupt officers, police shootings, and department scandals, and it may be understandable why people are shying away from police careers. To counter this declining interest, departments are accentuating the occupation's positive aspects: solid insurance, excellent retirement plans, long vacations, and opportunities to advance.[17]

Recruiting and retaining women in police service remain particularly problematic. Gender bias (reflected in the absence of women being hired and promoted to policy-making positions) and sexual harassment concerns prevent many women from applying and cause many female officers to leave—and quickly: About 60 percent of female officers who leave their agency do so during their second to fifth years on the job.[18] (Problems associated with bringing women into policing—and retaining them—are discussed more fully below.)

EXHIBIT 1

Diversity Expansion Within the NYPD Ranks

A mid-2007 academy class at the New York City Police Department (NYPD), consisting of about 1,100 graduates, was a "United Nations" of law enforcement: 264 of the rookies were born in 49 foreign countries, including Turkey, Azerbaijan, Venezuela, Albania, and Burma. Today the NYPD has about 40 officers assigned full-time to recruit from all corners of the city and its immigrant communities. It budgets millions of dollars for advertising and hired a top Manhattan firm to mount a campaign that emphasizes diversity—which is viewed as essential for serving this highly diverse city and building trust. More than 400 officers and civilian employees of NYPD speak about three dozen languages; in addition to having an abundance of Spanish- and Italian-speaking officers, the department has personnel who can also speak Kurdish, Pasto, and Cambodian.

Source: Adapted from Tom Hays, "Diversity Grows in NYPD Ranks," Associated Press, *Reno Gazette-Journal*, July 19, 2007, p. 2C.

But some agencies have successfully addressed the recruitment dilemma. For example, the New York State Police (NYSP) recently swore in its largest class in thirty years. Using an academic survey developed by a high-ranking trooper with a doctorate, the agency asked people what would make them consider joining the state police. (Their answer: job enrichment or more interesting work.) The survey also revealed that the two factors playing a key role in a person's decision to enter police work were the ability to help others and the opportunity to serve the community—two factors that the NYSP stresses in its mission and values statements and in its recruitment drives. Also emphasized in recruitment literature and television announcements are how female troopers can balance family and career as well as the various specialized jobs—foreign language proficiency or scuba diving, for example—that are available within the NYSP. The organization enlisted the entire force as recruiters and sought applicants at nontraditional locations, such as women's road races and health clubs.[19]

Other methods employed by police agencies in their attempts to develop a bigger pool of applicants include seeking applicants far from home (for example, Los Angeles recruits in Chicago, and Chicago recruits in Wisconsin), having downloadable application forms on the Web, lowering the minimum age from twenty-two to twenty-one, and allowing some applicants to substitute work experience for college credits.[20] Exhibit 1 shows the recruiting successes of the New York Police Department.

Testing: The Hurdle Process for New Personnel

Even though a person meets the minimum qualifications for being a police officer (age, education, no disqualifying criminal record), much work still remains to be done before he or she is ready to be put to work as a police officer. The new recruit must successfully complete what is known as the **hurdle process**. In this section, we consider some kinds of tests that are used to weed out undesirable candidates.

mycrimekit™
Evidence: *Background Investigation.*

Tables 1 and 2 show the kinds of tests and background checks that are used in selecting new officer recruits. Both tables are organized by agency size, from under 2,500 to more than 1 million. A study by the federal Bureau of Justice Statistics (see Tables 1 and 2) found that nearly all local police agencies (99 percent) use criminal record checks, background investigations (98 percent), and driving record checks (96 percent) to screen applicants. Personal interviews (98 percent), psychological evaluations (67 percent), written aptitude tests (43 percent), physical agility tests (50 percent), personality inventory (26 percent), drug tests (73 percent), and medical exam (85 percent) are also commonly used.[21]

Certainly not all types of tests shown in Figure 1 are employed by all of the seventeen thousand police agencies in America, nor are these tests necessarily given in the sequence shown. Under affirmative action laws and court decisions, a burden rests with police administrators to demonstrate that the tests used are job related. The hiring sequence shown in Figure 1, called the "multiple hurdle procedure,"[22] may take longer than three months to complete, depending on the number and types of tests used and the ease of scheduling and performing them.

Table 1
INTERVIEWS, TESTS, AND EXAMINATIONS USED IN SELECTION OF NEW OFFICER RECRUITS IN LOCAL POLICE DEPARTMENTS, BY SIZE OF POPULATION SERVED

	Interviews, Tests, and Examinations Used to Select New Officer Recruits									
Population Served	Personal Interview	Medical Exam	Drug Test	Psychological Evaluation	Physical Agility Test	Written Aptitude Test	Personality Inventory	Polygraph Exam	Voice Stress Analyzer	Second-Language Ability Test
All sizes	98%	85%	73%	67%	50%	43%	26%	25%	4%	1%
1,000,000 or more	94	100	100	100	94	81	56	81	0	0
500,000–999,999	100	100	95	100	86	84	48	64	11	11
250,000–499,999	95	93	98	98	93	83	51	78	10	2
100,000–249,999	95	97	86	95	88	82	50	77	11	1
50,000–99,999	99	97	90	97	83	80	47	57	7	3
25,000–49,999	99	99	88	96	76	76	45	47	12	2
10,000–24,999	99	98	88	89	71	72	40	42	6	1
2,500–9,999	99	91	74	71	52	48	26	25	3	—
Under 2,500	98	73	63	47	31	20	16	11	2	—

Note: List of selection methods is not intended to be exhaustive.

— indicates less than 0.5%.

Source: U.S. Department of Justice, Bureau of Justice Statistics, *Local Police Departments, 2003* (Washington, DC: Author, May 2006), p. 8.

Table 2
BACKGROUND CHECKS USED IN SELECTION OF NEW OFFICER RECRUITS IN LOCAL POLICE DEPARTMENTS, BY SIZE OF POPULATION SERVED

	Background Checks Used to Select New Officer Recruits				
Population Served	Criminal Record Check	Background Investigation	Driving Record Check	Credit History Check	Volunteer Service Check
All sizes	99%	98%	96%	55%	8%
1,000,000 or more	100	100	100	81	0
500,000–999,999	100	100	100	89	19
250,000–499,999	100	100	98	88	7
100,000–249,999	100	99	98	88	12
50,000–99,999	99	100	99	87	8
25,000–49,999	100	100	99	83	11
10,000–24,999	99	99	99	76	8
2,500–9,999	99	98	99	55	9
Under 2,500	98	97	92	39	6

Note: List of selection methods is not intended to be exhaustive.
Source: U.S. Department of Justice, Bureau of Justice Statistics, *Local Police Departments, 2003* (Washington, DC: Author, May 2006), p. 8.

Written Examinations: General Knowledge and Psychological Tests

Measures of general intelligence and reading skills are the best means a police agency can use for predicting who will do well in the police academy.[23] Of course, any such test must be reliable and valid. To achieve reliability and validity, many (if not most) police agencies purchase and use "canned" test instruments—those prepared by professional individuals or companies.

Larger police departments and state police agencies use four types of written tests: cognitive tests (measuring aptitudes in verbal skills and mathematics, reasoning, and related perceptual abilities), personality tests (predominantly the Minnesota Multiphasic Personality Inventory [MMPI]), interest inventories (the Strong-Campbell, the Kuder, and the Minnesota Interest tests), and biographical data inventories.[24]

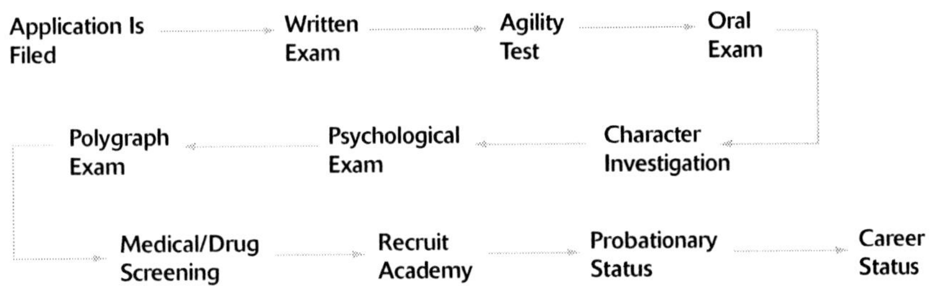

Figure 1
Major Elements of the Police Hiring Process

Over time, research findings have been mixed concerning the implications of written examinations. For example, a 1962 study of deputy sheriffs found that candidates with written test scores above the 97th percentile were most apt to be successful in their careers.[25] However, a study of the Tucson, Arizona, Police Department determined that the IQ scores of officers who dropped out of the force were significantly higher than those of a norm group. The study concluded that one can be too bright to be a cop, unless an alternate career development program can be developed to challenge and use highly intelligent people.[26] Of course, there is much more to police work than reading skills.

General intelligence tests are often administered and scored by the civil service or the central personnel office. Most frequently, those who fail the entrance examination (that is, they do not make the minimum score, which is usually set at 70 percent) will go on to other careers, although most jurisdictions allow for a retest after a specified period of time. The names of those who pass are forwarded to the police agency for any further in-house testing and screening.[27]

Another form of written examination for police applicants is the psychological screening test. There are two major concerns in using such tests to screen out applicants: stability and suitability. Candidates must be carefully screened in order to exclude those who are emotionally unstable, overly aggressive, or suffering from some personality disorder. The two primary tests of suitability of police candidates are the MMPI and the California Personality Inventory (CPI).[28] Stability is a major legal concern. If an officer commits a serious, harmful, and inappropriate act, the question of his or her stability will be raised, and the police agency may be asked to provide documentation about why the officer was deemed stable at the time of employment. It has been found that 2 to 5 percent of the police applicant pool may be eliminated due to severe emotional or mental problems.[29]

Physical Agility Test

Entry-level physical examinations range from a minimally acceptable number of push-ups to timed running and jumping tests to tests of strength and agility, such as dragging weights, pushing cars, leaping over six-foot walls, walking on horizontal ladders, crawling through tunnels, and negotiating monkey bars. The problem is that very few of these activities are actually performed by police officers on the job.

The challenge for police executives, and an area of lawsuit vulnerability, is selecting a truly job-related physical agility test. Police agencies must determine the nature and extent of physical work performed by police officers and use that information to develop an instrument to measure applicants' ability to perform that work. One such test is based on the theory that police officers must perform three basic physical functions: getting to the problem (possibly needing to run, climb, vault, and so forth), resolving the problem (perhaps needing to fight or wrestle with an offender), and removing the problem (often requiring that the officer carry heavy weights). To establish the testing protocol for a given jurisdiction, the officers fill out written forms concerning the kinds of physical work that they performed each workday for one month. Information from the forms is then analyzed by computer and used to develop a physical agility test that accurately measures the recruit's ability to do the kinds of work performed by police officers in that specific locale.[30] If challenged in court, agencies using such tests can show that they test for the actual job requirements of their jurisdiction and do not discriminate on the basis of gender, race, height, age, and physical condition.

Personal Interview

As noted in Table 1, the personal interview is used by 98 percent of all police agencies as part of the selection process.[31] Candidates appear individually before one or more boards that are composed of members of the police agency and often the community. Candidates may also be asked to participate in a clinical interview with a psychologist; studies have indicated that the clinical interview complements the written psychological test.[32]

The purpose of the interview is to assess aspects of the candidate that cannot be measured on other tests, such as appearance, ability to communicate and reason (often using situational questions), and general poise and bearing. The interview is not normally well suited for judging character, dependability, initiative, or other such factors.

A primary advantage of the interview is that evaluators can ask applicants to explain how they would behave and use force in given situations because any number of possible scenarios exist. Following are five examples of the kinds of situations that might be posed to police applicants to see how well they think on their feet, develop appropriate responses, and prioritize their actions:

1. You are dispatched to a neighborhood park to check out a young man who is acting strangely. Upon arrival, you see the youth standing near a group of children playing on a merry-go-round. He is holding a .22-caliber rifle. What is your next action?
2. You are in the men's locker room at the end of your shift. You hear another male officer talking about a female officer's body. What do you do?
3. You are at home watching a football game on a weekend. Your neighbor comes to your door and frantically claims that his door has been kicked in and that he believes someone is inside. What do you do? What if the neighbor tells you that his daughter is upstairs in his house? How would you proceed?
4. You are in a downtown area making an arrest. A crowd gathers and you begin to hear comments about "police harassment." Soon the crowd becomes angry. How do you react?
5. You and another officer are responding to a burglary call at an office building. While searching the scene, you observe the other officer remove an expensive fountain pen from the top of a desk and put it in his pocket. What do you do?

Character Investigation

As indicated earlier, nearly all local police departments use background checks or character investigations—probably the most important element of the selection process. If done properly, the character investigation will also be one of the most time-consuming and costly elements of the process.

Character is one of the most subjective yet most important factors an applicant brings to the job, and it cannot be measured with data and interviews. A character investigation involves talking to the candidate's past and current friends, co-workers, teachers, neighbors, and employers. The applicant should be informed that references will be checked and that in the course of reviewing them, the investigation may spread to other references and others who are known to the applicant. No expense should be spared in talking with anyone who has personal knowledge of the candidate and can provide crucial information; if the job is done properly, the investigator will not only have a complete knowledge of the person's character but will also know where any skeletons may be buried in the applicant's background.

Polygraph Examination

As shown in Table 1, 25 percent of the nation's police agencies—including 77 percent of those that serve populations of 100,000 or more—conducted polygraph examinations as part of their selection process.[33] These agencies are willing to devote the extra resources necessary to help them determine that their applicants are honest and to secure higher-quality employees.

A survey of the benefits of polygraph examinations for police applicants by Richard Arther, director of the National Center of Lie Detection, supported the need for the polygraph for police recruitment:[34]

- An applicant for a police position in Lower Merion, Pennsylvania, came to that agency highly recommended by a police lieutenant and his employer at a home for blind, retarded children. During the polygraph examination, however, the applicant admitted to at least fifty instances of sexually abusing the children under his care.
- An applicant with the Wichita, Kansas, Police Department admitted to the polygraphist that he had been involved in many burglaries. The detective division was able to clear eight unsolved crimes as a result of the applicant's confession.
- A police officer in one California police department applied for employment in the Salinas, California, Police Department. He appeared to be a model police officer, was in excellent physical condition, and was familiar with state codes. His previous experience made him a potentially ideal candidate. However, during the polygraph exam, he admitted to having committed over a dozen burglaries while on duty and to having used his patrol car to haul away the stolen property. He also admitted to planting stolen narcotics on innocent suspects in order to make arrests and to having had sexual intercourse with girls as young as sixteen in his patrol car.
- An applicant for the San Diego Sheriff's Department admitted to that agency's polygraphist that on weekends he would go from bar to bar pretending to be drunk. He would then seek out people to pick fights with, since he could only have an erection and orgasm while inflicting pain on others. In addition to these

sadistic tendencies, he also admitted that he got rid of his frustrations by savagely beating "niggers, Chicanos, and long-haired pukes who cause all the trouble."

These are but a few examples of how the investment of time and money for polygraph examinations can spare the public and police agencies a tremendous amount of trouble and expense later. It is doubtful that few (if any) of these behaviors would have surfaced during the course of a personal interview or a background investigation.

Medical Examination and Drug Screening

Someone once said that some police medical examinations are often of the "Can you hear thunder/see lightning?" variety—meaning that they are cursory at best. It is also widely believed that policing is only for those young people who are in peak physical condition. Whether these statements are facetious or not, it is certainly true that policing is no place for the physically unfit. Such officers would be a hazard not only to themselves but also to their co-workers. The job, with its stress, shift work, many hours of inactivity during patrol time, and other factors, can be physically debilitating even for veteran officers, especially those who fail to exercise and eat properly, so police administrators certainly do not want applicants who are unfit. The Federal Bureau of Investigation (FBI), for example, will not consider applicants whose weight exceeds the norm for their height and body type. Unfit personnel are thought to have lower energy levels, to give less attention to duty, and to take more sick days. Early retirement and disability often result, as do increased operating expenses for replacing ill officers and hiring and training new permanent replacements.

More and more often, police agencies, like private-sector businesses, the military, and other sensitive government agencies, are compelling prospective employees to submit to a drug test. Substance abuse remains a very real problem in the workplace, resulting in poor productivity, lowered agency morale, and increased accidents and injuries.

Assessment Center

Recently, the use of an **assessment center** has become more popular with police agencies. While used by many departments for promotional testing and for hiring a chief executive, some agencies also use this method for hiring new personnel. An assessment center may include interviews; psychological tests; in-basket exercises; management tasks; group discussions; role-playing exercises, such as simulations of critical incidents or interviews with subordinates, the public, and news media; fact-finding exercises; oral presentation exercises; and written communication exercises. Behaviors and skills that are important to the successful performance of the position are identified and possibly weighted, and each candidate is evaluated on his or her ability to perform them.

Individual and group role-playing provides a hands-on atmosphere during the selection process. For example, candidates may be required to perform in simulated police–community problems (such as having candidates conduct a "meeting" to hear concerns of local minority groups), react to a major incident (such as a simulated shooting or riot situation), hold a news briefing, or participate in other such exercises. They may be given an in-basket situation, for example, assuming the role of the new chief or captain who receives an abundance of paperwork, policies, and problems to be prioritized and dealt with in a prescribed amount of time. To evaluate candidates' writing abilities, they may be given a specified amount of time (thirty minutes, for example) to develop a new use-of-force policy for a hypothetical or real police agency, allowing raters to assess candidates' written communication skills and their understanding of the technical side of police work, as well as the ways they think and build a case.

During each exercise, several assessors or raters analyze each candidate's performance and record some type of quantitative or qualitative evaluation score, which is then turned over to the hiring or promoting authority. Raters are typically selected who have held and now supervise the position for which candidates are testing. For example, if the assessment center is used to hire new officers, it would minimally be best that sergeants serve as raters (for promotion to sergeant, lieutenants should be raters, and so on).

Assessment centers are obviously more difficult logistically to conduct and are normally more labor-intensive and costly than traditional (mere interviewing) procedures, but they are well worth the extra investment. Monies invested at the early stages of a hiring or promotional process can help the agency to make the best hiring decisions and save untold problems for years to come.

Formal Entry into Policing: Academy Training

Training Nature and Topics

Receiving an offer of employment in policing obviously is not immediately accompanied by a badge, uniform, and set of keys to your new cruiser. Completion of an academy and field training program will be one's final hurdles to becoming a full-fledged officer.

The following Career Profile briefly discusses the views and experiences of a former chief of police concerning the need to be trained and educated for the job.

Each state and each jurisdiction has different training requirements. In some areas, one can attend basic law enforcement training at the local community college or other state-sponsored institution first and then apply to the agency of his or her choice. Other jurisdictions may require individuals to complete their in-house training program after successful completion of their hiring process or sponsor them to attend an academy elsewhere. Still others may accept one's external academy certificate but also require completion of an abbreviated version of their academy. Regardless, people must receive extensive training prior to working alone on patrol. The majority of their initial training will be classroom based, supplemented by practical exercises and scenarios. They will hold the rank of "cadet" or "police trainee" during this time, and if sponsored by a hiring agency, receive their first paycheck and be eligible to receive benefits.

There is no standard national academy curriculum, but the state may guide agencies in developing training programs. Each state has a Commission on Peace Officers Standards and Training (POST) or similar entity that establishes minimum

CAREER PROFILE

METRO STATE

Name: Hal Nees

Position: Professor of Criminal Justice and Criminology, Metropolitan State College of Denver

Colleges attended: University of Colorado at Denver, University of Northern Colorado, Metropolitan State College of Denver, and Northern Arizona University

Degrees: Doctor of Public Administration, M.A. in Criminal Justice and Public Administration, B.A. in Criminal Justice, B.A. in History and Economics

Current teaching position: Metropolitan State College of Denver

What CJ-related jobs have you held and when?

1970–1993 Law Enforcement, Officer to Police Chief (two departments)

1993–1998 Director of Community Correction (county program)

1998–present Professor of Criminal Justice and Criminology

What positions did you like most?

I enjoyed them all. From being a police officer to police chief, to managing community corrections, to teaching, they have all been good, and I am glad that I had the opportunity to do many different types of work.

What qualities/characteristics most helped you succeed in the field?

Drive, tenacity, and willingness to take a chance. A drive to improve myself, to learn and attend college; tenacity to stick with the work and the college; and a willingness to take a chance on the job and with new jobs.

What are the typical salary ranges students can expect entering these fields?

Salaries typically start from $40,000 to $50,000, but salary depends on the area, the education, and the type of job. Some will start at $10 per hour, but these are learning jobs and should be considered internship positions that teach you a lot.

What advice would you give students early in their college career to help them find a rewarding job in criminal justice?

Learn what area you wish to work in, find out the requirements, and gain those skills and abilities. An ability to speak a second language is a good skill, and minoring in psychology, sociology, or human services can also help you do a better job. Prepare yourself for the future of your career, not just for today.

In addition to classroom instruction, academy recruits are trained in such areas as felony car stops, use of less-lethal tools, physical training, and use of firearms. *(Western Nevada State Police Officer Academy)*

selection standards for law enforcement officers, sets minimum education and training standards, and serves as the certification or licensing authority for sworn personnel. These agencies may be helpful in obtaining an idea of the state's approach to law enforcement training.

(Western Nevada State Police Officer Academy)

(Mark Ide)

(Mark Ide)

(Mark Ide)

According to the Bureau of Justice Statistics,[35] about 648 state and local law enforcement academies are operating in the United States and offering basic law enforcement training to individuals recruited or seeking to become law enforcement officers. These include local police officers, sheriff's deputies, campus police officers, state police or highway patrol officers, constables, and tribal police officers. Some academies also provide training for jail and corrections officers, probation and parole officers, fire marshals and arson investigators, private security officers, firefighters, emergency medical technicians, and animal control officers. About 40 percent of academies provided preservice training for individuals not sponsored by an employing agency and nearly 90 percent provide **in-service training**, especially for such units as K-9 or special weapons and tactics (SWAT) units. Some also train first-line (e.g., sergeant) or higher supervisors and field training instructors.

The median duration of basic recruit training is 19 weeks. Seventy percent of academies trained and certified sheriff's deputies, 50% trained and certified campus police officers, 21% trained and certified state police or highway patrol officers, and 15% trained and certified tribal police officers. The median class size among all academies was 18 recruits.

Table 3 includes a summary of training topics, the percentage of academies providing each topic, and the median number of hours of instruction per topic.

New Demeanor and Uniform

As **academy training** begins, recruits adopt a new identity and a system of discipline in which they learn to take orders and not to question authority. They learn that loyalty to fellow officers, a professional demeanor and bearing, and respect for authority are all highly valued in this occupation. The classroom teaches the recruit how to approach situations. Outside the classroom, as recruits share war stories discussed with academy staff, they informally transmit the proper attitudes to one another. Thus the recruits begin to form a collective understanding of policing and how they are supposed to function, and they gradually develop a common language and demeanor. Many people also believe that the police develop a swagger: a confident, authoritarian way of walking and presenting themselves. This is the beginning of the police officer's **working personality**.[36]

Recruits may wear a uniform for the first time during academy training, which is typically an awe-inspiring experience for them. The uniform sets recruits apart from society at large and conveys a sense of authority and responsibility to them and to the public. "Image is everything," according to a popular saying, and the choice of agency uniform can go a long way toward setting the image and tone of the department. Police uniforms come in various colors, styles, and fabrics. Some agencies even have their officers wearing blue jeans or shorts and T-shirts (e.g., for beach patrol).

The belt is one of the most important components of the patrol uniform and is certainly one of the heaviest. It often exceeds twenty pounds when laden with weapon, cuffs, baton, radio, flashlight, extra ammunition, chemical weapons, and so on. The uniform hat comes in several styles and is probably the piece of equipment that most readily identifies the officer and the department's image; each type of hat makes a certain statement to the public about the officer and his or her authority. The officer's badge also conveys a tremendous sense of authority; the most popular are customized shields, incorporating everything from the state motto and seal to symbols that convey the agency's image and philosophy. When designing its badge, a police department considers its tradition and history as well as those of the community.[37]

Table 3
TOPICS INCLUDED IN BASIC TRAINING OF STATE AND LOCAL LAW ENFORCEMENT TRAINING ACADEMIES

Topics	Percentage of Academies with Training	Median Number of Hours of Instruction
Operations		
Report writing	100%	20 hrs.
Patrol	99	40
Investigations	99	40
Basic first aid/CPR	99	24
Emergency vehicle operations	97	40
Computers/information systems	58	8
Weapons/self-defense		
Self-defense	99%	51 hrs.
Firearms skills	98	60
Non-lethal weapons	98	12
Legal		
Criminal law	100%	36 hrs.
Constitutional law	98	12
History of law enforcement	84	4
Self-improvement		
Ethics and integrity	100%	8 hrs.
Health and fitness	96	46
Stress prevention/management	87	5
Basic foreign language	36	16
Community policing		
Cultural diversity/human relations	98%	11 hrs.
Basic strategies	92	8
Mediation/conflict management	88	8
Special topics		
Domestic violence	99%	14 hrs.
Juveniles	99	8
Domestic preparedness	88	8
Hate crimes/bias crimes	87	4

Source: U.S. Department of Justice, Bureau of Justice Statistics, *State and Local Law Enforcement Training Academies, 2006* (February 2009), bjs.ojp.usdoj.gov/content/pub/pdf/slleta06.pdf (accessed July 15, 2010), p. 6.

mycrimekit™
Review: *Methods Used to Train Law Enforcement.*

Suspicion: The "Sixth Sense"

Police recruits are taught to nurture a **sixth sense**: suspicion. A suspicious nature is as important to the street officer as a fine touch is to a surgeon. The officer should not only be able to visually recognize but also be able to physically sense when something is wrong or out of the ordinary. A Chicago Police Department bulletin stated the following:

> Actions, dress, [and] location of a person often classify him as suspicious in the mind of a police officer. Men loitering near schools, public toilets, playgrounds and swimming pools may be sex perverts. Men loitering near . . . any business at closing time may be robbery suspects. Men or youths walking along looking into cars may be car thieves or looking for something to steal. Persons showing evidence of recent injury, or whose clothing is disheveled, may be victims or participants in an assault or strong-arm robbery.[38]

Officers are trained to be observant, to develop an intimate knowledge of the territory and people, and to "notice the normal. . . . . Only then can [they] decide what persons or cars under what circumstances warrant the appellation 'suspicious.'"[39] They must recognize when someone or something needs to be checked out. The following observations often warrant a field investigation:[40]

- People who do not "belong" where they are observed
- Automobiles that do not "look right" (such as dirty cars with clean license plates or a vehicle with plates attached with wire or in another unusual fashion)
- Businesses that are open at odd hours or that are not operating according to routine or custom
- People who exhibit exaggerated unconcern over contact with the officer or who are visibly "rattled" when near the officer
- Solicitors or peddlers who are in a residential neighborhood
- Lone males who sit in cars near a shopping center or near a school while paying unusual attention to women or children
- Persons who are hitchhikers
- Persons who wear a coat on a hot day

The academy also teaches neophyte officers that their major tool is their body; like mountain climbers, acrobats, or athletes, their body is an essential tool for the performance of their trade. The gun and nightstick initially fascinate the recruits, but until they are adequately trained, officers using them would be more a menace to society than a protector. Proper handling and safety measures are drilled into the recruits—the message is unequivocal that recruits will not be trusted with these potentially lethal weapons until they become proficient in their use. The new officers must be taught to measure their capacity to do the job, to assess carefully the physical capabilities of people they confront on the street, and to determine whether someone can be subdued without assistance or the risk of injury if a physical altercation should develop.[41]

The officers are also told, however, that they cannot approach every situation with the holster unsnapped or baton raised or twirling; they must demonstrate poise and not be eager to use force. The fact that the days of the club-swinging cop are gone is constantly instilled in officers. Thus, knowing that the body is a tool, the recruits are taught how to position themselves unobtrusively, whether at a vehicle stop or while engaged in a discussion on the street, in order to gain a physical advantage should trouble arise. They are taught when to use force and when to relent, to always keep control of the situation, and to feel that they would emerge victorious should force be required. Thus, in addition to weapons training, they may be given some weaponless defense training, including some holds that can be applied to subjects to bring them into compliance.

Recruits are taught some aspects of human nature and are encouraged not to be prejudicial in their actions or speech. They learn to deal with criminal suspects, offenders, victims, and witnesses and to be suspicious of "eyewitness" accounts. (For example, twenty-five "witnesses" claimed that they helped carry Abraham Lincoln from the Ford Theater into the little house where he died; eight different people said they held his head, and eighty-four people said they were in the room that night.[42])

Recruits often participate in hands-on training, practicing their new techniques in the field in simulated situations. Quite possibly the ultimate in hands-on training occurs at the Hogan's Alley complex at the FBI Academy in Quantico, Virginia, which opened in 1987 and covers almost thirty-five acres. This facility combines training, office, and classroom space on one site, increasing training effectiveness. Hogan's Alley (the name given many early-twentieth-century training facilities, apparently after an old comic strip about mischievous Irish kids) resembles a fully developed urban area. The set includes a business area and a residential street with townhouses and apartments. The use of movie-set techniques gives the illusion of depth and space. All furnishings—including a fleet of cars, furniture, desks, and even a pool table—were forfeited by convicted criminals. Federal agents are trained in the practical skills of crime-scene investigation and photography, surveillance techniques, arrest mechanics, and investigative skills. Trainees participate in paintball gunfights with persons role-playing criminals.

Other methods of police training that are currently used include **computer-based training (CBT)**, electronic bulletin boards, satellite training and teleconferencing, online computer forums, and correspondence courses. With computer costs declining, CBT is becoming increasingly popular and has been shown to be very effective. As CBT simulates real-life situations through the use of computer-modeled problems, it closely duplicates the way we think. One study found that police officers who learned about the exclusionary rule through CBT understood the material significantly better than the non-CBT control group.[43]

Virtual reality is another available (although very costly) form of police training. Trainees wear a head-mounted device that restricts their vision to two monitors and projects a computer-generated three-dimensional illusion that engulfs the senses of

The FBI's Hogan's Alley. *(Courtesy Federal Bureau of Investigation)*

sight, sound, and touch. Virtual reality may one day be commonly used for training police officers in such areas as pursuit driving, firearms training, critical-incident management, and crime-scene processing.

Finally, graduation day arrives, and the academy experience becomes a rite of passage. Graduation also means new uniforms, associates, and responsibilities and a raise in pay and status. As Arthur Niederhoffer observed, for many officers academy graduation is a worthy substitute for a college education. But "the very next morning the graduate is rudely dumped into a strange precinct where he must prove himself."[44]

Postacademy Field Training

Field Training Officer (FTO) Program

Once the recruits leave the academy, their knowledge of and acceptance into the police subculture are not yet complete. Another very important part of this acquisition process is assignment to a veteran officer for initial field instruction and observation in what is sometimes called a **field training officer (FTO) program**. The oldest formal FTO program began in the San Jose, California, Police Department in 1972.[45] This training program provides recruits with an opportunity to make the transition from the academy to the streets under the protective arm of a veteran officer. Recruits are on probationary status, normally ranging from six months to one year; they understand that they may be immediately terminated if their overall performance is unsatisfactory during that period. Figure 2 is a flowchart of the San Jose FTO program.

Most FTO programs consist of four identifiable phases: an introductory phase (the recruit learns agency policies and local laws), the training and evaluation phases (the recruit is introduced to more complicated tasks that patrol officers confront), and a final phase (the FTO acts strictly as an observer and evaluator while the recruit performs all the functions of a patrol officer).[46] The National Institute of Justice (NIJ), surveying nearly six hundred police agencies, found that 64 percent had an FTO program and that such programs had reduced the number of civil liability suits filed against their officers and against standardized training programs.[47] The length of time rookies are assigned to FTOs will vary; a formal FTO program might require close supervision for a range of one to twelve weeks.

Police Training Officer (PTO) Program

Another new approach to training new officers is slowly gaining traction across the nation; as with the FTO program discussed above, it is multifaceted and is an in-depth method: the **police training officer (PTO) program**. A PTO program seeks to take the traditional FTO program to a higher level, one that embraces new officers and evaluates them on their understanding and application of community-oriented policing and problem solving.

With a half million dollars in federal assistance, training needs were assessed and a new PTO program was recently initiated in the Reno, Nevada, Police Department and at five other national sites. Its theoretical underpinnings include

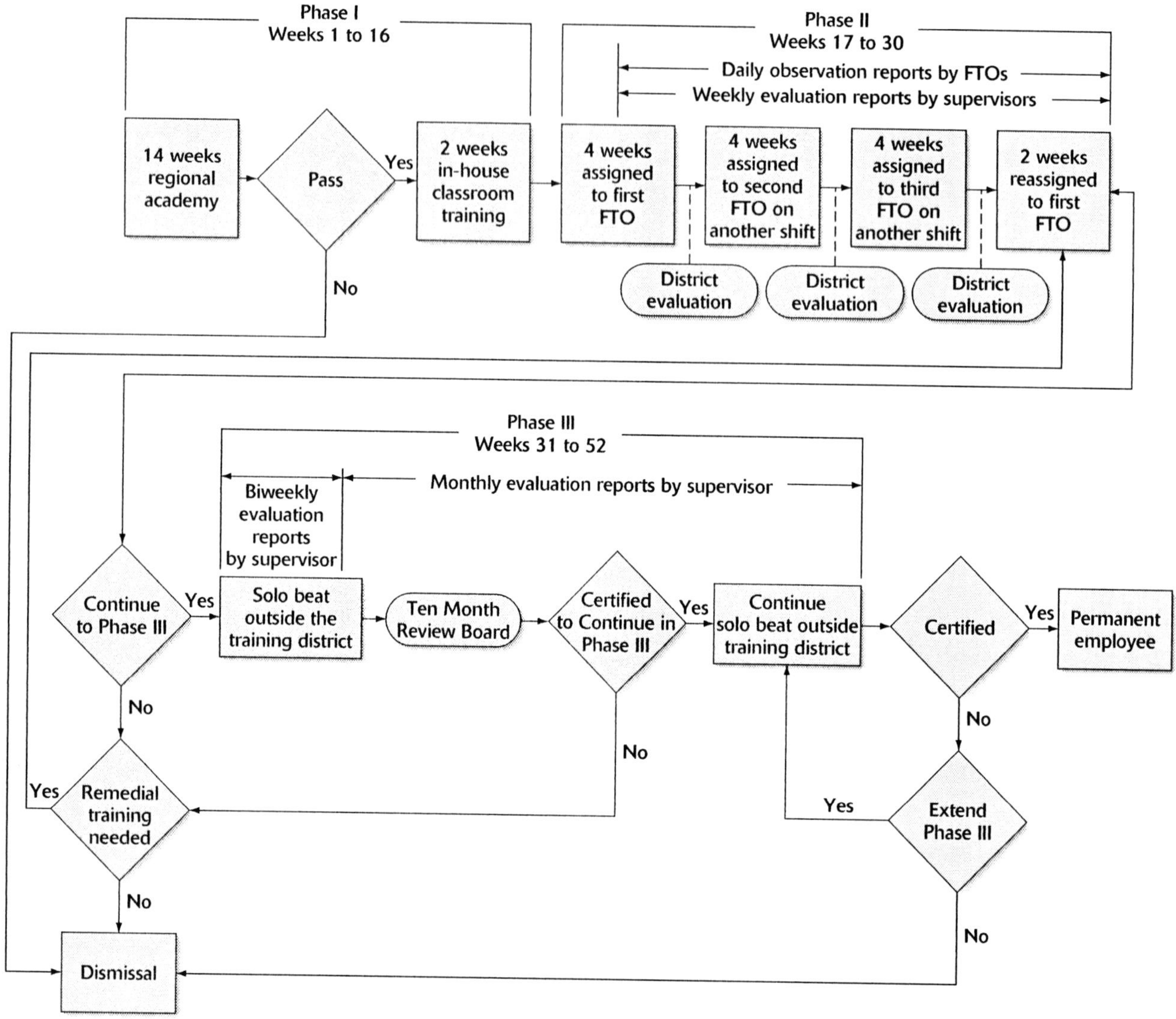

Figure 2

Flow Chart of the San Jose, California, FTO Training Program

Source: Michael McCampbell, *Field Training for Police Officers: The State of the Art*, www.ncjrs.gov/pdffiles1/nij/105574.pdf

adult and problem-based learning. The PTO program covers two primary training areas: substantive topics (the most common policing activities) and core competencies (the required common skills that officers engage in and that are required in the daily performance of their duties). New officers must successfully pass fifteen core competencies, specific skills, knowledge, and abilities that have been identified as essential for good policing. A learning matrix serves as a guide for trainees and trainers during the training period and demonstrates the interrelationships between the daily policing activities and core competencies during the eight phases of the PTO program.[48]

New Technology

New technology in the training function includes software known as ADORE (for Automated Daily Observation Report and Evaluation). FTOs in several agencies now field-testing the software find that it saves them time because they do not have to write reports by hand for each recruit. ADORE, which can be accessed through either a laptop or a Palm Pilot, allows FTOs to take computerized notes while watching trainees at work; it also reduces paperwork by allowing trainers to easily compile numbers for evaluating performance in dozens of categories. The software is credited with reducing FTO burnout, which is often a part of the paper-intensive evaluation process.[49]

Another new form of technology for police training that is being tested involves pursuit simulation. The training simulator is thought to be an effective means of determining how and when a vehicle pursuit should be halted. In one scenario, trainees in a simulated pursuit swerve around computerized images of a transit bus, a produce truck, a minivan, and a child on a skateboard before the chased vehicle enters a school zone, where the officer should end the hot pursuit. These simulated pursuits also allow supervisors to see how well trainees conduct themselves in accordance with their agency's pursuit policy, which is often several pages long.[50]

In-Service Training

Changes in departmental policies and procedures, court decisions, the specter of liability, and operational strategies and techniques demand that training be an ongoing process throughout a police officer's career. It is simply unreasonable to expect that the

Officer using a driving simulator.
(Courtesy WCSO Reno)

Officer in SWAT training.
(Courtesy WCSO Reno)

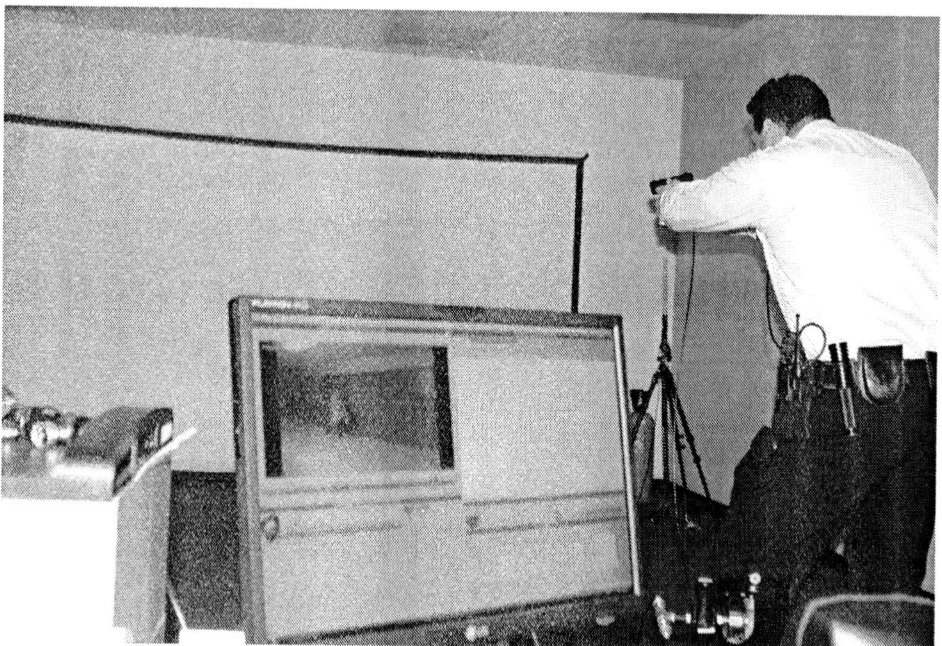

Officer training in indoor range.
(Courtesy Kenneth Peak)

knowledge gained during basic academy training or specialized training can serve an officer for an entire career. As Roger Dunham and Geoffrey Alpert put it, "Whether an officer is overweight or out of shape, a poor shot, uses poor judgment, or is too socialized into the police subculture to provide good community policing, in-service training can be used to restore the officer's skills or to improve his attitude."[51]

In-service training is used to recertify, refresh, or provide new information to officers in the most critical areas of their job, including weapons qualification, driving, defensive tactics, first aid, and changes in the law. Most states require a minimum number of hours of in-service training for police officers, and many departments exceed the minimum requirement. News items, court decisions, and other relevant information can be covered at roll call before the beginning of each shift. Short courses ranging from a few hours to several weeks are available for in-service officers through several means, such as videos and nationally televised training programs.

Working Personality: Having the "Right Stuff"

Development and Use of a Police Personality

Since William Westley first wrote about the police subculture in 1950, the notion of a police personality has become a popular area of study. In 1966, Jerome Skolnick[52] described what he termed the *working personality* of the police. He determined that the police role contained two important variables: danger and authority. Danger is a constant feature of police work. Police officers, constantly facing potential violence, are warned at the academy to be cautious and are told many war stories of officers shot and killed at domestic disturbances or traffic stops. Consequently, they develop a "perceptual shorthand," Skolnick said, that they use to identify certain kinds of people as "symbolic assailants"—individuals whom the officer has come to recognize as potentially violent based on their gestures, language, and attire.

The police, as Skolnick stated, represent authority, but unlike doctors, ministers, and the like, they must establish their authority. The symbols of that authority—the gun, the badge, and the baton—assist them, but officers' behavior and confidence are more important in social situations. As William Westley said, an officer "expects rage from the underprivileged and the criminal but understanding from the middle classes: the professionals, the merchants and the white-collar workers. They, however, define him as a servant, not as a colleague, and the rejection is hard to take."[53] Thus officers cannot even depend on their symbols and position of authority in dealing with the public; they are often confused when the public does not automatically observe and accept their authority.

Considerable research has compared the personality characteristics of the police with those of the general public,[54] and a number of differences have been discovered. One study found the average officer to be more intelligent, assertive, dependable, straightforward, and conscientious than civilians.[55] Other researchers who recently studied state traffic officers and deputy sheriffs using the MMPI and CPI scales reported that the officers scored high on the values of achievement, strong work ethic, ambition, leadership potential, and organizational skills.[56] Studies have also found conservatism and a high degree of cynicism among officers, although those traits are found to be present in much of the society at large. The late LAPD Chief William Parker asserted that police were "conservative, ultraconservative, and very right wing."[57]

Niederhoffer reported his classic study of **police cynicism** in 1967, using the NYPD as the site of a longitudinal study.[58] He found that although typical recruits begin their career without a trace of cynicism, police cynicism spikes most dramatically immediately after they leave the basic academy. This is probably because they confront the reality of the streets—the pain and criminality of society—and perhaps lose friends. Cynical veteran peers frequently reinforce the worst aspects of the job. In the period of about two to six years of service, the cynicism level continues to increase, but at a slower rate. The recruit has begun to adapt to the occupation and the people to be dealt with every day. At about mid-career (about eight to thirteen years of service), the cynicism level actually begins to decline, possibly because the officer has accepted the job and has been promoted, earns a decent salary and benefits, and realizes that he or she is about halfway to retirement. Toward the end of the career, the degree of cynicism levels off; for many officers, this is a period of coasting toward retirement.

A police officer's view of humanity may become distorted and cynical because many of the people the police deal with are offenders. They see what they feel are miscarriages of justice, such as improper or lenient court decisions, perjury on the witness stand, plea bargaining (where defendants are allowed to plead guilty to less serious offenses than charged or to fewer counts than charged, and observe fellow officers who do not live up to their code of ethics). Cynicism does have a protective feature, however: It can help to make the officer callous, allowing him or her to observe things that would sicken or horrify the average citizen without becoming mentally debilitated.

John Broderick[59] presented another view of the working personality of the police. He believed that there are actually four types of police personalities: enforcers, idealists, realists, and optimists.

Enforcers are officers who believe that the job of the police consists primarily of keeping their beats clean, making good arrests, and sometimes helping people. These officers have sympathy for vagrants, the elderly, the working poor, and others whom they see as basically good people. However, drug users, cop haters, and others frustrate the efforts of enforcers to make them "good," which makes the enforcers very unhappy. Thus they have high job dissatisfaction and an attitude of resentment, feeling that a lot of people are hostile toward them.

Idealists, according to Broderick, are officers who put high value on individual rights and due process. They also believe that it is their duty to keep the peace, protect citizens from criminals, and generally preserve the social order. With a high percentage of college graduates, idealists' commitment to the job is the lowest of the four groups, and they are less likely to recommend the job to a son or daughter.

Realists place relatively little emphasis on either social order or individual rights, Broderick says. They seem less frustrated, having found a way to come to terms with a difficult job. For them, the reality of the job consists of manila envelopes and properly completed forms. Realists see many problems in policing, such as special privileges given to politicians. Reality is not warm bodies to be dealt with but rather the paperwork that the bodies leave behind. They work well in the ordered, predictable environment of a police records room.

Broderick's last group, the *optimists*, also places a relatively high value on individual rights. Like idealists, they see their job as people oriented instead of crime oriented. They see policing as providing opportunities to help people; they view the television version of policing as totally unrealistic and find it rewarding to spend the majority of their time in service activities. Optimists have the lowest amount of job resentment, are committed to the job, and would choose policing as a career all over again. They enjoy the mental challenge of problem solving.

What Traits Make a Good Cop?

It is not too difficult to identify a bad cop through his or her unethical or criminal behavior. It is probably more difficult for the average person to identify the **traits of good officers**. How can a quantitative measure assess the work of police? Is it possible to judge the quality of an officer's work? These are challenging questions for police supervisors.

A major obstacle to assessing police performance rests with the nature of police work generally and the variation in the kinds of work performed by different shifts. The police role varies according to whether the officer is assigned to the day shift, evening (swing) shift, or night (graveyard) shift.

Dennis Nowicki[60] acknowledged that while certain characteristics form the foundation of a police officer—honesty, ethics, and moral character—no scientific formula can be used to create a highly effective officer. However, he compiled twelve qualities that he believes are imperative for entry-level police officers:

1. *Enthusiasm.* Believing in what one is doing and going about even routine duties with a certain vigor that is almost contagious.
2. *Good communication skills.* Having highly developed speaking and listening skills and interacting equally well with a wealthy person or someone lower on the socioeconomic ladder.
3. *Good judgment.* Having wisdom and the ability to make good analytic decisions based on an understanding of the problem.
4. *Sense of humor.* Being able to laugh and smile in order to help oneself cope with regular exposure to human pain and suffering.
5. *Creativity.* Using creative techniques to place oneself in the mind of the criminal and accomplish legal arrests.
6. *Self-motivation.* Making things happen, proactively solving difficult cases, and creating one's own luck.
7. *Knowing the job and the system.* Understanding the role of a police officer and the intricacies of the justice system, knowing what the administration requires, and using both formal and informal channels to be effective.
8. *Ego.* Believing one is a good officer and having the self-confidence that enables one to solve difficult crimes.

9. *Courage.* Being able to meet physical and psychological challenges, thinking clearly during times of high stress, admitting when one is wrong, and standing up for what is right.
10. *Discretion.* Enforcing the spirit of the law (not the letter of the law), giving people a break, showing empathy, and not being hard-nosed, hardheaded, or hard-hearted.
11. *Tenacity.* Staying focused, seeing challenges rather than obstacles, and viewing failure not as a setback but as an experience.
12. *Thirst for knowledge.* Being aware of new laws and court decisions and always learning (from the classroom but also via informal discussions with other officers).

Roles, Functions, and Styles of Policing

Definition and Knowledge of the Police Role

Why do the police exist? What are they supposed to do? Often these questions are given oversimplified answers such as "They enforce the law" or "They 'serve and protect.'"[61]

But policing is much more complex. As Herman Goldstein put it, "Anyone attempting to construct a workable definition of the police role will typically come away with old images shattered and with a newfound appreciation for the intricacies of police work."[62] Even with all of the movies and television series depicting police in action, most Americans probably still do not have an accurate idea of what the police really do. This confusion is quite understandable because the police are called on to perform an almost countless number of tasks. Police are even used as prosecutors in some states, such as New Hampshire.

Who defines the police role? There are several groups and individuals who do:[63]

- Private citizens influence the nature of the police role through their contacts with the police, by participation in COPPS groups, and through the election of public officials who set policy and appoint police administrators.
- Legislative bodies influence the role of the police by enacting statutes, both those that govern the police and those that the police use to govern others. In addition, legislative bodies determine police department budgets.
- The courts actively "police the police" by handing down decisions that regulate police conduct.
- Executives such as city managers and prosecutors help to define the police role by determining the types of cooperative agreements and evidence necessary for a prosecutable case.
- Police officers themselves define their roles by choosing to intervene in some incidents while ignoring others.

One of the greatest obstacles to understanding the American police is the crime fighter image. Many people believe that the role of the police is confined to law enforcement: the prevention and detection of crime and the apprehension of criminals. This is not an accurate view of contemporary policing.[64] It does not describe what the police do on a daily basis. First, only about 20 percent of the police officer's typical day is devoted to fighting crime per se.[65] As Jerome Skolnick and David Bayley point out, the crimes that terrify Americans the most—robbery, rape, burglary, and homicide—are rarely encountered by police on patrol: "Only 'Dirty Harry' has his lunch disturbed by a bank robbery in progress. Patrol officers individually make few important arrests. The 'good collar' is a rare event. Cops spend most of their time passively patrolling and providing emergency services."[66]

The crime fighter image persists, although it is extremely harmful to the public and individual officers.[67] The public suffers from this image because it gives rise to unrealistic expectations about the ability of the police to catch criminals. The image harms individual officers, who believe that rewards and promotions are tied only to success in capturing criminals. Also, many individuals enter policing expecting it to be exciting and rewarding, as depicted on television and in the movies. Later they learn that much of their time is spent with boring, mundane tasks that are anything but glamorous, that much of the work is trivial, and that paperwork is seldom stimulating.

Role Conflicts

Role conflicts may develop with officers and their departments. A family disturbance is a good example. Assume that Jane Smith reports to the police that her husband, John, is assaulting her. Police officers must respond to the disturbance, and the law empowers them to intervene, to enforce the law, and to maintain order. For the combatants, it is a very trying experience, not only because their family is dysfunctional but also because the police have been summoned to their home. Veteran officers might view the domestic call as trivial and inconvenient, leaving the scene as quickly as possible to go perform "real" police duties.

By the same token, the role of the police is often in the eye of the beholder. For example, the domestic argument just described might seem to fit best the category of maintaining order. However, if the responding officers are trained in crisis intervention or if they refer the couple to counseling, they are providing a social service. On the other hand, if John is found to have assaulted Jane, it is likely a criminal matter. If the police make an arrest or even just assist Jane in swearing out a warrant, the matter becomes a law enforcement issue. The category to which this incident is assigned will vary greatly from agency to agency, officer to officer, and researcher to researcher, making it difficult to draw any solid conclusions about the police role.

Still, it is important to be as explicit as possible about the police role for several reasons. First, we can recruit and select competent police personnel only when we have a clear vision of what the police are supposed to accomplish. Second, evaluation for retention and promotion is useful only to the extent that we evaluate in terms of what the police are supposed to do. Third, budgetary decisions should be based on an accurate analysis of police roles. Fourth, efficiency and effectiveness in police organizations depend on accurate task descriptions. Fifth, public cooperation with the police depends on developing reasonable expectations of the roles of the police and the public.[68]

The police must identify those crimes on which police resources should be concentrated, focusing on the crimes that generate the most public fear and economic loss. The chief executive should have written policies to ensure that the police mission and the objectives used to achieve that mission are maintained by the police department. In other words, it is not enough for the police to "maintain order" or "provide justice." A police department may use many methods to maintain order and provide justice. In China or Saudi Arabia, those methods would be far different from those generally employed in the United States. But would "justice" result? In America, the police must maintain order without resorting to extralegal means or violating human rights.

Policing Functions and Styles

Officers may be said to perform four basic **policing functions**: (1) enforcing the law, (2) performing services (such as maintaining or assisting animal-control units, reporting burned-out street lights or damaged traffic signs, delivering death messages, checking the welfare of people in their homes, delivering blood), (3) preventing crime (patrolling, providing the public with information on crime prevention), and (4) protecting the innocent (by investigating crimes, police are systematically removing innocent people from consideration as crime suspects).

James Q. Wilson[69] looked at the functions of the police differently, determining that the police perform two basic functions: maintaining order (peacekeeping) and enforcing the law. Maintaining order constitutes most of the activities of the police; as noted earlier, less than 20 percent of the calls answered by police are directly related to crime control or law enforcement. Much of an officer's time is spent with such service activities as traffic control and routine patrol. Indeed, in some cases the police deliberately avoid enforcing the law in an attempt to maintain order. For example, if the police know of a busy street where many drivers speed, they may desist from setting up a speed trap during rush hours so as not to impede the flow of traffic and possibly cause accidents.

Enforcing the law means upholding the statutes, but this is not as simple and straightforward a function as it might seem. First, the police are really not very good at performing the law enforcement function; they have not traditionally been successful at preventing crime or providing long-term solutions to neighborhood disorder (although the relatively new community-policing and problem-solving concepts are addressing this shortcoming). Second, there are several types of crime—such as white-collar crime—with which the local police seldom deal. Third, the police, representing only about 2.3 officers per 1,000 population in the United States, cannot effectively control the public alone. Finally, the police are successful in solving only a fraction of the property and personal crimes that occur.[70]

Wilson also maintained that there are three distinctive **policing styles**:[71]

Review: *Policing Styles.*

1. *Watchman style.* The watchman style involves the officer as a "neighbor." Here, officers act as if order maintenance (rather than law enforcement) is their

primary function. The emphasis is on using the law as a means of maintaining order rather than regulating conduct through arrests. Police ignore many common minor violations, such as traffic and juvenile offenses. These violations and so-called victimless crimes, such as gambling and prostitution, are tolerated and will often be handled informally. Thus the individual officer has wide latitude concerning whether to enforce the letter or the spirit of the law; the emphasis is on using the law to give people what they "deserve." It assumes that some people, such as juveniles, are occasionally going to "act up."

2. *Legalistic style.* A legalistic style casts the officer as a "soldier." This style takes a much harsher view of law violations: Police officers issue large numbers of traffic citations, detain a high volume of juvenile offenders, and act vigorously against illicit activities, and large numbers of other kinds of arrests occur as well. Chief administrators want high arrest and ticketing rates not only because violators should be punished but also because it reduces the opportunity for their officers to engage in corrupt behavior. This style of policing assumes that the purpose of the law is to punish.
3. *Service style.* The service style views the officer as a "teacher." This style falls between the watchman and legalistic styles. The police take seriously all requests for either law enforcement or order maintenance (unlike in the watchman-style department) but are less likely to respond by making an arrest or otherwise imposing formal sanctions. Police officers see their primary responsibility as protecting public order against the minor and occasional threats posed by unruly teenagers and "outsiders" (tramps, derelicts, out-of-town visitors). The citizenry expects its service-style officers to display the same qualities as its department store salespeople: They should be courteous, neat, and deferential. The police will frequently use informal sanctions instead of making arrests.

Which Role, Function, and Style Are Typically Employed?

As we have seen, the role, function, and style of the police will differ by time and place. They will also be fluid within the agency, changing with the times, the political climate, and the problems of the day. Most police agencies do not determine which problems they address; rather, they respond to the problems that citizens believe are important, and the police agencies depend on the goals set by the community, the chief executive, and the individual officers. Sometimes roles, functions, and styles overlap, but most of the time they are distinct.

Bringing Down the Walls: Women and Minorities Wearing the Badge

Over the last thirty years, the proportion of **women police officers** has grown steadily. During the 1970s, some formal barriers to hiring women were eliminated, such as height requirements; in addition, subjective physical agility tests and oral

Female officers. (Courtesy Reno, Nevada, Police Department)

interviews were modified.[72] Some job discrimination suits further expanded women's opportunities.

Women as Officers and Chief Executives

Women represent about 14.5 percent of the sworn personnel in municipal agencies, 13.5 percent of sworn personnel in county agencies, and 8.2 percent in small agencies.[73] State agencies as a whole have a much lower percentage of female officers than either local or federal law enforcement agencies, 6.8 percent.[74] Women account for 14.8 percent of all federal officers, which is a bit higher than local agencies.[75]

Although this representation of women officers is low compared to their overall proportion in the total population, it becomes even more evident in the leadership ranks, where women number only 1 percent of the police chiefs in the United States.[76] The number of women serving as chiefs has expanded considerably, however, since Penny Harrington took over as chief in 1985 in Portland, Oregon (becoming the first woman chief in a large agency), and Elizabeth (Betsy) Watson assumed the helm in 1990 in Houston, Texas (becoming the first in a city of more than 1 million population). As examples, in early 2004, newly appointed women were serving as chiefs of police in San Francisco, Boston, Detroit, and Milwaukee, providing further evidence that today's "mayors are looking for sophisticated CEOs who can oversee large budgets, negotiate thorny management problems, and set sound department-wide policy."[77]

One survey[78] identified 157 women serving as chiefs of police and 25 who were sheriffs; 96 of these chiefs participated in a survey intended to establish a demographic profile of the women. Of these chief executives 48 (49 percent) were in charge of municipal police departments, whereas 40 (42 percent) led college and university police departments. Only 7 of the respondents led agencies with more than 100 sworn officers (5 being municipal, 1 a campus police agency, and 1 a tribal agency). Conversely, 23 (25.8 percent) were in agencies with 10 or fewer officers. These women CEOs reflect the increasing levels of education achieved by today's chiefs, with three-fourths having either a bachelor's or a master's degree. About one-third had a partner who was also in policing.[79]

Certainly, a large enough proportion of women have now been employed in policing long enough to be considered for promotion. A number of researchers question the commitment of police agencies and their male administrators in promoting women and have made recommendations for changing the evaluation and promotional process.[80]

Key Issues

Peter Horne identified several key issues that need to be addressed:[81]

1. *Recruitment.* Unfocused, random recruiting is unlikely to attract diversity. Literature such as flyers, posters, and brochures should feature female officers working in all areas of policing. Furthermore, agencies should go anywhere (local colleges, women's groups, female community leaders, gyms, martial arts schools) and use all types of media to attract qualified applicants.[82]
2. *Pre-employment physical testing.* Historically, women have been screened out disproportionately in the pre-employment screening physical testing used by many agencies. Tests that include such components as scaling a six-foot wall, bench-pressing one's own weight, and throwing medicine balls are likely to have an adverse impact on female applicants, so agencies should examine their physical tests to determine the reasons women are disproportionately screened out. In addition, agencies should permit all candidates to practice for the pre-employment physical exam.
3. *Academy training.* Recruits must be trained in sexually integrated academy classes to ensure full integration between female and male officers. Female instructors are especially important during academy training because they are positive role models and help female rookies to develop skills and confidence. Involving female instructors in firearms and physical/self-defense training will send a message that trained, veteran female officers can effectively handle the physical aspects of policing.
4. *Field training.* FTOs play a crucial role in transforming the academy graduate into a competent field officer. FTOs should be both supportive of female rookies and effective evaluators of their competence. Women should also serve as FTOs.
5. *Assignments.* Agencies should routinely review the daily assignments of all probationary officers to ensure they have equal opportunity to become effective patrol officers. If women are removed from patrol early in their careers (for any reason), they will miss vital field patrol experience. The majority of supervisory

positions exist in the patrol division, and departments generally believe that field supervisors must have adequate field experience to be effective and respected by subordinates.

6. *Promotions.* The so-called glass ceiling continues to restrict women's progress through the ranks. Performance evaluations and the overall promotional system utilized by agencies should be scrutinized for gender bias. For example, studies show that the more subjective the promotion process, the less likely women are to pass it. To provide more objectivity (in terms of ability to measure aptitude), the process may include more hands-on (practical, applied) tasks and the selection of board members of both genders.
7. *Harassment and discrimination.* Where they exist, sexual discrimination and harassment exact a human cost from the women involved—including a negative impact on their performance and careers (and, probably, a negative impact on the recruitment of other women into policing). A Police Foundation study found that "most women officers have experienced both sex discrimination and harassment on the job."[83] Departments need policies in place concerning sexual harassment and gender discrimination—and they must enforce them.
8. *Mentoring.* The employee's experience as he or she transitions into the organization can be a deciding factor in whether the employee remains with the organization. Formal mentoring programs—which can begin even before the rookie enters the academy—have helped some agencies raise their retention rates for women; such programs can include having a veteran employee provide new hires with information concerning what to expect at the academy and beyond during field training and the probationary period.
9. *Career and family.* Police work can create a considerable amount of conflict between one's work life and one's family life. Police agencies should have a leave policy covering pregnancy and maternity leave. Light- or limited-duty assignments (e.g., desk, communications, records) can be made available to female officers when reassignment is necessary. Other issues include the availability of quality child care and shift rotation (which can more heavily burden single parents) and uniforms, body armor, and firearms that fit women.

As the community-oriented policing and problem-solving concept continues to expand, female officers can play an increasingly vital role. Experts also maintain that the verbal skills many women possess often have a calming effect that defuses potentially explosive situations.

Still, this clearly remains an area in which law enforcement must change. For women to serve effectively as police officers, executives must see the value of utilizing and vigorously recruiting, hiring, and retaining them. A basic task for the chief executive is to consider how departmental policies impact female officers with respect to selection, training, promotion, sexual harassment, and family leave. Most important, executives must set a tone of welcoming women into the department.

Minorities as Law Enforcement Officers

The recruitment of **minority police officers** also remains a difficult task. Probably the most difficult barrier has to do with the image that police officers have in the minority communities. Unfortunately, police officers have been seen as symbols of oppression and have been charged with using excessive brutality; they are often seen as an army of occupation.

African American police officers face problems similar to those of women who attempt to enter and prosper in police work. Until more African American officers are promoted and can affect police policy and serve as role models, they are likely to be treated unequally and have difficulty being promoted—a classic catch-22 situation. African Americans considering a police career may be encouraged by a survey of African American officers, which found that most believed their jobs were satisfying and offered opportunities for advancement.[84]

An influential coalition of African Americans is the National Organization of Black Law Enforcement Executives (NOBLE), which was founded in 1976 and has 57 chapters in the United States. Its purposes are to unify African American law enforcement officers at executive and command levels; to conduct research in relevant areas of law enforcement; to recommend legislation relating to the criminal justice process; to establish means and strategies for dealing with racism in the field of criminal justice; to sensitize people to the problems of the African American community; to facilitate the exchange of information among African American police executives; and to articulate the concerns of African American executives in law enforcement.[85]

Officers on patrol. *(Courtesy Michael Newman, PhotoEdit.)*

SUMMARY

We began this chapter with a look at the officer's world and an explanation of how private citizens are socialized into their role as police officers and prepared for working the street; an emphasis was placed on viewing these officers as individuals rather than in the aggregate, as is often the case. The reader has seen how people are recruited, tested, and trained for their role as police officers through a series of "hurdles"; during this process they are transformed psychologically, physically, and emotionally to become competent and to function in the very challenging world of the police.

We have established that a working personality develops in police officers. Both formal training and peer relations are instructive and helpful in teaching the novice officer how to act, think, and view certain elements of the job. Unfortunately, it was shown that danger, suspicion, constantly witnessing the seedy side of humanity, and other factors also tend to inculcate in police officers another common trait: cynicism.

This chapter also examined the roles, functions, and styles of the local police in America. More than a century and a half after the adoption of the early British model of policing, disagreement, conflict, and debate are still widespread concerning what we truly want our police to do, represent, and become.

The hiring process described in this chapter is certainly the ideal rather than the real. Probably few of the seventeen thousand American police agencies compel their applicants to successfully complete the entire battery of tests and screening examinations described here, nor do all departments have the inclination or resources to engage in a full-fledged FTO or PTO program that would monitor and further train new recruits. It is also doubtful that formal education requirements are being elevated for or acquired by police at the rate of the society at large. Yet the present recruitment and training process seems to work well overall, except in those instances where a jurisdiction, sorely needing personnel, engages in rapid hiring and can easily bring substandard people into the field.

Women and minorities in policing also were discussed. The incorporation of community-oriented, problem-solving strategies of policing has changed the focus of policing from a highly physical, quantitative, and hardware-oriented field to one that requires officers with communication skills, an understanding of our diverse society, and problem-solving capabilities. Women and minorities, in both philosophical and quantitative terms, have yet to be accepted in this occupation, even though studies have shown their tremendous value to the field. The argument seems compelling that until enough women and minorities are employed at all levels of a police force, policy decisions about hiring and promoting them will be ineffective or nonexistent. Strategies to encourage them to enter the field are still being developed; much more can obviously be done toward enhancing their visibility, presence, and usefulness in this occupation.

KEY TERMS

academy training
assessment center
computer-based training (CBT)
field training officer (FTO) program
hurdle process
in-service training
minority police officers
police cynicism
police training officer (PTO) program
policing functions
policing styles
recruiting
sixth sense
traits of good officers
women police officers
working personality

REVIEW QUESTIONS

1. What are some of the problems confronting today's police recruiters and some of the unique measures they use to obtain a viable applicant pool?
2. What is generally the hiring process for new police officers and the kinds of tests that are commonly given to applicants?
3. Which kinds of skills and knowledge are imparted to police trainees during their academy training, and what are the typical subjects that are taught in a police academy curriculum?
4. What are the methods and purposes of the FTO and PTO programs?
5. What is meant by the term *working personality*, how was the concept developed, and what is its function?
6. What is police cynicism, and how does it operate?
7. What are the ideal traits of police officers?
8. Why is the crime fighter image the greatest obstacle in accepting a realistic view of the police role?
9. What are the primary functions and styles of policing?
10. What are some challenges facing the recruitment and retention of women and minorities in policing, as well as those women and minorities who are employed in the field?

LEARN BY DOING

1. You are consulting with a medium-size police department that has been criticized in the media for its high levels of recruit dropouts from the basic academy as well as high percentages of recruits being failed by their field training officers (FTOs) during their probationary period. It appears at first glance that local police–community relations are

such that there are not large pools of police applicants. You are to recommend better recruitment methods that will overcome these academy and FTO problems. What would you recommend?

2. Assume the same scenario as above, in #1. Now, however, the emphasis shifts to the kinds of tests that should be employed during the initial hurdle process or hiring phase. While admitting the need for improvement, the chief of police argues that there simply is not enough time, money, or other resources to employ the full range of test methods, one that would include for each recruit in a *large* agency a written examination, psychological test, physical agility test, personal interview, character investigation, polygraph examination, medical examination, and drug screening. The chief asks you to consider each type of entry-level examination in terms of its contribution to the hiring process and the overall mission of the agency, and then—due to cost limitations—make recommendations for *six* forms of testing that should minimally be employed for hiring new officers. Which six types of tests would you recommend (defend your choices)?
3. Still assuming the same scenario as in #1 and #2, the emphasis now shifts to training. Due to a number of recent incidents involving police errors in procedure and revelations of inappropriate use of force, the department has been criticized in the media for its recruit training requirements. Looking at the nature of the curriculum and topics included in Table 3, which training topics do you think might be added to the curriculum? Expanded in their duration? Deleted? Defend your answers.

mycrimekit™

Go to MyCrimeKit.com and discover additional study tools and resources related to this chapter.

- Key Terms
- Review Questions
  - Multiple Choice Questions
  - True/False
  - Fill in the Blank
  - Essay
- MEDIA REVIEW: where you can review the *traits of a good law enforcement officer, methods used to train law enforcement*, and *policing styles* covered in this chapter.
- FLASHCARDS: to test your knowledge of this chapter.
- *NEW YORK TIMES:* where you can read the latest articles related to criminology and criminal law.
- THE CAREER CENTER: where you can explore career opportunities in criminal justice and criminology.
- THE ONLINE RESEARCH LIBRARY: where you can explore the Cybrary and Research Navigator

NOTES

1. William A. Westley, *Violence and the Police* (Cambridge, MA: MIT Press, 1970).
2. Geoffrey P. Alpert and Roger G. Dunham, *Policing Urban America,* 2nd ed. (Prospect Heights, IL: Waveland Press, 1992), p. 80; for an excellent description of the evolving police role, also see Roger G. Dunham and Geoffrey P. Alpert, *Critical Issues in Policing: Contemporary Readings,* 5th ed. (Long Grove, IL: Waveland Press, 2005), pp. 1–9.
3. Quoted in V. A. Leonard and Harry W. More, *Police Organization and Management,* 3rd ed. (Mineola, NY: Foundation Press, 1971), p. 128.
4. Joel Lefkowitz, "Industrial-Organizational Psychology and the Police," *American Psychologist* (May 1977): 346–364.
5. R. B. Mills, "Use of Diagnostic Small Groups in Police Recruit Selection and Training," *Journal of Criminal Law, Criminology and Police Science* 60 (1969): 238–241; John Van Maanen, "Police Socialization: A Longitudinal Examination of Job Attitudes in an Urban Police Department," *Administrative Science Quarterly* 20 (1975): 207–228.
6. C. Gorer, "Modification of National Character: The Role of the Police in England," *Journal of Social Issues* 11 (1955): 24–32; Arthur Niederhoffer, *Behind the Shield: The Police in Urban Society* (New York: Anchor, 1967), p. 140.
7. M. Steven Meagher and Nancy A. Yentes, "Choosing a Career in Policing: A Comparison of Male and Female Perceptions," *Journal of Police Science and Administration* 14 (1986): 320–327.
8. Lefkowitz, "Industrial-Organizational Psychology and the Police."
9. J. D. Matarazzo, B. V. Allen, G. Saslow, and A. N. Wiens, "Characteristics of Successful Policemen and Firemen Applicants," *Journal of Applied Psychology* 48 (1964): 123–133.
10. Bruce N. Carpenter and Susan M. Raza, "Personality Characteristics of Police Applicants: Comparisons Across Subgroups and with Other Populations," *Journal of Police Science and Administration* 15 (1987): 10–17.
11. Carpenter and Raza also compared police applicants with other similar occupational groups and found that police applicants appear to be most like nuclear submariners and least like air force trainees and security guards.
12. Lawrence S. Wrightsman, *Psychology and the Legal System* (Monterey, CA: Brooks/Cole, 1987), pp. 85–86.
13. Al Seedman and P. Hellman, *Chief!* (New York: Arthur Fields, 1974), pp. 4–5.
14. Jeremy M. Wilson and Clifford A. Grammich, *Police Recruitment and Retention in the Contemporary Urban Environment: A National Discussion of Personnel Experiences and Promising Practices from the Front Lines* (Santa Monica, CA: RAND Corporation, 2009), p. 5; also available at www.rand.org/pubs/conf_proceedings/2009/RAND_CF261.pdf (accessed July 14, 2010).
15. Ibid., p. 2.

16. Stephanie Slahor, "RAND Study Suggests Strategies to Address Recruiting Shortage," *Law and Order*, December 8, 2008, p. 32.
17. Dizon, "Searching for Police."
18. "Plenty of Talk, Not Much Action," *Law Enforcement News*, January 15/31, 1999, p. 1.
19. "Hiring Problem? What Hiring Problem? NYSP Has Answers to Recruiting Slump," *Law Enforcement News*, November 30, 2000, p. 1.
20. "Police Chiefs Try Many Recruiting Strategies to Boost Applicant Pool," *Crime Control Digest*, February 2, 2001, pp. 1–2.
21. U.S. Department of Justice, Bureau of Justice Statistics, *Local Police Departments, 2003* (Washington, DC: Author, May 2006), p. 8.
22. Alfred Stone and Stuart DeLuca, *Police Administration* (New York: John Wiley and Sons, 1985).
23. Hans Toch, *Psychology of Crime and Criminal Justice* (Prospect Heights, IL: Waveland Press, 1999), p. 44.
24. Philip Ash, Karen B. Slora, and Cynthia F. Britton, "Police Agency Officer Selection Practices," *Journal of Police Science and Administration* 17 (December 1990): 259–264.
25. S. H. Marsh, "Validating the Selection of Deputy Sheriffs," *Public Personnel Review* 23 (1962): 41–44.
26. William H. Thweatt, "A Vocational Counseling Approach to Police Selection" (unpublished dissertation, University of Arizona).
27. W. Clinton Terry III, *Policing Society* (New York: John Wiley and Sons, 1985), p. 194.
28. George E. Hargrave, "Using the MMPI and CPI to Screen Law Enforcement Applicants: A Study of Reliability and Validity of Clinicians' Decisions," *Journal of Police Science and Administration* 13 (1985): 221–224.
29. Roger G. Dunham and Geoffrey P. Alpert, *Critical Issues in Policing: Contemporary Readings* (Prospect Heights, IL: Waveland Press, 1989), p. 80.
30. For a complete discussion of the Sparks Police Officers Physical Abilities Test (POPAT), see Ken Peak, Douglas Farenholtz, and George Coxey, "Physical Abilities Testing for Police Officers: A Flexible, Job Related Approach," *Police Chief* (January 1992): 51–56.
31. Terry Eisenberg, D. A. Kent, and C. R. Wall, *Police Personnel Practices in State and Local Governments* (Gaithersburg, MD: International Association of Chiefs of Police, 1973), p. 15.
32. George E. Hargrave and Deirdre Hiatt, "Law Enforcement Selection with the Interview, MMPI, and CPI: A Study of Reliability and Validity," *Journal of Police Science and Administration* 15(2) (1987): 110–117.
33. U.S. Department of Justice, Bureau of Justice Statistics, *Local Police Departments, 2003*, p. 8.
34. Quoted in Charles R. Swanson, Leonard Territo, and Robert W. Taylor, *Police Administration*, 2nd ed. (New York: Macmillan, 1988), pp. 202–203.

35. U.S. Department of Justice, Bureau of Justice Statistics, *State and Local Law Enforcement Training Academies, 2006* (February 2009), http://bjs.ojp.usdoj.gov/index.cfm?ty=tp&tid=77 (accessed August 21, 2010); also see U.S. Department of Justice, Bureau of Justice Assistance, "Discover Policing: Training/Academy Life," discoverpolicing.org/what_does_take/?fa=training_academy_life (accessed July 15, 2010).
36. Ibid., pp. 6, 8.
37. Lois Pilant, "Enhancing the Patrol Image," *Police Chief* (August 1992): 55–61.
38. Wrightsman, *Psychology and the Legal System*, p. 86.
39. Quoted in Jerome Skolnick, "A Sketch of the Policeman's Working Personality," in *The Police Community*, ed. Jack Goldsmith and Sharon S. Goldsmith (Pacific Palisades, CA: Palisades Publishers, 1974), p. 106.
40. Thomas F. Adams, "Field Interrogation," *Police* (March–April 1963): 1–8.
41. Jonathan Rubenstein, "Cop's Rules," in *Police Behavior: A Sociological Perspective*, ed. Richard J. Lundman (New York: Oxford University Press, 1980), pp. 68–78.
42. Bruce Catton, "Eyewitness Reports on the Assassination of Abraham Lincoln," in *Criminal Justice: Allies and Adversaries*, ed. John R. Snortum and Ilana Hader (Pacific Palisades, CA: Palisades Publishers, 1978), pp. 155–157.
43. Tom Wilkenson and John Chattin-McNichols, "The Effectiveness of Computer-Assisted Instruction for Police Officers," *Journal of Police Science and Administration* 13 (1985): 230–235.
44. Niederhoffer, *Behind the Shield*, p. 51.
45. Dunham and Alpert, *Critical Issues in Policing*, p. 112.
46. Ibid., p. 111.
47. Ibid., pp. 112–115.
48. Kenneth J. Peak, Steven Pitts, and Ronald W. Glensor, "From 'FTO' to 'PTO': A Contemporary Approach to Post-Academy Recruit Training" (paper presented at the annual conference of the Academy of Criminal Justice Sciences, Seattle, WA, March 22, 2007).
49. "Field Trainers Have Reports Well in Hand," *Law Enforcement News*, November 15, 2000, p. 5.
50. "Pursuit Simulation Training Is No Ordinary Crash Course," *Law Enforcement News*, November 15, 2000, p. 6.
51. Alpert and Dunham, *Policing Urban America*, p. 58.
52. Jerome Skolnick, "A Sketch of the Policeman's Working Personality," quoted in *The Police Community*, eds. Jack Goldsmith and Sharon S. Goldsmith (Pacific Palisades, CA: Palisades Publishers, 1974), p. 106.
53. William Westley, *Violence and the Police* (Cambridge, MA: MIT Press, 1970), p. 56.
54. Elizabeth Burbeck and Adrian Furnham, "Police Officer Selection: A Critical Review of the Literature," *Journal of Police Science and Administration* 13 (1985): 58–69.
55. Joseph D. Matarazzo, B. V. Allen, George Saslow, and Arthur N. Wiens, "Characteristics of Successful Policemen and Firemen Applicants," *Journal of Applied Psychology* 48 (1964): 123–133.

56. George E. Hargrave, Deirdre Hiatt, and Tim W. Gaffney, "A Comparison of MMPI and CPI Profiles for Traffic Officers," *Journal of Police Science and Administration* 14 (1986): 250–258.
57. Quoted in Seymour M. Lipset, "Why Cops Hate Liberals—and Vice Versa," *Atlantic Monthly* 223 (March 1969): 76.
58. Niederhoffer, *Behind the Shield*, p. 140.
59. John J. Broderick, *Police in a Time of Change* (Prospect Heights, IL: Waveland Press, 1987), p. 215.
60. Adapted from Dennis Nowicki, "Twelve Traits of Highly Effective Police Officers," *Law and Order*, October 1999, pp. 45–46.
61. Samuel Walker, *The Police in America: An Introduction*, 2nd ed. (New York: McGraw-Hill, 1992), p. 61.
62. Herman Goldstein, *Policing a Free Society* (Cambridge, MA: Ballinger, 1977), p. 21.
63. Steven M. Cox, *Police: Practices, Perspectives, Problems* (Boston: Allyn & Bacon, 1996), pp. 18–19.
64. Ibid., p. 61.
65. See Albert Reiss, *The Police and the Public* (New Haven, CT: Yale University Press, 1971), p. 96.
66. Jerome H. Skolnick and David H. Bayley, *The New Blue Line: Police Innovation in Six American Cities* (New York: Free Press, 1986), p. 4.
67. Patrick V. Murphy and Thomas Plate, *Commissioner: A View from the Top of American Law Enforcement* (New York: Simon and Schuster, 1977). Also see Walker, *The Police in America*, pp. 55–56.
68. Cox, *Police*, pp. 18–19.
69. James Q. Wilson, *Varieties of Police Behavior* (Cambridge, MA: Harvard University Press, 1968), pp. 140–226.
70. Cox, *Police*, pp. 18–19.
71. Wilson, *Varieties of Police Behavio*r, pp. 140–226.
72. Barbara Raffel Price, "Sexual Integration in American Law Enforcement," in ed. William C. Heffernan and Timothy *Police Ethics: Hard Choices in Law Enforcement*, (New York: John Jay Press, 1985), see also Vivian B. Lord and Kenneth J. Peak, *Women in Law Enforcement Careers: A Guide for Preparing and Succeeding* (Upper Saddle River, NJ: Prentice Hall, 2005).
73. U.S. Department of Justice, Bureau of Justice Statistics, *Local Police Departments, 2003* (Washington, DC: Author, 2006), p. iii; U.S. Department of Justice, Bureau of Justice Statistics, *Sheriff's Offices, 2003* (Washington, DC: Author, 2006), p. iii.
74. National Center for Women and Policing, *Equality Denied: The Status of Women in Policing* (Washington, DC: Feminist Majority Foundation, 2001), p. 5.
75. Department of Justice, Bureau of Justice Statistics, *Federal Law Enforcement Officers, 2004* (Washington, DC: Author, July 2006), p. 1.
76. Dorothy Moses Schulz, "Women Police Chiefs: A Statistical Profile," *Police Quarterly* 6(3) (September 2003): 330–345.
77. Peg Tyre, "Ms. Top Cop," *Newsweek* (April 12, 2004), p. 49.

78. Schulz, "Women Police Chiefs," p. 333.
79. Ibid.
80. Ibid.
81. Peter Horne, "Policewomen: 2000 A.D. Redux," *Law and Order* (November 1999), p. 53.
82. For information about successful recruiting efforts as well as the diverse kinds of assignments women now occupy in law enforcement, see Vivian B. Lord and Kenneth J. Peak, *Women in Law Enforcement Careers: A Guide for Preparing and Succeeding* (Upper Saddle River, NJ: Prentice Hall, 2005).
83. Quoted in Horne, "Policewomen," p. 59.
84. Lena Williams, "Police Officers Tell of Strains of Living as a 'Black in Blue,'" *New York Times*, February 14, 1988, pp. 1, 26.
85. National Organization of Black Law Enforcement Executives, "About NOBLE," www.noblenatl.org/index.php?option=com_content&view=section&id=4&Itemid=41 (accessed July 15, 2010).

Personnel Issues and Practices

Personnel Issues and Practices

STRESS, LABOR RELATIONS, HIGHER EDUCATION, PRIVATE POLICE

Debate on public issues should be uninhibited, robust, and wide open.
—*Justice William Brennan*

History has many cunning passages, contrived corridors, and issues.
—*T. S. Eliot*

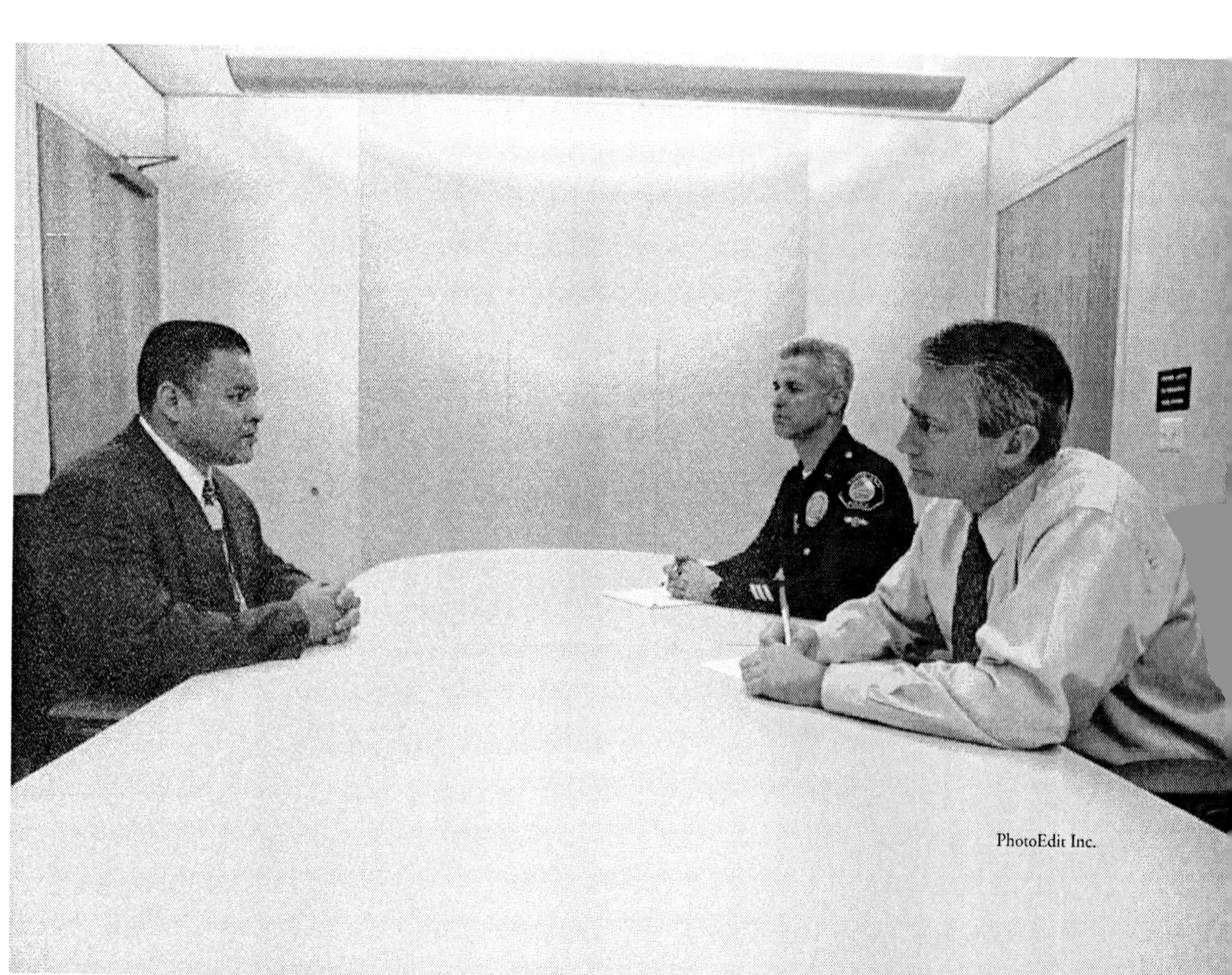

PhotoEdit Inc.

Learning Objectives

As a result of reading this chapter, the student will:

- Understand the nature and causes of stress in policing, to include the primary stressors for officers, and ways in which officers may reduce stress levels
- Understand the employment rights of police officers, including the provisions of the Peace Officer Bill of Rights
- Be able to explain the development of police unions and their influence today
- Know the three models of collective bargaining
- Be able to describe the four kinds of job actions
- Understand the Fair Labor Standards Act and how it operates in policing
- Be able to delineate the major arguments for and against police officers possessing higher education
- Understand how and why private policing/security evolved, some issues and concerns that it poses, and the current legal status of the field

Introduction

This chapter addresses a number of important policing matters. Because of their common nature—all represent a substantial degree of change, controversy, and/or influence within society and the operations of their agencies—they are consolidated and set apart here for discussion.

First we examine police stress, which can certainly be debilitating to those who are engaged in police service as well as their peers, supervisors, and the public; included in this discussion are its myriad causes and physical and emotional effects. Next we look at the broad area of labor relations, which includes police officers' rights, unionization, and collective bargaining, It will be seen in this chapter section that, over time, the balance of power has shifted considerably in the direction of the police with regard to their employment and bargaining rights.

Then we consider the topic of higher education for police. Although it may seem quite odd—given the gravity of their roles, the challenges posed by increasingly sophisticated criminals (especially with computer and financial crimes), and the creative demands of community policing and problem solving and increasing educational levels of society in general—that not only are the police lagging in terms of higher education, but there are actually leaders in the field who oppose raising entry-level educational standards for their officers; we will examine the reasons for and against doing so. Finally, we examine the extent and nature of private police/security forces—forces that provide a valuable service but about which there are several significant issues and concerns. A summary, key terms, review questions, and several scenarios and activities that provide opportunities for you to learn by doing conclude the chapter.

The Silent Epidemic: Stress

We would prefer to ignore one side of policing—the **stress** that is induced by the job—and its supervision and management. Indeed, Sir W. S. Gilbert observed that "When constabulary duty's to be done, the policeman's lot is not a happy one."[1] Furthermore, William A. Westley observed that "The policeman's world is spawned of degradation, corruption and insecurity. He walks alone, a pedestrian in Hell."[2]

Many people with whom the police interact are heavily armed and arrogant. The job of policing has never been easy, but the danger, frustration, and family disruption of the past have been made worse by the drug war and violent criminals who have more contempt for the police than ever before. Furthermore, as will be seen later in this chapter, compounding this situation is that the officer's own organizational policies and practices often generate more stress than the streets.

Nature and Types of Stress

The police work environment itself can and does have adverse effects on police officers. It creates stress, which may be defined as a force that is external in nature that causes both physical and emotional strain upon the body. The late Hans Selye, who is known as "the father of stress research," defined stress as a nonspecific response of a body to demands placed on it. Succinctly, stressors are situations or occurrences outside of ourselves that we allow to turn inward and cause problems.[3]

A police officer at a road block in Manhattan, New York, on September 11, 2001. *(Courtesy PhotoEdit Inc.)*

Stress can be positive or negative. Positive stress is referred to as *eustress,* while negative stress is called *distress.* When people think about stress, they usually focus on negative stress and negative situations; however, positive events in our lives can create stress. For example, an officer's promotion to sergeant is a positive experience, but at the same time it creates stress. The officer has to react and adjust to the new position. The promotion, although positive for the officer's career, is somewhat psychologically disruptive.

Traumatic stress is the result of an extremely stressful event, such as a line-of-duty shooting or a hostage situation. This stress is immediate and has a significant and profound impact on the officer. *Chronic stress,* on the other hand, generally represents the accumulation of the effects of numerous stressful events over time. Each can adversely affect a police officer and result in physical, emotional, and psychological problems. Traumatic stress may subside over time, but chronic stress for many police officers is ever present. If an officer cannot cope with a traumatic stressful event or manage the long-term effects of chronic stress, he or she may suffer from its consequences.

No human being can exist in a continuous state of stress. The body strives to maintain its normal state, **homeostasis**, and to adapt to the alarm, but it can actually develop disease in the process. Thus, it is extremely important for police agencies to recognize stress and its impact on officers and their productivity.

Sources of Stress

Stress can come from a number of directions, so police officers can experience job stress as the result of a wide range of problems and situations. The four general categories of stress are (1) organizational and administrative practices, (2) the criminal justice system, (3) the public, and (4) stress intrinsic to police work itself.

Organizational and Administrative Practices

A primary source of stress is the police organization itself. Police departments typically are bureaucratic and authoritarian in nature, and this type of organization creates stress for individual officers in at least two ways. First, police departments follow strict rules and regulations that are dictated by top management. Line officers and first-line supervisors seldom have direct input into their formulation, resulting in officers feeling powerless and alienated about the decisions that directly affect their jobs. Second, these rules dictate how officers specifically perform many of their duties and responsibilities. They are created to provide officers with guidance and direction. Police officers, however, sometimes view them as mechanisms used by management to restrict their freedom and discretion or to punish them. Officers also view rules as protection for the department when officers make incorrect decisions or errors. In these instances, departments sometimes use rules to avoid liability when officers' actions are challenged in civil actions.

Problems are also faced by female police officers. Because policing has traditionally been a male-dominated occupation, in many agencies female officers do not have the same standing as their male counterparts. The primary sources of stress for female officers are sexual harassment and treatment different from that which males receive in the workplace. Some women officers have reported that they were given different assignments, were the object of jokes (often concerning sexual orientation), were propositioned by male officers, and were generally victimized by gender stereotyping in the department.[4]

The Criminal Justice System

Each component of the criminal justice system affects the other components. For example, judges have openly displayed hostile attitudes toward the police, or prosecutors have not displayed proper respect to officers, arbitrarily dismissing cases, having them appear in court during regularly scheduled days off, and advocating rulings restricting police procedures.[5] Another example occurs when parole officers and probation officers do an inadequate job of supervising parolees, which results in their being involved in an inordinate amount of crime. The courts have the most direct impact on police officers and probably are the greatest source of stress from the criminal justice system.

The Public

When police officers perform community services, they also become involved in conflicts or negative situations. They arrest citizens; they write tickets; and they give citizens orders when intervening in domestic violence or disorder situations. Often, to resolve problems, they make half of the participants happy, but the other half are unhappy. The problem is that police officers develop unrealistic or inaccurate ideas about citizens as a result of their negative encounters. Officers must keep their relationship with citizens in proper perspective. This is achieved by open, straightforward discussions of public attitudes and encounters with citizens. It also means that managers must emphasize the importance of good police–public relations and of the majority of citizens supporting and respecting the police.

Stressors Intrinsic to Police Work

Police work is fraught with situations that pose physical danger to officers. Domestic violence, felonies in progress, and fight calls often require officers to physically confront suspects. It would seem that police work itself, since it includes dealing with dangerous police activities and dangerous people, would be the most stressful part of police work. Certainly traumatic incidents can require long-term follow-up support for law enforcement personnel.

Another major job-related stressor involves undercover work. The glamorous depiction of undercover officers in books, movies, and other media does not adequately portray the stress that is caused by the overall nature of the work—the isolation, danger, relationships with suspects, loss of personal identity, protracted periods of removal from family and friends, and fear of discovery.[6]

Incidents that Provoke Stress

Some events or conditions are more stressful for officers than others. Table 1 lists twenty-five stressful situations based on previous surveys categorized using the preceding sources of police stress. Table 1, which shows a number of stressful life events for police personnel, reveals that the majority of stressors are organizational or intrinsic to police work. It should be noted that the most stressful events in the intrinsic

Table 1
Twenty-Five Stressful Law Enforcement Critical Life Events

1. Violent death of a partner in the line of duty
2. Dismissal from the force
3. Taking a life in the line of duty
4. Shooting someone in the line of duty
5. Suicide of an officer who is a close friend
6. Violent death of another officer in the line of duty
7. Murder committed by a police officer
8. Duty-related violent injury (shooting)
9. Violent job-related injury to another officer
10. Suspension
11. Passed over for promotion
12. Pursuit of an armed suspect
13. Answering a call to a scene involving violent nonaccidental death of a child
14. Assignment away from family for a long period of time
15. Personal involvement in a shooting incident
16. Reduction in pay
17. Observing an act of police corruption
18. Accepting a bribe
19. Participating in an act of police corruption
20. Hostage situation resulting from aborted criminal action
21. Response to a scene involving the accidental death of a child
22. Promotion of inexperienced/incompetent officer over you
23. Internal affairs investigation against you
24. Barricaded suspect
25. Hostage situation resulting from a domestic disturbance

Source: J. Sewell, *FBI Law Enforcement Bulletin*, 50(4), 1981.

category occur very infrequently, and indeed, the average officer will experience very few of these events in his or her career. On the other hand, many of the organizational stressors occur very frequently. This may be why research shows that organizational stressors result in the most concern for officers.

Effects of Stress

It has been estimated that 15 percent of a department's officers will be in a burnout phase at any time. These officers account for 70 to 80 percent of all the complaints against their department, including physical abuse, verbal abuse, and misuse of firearms. If officers do not relieve the pressure, they eventually may suffer heart attacks, nervous breakdowns, back problems, headaches, psychosomatic illnesses, and alcoholism. They may also manifest excessive weight gain or loss; combativeness or irritability; excessive perspiration; excessive use of sick leave; excessive use of alcohol, tobacco, or drugs; marital or family disorders; inability to complete an assignment; loss of interest in work, hobbies, and people in general; more than the usual number of "accidents," including vehicular and other types; and shooting incidents.[7] An extreme reaction to stress is suicide. Police are at a higher risk for committing suicide because of their access to firearms, continuous exposure to human misery, shift work, social strain, marital difficulties, physical illness, and alcohol addiction.

It is imperative that officers learn to manage their stress before it causes deep physical and/or emotional harm. One means is to view the mind as a "mental bucket" and strive to keep it full through hobbies or activities that provide relaxation. Exercise, proper nutrition, and positive lifestyle choices (such as not smoking and moderation with alcohol) are also essential for good health.

Employee Assistance Programs

To help officers deal with stress and its effects, a comprehensive wellness program is needed that should include five elements: (1) physical fitness, (2) stress management, (3) psychological and mental health, (4) nutrition and dietary-related behaviors, and (5) alcohol/chemical dependency. Police agencies need a comprehensive wellness program to assist officers in coping with stress, but if that fails or is absent, an **employee assistance program (EAP)** should be available to help officers to cope with alcohol and substance abuse, psychological problems such as depression, or family management problems.

Excessive drinking and alcoholism remain a problem in policing. When officers' drinking becomes excessive, other officers and frequently supervisors and the department cover up for them. In the end, however, covering up drinking problems postpones officers' seeking or being required to obtain assistance. Drug abuse can also be present among officers, although it is not known if it is a significant problem. What is known, however, is that drug testing reduces the incidence of drug usage among police officers. If officers know they are going to be tested, they are less likely to use drugs. A number of departments require officers in selected assignments such as narcotics or special response teams to submit to drug testing, and some departments require testing of officers being transferred to such units.

If an officer is found to be using illegal drugs, what should be done with the employee? A number of arguments can be made for immediate termination. First, the police officer has committed a crime. Second, the officer has associated with known criminals when obtaining the illegal drugs. And third, the officer's drug use poses a liability problem for the police department. Immediate termination is counter to a humane view of police personnel administration, however. It should be realized that job stress may be the primary contributing factor to the drug usage. Second, the department has a significant investment in each of its officers, and a termination decision should not be taken lightly; problem officers can be salvaged and returned to work. Thus, termination, although an acceptable choice for officers with chronic drug problems, may not be the best solution for officers who had not previously caused the department any problems or had not otherwise been in trouble. Factors considered in making this decision include the severity of the offense (type and amount of drug used and whether or not the officer went beyond mere usage), prior drug and disciplinary problems, and the probability of the officer's being rehabilitated.

Labor Relations: Officers' Rights, Unionization, and Collective Bargaining

In an earlier time, police supervisors, middle managers, and chief executives were largely unrestricted and unchallenged in their treatment of rank-and-file officers. Disciplinary action was subjective, and the prevailing theme was often "Do as I say, not as I do." Employees served "at will," or until their employer (for whatever reason) no longer had need of their services. Today the labor–management relationship has changed significantly. First and foremost is the fact that a long line of court cases has established the legal view that public employees have a property interest in their employment. This flies in the face of the old view, mentioned above, that employees served at will and could be terminated for little cause. The U.S. Supreme Court has provided some general guidance on how the question of a constitutionally protected property interest is to be resolved:

> To have a property interest in a benefit, a person . . . must have a legitimate claim of entitlement to it. It is a purpose of the ancient institution of property to protect those claims upon which people rely in their daily lives, reliance that *must not be arbitrarily undermined* [emphasis added].[8]

Labor relations—a broad term that includes officers' employment rights and the related concepts of unionization and collective bargaining—has become an important issue in policing. This section explores these topics.

Police Officers' Rights

There are several restrictions that are placed on the rights of police officers (such as place of residence, religious practices, freedom of speech, and search and seizure). Given those numerous restrictions, in this section we look at some measures the police have taken to maintain their rights on the job to the extent possible.

In the 1980s and 1990s, police officers began to insist on greater procedural safeguards to protect themselves against what they perceived as arbitrary infringements on their rights. These demands have been reflected in a statute enacted in many states, generally known as the **Peace Officer Bill of Rights**. This legislation confers on police employees a property interest in their position and mandates due process rights for peace officers who are the subject of internal investigations that could lead to disciplinary action. The legislation identifies the type of information that must be provided to the accused officer, the officer's responsibility to cooperate during the investigation, the officer's rights to representation during the process, and the rules and procedures concerning the collection of certain types of evidence. Following are some provisions of the Peace Officer Bill of Rights:

- *Written notice.* The department must provide the officer with written notice of the nature of the investigation, a summary of the alleged misconduct, and the name of the investigating officer.

- *Right to representation.* The officer may have an attorney or a representative of his or her choosing present during any phase of questioning or any hearing.
- *Polygraph examination.* The officer may refuse to take a polygraph examination unless the complainant submits to an examination and is determined to be telling the truth. In this case, the officer may be ordered to take a polygraph examination or may be subject to disciplinary action.

Officers expect to be treated fairly, honestly, and respectfully during the course of an internal investigation. In turn, the public expects that the agency will develop sound disciplinary policies and will conduct thorough inquiries into allegations of misconduct. It is imperative that supervisors be thoroughly familiar with statutes, contract provisions, and existing rules between employer and employee to ensure that procedural due process requirements are met, particularly in disciplinary cases in which an employee's property interest is affected.

Police officers today are also more likely to file a **grievance** when they believe their rights have been violated. Grievances may cover a broad range of issues, including salaries, overtime, leaves, hours of work, allowances, retirement, opportunities for advancement, performance evaluations, workplace conditions, tenure, disciplinary actions, supervisory methods, and administrative practices. The preferred method for settling an officer's grievance is through informal discussion during which the employee explains his or her grievance to the immediate supervisor, and most complaints can be handled this way. Complaints that cannot be dealt with informally are usually handled through a more formal grievance process, which may involve several different levels of action.

Unionization

Probably as a result of their often difficult working conditions and traditionally low salary and poor benefits packages, police have often elected for **unionization**, banding together to fight for improvement. Another major force in the development and spread of unionization was the aforementioned authoritarian, unilateral "Do as I say, not as I do" management style that characterized many police administrators of the past.

The first campaign to organize the police started shortly after World War I when the American Federation of Labor (AFL) reversed a long-standing policy and issued charters to police unions in Boston, Washington, D.C., and about thirty other cities. Many police officers were suffering from the rapid inflation following the outbreak of the war and believed that if their chiefs could not get them long-overdue pay raises, then perhaps unions could. Capitalizing on their sentiments, the fledgling unions signed about 75 percent of all officers in Boston, 60 percent in Washington, D.C., and a similar proportion in other cities.[9]

The unions' success was short-lived, however. The Boston police commissioner refused to recognize the union, forbade officers to join it, and filed charges against several union officials. Shortly thereafter, on September 9, 1919, the Boston police initiated a famous strike of three days' duration, causing major riots and a furor against the police all across the nation; nine rioters were killed, and twenty-three were seriously injured. During the strike, Massachusetts Governor Calvin Coolidge uttered his now-famous statement: "There is no right to strike against the public safety by anybody, anywhere, anytime." Then, during World War II, the unionization effort was reignited. Unions issued charters to a few dozen locals all over the country even though most police chiefs continued speaking out against unionization. But in a series of rulings, the courts upheld the right of police authorities to ban police unions. Then in the early 1950s, many benevolent and fraternal organizations of police were formed in cities such as Chicago, New York, and Washington, D.C.; others were fraternal orders of police (FOPs). Soon a new group of highly vocal rank-and-file association leaders came into power, supporting higher salaries and pensions, free legal aid, low-cost insurance, and other benefits.[10]

Since the 1970s, the unionization of the police has continued to flourish. Today the majority of U.S. police officers belong to unions.[11] The International Brotherhood of Police Officers touts itself as the largest police union, but it is rivaled by the American Federation of State, County, and Municipal Employees union, which represents about 1.4 million workers and one hundred affiliated associations.[12] This dramatic rise in union membership was fomented by several factors: the job dissatisfaction that was experienced by police officers, the belief that the public was hostile to police needs, and an influx of younger officers who held less traditional views on relations between officers and the department hierarchy.[13]

Collective Bargaining

In this section, different models, relationships, negotiations, and impasses associated with **collective bargaining** (the process of negotiations between employer and employees) are covered.

Three Models. Each state is free to decide which public-sector employees (if any) will have collective-bargaining rights and under what terms, so there is considerable variety in collective-bargaining arrangements across the United States. In states with comprehensive public-sector bargaining laws, the administration of the statute is the responsibility of a state agency, such as a public employee relations board (PERB) or a public employee relations commission (PERC). Three basic models are used in the states: (1) binding arbitration, (2) meet and confer, and (3) bargaining not required.[14]

Under the binding-arbitration model, used in twenty-five states, public employees are given the right to bargain with their employers. If the bargaining reaches an impasse, the matter is submitted to a neutral arbiter, who decides what the terms and conditions of the new collective-bargaining agreement will be.[15]

Only three states use the meet-and-confer model, which grants very few rights to public employees. As with the binding-arbitration model, police employees in meet-and-confer states have the right to organize and to select their own bargaining representatives.[16] However, when an impasse is reached, employees are at a distinct disadvantage: Their only legal choices are to accept the employer's best offer, try to influence the offer through political tactics (such as appeals for public support), or take some permissible job action.[17]

The twenty-two states that follow the bargaining-not-required model have statutes that either do not require or do not allow collective bargaining by public employees.[18] In the majority of these states, laws permitting public employees to engage in collective bargaining have not been passed.

Bargaining Relationships. In those states and agencies seeking to organize for collective bargaining, the process goes as follows. First, a union will begin an organizing drive, trying to get a majority of the classes of employees it seeks to represent to sign authorization cards; at this point, agency administrators may attempt to convince employees that they are better off without the union. Questions may also arise, such as whether certain employees (e.g., police lieutenants) are part of management and therefore ineligible for union representation.

Once a majority of the eligible employees have signed cards, the union notifies the criminal justice agency. If management believes that the union has obtained a majority legitimately, it will recognize the union as the bargaining agent of the employees it seeks to represent. Once recognized by the employer, the union will petition the PERB or another body responsible for administering the legislation for certification.

Negotiations. Figure 1 depicts a typical configuration of the union and management bargaining teams. Positions shown in dashed boxes typically serve in a support role and may or may not actually partake in the bargaining. The management's labor relations manager (lead negotiator) is often an attorney assigned to the human resources department who reports to the city manager or assistant city manager and represents the city in grievances and arbitration matters. The union's chief negotiator will normally not be a member of the bargaining unit; rather, he or she will be a

Figure 1
Union and Management Collective Bargaining Teams
Source: Reno, Nevada, Police Department

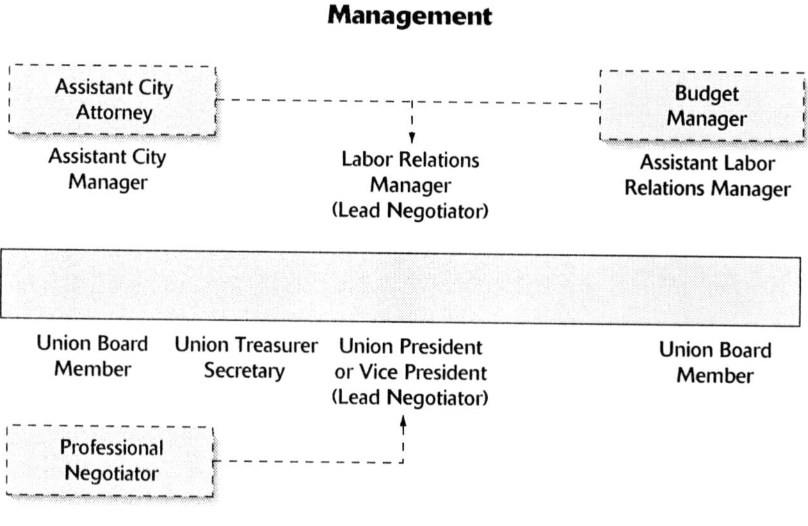

specialist brought in to represent the union's position and to provide greater experience, expertise, objectivity, and autonomy. The union's chief negotiator may be accompanied by individuals who have conducted surveys on wages and benefits, trends in the consumer price index, and so on.[19]

Management's chief negotiator may be the director of labor relations or the human resources director for the unit of government involved or a professional labor relations specialist. The agency's chief executive should not appear at the table personally—it is extremely delicate for the chief to represent management one day and then return to work among the employees the next. Management is represented by a key member of the command staff who has the executive's confidence.

Impasses. The purpose of bargaining is to produce a bilateral written agreement to which both parties will bind themselves during the lifetime of the agreement. Even parties bargaining in good faith may not be able to resolve their differences by themselves, and an **impasse** may result. In such cases, a neutral third party may be appointed to facilitate, suggest, or compel an agreement. Three major forms of impasse resolution are mediation, fact-finding, and arbitration:

1. *Mediation.* Mediation occurs when a third party, called the mediator, comes in to help the adversaries with the negotiations.[20] This person may be a professional mediator or someone in whom both parties have confidence. In most states, mediation may be requested by either labor or management. The mediator's task is to build agreement about the issues involved by reopening communication between the two sides. The mediator has no way to compel an agreement, so an advantage of the process is that it preserves the nature of collective bargaining by maintaining the decision-making power in the hands of the parties involved.[21]
2. *Fact-finding.* Fact-finding primarily involves the interpretation of facts and the determination of what weight to attach to them. Appointed in the same way as mediators, fact-finders also do not have a way to impose a settlement of the dispute. Fact-finders may sit alone or as part of a panel, which normally consists of three people. The fact-finding hearing is quasi-judicial, although less strict rules of evidence are applied. Both labor and management may be represented by legal counsel, and verbatim transcripts are commonly made. In most cases, the fact-finder's recommendations are made public at some point.[22]
3. *Arbitration.* Arbitration parallels fact-finding but differs in that the "end product of arbitration is a final and binding decision that sets the terms of the settlement and with which the parties are legally required to comply."[23] Arbitration may be compulsory or voluntary: It is compulsory when mandated by state law and binding on the parties even if one of them is unwilling to comply; it is voluntary when the parties of their own volition decide to use the procedure. Even when entered into voluntarily, arbitration is binding on the parties who have agreed to it.

Grievances. The establishment of a working agreement between labor and management does not mean that the possibility for conflict no longer exists; the day-to-day administration of the agreement may also be the basis for strife. Questions can arise about the interpretation and application of the document and its various clauses. Grievances—complaints or expressions of dissatisfaction by an employee concerning some aspect of employment—may arise. The grievance procedure is a formal process that involves the seeking of redress of the complaints through progressively higher channels within the organization. The sequence of the grievance process will be spelled out in the collective-bargaining agreement and will typically include the following steps: The employee presents the grievance to his or her immediate supervisor; if the employee does not receive satisfaction, a written grievance is presented to the division commander, then to the chief executive officer, then to the city or county manager, and finally to an arbiter, who is selected according to the rules of the American Arbitration Association.[24]

The burden of proof is on the grieving party except in disciplinary cases, in which it is always on the employer. The parties may be represented by counsel at the hearing, and the format will include opening statements by each side, examination and cross-examination of any witnesses, and closing arguments in the reverse order in which opening arguments were made.[25]

Job Actions. A **job action** is an activity in which employees engage to express their dissatisfaction with a particular person, event, or condition or to attempt to influence the outcome of some matter pending before decision makers.[26] Job actions are of four types: vote of confidence, work slowdown, work speedup, and work stoppage.

1. *Vote of confidence.* The vote of confidence is used sparingly. A vote of no confidence signals employees' collective displeasure with the chief administrator of the agency. Although such votes have no legal standing, they may have high impact due to the resulting publicity.
2. *Work slowdown.* In work slowdowns, employees continue to work, but they do so at a leisurely pace, causing productivity to fall. As productivity declines, revenues decline (through fewer citations being issued), and the public may pressure government officials to bring about normal operations (e.g., to slow down speeders in school zones, and so forth).[27]
3. *Work speedup.* A work speedup involves accelerated activity in the level of services. For example, a police department may conduct a "ticket blizzard" to pressure public officials into granting pay increases, to make more concessions at the bargaining table, or to abandon some policy change that affects their working conditions. In any case the idea is to raise public ire by the police doing their jobs—with too much gusto, and with an impact on wallets and purses.
4. *Work stoppage.* Work stoppages constitute the most severe job action. The ultimate work stoppage is the strike, or the withholding of all employee services. This tactic is most often used by labor to force management back to the

bargaining table when negotiations have reached an impasse. However, criminal justice employee strikes are now rare. Briefer work stoppages, which do not involve all employees and are known in policing as "blue flu," last only a few days.

Fair Labor Standards Act. An area of policing that is at the heart of management–labor relations is the **Fair Labor Standards Act (FLSA)**. For some police administrators, the FLSA has become a budgetary and operational nightmare. Indeed, one observer referred to the FLSA as the criminal justice administrator's "worst nightmare come true."[28] The act provides minimum pay and overtime provisions covering both public- and private-sector employees and contains special provisions for firefighters and police officers. Although Congress has often debated whether or not to repeal or modify this act, it is still a legislative force with which administrators, mid-level managers, and supervisors must reckon.

The FLSA was passed in 1938 to protect the rights and working conditions of employees in the private sector. During that time, long hours, poor wages, and substandard work conditions plagued most businesses, and the FLSA placed a number of restrictions on employers to improve these conditions. In 1985, the U.S. Supreme Court brought local police employees under the coverage of the FLSA. In this major (and very costly) decision, *Garcia* v. *San Antonio Transit Authority*,[29] the Court held, 5 to 4, that Congress imposed the requirements of the FLSA on state and local governments.

Police operations, which take place twenty-four hours a day, seven days a week, often require overtime and participation in off-duty activities such as court appearances and training sessions. The FLSA comes into play when overtime salaries must be paid. It provides that an employer must generally pay employees time and a half for all hours worked over 40 per week; overtime must also be paid to personnel for all work in excess of 43 hours in a seven-day cycle or 171 hours in a twenty-eight-day period. Public-safety employees may accrue a maximum of 480 hours of "comp" (compensation) time, which, if not utilized as leave, must be paid off upon separation from employment at each employee's final rate of pay or at the average pay over the last three years, whichever is greater.[30] Furthermore, employers usually cannot require employees to take comp time in lieu of cash. The primary issue with the FLSA is the rigidity of application of what is compensable work because the act prohibits an agency from taking "volunteered time" from employees.

Today an officer who works the night shift must receive pay for attending training or testifying in court during the day. Furthermore, officers who are ordered to remain at home in anticipation of emergency actions must be compensated. Notably, however, FLSA's overtime provisions do not apply to those who are employed in a bona fide executive, administrative, or professional capacity. In criminal justice, the act has generally been held to apply to detectives and sergeants but not to those of the rank of lieutenant and above.

Garcia prompted an onslaught of litigation by police and fire employees of state and local government entities. The issues are broad but may include paying overtime compensation to K-9 and equestrian officers who care for department animals while "off duty," overtime pay for officers who access their work computer and conduct business from home, pay for academy recruits who are given mandatory homework assignments, and standby and on-call pay for supervisors and officers who are assigned to units that require their unscheduled return to work. These are just a few of the many FLSA issues that have been litigated in courts across the nation.

Higher Education

An Enduring Controversy

Today a relatively small proportion of police officers have (or are required to have) a college degree. Indeed, of all local police agencies, only 8 percent require officers to have some college; 9 percent require a two-year college degree, and only 1 percent require a four-year degree[31] (a statistic that becomes more poignant when one considers that 27 percent of U.S. adults age twenty-five and older hold at least a bachelor's degree[32]). These low percentages are certainly surprising in light of the reports of numerous studies, courts, and national commissions (some of which are discussed below) that have concluded that **higher education** is essential for police officers. As will be seen, this remains one of policing's most enduring and controversial issues.

Efforts to involve college-educated personnel in police work were first made by August Vollmer in 1917 when he recruited University of California students as part-time police officers in Berkeley.[33] However, few departments elsewhere in the country took any immediate steps to follow Vollmer's example. Rank-and-file officers strongly resisted the concept of college-level studies for police, and officers with a college education remained very much an exception; they were often referred to disparagingly as "college cops."[34]

However, the movement toward higher education for police continued to spread: By 1975, there were 729 community college and 376 four-year applicable programs.[35] The Law Enforcement Education Program (LEEP) provided tuition assistance for in-service police officers and preservice students. In 1973, ninety-five thousand college and university students were receiving LEEP assistance—unquestionably the "glory days" of higher education in criminal justice.[36] Many patrol officers who otherwise could not have afforded it received quality higher education.

The accompanying Career Profile is provided by an individual who has devoted her professional career to higher education in criminal justice.

Rationales For and Against Higher Education for Police

The issue of higher education for police officers has been addressed by a number of notable entities, going back more than forty years. First, the President's Commission on Law Enforcement and the Administration of Justice made this statement in 1967:

> It is nonsense to state or assume that the enforcement of law is so simple that it can be done by those unencumbered by the study of liberal arts.

CAREER PROFILE

Name: Dr. Wendy L. Hicks

Position: Associate Professor

College attended: Illinois State University and Michigan State University

Degrees: B.A. and M.A. in Psychology, M.A. and Ph.D. in Criminal Justice

Current teaching position: Loyola University, New Orleans

What CJ-related jobs have you held and when?

I have always worked in academia as a university professor. Academia is the best job in the world!

What qualities/characteristics most helped you succeed in the field?

Tenacity, intelligence, and a good sense of work have enabled me to prosper in the academic world.

What are the typical salary ranges students can expect entering this field?

In academia, assistant professors start in the mid to lower $40,000 range, although some schools start in the mid $30,000 range.

What advice would you give students early in their college career to help them find a rewarding job in criminal justice?

Take a good, hard, honest look at yourself. Finding areas of interest, unique abilities, or possible weaknesses will assist you in the job search. In my experience, students who have prospered in criminal justice have had a very realistic perception of the world in which they live, and they have been honest with themselves regarding the possible impact they might conceivably have working within criminal justice. I would also suggest investigating various fields within criminal justice to see what avenues for employment might exist. If some specific field is of interest, a student would be wise to investigate the nuances of that field.

> Officers of any department should certainly be conversant with the structure of government, [and] be well grounded in sociology, criminology, and human relations in order to understand the ramifications of the problems which confront them daily.[37]

Shortly afterward, in 1972, the American Bar Association provided more accolades for higher education for police:

> Police need personnel in their ranks who have the characteristics a college education seeks to foster: intellectual curiosity, analytical ability, articulateness, and a capacity to relate the events of the day to the social, political, and historical context in which they occur.[38]

In 1973, the National Advisory Commission on Criminal Justice Standards and Goals, concurring that college-educated officers were needed, recommended that all police officers have a four-year college education by 1982,[39] a goal that obviously went unmet. Nevertheless, from 1967 to 1986, every national commission that studied crime, violence, and policing in America came to the conclusion that a college education could help the police do their jobs better.[40] Advocates of higher education for the police maintain that it will improve the quality of policing by making officers more tolerant of people who are different from themselves; in this view, college-educated officers are more professional, communicate better with citizens, are better decision makers, and have better written and verbal skills than less educated officers.

A ringing endorsement for higher education for the police also came in 1985 when a lawsuit challenged the Dallas, Texas, Police Department's requirement that all applicants for police officer positions possess forty-five credit hours and at least a C average at an accredited college or university. The Fifth Circuit Court of Appeals, and eventually the U.S. Supreme Court, upheld the educational requirement. The circuit court said:

> Even a rookie police officer must have the ability to handle tough situations. A significant part of a police officer's function involves his ability to function effectively as a crisis intervenor, in family fights, teen-age rumbles, bar brawls, street corner altercations, racial disturbances, riots and similar situations. Few professionals are so peculiarly charged with individual responsibilities as police officers. Mistakes of judgment could cause irreparable harm to citizens or even to the community. The educational requirement bears a manifest relationship to the position of police officer. We conclude that the district court's findings . . . are not erroneous.[41]

Many proponents of higher education requirements in policing (including many police executives and sheriffs themselves) bemoan the fact that local police have the lowest standards for education and training in the criminal justice system. They find it incomprehensible that in more than 80 percent of all agencies someone can enter policing with only a General Education Diploma (GED) or a high school diploma. Then, after attending a training academy of less than six months' duration followed by field training, the officers are expected to "guide people through complex, life-threatening situations far beyond their abilities and training" and interact daily with highly educated people in the community.[42] They also wonder—at the expense of the candidate—how policing can be deemed a profession when a hallmark of professionalism is high educational requirements.[43]

Abundant empirical evidence also indicates that college-educated police officers are better officers. Compared to less educated officers, they have significantly fewer founded citizen complaints[44]; have better peer relationships[45]; are likelier to take a leadership role in the organization[46]; tend to be more flexible[47]; are less dogmatic and less authoritarian[48]; take fewer leave days, receive fewer injuries, have less injury time, have lower rates of absenteeism, use fewer sick days, and are involved in fewer traffic accidents[49]; and have a more desirable system of personal values.[50] Furthermore, college graduates are significantly less likely to violate their department's internal regulations regarding insubordination, negligent use of a firearm, and absenteeism than officers who lack a college degree.[51]

A major argument by police administrators against requiring a college degree for entry-level officers is that the recruitment of minorities will greatly suffer, which is particularly problematic at a time when agencies seek to diversify their ranks. However, a number of jurisdictions argue just as strongly that this is not a problem and offer evidence (albeit anecdotal) that the reverse is actually true and that maintaining the college requirement has a number of benefits:[52]

- The Arlington, Texas, Police Department (APD) has required police officers to have bachelor's degrees since about 1983 and has successfully recruited officers, even protected-class officers. In fact, people from these protected classes have made up about two-thirds of each of its recruit classes since 1986. Colleges with higher minority and female enrollment, directors of female athletic programs, community referrals—all are sources for college-educated recruits and are heavily targeted.
- Dover Township, New Jersey, has required a two-year associate's degree since 1978 and a four-year degree since 1994; it also recruits heavily on college campuses and advertises widely in the mainstream media, including cable television. Dover has also found that many applicants are from other departments who are seeking the opportunity to work in the professional atmosphere of a college-educated agency.
- The Lakewood, Colorado, Police Department (LPD) has required bachelor's degrees for its officers (known as agents) since 1970, and today many agents have graduate degrees, including law degrees. LPD street officers are generalists who, the LPD feels, amass more experience in a few years than officers in other departments obtain in their entire careers; officers are given the authority to take creative approaches in their daily assignments and are among the highest-paid officers in the state. Sixty LPD agents have become chiefs of police and sheriffs in other agencies across the nation.
- The Tulsa, Oklahoma, Police Department (TPD) instituted a bachelor's degree requirement in 1996. Uniquely, if a young black man or woman met all the criteria for employment except for education, the TPD would lend him or her the money for books and tuition (with donated funds); then, after meeting the educational requirement, he or she would be employed as an apprentice police officer and enter the academy, later becoming a full-fledged officer. (This program was very successful, but claims of reverse discrimination caused it to be terminated.) Educational incentives are offered today, and the higher education requirement has not made recruiting more difficult. The TPD has also found that its educated officers maintain a much higher degree of community involvement—coaching, mentoring, teaching, volunteering, serving on boards and committees, and having a lifelong-learning mentality.
- Redlands, California, requires sixty credit hours upon hiring, but most officers have bachelor's degrees; educational requirements become higher as officers are promoted up through the ranks. To make it easier for officers to complete their education, the department offers flexible schedules and will pay for the officers' education.

- Charleston, South Carolina, and Burnsville, Minnesota, have a surplus of well-qualified applicants with bachelor's and higher degrees; attracting college-educated personnel has meant retooling the traditional recruiting techniques through extensive outreach to all colleges in the southeastern United States.

Some studies, however, have identified some negative effects of higher education. Critics believe that educated officers are more likely to become frustrated with their work and that their limited opportunities for advancement will cause them to leave the force early. Furthermore, they argue that police tasks that require mostly common sense or street sense are not performed better by officers with higher education.[53] These studies found that it had no positive effect on officers' public-service orientation (those with a degree displayed less orientation toward public service than those without a degree)[54] and that college-educated officers attach less value to obedience to supervisors than do officers without a college education.[55]

It seems paradoxical—given the research, the increase in educational level of society in general, and the need for police agencies to recruit the best people—that in this new millennium our society still does not require higher educational standards for police officers. No true profession requires less than a college degree, and police, in their quest for greater professionalism, should take notice.

On Guard: The Private Police

Types, Roles, and Some Concerns

Much has certainly changed in society and the private security industry since 1851, when Allan Pinkerton initiated the Pinkerton National Detective Agency, which specialized in railroad security. Pinkerton established the first private security contract operation in the United States. His motto was "We Never Sleep," and his logo, an open eye, was probably the genesis of the term private eye.

Today, according to the late loss-prevention expert Saul Astor, "We are a nation of thieves"[56]—and, it might be added, a nation that needs to be protected against would-be terrorists, rapists, robbers, and other dangerous people. There are about 5.2 million violent-crime victimizations and 17.5 million property crime victimizations each year in this nation.[57] As a result, and especially since 9/11, this nation has become highly security minded concerning its computers, lotteries, celebrities, college campuses, casinos, nuclear plants, airports, shopping centers, mass transit systems, hospitals, and railroads. Such businesses, industries, and institutions have recognized the need to conscientiously protect their assets against threats of crime and other disasters—as well as the limited capabilities of the nation's full-time sworn officers and agents to protect them—and have increasingly turned to the "other police"—those of the private sector—for protection.

Estimates are that more than ten thousand private security companies are now operating in the United States, employing over seven hundred thousand uniformed officers as well as about one hundred thousand managers and store detectives.[58]

William A. Pinkerton, principal of the western branch of Pinkerton's National Detective Agency.
(Reprinted from The Blue and the Brass: American Policing, 1890–1976. *Copyright held by the International Association of Chiefs of Police, 515 North Washington Street, Alexandria, VA 22314. Further reproduction without express written permission from IACP is strictly prohibited.)*

If accurate, the private policing field is larger in both personnel and resources than the federal, state, and local forces combined.[59]

In-house security services, directly hired and controlled by the company or organization, are called **proprietary services**; **contract services** are those outside firms or individuals hired by the individual or company to provide security services for a fee. The most common security services provided include contract guards, alarm services, private investigators, locksmith services, armored-car services, and security consultants.

Although some of the duties of the security officer are similar to those of the public police officer, their overall powers are entirely different. First, because security officers are not police officers, court decisions have stated that the security officer is not bound by the *Miranda* decision concerning suspects' rights. Furthermore, security officers generally possess only the same authority to effect an arrest as does the common citizen (the exact extent of citizen's arrest power varies, however, depending on the type of crime, the jurisdiction, and the status of the citizen). In most states, warrantless arrests by private citizens are allowed when a felony has been committed and reasonable grounds exist for believing that the person arrested committed it. Most states also allow citizen's arrests for misdemeanors committed in the arrester's presence.

The tasks of the **private police** are very similar to those of their public counterparts: protecting executives and employees, tracking and forecasting security threats, monitoring alarms, preventing and detecting fraud, conducting investigations, providing crisis management and prevention, and responding to substance abuse.[60]

Still, there are concerns about the field: as one author noted, "Of those individuals involved in private security, some are uniformed, some are not; some carry guns, some are unarmed; some guard nuclear energy installations, some guard golf courses; some are trained, some are not; some have college degrees, some are virtually uneducated."[61] Studies have shown that security officer recruits often have minimal education and training; because the pay is usually quite low, the jobs often attract only those people who cannot find other jobs or seek temporary work. Thus much of the work is done by the young and the retired, and the recruitment and training of lower-level private security personnel can present a real concern.[62] Clearly, today's security officer needs to be highly trained and competent.

Because so many security officers are ill-trained and low-paid (often little more than restaurant cooks or janitors), another issue that has surfaced concerns preemployment screening. A bill (H.R. 4022) introduced in September 2004 would have allowed the owners of private security companies to access the FBI's criminal database through the National Crime Information Center, and owners of contract security companies would have been required to check the database for any criminal activity committed by prospective employees. However, the bill never made it out of committee. That may be unfortunate, because the industry is governed by "a maze of conflicting rules," whereby wide chasms exist among the states in requirements for background checks and training. Indeed, in states that keep such records, tens of thousands of security guard applicants have been turned down for having criminal histories. A more bothersome figure cannot be determined, however: the number of individuals who have been convicted of serious offenses and have been hired in states without background checks. One federal investigation found at two military bases eighty-nine private guards working though they had histories including assault, larceny, possession and use of controlled substances, and forgery. Clearly more needs to be done to tighten and upgrade the industry—and, as a result, increasing salaries by weeding out many persons whose criminal histories compel them to accept the low salaries.[63]

Finally, a question that arises is whether the private police should be armed. In the past, much has been made about security officers who have received little or no prior training or have undergone no checks on their criminal history records but are carrying a weapon. Twenty-three hours of firearms instruction is recommended for all security personnel, as well as another twenty-four hours on general matters and proper legal training.[64]

SUMMARY

This chapter has examined several contemporary trends and issues in policing. Despite its 180-year-plus history and many advances, policing still has many issues that have not been resolved.

First, this chapter addressed police officer stress, where it was demonstrated that police agencies must recognize and address the needs of their human resources just as they plan for the purchase of capital equipment or for operations. Too often, police departments neglect or take their personnel for granted. People are a department's most important asset.

Certainly the section on collective bargaining and the discussion of officers' rights would be completely foreign to the major figures (Peel, Vollmer, Parker, and so on) instrumental in the development and maintenance of the reform era of policing. It was shown that the balance of power is certainly different today, as compared with the earlier unilateral, serve-at-the-pleasure-of-the-boss era, when officers had little protection against the whims of their leadership or complaints by the public; furthermore, their employment and ability to negotiate for better working conditions and benefits have greatly increased over time.

Higher education also remains a questionable element of policing for many people—notwithstanding that several major national commissions and court decisions as well as other entities and police executives have been advocating this requirement for nearly three decades. The major argument against having a college education requirement—that it greatly diminishes the minority hiring pool—was also brought into question in this chapter.

In sum, this chapter lays bare some elements of policing that have vastly changed, some that have largely remained the same, and some that are likely to be around for a long time. Whether or not they prove to be a blessing or a curse for the police remains largely to be seen—perhaps to be determined the police themselves.

KEY TERMS

collective bargaining
contract services
employee assistance program (EAP)
Fair Labor Standards Act (FLSA)
grievance
higher education
homeostasis
impasse
job action
labor relations
Peace Officer Bill of Rights
private police
proprietary services
stress
unionization

REVIEW QUESTIONS

1. How would you define stress, and what are the four general areas of police work that contribute to stress?
2. How may police personnel attempt to manage their stress levels?
3. What are the functions of an employee assistance program?

4. What employment rights do today's police officers possess, and what are some of the common provisions of the Peace Officer Bill of Rights?
5. What are the major reasons for the development and expansion of police unions, and what is their impact today?
6. What are the three models of collective bargaining, and what happens under each model when there is an impasse?
7. What are the four kinds of job actions?
8. How would you describe the Fair Labor Standards Act and the way it operates in policing?
9. Why is the possession of higher education by police officers controversial, and what are some rationales given for and against officers having such education?
10. How did private policing evolve, how does it differ from public policing, and what are some issues and concerns it presents to the public?

LEARN BY DOING

1. Unquestionably, the best way for you to determine the kinds of stressors that exist in policing is to interview a municipal police officer or county deputy sheriff. Encourage your interviewee to identify the degrees of stress that are caused by the stressors described in this chapter; the stressors caused by personnel; the issues that originate both inside and outside the organization; which type of calls for service create the most stress; and how he or she attempts to cope with stress.
2. Your criminal justice professor assigns a project in class wherein you are to debate the pros and cons of police officers and higher education—specifically, whether or not they should be required to possess a four-year or graduate degree. Taking either a pro or con side, develop your debating points.
3. Recently there has been a movement in your tourism-based community to examine the field of private policing. Today while you are guest lecturing before a local civic group's luncheon, a member of the audience asks you to describe the kinds of duties, rights, and training that should exist under the law for the private police. Also of interest to the audience is the interface between the public and private police—advantages and disadvantages of one as compared with the other. With what specifics do you respond?

mycrimekit

Go to MyCrimeKit.com and discover additional study tools and resources related to this chapter.

- Key Terms
- Review Questions
  - Multiple Choice Questions
  - True/False

- Fill in the Blank
- Essay
- FLASHCARDS: to test your knowledge of this chapter.
- *NEW YORK TIMES*: where you can read the latest articles related to criminology and criminal law.
- THE CAREER CENTER: where you can explore career opportunities in criminal justice and criminology.
- THE ONLINE RESEARCH LIBRARY: where you can explore the Cybrary and Research Navigator.

NOTES

1. Quoted in J. Bartlett, ed., *Familiar Quotations,* 16th ed. (Boston: Little, Brown, 1992).
2. William A. Westley, *Violence and the Police* (Cambridge, MA: The MIT Press, 1970), p. 3.
3. Hans Selye, *Stress Without Distress* (Philadelphia: Lippincott, 1981).
4. Merry Morash and Robin Haarr, "Gender, Workplace Problems, and Stress in Policing." Paper presented at the annual meeting of the Academy of Criminal Justice Sciences, Nashville, TN (March 12, 1991).
5. L. Brooks and N. Piquero, "Police Stress: Does Department Size Matter?" *Policing: An International Journal of Police Strategies and Management* 21(1)(1998): 600–617.
6. S. R. Band and D. C. Sheehan, "Managing Undercover Stress: The Supervisor's Role," *FBI Law Enforcement Bulletin* (February 1999): 1–6.
7. G. L. Fishkin, *Police Burnout: Signs, Symptoms and Solutions* (Gardena, CA: Harcourt Brace Jovanovich, 1988).
8. *Board of Regents v. Roth,* 408 U.S. 564 (1972), at 578.
9. W. Clinton Terry III, *Policing Society: An Occupational View* (New York: Wiley, 1985), p. 168.
10. Ibid., pp. 170–171.
11. Samuel Walker, *The Police in America: An Introduction,* 3rd ed. (Boston: McGraw-Hill, 1999), p. 368.
12. American Federation of State, County and Municipal Employees, "About AFSME," www.afscme.org/about/aboutindex.cfm (accessed July 28, 2010).
13. Ibid., p. 318.
14. Will Aitchison, *The Rights of Police Officers,* 3rd ed. (Portland, OR: Labor Relations Information System, 1996), p. 7.
15. Ibid.
16. Ibid.
17. Ibid., p. 8.
18. Ibid., p. 9.
19. Charles R. Swanson, Leonard Territo, and Robert W. Taylor, *Police Administration: Structures, Processes, and Behavior,* 6th ed. (Upper Saddle River, NJ: Prentice Hall, 2005), p. 517.

20. Arnold Zack, *Understanding Fact-Finding and Arbitration in the Public Sector* (Washington, DC: U.S. Government Printing Office, 1974), p. 1.
21. Thomas P. Gilroy and Anthony V. Sinicropi, "Impasse Resolution in Public Employment," *Industrial and Labor Relations Review* 25 (July 1971): 499.
22. Robert G. Howlett, "Fact Finding: Its Values and Limitations—Comment," in *Arbitration and the Expanded Role of Neutrals* (Proceedings of the Twenty-Third Annual Meeting of the National Academy of Arbitrators) (Washington, DC: Bureau of National Affairs, 1970), p. 156.
23. Zack, *Understanding Fact-Finding and Arbitration in the Public Sector,* p. 1.
24. Charles W. Maddox, *Collective Bargaining in Law Enforcement* (Springfield, IL: Charles C Thomas, 1975), p. 54.
25. Swanson, Territo, and Taylor, *Police Administration,* p. 530.
26. Ibid., p. 423.
27. Ibid.
28. L. Lund, "The 'Ten Commandments' of Risk Management for Jail Administrators," *Detention Reporter* 4 (June 1991): 4.
29. *Garcia v. San Antonio Transit Authority,* 469 U.S. 528 (1985).
30. Swanson, Territo, and Taylor, *Police Administration,* p. 392.
31. U.S. Department of Justice, Bureau of Justice Statistics, *Local Police Departments, 2003* (Washington, DC: Author, 2006), p. 9.
32. U.S. Census Bureau, "Educational Attainment in the United States: 2007," January 2009, www.census.gov/prod/2009pubs/p20-560.pdf (accessed July 28, 2010).
33. Albert Deutsch, *The Trouble with Cops* (New York: Crown, 1955), p. 122.
34. Herman Goldstein, *Policing a Free Society* (Cambridge, MA: Ballinger, 1977), pp. 283–284.
35. Deutsch, *The Trouble with Cops,* p. 213; *Law Enforcement and Criminal Justice Education: Directory, 1975–76* (Gaithersburg, MD: International Association of Chiefs of Police, 1975), p. 3.
36. Law Enforcement Assistance Administration, *Fifth Annual Report, Fiscal Year 1973* (Washington, DC: Government Printing Office, 1973), p. 119.
37. President's Commission on Law Enforcement and the Administration of Justice, *The Police* (Task Force Report) (Washington, DC: Government Printing Office, 1973), p. 155.
38. American Bar Association, *Standards Relating to the Urban Police Function* (Chicago: Institute of Judicial Administration, 1972).
39. National Advisory Commission on Criminal Justice Standards and Goals, *Police* (Washington, DC: Government Printing Office, 1973), p. 369.
40. Gerald W. Lynch, "Why Officers Need a College Education," *Higher Education and National Affairs* (September 20, 1986): 11.
41. *Davis v. City of Dallas,* 777 F.2d 205 (5th Cir. 1985).
42. Reuben M. Greenberg, Police Chief (Ret'd.), Charleston, South Carolina, quoted in Louis Mayo, "College Education and Policing" Proceedings of the 110th Annual Conference of the International Association of Chiefs of Police, October 18–23, 2003.
43. Ibid.

44. Victor E. Kappeler, Allen D. Sapp, and David L. Carter, "Police Officer Higher Education, Citizen Complaints and Departmental Rule Violations," *American Journal of Police* 11 (1992): 37–54. Also see Mayo, "College Education and Policing."
45. Charles L. Weirman, "Variances of Ability Measurement Scores Obtained by College and Non-College Educated Troopers," *Police Chief* 45 (August 1978): 34–36.
46. Ibid.
47. Robert Trojanowicz and T. Nicholson, "A Comparison of Behavioral Styles of College Graduate Police Officers Versus Non-College Going Police Officers," *Police Chief* 43 (August 1976): 56–59.
48. A. F. Dalley, "University and Non-University Graduated Policemen: A Study of Police Attitudes," *Journal of Police Science and Administration* 3 (1975): 458–468.
49. Wayne F. Cascio, "Formal Education and Police Officer Performance," *Journal of Police Science and Administration* 5 (1977): 89–96; Bernard Cohen and Jan M. Chaiken, *Police Background Characteristics and Performance* (New York: RAND, 1972); B. E. Sanderson, "Police Officers: The Relationship of College Education to Job Performance," *Police Chief* (August 1977): 62–63.
50. James W. Sterling, "The College Level Entry Requirement: A Real or Imagined Cure-All?" *Police Chief* 41 (April 1974): 28–31.
51. Gerald W. Lynch, "Cops and College," *America,* April 4, 1987, pp. 274–275.
52. Mayo, "College Education and Policing," n.p.
53. Robert E. Worden, "A Badge and a Baccalaureate: Policies, Hypotheses, and Further Evidence," *Justice Quarterly* 7 (September 1990): 565–592.
54. Jon Miller and Lincoln Fry, "Reexamining Assumptions About Education and Professionalism in Law Enforcement," *Journal of Police Science and Administration* 4 (1976): 187–198.
55. John K. Hudzik, "College Education for Police: Problems in Measuring Component and Extraneous Variables," *Journal of Criminal Justice* 6 (1978): 69–81.
56. Saul D. Astor, "A Nation of Thieves," *Security World* 15 (September 1978).
57. Department of Justice, Bureau of Justice Statistics, *Criminal Victimization in the United States, 2007 Statistical Tables,* February 2010, p. 13, bjs.ojp.usdoj.gov/content/pub/pdf/cvus07.pdf (accessed July 28, 2010).
58. Mahesh K. Nalla and Cedrick G. Heraux, "Assessing Goals and Functions of Private Police," *Journal of Criminal Justice* 31 (2003): 237.
59. Ibid.
60. Ibid., p. 238.
61. Lawrence J. Fennelly, ed., *Handbook of Loss Prevention and Crime Prevention,* 2nd ed. (Boston: Butterworths, 1989), in foreword.
62. George F. Cole and Christopher E. Smith, *The American System of Criminal Justice,* 11th ed. (Belmont, CA: Thomson Wadsworth, 2007), p. 253.
63. Larry Margasak, "Private Security Guards a Weak Link in Protection," Associated Press, *The Washington Post,* www.washingtonpost.com/wp-dyn/content/article/2007/05/29/AR2007052900650.html (accessed July 28, 2010).
64. National Advisory Commission on Criminal Justice Standards and Goals, Private Security (Washington, DC: U.S. Government Printing Office, 1976), p. 99.

On Patrol

On Patrol

METHODS AND MENACES

The wicked flee when no man pursueth, but the righteous are bold as a lion.

—*Inscription on the National Law Enforcement Officers Memorial, Washington, D.C., from Proverbs 28:1*

It is not the critic who counts. The credit belongs to the man in the arena, whose face is marred by dust and sweat and blood, who strives valiantly, who errs and comes up short again and again. [H]e who . . . spends himself in a worthy cause . . . knows his place shall never be with those timid and cold souls who know neither victory nor defeat.

—*Theodore Roosevelt*

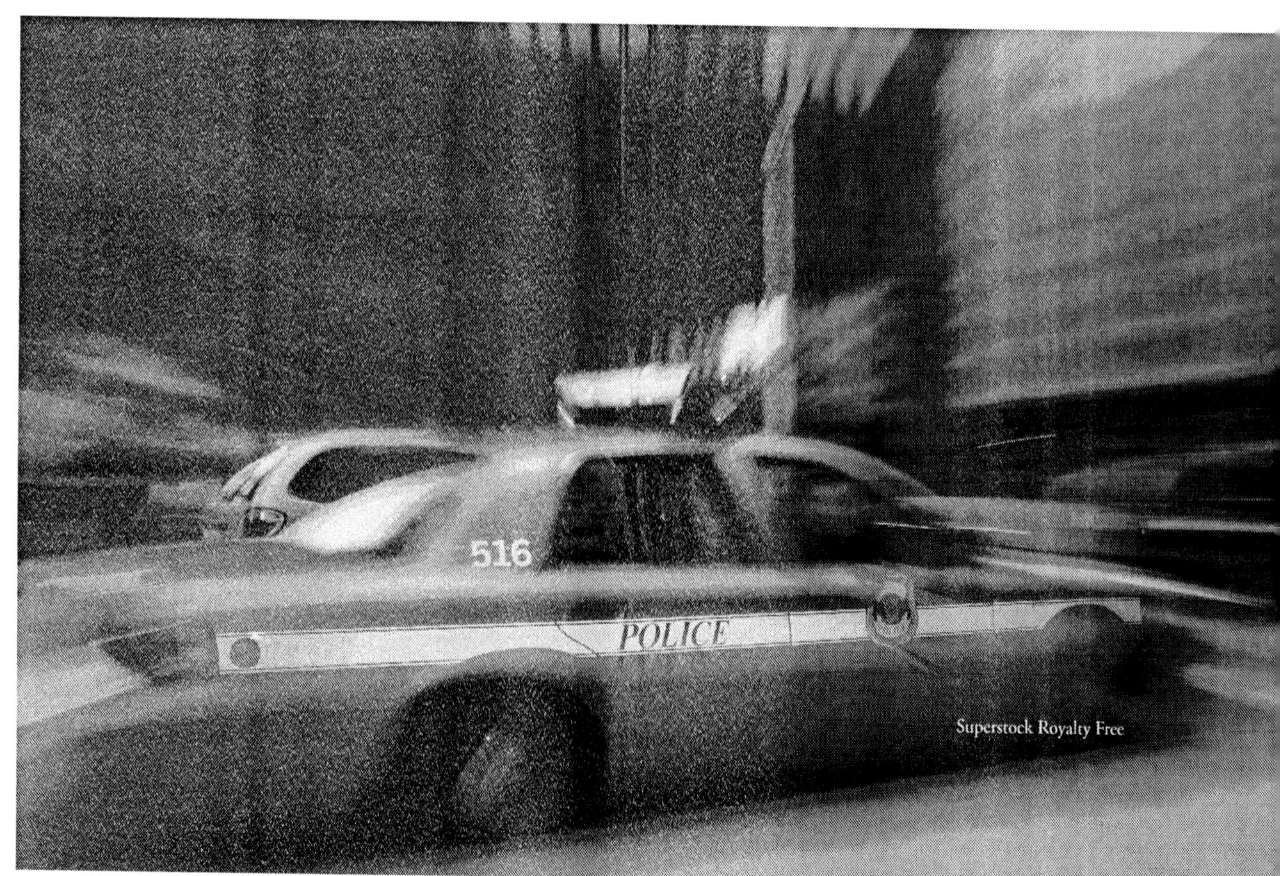

Superstock Royalty Free

Learning Objectives

AS A RESULT OF READING THIS CHAPTER, THE STUDENT WILL:

- Understand the general nature of patrol, including how the patrol function is affected by the officer's shift assignment and the nature of the beat to which he or she is assigned
- Be aware of some of the hazards that are inherent in police work and patrol functions, and know the newly enacted piece of legislation that allows retired officers to carry their weapons
- Know the functions of different types of patrol vehicles, how they are used, and how the recent economic downturn affected traditional patrol functions
- Be able to list several of the major studies and findings of the patrol function
- Be able to define what is meant by police discretion, and understand some of its advantages and disadvantages as well as the factors that can enter into the officer's decision-making process
- Know the nature and importance of the traffic function in patrol work
- Comprehend the legal and psychological aspects of police officers' uniforms and their general appearance, and the nature and purpose of an agency dress code (and why officers are filing civil actions against their employees in this regard)
- Be able to explain the importance—the "lifeline"—that police dispatchers provide to patrol officers

Introduction

The patrol function has long been viewed as the backbone of policing, the most important and visible part of police work. It is the primary means by which the police fulfill their mission. Patrol officers are the eyes and ears of the police organization, the worker bees of community policing and problem solving, the initial responders and protectors of the crime scene, and typically the first police representative whom citizens meet. All other specialized units either directly or indirectly support the patrol function. Patrol is where the art of policing is learned, citizens go to lodge concerns and complaints, and needs of the community are met. Significantly, all police chiefs, sheriffs (unless elected without prior experience) and other high-ranking personnel began their careers as patrol officers.

Indeed, this chapter serves as a prologue to many different kinds of police activities, all of which branch off from the patrol function. Because patrol duties normally involve 60 to 70 percent of a police agency's workforce, this task has been a topic of considerable interest and analysis.

In addition to the patrol function, the work of policing also revolves around the discretionary use of authority. Patrol officers possess a wide range of options as they go about the business of patrolling, including whether or not to stop and question or cite someone, to arrest, to use force, or to shoot. From the relatively innocuous traffic stop to the use of lethal force, many choices are involved, including some with serious consequences.

This chapter begins by describing the culture of the beat; included are sections concerning the purposes and nature of patrol, patrol work as a function of shift and beat assignment, and the extent and kinds of violence and occupational hazards that may be confronted while officers are on patrol. Then we consider an often overlooked yet extremely important tool for patrol: the patrol vehicle; included in this section are some modifications of patrol methods that were forced on the police by the recent economic downturn. Next is an overview of what research has revealed concerning the patrol function. Following that is an examination of the discretionary use of police authority, a review of the factors and political considerations that can enter into an officer's decision-making process, and the advantages and disadvantages of such discretionary authority. Then we discuss another function that is closely related to patrol: traffic. Next, we examine two very important aspects of patrol that are seldom considered: the legal and psychological aspects of police officers' uniforms and their general appearance (to include agency dress codes and litigation involving the codes), and the relationship to and importance of police dispatchers—the lifeline—to patrol officers. The chapter concludes with a summary, key terms, review questions, and several scenarios and activities that provide opportunities for you to learn by doing.

Two closely related topics that are at the heart of the patrol function are discussed in later chapters: community-oriented policing and problem solving and the tools and high technology used by patrol officers in the performance of their duties, including less lethal weapons.

Patrol as Work: Culture of the Beat

Purposes and Nature of Patrol

Earlier, we discussed the role and functions of the police, including the four basic tasks of policing: preventing crime, enforcing the laws, protecting the innocent, and providing services. In this section, we expand that discussion by looking at the **beat culture**, or some of the methods and problems that are connected with the **patrol function**.

Police work has certainly changed since 1910, when Leonard Fuld observed that "the policeman's life is a lazy life in as much as his time is spent doing nothing."[1] Today the patrol officer performs myriad duties, and danger is a constant adversary.

When not handling calls for service, today's officers frequently engage in problem-solving activities and in random preventive patrol, hoping to deter crime with a police presence. The various forms of preventive patrol include automobile, foot, bicycle, horse, motorcycle, marine, helicopter, and even snowmobile patrols. During all of these duties, the officer is alert for activities and people who seem out of the ordinary. The traditional method of **deployment** of patrol officers should take into account where and when crimes occur, attempting to distribute available personnel at the places and the times of day and days of the week when trouble and crime seem to occur with greatest frequency. Unfortunately, many departments still deploy their patrol officers in their jurisdictions by using convenient beat dividers, such as major streets or rivers, instead of analyzing when and where crime and other disturbances are taking place.

Patrol officers also attempt to effect good relations with the people on their beat, realizing that they cannot apprehend criminals or even maintain a quiet sector without public assistance. In many ways, the success of the entire police agency depends on the skill and work of the patrol officers. For example, upon arriving at a crime scene, police must protect and collect evidence, treat and interview victims, locate and interview suspects and witnesses, and make important discretionary decisions such as whether to arrest someone and even perhaps whether to use their weapons.

The American Bar Association offered the following major purposes of police patrol:[2]

- To deter crime by maintaining a visible police presence
- To maintain public order
- To enable the police department to respond quickly to law violations or other emergencies
- To identify and apprehend law violators
- To aid individuals and care for those who cannot help themselves
- To facilitate the movement of traffic and people
- To create a sense of security in the community

The accompanying Career Profile describes the views of the patrol function as seen by one who has served as a patrol commander.

Officers must become very knowledgeable about their **beat assignment**: They must be familiar with such details as where the doors and windows of buildings are, where the alleys are, where smaller businesses are located, and how the residential areas they patrol are laid out. Officers must learn what is normal on their beat and thus be able to discern people or things that are abnormal; in short, they should develop a kind of sixth sense that is grounded on suspicion—an awareness of something bad, wrong, harmful, without solid evidence. This is often termed "JDLR" (things "Just Don't Look Right").

Patrol officers may also develop certain informal rules pertaining to their beat. For example, they may adopt the belief that "after midnight, these alleys belong to me." In other words, an officer may take the position that any person who is observed in "his" or "her" alley after midnight must be checked out—especially if that person is wearing dark clothing or is acting in a furtive or surreptitious manner.

Several authors have described, often in colorful but realistic terms, the kinds of situations encountered by officers on patrol. For example, as W. Clinton Terry III put it:

> Patrol officers respond to calls about overflowing sewers, reports of attempted suicides, domestic disputes, fights between neighbors, barking dogs and quarrelsome cats, reports of people banging their heads against brick walls until they are bloody, requests to check people out who have seemingly passed out in public parks, requests for more police protection from elderly ladies afraid of entering their residence, and requests for information and general assistance of every sort.[3]

CAREER PROFILE

Name: Marcel F. Beausoleil

Position: Assistant Professor of Criminal Justice and Director of the Undergraduate Criminal Justice Program, Anna Maria College

Colleges attended: Bryant College and Salve Regina University

Degrees: B.S. in Criminal Justice, M.S. in Administration of Justice, and Ph.D. in Humanities

What CJ-related jobs have you held and when?

Reserve police officer, 1978 to 1979. Patrol officer, Rhode Island Park Police Department, 1979. Woonsocket Police Department, 1979 to 2000. While a member of the Woonsocket Police Department, I held the positions of patrol officer, sergeant, lieutenant, captain, and commander. As commander, I commanded the patrol bureau, then the administrative bureau, and at retirement was the executive officer of the department. On several occasions I served as Acting Chief of Police of the department.

What positions did you like most?

I liked the positions of patrol sergeant and patrol commander the most. Patrol work was always challenging and interesting; it was usually unpredictable, something different every day. I also enjoyed being with and working with the public—that, for me, was what policing was really all about.

What qualities/characteristics most helped you succeed in the field?

The ability to relate well to people and talk with them. Having an open and inquisitive mind was also a plus. When it came to career advancement I truly believe that my college education was a plus. Not only did it help me to do well in promotional examinations, but the knowledge and skills learned enabled me to excel in my new assignments and helped to pave the way for new ones.

What are the typical salary ranges students can expect entering these fields?

Salary ranges for patrol officers will vary geographically and are usually related to the cost of living in the area. In Rhode Island and Massachusetts, new officers can expect approximately $35,000 to $40,000 their first year. After that, typical salaries may range from $45,000 to $60,000, and may be increased through overtime and outside details.

What advice would you give students early in their college career to help them find a rewarding job in criminal justice?

Pay serious attention to your studies and learn how to communicate well both verbally and in writing. These skills are extremely important for today's police officer. Try to get jobs with local police departments, if possible, as part-time dispatchers or part-time (reserve) police officers. These positions give you experience and exposure to the field, which will be helpful later. Seize opportunities to volunteer in the community, since this helps you learn the community and again gives you exposure. Attend job fairs and circulate your name, as name recognition is important when applying for jobs.

A former police chief described patrol duties as follows:

> Cops on the street hurry from call to call, bound to their crackling radios, which offer no relief—especially on summer weekend nights. That is the time when the [city] throbs with noise, booze, violence, drugs, illness, blaring TVs, and human misery. The cops jump from crisis to crisis, rarely having time to do more than tamp one down sufficiently and leave for the next. Gaps of boredom and inactivity fill the interims, although there aren't many of these in the hot months.[4]

Indeed, patrolling officers will encounter all manner of things while engaged in routine patrol—things they discover as well as problems phoned in by citizens. They are assigned "attempt to locate" calls (usually involving missing persons, ranging from juveniles who have not returned home on time to elderly people who have wandered away from nursing homes); "attempt to contact" and "be on the lookout" calls (e.g., an out-of-town individual asks police to try to locate someone in order to deliver a message); and "check the welfare of" calls (involving a person who has not been seen or heard from for some time).

One type of call is said to have broken the back of many police agencies: nonemergency calls to 911. Several hundred thousand 911 calls are made each day across the United States—and 90 percent of them are for nonemergencies. Departments must find ways to free patrol officers from what has been called the "tyranny of 911": nonstop calls that send officers bouncing from one nonemergency call for service to the next. (The author witnessed one such call to a 911 dispatcher in the Midwest. The caller was reporting a goat standing on the front porch.) Indeed, the range of "emergencies" 911 callers report boggles the mind: Some people call because they want to know when the National Football League game begins that day, some people want to know the weather report, and some want help to exorcise the alien who entered their kitchen through the refrigerator's electrical cord. Nonemergency 911 calls leave officers little time for community-oriented policing and problem-solving (COPPS) activities.[5] (Exhibit 1 describes the complex nature of a patrol officer's work.)

Activities During Occasional Hours of Boredom

As noted, contrary to the image that is portrayed on television some (or even much) of the time officers devote to patrolling consists of gaps of inactivity. During those periods of time (particularly on the graveyard shift, when even late-night people and partygoers submit to fatigue and go home to sleep), patrol officers engage in a variety of activities to pass the time:

- They create "private places" for themselves—fire stations, hospitals, and other places where they can wash up, have a cup of coffee, make a phone call, or simply relax for a few moments.

Today's police patrol function involves many methods of transportation other than the automobile.
(Courtesy Ft. Lauderdale, Florida, P.D.)

EXHIBIT 1

Police Patrol: A Job Description

This behavioral analysis of a patrol officer's job provides one of the few empirical descriptions of the complex and varied demands of patrol work. Based on extensive field observations, the findings are reported as a list of the attributes that are required for successful performance in the field. Although completed more than three decades ago, the findings appear to conform well to the patrol activities of today. The researchers concluded that patrol officers must do the following:

1. Endure long periods of monotony in routine patrol, yet react quickly (almost instantaneously) and effectively to problem situations observed on the street or to orders issued by the radio dispatcher.
2. Gain knowledge of the patrol area, not only of its physical characteristics but also of its normal routine of events and the usual behavior patterns of its residents.
3. Exhibit initiative, problem-solving capacity, effective judgment, and imagination in coping with the numerous complex situations they are called on to face, such as a family disturbance, a potential suicide, a robbery in progress, an accident, or a disaster.
4. Make prompt and effective decisions, sometimes in life-and-death situations, and be able to size up a situation quickly and take appropriate action.
5. Demonstrate mature judgment (e.g., when deciding whether an arrest is warranted by the circumstances or whether a warning is sufficient or when facing a situation in which the use of force may be needed).
6. Demonstrate critical awareness in discerning signs of out-of-the-ordinary conditions or circumstances that indicate trouble or a crime in progress.
7. Exhibit a number of complex psychomotor skills, such as driving a vehicle in normal and emergency situations; firing a weapon accurately under extremely varied conditions; maintaining agility, endurance, and strength; and showing facility in self-defense and apprehension (for example, taking a person into custody with a minimum of force).
8. Perform the communication and record-keeping functions of the job, including oral reports, formal case reports, and departmental and court forms.
9. Have the facility to act effectively in extremely divergent interpersonal situations. Police officers constantly confront people who are violating the law, ranging from curfew violators to felons. They constantly confront people who are in trouble or who are victims of crimes. At the same time, officers must relate to law-abiding citizens such as businesspeople, residents, school officials, and visitors on their beat. Their interpersonal relations must range up and down a continuum defined by friendliness and persuasion on one end and by firmness and force on the other.
10. Endure verbal and physical abuse from citizens and offenders (as when placing a person under arrest or facing day-in and day-out race prejudice) while using only necessary force in the performance of their job.
11. Exhibit a self-assured professional presence and a self-confident manner when dealing with offenders, the public, and the courts.
12. Be capable of restoring equilibrium to social groups (e.g., restoring order in a family fight, in a disagreement between neighbors, or in a clash between rival youth groups).
13. Be skillful in questioning suspected offenders, victims, and witnesses of crimes.
14. Take charge of situations, such as a crime or accident scene, yet not unduly alienate participants or bystanders.
15. Be flexible enough to work under loose supervision in most day-to-day patrol activities and also under direct supervision in situations where large numbers of officers are required.
16. Tolerate stress in a multitude of forms (e.g., meeting the violent behavior of a mob, coping with the pressures of a high-speed chase or a weapon being fired, or assisting a woman bearing a child).
17. Exhibit personal courage in the face of dangerous situations that may result in serious injury or death.
18. Maintain objectivity while dealing with a host of special-interest groups, ranging from relatives of offenders to members of the press.
19. Maintain a balanced perspective in the face of constant exposure to the worst side of human nature.
20. Exhibit a high level of personal integrity and ethical conduct (e.g., refraining from accepting bribes or favors and providing impartial law enforcement).

Source: Adapted from M. E. Baehr, J. E. Furcon, and E. C. Froemel, *Psychological Assessment of Patrolman Qualifications in Relation to Field Performance* (Washington, DC: Department of Justice, 1968), pp. 11–3 to 11–5.

comparative CLOSEUP ▸▸ Little to Do on Patrol: Saudi Arabia

New measures adopted in mid-2009 require that Saudi Arabia's religious police, also known as the Committee for the Promotion of Virtue and the Prevention of Vice, must have long beards, Islamic attire, and a degree in Islamic Sharia law in order to serve in the corps.[1] Those are not the only areas where Saudi police differ greatly from their Western counterparts, however. For example, the police in Saudi Arabia assist with enforcing the very cruel (by Western standards) Islamic law, which is governed by the Koran—including the so-called chop-chops (a beheading or hacking off of an offender's limb), which are conducted in many cities. Because there is a near total absence on Saudi Arabian streets of gangs, drive-by shootings, purse snatchings, and contraband, the police patrol the streets in Chevrolets, BMWs, and Volvos, looking for minor infractions of the law.[2] Owing to its harsh criminal code, there is little for the Saudi police to do in terms of crime prevention or investigation. The religious police—the Mutawin— patrol and stroll in their white cotton robes and sandals and look, as one writer observed, like "desert nomads who have stumbled unexpectedly into the 20th century."[3] They look for people who are improperly dressed or women who have a loose strand of hair falling across their face or who need to adjust their *tarhas* (head coverings). Around-the-clock patrols ensure that shops are closed in time for daily prayers and that only married couples are sitting in family sections of restaurants. The patrols often follow persons suspected of being involved in what is deemed immoral behavior, such as drug use, homosexuality, gambling, and begging. Teams of religious police will also destroy home satellite dishes, which bring uncensored Western television broadcasts into Saudi homes.[4]

Note: Saudi police are discussed more in Chapter 9 in regard to enforcing the Koran and the harsh Law of Sharia.

Sources: 1. Adnkronos International, "Saudi Arabia: New Rules for the Religious Police," www.adnkronos.com/AKI/English/Security/?id=3.0.3552134122 (accessed July 21, 2010). 2. Personal communication with a former American residing in Saudi Arabia, July 27, 1994. 3. Chris Hedges, "Everywhere in Saudi Arabia, Islam Is Watching," *New York Times*, January 6, 1993, p. A4(N), col. 3. 4. Ibid.

- They engage in police-related activities, such as completing reports, checking license plates of vehicles that are parked at motels (to locate stolen vehicles or wanted persons), or meeting with other officers. Other more relaxing activities might include exercising in the station house workout room.
- The officer is often encouraged (beginning during recruit training) to make good use of this slack time, even while engaged in routine patrol, by engaging in "what-if" mental exercises: "What if an armed robbery occurred at (location)? How would I get there most rapidly? What would I do after arrival? Where would I find available cover?" Of course, officers can concoct any number of scenarios and types of calls for service to keep themselves mentally honed and ready to respond in the most efficacious manner.
- An often overlooked part of policing is that patrol officers must also spend a lot of time—especially during the early part of their careers—memorizing many things: the "Ten Code," for example, and the numbering systems of streets and highways within their jurisdiction. (Indeed, new recruits can and do "wash out" during the field training phase of their careers because of their inability to read an in-car map of the city, thus preventing them from arriving at their destination promptly.)

Patrol Work as a Function of Shift Assignment

Although the following analysis does not apply to all jurisdictions, the nature of patrol work is very closely related to the officer's particular **shift assignment**. Following are general descriptions of the nature of work on each of the three daily shifts.

Officers working the day shift (approximately 8:00 A.M. to 4:00 P.M.) probably have the greatest contact with citizens and provide traffic control. Officers may start their day by watching school crossings and unsnarling traffic jams. Speeding and traffic accidents are more common as people hurry to work in the morning. Officers also participate in school and civic presentations and other such programs. Most errands and nonpolice duties assigned to the police are performed by day-shift officers, such as unlocking parking lots, escorting people, delivering agendas to city council members, transporting evidence to court, and seeing that maintenance is performed on patrol vehicles. Day-shift officers are more likely to be summoned to such major crimes as armed robberies and bomb threats. This shift often has lulls, as most people are at work or in school. Usually, the officers with the most seniority work the day shift.

Officers of the swing, or evening, shift (4:00 P.M. to 12:00 A.M.) report to duty in time to untangle evening traffic jams and respond to a variety of complaints from the public. Youths are out of school, and shops are beginning to close; as darkness falls, officers must begin checking commercial doors and windows on their beat (new officers are amazed at the frequency with which businesspeople leave their buildings unsecured). Warm weather brings increased drinking and partying, along with noise complaints. Domestic disturbances begin to occur, and the action at bars and nightclubs is beginning to pick up—soon fights will break out. Many major events, such as athletic events and concerts, occur in the evenings, so officers often perform crowd and traffic control duties. Toward the end of the shift, fast-food restaurants and other businesses begin complaining about loitering and littering by teenagers. Arrests are much more frequent than during the day shift, and officers must attempt to take one last look at the businesses on the beat before ending their shift to ensure that none have been burglarized during the evening and night hours. That done, arrest and incident reports must be completed before officers may leave the station house for home.

The night shift (12:00 A.M. to 8:00 A.M.), known throughout history as the graveyard shift, is an entirely different world. Because of its adverse effects on officers' sleeping and eating habits, this shift is usually worked by newer officers (who also must work most weekends and holidays because of low seniority)—but only long enough for the officers to build enough seniority to transfer to another shift. Few officers actually like the shift enough to want to devote much of their career working it. (Many agencies also have shift rotation, transferring their officers from one shift to another at fixed intervals.)

Officers on this shift come on duty fresh and ready for action. From about midnight to 3:00 A.M., the night shift is quite busy as bars and taverns close. Traffic is relatively heavy for several hours and then normally drops off to a trickle. The "night people" begin to come out—those who sleep in the daytime and prowl at night, including the burglars. The nightly cat-and-mouse game begins between the cops and the robbers. Night-shift officers come to know who these people are and what vehicles they drive, what crimes they prefer, what their habits are, and where they hang out. Night-shift officers spend much of the night patrolling alleys and businesses, working their spotlight as they seek signs of suspicious activity such as open doors and windows in businesses or signs of unlawful entry. They also watch the residential areas, performing courtesy checks of homes in general and with greater scrutiny when people are away on vacation and have asked the police for a periodic check of their property.

Such patrol work is inevitably eerie in nature. Officers typically work alone under cover of darkness, often without hope of rapid backup units, although greater attention is given where possible to providing backup to night-shift officers, even during traffic stops. The police never know who or what awaits them around the next dark corner. The protective shroud of darkness given to the offenders makes the night-shift officers more wary. As noted, after midnight graveyard officers view alleys as theirs alone; anyone violating the peace of "their" alleys—especially one of the known "night people" or anyone wearing dark clothing or engaging in other suspicious activity—should be prepared to explain his or her actions and presence. Such individuals may also be compelled to undergo a stop-and-frisk (pat-down) search.

Once the alleys and buildings have been checked, the officers begin rechecking them, avoiding any routine pattern that burglars may discern. Some burglars can tell which beats are "open"—that is, wide open for burglarizing—by observing which patrol vehicles are parked at the station or at restaurants; therefore, officers should vary their patrol routine each night. At two or three o'clock in the morning, boredom can set in. Some officers welcome this change of pace, while others loathe it and look for ways to fight the monotony of the "dog watch." For them, the occasional high-speed chase may bring a welcome adrenaline rush, as does a crime in progress. Other means of staying alert include meeting and chatting with other officers who are also bored with patrol and stopping for coffee. But these officers must be mentally prepared for action; they know that while this is normally a quiet shift after the initial activity, when something does occur on the night shift, it is often a major incident or crime.

Influence of an Assigned Beat

Just as the work of the patrol officer is influenced by his or her shift assignment, the nature of that work is determined by the beat assignment. Each beat has its own personality, which may be quite different from other contiguous beats in terms of its structure and demographic character, as seen in the following hypothetical examples:

- Beat A contains a university with many large crowds that attend athletic and concert events; it also contains a number of taverns and bars where students congregate, resulting in an occasional need for police presence. A large hospital is located in this sector. Residents here are predominantly middle class. A large number of shopping malls and retail businesses occupy the area. The crime rate is quite low here, as are the number of calls for service. The university commands a considerable amount of officer overtime for major events as well as general officer attention for parking problems. During university homecoming week and other major events, officers in this beat will be going from call to call while officers assigned to other beats may find themselves completely bored. One portion of the beat contains several bars that attract working-class individuals and generate several calls for service each week due to fights, traffic problems, and so forth.

- Beat B is almost totally residential in nature and is composed of the "old money" people of the community: upper- and upper-middle-class people who "encourage" routine patrols by the police. Some of the community's banks, retail businesses, and industrial complexes are also located in this area. Most people have their homes wired for security, either to a private security firm or to the local police department. The crime rate and calls for service are relatively low in this beat, but patrol covers a large amount of territory, and a major thoroughfare runs along the beat's perimeter, generating some serious traffic accidents.
- Beat C is composed primarily of blue-collar working-class residents. It generates a low to medium number of calls for service relative to the other beats, and much of its geographic area is consumed by a small airport and a large public park with a baseball diamond/golf course complex.
- Beat D is the worst in the city in terms of quality of life, residents' income levels, and police problems. Though smaller in size than the other beats, it generates a very high number of calls for service. It contains a large number of residents living on the margins of the economy, lower-income housing complexes, older mobile home parks and motels, taverns, barely surviving retail businesses, and a major railroad switching yard. Officers are constantly driving from call to call, especially during summer weekend nights. At night, officers who are engaged in calls for service—even traffic stops—are given backup by fellow officers whenever possible.

Of course, even the normal ebb and flow of beat activity is greatly altered when a critical incident occurs; for example, an act of nature (such as a tornado, an earthquake, or a fire) or a major criminal event (such as a bank robbery or a kidnapping) can wreak havoc on a beat that is normally the most placid in nature.

Three "cops' rules" are part of the beat culture:

1. Don't get involved in another officer's sector; "butt out" unless asked to come to a beat to assist. Each officer is accountable for his or her territory, and each officer must live with the consequences of decisions that pertain to his or her beat.
2. Don't leave work for the next duty shift; take care of such practical matters as putting gas in the patrol car and taking all necessary complaints before leaving the station house.
3. Hold up your end of the work: Don't slack off.[6]

mycrimekit
Simulation: *Anticipating Danger.*

Where Danger Lurks: Occupational Hazards of Patrol

At Their Peril

Although several occupations—commercial fishing, logging, and piloting airplanes in particular—have workers dying at much higher rates than policing,[7] police officers' lives are still rife with **occupational hazards**. Police officers never know if the citizen they are about to confront is armed, is high on drugs or alcohol, or plans to engage in a relatively

Policing can be perilous. Each year many officers attend ceremonies at the National Law Enforcement Officers Memorial, Washington, D.C. *(Courtesy Washoe County, Nevada, Sheriff's Office)*

recent phenomenon known as "suicide by cop" (discussed below). Certainly an entire community, not only its police agency, is stunned when one of its officers is murdered; probably few were more shocked than the residents of Oakland, California, when four of their officers were murdered in a single day in March 2009 by a convicted felon.[8]

Because police officers are killed by both criminal and noncriminal (i.e., traffic accidents) means, the number of officers losing their lives in a given year will fluctuate wildly; in fact, during the past decade the number of officer fatalities has ranged from 240 in 2001 to 116 in 2009; approximately 19,000 police officers have lost their lives since 1792.[9]

Although the number of officers killed annually has generally declined since 2001, the United States remains a dangerous nation (but see the "Comparative Closeup" later in this chapter, which concerns killings of Iraqi police and security officers), and today's police officer would be very unwise to go on patrol without wearing body armor, although wearing body armor is certainly no guarantee that he or she will survive a shooting. (Exhibit 2 provides a profile and circumstances of police officers who were murdered during a recent year.)

An area in which better efforts must be made for officer safety is traffic accidents. Experts fear (but it has not been proven) that a contributing factor may be that more officers are driving without seatbelts in order to have quicker access to their sidearms in the event someone begins shooting at them. However, traffic accidents alone may explain a good proportion of police fatalities; over the past thirty years, the number of officers killed in traffic crashes has jumped by 40 percent while the number shot to death has declined by about the same amount.[10]

EXHIBIT 2

Officers Killed in the United States: A Profile

Following is a profile of the 41 police officers who were feloniously killed during a recent year:

- The average age of the officers was 39 years.
- They had worked in law enforcement for about 10 years.
- They were assigned to patrol (27).
- They were murdered with firearms (35); of these, 25 were slain with handguns.
- They were wearing body armor (32).
- They were disproportionately employed in the South (20).

Source: Adapted from the Federal Bureau of Investigation, Uniform Crime Reports, *Law Enforcement Officers Killed and Assaulted 2008*, www.fbi.gov/ucr/killed/2008/feloniouslykilled.html (accessed July 23, 2010).

The patrol function often takes officers to places that are "brutish" and dangerous.
(Courtesy Washoe County, Nevada, Sheriff's Office)

Suicide by Cop

A type of incident that certainly poses serious potential for danger to the police is **suicide by cop**, which is defined as "an act motivated in whole or in part by the offender's desire to commit suicide that results in a justifiable homicide by a law enforcement officer."[11]

Presently, the extent of the suicide by cop phenomenon remains unknown for two reasons:

1. Lack of both a clear definition and established reporting procedures
2. Immediate removal of suicide attempts from the criminal process and placement within the mental health arena, causing the police investigation to cease and preventing an agency from identifying a potential threat to its officers

Although it is difficult to measure, one study by a medical organization of deputy-involved shootings in the Los Angeles County, California, Sheriff's Department found that suicide by cop incidents accounted for 11 percent of all deputy-involved shootings and 13 percent of all deputy-involved justifiable homicides. The report concluded that suicide by cop constitutes an actual form of suicide.[12]

Case Study

While each case of suicide by cop is different, following is an example of how such an incident might occur:

> An officer is dispatched to an apartment building in response to a woman yelling for help. Upon arriving at the location, the officer observes a woman standing on the front steps. The officer is waved inside, and as she enters the apartment she hears a man yelling, then sees him standing in the kitchen area. When the male observes the female officer, he produces a large butcher knife and holds the blade of the knife firmly against his stomach with both hands; he appears highly intoxicated, agitated, and angry. The officer draws her service weapon and orders the man to put down the knife. The offender responds by stating, "[Expletive] you, kill me!" The officer attempts to talk with the offender, who responds by turning around and slicing himself severely on his forearm, bleeding profusely. The officer repeatedly asks him to drop the knife. The offender begins to advance toward the officer, telling her to shoot him while still ignoring her commands to drop the knife. From a distance of approximately 12 feet, he raises the knife in a threatening manner and charges the officer; she fires her weapon, striking him in the chest and hand, killing him.[13]

Two-Tiered Investigation

At minimum, to establish what happened and to track the incidents of suicide by cop, it is recommended that the following two investigative steps ensue when such an incident appears to have occurred: reporting procedure and classifying procedure.

Reporting Procedure. The reporting officer should list in detail in the initial offense report the specific elements observed at the scene:

- Statements made by the offender, including the names of any witnesses to the statements
- Type(s) of weapon possessed by the offender
- Offender's specific actions that resulted in the use of deadly force
- Offender's conduct that the officer deemed bizarre or inappropriate
- Circumstances indicating that the offender's motivation may have been suicide

A trained individual or unit must then sift carefully through the facts and circumstances, using stringent criteria to determine if the incident probably was motivated by the offender's *will* to commit suicide, noting items such as the following:

- Notes or recent correspondence, such as e-mails and other computer files, left at the scene or any other place the offender frequented
- Detailed verbatim statements from family members, friends, and associates
- Forensic evidence pertinent to the investigation (if the offender used a firearm, whether it was loaded with proper ammunition and capable of firing ammunition)
- Personal history of the offender, including medical and psychiatric information, credit reports, insurance policies, employment records, history of significant relationships, prior suicides of family members, and prior attempted suicides (particularly attempts that involved confrontations with law enforcement officers)
- Criminal history, including sentencing information, presentence reports, psychiatric evaluations, and prison records

As an example, the follow-up investigation of the preceding case study would reveal the following:

- The offender possessed a weapon capable of inflicting serious bodily injury or death.
- He used the weapon to seriously injure himself and attacked the officer with the weapon.
- During the attack, he demanded that the officer kill him.

Following those findings, a classifying procedure should be initiated.

Classifying Procedure. An officer or unit with expertise in the use of deadly force renders the final determination of whether a suicide by cop incident has occurred, focusing on the subject's motivation. The classification should include indicators that can help establish motivations and behavior patterns of the offender, for later tabulation and analysis.[14] The investigation of the preceding case study would thus demonstrate that the elements of a suicide by cop event were present, so the case would be classified as such.

Arms and Armor for Duty

Jerome Skolnick and David Bayley describe how officers prepare to face the beat's dangers on their tour of duty:

> Policing in the United States is very much like going to war. Three times a day in countless locker rooms, large men and a growing number of women carefully arm and armor themselves for the day's events. They begin by strapping on [body armor]. Then they pick up a wide, heavy, black leather belt and hang around it the tools of their trade: gun, mace, handcuffs, bullets. When it is fully loaded they swing the belt around their hips with the same practiced motion of the gunfighter in Western movies, slugging it down and buckling it in front. Inspecting themselves in a full-length mirror, officers thread their night sticks into a metal ring on the side of their belt.[15]

As John Crank states, "This is not a picture of American youth dressing for public servitude. These are warriors going to battle, the New Centurions, as Wambaugh calls them. In their dress and demeanor lies the future of American policing."[16] As Crank also observes, police recognize many citizens for what they are: "Dangerous, unpredictable, violent, savagely cunning . . . in a world of capable and talented reptilian, mammalian . . . predators."[17]

This depiction of the people officers confront on the beat may seem overly contrived, exaggerated, or brusque. Most patrol officers with any length of service, however, can attest to the fact that certain members of our society are, as one officer put it, "irretrievable predators that just get off . . . on people's pain and on people's crying and begging and pleading. They don't have any sense of morality, [and] they don't have any sense of right and wrong."[18] During their careers, most patrol officers are verbally threatened by such individuals; they take the great majority of such threats with a grain of salt. Occasionally, however, the "irretrievable predator" who possesses no sense of morality will issue such a threat, which the officer will (and must) take quite seriously. This is a very disconcerting part of the job.

The importance of patrol officers providing backup to one another—especially during the hours of darkness—cannot be overstated, as described by Anthony Bouza:

> The sense of "us vs. them" that develops between cops and the outside world forges a bond between cops whose strength is fabled. It is widened by the dependence cops have on each other for safety and backup. The response to help is a cop's life-line. An "assist police officer" is every cop's first priority. The ultimate betrayal is for one cop to fail to back up another.[19]

In this same vein, patrol officers quickly come to know on whom they can count when everything "hits the fan"—which officers will race to assist another officer at a barroom brawl, a felony in progress, and so on—and which will not.

H.R. 218

A relatively new legislative enactment, the **Law Enforcement Officers Safety Act of 2004 (H.R. 218)**, exempts qualified police officers from state laws prohibiting the carrying of concealed weapons and allows retired officers having at least fifteen years of service to carry a firearm.[20] The purpose of the act, its supporters state, is to afford these retired officers "protection of themselves, their families and our nation's communities." Retired officers who carry weapons under this law do not possess any police powers or immunities in other states, however, and are personally responsible for checking and understanding the laws of any jurisdictions they visit while armed.[21]

comparative CLOSEUP ▸▸ The World's Most Dangerous Venue: Iraq

Iraqi police offices secure the site of a car bomb that exploded in the southern Iraqi city of Basra.
(Courtesy AP World Wide Photos)

Undoubtedly, the most dangerous international venue in which to be a police officer in recent years is Iraq, where 7,348 Iraqi police and security forces died from mid-2005 to mid-2009.[1] This carnage is, of course, a result of the country's rampant terrorist acts. Following are but a few examples of the attacks upon Iraqi police—attacks that are all too commonplace there but would bring shock and horror to Americans if committed but once in the United States:

- Suspected Sunni insurgents attacked a minibus carrying police recruits in May 2008, killing all 11 recruits near Iraq's border with Syria.[2]
- An al-Qaida–linked Sunni group kidnapped eighteen soldiers and police of the Shiite-dominated police force in March 2007; hours later, the government said the bodies of 14 police officers had been found.[3]
- Twelve Iraqi police officers were killed by a suicide bomber and explosions in one weekend in Baghdad in December 2006.[4]
- Six Iraqi police officers were killed and 12 others wounded in November 2005 in a gun battle at a checkpoint north of Baghdad. At least 40 gunmen in three vehicles began shooting at the checkpoint near Baquba; the battle continued for about 30 minutes.[5]
- A suicide attacker detonated a car bomb outside the Iraqi police academy in Kirkuk in September 2004 as hundreds of trainees and civilians were leaving, killing 20.[6]
- Insurgents using rocket-propelled grenades, machine guns, and mortars staged a brazen daylight attack on a Fallujah police station in February 2004, freeing dozens of prisoners in a battle that killed 23 people.[7] A truck bomb also exploded at a police station south of Baghdad as dozens of police recruits lined up to apply for jobs, killing at least 54 people and wounding 60 others.[8]

Indeed, the high number of Iraqi police deaths prompted several members of a U.S. House Select Committee on Intelligence to pay tribute in Baghdad to these murdered officers.[9]

Sources: 1. Congressional Research Service, *Iraq Casualties: U.S. Military Forces and Iraqi Civilians, Police, and Security Forces,* p. 4, www.fas.org/sgp/crs/mideast/R40824.pdf (accessed July 21, 2010). 2. Associated Press, 11 Iraqi Police Recruits Killed, Police Say, www.gmanews.tv/story/96232 (accessed July 26, 2010). 3. Associated Press, 14 Iraqi Police Killed Following Kidnapping," www.msnbc.msn.com/id/17413060/Press (accessed August 24, 2009). 4. Lauren Frayer, Associated Press, "12,000 Iraqi Police Killed Since 2003," December 25, 2006), www.boston.com/news/world/middleeast/articles/2006/12/25/12000_iraqi_police_reported_killed_since_03 (accessed July 21, 2010). 5. "Officials: Iraqi Police Killed in Checkpoint Battle," November 4, 2005, www.cnn.com/2005/WORLD/meast/11/04/iraq.main (accessed July 21, 2010). 6. Yehia Barzanji, "Car Bomb Kills 20 in Kirkuk: Explosion Outside Iraqi Police Academy," Associated Press, September 4, 2004, www.thefreelibrary.com/Car+bomb+kills+20+in+Kirkuk+36+wounded+Explosion+outside+Iraqi+police...-a0121676107 (accessed July 26, 2010). 7. Anthony Shadid, "Insurgents Storm Iraq Police Station, 23 Die in Fighting," *Washington Post* (February 15, 2004), p. 1A. 8. CBS News, "Timeline: December 2004," 911research.wtc7.net/cache/post911/attacks/iraq/cbc_timeline.html (accessed January 3, 2007). 9. "Lawmakers Honor Slain Iraqi Officers," Associated Press, *Reno Gazette-Journal,* February 17, 2004.

Cycles, Segways, and Automobiles: Diverse Patrol Vehicles

A Sanctuary and "Rolling Office"

mycrimekit
Review: *Importance of the Patrol Car.*

The **patrol vehicle** is perhaps the most underappreciated and ignored aspect of police work—by both scholars and officers themselves. The patrol vehicle warrants greater attention because it is not only a place where officers on patrol spend a great deal of their time but also their sanctuary. It contains the myriad vital tools for accomplishing their work and, to a great extent, represents their authority.

The patrol vehicle is generally safe and comfortable, containing several essential accoutrements (a radio, spotlight, and weapons such as a shotgun or rifle) that contribute to the officer's safety. It is a mobile haven, providing comfort from inclement climates as well as against humans who would hurt the officer. The patrol car provides access to the tools of defense and is a safe place to deposit combative prisoners for transport.

Vital tools can also be stored in or mounted on the vehicle, which serves as a virtual office: the radio (for summoning assistance), warning lights and siren, defensive weapons (e.g., a shotgun or other firearm as well as a TASER electronic control device [ECD], baton, or other less lethal tool), possibly an onboard computer and video recorder, flares, cameras, and other evidence-gathering equipment. In addition, on the graveyard shift, the vehicle's spotlight can be one of the officer's greatest assets.

The police vehicle also is a rolling symbol of authority. For this reason, few people enjoy seeing a police vehicle appear in their rearview mirror; for some, it is a prelude to being issued a traffic citation or, worse, being taken to jail. Still, it can be stated that since the first police car appeared, citizens have been fascinated with the speed and imposing appearance of these vehicles.

In addition to the traditional beefed-up engines, heavy suspension, and upgraded electrical systems, some patrol cars contain additional features that mean a lot to the officers on patrol. For example, new models come with plates in the driver's seatback to protect against assault from the rear, cutouts in the driver's seat for a holster, extra-long safety belts, reinforced front steel beams and higher-rated tires for high-speed pursuits, a voice-recognition system for accessing onboard computers, a camera mounted in the overhead light bar with output to a laptop computer, an aircraft-style "blue box" accident data recorder, and crush-resistant bumpers.[22]

Patrolling on Two Wheels

The escalating costs of gasoline that began in mid-2008—climbing to $4 per gallon—caused police agencies to rethink their vehicle patrol methods. Following are some of the changes that were put into effect as gas prices escalated across the United States; many of these modifications will be continued now and into the future, given the ongoing increases and unstable nature of U.S. fuel costs:

- Many officers lost the right to take their patrol cars home, or they were forced to pay for the privilege.

An in-car computer. A GPS is mounted on the top-right of the monitor.

- Officers in some communities were told to turn off their ignition whenever they are stopped and idling for more than a minute.[23]
- Some departments switched to lower octane gasoline and installed GPS receivers in patrol cars to make dispatching more efficient.
- Some state troopers have begun sitting and monitoring traffic rather than cruising the highways, and they have increased their use of single-engine airplanes to look for speeders.[24]

Regarding the use of police motorcycles, with more than 41,000 people killed and three million injured each year on U.S. roadways, costing the economy $150 billion annually, motorcycle traffic enforcement is increasingly used to assist in attempts to reduce the incidences of aggressive driving, impaired driving, speeding, and red-light running. The use of motorcycle patrol units dates to 1909, when mounted officers abandoned their horses in lieu of transportation that could keep up with the rapidly evolving motor vehicle. These specialized enforcement units are capable of diverse assignments and, due to their build, can reach a crash scene more quickly than their four-wheeled counterparts. Motorcycle patrol officers also assume a community-policing role because citizens typically tend to be more comfortable approaching an officer on a motorcycle without the perceived barrier of an enclosed vehicle. Motorcycle patrol officers are also called upon to conduct traffic safety presentations to various civic groups and organizations and are frequently used for dignitary escort and ceremonial duties.[25]

Bicycle patrol is also being increasingly used. Although a 2003 federal Bureau of Justice Statistics survey found that 38 percent of police agencies of all sizes used bicycles,[26] and a 2008 study by Chris Menton found that more than 82 percent of all agencies service populations of 25,000 or more had patrol bicycles.[27] Further indications of the popularity of bike patrol are seen in the Federal Law Enforcement Training Center now providing a Police Bicycle Training Program to officers from the 85 agencies it trains[28] and in the existence of two national associations for bike officers, the Law Enforcement Bicycle Association and the International Police Mountain Bike Association.[29]

Concerning the uses and benefits of police bicycles, Menton also determined the following:

- Bike patrols had more than double the number of contacts with people, per hour, as officers patrolling in cars
- Bicycle officers did essentially the same level of serious and non-serious work as motor patrols.
- Incidents of public drinking, urination, and drug use were more readily discovered and dealt with by bicycle officers (the issue of stealth is important here; there is often no time for offenders to hide their drugs or open containers of alcohol).
- Bike officers have enhanced access, using alternative routes (including closed roads, sidewalks, alleyways, footpaths, and so on).[30]

Today hundreds of venues are also patrolling on their battery-powered Segways. Launched in 2001, the battery-powered Segway is, of course, much cheaper to operate than a patrol car, but it is are also marketed as providing officers with more mobility than a bicycle and the ability to negotiate large crowds quickly and easily. Models come equipped with a siren, saddle bags to carry forms and other materials, and even an alarm that allows officers to park the machine while tending to business without fear of it being stolen.[31]

Also worthy of mention regarding police vehicles is a new siren that is being tested in several cities. With high-output speakers and subwoofers, it is designed to be more effective with distracted drivers (or those with air conditioning, stereo, or cell phones in use). It bounces low-frequency waves off buildings and vehicles. A side benefit is that studies indicate people respond and get out of the way, rather than ignore the usual, commonly heard siren's wail.[32]

Studies of the Patrol Function

Because of the vast resources devoted to the patrol function and a desire to make patrolling more productive and pleasant for officers, many patrol studies have been conducted. Several have uncovered deficiencies and exposed myths about preventive patrol. These studies have helped us understand how the professional policing model put up walls between the public and the police, whom many people began to view as an occupying force.[33] As the Police Foundation said, "Isolated in their rolling fortresses, police seem[ed] unable to communicate with the citizens they presumably served."[34]

The best-known study of patrol efficiency, the **Kansas City Preventive Patrol Experiment**, was conducted in Kansas City, Missouri, in 1973, by George Kelling and a research team at the Police Foundation. The researchers divided the city into fifteen beats, which were then categorized into five groups of three matched beats each. Each group consisted of neighborhoods that were similar in terms of population, crime characteristics, and calls for police services. Patrolling techniques used in the three beats varied: There was no preventive patrol in one beat (police only responded to calls for service), increased patrol activity in another (two or three times the usual amount of patrolling), and the usual level of service in the third. Citizens were interviewed and crime rates were measured during the year the experiment was conducted. This experiment challenged several traditional assumptions about routine police patrol. The study found that the deterrent effect of policing was not weakened by the elimination of routine patrolling. Citizens' fear of crime and their attitudes toward the police were not affected, nor was the ability of the police to respond to calls.

The Kansas City Preventive Patrol Experiment (depicted in Figure 1) indicated that the old sacrosanct patrol methods were subject to question. As one of the study's authors stated, "[It showed] that the traditional assumptions of 'Give me more cars and more money and we'll get there faster and fight crime' is probably not a very viable argument."[35]

Figure 1
Schematic Representation of the Kansas City Preventive Patrol Experiment

Source: George L. Kelling, Tony Pate, Duane Dieckman, and Charles E. Brown, The Kansas City Preventive Patrol Experiment: Final Report *(Washington, DC: Police Foundation, 1974), p. 9. Used with permission of the Police Foundation.*

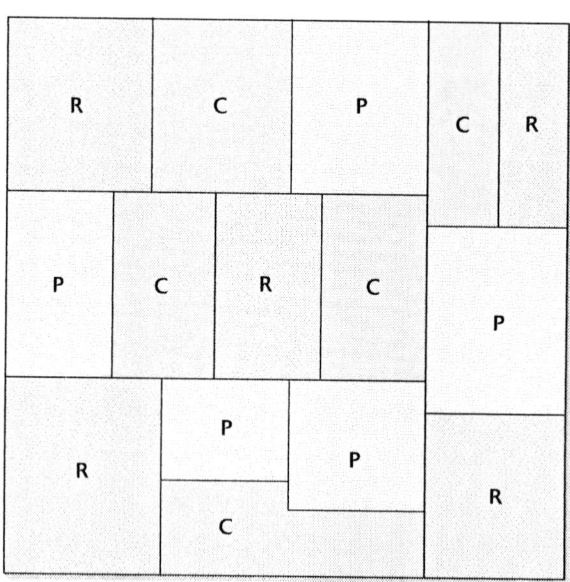

P = proactive
C = control
R = reactive

In the mid-1970s, it was suggested that the performance of patrol officers would improve by redesigning the job based on motivators rather than by attempting to change the individual officer selected for the job (by such means as increasing education requirements).[36] This suggestion later evolved into a concept known as "team policing," which differed from conventional patrol in several areas. Officers were divided into small teams that were assigned permanently to small geographic areas or neighborhoods. Officers were to be generalists, trained to investigate crimes and to attend to all the problems in their area. Communication and coordination between team members and the community were to be maximized; team involvement in administrative decision making was emphasized as well. This concept, later abandoned by many departments (apparently because of its strain on resources), was the beginning of the 1980s movement to return to community-oriented policing.

Two more attempts to increase patrol productivity, generally referred to as "directed patrol," occurred in 1975. The New Haven, Connecticut, Police Department used computer data of crime locations and times to set up deterrent runs (D-runs) to instruct officers on how to patrol. For example, the officer might be told to patrol around a certain block slowly, park, walk, get back in the car, and cruise down another street. A D-run took up to an hour, with each officer doing two or three of them per shift. Support for patrol officers was generally low, and the program did not reduce crime but rather displaced it. After a year, the experiment quietly died.[37] Wilmington, Delaware, instituted a split-force program, whereby three-fourths of the 250 patrol officers were assigned to a basic patrol unit to answer prioritized calls. The remaining officers were assigned to the structured unit and were deployed in high-crime areas, usually in plainclothes, to perform surveillances, stakeouts, and other tactical assignments. An evaluation of the project found that police productivity increased 20 percent and crime decreased 18 percent in the program's first year.[38]

In the late 1970s, a renewed interest in foot patrol—in keeping with Peel's view that police officers should walk the beat—compelled the Police Foundation to evaluate the effectiveness of foot patrol in selected New Jersey cities between 1977 and 1979. It was found that, for the most part, crime levels were not affected by foot patrol, but it did have a significant effect on the attitudes of area residents. Specifically, residents felt safer, thinking that the severity of crimes in their neighborhoods had diminished. Furthermore, evaluations of the Neighborhood Foot Patrol Program in Flint, Michigan, in 1985 found that foot officers had a higher level of job satisfaction[39] and felt safer on the job than motor officers.[40]

Other studies have illuminated the patrol function as well. A long-standing assumption was that as police response time increased, the ability to arrest perpetrators proportionately decreased. Thus, conventional wisdom held, more police were needed on patrol in order to get to the crime scene more quickly and catch the criminals. In 1977, a study examined police response time in Kansas City, Missouri, and found that response time was unrelated to the probability of making an arrest or locating a witness. Furthermore, neither dispatch nor travel time was strongly associated with citizen satisfaction. The time it takes to report a crime, the study found, is the

EXHIBIT 3

Police Stops of Pedestrians: Cops Cheer, Citizens Complain

An Associated Press study reported in late 2009 that police in major U.S. cities now stop and question more than one million citizens each year—a number that is sharply higher than just a few years before and still rising. Most who are questioned are Hispanic and black, many are frisked, and few are arrested (about 15 percent, according to one study). Civil liberties groups say the practice is racist and fails to deter crime; the police, conversely, argue that it is a necessary tool—that officers being drawn to people who act suspiciously turns up illegal weapons and drugs and prevents more serious crime. Not all stops are the same. Some people are merely stopped and questioned; others have their bag or backpack searched, while others are given a pat-down frisk. When officers make a stop, they are typically required to fill out a form to describe the person stopped, whether the person was frisked, why the police were suspicious, and the time, location, and purpose of the stop. The RAND Corporation found little racial profiling in looking at the stops in New York City, where more than ten million people work every day, and more than a half million people are stopped each year. The practice is quite legal: the U.S. Supreme Court established, in its 1968 decision in *Terry v. Ohio* (discussed in Chapter 9) the benchmark of "reasonable suspicion"—a standard that is lower than the "probable cause" standard needed to justify an arrest.

Source: Adapted from Colleen Long, "Police Stop More than 1 Million People on Street," abcnews.go.com/US/wireStory?id=8784669 (accessed July 23, 2010).

major determining factor of whether an on-scene arrest takes place and whether witnesses are located.[41] It has also been found that two-person patrol cars are no more effective than one-person cars in reducing crime or catching criminals. Furthermore, injuries to police officers are not more likely to occur in one-person cars. In addition, most officers on patrol do not stumble across felony crimes in progress.[42]

While these studies should not be viewed as conclusive—different results could be obtained in different communities—they do demonstrate that old police methods should be viewed very cautiously. Many police executives have had to rethink the sacred cows of patrol functions.

Discretionary Use of Police Authority

Myth of Full Enforcement

The municipal police chief or county sheriff is asked during a civic club luncheon speech which laws are and are not enforced by his or her agency. The official response will inevitably be that *all* of the laws are enforced equally, all of the time. Yet the chief or sheriff knows that full enforcement of the laws is a myth—that neither the resources nor the desire to enforce them all is available, nor are all laws enforced impartially. It is neither prudent nor politically wise to list the offenses for which the police treat some offenders more harshly or more leniently or for which they look the other way (and *non*enforcement of laws is a form of discretion). There are legal concerns as well. For example, releasing some offenders (e.g., to get information about other crimes or because of a good excuse) cannot be the official policy of the agency; however, the chief or sheriff cannot broadcast that fact to the public.

Indeed, it has been stated that the "single most astonishing fact of police behavior is the extent to which police do *not* enforce the law when they have every legal right to do so."[43] As an example, police scholar George Kelling described a Newark, New Jersey, street cop with whom he spent many hours walking a beat:

> As he saw his job, he was to keep an eye on strangers, and make certain that the disreputable regulars observed some informal but widely understood rules. Drunks and addicts could sit on the stoops, but could not lie down. People could drink on side streets, but not at the main intersection. Bottles had to be in paper bags. Talking to, bothering or begging from people waiting at the bus stop was strictly forbidden. Persons who broke the informal rules, especially [the latter], were arrested for vagrancy. Noisy teenagers were told to keep quiet.[44]

This quote points out the inextricable link between the patrol function and **discretionary use of police authority**: We cannot have one without the other.

Attempts to Define Discretion

Scholarly knowledge about the way police make decisions is limited. What is known, however, is that when police observe something of a suspicious or illegal nature, two important decisions must be made: (1) whether to intervene in the situation and (2) how to intervene. The kind, number, and possible combination of interventions are virtually limitless. What kinds of decisions are available for an officer who makes a routine traffic stop? David Bayley and Egon Bittner observed long ago that officers have as many as 10 actions from which to select at the initial stop (e.g., order the driver out of the car), 7 strategies appropriate during the stop (e.g., a roadside sobriety test), and 11 exit strategies (e.g., releasing the driver with a warning), representing a total of 770 different combinations of actions that might be taken![45]

Criminal law has two sides: the formality and the reality. The formality is found in the statute books and opinions of appellate courts; the reality is found in the practices of enforcement officers. In some circumstances, the choice of action to be taken is relatively easy, such as arresting a bank robbery suspect, but in other situations, such as quelling a dispute between neighbors, the choice is more difficult. Drinking in the park is a crime according to many local ordinances, but quietly drinking at a family picnic without disturbing others is not a crime according to the reality of the law because officers uniformly refuse to enforce the ordinance in such circumstances. When the formality and the reality differ, the reality prevails.[46]

These examples demonstrate why the use of discretion is one of the major challenges facing U.S. police today. The system tends to treat people as individuals: One person who commits a robbery is not the same as another person who commits a robbery because the system takes into account why and how a person committed a crime (his or her intent, or *mens rea*). With the U.S. judicial process, when one person shoots another, a variety of possible outcomes can occur. The most important decisions take place on the streets, day or night, generally without the opportunity for the officer to consult with others or to carefully consider all the facts.

Determinants of Officer Discretion

The U.S. government is supposed to be based on laws, not on people. That axiom is simply a myth—at least in the manner in which the law is applied. Official discretion pervades all levels and most agencies of government. The discretionary power of the police is awesome. Kenneth Culp Davis, an authority on police discretion, writes, "The police are among the most important policy makers of our entire society. And they make far more discretionary determinations in individual cases than does any other class of administrators; I know of no close second."[47]

What determines whether the officer will take a stern approach (enforcing the letter of the law with an arrest) or will be lenient (issuing a verbal warning or some other outcome short of arrest)? Several variables enter into the officer's decision:

1. The *law* is indeed a factor in discretionary use of police authority. For example, many state statutes and local ordinances now mandate that the police arrest for certain suspected offenses, such as driving under the influence or committing domestic violence.
2. The *officer's attitude* can also be a factor. First, some officers are more willing to empathize with offenders who feel they deserve a break than others. Also, as Carl Klockars and Stephen Mastrofski observed, although violators frequently offer what they feel are very good reasons for the officer to overlook their offense, "every police officer knows that, if doing so will allow them to escape punishment, most people are prepared to lie through their teeth."[48] What also makes situations awkward is that the officer cannot comfortably acknowledge the real reasons for denying a citizen's appeal for discretion. Imagine a police officer saying to a traffic violator, "The city depends on traffic fines for revenue," "Sorry, I don't like people like you," "Sorry, I don't think your excuse is good enough," or "Sorry, but I don't believe you."[49] Furthermore, police officers, being human, can bring to work either a happy or an unhappy disposition. If, on the same day as reporting for duty, the officer received an IRS notice saying back taxes were owed, had a nasty spat with a significant other, and was bitten while picking up the family pet shortly before leaving for work, he or she might naturally be more inclined to enforce the letter of the law rather than dispense leniency. Personal views toward specific types of crimes also play a role; for example, perhaps the officer is fed up with juvenile crimes that have been occurring of late and thus will not give any leniency to youths he or she confronts who are involved in even minor crimes.
3. Another major consideration in the officer's choice among various options is the *citizen's attitude*. If the offender is rude and condescending, denies having done anything wrong, or uses some of the standard clichés that are almost guaranteed to rankle the officer—such as "You don't know who I am" (someone who is obviously very important in the community), "I'll have your job," "I know the chief of police," "I'm a taxpayer, and I pay your salary"—the probable outcome is obvious. On the other hand, the person who is honest with the officer, avoids attempts at intimidation and sarcasm, and does not try to "beat the rap" may fare better.

Several studies have found that not only a citizen's demeanor but also his or her social class, sex, age, and race influence the decisions made by patrol officers.[50] This possible discrimination on the part of officers points out that the police—like other citizens—are subject to stereotypes and biases that will affect their behavior.

Pros, Cons, and Politics of Discretionary Authority

Several ironies are connected with the way in which the police apply discretion. First is the inverse relationship between the officers' rank and the amount of discretion that is available. In other words, as the rank of the officer increases, the amount of discretion that he or she can employ normally decreases. The street officer makes discretionary decisions all the time, including decisions about whether to arrest, search, seize property, and so forth. But the chief of police, who does very little actual police work, may be very constrained by department, union, affirmative action, or governing board guidelines and policies. Furthermore, the chief of police knows that neither the resources nor the desire are readily available to enforce all the laws that are broken.

In addition, the issue of police discretion is shrouded in controversy. Various arguments are made both for and against discretion. Advantages include that it allows the officer to treat different situations in accordance with humanitarian and practical goals. For example, an officer pulls over a speeding motorist, only to learn that the car is en route to the hospital with a woman who is about to deliver a baby. While the agitated driver is endangering everyone in the vehicle as well as other motorists on the roadway, discretion allows the officer to be compassionate and empathetic, giving the car a safe escort to the hospital rather than issuing a citation for speeding. In short, discretionary use of authority allows the police to employ a philosophy of justice tempered with mercy.

Conversely, discretion can also carry the specter of impartiality—the ability of officers to treat different people differently for committing essentially the same offense. Critics of discretion also argue that such wide latitude in decision making may serve as a breeding ground for police corruption; for example, an officer may be offered a bribe to overlook an offense. And as Lawrence Sherman observed, another problem is that the police do not know the consequences of their discretionary decisions. He contrasted the police with artisans and navigators who receive feedback on the effects of their decisions. The police, however, have failed to create a feedback information system that tells them what happens after they leave a call or even after they make an arrest. Thus police lack knowledge about the effects of their discretionary actions on suspects, victims, witnesses, and potential criminals.[51]

Certain aspects of policing will never be completely free of discretion, however; to a large extent, the work of a police officer is unsupervised and unsupervisable. As the police strive to achieve professionalism, they will remember that discretion is a key element of a profession.

Police discretion is also part of the American political process.[52] As Kenneth Culp Davis observed, a major contributing factor to police discretion is that state legislative commands are ambiguous. Legislatures speak with three voices: (1) they enact state statutes that seemingly require full enforcement of the laws, (2) they provide only enough resources for limited enforcement of them, and (3) they consent to such limited enforcement.[53] Some observers have even questioned the legality and morality of police discretion.[54] It might also be added that the statute books are often treated as society's "trash bins." A particular behavior is viewed negatively, so a law is passed against it, and the police are stuck with the dilemma of having to enforce or ignore what may be an overly broad or unpopular law.

Other aspects of politics are found in police discretion. For example, several state and local governments restricted police use of deadly force long before the U.S. Supreme Court did away with the common law "fleeing felon" doctrine in *Tennessee* v. *Garner* (1985).[55]

A Related Function: Traffic

A major figure in policing in the mid-1900s, O. W. Wilson, reportedly said that "the police traffic function overshadows every other function." That may be an overstatement today, but a strong link still exists between the patrol function and **traffic control**. Traffic stops account for about half (52 percent) of the contact Americans have with the police.[56] Therefore, the importance of a seemingly trivial traffic stop cannot be overstated because the manner in which the officer conducts the stop may in large measure determine the citizen's view of the police for many years to come.

Enforcement of Traffic Laws: Triumph and Trouble

A report by the Federal Bureau of Justice Statistics stated that there are 193 million drivers in the United States and that each year about 16.8 million, or 8.7 percent, of

Officer at accident scene. *(Courtesy Western Nevada State Peace Officer Academy, Carson City, Nevada)*

those who are over age sixteen will be stopped by the police. Although the number of drivers is evenly divided between males and females, males (60.8 percent) are stopped by police at a much higher rate than females (39.2 percent); furthermore, young drivers (ages sixteen to twenty-four) are more likely to be stopped by the police (26 percent of the total). About six in ten persons who are stopped are ticketed for a violation.[57]

Police endeavor to reduce traffic deaths and injuries through the enforcement of traffic laws, and on its face, this is a noble undertaking. But this is a very delicate area of contact between citizens and their police. Indeed, citizens may have their one and only contact with a police officer because of some traffic-related matter; therefore, the extent to which the officer displays a professional demeanor—and the attitude and demeanor projected by the citizen—may well have long-term effects for both and carry long-term significance for both community policing (which relies heavily on community teamwork) and public relations. More than a few bond issues to hire new officers, purchase new equipment, or build a new station house have been defeated at the ballot box because of ill will created by the police traffic function.

Levels of traffic enforcement differ, too. Some departments are relatively lenient, but others have initiated ticket quotas, and some jurisdictions pressure their officers to have a "ticket blizzard" to generate revenue. Aside from often being rankled by having to pay a fine, many citizens also believe the police should be engaged in other "more important" functions ("Why aren't you out catching bank robbers?"). Therefore, traffic stops can be a major source of friction between police officers and citizens, and strict traffic enforcement policies can negatively impact police–community relations.[58] Furthermore, because of "extinction"—the process of people forgetting about the traffic citation they received and the need to obey traffic laws—the long- and even short-term deterrent effects of handing out traffic citations have been called into question.[59]

Despite citizen disgruntlement with traffic enforcement, traffic stops and citations generally remain an integral part of police work. Police administrators find such work to be easily verifiable evidence that their officers are working.[60] Traffic enforcement has even gone high tech with the advent of the traffic camera, which has been nicknamed "the photocop." Traffic cameras, either mounted on a mobile tripod or permanently fixed on a pole, emit a narrow beam of radar that triggers a flash camera when the targeted vehicle is exceeding the speed limit by a certain amount, usually ten miles per hour.

Police in Berkeley, California, have applied a new twist to the traffic function. Drivers who are "caught" driving safely and courteously are stopped and issued coupons good for movies or free nonalcoholic beverages at a local cafe. This Good Driver Recognition Program, which began with officers' donations, now receives city funding.[61]

Traffic Crash Investigation

Patrol officers have long been required to investigate traffic crashes. (*Note:* The long-used term *traffic accident* is increasingly being replaced with *traffic crash* or *collision* because *accident* implies that the crash was unintended, but with the increase in road rage incidents and other uses of motor vehicles as weapons, *collision* can include both intended and unintended crashes.) In this era of accountability and litigation, and due to the vast amount of damage done to people and property each year as a result of traffic crashes, it is essential that officers understand this process of investigation and cite the guilty party—not only from a law enforcement standpoint but also in the event that the matter is taken to civil court. Until officers receive formal training in this complex field, they are in a very precarious position.

In addition to basic traffic crash investigation (TAI) training normally provided at the police academy, several agencies offer good in-service courses, and Northwestern University has a renowned crash investigation program. The process of analyzing road and damage evidence, estimating speeds, reconstructing what occurred and why, issuing citations properly, drawing a diagram of the scene, and explaining what happened in court is too important to be left to untrained officers. The public demands skilled crash investigations.

Pursuit of the "Phantom" Driver

One of the traffic-related areas in which the police enjoy wide public support is their efforts to identify, apprehend, and convict the hit-and-run (or "phantom") driver. No one thinks highly of these drivers (who are often intoxicated) who collide with another vehicle or person and leave the scene. This matter requires more of a criminal investigation than a crash investigation for the police. In some states, the killing of a human being by someone driving under the influence (DUI) is a felony. Physical evidence and witness statements must be collected in the same fashion as in a conventional criminal investigation; paint samples and automobile parts left at the scene are sent to crime laboratories for examination. The problem for the police is that unless the driver of the vehicle is identified—by physical evidence, an eyewitness, or a confession—the case can be lost. If the phantom vehicle is located, the owner can simply tell the police that his or her vehicle was stolen or is on loan. Thus, the police often must resort to psychology to get a confession by convincing the suspect that incriminating evidence exists.

Officers on Display: Appearance, Uniforms, and Dress Codes

The police are paramilitary in nature; as such, in addition to being hierarchical in organization, with rank and chain of command, they are typically uniformed (unless assigned to undercover work). And, as two authors stated, "The uniform stands out as one of the most important visual representations of the law enforcement profession."[62]

From the moment a neophyte officer puts on a **uniform**, his or her world changes; the officer is immediately and uniquely set apart from society. For some, the uniform seems to be a target for all kinds of verbal abuse and even fists or bullets; for others, it is a welcome symbol of legal authority. In any case, the uniform and overall appearance of police officers have several psychological and legal aspects, as we will see in this chapter section.

Legal Aspects

Succinctly put, police administrators have long been able to regulate the appearance of their officers. In *Kelley v. Johnson*[63] (1976), the U.S. Supreme Court held that police agencies have a legitimate, "rational" interest in establishing such rules and regulations. There, the Suffolk County (New York) Police Department's hair-grooming standards applicable to male members of the police force (governing the style and length of hair, sideburns, and mustaches and prohibiting goatees) were attacked as violating officers' First and Fourteenth Amendments rights of expression and liberty. The Supreme Court upheld such regulations, on the grounds they:

> may be based on a desire to make police officers readily recognizable to the members of the public, or a desire for the esprit de corps which such similarity is felt to inculcate within the police force itself. Either one is a sufficiently rational justification for regulations.[64]

Therefore, police administrators can dictate how the uniform will be worn—as well as other aspects of personal appearance (discussed below).

Psychological Aspects of the Uniform

Why do most agencies insist that patrol officers dress in uniforms? Certainly officers' uniforms convey power and authority; in addition, the uniform elicits stereotypes about that person's status, attitudes, and motivations. The uniform identifies a person with powers to arrest and use force and establishes order, as well as conformity within the ranks of those who wear it by suppressing individuality.[65]

Research has consistently supported suggestions about the police uniform's power and authority. In one study, individuals ranked 25 different occupational uniforms by several categories of feelings. The test subjects consistently ranked the police uniform as the one most likely to induce feelings of safety. Studies have also shown that people consistently rate models as more competent, reliable, intelligent, and helpful when pictured in a police uniform, rather than in casual clothes.[66]

Details about a police officer's uniform, such as the style of hat or the tailoring, can also influence the level of authority emanating from the officer. For example, studies show that the traditional "bus driver" garrison cap and the "Smoky the Bear" campaign hat conveyed more authority than the baseball cap or no hat at all.[67]

An interesting experiment in deviation from the conventional police uniform occurred in 1969, in the Menlo Park, California, Police Department (MPPD). There, hoping to improve police–community relations, the police discontinued their traditional navy blue, paramilitary-style uniforms and adopted a uniform that consisted of a forest green blazer worn over black slacks, a white shirt, and a black tie. Officers displayed their badges on the blazer and concealed their weapons under the coat. Eventually, more than four hundred other police departments in the United States also experimented with a blazer-style uniform.[68]

The initial results were promising: after wearing the new uniforms for eighteen months, MPPD officers displayed fewer authoritarian characteristics when compared to officers in the surrounding jurisdictions. Also, after wearing the uniforms for about a year, assaults on MPPD officers decreased by 30 percent and injuries to civilians by the police dropped 50 percent (however, other variables were deemed to be responsible for these decreases as well). The number of college-educated officers in the department increased dramatically, and the agency abolished its traditional autocratic management style during this same time period.[69]

After eight years of officers wearing blazers, however, the MPPD dropped the blazer concept, determining that it did not command respect, and returned to a traditional, paramilitary-style uniform. A final evaluation showed that, although assaults on officers had dropped during the first eighteen months of the new uniform implementation, the number of assaults steadily began to rise again until it doubled the amount of the year before the uniform change occurred. During the initial four-year period after MPPD officers returned to a traditional uniform, the number of assaults on their officers dropped steadily.[70]

Instituting (and Enforcing) a Dress Code

Many, if not most, police agencies have general orders or policies constituting a **dress code**—how their officers will dress and their general appearance—so as to:

> promote a professional image to the community served; have uniformed officers be consistently attired to reflect their authority, respective assignment, and rank within the agency; require the wearing of agency approved uniforms, and to have officers be properly groomed and his/her uniform clean, pressed and in proper condition.[71]

Such dress codes might address such matters as the length of hair, sideburns, beards, and goatees (whether or not they are permitted); types of sunglasses to be worn (mirrored, for example, are often banned); and tattoos (whether or not any body art is to be permitted for officers, and if they are to be covered while on duty).

The wearing of uniforms and displaying of tattoos, bodily hair, and beards are only the tip of the iceberg, however. Regulations might also spell out, for example, when officers are to begin wearing their summer and winter uniforms (specified dates normally occurring in spring and fall) and the proper components of each uniform (the list can specify certain types of socks, shoes, turtleneck, patches and insignia, and prohibitions against wearing items of clothing with an identifying logo—so the jurisdiction will not be seen as endorsing a particular name brand).

Imposing the will of the police administration concerning officers' appearance and attire is not always as easy as it might appear, however; today officers show little reluctance to file lawsuits if feeling that such codes violate their rights to freedom of expression:

- A northeastern Pennsylvania man sued in late 2009, claiming his rights were violated when he was not hired with the state police because he would not have his arm tattoo removed. Applicants' tattoos are subject to review by the Tattoo and Replica Review Committee, which can insist they be removed before a job will be offered. The lawsuit seeks to determine whether "the government can require you to physically alter your body in exchange for employment," and infringes on the applicant's "freedom of choice in personal matters."[72]
- The Houston City Council voted to spend up to $150,000 to hire outside lawyers to defend the city's no-beard policy for police. Four black officers filed a federal civil rights lawsuit against the city, claiming discrimination because shaving exacerbates a skin condition that disproportionately affects black men; officers with beards are barred from wearing the Houston Police Department uniform.[73] In March 2010 a federal appeals court upheld the city's policy, saying it was not racially discriminatory.
- Des Moines, Iowa, police policy states that any tattoos, branding and intentional scarring on the face, head, neck, hands, and exposed arms and legs are prohibited. Employees who already have tattoos are exempt. The police union says the policy is unreasonable and has filed a grievance.[74]
- Other agencies have implemented or are considering policies that would require officers to either not be tattooed, or to cover the tattoos completely when on duty.[75]

As mentioned, there are certainly several legal and psychological aspects of police uniforms and dress codes. This is an area where the views of administrators toward officers' uniforms and appearance may well inherently clash with the street officers' viewpoints, as the latter tries to be more "expressive" in an era when tattoos and facial hair are more commonplace and less stigmatized.

However, this is also an area of importance to the public, and studies show that the American public does not support relaxed grooming standards; one study found that 88 percent of Americans believe that public respect for police would drop if officers deviated from strict grooming standards.[76]

The Patrol Lifeline: Dispatchers and Communications

One group of police employees—often civilians—that a majority of police officers would no doubt say qualifies as their "unsung heroes" are police **dispatchers**, also called communications specialists. Neophyte police officers soon learn to highly value and rely on the knowledge, insight, and assistance of their dispatchers; they know their lives and safety may literally depend on the dispatcher's ability to determine the type, seriousness, and location of calls for service. In fact, their role is so critical that many agencies require

Computer-aided dispatch (CAD) systems help dispatchers to provide vital information—and be a "lifeline"—to officers responding to calls for service. *(Courtesy Citrus Heights, Calif., P.D.)*

their dispatchers to have first worked as patrol officers for a substantial amount of time in order to fully understand what the officers are facing and feeling while on patrol.

Dispatchers generally work in a centralized communications center. When handling calls, the information obtained is posted either electronically by computer or, with decreasing frequency, by hand. The dispatcher then quickly decides the priority of the incident, the kind and number of units needed, and the location of the closest and most suitable units available.

Dispatchers often are the first people the public contacts when emergency assistance is required. If certified for emergency medical services, the dispatcher may also provide medical instruction to those on the scene of the emergency and to citizens at home before the emergency personnel arrive. Particularly where communications services are combined or regional, a single dispatcher may also be responsible to take citizens' calls for, and to dispatch, fire fighters, ambulance personnel, sheriff's deputies, other outlying police department units, state troopers, and fish and game wardens.[77]

SUMMARY

This chapter has examined several issues related to the patrol function, which can be fairly stated as being the essence of policing. It discussed the purposes and nature of patrol; the influence of an officer's shift and beat; some hazards involved with patrol duties; the discretionary authority of patrol officers; the traffic function; the nature and purposes of various patrol vehicles; the legal and psychological significance of the patrol uniform; and the vital importance of the dispatch or communications function.

It was demonstrated that the patrol function is truly the backbone of policing, the primary means by which the police fulfill their mission. As noted, patrol officers do the work of community policing and problem solving, and they are the eyes and ears of the police organization. Patrol is the beginning point for all other specialized and administrative assignments, where citizens go to lodge concerns and complaints and where the needs of the community are met.

Because of the importance of patrol, researchers have tried to determine what works on patrol, and research findings on the patrol function were also presented—clearly it concerns more than just "driving around." Perhaps we have not yet reached the point of understanding how to best deploy patrol officers to their maximum effect, but research is demonstrating that some patrolling methods, which for decades were felt to be "tried and true," are myths and do not work. Ongoing research on the patrol function is needed. The fundamental—and seemingly simple—police task of seeing and being seen is indeed complicated and challenging. Knowledge of patrol utilization and effectiveness becomes more crucial because research has shown the crime-solving ability of detectives to be overrated. We have also seen that the street cop performs a variety of duties while using wide discretion in deciding how to handle problems. In essence, this chapter has attempted to put readers in the patrol officer's position by giving them a sense of what's involved in that profession.

KEY TERMS

beat assignment
beat culture
deployment
discretionary use of police authority
dispatcher
dress code
Kansas City Preventive Patrol Experiment
Law Enforcement Officers Safety Act of 2004 (H.R. 218)
occupational hazards
patrol function
patrol vehicle
shift assignment
suicide by cop
traffic control
uniform

REVIEW QUESTIONS

1. How is the patrol function affected by the officer's shift assignment and the nature of the beat to which he or she is assigned?
2. What are some of the occupational hazards that are inherent in beat patrol? What does H.R. 218 permit?
3. What is meant by suicide by cop, and what is the two-step investigative process that must take place to determine when it has occurred and to analyze the phenomenon?

4. What are some of the major findings of studies of the patrol function? (Emphasize in your answer the Kansas City Preventive Patrol Experiment.)
5. What is meant by discretionary use of police authority, and what are some of its advantages, disadvantages, and factors that enter into the officer's decision-making process?
6. Why is the traffic function important in patrol work, and how can it bring about bad citizen–police relations?
7. Why is the patrol vehicle so important in the lives and duties of patrol officers?
8. In what ways did the recent downturn in the economy affect normal, traditional patrol function, and how was patrolling "on two wheels" implicated in these difficult economic times?
9. What are the legal and psychological aspects of police officers' uniforms and their general appearance, and the nature and purpose of an agency dress code? What types of lawsuits are officers filing in regard to dress codes?
10. How would you describe the relationship between patrol officers and police dispatchers?

LEARN BY DOING

1. You are a patrol sergeant, lecturing to your agency's Citizens' Police Academy about the patrol function. Someone raises her hand and asks, "Sergeant, your officers obviously can't enforce all of the laws all of the time. Which laws are always enforced, and which ones are not? What factors determine how police discretion is used?" How do you respond (without saying something like "We enforce all of the laws, all of the time," which of course would be untrue)? How would you fully explain police discretion to the citizens' group?
2. The concepts of police discretion and ethics are obviously intertwined because all ethical dilemmas involve making a choice. As a new lieutenant in your professional standards unit, which has had ethical problems prior to your being promoted, what measures would you take to foster good ethical decision making on the part of your subordinates?
3. As a police consultant, you are hired by a nearby police agency to develop a new police uniform and dress code for all sworn officers, paying attention to legal and practical aspects. Develop a dress code as well as a description of the new uniform (color, accoutrements, etc.) that you would recommend, with arguments in defense of both.
4. For a practical view of traffic problems and solutions, go to www.popcenter.org/problems/street_racing (Guide No. 26) and/or to www.popcenter.org/problems/drunk_driving (Guide No. 28). These guides are published by the federal Center for Problem-Oriented Policing. Read and describe the kinds of problems that are caused by illegal street racing and/or drunk driving. Consider the efforts described in the guides that police are using to successfully address these problems.

mycrimekit

Go to MyCrimeKit.com and discover additional study tools and resources related to this chapter.

- Key Terms
- Review Questions
  - Multiple Choice Questions
  - True/False
  - Fill in the Blank
  - Essay
- MEDIA REVIEW: where you can review the *importance of the police car.*
- MEDIA SIMULATION: with a focus on *anticipating danger.*
- FLASHCARDS: to test your knowledge of this chapter.
- *NEW YORK TIMES:* where you can read the latest articles related to criminology and criminal law.
- THE CAREER CENTER: where you can explore career opportunities in criminal justice and criminology.
- THE ONLINE RESEARCH LIBRARY: where you can explore the Cybrary and Research Navigator.

NOTES

1. Quoted in John A. Webster, "Patrol Tasks," in *Policing Society: An Occupational View,* ed. W. Clinton Terry III (New York: Wiley, 1985), pp. 263–313.
2. American Bar Association, *Standards Relating to Urban Police Function* (New York: Institute of Judicial Administration, 1974), Standard 2.2.
3. W. Clinton Terry III, ed., *Policing Society: An Occupational View* (New York: Wiley, 1985), pp. 259–260.
4. Anthony V. Bouza, *The Police Mystique: An Insider's Look at Cops, Crime, and the Criminal Justice System* (New York: Plenum, 1990), p. 27.
5. See U.S. Department of Justice, Office of Community Oriented Policing Services, *311 for Non-Emergencies* (August 2006).
6. Elizabeth Reuss-Ianni, *Two Cultures of Policing: Street Cops and Management Cops* (New Brunswick, NJ: Transaction Books, 1983).
7. CNNMoney.com, "America's Most Dangerous Jobs," August 17, 2006. money.cnn.com/2006/08/16/pf/2005_most_dangerous_jobs/index.htm (accessed July 21, 2010).

8. See CNN.com, "Oakland Police Officer Pronounced Brain Dead After Shootings," www.cnn.com/2009/CRIME/03/22/california.officers/index.html (accessed July 21, 2010).
9. National Law Enforcement Memorial Fund, "Officer Deaths by Year: Year-by-Year Breakdown of Law Enforcement Deaths Throughout U.S. History," www.nleomf.org/facts/officer-fatalities-data/year.html (accessed July 23, 2010).
10. Associated Press, "More Police Dying in Traffic Accidents," www.msnbc.msn.com/id/16362182 (accessed July 21, 2010).
11. Anthony J. Pinizzotto, Edward F. Davis, and Charles E. Miller III, "Suicide by Cop Defining a Devastating Dilemma," *FBI Law Enforcement Bulletin* 74, no. 2 (February 2005), www.fbi.gov/publications/leb/2005/feb2005/feb2005.htm#page8 (accessed July 21, 2010).
12. H. Range Huston and Diedre Anglin, "Suicide by Cop," *Annals of Emergency Medicine* 32, no. 6 (December 1998).
13. Adapted from Pinizzotto, Davis, and Miller, "Suicide by Cop Defining a Devastating Dilemma."
14. Ibid.
15. Jerome H. Skolnick and David H. Bayley, *The New Blue Line: Police Innovation in Six American Cities* (New York: Free Press, 1986), pp. 141–142.
16. John P. Crank, *Understanding Police Culture* (Cincinnati OH: Anderson, 1998), p. 83.
17. Ibid., p. 254.
18. Quoted in Mark Baker, *Cops: Their Lives in Their Own Words* (New York: Pocket Books, 1985), p. 298.
19. Bouza, *The Police Mystique,* p. 74.
20. See the full text of the law at www.sdsos.gov/adminservices/adminpdfs/h218enr.pdf (accessed July 21, 2010).
21. Law Enforcement Alliance of America, "President Bush Signs Historic 'National Concealed Carry for Cops' into Law," www.leaa.org/218/218release0722.html (accessed July 21, 2010).
22. Dawson, "The Evolution of the Cop Car," p. 72.
23. Ibid.
24. Shaila Dewan, "As Gas Prices Rise, Police Turn to Foot Patrols," *The New York Times* (July 20, 2008), http://www.nytimes.com/2008/07/20/us/20patrol.html (accessed June 29, 2009).
25. U.S. Department of Transportation, National Highway Traffic Safety Administration, "Motorcycle Traffic Enforcement," www.nhtsa.dot.gov/people/injury/pedbimot/motorcycle/motorcycle_traffic03/preface.htm#2 (accessed July 22, 2010).
26. U.S. Department of Justice, Bureau of Justice Statistics, "Local Police Departments, 2003," p. iii, bjs.ojp.usdoj.gov/content/pub/pdf/lpd03.pdf (accessed July 26, 2010).
27. Chris Menton, "Bicycle Patrols: An Underutilized Resource," *Policing: An International Journal of Police Strategies & Management* 31 (1)(2008): 93–108.
28. Ibid, p. 94.

29. See Law Enforcement Bicycle Association, "Frequently Asked Questions," www.leba.org/faq.html (accessed July 22, 2010); and Kirby Beck, "The Case for Bicycle Law Enforcement," International Mountain Bike Association, www.ipmba.org/newsletter-0206-safety.htm (accessed July 22, 2010).
30. Chris Menton, "Bicycle Patrols: An Underutilized Resource," p. 98–103.
31. See Officer.com, "Vehicles and Equipment," directory.officer.com/list/Vehicles_Equipment (accessed July 29, 2009).
32. Jim McKay, "It's a . . . Car?" *Government Technology* (October 2008), pp. 48–49.
33. Joel Samaha, *Criminal Justice*, 2nd ed. (St. Paul, MN: West, 1991), pp. 163–164.
34. Police Foundation, *The Newark Foot Patrol Experiment* (Washington, DC: Author, 1981), p. 9.
35. Quoted in Kevin Krajick, "Does Patrol Prevent Crime?" *Police Magazine* 1 (September 1978): 4–16.
36. T. J. Baker, "Designing the Job to Motivate," *FBI Law Enforcement Bulletin* 45 (1976): 3–7.
37. Krajick, "Does Patrol Prevent Crime?" p. 10.
38. Ibid., pp. 11–13.
39. Robert C. Trojanowicz and Dennis W. Banas, *Job Satisfaction: A Comparison of Foot Patrol Versus Motor Patrol Officers* (East Lansing: Michigan State University, 1985).
40. Ibid.
41. Ibid., p. 235.
42. Skolnick and Bayley, *The New Blue Line*, p. 4.
43. Carl B. Klockars and Stephen D. Mastrofski, "Police Discretion: The Case of Selective Enforcement," in *Thinking About Police: Contemporary Readings*, 2nd ed., ed. Carl B. Klockars and Stephen D. Mastrofski (Boston: McGraw-Hill, 1991), p. 330.
44. James Q. Wilson and George L. Kelling, "'Broken Windows': The Police and Neighborhood Safety," *Atlantic Monthly*, March 1982, pp. 28–29.
45. David H. Bayley and Egon Bittner, "Learning the Skills of Policing," in *Critical Issues in Policing: Contemporary Readings*, ed. Roger G. Dunham and Geoffrey P. Alpert (Prospect Heights, IL: Waveland Press, 1989), pp. 87–110.
46. Kenneth Culp Davis, *Police Discretion* (St. Paul, MN: West, 1975), p. 73.
47. Kenneth Culp Davis, *Discretionary Justice* (Urbana: University of Illinois Press, 1969), p. 222.
48. Klockars and Mastrofski, "Police Discretion," p. 331.
49. Ibid.
50. Richard J. Lundman, "Routine Police Arrest Practices: A Commonweal Perspective," *Social Problems* 22 (1974): 127–141; Donald Petersen, "Informal Norms and Police Practices: The Traffic Quota System," *Sociology and Social Research* 55 (1971): 354–361.
51. Lawrence W. Sherman, "Experiments in Police Discretion: Scientific Boon or Dangerous Knowledge?" *Law and Contemporary Problems* 47 (1984): 61–82.
52. For a thorough discussion, see Gregory Howard Williams, "The Politics of Police Discretion," in *Discretion, Justice and Democracy: A Public Policy Perspective*, ed.

Carl F. Pinkele and William C. Louthau (Ames: Iowa State University Press, 1985), pp. 19–30.

53. Davis, *Police Discretion*, p. 22.
54. See James F. Doyle, "Police Discretion, Legality, and Morality," in *Police Ethics: Hard Choices in Law Enforcement*, ed. William C. Heffernan and Timothy Stroup (New York: John Jay Press, 1985), pp. 47–68.
55. *Tennessee v. Garner*, 471 U.S. 1 (1985).
56. U.S. Department of Justice, Bureau of Justice Statistics, *Characteristics of Drivers Stopped by Police, 2002* (Washington, DC: Author, 2006), pp. 1–2, 5.
57. Ibid.
58. See, for example, Terry C. Cox and Mervin F. White, "Traffic Citations and Student Attitudes Toward the Police: An Examination of Selected Interaction Dynamics," *Journal of Police Science and Administration* 16, no. 2 (fall 1988): 105–121.
59. Adam F. Carr, John F. Schnelle, and John F. Kirchner, "Police Crackdowns and Slowdowns: A Naturalistic Evaluation of Changes in Police Traffic Enforcement," *Behavioral Assessment* 2 (Spring 1980): 33–41; Tom Robinson, "Extinction Rate Measurement of the Mobile Radar Display Trailer" (unpublished manuscript, Department of Political Science, University of Nevada, Reno, 1993).
60. Richard J. Lundman, "Working Traffic Violations," in *Policing Society: An Occupational View*, ed. W. Clinton Terry III (New York: Wiley), pp. 327–333.
61. City of Berkeley City Council, "Agenda: June 27, 2000," www.ci.berkeley.ca.us/citycouncil/2000citycouncil/agenda/062700A.html (accessed July 22, 2010).
62. Paul N. Tinsley and Darryl Plecas, "Studying Public Perceptions of Police Grooming Standards," *The Police Chief*, November 2003, policechiefmagazine.org/magazine/index.cfm?fuseaction= display_arch&article_id=152&issue_id=112003 (accessed July 22, 2010).
63. 425 U.S. 238 (1976).
64. Ibid., at pp. 247–248.
65. Richard R. Johnson, "The Psychological Influence of the Police Uniform," *FBI Law Enforcement Bulletin*, March 2001, pp. 27–32; Tinsley and Plecas, "Studying Public Perceptions of Police Grooming Standards," p. 2.
66. Ibid., p. 29.
67. Ibid., p. 3.
68. Ibid., p. 2.
69. Ibid., p. 3.
70. Ibid., p. 3.
71. Adapted from the Watertown (South Dakota) Police Department General Order A-170, Effective Date: February 1, 2007, www.watertownpd.com/images/pdf_files/a-170%20personnel%20dress%20code%20and%20uniform%20regulations.pdf (accessed July 22, 2010).
72. "Tattooed State Police Job Applicant Sues Over Policy," www.wpxi.com/news/20567045/detail.html (accessed September 6, 2009).

73. Carolyn Feibel, "Ban on Beards at HPD Could Grow Costly," *Houston Chronicle*, May 29, 2008, www.chron.com/disp/story.mpl/metropolitan/5806843.html (accessed July 23, 2010).
74. Des Moines Police Ban New Tattoos," http://www.foxnews.com/story/0,2933,379203,00.html (accessed September 6, 2009).
75. Park, "HPD Weighs Tattoo Cover-up," p. 1.
76. Tinsley and Plecas, "Studying Public Perceptions of Police Grooming Standards," p. 4.
77. U.S. Department of Labor, Bureau of Labor Statistics, "Police, Fire, and Ambulance Dispatchers," www.bls.gov/oco/ocos138.htm (accessed July 22, 2010).

Criminal Investigation

Criminal Investigation

THE SCIENCE OF SLEUTHING

And the Lord said unto Cain, Where is thy brother Abel? [The first recorded instance of a criminal interrogation]
And he said. I know not: am I my brother's keeper? [The first recorded instance of perjury]
And He said, what hast thou done? The voice of thy brother's blood crieth unto me from the ground. [The first recorded instance of criminal evidence]

—*Genesis 4:9–10*

Murder though it hath no tongue will speak.

—*Shakespeare,* Hamlet, *Act II, Scene 2*

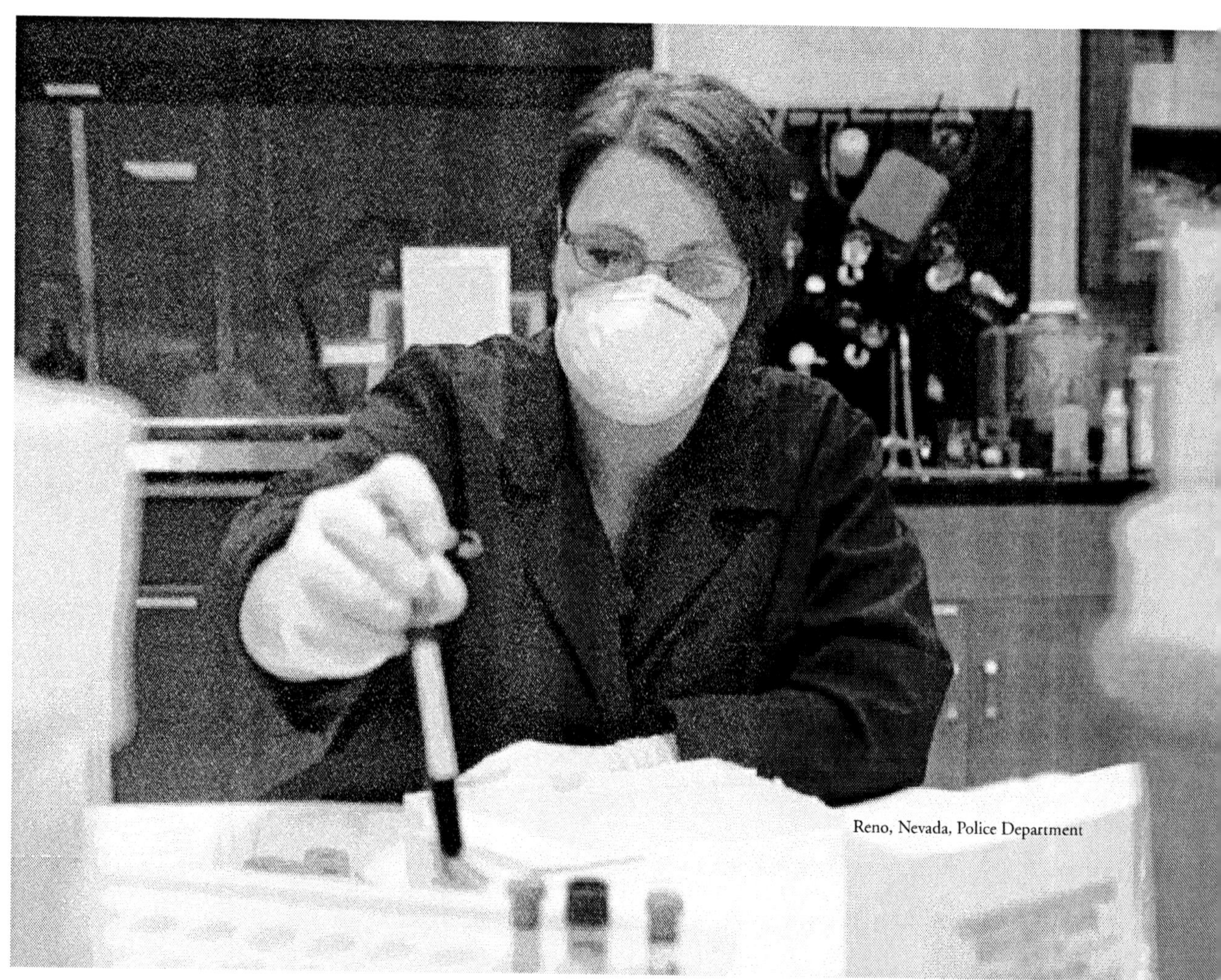

Reno, Nevada, Police Department

Learning Objectives

AS A RESULT OF READING THIS CHAPTER, THE STUDENT WILL:

- Be able to distinguish between *forensic science* and *criminalistics*
- Understand the origins of criminalistics as well as the types of information that physical evidence can provide
- Be able to compare anthropometry and dactylography
- Understand how August Vollmer and others contributed to the development of criminal investigation techniques
- Know the kinds of qualities that detectives and undercover officers need to possess
- Be able to explain the basic functions of the polygraph and its legal status in the courts
- Understand how DNA analysis operates as well as recent developments and some legal and policy issues concerning its use
- Know the contributions of insects and dogs to the investigative process
- Understand the nature of investigating stalking
- Be able to explain the nature of Internet crimes and how social networking sites are being used in criminal investigations
- Know the purpose and operation of a cold case squad
- Understand the investigative benefits that are provided by the regional computer forensics laboratory program

Introduction

The challenges involved with investigating crimes may well be characterized by a quote from Ludwig Wittgenstein: "How hard I find it to see what is right in front of my eyes!" Investigating crimes has indeed become a complicated art as well as a science, as will be seen in this chapter.

The art of sleuthing has long fascinated the American public. Certainly the expanding uses of DNA in the news, such television series as *CSI: Crime Scene Investigation,* and books and movies describing real-life serial killers such as the "Zodiac," "BTK," the "Green River Killer," and the "Night Stalker" have done much to capture the public's fascination with criminal investigation and forensic science in the twenty-first century. This interest in sleuthing is not a recent phenomenon, however; for decades, Americans have feasted on the exploits of dozens of fictional masterminds, including Sherlock Holmes, Agatha Christie's Hercule Poirot, Clint Eastwood's portrayal of Detective "Dirty Harry" Callahan, and Peter Falk's Columbo, to name a few.

In reality, investigative work is largely misunderstood, often boring, and overrated; it results in arrests only a fraction of the time; and it relies strongly on the assistance of witnesses and even some luck. Nonetheless, the related fields of forensic science and criminalistics are the most rapidly developing areas of policing—and probably in all of criminal justice. This is an exciting time to be in the investigative or forensic disciplines.

This chapter begins by defining forensic science and criminalistics and by looking at their origins; included is a brief discussion of crime scenes. Then we review the evolution of criminal investigation, emphasizing the identification of people and firearms. Next we analyze the application of forensic science within the larger context of the criminal justice system, followed by a review of the qualities detectives and undercover officers should have. We then briefly touch on the use of polygraph testing.

The status of DNA analysis is covered next; here we consider some new policy and legal developments—whether DNA testing should be employed for property crimes as well as for convicted offenders; also in this connection we consider what reputable sources are finding about the status of the nation's crime labs. We then look at the contributions to investigations made by behavioral science (including criminal profiling, psychics, and hypnosis) insects, and dogs; following that we examine the nature and investigation of two serious and growing crime problems: stalking and crimes involving the Internet. Next are discussions of the handling of cold cases and an expanding (and much needed) program known as the Regional Computer Forensics Laboratory. The chapter concludes with a summary, key terms, review questions, and several scenarios and activities that provide opportunities for you to learn by doing.

Scope of Forensic Science and Criminalistics

Definitions of Terms

The terms *forensic science* and *criminalistics* are often used interchangeably. **Forensic science** is the broader term and is that part of science used to answer legal questions. It is the examination, evaluation, and explanation of physical evidence in law. Forensic science encompasses pathology, toxicology, physical anthropology, odontology (the study of tooth anatomy and development and diseases of the teeth and related structures), psychiatry, questioned documents, ballistics, tool work comparison, and serology (the study of reactions and properties of serums), among other fields.[1] **Criminalistics** is one branch of forensic science; it deals with the study of physical evidence related to crime. From such a study, a crime may be reconstructed.

Criminalistics is interdisciplinary, drawing on mathematics, physics, chemistry, biology, anthropology, and many other scientific fields[2] (see Exhibit 1).

Basically, the analysis of physical evidence is concerned with identifying traces of evidence, reconstructing criminal acts, and establishing a common origin of samples

EXHIBIT 1

Where the Coursework Is Corpses: "Body Farms"

At times when the wind shifts in the spring, the bucolic region of east Tennessee carries the smell of human decomposition. That is because a two-acre plat at the University of Tennessee Anthropological Research Facility—unofficially termed the "body farm"—is the final resting place for nearly two hundred corpses under study. Some are buried, others lie on the grass or in the woods, in various stages of decay. Since 1981 the facility has studied hundreds of such corpses to determine what happens to the human body postmortem. This is the first facility of its kind (several others will open soon), and its findings have revolutionized forensic anthropology. It has even been mentioned in novels as well as on popular crime-scene television programs. As the facility's reputation has spread, a waiting list has grown to more than twelve hundred people wishing to be donated and used for analysis. The facility has provided a storehouse of knowledge concerning the determination of time of death as well as what happens when bodies are burned, dismembered, or invaded by a variety of insects and mammals; researchers there have also developed a software program that will assist with determining—from human remains—sex, race, height, and age. But much work is yet to be completed: current projects include calculating how long DNA lasts in tissue and how bones from the nuclear age are different from those of people who died before Hiroshima.

Source: Adapted from Raina Kelley, "Bodies Wanted," *Newsweek*, June 11, 2007, pp. 50–52.

of evidence. Peter DeForest and colleagues described the types of information that physical evidence can provide:[3]

- *Information on the* **corpus delicti** (body of the crime). Physical evidence, such as tool marks, a broken door or window, a ransacked home, missing valuables in a burglary, a victim's blood, a weapon, or clothing torn in an assault, shows that a crime was committed.
- *Information on the* **modus operandi** (method of operation). Physical evidence points to the means used by the criminal to gain entry, the tools used in the crime, the types of items taken, and other signs, such as urine left at the scene, an accelerant used at an arson scene, and the way crimes are committed. Many well-known criminals have left their "calling card" at their crimes, in terms of either what they did to their victims or the physical condition of the crime scene.
- *Linking of a suspect with a victim.* One of the most important linkages, particularly with violent crimes, is the connection to the suspect. This can include hair, blood, clothing fibers, and cosmetics that may be transferred from the victim to the perpetrator. Items found in a suspect's possession, such as bullets or a bloody knife, can also be linked to a victim.
- *Linking of a person to a crime scene.* Also a common and significant type of linkage, this includes fingerprints, glove prints, blood, semen, hairs, fibers, soil, bullets, cartridge cases, tool marks, footprints or shoe prints, tire tracks, and objects that belonged to the criminal. Stolen property is the most obvious example.
- *Disproving or supporting of a witness's testimony.* Evidence can indicate whether or not a person's version of events is true. An example is a driver whose car matches the description of a hit-and-run vehicle. If blood is found on the

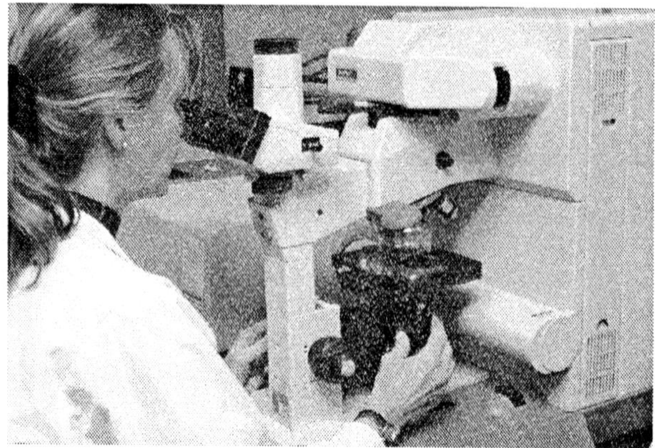

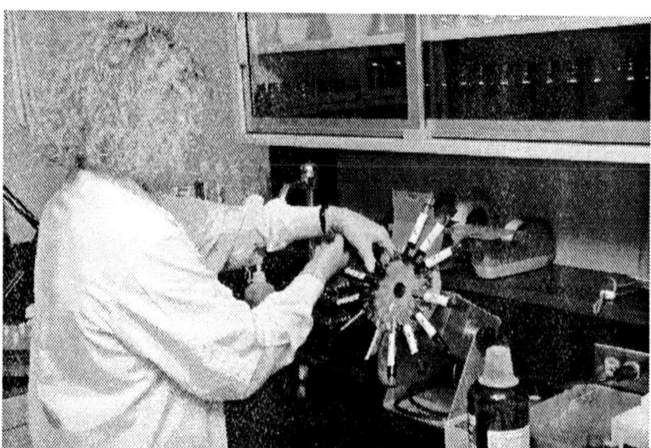

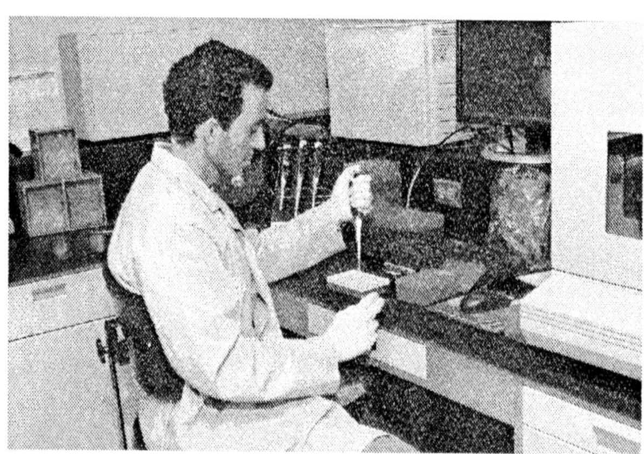

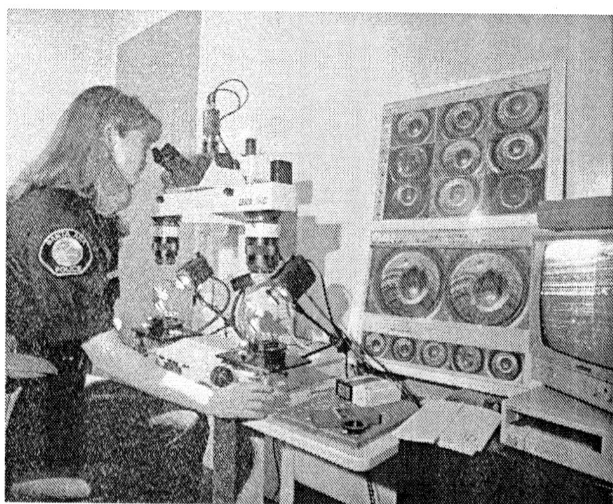

Technology is rapidly advancing in forensic laboratories. Shown here are lab technicians performing a variety of analyses. *(Courtesy Washoe County, Nevada, Sheriff's Office; © Spencer Grant (lower right)*

underside of the car and the driver claims that he hit a dog, tests on the blood can determine whether the blood is from an animal or from a human.

- *Identification of a suspect.* One of the best forms of evidence for identifying a suspect is fingerprints, which prove "individualization." Without a doubt, that person was at the crime scene.

A Word About Crime Scenes

On the subject of the **crime scene**, we will not go into detail concerning the roles of patrol officers, crime-scene technicians, and investigators; however, it should be emphasized that the protection of the crime scene and all evidence contained therein is of utmost importance for these personnel if the scene is to be properly preserved and evidence properly collected and analyzed. It is critical that at the moment they arrive, responding personnel are trained to (1) describe vehicles (make, model, color, condition, license plate number) and individuals (height, weight, race, age, clothing, sex, distinguishing features), including their direction of travel from first observation; (2) assess the scene for officer safety (downed power lines, animals, biohazards, chemicals, weapons); (3) watch for violent persons and attend to any emergency medical needs; and (4) prevent any unauthorized persons from entering the scene. A very good resource for crime-scene investigation, published by the National Institute of Justice, is titled *Crime Scene Investigation: A Reference for Law Enforcement Training.*[4]

Origins of Criminalistics

mycrimekit™
Review: *History of Criminal Investigation.*

The study of criminalistics began in Europe. The first major book describing the application of scientific disciplines to criminal investigations was written in 1893 by Hans Gross, a public prosecutor and later a judge from Graz, Austria.[5] Translated into English in 1906, the book remains a highly respected work in the field. Two prominent aspects of criminalistics, personal identification and firearms analysis, are covered next, followed by a discussion of individual contributions, investigative techniques, and state and federal developments in the field.

Personal Identification: Anthropometry and Dactylography

Anthropometry

Historically, two major systems for personal identification of criminals have been used: *anthropometry* and *dactylography.* **Dactylography**, better known as fingerprint identification, is widely used throughout the world today.

Anthropometry, a system that did not survive long, was developed in 1882 by Alphonse Bertillon (1853–1914). The **Bertillon system**, the first attempt at criminal identification that was thought to be reliable and accurate, was based on the theory that human beings differ from each other in the exact measurements of their bodies and that the sum of these measurements yields a characteristic formula for each individual.[6]

Bertillon performed menial tasks in 1879 for the Paris Police Department, filing cards that described criminals so vaguely as to have little meaning—"stature: average . . . face: ordinary."[7] He began comparing photographs of criminals and taking measurements of those who had been arrested, and eventually he concluded that if eleven physical measurements of a person were taken, the chances of finding another person with the same eleven measurements were 4,191,304 to 1.[8] Bertillon's report of his findings to his superiors was treated as a "joke," however[9]; but in 1883 his "joke" was given worldwide attention when it was implemented on an experimental basis and Bertillon correctly made his first criminal identification.[10]

Around the start of the twentieth century, many countries abandoned anthropometry, or the Bertillon system, adopting the simpler and more reliable system of fingerprint identification.[11] Still, Bertillon's pioneering work in personal identification has earned him a place in history, and today he is considered the "father of criminal investigation."[12]

L'ANTHROPOMÉTRIE. — Mesure de l'oreille (p. 295, col. 1).

A police officer taking Bertillon measurements. *(Courtesy St. Louis, Missouri, Police Department.)*

The major breakthrough for fingerprints was made by Edward Henry (1850–1931), who developed a fingerprint-classification system in 1897 that was adopted throughout British India. In 1901, Henry published his *Classification and Use of Finger Prints* and was appointed assistant police commissioner of London, rising to the post of commissioner two years later.[13]

The Jones Case. In 1904, Detective Sergeant Joseph Faurot of New York City was sent to England to study fingerprints. Upon his return to New York, Faurot was told by his superiors to forget such scientific nonsense, and he was transferred to a walking beat. In 1906, Faurot arrested a man who was creeping out of a suite at the Waldorf-Astoria Hotel; the man claimed to be a respected citizen named James Jones, but Faurot sent the man's fingerprints to Scotland Yard and learned that "James Jones" was actually Daniel Nolan, who had twelve prior convictions for hotel thefts. Nolan confessed to several thefts in the Waldorf-Astoria and was sent to prison for seven years. Publicity surrounding this case greatly advanced the credibility of fingerprinting in America.[14]

The West Case. An even more important incident that furthered the use of fingerprints in America occurred in 1903 when Will West arrived at the federal penitentiary in Leavenworth, Kansas. While West was being processed into the institution, a staff member said that a photograph was already on file for him, along with Bertillon

FEDERAL BUREAU OF INVESTIGATION
UNITED STATES DEPARTMENT OF JUSTICE
J. Edgar Hoover, Director

History of the "West Brothers" Identification..

Bertillon Measurements are not always a Reliable Means of Identification

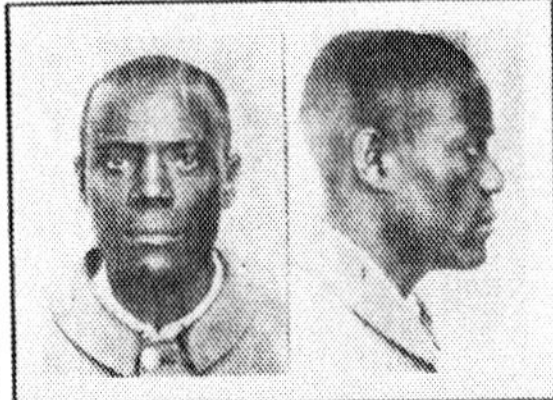

In 1903, one WILL WEST was committed to the U. S. Penitentiary at Leavenworth, Kansas, a few days thereafter being brought to the office of the record clerk to be measured and photographed. He denied having been in the penitentiary before, but the clerk doubting the statement, ran his measuring instruments over him, and from the Bertillon measurements obtained went to his files, returning with the card the measurements called for properly filled out, accompanied with the photograph and bearing the name WILLIAM WEST. Will West, the new prisoner, continued to deny that the card was his, whereupon the record clerk turned it over and read that William West was already a prisoner in that institution, having been committed to a life sentence on September 9, 1901, for murder.

The Bertillon measurements of these, given below, are nearly identical whereas the fingerprint classifications given are decidedly different.

The case is particularly interesting as indicating the fallacies in the Bertillon system, which necessitated the adoption of the fingerprint system as a medium of identification. It is not even definitely known that these two Wests were related despite their remarkable resemblance.

Their Bertillon measurements and fingerprint classifications are set out separately below:

177.5; 188.0; 91.3; 19.8; 15.9; 14.8; 6.5; 27.5; 12.2; 9.6; 50.3
15- 30 W OM 13 Ref: 30 W OM 13
28 W I 26 U OO

178.5; 187.0; 91.2; 19.7; 15.8; 14.8; 6.6; 28.2; 12.3; 9.7; 50.2
10- 13 U O O Ref: 13 U O 17
32 W I 18 28 W I 18

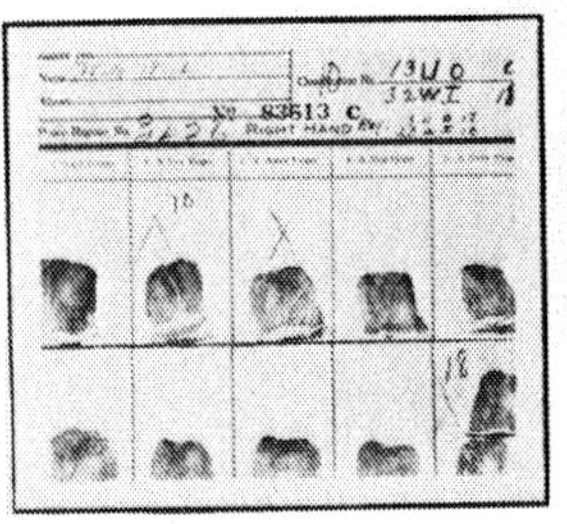

The "West Brothers" Case.
(Courtesy FBI)

measurements. West denied ever having been in Leavenworth. A comparison of fingerprints showed that despite nearly identical physical appearance and Bertillon measurements, the identification card on file belonged to a William West who had been in Leavenworth since 1901. The incident served to establish the superiority of fingerprints over anthropometry as a system of personal identification.

Firearms Identification

Firearms are involved in about 300,000 incidents per year in this country, resulting in nearly 344,000 firearms victims. Those figures are bad enough, but they actually compare favorably with more than a million incidents and about 1.3 million victims per year in the early 1990s.[15] The frequency of shootings in this country has obviously made firearms identification very important.

Chicago witnessed the St. Valentine's Day Massacre in 1929. A special grand jury inquiring into the matter noted that there were no facilities for analyzing the numerous bullets and cartridge cases that had been strewn about. As a result, several influential jury members raised funds to establish a permanent crime laboratory. Colonel Calvin Goddard (1858–1946) was appointed director of the lab and is the person most responsible for raising the status of firearms identification to a science and for perfecting the bullet comparison microscope.[16]

mycrimekit
Review: *Functions of the Crime Lab.*

Firearms identification goes beyond comparing a bullet found in the victim and a test bullet fired from the defendant's weapon. It also includes identifying types of ammunition, designing firearms, restoring obliterated serial numbers on weapons, and estimating the distance between a gun's muzzle and a victim when the weapon was fired.[17]

Contributions of August Vollmer and Others

The contributions of August Vollmer to the development of criminalistics and investigative techniques should not be overlooked. In 1907, as police chief of Berkeley, California, he enlisted the services of a University of California chemistry professor named Loeb to identify a suspected poison during a murder investigation. Vollmer instituted a formal training program to ensure that his officers properly collected and preserved criminal evidence. He also called on scientists on campus on several other occasions, and his support helped John Larson produce the first workable polygraph in 1921.

Vollmer also established in Los Angeles in 1923 the first full forensic laboratory; the concept soon spread to other cities, including Sacramento (a state laboratory), San Francisco, and San Diego. Because Vollmer's subsequent efforts to establish a relationship between his police department and the university led other scientists to get involved in forensic science, eventually courses in forensics were offered as part of the biochemistry curriculum at the University of California at Berkeley,[18] with many graduates of that program becoming criminalists.

Other early major contributors included Albert Osborn, who in 1910 wrote *Questioned Documents,* a definitive work; Edmond Locard, who maintained a central interest in locating microscopic evidence; and Leone Lattes, who in 1915 developed a blood-typing procedure from dried blood, a key event in serology.[19]

The forerunner of what was to become the Federal Bureau of Investigation was created in 1908. In 1924, J. Edgar Hoover assumed leadership of the Bureau of Investigation; eleven years later, Congress enacted legislation giving the FBI its present designation. Under Hoover, who understood the importance and uses of information, records, and publicity, the FBI became known for investigative efficiency. In 1932, the FBI established a crime laboratory and made its services free—they remain free of charge today to state and local police. In 1935, it opened its National Academy, providing training courses for state and local police as well as federal officers. And in 1967, the National Crime Information Center (NCIC) was made operational by the FBI, providing data on wanted persons and stolen property in all fifty states. These developments gave the FBI considerable influence over policing in America; Hoover and the FBI vastly improved policing practices in the United States, keeping crime statistics and assisting investigations.[20]

Forensic Science and the Criminal Justice System

Investigative Stages and Activities

The police (more specifically, investigators and criminalists) operate on the age-old theory that there is no such thing as a perfect crime: Criminals either leave a bit of themselves (such as a hair or clothing fiber) at the crime scene or take a piece of the crime scene away with them. Thus it is the job of the police and the crime lab to unify their efforts and to find that incriminating piece of evidence, which they can use in conjunction with other pieces of evidence to determine "whodunit" and to bring the guilty party to justice.

In the apprehension process, when a crime is reported or discovered, police officers respond, conduct a search for the offender (it may be a "hot" crime-scene search where the offender is likely present, a "warm" search in the general vicinity, or a "cold" investigative search), and check out suspects. If the search is successful, evidence for charging the suspect is assembled, and the suspect is apprehended.[21] Cases not solved in the initial phase of the apprehension process are assigned either to an investigative specialist or, in smaller police agencies, to an experienced uniformed officer who functions as a part-time investigator. According to Paul Weston and Kenneth Wells, what follows are the basic **investigative stages**:[22]

Review: *Investigation.*

Preliminary investigation. The work of the preliminary investigation is crucial, involving the first police officer at the scene. Duties to be completed include establishing whether a crime has been committed; securing from any witnesses a description of the perpetrator and his or her vehicle; locating and interviewing the victim and all witnesses; protecting the crime scene (and searching for and collecting all items of possible physical evidence); determining how the crime was committed and what the resulting injuries were, as well as the nature of property taken; recording in field notes and sketches all data about the crime; and arranging for photographs of the crime scene.

Continuing investigation. The next stage, which begins when preliminary work is done, includes conducting follow-up interviews; developing a theory of the crime; analyzing the significance of information and evidence; continuing the search for witnesses; beginning to contact crime lab technicians and assessing their analyses of the evidence; conducting surveillances, interrogations, and polygraph tests, as appropriate; and preparing the case for the prosecutor.

Reconstruction of the crime. The investigator seeks a rational theory of the crime. Most often, inductive reasoning is used: The collected information and evidence are carefully analyzed to develop a theory. Often, a rational theory of a crime is developed with some assistance from the careless criminal. *Verbrecherpech,* or "criminal's bad luck," is an unconscious act of self-betrayal. One of the major traits of criminals is vanity; their belief in their own cleverness, not chance, is the key factor in their leaving a vital clue. Investigators look for mistakes.

Focus of the investigation. When the last stage is reached, all investigative efforts are directed toward proving that one suspect (perhaps with accomplices) is guilty of the crime. This decision is based on the investigator's analysis of the connections between the crime, the investigation, and the habits and attitudes of the suspect.

Arrest and Case Preparation

A lawful arrest brings the investigation into even greater focus and provides the police with several investigative opportunities. The person arrested can be searched and booked at the police station, and fingerprints can be taken for positive identification and possible future use. Evidence may be found at these stages. The prisoner may wish to talk to the police. Here, the officer must obviously know and understand the laws of arrest and search and seizure as well as the laws of evidence (especially the "chain of custody"). Any evidence found during the arrest must be collected, marked, transported, and preserved as carefully as that found at a crime scene.

"Case preparation is organization."[23] For an investigation to succeed at trial, all reports, documents, and exhibits must be arrayed in an orderly manner. This package must then be forwarded to the prosecutor. At this point, the investigator never injects personal opinions or conclusions into the case. The identification of the accused leads to an array of witnesses and physical evidence. The corpus delicti of the crime has been established, and the combination of "what happened" and "who did it" has occurred, at least in the mind of the investigator. The investigator must also prepare for the almost inevitable negative evidence that must be countered at trial, where the accused may contend that he or she did not commit the crime. (He or she may try to attack the investigative work, use an alibi, or get the evidence suppressed.) The defendant may offer an affirmative defense, admitting that he or she committed the acts charged but claiming that he or she was coerced, acted in self-defense, was legally insane, and so forth. Or the defendant may attack the corpus delicti, contending that no crime was committed or that there was no intent present.[24]

In the prosecutor's office, the case is reviewed, assigned for further investigation, and (if warranted) prepared for trial. Conferences with the investigator and witnesses are usually held. The prosecutor may waive prosecution if the case appears to be too weak to result in a conviction; if the accused will inform on other (usually more serious) offenders; if a plea bargain is more attractive than a trial; or if there are mitigating circumstances in the case (such as emotional disturbance).

An investigation is successful when the crime being investigated is solved and the case closed. Often a case is considered cleared even if no arrest has been made, as when the offender dies, the case is found to be a murder–suicide, the victim refuses to cooperate with the police or prosecutor, or the offender has left the jurisdiction and the cost of extradition is not justified.[25]

Detectives: Qualities, Myths, and Attributes

The **detective** function is now well established within the police community. A survey by the RAND Corporation revealed that every city with a population of more than 250,000, along with 90 percent of the smaller cities, has officers specifically assigned to investigative duties.[26]

Several myths surround police detectives, who are often portrayed in movies as rugged, confident (sometimes overbearing), independent, streetwise individualists who bask in glory, are rewarded with big arrests, and are adorned by beautiful women. Detective work carries a strong appeal for many patrol officers, young and veteran alike. In reality, detective work is seldom glamorous or exciting. Investigators, like their bureaucratic cousins, often wade in paperwork and spend many hours on the telephone. Furthermore, studies have not been kind to detectives, showing that their vaunted productivity is overrated. Not all cases have a good or even a 50–50 chance of being cleared by an arrest. Indeed, in a study of over 150 large police departments, a RAND research team learned that only about 20 percent of their crimes could have been solved by detective work.[27] Another study, involving the Kansas City, Missouri, Police Department, found that fewer than 50 percent of all reported crimes received more than a minimal half hour's investigation by detectives. In many of these cases, detectives merely reported the facts discovered by the patrol officers during the preliminary investigations.[28]

Yet the importance and role of detectives should not be understated. Detectives know that a criminal is more than a criminal. As Weston and Wells said:

> John, Jane and Richard are not just burglar, prostitute and killer. John is a hostile burglar and is willing to enter a premises that might be occupied. Jane is a prostitute who wants a little more than pay for services rendered and is suspected of working with a robbery gang and enticing her customers to secluded areas. Richard is an accidental, a person who, in a fit of rage, killed the girl who rejected him.[29]

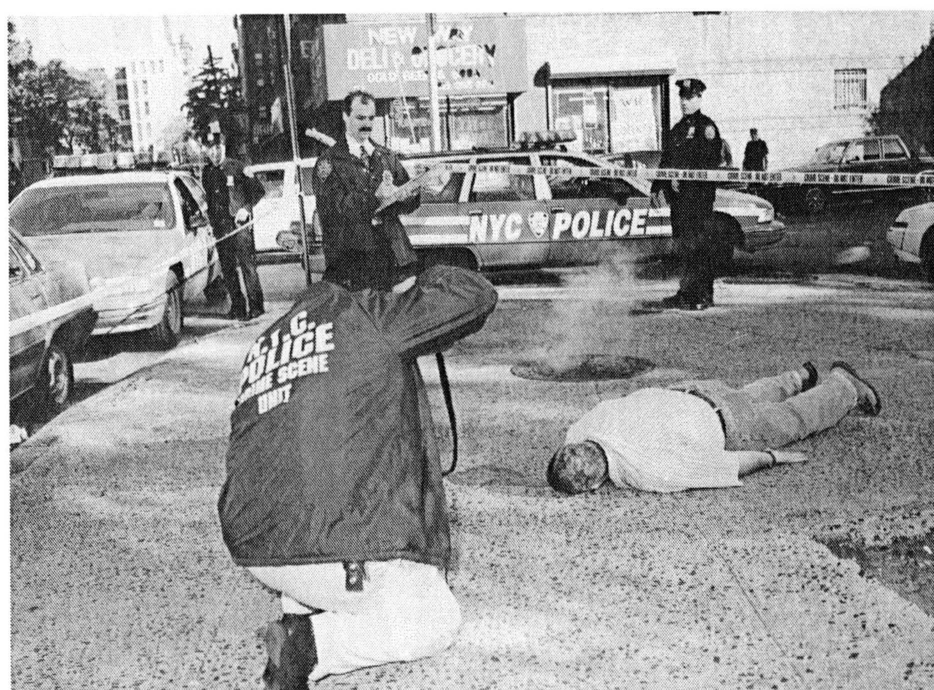

Homicide investigation is the most important and challenging work performed by detectives.
(Courtesy NYPD Photo Unit)

mycrimekit
Review: *Criminal Investigator Role.*

To be successful, the investigator must possess four personal attributes to enhance the detection of crime: an unusual capability for observation and recall; an extensive knowledge of the law, rules of evidence, scientific aids, and laboratory services; a powerful imagination; and a working knowledge of social psychology.[30] Successful detectives (and even patrol officers) also appear to empathize with the suspect; if a detective can appear to understand why a criminal did what he or she did ("You robbed that store because your kids were hungry, right?"), a rapport is often established that results in the suspect's telling the officer his or her life history—including how and why he or she committed the crime in question. Perhaps first and foremost, however, detectives need logical skills, the ability to exercise deductive reasoning, to assist in their investigative work.

The accompanying Career Profile briefly expresses the viewpoints of a former detective.

Officers Who "Disappear": Working Undercover

Undercover work is a highly sought after and valued type of investigative police work. Undercover work can be defined as the assignment of police officers to investigative roles in which they adopt fictitious civilian identities for a sustained period of time in order to uncover criminal activities that are not usually reported to police.[31]

Undercover police operations have increased greatly since the 1970s, owing largely to expanded drug investigations. The selection process typically is intense and very competitive. Since only a few officers are actually selected for undercover assignments, these officers enjoy a professional mystique, in large measure because of wide discretionary and procedural latitude in their roles, minimal departmental supervision, ability to exercise greater personal initiative, and higher degree of professional autonomy than regular patrol officers.[32]

Problems with the Role

The conditions of undercover work, however, may lessen officer accountability and lower adherence to procedural due process and confidence in the rule of law.[33] One of the most important requirements is the ability to cultivate informants for information on illegal activities and for contacts with active criminals. Deals and bargains must be struck and honored. Therefore close association with criminals—both the informants and the targeted offenders—heightens the challenges of the undercover role considerably. Undercover officers must sustain a deceptive front over extended periods, thereby facing increased risk of stress-induced illness, physical harm, and corruption. One study determined that the greater the number of undercover assignments undertaken, the more drug, alcohol, and disciplinary problems federal officers had during their careers.[34]

Undercover agents can experience profound changes in their value systems, often resulting in an overidentification with criminals and a questioning of certain

CAREER PROFILE

Name: Donald F. Pussehl, Jr.

Position: Chief of Police, Saginaw Township Police Department, Saginaw, Michigan.

College attended: Delta College and Saginaw Valley State University

Degrees: Associate's Degree in Criminal Justice, B.A. in Criminal Justice, and M.A. in Criminal Justice/Political Science.

Current teaching position: Delta College and Saginaw Valley State University

What CJ-related jobs have you held and when?

Patrol Officer	1978–1987 Bridgeport Township Police Dept./Saginaw Police Dept.
Detective	1987–1993 Saginaw Police Dept.
Sergeant	1993–1995 Saginaw Police Dept.
Lieutenant	1995–1997 Saginaw Police Dept.
Deputy Chief	1997–2000 Saginaw Police Dept.
Chief of Police	2000–2004 Saginaw Police Dept.
Chief of Police	2004–Present Saginaw Township Police Dept.
SWAT Team	1987–1995 Saginaw Police Dept.
Adjunct Professor at Delta College and Saginaw Valley State University	1995–present

What positions did you like most?

The most rewarding position was the detective's position, especially investigating homicides. I found it challenging to gather information from witnesses and then put the puzzle together in order to charge the person responsible for the crime. I enjoy working with people on a daily basis in an effort to resolve the issues that they may have.

What qualities/characteristics most helped you succeed in the field?

Being firm yet compassionate with people, and trying to put myself into their shoes to see what they were experiencing at that moment in their life. An important characteristic is being able to listen attentively to gather all the information that is important to the case.

What is the typical salary students can expect entering this field?

Starting wage for a patrol officer is approximately $38,000 per year and may increase to $58,000 after approximately fifteen years of service.

What advice would you give students early in their college career to help them find a rewarding job in Criminal Justice?

Participate in internships or volunteer work within different criminal justice agencies to see what each agency has to offer. This may help you determine which criminal justice field you may wish to enter after graduating. Integrity and honesty are extremely important in the criminal justice profession. Holding yourself to high standards will help make you marketable when you begin searching for employment.

criminal statutes they are sworn to enforce.[35] These isolated assignments may also involve a separation of self, disrupting or interfering with officers' family relationships and activities and perhaps even leading to a loss of identity and the adoption of a criminal persona as they distance themselves from a conventional lifestyle.[36] Author Gary Marx cites one instance:

> A good example of this is the case of a Northern California police officer who participated in a "deep cover" operation for eighteen months, riding with the Hell's Angels. He was responsible for a very large number of arrests, including previously almost untouchable higher-level drug dealers.

But this was at the cost of heavy drug use, alcoholism, brawling, the break-up of his family, an inability to fit back into routine police work, resignation from the force, several bank robberies, and a prison term.[37]

Return to Patrol Duties

Ending an undercover assignment, and then returning to patrol duty, is an awkward experience for the many officers who have difficulty adjusting to the everyday routine of traditional police work. These officers may suffer from such emotional problems as anxiety, loneliness, and suspiciousness, and they may experience marital problems. Officers will quickly have less autonomy and diminished initiative in job performance; they are no longer working in a tight-knit unit with expanded freedom and control and no longer feel as though they are behind enemy lines in the battle against crime, where their work experiences are intense and inherently dangerous. The return to routine patrol may be analogous to coming down from an emotional high, and officers in this position may feel depressed and lethargic.[38]

Uses of the Polygraph

In terms of its use in police recruiting and hiring, the polygraph has also been used by the police in the investigation of serious crimes since at least the early 1900s. The modern polygraph is a briefcase-size device or computerized model that records changes in skin resistance (perspiration), blood pressure, pulse rate, and breathing. Activity in each of these physiological measurements is monitored and recorded on a paper chart.[39]

The polygraph, commonly referred to as a lie detector, cannot actually detect when a lie is told; therefore, the **polygraph examination** is an inferential process in which "lying" is inferred from comparisons of the aforementioned physiological responses to questions that are asked during polygraph testing. In police work, the two major uses of polygraph testing are specific issue testing and preemployment screening. In specific issue testing, the polygraph is used to investigate whether a particular person is responsible for or involved in the commission of a specific offense. The use of the polygraph for preemployment screening is very controversial and is, in fact, illegal in some jurisdictions. When used, however, polygraph testing can help to verify information collected during traditional background investigations and to uncover information not otherwise available. Studies show that polygraph procedures may yield an accuracy of about 90 percent.[40]

The commonly held belief that polygraph examination results are not admitted into evidence in court is untrue. Some courts admit polygraph evidence even over the objection of counsel; in other jurisdictions, polygraph results are admitted by stipulation. At the federal level, no single standard governs admissibility. It is also common for prosecutors to use polygraph results to decide which charges to file, if any, and defense attorneys rely on polygraph testing to plan their defense and to negotiate pleas. Some judges also use polygraph results in sentencing decisions.[41]

DNA Analysis

Discovery and Types of Analyses

Deoxyribonucleic acid (DNA) is the basic building code for all the human body's chromosomes and is the same for each cell of an individual's body, including skin, organs, and all body fluids.[42] Developed in England in 1984 by Alec Jeffreys,[43] we know that portions of the DNA structure are as unique to each individual as fingerprints and that inside each of the sixty trillion cells in the human body are strands of genetic material—chromosomes. Arranged along the chromosomes, like beads on a thread, are nearly a hundred thousand genes, which are the fundamental unit of heredity; they instruct the body cells to make proteins that determine everything from hair color to susceptibility to diseases, and they pass genetic instructions from one generation to the next.[44]

DNA profiling, also called genetic fingerprinting or DNA typing, has shown much promise in helping investigators to solve crimes and to ensure that those guilty of crimes are convicted in court by the examination of DNA samples from body fluid, hair, and bones to determine whether they came from a particular subject. For example, semen on a rape victim's jeans can be positively or negatively compared with a suspect's semen. DNA is thus powerful evidence. Indeed, in April 2007 it was reported that the two-hundredth person—a former Army cook who spent nearly twenty-five years in prison for a rape he did not commit—was exonerated by DNA evidence (the tenth exoneration since January 2002).[45]

The FBI's DNA Analysis Unit and many other forensic laboratories in the U.S. examine items of evidence from a wide variety of alleged crimes including counterterrorism and intelligence gathering efforts, threatening letters (e.g. anthrax threat letters), violent crimes such as homicides and sexual assaults, bank robberies, extortion and organized crime cases, and many other violations. The DNA analysis method currently used by the FBI Laboratory is termed the "polymerase chain reaction-based–Short Tandem Repeat" typing technique. This (PCR–STR) technique allows for the analysis of extremely small body fluid stains, as well as the analysis of samples with no visible staining (e.g., envelopes in an extortion case or a ski mask from a bank robbery). The results of the DNA analyses on evidentiary items are then compared to the results obtained from known blood or saliva samples submitted from the victims and/or suspects potentially involved in the alleged incident.[46] Also used is mitochondrial DNA—a tiny ring-shaped molecule that is much smaller than the more familiar nuclear DNA—that can be extracted from hair, bones, and teeth when little else remains of a body.[47]

CODIS

Another recent DNA innovation is the **Combined DNA Index System (CODIS)**. CODIS contains DNA profiles obtained from subjects convicted of homicide, sexual assault, and other serious felonies. Investigators are able to search and compare evidence from their individual cases against the system's extensive national file of DNA genetic markers.

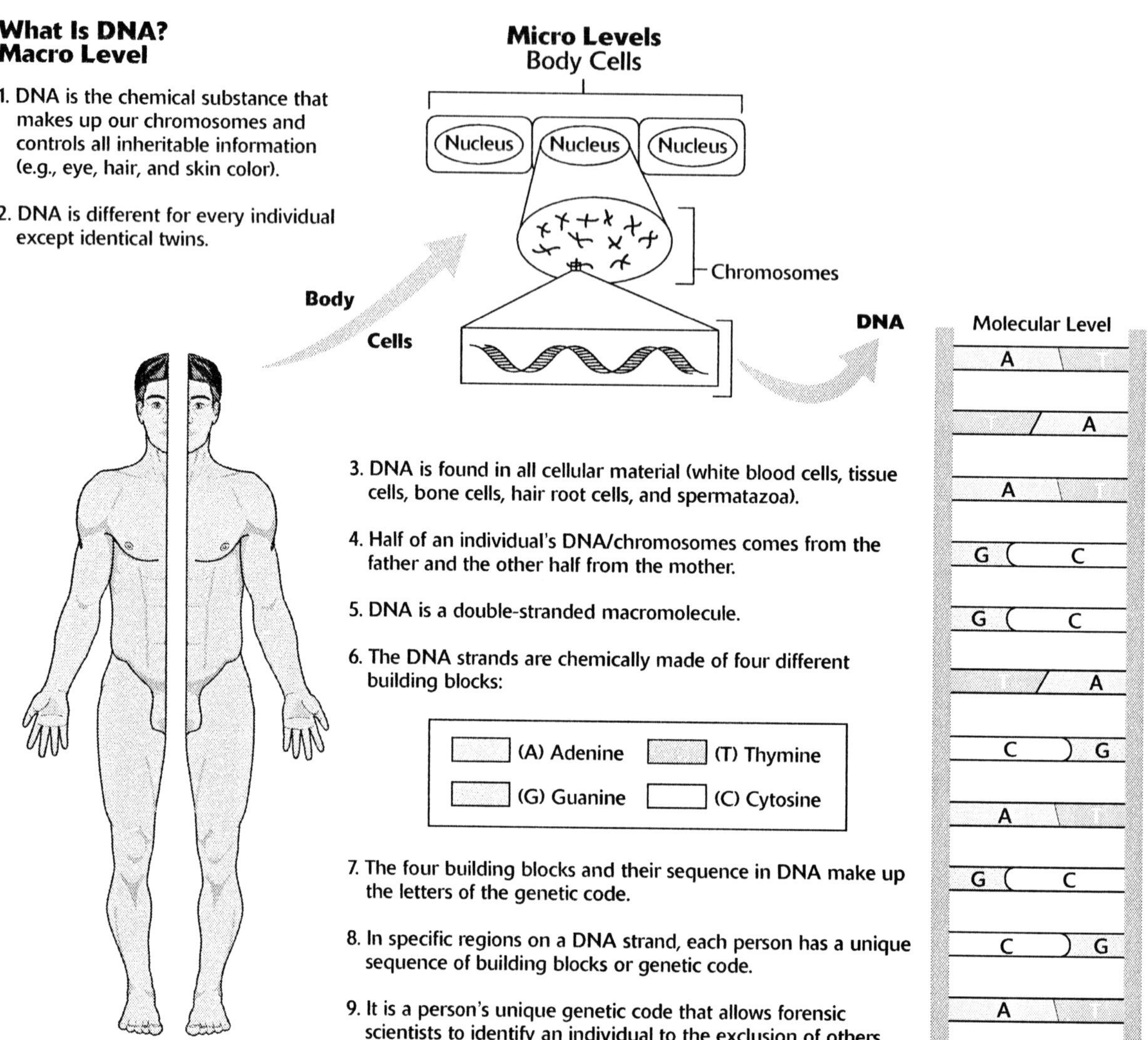

What Is DNA?
Macro Level
1. DNA is the chemical substance that makes up our chromosomes and controls all inheritable information (e.g., eye, hair, and skin color).
2. DNA is different for every individual except identical twins.
Micro Levels
Body Cells
Nucleus
Nucleus
Nucleus
Chromosomes
Body
Cells
DNA
Molecular Level
A
A
A
G C
G C
A
C G
A
G C
C G
A
3. DNA is found in all cellular material (white blood cells, tissue cells, bone cells, hair root cells, and spermatazoa).
4. Half of an individual's DNA/chromosomes comes from the father and the other half from the mother.
5. DNA is a double-stranded macromolecule.
6. The DNA strands are chemically made of four different building blocks:
(A) Adenine
(T) Thymine
(G) Guanine
(C) Cytosine
7. The four building blocks and their sequence in DNA make up the letters of the genetic code.
8. In specific regions on a DNA strand, each person has a unique sequence of building blocks or genetic code.
9. It is a person's unique genetic code that allows forensic scientists to identify an individual to the exclusion of others.

Figure 1
What Is DNA?
Source: Federal Bureau of Investigation, Laboratory Division

CODIS provides software and support services so that state and local laboratories can establish databases of convicted offenders, unsolved crime scenes, and missing persons. It allows these forensic laboratories to exchange and compare DNA profiles electronically, thereby linking serial violent crimes, especially sexual assaults, to each other and identifying suspects by matching DNA from crime scenes to convicted offenders.[48]

DNA Policy Nightmare: Solving Property Crimes

A recent study compared burglary investigations in which traditional police practices were used to collect and analyze DNA in the usual manner, as well as through "touch"

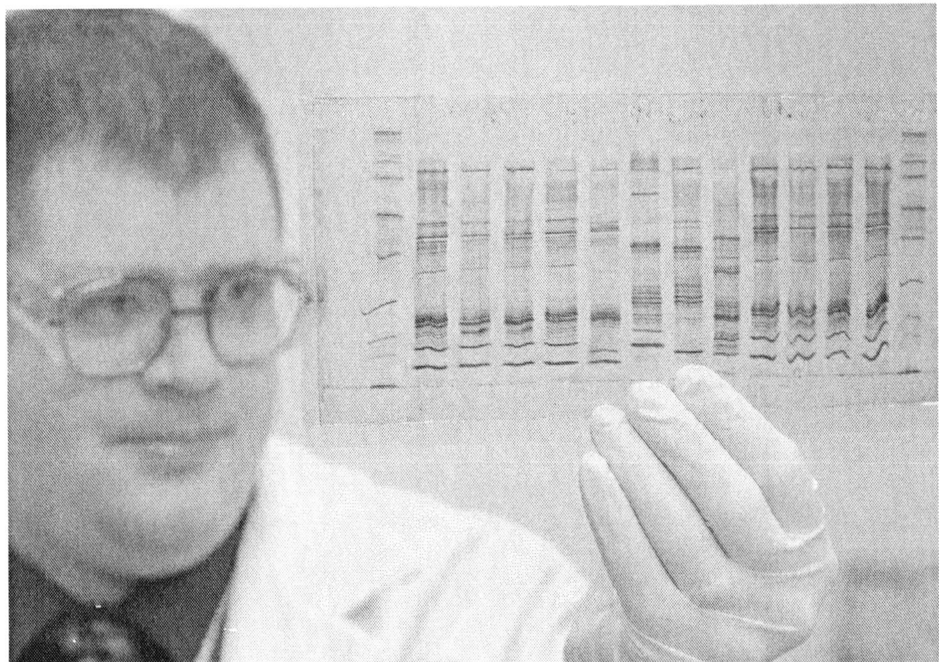

A chemist reads a DNA profile.
(Courtesy U.S. Customs and Border Protection, photographer James Tourtellotte)

DNA. The latter process has been available for several years and is so-named because DNA profiles can be obtained from such nontraditional sources of evidence as computer cords, jewelry boxes, and door handles. The study revealed that when DNA was analyzed:[49]

- more than twice as many suspects were identified,
- twice as many suspects were arrested,
- more than twice as many cases were accepted for prosecution, and
- suspects were five times as likely to be identified through DNA evidence as through fingerprints.[50]

The question as to whether DNA should be applied to property crimes should be a no-brainer—right? Unfortunately, the answer is not an emphatic yes, and the whole matter has the potential to turn the criminal justice system on its head.

First, consider that in a given year more than 2.2 million burglaries are reported to the police[51] and that only about one in eight of them will be solved. Lurking in this question of using DNA in property offenses are some huge policy decisions, such as the following:

- How will U.S. crime laboratories process the increase in evidence? And how many new labs would need to be built to accommodate the log of new cases?
- Are we willing to hire more prosecutors and public defenders to handle an increased volume of cases?

- How can we ensure that using DNA to solve burglaries will not pull investigative resources away from other criminal investigations, such as sex crimes, robbery, and domestic violence?
- Even if the preceding issues were addressed, do we need to revisit sentencing guidelines—or are we going to pay the cost to build many more prisons and jails that would be needed to handle these newly arrested property offenders?[52]

Perhaps the major policy implication surrounding this matter would be how to reduce the current backlog of evidence needing to be analyzed in U.S. crime labs. Would Americans be willing to have a large measure of cases outsourced to for-profit DNA labs?[53] Such questions would need to first be answered in determining whether or not to extend the reach of DNA testing. The truth is, DNA works, but it costs a lot of money.[54]

Postconviction DNA Tests: The Supreme Court Speaks

A major issue involving DNA has concerned **postconviction testing**. Because the speed and accuracy of testing have improved and because there are stories of convicted people who were exonerated because of DNA tests, many inmates want to be tested if there is any evidence from which DNA can be extracted. They have everything to gain and nothing to lose.

In June 2009 the U.S. Supreme Court addressed the question of whether or not convicts enjoyed a constitutional right to such testing in hopes of proving their innocence; in a 5–4 decision, the Court said such persons had *no* such right. (The plaintiff in this case, William Osborne, was an Alaska citizen who had been convicted of a brutal attack on a prostitute sixteen years ago.[55]) The decision, however, was seen as having limited impact because the federal government and forty-seven states already had laws allowing convicts some access to genetic evidence.

A Wider Net: New Law Expands DNA Gathering

In early 2007, the U.S. Department of Justice finalized guidelines for allowing the collection of DNA from most people arrested or detained by federal authorities, a vast expansion that will include hundreds of thousands of illegal immigrants each year. The new forensic DNA sampling was authorized by Congress in the January 2006 renewal of the Violence Against Women Act, and it permits DNA collection from anyone under arrest by federal authorities and from illegal immigrants detained by federal agents.

Labs and DNA Storage Under Fire

Recent heightened concerns about problems in forensic laboratories as well as police preservation of DNA have come under greater scrutiny. Next we briefly look at both areas.

Because of what were perceived as "critical problems"—including allegations of misconduct in death-penalty cases—several states launched oversight boards to investigate misconduct in crime labs. Crime lab problems (falsified tests, misplaced evidence, scientific mistakes) have surfaced across the United States in recent years, leading to lawsuits and sometimes audits of examinations. Unfortunately, this is not a "witch hunt"—there are strong indicators of serious problems in this nation's crime labs. Indeed, the National Academy of Sciences (NAS) found in 2009 that, because of crime lab deficiencies, criminals going free, and improper convictions, only a "massive overhaul" can improve the system.[56] NAS found nearly 400 publicly funded crime labs that were underfunded, underequipped, and detached from scientific standards; only DNA examinations were dependable enough to allow police officers to testify in court. The root of the problem, NAS argued, is the lack of strict standards, which it called on Congress to correct by establishing a national institute of forensic sciences to accredit crime labs.[57]

Another recent controversy concerns DNA preservation. Half of the states lack requirements to preserve DNA evidence, despite a series of exonerations based on this evidence. However, disagreement is extensive concerning how the evidence should be maintained—and whether or not the police have enough room to store it (see the preceding discussion concerning use of DNA analysis with property crimes). Very few states have enacted legislation mandating that biological evidence be maintained for as long as the offender remains in prison.[58]

Behavioral Science in Criminal Investigation

Criminal Profiling

The **criminal profiling** of serial killers has probably captured the public's fancy more than any other investigative technique used by the police. The success of profiling depends on the profiler's ability to draw on investigative experience, training in forensic and behavioral science, and empirically developed information about the characteristics of known offenders. It is more art than science. The focus of the analysis is the behavior of the perpetrator while at the crime scene.[59]

There are various types of investigative profiles. Drug-courier profiles have been developed from collections of observable characteristics that experienced investigators believe indicate a person who is carrying drugs. Other types of profiles include loss-control specialists' profiles of shoplifters as well as threat assessments, such as the Secret Service's profiles of potential presidential assassins. Criminal profiling of violent offenders, however, is the area for which the most descriptive information has been collected and analyzed and the most extensive training programs have been developed.[60] Unfortunately, most people associate criminal profiling with the psychic profiler on television's *The Profiler* or with Agent Starling in the film *The Silence of the Lambs*—both of which are inaccurate portrayals.[61]

Profiling is not a new discovery; indeed, Sir Arthur Conan Doyle's fictional character Sherlock Holmes often engaged in profiling. For example, in "A Study in Scarlet," published in 1887, Holmes congratulated himself on the accuracy of his psychological profile: "It is seldom that any man, unless he is very full-blooded, breaks out in this way through emotion, so I hazarded the opinion that the criminal was probably a robust and ruddy-faced man. Events proved that I had judged correctly."[62] Profiling was used by a psychiatrist to study Adolph Hitler during World War II and to predict how he might react to defeat.[63]

Psychological profiling, while not an exact science, is obviously of assistance to investigators; however, it does not replace sound investigative procedures. Profiling works in harmony with the search for physical evidence. Victims play an important role in the development of a profile, as they can provide the investigator with the offender's exact conversation. Other items needed for a complete profile include photographs of the crime scene and any victims, autopsy information, and complete reports of the incident, including the weapon used. From this body of information the profiler looks for motive.[64]

Serial murderers—killers who are driven by a compulsion to murder again and again—are also profiled. Many psychologists believe that serial murderers fulfill violent sexual fantasies they have had since childhood. They satisfy their sexual needs by thinking about their killings, but when the satisfaction wears off they kill again. Most serial murderers, the FBI has learned, are solitary males; an alarming number are doctors, dentists, or other health-care professionals. Almost one-third are ex-convicts and former mental patients. Many, like Kenneth Bianchi, the Los Angeles Hillside Strangler, are attracted to policing. (Bianchi, who was working as a security guard when he was finally caught in Washington State, often wore a police uniform during his crimes.) Serial killers seem normal, and they principally attack lone women, children, older people, homeless people, hitchhikers, and prostitutes.[65]

Another psychology-related investigative tool is **psycholinguistics**, which provides an understanding of those who use criminal coercion and strategies for dealing with threats. The 1932 kidnapping case of Charles Lindbergh's infant son (perpetrated by a German-born illegal alien, whose notes revealed his background and ethnicity) marked the beginning of this investigative method. Concentrating on evidence obtained from a message, spoken or written, the psycholinguistic technique microscopically analyzes the threats or messages for clues to the origins, background, and psychology of the maker. Every sentence, syllable, phrase, word, and comma is computer scanned. A "threat dictionary" containing more than 350 categories and 15 million words is consulted; these "signature" words and phrases are then used to identify possible suspects.[66]

Clearly, profiling can be useful in criminal inquiries in several ways: focusing the investigation on more likely types of offenders, suggesting proactive strategies, suggesting trial strategies, and preventing violent crimes. The FBI has trained dozens of state and local investigators in the profiling process. The program required twelve months of intensive training and hands-on profiling experience and consisted of an academic phase and an application phase.[67]

Psychics and Hypnosis

Psychics are also brought in from time to time, usually as a last resort when an investigation has stalled and no solution is imminent. Psychics are believed to possess extrasensory perception (ESP) or paranormal powers. National interest was focused on parapsychology—the discipline dealing with ESP, clairvoyance, and so forth—with the publicity accompanying the solving of three sex murders of youths in South Gate, California, in 1978. After two fruitless years of investigation, police resorted to the services of a local psychic, who helped an artist sketch a drawing of a face that had appeared to the psychic in a vision. With this information, police apprehended a suspect. However, Martin Reiser, a prominent Los Angeles Police Department (LAPD) psychologist, has studied the use of psychics and has found no support for the "contention that psychics can provide significant information leading to the solution of major crimes."[68]

In the early 1970s, policing turned to hypnosis as an investigative tool. A number of police practitioners were trained in how to place witnesses, victims, arresting officers, and even investigators in a hypnotic state.[69] Hypnosis has been used to help people recall license plate numbers, names, places, or details of an incident. Although a trend toward acceptance of hypnosis by appellate courts began to develop in the early and mid-1970s, a 1976 California ruling reflected current skepticism with the technique. Hypnosis was used in a murder case to secure details of the suspect's identity and to obtain his conviction.[70] Following this case, the courts, increasingly concerned with the suggestibility of potential witnesses while under hypnosis, began rendering adverse rulings against such testimony. It then became clear to police and prosecutors that witnesses whose recall had been enhanced through hypnosis could not be put on the witness stand. Today, hypnosis is used sparingly, generally for people who would otherwise be useless as material witnesses.

Today only two states—Nevada and Texas—expressly allow such evidence. Officials in those states believe that forensic hypnotists can help otherwise frustrated investigators to solve crimes and that investigators with information obtained through hypnotism are free to either confirm, corroborate, or refute that information through the use of other evidence.[71]

Developing Areas in Forensic Science and Investigation

Technological opportunities—as well as new scientific and investigative problems—are rapidly developing for federal, state, and local police practitioners. In this section, we discuss several of them.

Forensic Entomology: "Insect Detectives"

Forensic entomology has developed the use of new "investigators": insects. Anyone involved in death investigations is aware of the connection between dead bodies and insects, especially maggots. As one forensic entomologist stated, "Insects are major players in nature's recycling effort, and in nature a corpse is simply organic matter to be recycled. Left to its own devices, nature quickly populates a corpse with a diverse community of organisms, all dedicated to reducing the body to its basic components."[72]

The application of insect evidence to criminal investigations is not a new idea. In 1255, a Chinese "death investigator" named Sung Ts'u wrote a book titled *The Washing Away of Wrongs*. Sung tells of a murder in a Chinese village in which the victim was repeatedly slashed. The local magistrate thought the wounds might have been inflicted by a sickle and ordered all the village men to assemble, each with his own sickle. In the hot summer sun, flies were attracted to one sickle because of the residue of blood and small tissue fragments still clinging to the blade and handle. The owner of the sickle confessed.[73]

Unfortunately, it was not until much later, in 1855, that this discovery would be used in a forensic investigation. During a remodeling of a house outside Paris, the mummified body of an infant was discovered behind a mantelpiece. An autopsy determined that a flesh fly had exploited the body during the first year and that mites had laid their eggs on the dried corpse the following year. The logical suspects were people who were the occupants of the house in 1848—a young couple—who were subsequently arrested and convicted.[74]

In the mid-1930s, entomological evidence came to the fore in a brutal murder case. A woman saw a severed human arm while looking over a bridge spanning a small stream in Scotland. Ultimately, more than seventy pieces of two badly decomposed corpses—the wife of a local physician and her personal maid—were recovered from the area. Some maggots were discovered feeding on the decomposing body parts and were sent to the laboratory; they were identified as belonging to a type of blow fly and were thought to be between twelve and fourteen days old. For a number of reasons, suspicion fell on the physician: the entomological estimate of the time of death, the skillful manner of the dismemberment, and the fact that the doctor had been seen with a cut finger. He was convicted of both murders.[75]

Today forensic entomology can be of tremendous assistance to investigators. When a person dies, hundreds of species of insects descend on the corpse and the crime scene. Attracted by what scientists think may be a "universal death scent," common green flies, ground beetles, and other insects that thrive on flesh migrate to a corpse to lay eggs or to feast. The death of a human triggers very predictable patterns of insect activity that can be traced backward through time. There are several waves of insects, and their presence is informative. The life cycles of these creatures are so fixed and precise that they act as a natural clock to the trained eye.[76]

The phenomenon of succession is also telling: As each organism feeds on a body, it changes the body; this change in turn makes the body attractive to another group of organisms, which changes the body for the next group, and so on until the body has been reduced to a skeleton. This is a predictable process,[77] and it is now being studied scientifically at several so-called "body farms" (see Exhibit 1).

Often the strongest circumstantial evidence in a criminal prosecution is the fact that the victim and a suspect were seen together. For example, the body of a nine-year-old girl who had been missing for three weeks was found in Kenosha, Wisconsin. Insect evidence put her death at midnight twenty-one days before—the exact day she had gone to a carnival with the suspect, who was eventually convicted.

Insects are also used in other ways. A Florida murderer who dropped his victim in a swamp was convicted when mayflies, only active in a swamp region a few days of the year, were found in his car radiator. In a rape case, the offender was convicted when his ski mask was found to contain larvae from caterpillars that emerged only in late summer and were known to dwell in the woods next to the rape scene. Furthermore, insects feeding on infected tissues where children's diapers were not changed or under bandages and bedsheets that were used by the elderly have often been the only evidence that neglect has occurred.[78]

A forensic entomology laboratory has been established at Simon Fraser University in British Columbia. It is the first university lab in North America founded for the sole purpose of refining the ways in which insect biology can help solve crimes.[79]

Use of "Nonhuman Detectives": Dogs

Police dogs now also play an increasingly vital role in investigative work and are used around the world. In addition to their historical use for tracking and catching criminals and controlling crowds, because of their keen sense of smell and agility they are now being used by the police for finding drugs, explosives, and human remains. They are taught how to bark continuously when they find what they are looking for and how to chase and attack, even when they are being threatened with weapons.

The most popular breed for police work is the German shepherd. Chosen for its intelligence and highly developed senses, this breed tends to be more instinctively suspicious of strangers than other breeds. However, springer spaniels and Labrador retrievers are often used for police work as well because of their natural tracking abilities.

As the threat of terrorism has increased, these specialist police dogs have become even more important to the police. Just as police work is making increasing use of

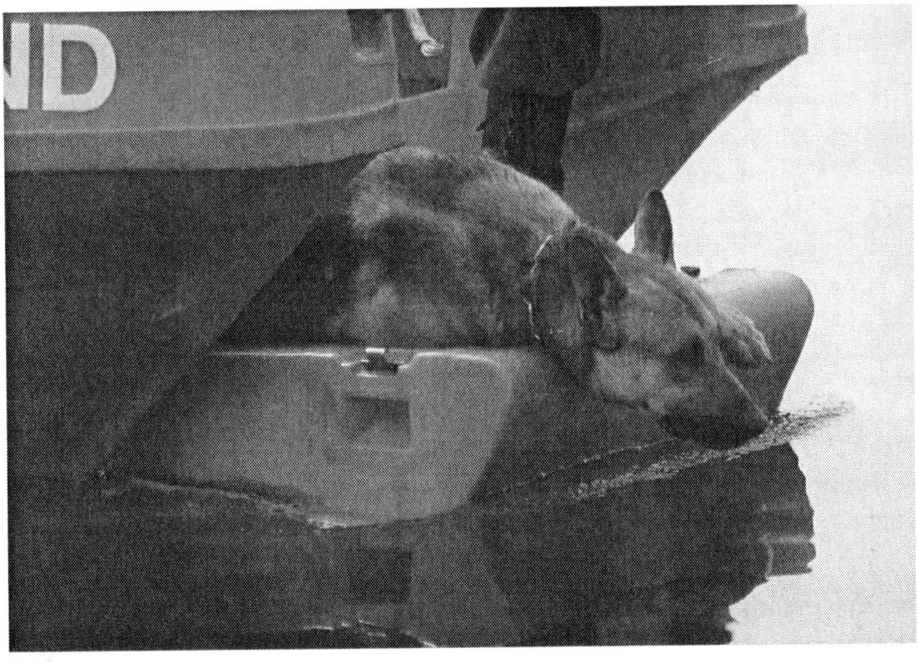

Police dogs occupy vital roles in investigative work, being used to find drugs, explosives, and human remains. Here, an underwater corpse-sniffing police dog rides on a police boat. *(Courtesy Photolibrary/Peter Arnold, Inc.)*

new technology, so is the training police dogs receive. Police dogs are now being trained to work with cameras attached to their heads, enabling them to enter dangerous places and send pictures back to officers.[80]

Stalking Investigations

Stalking, defined as conduct that would cause a reasonable person on at least two separate occasions to feel fear, remains a pervasive problem in our society. In fact, the U.S. Department of Justice reports that stalking is on the rise and now affecting about 3.4 million Americans per year. Stalking is generally not a random act: nearly three-fourths of all victims know their stalker in some capacity.[81]

In addition to the increase in such acts, many stalkers are also now "cyberstalking" their victims: about one-fourth of stalking victims report their stalker had used some form of cyberstalking, such as cell phone "textual harassing" or e-mail. To date, only four states specifically prohibit using cyberstalking methods to instill fear in stalking victims.[82]

There are four types of stalking situations:

1. *Erotomanic stalking.* The erotomanic stalker has a delusional disorder in which the victim, usually a person of higher status and opposite gender (often a celebrity or a public figure), is believed to be in love with the stalker. In fact, the victim does not know the stalker, and the stalking is usually short-lived, lasting one to four months.
2. *Love obsessional stalking.* Similar to the erotomanic stalker, the love obsessional type does not know the victim except through the media and has a psychiatric diagnosis. These stalkers usually write letters and make telephone calls in a campaign to make their existence known to the victim. This behavior lasts much longer, often exceeding ten years.
3. *Simple obsessional stalking.* In this type of incident, the simple obsessional stalker had a prior relationship with the victim (e.g., as a former spouse or employer), and the stalking began after the relationship soured. The stalking usually lasts about five months. (*Note:* Stalking is most often perpetrated against current or former intimate partners, with young women between ages eighteen and twenty-nine as the primary targets; therefore, stalking is closely related to the national problem of domestic violence.[83])
4. *False victimization syndrome.* The rarest form, a person with false victimization syndrome claims that someone is stalking him or her in order to gain attention as a victim. There is no stalker, and this phenomenon is similar to Münchausen syndrome by proxy, in which people intentionally produce physical symptoms of illness in their children in order to gain attention and sympathy.[84]

Evidence collection for crimes of stalking begins with the victims. Victims should record each time they see the stalker or when any contact is made and should document specific details, such as time, place, location, and any witnesses. Messages on answering machines, faxes, letters, and computer e-mails provide useful evidence for building a case against the offender. Police agencies should also consider providing victims with a small tape recorder to facilitate the collection of this information and should encourage victims to report in a journal how the stalking has affected them and their lifestyle, to later help convince juries of the victims' fear and trauma. Another investigative strategy is doing surveillance on suspects at times when they are likely to stalk their victims. Executing a search warrant for the suspect's personal and work computers, residence, and vehicle can prove useful in many circumstances; officers should look for spying equipment (such as binoculars and cameras), photos, and any property belonging to the victim.[85]

Investigating Internet Crimes and Using Social Networking Sites

The Internet has obviously revolutionized the way people communicate, shop, entertain themselves, learn, and conduct business. But as the saying goes, "The fleas come with the dog." This high-tech revolution in our homes and offices has opened a whole new world for the criminal element, creating a new type of criminal—the **cybercrook**. Often termed **cybercrimes**, these are criminal activities that involve the use of computers and the Internet; a variety of activities are included under this heading, from downloading illegal music files to stealing millions of dollars from online bank accounts. Pornographers and pedophiles (discussed below) are also on the Web, as are other, newer types of criminals: better educated, upscale, older, and increasingly female. Today's computer crimes include identity theft; cyberterrorism; software piracy; industrial espionage; credit card, consumer, and stock market fraud; baby adoption scams; and embezzlement.

The vast majority of **Internet crime** cases involve some form of fraud, and average about $930 per complaint; cases typically include undelivered merchandise and/or payment, comprising one-third of all complaints; Internet auction fraud accounts for about one-fourth of such cases. E-mail (about three-fourths of the cases) and Web pages (about one-fourth) were the two most primary mechanisms by which the fraudulent contacts take place.[86]

The above types of crimes compel the development of new investigative techniques, specialized and ongoing training for police investigators, and the employment of individuals with strong technical backgrounds (and an ability to "follow the money"). Concerning police futures, the police must become better educated, better equipped, and more adaptable.

Social networking sites such as MySpace and Facebook are also becoming one of the most dangerous places on the Internet. According to Reuters, "scammers break into accounts posing as friends of users, sending spam that directs them to Web sites that steal personal information and spread viruses." Since Facebook alone has, by some measures, more than 200 million members, the problem is extremely serious.[87]

But such sites are also yielding character evidence to detectives and police who find damaging Internet photos of defendants to use against them. For example, two weeks after a twenty-year old Rhode Island man was charged with driving while intoxicated for seriously injuring a woman, he attended a Halloween Party dressed as a prisoner; pictures from the party showed him in an orange jumpsuit labeled "Jail Bird"; the prosecutor, tipped off to the picture, argued for incarceration, and the young man was sentenced to two years in prison.[88]

No Stone Unturned: Cold Cases

Many jurisdictions plagued by a significant number of unsolved murders, or **cold cases**, have created a cold case squad. These squads can be especially useful in locating and working with past and potential witnesses and in reviewing physical evidence to identify suspects.

The most important component of cold case squads is personnel—the squads must have the right mix of investigative and supervisory talent. Squads may also use, as needed, the services of federal law enforcement agencies, medical or coroners' offices, retired personnel, criminalists or other specialists, or college or student interns. Cold cases selected for investigation are usually at least a year old and cannot be addressed by the original investigative personnel because of workload, time constraints, or the lack of viable leads. Cases are prioritized on the basis of the likelihood of an eventual solution. The highest-priority cases are those in which there is an identified homicide victim, suspects were previously named or identified through forensic methods, an arrest warrant was previously issued, significant physical evidence can be reprocessed, newly documented leads have arisen, and critical witnesses are available and willing to cooperate.[89] See Exhibit 2 for information on a new institute focusing on cold cases.

EXHIBIT 2

Looking at "Cold" Cases

At the new Institute for Cold Case Evaluation (ICCE) at West Virginia University, a nonprofit consulting center, law-enforcement agencies will have at their disposal a diverse array of scientists in fields ranging from anthropology to entomology, according to the institute's creator, Max Houck, a forensic anthropologist who previously worked at the FBI crime laboratory.

Each year, the number of cold cases in the nation grows by about another 6,000, on top of the 200,000 unsolved murder cases that have accumulated since 1960.

"At other agencies, they just take the last retiree, hire him back as a contractor and give him a desk and a phone because that's all they have," Houck told the Associated Press. "Then they put a stack of files in front of him . . . with no resources."

Houck, who teaches at the university, said the ICCE will provide departments with free or discounted services from at least two dozen scientists. It will launch a Web site as well, with a free electronic newsletter and a secure chat room for investigators. The public can browse the site, searching through cases and making donations that will help fund the center.

Source: "Case Studies," *Law Enforcement News,* November 15/30, 2003, p. 7. John Jay College of Criminal Justice, CUNY, 899 Tenth Avenue, New York, NY 10019.

Modern Day "Cavalry": Regional Computer Forensics Laboratory Program

New developments in technology will create—and have already created—a need for investigators who can cope with the criminal uses of those technologies.

Fortunately, for investigative personnel who now confront digital crimes, the future is here; help is available in the form of the **Regional Computer Forensics Laboratory (RCFL)** program. This program, which began in 1999 in San Diego, California, is now a national network of fourteen digital evidence laboratories and training centers sponsored by the FBI; the FBI provides start-up and operational funding, training, staff, and equipment, while state, local, and other federal law enforcement agencies assign personnel to staff the laboratories.

Each RCFL is devoted to the examination of digital evidence at all levels of government and in a wide variety of investigations, from terrorism to child pornography, fraud, homicide, and more. Digital media of all kinds are examined (see Table 1),[90]

Table 1
Types of Media Analyzed by RCFLs, Fiscal Year 2009

Media Type	Total Media Processed for FY09	Compared with FY08
CD/DVD	14,028	↓
Cellular Telephone	1,690	↓
*iPhone®	263	N/A
CPUs	684	↑
Digital Camera	148	↑
Digital Media Player	95	↑
Flash Media	2,820	↓
Floppy Disk	4,104	↓
Global Positioning System (GPS)	54	↔
Hard Disk Drive	15,630	↓
Personal Digital Assistant (PDA)	96	↓
Tape	586	↑
Total Media Processed	40,198	↓

Source: U.S. Department of Justice, Federal Bureau of Investigation, *Regional Computer Forensics Laboratory: Annual Report for Fiscal Year 2009*, pp. 12–13, www.rcfl.gov/downloads/documents/RCFL_Nat_Annual09.pdf (accessed July 28, 2010).

and each year RCFLs conduct about 4,500 forensic examinations and train nearly 5,000 law enforcement officers in digital forensics techniques.[91]

Following are some high-profile cases in which RCFLs were recently involved:

- Christopher Paul, who pled guilty to conspiring to use a weapon of mass destruction against targets in Europe and the United States
- A civil rights investigation into abuses against inmates by five Fayette County, Kentucky, detention center corrections officers
- Lisa Montgomery, charged with the murder of a twenty-three-year-old pregnant woman and the kidnapping of the woman's unborn child
- Corruption charges against former Newark, New Jersey, Mayor Sharpe James
- Identify thief Jocelyn Kirsch, who stole personal information from fifty friends, co-workers, and neighbors[92]

SUMMARY

This chapter has presented the evolution of criminal investigation, including definitions of key terms, identification of people and firearms, ways investigators work within the larger context of the criminal justice system, qualities needed by detectives, undercover police work, polygraph testing, DNA analysis, profiling, recent investigative developments (e.g., use of behavioral science, insects, dogs), and special investigations such as stalking, cybercrimes, cold cases, social networking sites, and RCFLs.

The evolution of forensic evidence, criminalistics, and criminal investigation is the product of a successful symbiosis of science and policing. This chapter has shown the truly interdisciplinary nature of police work; we discussed not only the influence of the so-called hard sciences—computer science, chemistry, biology, and physics—but also the assistance of psychology.

Forensic science is arguably the most rapidly progressing area of criminal justice, and there is little doubt that the future holds even greater advances in this realm. This discipline has traveled a great distance, especially in laboratory processes, in DNA analysis and application, and in ever-expanding uses of the computer. The potential of the computer to assist in solving crimes is limited only by our funds and imagination. Thus policing should continue indefinitely to reap the benefits of applying scientific aids to criminal justice matters.

Certainly this area of policing carries with it a high degree of fascination and mystique for the public, and rightfully so. Although policing certainly has its limitations, such as paperwork, boredom, failures, and other liabilities, there is nothing quite like using "gee whiz" investigative tools and techniques to catch bad guys—at least in the public's mind.

KEY TERMS

anthropometry
Bertillon system
cold cases
Combined DNA Index Systems (CODIS)
corpus delicti
crime scene
criminalistics
criminal profiling
cybercrimes
cybercrook
dactylography
detective
forensic entomology
forensic science
Internet crime
investigative stages
modus operandi
polygraph examination
postconviction testing
psycholinguistics
Regional Computer Forensic Laboratory (RCFL)
stalking

REVIEW QUESTIONS

1. How would you differentiate the terms *forensic science* and *criminalistics*?
2. What are the origins of criminalistics, and what are the differences between anthropometry and dactylography?
3. What types of information can physical evidence provide?
4. What does a "body farm" do?
5. What contributions did August Vollmer and other pioneers in law enforcement make to the development of criminal investigation techniques?
6. What qualities do detectives and undercover officers need and use?
7. What are the basic functions of the polygraph and its legal status in the courts?
8. In lay terms, how does DNA analysis operate?
9. What policy implications are involved with the use of DNA analysis for investigation of property offenses?
10. What was the purpose of the U.S. Supreme Court rule concerning the right of prison inmates to receive a DNA analysis?
11. What contributions have behavioral science, insects, and dogs made to criminal investigation?
12. What are the four types of stalking situations, and what new form of stalking is being employed by stalkers?
13. How has the Internet provided new opportunities for criminals?
14. How are social networking sites being used by investigators against offenders?
15. What is the purpose of a cold case squad, and how does it operate?

16. What concerns have been raised about forensic labs and DNA preservation, and what is being done to address those concerns?
17. What is the RCFL program, and how is it serving criminal investigators?

LEARN BY DOING

1. Unequivocally, the best means of learning about investigative techniques and forensic methods/equipment is to tour a modern forensics laboratory. A related aspect of investigation that should not be overlooked is that agency's means of safeguarding the chain of evidence and its storage prior to and following trial. If, for security or other reasons, you are unable to personally (or as a class) tour a forensic laboratory, then attempt to interview one or more detectives who work with crimes against persons and/or property concerning their methods, training and education; primary obstacles in successfully bringing a case to trial; greatest challenges in their work; methods employed in interviewing suspects; constitutional and other legal aspects of their role; recent changes in the investigative field; and so on.
2. To fully understand what kinds of investigative efforts are being made by police to address real-world problems, go to www.popcenter.org/Problems/?action=alpha&type=pdf#webguides. There you will find a selection of individual problem-solving guides—now more than fifty in number—published by the federal Center for Problem-Oriented Policing. Select two guides and describe what they say police are using to succeed in their investigative and problem-solving efforts.

mycrimekit™

Go to MyCrimeKit.com and discover additional study tools and resources related to this chapter.

- Key Terms
- Review Questions
  - Multiple Choice Questions
  - True/False
  - Fill in the Blank
  - Essay
- MEDIA REVIEW: where you can review topics such as the *history of criminal investigation, investigation, the criminal investigator's role,* and the *functions of a crime lab.*
- MEDIA VIDEO: where you can learn about a career as a criminalist and a fire investigator.

- FLASHCARDS: to test your knowledge of this chapter.
- *NEW YORK TIMES*: where you can read the latest articles related to criminology and criminal law.
- THE CAREER CENTER: where you can explore career opportunities in criminal justice and criminology.
- THE ONLINE RESEARCH LIBRARY: where you can explore the Cybrary and Research Navigator.

NOTES

1. Marc H. Caplan and Joe Holt Anderson, *Forensics: When Science Bears Witness* (Washington, DC: Government Printing Office, 1984), p. 2.
2. Charles R. Swanson, Neil C. Chamelin, Leonard Territo, and Robert W. Taylor, *Criminal Investigation,* 9th ed. (Boston: McGraw-Hill, 2006), p. 10.
3. Peter R. DeForest, R. E. Gaensslen, and Henry C. Lee, *Forensic Science: An Introduction to Criminalistics* (New York: McGraw-Hill, 1983), p. 29.
4. U.S. Department of Justice, National Institute of Justice, *Crime Scene Investigation: A Reference for Law Enforcement Training* (Washington, DC: Author, 2004).
5. Richard Saferstein, *Criminalistics: An Introduction to Forensic Science,* 9th ed. (Upper Saddle River, NJ: Prentice Hall, 2007), p. 8.
6. Jurgen Thorwald, *Crime and Science* (New York: Harcourt, Brace and World, 1967), p. 4.
7. Jurgen Thorwald, *The Century of the Detective* (New York: Harcourt, Brace and World, 1965), p. 7.
8. Ibid., pp. 9–10.
9. Ibid., p. 12.
10. Swanson, Chamelin, Territo, and Taylor, *Criminal Investigation,* p. 12.
11. Ibid., pp. 12–13.
12. Ibid., p. 12.
13. Thorwald, *The Century of the Detective,* p. 18.
14. Thorwald, *The Marks of Cain* (London, Thames & Hudson, 1965), pp. 78–79.
15. U.S. Department of Justice, Bureau of Justice Statistics, "Nonfatal Firearm-Related Violent Crimes, 1993–2008," bjs.ojp.usdoj.gov/content/glance/tables/firearmnonfataltab.cfm (accessed July 28, 2010).
16. Swanson, Chamelin, Territo, and Taylor, *Criminal Investigation,* p. 17.
17. Saferstein, *Criminalistics,* pp. 460–461.
18. DeForest, Gaensslen, and Lee, *Forensic Science,* pp. 13–14.
19. Ibid., p. 19.
20. Swanson, Chamelin, Territo, and Taylor, *Criminal Investigation,* pp. 8–9.

21. President's Commission on Law Enforcement and the Administration of Justice, *Task Force Report: Science and Technology* (Washington, DC: Government Printing Office, 1967), pp. 7–18.
22. Paul B. Weston and Kenneth M. Wells, *Criminal Investigation: Basic Perspectives,* 4th ed. (Englewood Cliffs, NJ: Prentice Hall, 1986), pp. 5–10.
23. Ibid., p. 207.
24. Ibid., pp. 207–209.
25. Ibid., p. 214.
26. Peter W. Greenwood and Joan Petersilia, *The Criminal Investigation Process,* vol. 1: *Summary and Policy Implications* (Santa Monica, CA: RAND, 1975). The entire report is found in Peter W. Greenwood, Jan M. Chaiken, and Joan Petersilia, *The Criminal Investigation Process* (Lexington, MA: D.C. Heath, 1977).
27. Ibid.
28. Ibid., p. 19.
29. Weston and Wells, *Criminal Investigation,* p. 5.
30. DeForest, Gaensslen, and Lee, *Forensic Science,* p. 11.
31. Mark R. Pogrebin and Eric D. Poole, "Vice Isn't Nice: A Look at the Effects of Working Undercover," *Journal of Criminal Justice* 21 (1993): 383–394.
32. Ibid., pp. 383–384.
33. Peter K. Manning, *The Narc's Game: Organizational and Informational Limits on Drug Enforcement* (Cambridge, MA: MIT Press, 1980).
34. M. Girodo, "Drug Corruption in Undercover Agents: Measuring the Risk," *Behavioral Sciences and the Law* 3 (1991): 299–308; also see David L. Carter, "An Overview of Drug-Related Conduct of Police Officers: Drug Abuse and Narcotics Corruption," in *Drugs, Crime, and the Criminal Justice System,* ed. Ralph Weisheit (Cincinnati, OH: Anderson, 1990).
35. U.S. Department of Justice, Federal Bureau of Investigation, *The Special Agent in Undercover Investigations* (Washington, DC: Author, 1978).
36. A. L. Strauss, "Turning Points in Identity," in *Social Interaction,* ed. C. Clark and H. Robboy (New York: St. Martin's, 1988).
37. Gary T. Marx, "Who Really Gets Stung? Some Issues Raised by the New Police Undercover Work," in *Moral Issues in Police Work,* ed. F. Ellison and M. Feldberg (Totowa, NJ: Bowman and Allanheld, 1988), pp. 99–128.
38. G. Farkas, "Stress in Undercover Policing," in *Psychological Services for Law Enforcement,* ed. J. T. Reese and H. A. Goldstein (Washington, DC: Government Printing Office, 1986).
39. Frank Horvath, "Polygraph," in *The Encyclopedia of Police Science,* 2nd ed., ed. William G. Bailey (New York: Garland, 1995), pp. 640–642.
40. Ibid., p. 643.
41. Ibid., p. 642.
42. John S. Dempsey and Linda S. Forst, *An Introduction to Policing,* 3rd ed. (Belmont, CA: Wadsworth, 2005), p. 373.

43. Massachusetts Institute of Technology, "Inventor of the Week Archive: Alec Jeffreys—DNA Fingerprinting," June 2005, web.mit.edu/invent/iow/jeffreys.html (accessed July 28, 2010).
44. Richard Saferstein, *Criminalistics,* pp. 382–383.
45. Richard Willing, "DNA to Clear 200th Person," www.usatoday.com/news/nation/2007-04-22-dna-exoneration_N.htm (accessed July 27, 2010).
46. U.S. Department of Justice, Federal Bureau of Investigation, "DNA—Nuclear," www.fbi.gov/hq/lab/html/dnau1.htm (accessed July 28, 2010).
47. U.S. Department of Justice, Federal Bureau of Investigation, "DNA—Mitochrondrial," www.fbi.gov/hq/lab/html/mdnau1.htm (accessed July 28, 2010).
48. Federal Bureau of Investigation, "Combined DNA Index System (CODIS)," www.fbi.gov/hq/lab/html/codis1.htm (accessed July 28, 2010).
49. U.S. Department of Justice, National Institute of Justice, *DNA Solves Property Crimes (But Are We Ready for That?)* (Washington, DC: Author, October 2008), p. 2.
50. Ibid., p. 3.
51. Federal Bureau of Investigation, "Crime in the United States, 2008: Burglary," www.fbi.gov/ucr/cius2008/offenses/property_crime/burglary.html (accessed July 28, 2010).
52. U.S. Department of Justice, *DNA Solves Property Crimes,* p. 10.
53. Ibid., p. 3.
54. Ibid., p. 10.
55. Adam Liptak, "Justices Reject Inmate Right to DNA Tests," *New York Times,* www.nytimes.com/2009/06/19/us/19scotus.html (accessed July 27, 2010).
56. Pete Williams, "Report: Crime Labs Seriously Deficient," NBC News, February 18, 2009, www.msnbc.msn.com/id/29258576 (accessed July 27, 2010).
57. Ibid.
58. Kevin Johnson, "DNA Not Kept in Half of States," *USA Today,* www.usatoday.com/news/nation/2008-08-05-dan-preservation_N.htm (accessed July 27, 2010).
59. Patrick E. Cook and Dayle L. Hinman, "Criminal Profiling: Science and Art," *Journal of Contemporary Criminal Justice* 15 (August 1999): 230.
60. Ibid., p. 232.
61. Steven A. Egger, "Psychological Profiling," *Journal of Contemporary Criminal Justice* 15 (August 1999): 243.
62. Ibid., p. 242.
63. Walter C. Langer, *The Mind of Adolph Hitler* (New York: World, 1978).
64. Swanson, Chamelin, and Territo, *Criminal Investigation,* 4th ed., pp. 601–602.
65. Brad Darrach and Joel Norris, "An American Tragedy," *Life,* August 1984, p. 58.
66. Swanson, Chamelin, and Territo, *Criminal Investigation,* pp. 606–607.
67. Cook and Hinman, "Criminal Profiling," p. 234.
68. Martin Reiser, Louise Ludwig, Susan Saxe, and Clare Wagner, "An Evaluation of the Use of Psychics in the Investigation of Major Crimes," *Journal of Police Science and Administration* 7 (1979): 18–25.

69. Joseph Deladurantey and Daniel Sullivan, *Criminal Investigation Standards* (New York: Harper and Row, 1980), p. 72.
70. *People v. Quaglino*, Cal. Ct. App., 2d Dist., 1977; cert. denied, 439 U.S. 875, 99 S. Ct. 212 (1978).
71. Bill O'Driscoll, "Hypnotist Keeping Busy Since Law Let His Evidence into State Courts," *Reno Gazette Journal*, June 21, 1999, p. 1c.
72. M. Lee Goff, *A Fly for the Prosecution: How Insect Evidence Helps Solve Crimes* (Cambridge, MA: Harvard University Press, 2000), p. 9. An excellent source of information concerning forensic entomology, this book contains not only the effects of insects but also the consequences of predators, air, fire, and water and provides a number of related case studies.
73. Ibid., p. 10.
74. Ibid., p. 11.
75. Ibid., pp. 12–13.
76. Joannie M. Schrof, "Murder, They Chirped," *U.S. News and World Report*, October 14, 1991, pp. 67–68.
77. Goff, *A Fly for the Prosecution*, p. 14.
78. Daniel Pedersen, "Down on the Body Farm," *Newsweek*, October 23, 2000, pp. 50–52.
79. S.M.F., "Dead Men Tell No Tales—But Bugs Do," *Time* (Special Edition: Criminal Justice, Issue 1, 2004), p. 24, www.time.com/time/magazine/article/0,9171,1956055,00.html (accessed July 28, 2010).
80. BBC: "Dog cameras to combat gun crime," news.bbc.co.uk/2/hi/uk_news/england/4497212.stm (accessed July 28, 2010).
81. U.S. Department of Justice, Bureau of Justice Statistics, *Stalking Victimization in the United States* (January 2009), p. 1, bjs.ojp.usdoj.gov/content/pub/pdf/svus.pdf (accessed July 28, 2010).
82. Carolyn Thompson, "Stalkers Turn to Cell Phones to 'Textually Harass,'" Associated Press, www.msnbc.msn.com/id/29493158 (accessed July 28, 2010).
83. U.S. Department of Justice, Violence Against Women Office, *Stalking and Domestic Violence: Report to Congress* (Washington, DC: Author, May 2001), p. 26.
84. Harvey Wallace, *Victimology: Legal, Psychological, and Social Perspectives* (Boston: Allyn and Bacon, 1998), pp. 333–334.
85. George E. Wattendorf, "Stalking: Investigation Strategies," *FBI Law Enforcement Bulletin* (March 2000): 10–15.
86. U.S. Department of Justice, Bureau of Justice Assistance, *2008 Internet Crime Report*, p. 1, www.ic3.gov/media/annualreport/2008_ic3report.pdf (accessed July 31, 2009).
87. Reuters, "Cybercrime Spreads on Facebook," www.reuters.com/article/idUSTRE55S55820090629 (accessed July 28, 2010); also see Jim McKay, "Cops on the Tweet to Solve Crimes and Educate the Public," www.govtech.com/gt/717300 (accessed July 28, 2010).
88. Eric Tucker, "Don't Drink and Drive, Then Post on Facebook," Associated Press, July 18, 2008, www.msnbc.msn.com/id/25738225 (accessed July 28, 2010).

89. Ryan Turner and Rachel Kosa, *Cold Case Squads: Leaving No Stone Unturned* (Washington, DC: U.S. Department of Justice, Bureau of Justice Assistance, July 2003), pp. 2–4.
90. U.S. Department of Justice, Federal Bureau of Investigation, *Regional Computer Forensics Laboratory: Annual Report for Fiscal Year 2008*, p. 3, www.rcfl.gov/downloads/documents/RCFL_Nat_Annual08.pdf (accessed July 28, 2010).
91. U.S. Department of Justice, Federal Bureau of Investigation, "Computer Forensics Labs: Making a Digital Difference," www.fbi.gov/page2/august09/rcfls_081809.html (accessed July 29, 2010).
92. Ibid.

Community-Oriented Policing and Problem Solving

Community-Oriented Policing and Problem Solving

CONFRONTING CRIME AND DISORDER

The benefits that come with community-oriented policing are numerous. Almost immediately, the police department establishes a better rapport with the community. When police officers become involved in the community at this level, they become community organizers, planners and educators. This not only benefits the community but it gives the individual police officer increased job satisfaction.

—*Internet Website for Rural Hall, North Carolina*

Courtesy of the City of Charlotte

Learning Objectives

AS A RESULT OF READING THIS CHAPTER, THE STUDENT WILL:

- Be able to define community-oriented policing and problem solving (COPPS) and to describe how this concept differs from traditional policing
- Know and understand the four parts of the SARA problem-solving process for police
- Be able to describe some important considerations for implementing and evaluating COPPS initiatives
- Know what is meant by the term *CompStat*, as well as how it functions and why it is now a rapidly growing tool for crime suppression
- Understand some methods, problems, and successes that are involved with evaluating COPPS efforts
- Know what is meant by crime prevention, and be able to describe how it relates to community policing and problem solving
- Be able to summarize some means by which COPPS can address neighborhood disorder, domestic violence, and juvenile problems (after reading the case study in the chapter)
- Understand the role of the patrol officer under COPPS

Introduction

This is a uniquely challenging time to be entering police work. A strategy that runs counter to the professional model of policing spreading across the country is **community-oriented policing and problem solving (COPPS)**. This chapter examines the rationale for and methods of that strategy, which represent a return to the philosophy and practices of policing of the early nineteenth century.

For the past several decades, the dominant police strategy emphasized motorized patrol, rapid response time, and retrospective investigation of crimes. Those strategies have some merit for police operations, but they were not designed to address root community problems but, rather, to detect crime and apprehend criminals—hence the image of the "crime fighter" cop. Current wisdom holds that the police cannot unilaterally attack the burgeoning crime, drug, and gang problems that beset our society, draining our federal, state, and local resources. Communities must police themselves. We also understand that it is time now for new police methods and measures of effectiveness.

This chapter begins by examining community-oriented policing (COP), and then it reviews a more recent development, which extends COP by using the community to address crime and disorder: problem-oriented policing (POP). Included is an overview of the scanning, analysis, response, assessment (SARA) problem-solving process. Following that, we look at how COP and POP, two interrelated and complementary concepts, work to engage the community in crime fighting through what has been termed community-oriented policing and problem solving (COPPS). We review how COPPS should be implemented and evaluated; a new and rapidly growing concept, CompStat; problems and methods involved with evaluating problem-solving efforts; and how this strategy relates to two elements of crime prevention: environmental design and repeat victimization. Next is an instructive case study of problem-solving efforts by police in Tulsa, Oklahoma, as concerned juvenile problems. A summary, key terms, review questions, and several scenarios and activities that provide opportunities for you to "learn by doing" conclude the chapter.

Also note that two related topics of discussion, intelligence-led policing (ILP) and predictive policing, could well be included here because they are essentially a part—and an extension—of the *analysis* phase of the problem-solving process discussed in this chapter. However, they are an essential tool that, when used as a tool of and in conjunction with fusion centers, can be applied to the problem of terrorism.

Review: *Community Policing.*

Basic Principles of Community Policing

Redefined Role

There is a growing awareness that the community can and must play a vital role in problem solving and crime fighting. A fundamental aspect of **community-oriented policing (COP)** has always been that the public must be engaged in the fight against crime and disorder. Robert Peel emphasized in the 1820s in his principles of policing that the police and community should work together.[1]

In the early 1980s, the notion of community policing emerged as the dominant model for thinking about policing. It was designed to reunite the police with the community.[2] No single program describes community policing. Community policing has been applied in various forms by police agencies in the United States and abroad and differs according to community needs, local politics, and available resources.

COP is much more than a police–community relations program; it attempts to address crime control through a working partnership with the community. Community institutions such as families, schools, and neighborhood and merchants' associations are seen as key partners with the police in creating safer, more secure communities. The views of community members have greater status under community policing than under the traditional policing model.[3]

COP is a long-term process that involves fundamental institutional change. This concept redefines the role of the officer on the street from crime fighter to problem solver and neighborhood ombudsman. It forces a cultural transformation of the entire department, including a decentralized organizational structure and

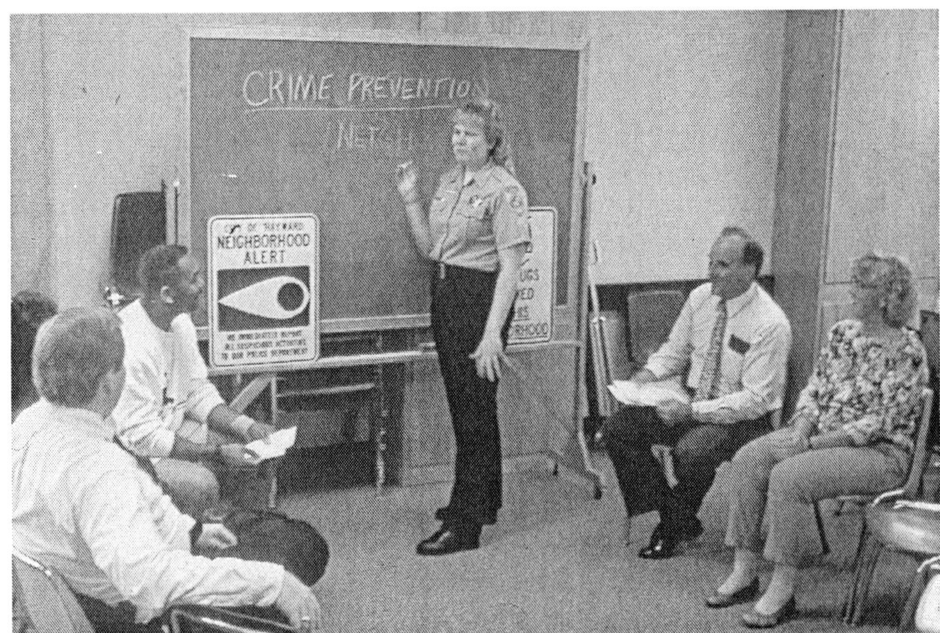

Citizen input is crucial to the police for crime detection and prevention.
(Courtesy Hayward, California, P.D.)

changes in recruiting, training, awards systems, evaluations, and promotions. This philosophy also requires officers to break away from the binds of incident-driven policing and to seek proactive and creative resolution to the problems of crime and disorder.

The major points at which COP departs from traditional policing are shown in Table 1.

Community Building in New Station House Design and Amenities

Even traditional monolithic police station houses are being changed in terms of design and amenities in some jurisdictions in order to better engage in community building. Generally, the public areas of most station houses are very stark, cold, unfriendly places. As is true for trips to the dentist, few people go to their police station voluntarily, but some jurisdictions are hoping to change that.

In the Los Angeles Police Department (LAPD) West Valley Station, in Reseda, California, residents will find ATMs in the light-filled lobby, kitchen-equipped meeting rooms for public use, and even an inviting outdoor courtyard with barbecue facilities. Gone from such "second-generation" station houses are the small windows that were located high off the ground to deter drive-by shootings but made the buildings look like bunkers and armed camps. These newer police stations also typically offer more areas that are open to the public (such as cafeterias where officers and civilians can eat together), bigger lobbies where people can comfortably sit, and community rooms where people can hold meetings and training sessions.[4]

Table 1
TRADITIONAL VERSUS COMMUNITY POLICING: QUESTIONS AND ANSWERS

Question	Traditional Policing	Community Policing
Who are the police?	A government agency principally responsible for law enforcement	The police are the public, and the public are the police: The police officers are those who are paid to give full-time attention to the duties of every citizen
What is the relationship of the police force to other public-service departments?	Priorities often in conflict	One department among many responsible for improving the quality of life
What is the role of the police?	To focus on solving crimes	To take a broader problem-solving approach
How is police efficiency measured?	By detection and arrest rates	By the absence of crime and disorder
What are the highest priorities?	Crimes that are high value (e.g., bank robberies) and those involving violence	Whatever problems disturb the community most
What, specifically, do police deal with?	Incidents	Citizens' problems and concerns
What determines the effectiveness of police?	Response times	Public cooperation
What view do police take of service calls?	Deal with them only if there is no real police work to do	View them as a vital function and a great opportunity
What is police professionalism?	Responding swiftly and effectively to serious crime	Keeping close to the community
What kind of intelligence is most important?	Crime intelligence (study of particular crimes or series of crimes)	Criminal intelligence (information about the activities of individuals or groups)
What is the essential nature of police accountability?	Highly centralized; governed by rules, regulations, and policy directives; accountable to the law	Emphasis on local accountability to community needs
What is the role of headquarters?	To provide the necessary rules and policy directives	To preach organizational values
What is the role of the press liaison department?	To keep the "heat" off operational officers so they can get on with the job	To coordinate an essential channel of communication with the community
How do the police regard prosecutions?	As an important goal	As one tool among many

Source: Malcolm K. Sparrow, Department of Justice, National Institute of Justice, "Implementing Community Policing" (Washington, DC: U.S. Government Printing Office, November 1988), pp. 8–9.

Major Step Forward: Problem-Oriented Policing

Problem solving is not new—police officers have always tried to solve problems. The difference is that officers in the past received little guidance, support, or technology from police administrators for dealing with problems, so the routine application of problem-solving techniques is new. It is premised on two facts: that problem solving can be applied by officers throughout the agency as part of their daily work and that routine problem-solving efforts can be effective in reducing or resolving problems.

Problem-oriented policing was grounded on different principles than COP, but they are complementary. **Problem-oriented policing (POP)** is a strategy that puts the COP philosophy into practice because it advocates that police examine the underlying causes of recurring incidents of crime and disorder. The problem-solving process helps officers identify problems, analyze them completely, develop response strategies, and assess the results.

Herman Goldstein is considered by many to be the principal architect of POP. Goldstein coined the term *problem-oriented policing* in 1979 out of frustration with the dominant model for improving police operations: "More attention [was] being focused on how quickly officers responded to a call than on what they did when they got to their destination."[5]

Goldstein argued for a radical change in the direction of efforts to improve policing. The first step in POP is to move beyond just handling incidents and to recognize that incidents are often overt symptoms of problems. It requires that officers take a more in-depth interest in incidents by acquainting themselves with some of the conditions and factors that cause them. (The expanded role of police officers under POP is discussed later.)

POP has at its nucleus a four-stage problem-solving process known as **scanning, analysis, response, assessment (SARA)**.[6]

Scanning: Problem Identification

Scanning involves problem identification. As a first step, officers should identify problems on their beats and look for a pattern or persistent repeat incidents. At this juncture, the question might well be asked "What is a problem?" *Problem* may be defined as a group of two or more incidents that are similar in one or more respects, causing harm and, therefore, being of concern to the police and the public. Incidents may be similar in various ways:

- *Behaviors.* People's behaviors are the most frequent indicator and include activities such as drug sales, robberies, thefts, and graffiti.
- *Locations.* Problems may occur in area hot spots, such as in downtown areas, in housing complexes plagued by burglaries, and in parks in which gangs commit crimes.
- *People.* Both repeat offenders and repeat victims account for a high proportion of crime.
- *Time.* Incidents may be similar in terms of the season, day of the week, or hour of the day; examples include rush hours, bar closing times, and tourist seasons.
- *Events.* Crimes may peak during events such as university spring break, rallies, and gatherings.

There appears to be no inherent limit on the types of problems patrol officers can face because all types of problems are candidates for problem solving.

Numerous resources are available to the police to help them identify problems, including calls for service (CFS) data, especially repeat calls from the same location or a series of similar incidents. Other means include citizen complaints, census data, data from other government agencies, newspaper and media coverage of community issues, officer observations, and community surveys.

The primary purpose of scanning is to conduct a preliminary inquiry to determine whether a problem really exists and whether further analysis is needed. During this stage, priorities should be established if multiple problems exist, and a specific officer or team of officers should be assigned to handle the problem. Scanning initiates the problem-solving process.

Analysis: Heart of Problem Solving

The second stage, analysis, is the heart of the problem-solving process. Crime analysis has been defined as "a set of systematic, analytical processes providing timely and pertinent information to assist operational and administrative personnel."[7]

Effective tailor-made responses cannot be developed unless people know what is causing the problem. Thus the purpose of analysis is to learn as much as possible about a problem in order to identify its causes. Complete analysis includes identifying the seriousness of the problem, knowing all the individuals or groups involved and affected, listing all the causes of the problem, and assessing current responses and their effectiveness.

Over time, several methods have been developed for analyzing crime and disorder. We examine some of them now: the problem-analysis triangle, mapping and offense reports, CFS analysis, and community surveys.

Problem-Analysis Triangle

One tool that may be used for analyzing problems is the **problem-analysis triangle**, which helps officers visualize the problem and understand the relationship between the three elements of the triangle (see Figure 1). In addition, it suggests where more information is needed and helps with crime control and prevention. Generally, three elements must be present before a crime or harmful behavior—a problem—can occur: an offender (someone who is motivated to commit harmful behavior), a victim (a desirable and vulnerable target), and a location (although the victim and offender are not always in the same place at the same time; locations is discussed later). If these three elements show up over and over again in patterns of recurring problems, removing one of these elements can stop the pattern and prevent future harm.[8]

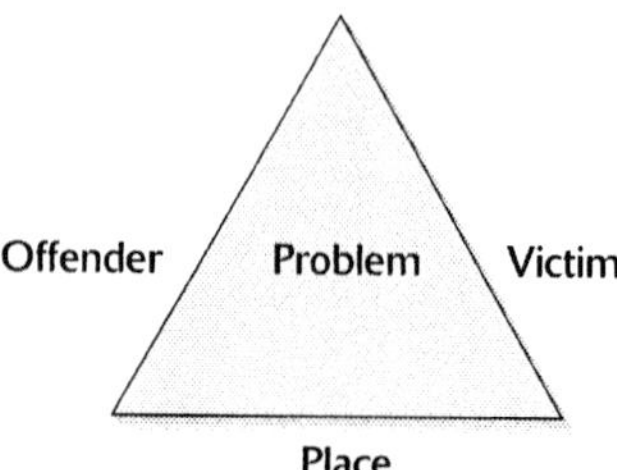

Figure 1
Problem-Analysis Triangle

Source: Department of Justice, Office of Community Oriented Policing Services, *Strategies to Address Gang Crime: A Guidebook for Local Law Enforcement*, April 2008, p. 11, www.cops.usdoj.gov/files/RIC/Publications/e060810142Gang-book-web.pdf (accessed July 27, 2010).

Mapping and Offense Reports

Computerized crime mapping also assists with crime analysis. Mapping combines geographic information from global positioning satellites with crime statistics gathered by the department's computer-aided dispatching (CAD) system and demographic data provided by private companies or the U.S. Census Bureau.

Police offense reports can also be useful, analyzed for suspect characteristics, modi operandi (MOs), victim characteristics, and many other factors. Offense reports are also a potential source of information about high-crime areas and addresses, since they capture exact descriptions of locations. In a typical department, however, patrol officers may write official reports on only about 25 to 30 percent of all calls to which they respond. Another limitation is that there may be a considerable lag between when the officer files a report and when the analysis is complete.[9]

Computer software now exists for COPPS to assist with profiling beats and demographics, finding patterns of problems, helping plan daily officer activities, balancing beat and officer workloads, and identifying current levels of performance. Such software can scan through hundreds of millions of pieces of data for patterns, trends, or clusters in beats and neighborhoods while ranking and reranking problems. In the field, the officer simply highlights the neighborhood, beat, or grid under consideration and then selects the problem or problems to be worked on from a menu on the computer.

CFS Analysis

With the advent of CAD systems, a more reliable source of data on CFS has become available. CAD systems, containing information on all types of CFS, add to information provided by offense reports, yielding a more extensive account of what the public reports to the police.[10] The data captured by CAD systems can be sorted to reveal hot

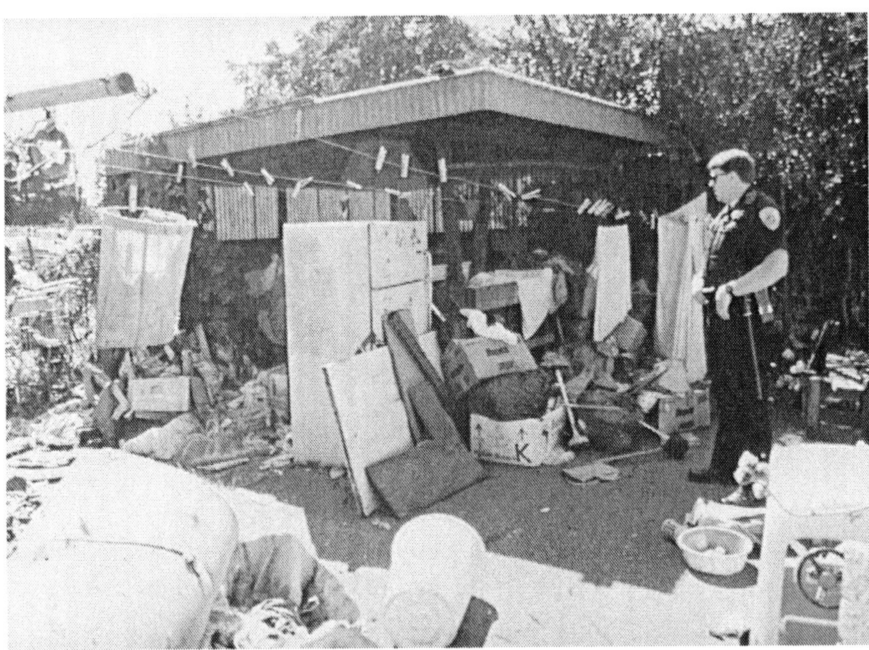

Once disorder begins to descend on a location, crime soon follows—and the police will become involved. *(Courtesy Reno, Nevada, P.D.)*

spots of crime and disturbances—specific locations from which an unusual number of calls to the police are made.

A study in Minneapolis on hot spots analyzed nearly 324,000 CFS for a one-year period over all 115,000 addresses and intersections. The results showed relatively few hot spots accounting for the majority of calls to the police:[11]

- In all the calls, 50 percent came from 3 percent of the locations.
- All robbery calls came from 2.2 percent of the locations.
- All rape calls came from 1.2 percent of the locations.
- All auto thefts came from 2.7 percent of the locations.

Many police agencies have the capability to use CAD data for repeat-call analysis (which is related to repeat victimization, discussed later). The repeat-call locations identified in this way can become targets of directed patrol efforts, including problem solving. For example, a precinct may receive printouts of the top twenty-five CFS areas to review for problem-solving assignments. In Houston, the police and Hispanic citizens were concerned about violence at cantinas (bars). Through repeat-call analysis, police learned that only 3 percent of the cantinas in the city were responsible for 40 percent of the violence. The data narrowed the scope of the problem and enabled a special liquor-control unit to better target its efforts.[12]

Repeat alarm calls are another example of how CAD data can be used to support patrol officer problem solving. In fact, when an experiment began in Baltimore County, Maryland, some commanders preferred that officers start with alarm projects. Data documenting repeat alarm calls by address were readily available, and commanders anticipated that solving alarm problems would be relatively simple and would bring considerable benefits compared to the investment of time.[13]

Community Surveys

Not to be overlooked in crime analysis is the use of community surveys to analyze problems. For example, an officer may canvass all the business proprietors in shopping centers on his or her beat. In Baltimore, an officer telephoned business owners to update the police department's after-hours business contact files. Although the officer did not conduct a formal survey, he used this task to inquire about problems the owners might want to bring to police attention.

On a larger scale, a team of officers may survey residents of a housing complex or neighborhood known to have particular crime problems. The survey could assist in determining residents' priority concerns, acquiring information about hot spots, and learning more about residents' expectations of police.[14] Residents are also more likely to keep the police abreast of future problems when patrol officers leave their business cards and encourage residents to contact them directly.

Many police agencies now provide citizens with crime analysis information via the Internet. As an example, Exhibit 1 shows the home page of the Tempe, Arizona, Police Department's Crime Analysis Unit.

EXHIBIT 1

The Home Page of the Tempe, Arizona, Police Department's Crime Analysis Unit

About Crime Analysis

Historically, the causes and origins of crime have been the subject of investigation by varied disciplines. Following are some factors known to affect the volume and type of crime occurring from place to place:

- Population density and degree of urbanization with size locality and its surrounding area
- Variations in composition of the population, particularly youth concentration
- Stability of population with respect to residents' mobility, commuting patterns, and transience
- Modes of transportation and highway system
- Economic conditions, including median income, poverty level, and job availability
- Cultural factors and educational, recreational, and religious characteristics
- Family conditions with respect to divorce and family cohesiveness
- Climate
- Effective strength of law enforcement agencies
- Administrative and investigative emphases of law enforcement
- Policies of other components of the criminal justice system (e.g., prosecutorial, judicial, correctional, and probational)
- Citizens' attitudes toward crime
- Crime-reporting practices of the citizenry

Definition of Crime Analysis

A set of systematic, analytical processes directed at providing timely and pertinent information relative to crime patterns and trend correlations to assist the operational and administrative personnel in planning the deployment of resources for the prevention and suppression of criminal activities, aiding the investigative process, and increasing apprehensions and the clearance of cases. Within this context, Crime Analysis supports a number of department functions including patrol deployment, special operations and tactical units, investigations, planning and research, crime prevention, and administrative services (budgeting and program planning).[1]

Types of Crime Analysis

Tactical. Provides information used to assist operations personnel (patrol and investigative officers) in identifying specific and immediate crime trends, patterns, series, sprees, and hot spots; investigating leads; and clearing cases. Analysis includes associating criminal activity by method of the crime, time, date, location, suspect, vehicle, and other types of information.

Strategic. Is concerned with long-range problems and projections of long-term increases or decreases in crime (crime trends). Strategic analysis also includes the preparation of crime statistical summaries, resource acquisition, and allocation studies.

Administrative. Focuses on provision of economic, geographic, or social information to administration.

Crime Analysis Personnel

The Tempe Police Department's Crime Analysis Unit consists of three full-time crime analysts and a full-time crime analysis clerk. The Tempe Police Department's Crime Analysis Unit performs all three types of crime analysis: tactical, strategic, and administrative.

Interesting Statistics

- The population of Tempe was 174,833 in 2009.
- A total of 170,315 citizen calls for service were generated in 2009 (a 1.5 percent decrease from 2005).
- The most common type of citizen-generated call for service is the "suspicious activity" call. These calls account for approximately 8.3 percent of the total number of citizen-generated calls for service.
- Approximately one police report is generated for every four calls for service (these are not necessarily criminal reports).
- In 2009 Tempe's crime rate was 57.0 Part I crimes per 1,000 persons.

To develop tailored responses, problem solvers should review their findings about the three sides of the crime triangle—victims, offenders, and locations—and develop creative solutions that will address at least two sides of the triangle. It is also important to remember that the key to developing tailored responses is making sure that the responses are very focused and directly linked to the findings from the analysis phase of the project.

Responses may be wide ranging and often require arrests, referral to social service agencies, or changes in ordinances. Note that apprehension is not always the most effective solution.

[1]See Steven Gottlieb Sharon Arenberg and Rag Singh, *Crime Analysis: From First Report to Final Arrest* (Montclair, CA: Alpha Publishing, 1994), pp. 11–13.

Source: Adapted from City of Tempe, Arizona, Police Department Crime Analysis Unit, "Tempe Crime and Calls for Service Information," www.tempe.gov/cau; see also "Statistics," www.tempe.gov/cau/CrimeStatistics.htm (accessed July 26, 2010).

Response: Formulation of Tailor-Made Strategies

After a problem has been clearly defined and analyzed, the officer confronts the ultimate challenge in POP: the search for the most effective way of dealing with it. The response may be quite simple (such as reprogramming a public telephone at a convenience store where drug dealers conduct their "business" so that it only makes outgoing calls) or quite involved (e.g., screening and evicting some tenants from a housing complex; cleaning up a neighborhood that is overcome with graffiti, debris, and junk cars; taking legal action to create a curfew; or condemning and razing a drug house).[15] (A number of examples of responses are provided in the COPPS case study.)

This stage of the SARA process focuses on developing and implementing responses to the problem. Before entering this stage, the police agency must overcome the temptation to implement a response prematurely and be certain that it has thoroughly analyzed the problem; attempts to fix problems quickly are rarely effective in the long term.

Assessment: Evaluation of Overall Effectiveness

In the assessment stage, officers evaluate the effectiveness of their responses. A number of measures have traditionally been used by police agencies and community members to assess effectiveness. These include numbers of arrests; levels of reported crime; response times; clearance rates; citizen complaints; and various workload indicators, such as CFS and the number of field interviews conducted.[16] Several of these measures may be helpful in assessing the impact of a problem-solving effort.

A number of nontraditional measures will also shed light on whether a problem has been reduced or eliminated:[17]

- Reduced instances of repeat victimization
- Decreases in related crimes or incidents
- Neighborhood indicators, including increased profits for businesses in the target area, increased usage of the area, increased property values, less loitering and truancy, and fewer abandoned cars
- Increased citizen satisfaction regarding the handling of the problem, determined through surveys, interviews, focus groups, electronic bulletin boards, and so on
- Reduced citizen fear related to the problem

Assessment is obviously key in the SARA process; knowing that we must assess the effectiveness of our efforts emphasizes the importance of documentation and baseline measurement. Supervisors can help officers assess the effectiveness of their efforts.

Exhibit 2 provides an example of the SARA process in action in Oakland, California.

EXHIBIT 2

A Winning Example: The Oakland Airport Motel Program

The Oakland Police Department (OPD) addressed a serious motel problem near its local airport. For the following efforts, the OPD won the coveted Herman Goldstein Award for Excellence in Problem-Oriented Policing, conferred at the annual International Problem Oriented Policing Conference:

- *Scanning.* Located along a major gateway to the city of Oakland, the Oakland Airport Motel is situated within a commercial area comprising lodging, restaurants, and fast-food outlets; it is also situated about two miles from Oakland's professional baseball, football, and basketball franchises. A complainant informed an Oakland officer that while working at the motel for several weeks, prostitutes soliciting sex had approached him nightly, that prostitutes "had the run of the place," and that there were loud parties and disturbances each night around the clock, junked vehicles littering the parking lot, and the smell of marijuana coming through his window nightly as well.
- *Analysis.* After consulting with city zoning and attorney offices concerning applicable laws, an officer reviewed the property owner information and determined that a large corporation owned the motel, there was not a policy of limiting the duration of guest stays, and a disproportionately high number of narcotics arrests had occurred over the previous two years. The officer made a site visit, photographing and documenting his observations and interviewing tenants and motel staff. He noted that a corner of the motel parking lot was used as a freelance and illegal auto repair business, that rooms were routinely rented to minors, and that prostitution activity was rampant. A review of police incidents over three years revealed that the motel had an astounding 900 percent higher number of police incidents than comparable area lodging facilities.
- *Response.* A response plan was developed. Phase One involved working with the motel manager to clean up the property and to deal with problem tenants. A policy was implemented to restrict renting rooms to persons age twenty-one or older, to evict problem tenants in a timely manner, to monitor the parking lot to prevent junked vehicles from being dumped there, and to fire employees caught renting out rooms "under the table" and using their passkeys. Corporate officials balked at several of these initiatives, however, so the officer sent a drug nuisance abatement notification letter to the motel. Police surveillance revealed that motel security guards were not taking affirmative steps to keep nuisances out of the parking lot, and frequent prostitution and open drug transactions continued to occur. An undercover officer rented rooms at the motel; on two occasions, motel managers changed the room lock and took the undercover officer's property left in the rooms so as to double-rent the rooms. Given this lack of improvement, Phase Two involved meeting with the motel's corporate officials. A document was prepared covering the criminal activity at the motel over a three-year period; descriptions and photographs of the prostitution and violent crimes occurring at the site; and the legal consequences and costs of not complying with relevant legal, health, and safety codes. It was requested that the motel be closed for ninety days to improve the physical aspects and to retrain motel staff in their proper duties and that the corporate officials post a $250,000 performance bond and repay OPD for investigative costs. Corporate officials promised swift change; again, however, there was little improvement in the conditions at the motel after two weeks had passed. Phase Three of the project was then launched: preparation of lawsuits and negotiations. Police continued surveillance of activities at the motel, and a drug nuisance abatement lawsuit was prepared for filing and sent to the chief executive officer at his home in France. Finally, after seven hours of negotiations, corporate officials agreed to post the performance bond and to pay the city $35,000 in fees and expenses incurred to date. Furthermore, barbed wire was installed along all fence lines to discourage fence climbing, area lighting was upgraded, room rates were increased by 50 percent to improve its clientele, room rentals for more than thirty days were prohibited, foot and vehicle traffic was stopped for identification by security guards, a "no-rent" list was developed for banned guests, cleaning and painting of the property was accomplished, rigorous background checks were performed on new employees, and problem employees were terminated.
- *Assessment.* Seven months after these activities were launched, calls for service to the motel dropped by 59 percent. Two years later, there had been only one call for police service. Overall crime and nuisance activity were also on par with the other five adjacent motels.

Source: Adapted from "The Oakland Airport Motel Program: Eliminating Criminal and Nuisance Behavior at a Motel," in U.S. Department of Justice, National Institute of Justice, *Best Practices in Problem-Oriented Policing: Winners of the 1999 Herman Goldstein Award for Excellence in Problem-Oriented Policing* (Oakland, CA: Oakland Police Department, 2003), pp. 1–7.

Collaborative Approach: Basic Principles of COPPS

The two concepts of COPPS (COP and POP) are separate but complementary notions that can work together. Both share some important characteristics: (1) decentralization (to encourage officer initiative and the effective use of local knowledge), (2) geographically defined rather than functionally defined subordinate units (to encourage the development of local knowledge), and (3) close interactions with local communities (to facilitate responsiveness to, and cooperation with, the community).[18] The following definition accurately captures the essence of this concept:

> Community-Oriented Policing and Problem Solving (COPPS) is a proactive philosophy that promotes solving problems that are criminal, affect our quality of life, or increase our fear of crime, as well as other community issues. COPPS involves identifying, analyzing, and addressing community problems at their source.[19]

For COPPS to succeed, the following measures are required:[20]

- Conducting accurate community needs assessments
- Mobilizing all appropriate players to collect data and brainstorm strategies
- Determining appropriate resource allocations and creating new resources where necessary
- Developing and implementing innovative, collaborative, comprehensive programs to address underlying causes and causal factors
- Evaluating programs and modifying approaches as needed

Implementation of COPPS

Principle Components

Since COPPS came into being, most police executives have implemented the strategy throughout the entire agency. Some executives, however, have attempted to introduce the concept in a small unit or an experimental district,[21] often in a specific geographic area of the jurisdiction.

It is strongly argued that a departmentwide implementation of COPPS be used. When COPPS is established as a distinct unit within patrol rather than departmentwide, the introduction of this "special unit" seems to exacerbate the conflict between community policing's reform agenda and the more traditional outlook and hierarchical structure of the agency. A perception of elitism is created—a perception that is ironic because COPPS is meant to close the gap between patrol and special units and to empower and value the rank-and-file patrol officer as the most important functionary of police work.

The key lesson from research in **implementation**, however, is that there is no golden rule or any universal method to ensure the successful adoption of COPPS. Two general propositions are important, however, for implementing the concept: the role of the rank-and-file officer and the role of the environment (or "social ecology") where COPPS is to be implemented.[22] The social ecology of COPPS includes both the internal/organizational and external/societal environments.

Moving an agency from the reactive, incident-driven mode to COPPS is a complex endeavor, often requiring a complete change in the culture of the police organization. Four principal components of implementation profoundly affect the way agencies do business: leadership and administration, human resources, field operations, and external relations.[23] These factors are discussed next.

Leadership and Administration

It is essential that the chief executive communicate the idea that COPPS is departmentwide in scope. To get the whole agency involved, the chief executive must adopt four practices as part of the implementation plan:[24]

1. Communicate to all department members the vital role of COPPS in serving the public. They must understand why handling problems is more effective than just handling incidents.
2. Provide incentives to all department members to engage in COPPS. This includes a new and different personnel evaluation and reward system as well as positive encouragement.
3. Reduce the barriers to COPPS that can occur. Procedures, time allocation, and policies all need to be closely examined.
4. Show officers how to address problems. Training is a key element of COPPS implementation. The executive must also set guidelines for innovation. Officers must know they have the latitude to innovate.

Human Resources

With regard to human resources, middle managers (captains and lieutenants) and first-line supervisors (sergeants) also play a crucial role in planning and implementing COPPS and in encouraging their officers to be innovative, take risks, and be creative.[25] First-line supervisors and senior patrol officers seem to generate the greatest resistance to community policing, largely because they have long-standing working styles cultivated from years of traditional police work and because these officers can feel disenfranchised by a management system that takes the best and brightest out of patrol and (they often believe) leaves them behind.

Field Operations

Furthermore, the mechanisms that motivate, challenge, reward, and correct employees' behaviors in the field must be compatible with the principles of COPPS. These include recruiting, selection, training, performance evaluation, promotion, honors and awards, and discipline, all of which should be reviewed to ensure that they promote and support the tenets of COPPS. First, recruiting literature should reflect the principles of COPPS. A job-task analysis identifying the new knowledge, skills, and abilities should be conducted and become a part of the testing process for entry-level employees. COPPS should also be integrated into academy training, field-training programs, and in-service training. Performance evaluations and reward systems should reflect new job descriptions and officers' application of their COPPS training. Also, promotion systems should be expanded from their usual focus on tactical decision making, should include knowledge of the research on community policing, and should test an officer's ability to apply problem solving to various crime and neighborhood problems.

External Relations

Collaborative responses to neighborhood crime and disorder are essential to the success of COPPS. This requires new relationships and the sharing of information and resources among the police and the community, local government agencies, service providers, and businesses. The media provide an excellent means for police to educate the community about COPPS and crime and disorder.

Political support is another essential consideration when implementing COPPS. The political environment varies considerably, say, with the strong mayor and council-manager forms of government. These and other rapidly changing political environments make the implementation of COPPS more difficult—especially when we add to the mix the at-will employment of most police executives.

Broader Role for the Street Officer

A major departure of POP from the conventional style lies with POP's view of the line officer, who is given much more discretion and decision-making ability and is trusted with a much broader array of responsibilities.

The accompanying Career Profile includes experiences of a former police officer with considerable experience in community policing and problem solving.

POP values "thinking" officers, urging that they take the initiative in trying to deal more effectively with problems in the areas they serve. This concept effectively uses the potential of college-educated officers, "who have been smothered in the atmosphere of traditional policing."[26] It also gives officers a new sense of identity and self-respect; they are more challenged and have opportunities to follow through on individual cases—to analyze and solve problems—which will give them greater job satisfaction. Using patrol officers in this manner allows the agency to provide sufficient challenge for both those who are better educated and those who remain patrol officers throughout their entire career.[27]

Under POP, officers continue to handle calls, but they also do much more. They combine the information gathered in their responses to incidents with information obtained from other sources to get a clearer picture of the problem. They then address the underlying conditions. If they are successful in ameliorating these conditions, fewer incidents may occur, and those that do occur may be less serious; the incidents may even cease. At the very least, information about the problem can help police

CAREER PROFILE

TRAINING ACADEMY INSTRUCTOR AND ASSOCIATE PROFESSOR

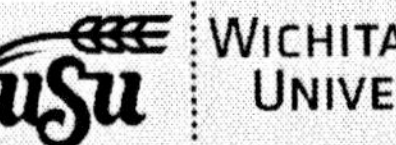

Name: Michael L. Birzer

Position: Associate Professor of Criminal Justice and Director, School of Community Affairs

College attended: Wichita State University and Oklahoma State University

Degrees: B.S. and M.A. in Criminal Justice and Ed.D. in Occupational and Adult Education

Current teaching position: Wichita State University

What CJ-related jobs have you held and when?

Lieutenant, Sedgwick County Sheriff's Department (1981–1999). I held assignments in detention, patrol, community policing, training, criminal investigations, DEA Task Force, and held supervisory and command positions in patrol, community policing, crime prevention, training, and the gang unit. In 1999 I entered into academia, where I have served on criminal justice faculties at East Central University (1999–2000), Washburn University (2000–2004), and Wichita State University (2004–present).

What positions did you like most?

As a practitioner, I most enjoyed the position of training academy instructor and also enjoyed my community policing assignments.

What qualities/characteristics most helped you succeed in the field?

The ability to show a sense of empathy when dealing with the general citizenry. This is important when dealing with citizen problems. It's easy for police officers to get into a routine mold when dealing with citizen concerns and this should be avoided. Further, the ability to engage in problem solving is also critical for the twenty-first-century police officer—that is the ability to look for the underlying causes of community- and crime-related problems—and identify the most effective resources to resolve these problems. My academic training in criminal justice and adult education, which provided a thorough grounding in criminological theory and adult learning theory, assisted me tremendously in training and leadership assignments as well as solving complex community crime-related problems.

What are the typical salary ranges students can expect entering these fields?

The salary range for entry-level police officers will vary by geographical location and the size of the police agency. However, the average income for police or deputy sheriff or patrol officer is generally in the upper $40,000 range.

What advice would you give students early in their college career to help them find a rewarding job in criminal justice?

Take advantage of internship opportunities as early as possible in your studies. Internships can assist you in honing your career interests in criminal justice and also can assist you in making invaluable contacts in the criminal justice enterprise.

design more effective ways of responding to each incident. Police administrators ought to be recruiting people as police officers who can "serve as mediators, as dispensers of information, and as community organizers."[28]

CompStat: Utilizing Information Technology to Manage Crime

A relatively new crime management tool used in the problem-solving process is known as **CompStat** (for "comparative or computer statistics"), which is designed for the collection and feedback of information on crime and related quality-of-life issues. This strategy is said to be "revolutionizing law enforcement management and practice,"[29] and some have called it "perhaps the single most important organizational/administrative innovation in policing during the latter half of the 20th century."[30]

Since the CompStat process was introduced by the New York City Police Department in 1994, it has been widely adopted: a national survey found that 58 percent of large agencies (those with 100 or more sworn officers) had either adopted or

COMPARATIVE CLOSEUP ▸▸ Community Policing in Japan

A Japanese koban.
(Courtesy Corbis NY)

Japan possesses the oldest and best-established community policing system in the world. Japan initiated its system immediately after World War II out of a combination of traditional culture and American democratic ideals. Four elements are at the core of this philosophy: (1) community-based crime prevention, (2) reorientation of patrol activities to emphasize nonemergency servicing, (3) increased accountability to the public, and (4) decentralization of command.[1]

Each of Japan's 47 prefectures has its own autonomous police force—together they employ about 220,000 officers—on densely populated islands totaling about 144,000 square miles and 150 million people.[2] The officers deal face-to-face with citizens daily and, therefore, have become a part of the community rather than being separated from the people in a vehicle. Also, Japanese neighborhood crime-prevention associations have generally cultivated a much closer relationship among neighbors.

Japanese police place heavy emphasis on order maintenance and crime prevention, aiding the community to resolve problems that could lead to disorder. Counseling services are part of every Japanese police station, provided by an experienced older officer and ranging from family disputes to questions about contracts and indebtedness. Trained in dispute resolution, the police are able to provide helpful informal conciliation.[3]

The urban police officer in Japan visits neighborhood households and does police business in what is termed the koban.[4] A koban may be found every few blocks, with about 15,000 kobans across the country—8,000 of which have officers who actually live inside. Police officers generally stand watch at the doorway of the koban or at nearby traffic intersections to help minimize crimes and traffic accidents, direct traffic, and make arrests when necessary. The Japanese police try to keep the number of people for which a koban is responsible to less than 12,000 and the area to less than four-tenths of a square mile.[5]

[1]Jerome H. Skolnick and David H. Bayley, *Community Policing: Issues and Practices Around the World* (Washington, DC: National Institute of Justice, 1988).
[2]Richard J. Terrill, *World Criminal Justice Systems: A Survey*, 5th ed. (Cincinnati, OH: Anderson, 2003), pp. 378–380.
[3]David H. Bayley, *Forces of Order: Police Behavior in Japan and the United States* (Berkeley: University of California Press, 1991), p. 87.
[4]*Community Police Activities of Japan* (Tokyo: National Police Agency of Japan, 1992), pp. 2, 9.
[5]David H. Bayley, *A Model of Community Policing: The Singapore Story* (Washington, DC: U.S. Department of Justice, National Institute of Justice, 1989), p. 8.

were planning to implement a CompStat-like program.[31] The key elements of CompStat are as follows:

- Specific objectives
- Accurate and timely intelligence
- Effective tactics
- Rapid deployment of personnel and resources
- Relentless follow-up and assessment[32]

CompStat pushes all precincts to generate weekly or monthly crime activity reports. Crime data are readily available, offering up-to-date information that is then compared at citywide, patrol, and precinct levels.

Under CompStat, police begin proactively thinking about ways to deal with crime in terms of suppression, intervention, and prevention. Commanders must explain what tactics they have employed to address crime patterns, what resources they have and need, and with whom they have collaborated. Brainstorming problem-solving sessions ensue about proactively responding to the crime problems, and

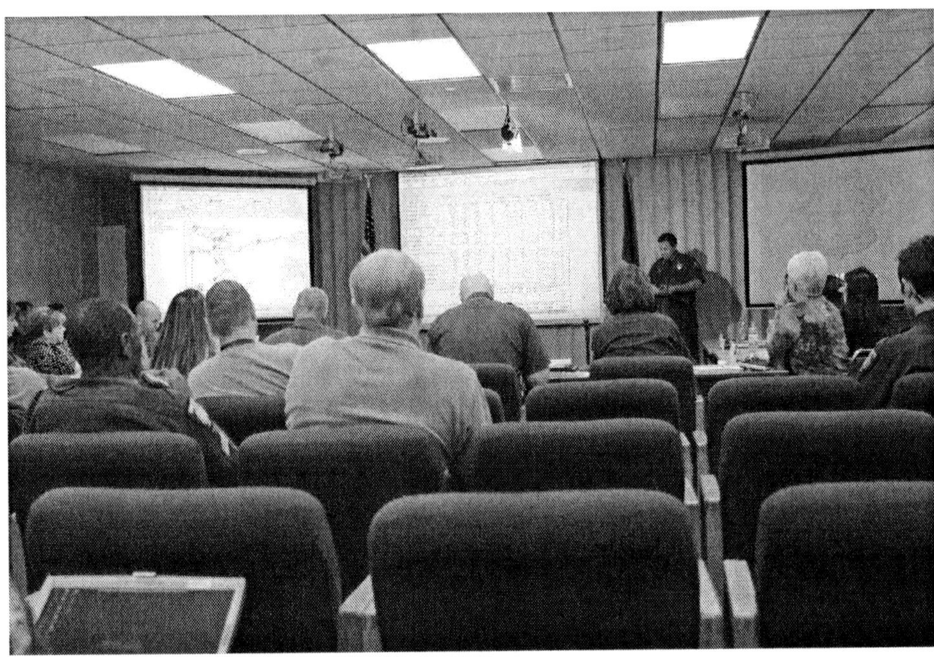

At CompStat meetings, police officials discuss crime patterns in their assigned area(s) and brainstorm about tactics and resources that might be used to address them. *(Courtesy Washoe County, Nevada, Sheriff's Office)*

suggestions for strategies are made at subsequent meetings, with relentless follow-up by top brass to further ensure accountability. Many scholars and practitioners believe that CompStat has played a prominent role in the significant crime reductions seen across the nation.

Does It Work? Evaluating COPPS

People consistently agree about two aspects of COPPS: first, there is a need for partnerships between the police and the public; second, there must be a focus on solving problems underlying criminal incidents.[33]

Empirical studies of COPPS also suggest that the impact of this strategy is twofold: first, community policing reduces disorder and increases positive community–police relations; second, community policing initiatives increase the positive attitudes that police officers have both toward their jobs and toward the community.[34]

Beyond these areas of agreement, however, studies of COPPS efforts have been scant and inconclusive. The first problem has been that, because COPPS serves to improve on several aspects of policing, its impact on crime has not always been the focus of **evaluations**; as one academic stated, "There needs to be an evaluation process/system that makes reality out of conjecture."[35] Studies have focused on fear of crime, public disorder, police response, and community support.[36]

Compounding this "scattergun" approach to evaluating COPPS are three additional issues:

1. The definition of community policing today is still ambiguous: What one department implements as a COPPS strategy may be very different from

other departments, resulting in very little consistency across implementations and evaluations.

2. COPPS is still implemented in a fractional manner: agencies that do not focus on complete departmental and institutional change will confound evaluations, because without that level of adoption, COPPS evaluations are limited to studying only those components that were implemented by the agency.
3. Studies have generally had a restricted focus on large cities: Evaluations have generally overlooked the potential success of a COPPS model when instituted in a sector or beat as opposed to the entire department jurisdiction.[37]

A 2008 study by Connell et al. sought to address these three issues by evaluating a clearly defined and comprehensive COPPS initiative where the initiative pervaded a single unit; the goal was to examine the effects of COPPS on violent, drug, and property crimes; and the initiative was situated in a suburban setting. Using a time-series design, the researchers' findings suggested that COPPS does have the capacity to affect crime rates. Indeed, the COPPS efforts resulted in an abrupt and permanent decline in the levels of violent and property crime in the treatment site (although the intervention may not have been as effective with drug crimes). The findings suggest that COPPS can be successful in reducing serious crimes and need not be limited to larger jurisdictions with greater resources.[38]

Attention must be paid in the future to the aforementioned problems and shortcomings of COPPS evaluations, which to this point have been very limited both in terms of their conclusions and generalizability. It is essential for this strategy—with emphasis on the fact that policing is now in the community policing *era*—that they, the public, and policy makers know unequivocally "what works."

Crime Prevention

An important corollary of COPPS—and a critical and rapidly developing concept that all police officers should understand—is crime prevention. It stands to reason that it is preferable as well as much less expensive (in terms of both financial and human resources) to prevent a crime from occurring in the first place than to try to solve the offense and arrest, prosecute, and possibly incarcerate the offender. A focus on crime prevention shifts a police organization's purpose. Once the question becomes "How can we prevent the next crisis?" all kinds of approaches become possible.[39]

Crime prevention once consisted primarily of exhorting people to "lock it or lose it" and giving advice to citizens about door locks and window bars for their homes and businesses. It typically was (and often still is) an add-on program for the police agency, which normally included a few officers who were trained to go to citizens' homes and perform security surveys or to speak publicly on the subject of target hardening. Times are rapidly changing in this regard.

Crime prevention and COPPS are close companions, attempting to define the problem, identify the contributing causes, seek out the proper people or agencies to assist in identifying potential solutions, and work as a group to implement the solution. The problem drives the solution.[40] At its heart, COPPS is about preventing crime.

Next we briefly discuss two important aspects of crime prevention—crime prevention through environmental design and repeat victimization—and briefly mention a drug-prevention program.

Crime Prevention Through Environmental Design

Crime prevention through environmental design (CPTED) is defined as the "proper design and effective use of the environment that can lead to a reduction in the fear and incidence of crime, and an improvement in the quality of life."[41] At its core are three principles that support problem-solving approaches to crime:[42]

1. *Natural access control.* Employ elements such as doors, shrubs, fences, and gates to deny access to a crime target and to create a perception among offenders that the target presents risk.
2. *Natural surveillance.* Place windows, lighting, and landscaping properly to increase the ability to observe intruders as well as regular users, allowing observers to challenge inappropriate behavior or to report it to the police or to the property owner.
3. *Territorial reinforcement.* Use elements such as sidewalks, landscaping, and porches to distinguish between public and private areas and to help users exhibit signs of ownership that send hands-off messages to would-be offenders.

Five types of information are needed for CPTED planning:[43]

1. *Crime-analysis information.* Crime mapping, police crime data, incident reports, and victim and offender statistics are all included.
2. *Demographics.* Statistics about residents, such as age, race, gender, income, and income sources, are used.
3. *Land use information.* Zoning information (such as residential, commercial, industrial, school, and park zones) and occupancy data for each zone are analyzed.
4. *Observations.* Information includes observations of parking procedures, maintenance, and residents' reactions to crime.
5. *Resident information.* Resident crime surveys and interviews with police and security officers are assessed.

Repeat Victimization

U.S. society—including the police—gives far greater attention to criminal offenders than to crime victims. Just as at the zoo, where more spectators seem to gather around the lions and tigers than around wildebeests and antelope, more attention is focused on the predators than on their prey. However, an evolving body of research in Great Britain suggests that crime victims should be placed on the national agenda. In the

United States—where POP has spread across the country—patterns of **repeat victimization (RV)** have not been examined or assimilated into problem solving. Police officers in the United States would benefit from this developing body of knowledge, which can play a major role in crime prevention and analysis.

The premise underlying RV is that if the police want to know where a crime will occur next, they should look at where it happened last. RV is not new; police officers have always been aware that the same people and places are victimized again and again. What is new, however, are attempts abroad to incorporate RV knowledge into formal crime-prevention efforts.

One in three burglaries reported in the United States is a repeat burglary of a household. Furthermore, a 48 percent RV rate was found for sexual incidents (including grabbing, touching, and assault), 43 percent for assaults and threats, and 23 percent for vehicle vandalism.[44] A study of white-collar crime indicated that the same people are victims of fraud and embezzlement time and time again and that banks that have been robbed also have high rates of RV.[45] These data show that providing crime-prevention assistance to potential victims is not only morally justifiable in most instances but also an efficient and practical way of allocating limited police resources.

Why would a burglar return to burgle the same household again? One could argue that, for several reasons, the burglar would be stupid not to return: Temporary repairs to a burgled home will make a subsequent burglary easier, the burglar is familiar with the physical layout and surroundings of the property, the burglar knows what items of value were left behind at the prior burglary, and the burglar also knows that items that were taken at an earlier burglary are likely to have been replaced through insurance policies.

RV is arguably the best single predictor routinely available to the police in the absence of specific intelligence information. A small number of victims accounts for a disproportionate number of victimizations.[46]

Drug Abuse Resistance and Education

A related attempt to prevent crime should be discussed briefly: the well-known Drug Abuse Resistance and Education (DARE) program. The program, launched in 1983 and now administered by police in 80 percent of schools, has not fared well among researchers. Beginning in the late 1990s, however, studies began establishing that the program did not keep kids from abusing drugs. Indeed, one such study's grim findings were that "20-year-olds who'd had DARE classes were no less likely to have smoked marijuana or cigarettes, drunk alcohol, used 'illicit' drugs like cocaine or heroin, or caved in to peer pressure than kids who'd never been exposed to DARE."[47] One of its key flaws, researchers allege, has been that students are taught that all drugs are equally dangerous; when students find that this is not true, the DARE message is undercut.[48]

Now DARE officials are admitting that the program needs a new direction. Officials are revamping the program, reducing the lecturing role of local officers and involving kids in a more active way. A new curriculum is being developed for use in some schools that will show brain scans after drug use to demonstrate the harm, shift officers into more of a coaching role, and have kids engage in role-playing about peer pressure.[49]

COPPS at Work

Ameliorating Juvenile Problems in Tulsa

Following is an excellent case study of COPPS efforts using the SARA model in Tulsa, Oklahoma.[50] Note that, instead of merely showing up at a crime scene, taking offense reports, and leaving the scene, the police employed a variety of responses to combat crime and disorder.

Scanning

North Tulsa experienced consistently higher crime rates than the rest of the city. Nearly half of the violent crimes that were reported occurred in this section of the city—a depressed low-income area lacking adequate services. The Tulsa Housing Authority was established to support the city's low-income public housing. In an attempt to determine the nature of the crime problem in North Tulsa, a special management team of Tulsa police officials conducted a study and decided to concentrate on five public-housing complexes where high crime rates and blatant street dealing existed.

Analysis

A residential survey conducted by patrol officers revealed that 86 percent of the occupants lived in households headed by single females. Officers in the target area noticed large groups of school-age youth in the housing complexes who appeared to be selling drugs during school hours. A comparison of the dropout and suspension rates in North Tulsa schools with those in other areas of the city determined that the city's northernmost high school, serving most of the high school–age youth in the five complexes, had the highest suspension (4.4 percent) and dropout (10 percent) rates of any school in the city. It also reported the highest number of pregnant teenagers in the school system. Few of the juveniles observed in the complexes had legitimate jobs, and most of them appeared to be attracted to drug dealing by the easy money.

Supervisors at Uniform Division North placed volunteers into two-officer foot teams, assigned to the complexes on eight-hour tours. The teams established a rapport with residents and assured them that police were present to ensure their safety. Within a month, officers verified juvenile involvement in drug trafficking. A strategy was needed to provide programs to deter youth from selling or using drugs.

Response

Officers S. and N., assigned to foot patrol at one of the complexes, believed that the youth needed programs that would improve their self-esteem, teach them values, and impart decision-making skills. Because 86 percent of the boys came from homes without fathers, the officers started a Boy Scout troop in the complex for boys between eleven and seventeen years of age to provide positive role models for them. Officer N., a qualified Boy Scout leader, and Officer S. began meeting with the boys on Saturdays in a vacant apartment.

Officers J. and E. also organized a Boy Scout troop. In addition, they started a group that worked to raise money for needy residents and police-sponsored youth activities. Officer J. spoke at civic group meetings and local churches throughout the city to solicit donations and increase awareness of the needs of young people on the city's north side. Volunteers came from the churches and the civic groups where Officer J. spoke.

Officers B. and F., foot patrol officers at another complex, developed plans for unemployed young people. Officer B. organized a group called the Young Ladies Awareness Group, which hosted guest speakers who taught different job-related skills each week. Programs instructed young women how to dress for job interviews and employment; role-playing officers demonstrated proper conduct during interviews. The women were also instructed in résumé writing, makeup, hair care, and personal hygiene. Officer F. worked with a government program that sponsored sessions on setting goals and building self-esteem to prepare young people to enter job-training programs. Officer F. also helped area youth apply for birth certificates and arranged for volunteers from the Oklahoma Highway Patrol and a local school to help teach driver's education. Officers even provided funds for young people who were unable to pay the fees to obtain birth certificates or driver's licenses. Officers F. and B. also tried to explain the value of an education and persuade youth in their complex to return to school. Unfortunately, parents too often appeared unconcerned when their children missed classes.

The foot patrol officers became involved in a day camp project conducted at "the Ranch," a twenty-acre northside property that the police had confiscated from a convicted drug dealer. The project used the property for a day camp for disadvantaged youth recruited from the target projects. Tulsa's mayor and chief of police came to the Ranch to meet with the youth, as did psychologists, teachers, ministers, and celebrities. Guests tried to convey the value of productive and drug-free lives, among other ethical values.

To combat dropout and suspension problems, a program called Adopt a School had police officers patrol the schools during classes, not to make arrests but rather to establish rapport with the students. The program was intended to reduce the likelihood of student involvement in illegal activities.

Assessment

The police noted a decline in street sales of illegal drugs in the five target complexes. Youth reacted positively to the officers' efforts to help them, and the programs seemed to deter them from drug involvement. The police department continued to address the problems of poor youth in North Tulsa. Foot patrol officers met with the Task Force for Drug Free Public Housing to inform the different city, county, and statewide officials of the needs of youth in public housing. Other social service agencies began working with the police department, establishing satellite offices on the north side of the city, scheduling programs, and requesting police support in their efforts.

SUMMARY

This chapter examined the basic principles and strategies of the current community era—the era in which policing now resides. It examined community policing and problem solving (COPPS), which is the best strategy for addressing neighborhood crime and disorder now and in the future. Blending the two concepts of community policing and problem-oriented policing results in a better, more comprehensive, and long-term approach to providing quality police service, combining the emphasis on forming a police–community partnership to fight crime with the use of the SARA problem-solving process. It was shown that two very important components of this philosophy are the expanded role of the street officer and the focus on crime analysis.

The associated strategy of crime prevention, including crime prevention through environmental design (CPTED) and repeat victimization (RV), is equally important. It is clear that the field of crime prevention has "matured" from its earlier forms, originally involving strategic placement of rocks by early cave dwellers and more recently having to do primarily with target hardening one's home with better locks. This chapter has shown the various elements of CPTED and RV as well as the results of research efforts concerning what good can occur when measures are taken to prevent crimes.

The overarching theme is that the police realize that they alone cannot prevent or address crime and disorder and that a partnership with the community is essential if the physical and social problems that plague communities are to be reduced or eliminated.

KEY TERMS

- community-oriented policing (COP)
- community-oriented policing and problem solving (COPPS)
- CompStat
- crime prevention through environmental design (CPTED)
- evaluations
- implementation
- problem-analysis triangle
- problem-oriented policing (POP)
- repeat victimization (RV)
- scanning, analysis, response, assessment (SARA)

REVIEW QUESTIONS

1. How would you define community policing, and what are some of the major ways this concept differs from traditional policing?
2. What are the four parts of the SARA problem-solving process?

3. Why are the implementation and evaluation phases of COPPS so critical?
4. What is CompStat? How does it function, and why is it now sweeping the nation's police agencies as a means toward crime suppression?
5. What are some methods, problems, and successes that are involved in evaluating COPPS itself?
6. What is meant by crime prevention, and how does it relate to COPPS?
7. What does the Tulsa case study demonstrate in terms of how COPPS functions and what this strategy accomplished with that city's juvenile problems?

LEARN BY DOING

1. Assume that for the past six months a small neighborhood market in the western part of the city has generated dozens of calls for service about drug dealing because of several drug dealers and users frequenting the area. Part I ("Index") crimes are beginning to increase in the area as well. A nearby drug house contributes heavily to the problem, and a T-shaped alley behind the store provides easy ingress and egress for buyers, both on foot and in vehicles. The lighting is poor, and pay telephones in front of the store are constantly in use by traffickers. You are assigned to launch a POP/SARA initiative at the location to effect long-term results. What kinds of information would you collect about the area and the drug problem? What kinds of responses might be considered? What types of assessment would you perform?
2. Using media reports or local crime data (oftentimes available from your local police agency Web site), identify a particularly crime-ridden neighborhood, beat, or area of your jurisdiction. Then, using techniques described in this chapter, including the problem-analysis triangle and SARA, explain what your approach would be to bringing a sense of order to that area through the use of a problem-solving exercise.
3. Your chief executive has assigned you, as head of the agency's research, planning, and analysis unit, the task of developing a comprehensive report containing recommendations for establishing a CompStat program. Explain what your report would contain.
4. Develop a one-hour course on the fundamentals of "Crime Prevention" for your area police academy (to include CPTED and repeat victimization).

mycrimekit

Go to MyCrimeKit.com and discover additional study tools and resources related to this chapter.

- Key Terms
- Review Questions

- Multiple Choice Questions
- True/False
- Fill in the Blank
- Essay

- MEDIA REVIEW: where you can review the topic of *community policing.*
- FLASHCARDS: to test your knowledge of this chapter.
- *NEW YORK TIMES*: where you can read the latest articles related to criminology and criminal law.
- THE CAREER CENTER: where you can explore career opportunities in criminal justice and criminology.
- THE ONLINE RESEARCH LIBRARY: where you can explore the Cybrary and Research Navigator.

NOTES

1. W. L. Melville Lee, *A History of Police in England* (London: Methuen, 1901), ch. 12.
2. Robert Trojanowicz and Bonnie Bucqueroux, *Community Policing: A Contemporary Perspective* (Cincinnati, OH: Anderson, 1990), p. 154.
3. Mark H. Moore and Robert C. Trojanowicz, *Corporate Strategies for Policing* (Washington, DC: Government Printing Office, 1988), pp. 8–9.
4. Sheila Muto, "Arresting Design: Police Stations Get a Lift," *Wall Street Journal*, January 5, 2005, p. B-1.
5. Herman Goldstein, "Problem-Oriented Policing" (paper presented at the Conference on Policing: State of the Art III, National Institute of Justice, Phoenix, June 12, 1987).
6. Ibid., pp. 43–52.
7. Noah Fritz, *Crime Analysis* (Tempe, AZ: Tempe Police Department, n.d.), p. 9.
8. John Eck, *A Dissertation Prospectus for the Study of Characteristics of Drug Dealing Places* (College Park: University of Maryland, November 1992).
9. Barbara Webster and Edward F. Connors, *Community Policing: Identifying Problems* (Alexandria, VA: Institute for Law and Justice, March 1991), p. 9.
10. See Lawrence W. Sherman, Patrick R. Gartin, and Michael E. Buerger, "Hot Spots of Predatory Crime: Routine Activities and the Criminology of Place," *Criminology* 27 (1989): 27.
11. Ibid., p. 36.
12. William Spelman, *Beyond Bean Counting: New Approaches for Managing Crime Data* (Washington, DC: Police Executive Research Forum, January 1988).
13. Webster and Connors, *Community Policing,* p. 11.
14. For an example of this type of survey process, see William H. Lindsey and Bruce Quint, *The Oasis Technique* (Fort Lauderdale: Florida Atlantic University/Florida International University Joint Center for Environmental and Urban Problems, 1986).

15. Rana Sampson, "Problem Solving," in *Neighborhood-Oriented Policing in Rural Communities: A Program Planning Guide* (Washington, DC: U.S. Department of Justice, Office of Justice Programs, Bureau of Justice Assistance, 1994), p. 4.
16. Darrel Stephens, "Community Problem-Oriented Policing: Measuring Impacts," in *Quantifying Quality in Policing,* ed. Larry T. Hoover (Washington, DC: Police Executive Research Forum, 1995).
17. U.S. Department of Justice, Office of Community Oriented Policing Services, *Problem-Solving Tips: A Guide to Reducing Crime and Disorder Through Problem-Solving Partnerships* (Washington, DC: Author, 2002), p. 20.
18. Moore and Trojanowicz, *Corporate Strategies for Policing,* p. 11.
19. Kenneth J. Peak and Ronald W. Glensor, *Community Policing and Problem Solving: Strategies and Practices,* 5th ed. (Upper Saddle River, NJ: Prentice Hall, 2008), p. 85.
20. Ibid.
21. Herman Goldstein, *Problem-Oriented Policing* (New York: McGraw-Hill, 1990), p. 172.
22. Gregory Saville and D. Kim Rossmo, "Striking a Balance: Lessons from Community-Oriented Policing in British Columbia, Canada" (unpublished manuscript, June 1993), pp. 29–30.
23. Ronald W. Glensor and Kenneth J. Peak, "Implementing Change: Community-Oriented Policing and Problem Solving," *FBI Law Enforcement Bulletin* 7 (July 1996): 14–20.
24. John E. Eck and William Spelman, *Problem-Solving: Problem-Oriented Policing in Newport News* (Washington, DC: Police Executive Research Forum, 1987), pp. 100–101.
25. Ibid., p. 9.
26. Herman Goldstein, "Toward Community-Oriented Policing," *Crime and Delinquency* 33 (1987): 6–30.
27. Ibid., p. 21.
28. Ibid.
29. Daniel DeLorenzi, Jon M. Shane, and Karen L. Amendola, "The CompStat Process: Managing Performance on the Pathway to Leadership," *The Police Chief* (September 2006), www.policechiefmagazine.org/magazine/index.cfm?fuseaction=display&article_id=998&issue_id=92006 (accessed July 27, 2010).
30. Ibid.
31. Ibid.
32. Heath B. Grant and Karen J. Terry, *Law Enforcement in the 21st Century* (Boston: Allyn & Bacon, 2005), pp. 329–330.
33. David M. Kennedy and Mark Moore, "Underwriting the Risky Investment in Community Policing: What Social Science Should Be Doing to Evaluate Community Policing," *Justice System Journal* 17(1995):271–289; Robert Trojanowicz and Bonnie Bucqueroux, "*Community Policing: A Contemporary Perspective* (Cincinnati, OH: Anderson, 1990).

34. A. Lurigio and D. P. Rosenbaum, "The Impact of Community Policing on Police Personnel," in *The Challenge of Community Policing: Testing the Promise,* ed. D. P. Rosenbaum, (Thousand Oaks, CA: Sage, 1994).
35. Donald S. Quire, "Models for Community Policing Evaluation: The St. Petersburg Experience," September 2008, p. 13, www.fdle.state.fl.us/Content/Florida-Criminal-Justice-Executive-Institute/Docs/Quire.aspx (accessed July 18, 2010).
36. Gary W. Cordner, "Community Policing: Elements and Effects," in *Critical Issues in Policing: Contemporary Readings* 4th ed., ed. Roger G. Dunham and Geoffrey P. Alpert, (Prospect Heights, IL: Waveland, 2001), pp. 493–510.
37. Nadine M. Connell, Kristen Miggans, and Jean Marie McGloin, "Can a Community Policing Initiative Reduce Serious Crime? A Local Evaluation," *Police Quarterly,* 11(2) (2008): 130–132.
38. Ibid., p. 146.
39. Jim Jordan, "Shifting the Mission: Seeing Prevention as the Strategic Goal, Not a Set of Programs," in *Subject to Debate* (Washington, DC: Police Executive Research Forum, December 1999), pp. 1–2.
40. Ibid., p. 8.
41. C. R. Jeffrey, *Crime Prevention Through Environmental Design* (Beverly Hills, CA: Sage, 1971).
42. National Crime Prevention Council, *Designing Safer Communities: A Crime Prevention Through Environmental Design Handbook* (Washington, DC: Author, 1997), pp. 7–8.
43. Ibid., p. 3.
44. G. Farrell and W. Sousa, "Repeat Victimization in the United States and Ten Other Industrialized Countries" (paper presented at the National Conference on Preventing Crime, Washington, DC, October 13, 1997).
45. Ibid.
46. G. Farrell, "Preventing Repeat Victimization," in *Building a Safer Society,* ed. M. Tonry and D. P. Farrington (Chicago: University of Chicago Press, 1995), pp. 469–534.
47. Jessica Reaves, "Just Say No to DARE," *Time.com,* February 15, 2001, www.time.com/time/nation/article/0,8599,99564,00.html (accessed July 27, 2010).
48. Rocky Anderson, quoted in Claudia Kalb, "DARE Checks into Rehab," *Newsweek,* February 26, 2001, p. 56.
49. Ibid.
50. U.S. Department of Justice, Bureau of Justice Assistance, *Problem-Oriented Drug Enforcement: A Community-Based Approach for Effective Policing* (Washington, DC: Police Executive Research Forum, October 1993), pp. 27–28.

Rule of Law

Rule of Law

EXPOUNDING THE CONSTITUTION

Let justice be done, though the heavens fall.

—Old Roman maxim

We must never forget that it is a constitution we are expounding.

—John Marshall, in McCulloch v. Maryland, *1819*

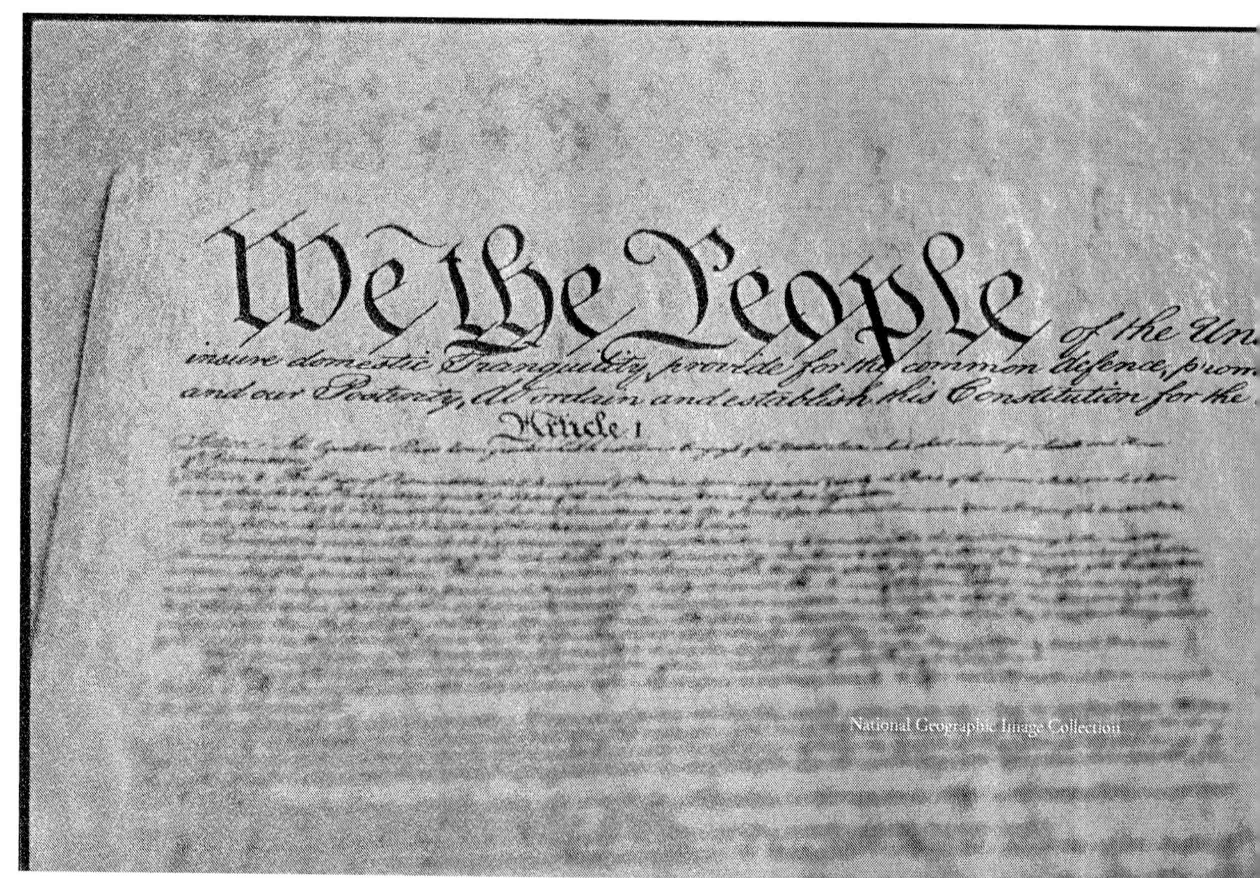

National Geographic Image Collection

Learning Objectives

AS A RESULT OF READING THIS CHAPTER, THE STUDENT WILL:

- Understand what is meant by the rule of law
- Be able to outline the protections afforded citizens by the Fourth, Fifth, and Sixth Amendments
- Know how to define and give examples of probable cause
- Be aware of the rationale for and ramifications of the exclusionary rule
- Be able to distinguish between arrests and searches and seizures with and without a warrant
- Know some significant ways in which the *Miranda* decision has been modified
- Be able to delineate the major rights of juveniles as well as the major philosophical differences in the law for treatment of juvenile and adult offenders

Introduction

The Bill of Rights—the first ten amendments to the U.S. Constitution—was passed largely to protect all citizens from excessive governmental power. The police are expected to control crime within the framework of these rights; they must conduct themselves in a manner that conforms to the rule of law as set forth in the U.S. Constitution, state constitutions, statutes passed by state legislatures, and the precedent of prior interpretations by the courts.

What is meant by the **rule of law**? This commonly used phrase was comprehensively defined in 1885 by Albert Venn Dicey in his now-classic *Introduction to the Study of the Law of the Constitution.*[1] Dicey identified three principles that together establish the rule of law:

1. Absolute supremacy or predominance of regular law as opposed to the influence of arbitrary power
2. Equality before the law or the equal subjection of all classes to the ordinary law of the land administered by the ordinary courts
3. Law of the U.S. Constitution as a consequence of the rights of individuals as defined and enforced by the courts

In other words, under the rule of law of the United States, the means are more important than the ends. A nation's democratic form of government would be of little value if the police could arrest, search, and seize its citizens and their property at will. If one considers the policing systems of some nondemocratic countries, it is readily apparent that from the citizen's standpoint, legal curbs on those who enforce the law are absolutely necessary.

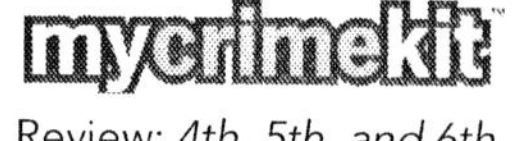

Review: *4th, 5th, and 6th Amendments.*

This chapter examines three constitutional amendments that regulate the police and prevent abuses of power: the Fourth Amendment (probable cause, exclusionary rule, arrest, search and seizure, electronic surveillance, and lineups), the Fifth Amendment (confessions, interrogation, and entrapment), and the Sixth Amendment (right to counsel and interrogation). To avoid overwhelming the reader with case titles, only better-known court cases—such as *Miranda v. Arizona*—are included in the body of the chapter; others are cited in the Notes section. Finally, we discuss a related yet in some ways very different area of law and procedure: the law pertaining to juvenile offenders. A summary, review questions, and several scenarios and activities that provide opportunities to learn by doing conclude the chapter.

Our Dynamic Legal System—and the Need to Act Accordingly

Contrary to what many people may believe, our nation's laws are dynamic—that is, like our society in general, they are constantly changing. Part of the reason for that flux in our legal system is the many *sources* of laws. Laws are enacted by courts and legislatures as well as by acts of Congress and treaties and are found in the U.S. and state constitutions and statutes, administrative laws (i.e., those laws involving the powers and duties of government agencies), and city and county ordinances; therefore, the laws are constantly in flux as new ones are created and old ones are repealed or overturned.

It is therefore quite challenging for the aspiring police officer, student of criminal justice, and of course judges, prosecutors, and defense attorneys to first learn the laws and then to understand how they are to be applied by the criminal justice system. Another equally challenging aspect of law is the need for those same persons to *remain* proficient with the changes in the laws and thus their application.

Although many police agencies will have the benefit of a legal advisor assigned by their city or county attorney's office to render legal advice for persons working in the field, most agencies probably do not have that luxury and thus must make an extra effort to read and understand new court decisions and other enactments. Many publications cover the major decisions that affect both the rights of the accused and the powers of the police. Among them are monthly police periodicals such as the *FBI Law Enforcement Bulletin* and *The Police Chief* magazine; other sources include the *Criminal Law Reporter*, *U.S. Law Week*, and the *Supreme Court Bulletin.*

The accompanying Career Profile briefly speaks to the need for police officers to constantly hone their knowledge of the legal aspects of their occupation.

Fourth Amendment

> The right of the people to be secure in their persons, papers, and effects, against unreasonable searches and seizures, shall not be violated, and no Warrants shall issue, but upon probable cause, supported by Oath or affirmation, and particularly describing the place to be searched, and the persons or things to be seized.

CAREER PROFILE

Name: Daniel J. Moeser

Position: Patrol Captain/Training Officer and Adjunct Professor

College attended: East Tennessee State University

Degrees: Bachelor's and master's in Criminal Justice and Criminology

Current teaching position: East Tennessee State University

What CJ-related jobs have you held and when?

1967–1998, United States Coast Guard (law enforcement)

2005–present, Adjunct Professor at ETSU

2005–present, Unicoi County Sheriff's Department (Patrol Captain/Training Officer)

What positions did you like most?

Teaching at the college level was what I wanted to accomplish in a second career. I wanted to pass on my experiences in the criminal justice field to as many students as possible. I had a strong desire to interact with others who were interested in the field.

What qualities/characteristics helped you succeed in the field?

Determination, work ethic, and desire to know all aspects of the CJ field. My years in the Coast Guard were very challenging, rewarding, and educational. After retiring I began my college education because I wanted to teach in the law enforcement field. As a graduate assistant I was able to teach and was offered a job as an adjunct professor. I was also hired by the county sheriff's department, where I served as training officer and captain of patrol. My additional academic education gave me a well-rounded background for teaching in the field. I feel strongly that instructors need to have field and academic background to fully understand the CJ field.

What advice would you give students early in their college career to help them find a rewarding job in criminal justice?

Learn the basics. The U.S. Constitution and Bill of Rights are the backbone of all laws, rules, and regulations. Read and ask as many questions as possible of those working in the field. Spend at least one summer volunteering with or employed by a law enforcement agency. Keep an open mind and always try to understand why someone takes an opposite view. Remember that others feel as strongly about their view as you do yours.

The **Fourth Amendment** is intended to limit overzealous behavior by the police. Its primary protection is the requirement that a neutral detached magistrate, rather than a police officer, issue warrants for arrest and **search and seizure**. Crime, though a major concern to society, is balanced by the concern that officers might thrust themselves unnecessarily into our homes. The Fourth Amendment requires that the necessity for a person's right of privacy to yield to society's right to search is best decided by a neutral judicial officer, not by an agent of the police.[2]

mycrimekit

Review: *The Fourth Amendment.*

mycrimekit

Review: *Search and Arrest Warrants.*

Probable Cause

The standard for a legal arrest is probable cause. This important concept is elusive at best; it is often quite difficult for professors to explain and even more difficult for students to understand. One way to define **probable cause** is to say that for an officer to make an arrest, he or she must have more than a mere hunch yet less than actual knowledge that the arrestee committed the crime. I often use the following example from my own experience to better explain the concept:

> At midnight, a fifty-five-year-old woman, having spent several hours at a city bar, wished to leave the bar and go to a nightclub in a rural part of the

county. A man offered her a ride, but rather than driving directly to the nightclub, he drove to a remote place and parked the car. There he raped the woman and forced her to orally sodomize him. She fought him and later told the police she thought she had broken the temples (side pieces) of his black glasses. After the act, he drove her back to town; when she got out of the car, she saw the license plate number and thought that the hood of the car was colored red. Her account of the crime and her physical description of the rapist immediately prompted a photograph lineup; a known rape/sodomy suspect's picture was shown to her, along with photos of several other men with a similar description. She tentatively identified the suspect in the mug shot but could not be certain; the suspect's mug shot had been taken several years earlier.

With this preliminary information, two police officers (one of whom was this author) hurried to the suspect's home to question him. They did not have a warrant. Upon entering the suspect's driveway, the officers observed a beige car—with a red hood. Probable cause was beginning to build. Next the officers noted that the vehicle's license plate number matched the one given by the victim; probable cause was now growing by leaps and bounds. Then the suspect exited the house and walked toward his car; the officers observed that the frame of his eyeglasses was black but that the temples were gold, indicating that the black temples had probably been broken and replaced by spare gold temples. The officers now had, by any standard, adequate probable cause to lead a "reasonable and prudent" person to believe that this suspect was the culprit; the failure to arrest him would have been a gross miscarriage of justice. The suspect was thus arrested and placed in an actual lineup, where the victim identified him. This was

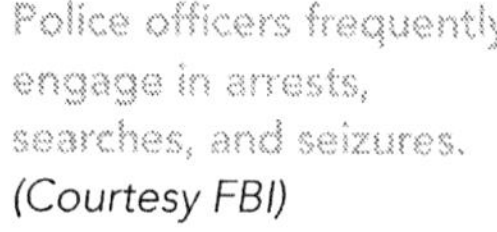
Police officers frequently engage in arrests, searches, and seizures. *(Courtesy FBI)*

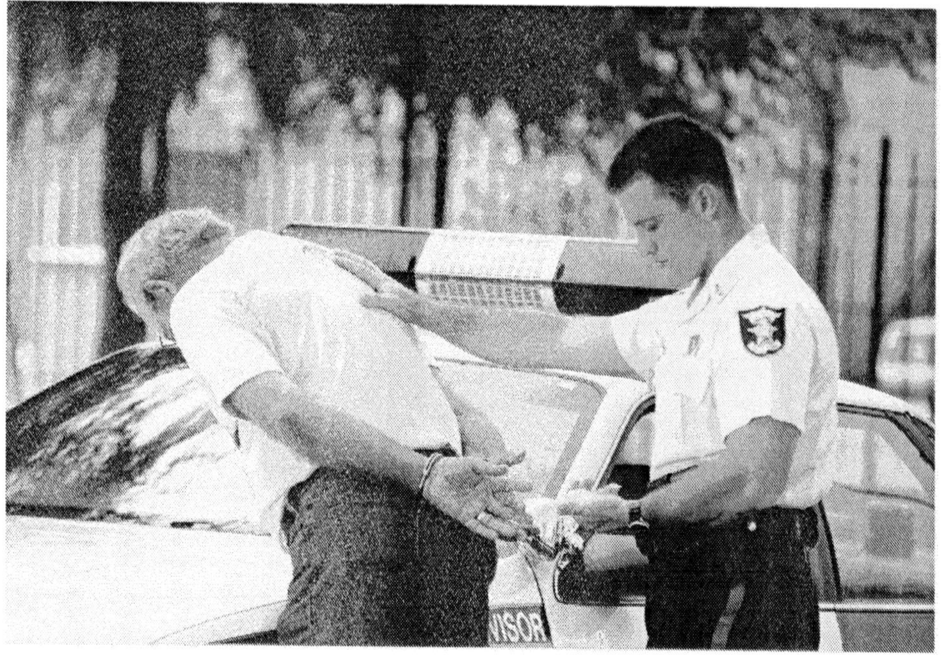

one of those rare cases where the evidence was so compelling that the defendant pleaded guilty at his initial appearance and threw himself on the judge's mercy.

Of course, the facts of each case and the probable cause present are different; the court will examine the type and amount of probable cause that the officer had at the time of the arrest. It is important to note that a police officer cannot add to the probable cause used to make the arrest after effecting the arrest; the court will determine whether there existed sufficient probable cause to arrest the individual based on the officer's knowledge of the facts at the time of the arrest.

The Supreme Court has upheld convictions when probable cause was provided by a reliable informant,[3] when it came in an anonymous letter,[4] and when a suspect fit a Drug Enforcement Administration profile of a drug courier.[5] The Court has also held that police officers who "reasonably but mistakenly conclude that probable cause is present" are granted qualified immunity from civil action.[6]

Exclusionary Rule

The Fourth Amendment recognizes the right to privacy, but its application raises some perplexing questions. First of all, not all searches are prohibited—only those that are unreasonable. Another issue has to do with how to handle evidence that is illegally obtained. Should murderers be released, Justice Benjamin Cardozo asked, simply because "the constable blundered"?[7] The Fourth Amendment says nothing about how it is to be enforced, a problem that has stirred a good amount of debate for a number of years. Most of this debate has focused on the wisdom of, and the constitutional necessity for, the so-called **exclusionary rule**, which requires that all evidence obtained in violation of the Fourth Amendment be excluded from government's use in a criminal trial.

The exclusionary rule has an interesting history. It first appeared in the federal criminal justice system in 1914, when the Supreme Court ruled in *Weeks v. United States* that all illegally obtained evidence was barred from use in federal prosecutions.[8] The practice has not existed in the state systems for nearly as long, however. Relatively few states employed the rule until 1950; indeed, as of 1949, only seventeen states followed the *Weeks* doctrine. There was considerable objection both within and outside the U.S. Supreme Court about the states being able to do what was forbidden to the federal government. The ludicrous nature of this situation becomes evident in that until 1960 any evidence illegally seized by state or local police officers could be turned over to and used by federal officers in federal courts; this was known as the "silver platter doctrine."[9]

In 1926, a police officer arrested a man in a hallway for stealing an overcoat—a misdemeanor. The officer then entered the defendant's room and searched it, discovering a bag containing a blackjack. Appealing his conviction for possessing the weapon, the defendant made a motion to suppress the blackjack as evidence, as it had been obtained through a warrantless search. Justice Benjamin Cardozo delivered a classic objection to the rule and considered its far-reaching effects:

> A room is searched against the law, and the body of a murdered man is found. The privacy of the home has been infringed, and the murderer goes

free. On the one side is the social need that crime shall be repressed. On the other hand, the social need that the law shall not be flouted by the insolence of office. There are dangers in any choice.[10]

Justice Oliver Wendell Holmes took an opposite view of the rule in his dissenting opinion in a wiretapping case.[11] Holmes said that we must consider two desirable objectives: that criminals should be detected and all available evidence used and that the government should not itself commit other crimes while gathering evidence. Holmes was repulsed by the manner in which government "dirtied" itself by engaging in snooping and wiretapping activities. In *Olmstead v. United States* (1928), Holmes made his classic statement: "For my part, I think it is a less evil that some criminals should escape than that the government should play an ignoble part."

The 1961 Supreme Court decision in *Mapp v. Ohio*[12] put an end to confusion over the admissibility of illegally seized evidence in the state courts (see Court Closeup: *Mapp v. Ohio*). But the Court's decision in *Mapp* did not end the controversy surrounding the exclusionary rule: Opponents of the rule are left with the suspicion that the rule is invoked only by someone—usually a guilty person—who does not want evidence of his or her crimes to be used at trial; furthermore, they believe that the suspect's behavior has been much more reprehensible than that of the police.[13]

The Supreme Court has objected to police behavior when it "shocks the conscience," excluding evidence, for example, that was obtained by forcible extraction (by stomach pump) from a man who had swallowed two morphine capsules in the police's presence.[14]

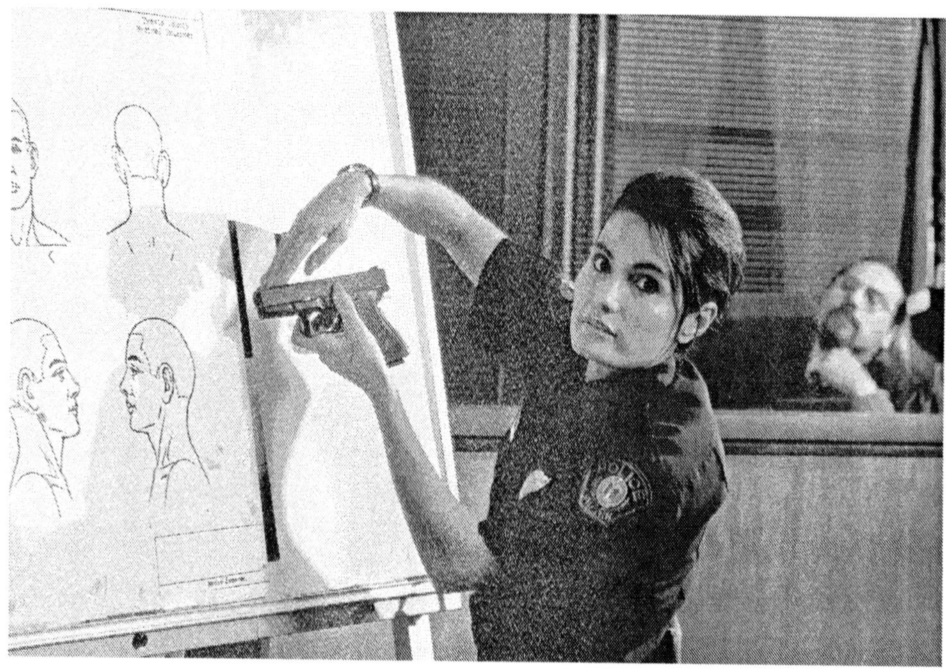

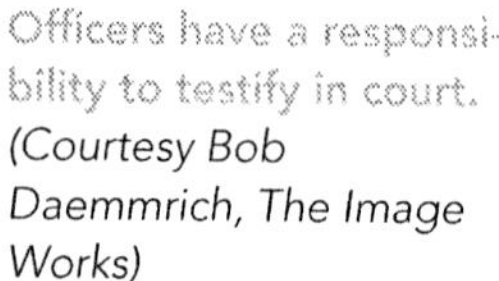

Officers have a responsibility to testify in court. *(Courtesy Bob Daemmrich, The Image Works)*

COURT CLOSEUP ▸▸ *Mapp v. Ohio*, 367 U.S. 643 (1961)

In May 1957, three Cleveland police officers went to the home of Dolree Mapp to follow up on an informant's tip that a suspect in a recent bombing was hiding there. They also had information that a large amount of materials for operating a numbers game would be found. Upon arrival at the house, officers knocked on the door and demanded entrance, but Mapp, after telephoning her lawyer, refused them entry without a search warrant.

Three hours later, the officers again attempted to enter Mapp's home, and again she refused them entry. They then forcibly entered the home. Mapp confronted the officers, demanding to see a search warrant; an officer waved a piece of paper at her, which she grabbed and placed in her bosom. The officers struggled with Mapp to retrieve the piece of paper, at which time Mapp's attorney arrived at the scene. The attorney was not allowed to enter the house or to see his client. Mapp was forcibly taken upstairs to her bedroom, where her belongings were searched. One officer found a brown paper bag containing books that he deemed to be obscene.

Mapp was charged with possession of obscene, lewd, or lascivious materials. At the trial, the prosecution attempted to prove that the materials belonged to Mapp; the defense contended that the books were the property of a former boarder who had left his belongings behind. The jury convicted Mapp, and she was sentenced to an indefinite term in prison.

In May 1959, Mapp appealed to the Ohio Supreme Court, claiming that the obscene materials were not in her possession and that the evidence was seized illegally. The court disagreed, ruling the evidence admissible. In June 1961, the U.S. Supreme Court overturned the conviction, holding that the Fourth Amendment's prohibition against unreasonable search and seizure had been violated:

> [Because] the right to be secure against rude invasions of privacy by state officers is . . . constitutional in origin, we can no longer permit that right to remain an empty promise. We can no longer permit it to be revocable at the whim of any police officer who, in the name of law enforcement itself, chooses to suspend its enjoyment.

Modifications of the Exclusionary Rule

Three major decisions during the 1983–1984 term of the Supreme Court served to modify the exclusionary rule. Then Associate Justice William Rehnquist (appointed Chief Justice in 1986) established a "public safety exception" to the doctrine. In that case, the defendant was charged with criminal possession of a firearm after a rape victim described him to the police. The officers located him in a supermarket, and upon questioning him about the weapon's whereabouts (without giving him the *Miranda* warning), they found it located behind some cartons. Rehnquist said that the case presented a situation in which concern for public safety outweighed a literal adherence to the rules. The police were justified in questioning the defendant on the grounds of "immediate necessity."[15]

Another 1984 decision announced the "inevitability of discovery exception." A ten-year-old girl was murdered and her body hidden. While transporting the suspect, detectives—who had promised the suspect's attorney that they would not question him while in transit—appealed to his sensitivities by saying it would be proper to find the body so that the girl's parents could give her a Christian burial. (This became known as the "Christian Burial Speech.") The suspect directed them to the body. In 1977, the Supreme Court ruled that the detectives had violated the defendant's rights by inducing him to incriminate himself without the presence of counsel. But the Court left open the possibility that the state could introduce evidence that the body would have been found even without the suspect's help. Using this "inevitability of discovery" opening, the Iowa courts found the defendant guilty, and in 1984 the Supreme Court upheld his conviction.[16]

Also in 1984, the Court ruled that evidence can be used even if obtained under a search warrant that is later found to be invalid. The Court held that evidence obtained by police officers acting in good faith on a reasonable reliance on a search warrant issued by a neutral magistrate could be used at trial even if the warrant was later found to be lacking in probable cause. This decision prompted a strong dissenting opinion by three justices, including William Brennan Jr., who said, "It now appears that the Court's victory over the Fourth Amendment is complete."[17]

Another ruling favorable to the police was handed down in 1988. Federal agents, observing suspicious behavior in and around a warehouse, illegally entered the building (with force and without a warrant) and observed marijuana in plain view. They left and obtained a search warrant for the building; then they returned and arrested the defendant for conspiracy to deliver illegal drugs. The Court allowed the evidence to be admitted at trial, saying that it ought not to have been excluded simply because of unrelated illegal conduct by the police. If probable cause could be established apart from their illegal activity, the Court said, evidence obtained from the search should be admitted.[18]

Views on the Exclusionary Rule

Today there are basically two schools of thought, or models, regarding the use of illegally seized evidence. The **crime-control model** holds that the police are going to make mistakes occasionally and that the victim is entitled to sue and have his or her complaint considered by a jury. Most important, this model holds, there is no reason why the evidence should not be used against the suspect at trial, even if obtained illegally. Proponents of the **due process model**, on the other hand, believe that the only way to deal with illegally obtained evidence is to suppress it before trial. When such evidence is allowed at trial, convictions based wholly or in part on it should be reversed. The victim of an illegal seizure usually is in no financial position to sue, and departmental discipline of officers is totally ineffective as a deterrent. Thus the only way to control the illegal collection of evidence is to take the profit out of it.[19]

The current trend is clearly toward the crime-control model, which weakens the impact of the exclusionary rule. Not only do many court watchers expect the Supreme Court to continue this trend, but a large number of law-and-order citizens also favor the rule's decline. Indeed, former Chief Justice Warren Burger openly criticized the rule. Acknowledging the primary reason for the rule to be controlling police misconduct, Rehnquist noted that since *Mapp* was decided, redress had become more easily obtainable by a defendant whose constitutional rights have been violated, given the *Bivens* decision and the long-dormant Section 1983 actions. Further, Rehnquist stated his belief that modern juries could be trusted to return fair awards to injured parties, saying, "I feel morally certain that the United States is the only nation in the world in which the most relevant, most competent evidence as to the guilt or innocence of the accused is mechanically excluded because of the manner in which it may have been obtained."[20]

EXHIBIT 1 ▶

Must Students "Shed Their Constitutional Rights at the Schoolhouse Gate"?

Rumors begin circulating among students in a high school that a senior possesses drugs and a gun in his locker. The school's principal questions the student, who denies the allegation. However, three other teachers report hearing "hallway chatter" of the same nature, so the principal conducts a search of the student's locker. She observes no gun but does find a stash of marijuana, a pipe, and other drug paraphernalia, as well as some photographs of other students engaged in drug activities. A digital camera is also found, but the principal does not look at its contents, being concerned that she might accidentally delete any photographic evidence. The principal contacts the local police and turns over the items to the responding officer. While in the principal's office, the officer turns on the digital camera and finds photographs involving child pornography. The student is charged with child pornography and drug violations. The defense argues that all evidence should be suppressed because both the principal and the officer violated the student's Fourth Amendment rights in their warrantless searches.

At issue is whether or not students in public institutions enjoy Fourth Amendment privileges and whether limits are placed on the police and school administrators regarding students' right of privacy. Even though parents transfer their authority for care and custody over their minor children to the school authorities while their children are in school, the school is an arm of government, which implicates constitutional concerns because Americans are generally protected against government's unreasonable searches and seizures.

The U.S. Supreme Court recognizes that schoolchildren have legitimate expectations of privacy while attending school, but schools also need to maintain a safe and secure learning environment. This latter interest dictates a different balancing scheme under the Fourth Amendment. Typically, prior to conducting a search, a police officer must be able to articulate that there was probable cause to believe that evidence of criminal activity exists in the place to be searched. However, where the interests of *public safety* are best served by a Fourth Amendment standard of reasonableness that stops short of probable cause, the Supreme Court has adopted such a standard. Therefore, for searches by officials in schools, the standard used is reasonable suspicion, which allows the school to achieve the goal of preserving order without invading the privacy interests of the students any more than necessary. Police officers, however, cannot automatically commence a search under the same standard applied to school authorities; officers are still held to a stricter Fourth Amendment standard because their government functions are different.

In the hypothetical case presented above, the principal's search of the student's locker was probably reasonable given the principal's reasonable suspicion. However, the police officer's warrantless search of the digital camera would be scrutinized under a different standard. A court would most likely suppress the digital photos discovered on the camera on the grounds that the officer should have secured the evidence and applied for a search warrant.

In sum, as the Court stated in 1969, students "do not shed their constitutional rights at the schoolhouse gate,"[1] and reasonableness remains the cornerstone by which the police and school officials' actions will be judged.

[1]This quote is from *Tinker v. Des Moines Independent Community School District*, 393 U.S. 503, 506, 89 S.Ct. 733 (1969).

Source: Adapted from Lucy Ann Hoover, "Getting Schooled in the Fourth Amendment," *FBI Law Enforcement Bulletin*, March 2007, pp. 22–32.

In summary, since the Warren Court expanded the rights of criminal defendants in the 1960s, a surge of cases to the Supreme Court has raised further questions concerning the exclusionary rule. Many observers expected the Court to overturn *Mapp*, yet the Court has not done so, apparently believing that without *Mapp* the flagrant abuses that occurred before it could resurface.

See Exhibit 1 for a discussion of the exclusionary rule as it pertains to school settings.

Arrests

A restriction on the right of the police to arrest is the hallmark of a free society. A basic condition of freedom is that one cannot be legally seized in an arbitrary and capricious manner at the discretion or whim of any government official. It is customary to refer to the writ of *habeas corpus*—the "Great Writ"—as the primary guarantee of personal freedom in a democracy. *Habeas corpus* is defined simply as a writ requiring an incarcerated person to be brought before a judge for an investigation of the restraint of that person's liberty. It should be noted that habeas corpus is the means of remedying wrongful arrest or other detention that has already occurred and that may have been illegal. The constitutional or statutory provisions for making an arrest are of crucial importance because they prevent police action that could be very harmful to the individual.[21]

Arrests with a Warrant

It is always best for a police officer to effect an arrest with a warrant. In fact, in 1980, the Supreme Court required police officers to obtain warrants when making felony arrests, should there be time to do so—that is, when there are no **exigent circumstances.**[22] To obtain an arrest warrant, the officer or a citizen swears in an **affidavit** (as an "affiant") that he or she possesses certain knowledge that a particular person has committed an offense. For example, a private citizen tells police or the district attorney that he or she attended a party at a residence where drugs or stolen articles were present, or (as is often the case) a detective gathers physical evidence or interviews witnesses or victims and determines that probable cause exists to believe that a particular person committed a specific crime. In any case, a neutral magistrate, if he or she agrees that probable cause exists, will issue the arrest warrant. Officers will execute the warrant, taking the suspect into custody to answer the charges.

Warrantless Arrests

An arrest without a warrant requires exigent circumstances and that the officer possess probable cause (as explained previously in the sodomy case). Street officers rarely have the time or opportunity to effect an arrest with a warrant in hand. Although the following real-life case involves a search preceding an arrest, it will make the point. One afternoon a police officer was sent to the residence of several college students. They reported that four men left their party and that soon afterward another guest discovered that a stereo had been taken from a car parked in the yard. A description of the men and their vehicle was given to the officer, who soon observed a vehicle and four men matching the description. The men were stopped in their vehicle, and the officer called for backup.

The law does not require that the officer ask the subjects to stay put while he speeds off to the courthouse to attempt to secure a search warrant. The doctrine of probable cause allows the officer to search the vehicle and arrest the occupants if stolen or contraband items are found (as in this case, where the stolen stereo was found under the driver's seat). Police officers encounter these kinds of situations thousands of times each day. Such searches and arrests without benefit of a warrant are legally permissible, provided the officer had probable cause (which can later be explained to a judge) for his or her actions.

Court Cases

In 1979, the Supreme Court rendered two decisions relating to arrests. Police, the Court said, must have probable cause to take a person into custody and to the police station for **interrogation.**[23] Police may not randomly stop a single vehicle to check the driver's license and registration; there must be probable cause for stopping the driver.[24] However, in 1990 the Court ruled that the stopping of all vehicles passing through sobriety checkpoints—a form of seizure—did not violate the Constitution, although singling out individual vehicles for random stops without probable cause is not authorized.[25] Several days later, it ruled that police were not required to give drunk-driving suspects a *Miranda* warning and could videotape their responses.[26]

In related decisions in the 2003–2004 term, the Supreme Court held that police may arrest *everyone* in a vehicle in which drugs are found. A Baltimore officer, stopping a speeding car and finding cocaine in an armrest in the backseat, was told by the driver and the two passengers that none of them owned the contraband; he arrested all three. Chief Justice Rehnquist wrote that in a small space like a car, officers can reasonably infer "a common enterprise" among a driver and passengers and would have probable cause to suspect that the drugs might belong to any or all of them.[27] A few months later, the Court ruled that police may set up roadblocks to collect information from motorists about crime. Short stops, "a very few minutes at most," are not too intrusive considering the value in crime solving; police may also hand out fliers or ask drivers to volunteer information, the Court noted.[28]

Finally, since 1975 police practice has been to ensure that a person arrested without a warrant receives a "prompt" initial appearance for a probable cause determination to see if the police were justified in arresting and holding the detainee. In its 1990–1991 term, the Supreme Court said that "prompt" does not mean "immediate" and that within forty-eight hours is generally soon enough.[29]

See the "Comparative Closeup" in this chapter, which discusses the rule of law in Saudi Arabia.

Search and Seizure

Because of the serious nature of police invasion of private property, the Supreme Court has had to examine several issues, particularly as they relate to searches of suspects' homes. In late 2003, the Court clarified how long police must wait before breaking into a home to serve a warrant, ruling unanimously that it was constitutional for police to wait fifteen to twenty seconds before knocking down the door of a drug suspect because to wait any longer would give the suspect time to flush evidence down the toilet. (The justices refused, however, to state exactly how long is reasonable in serving warrants.)[30] However, in 1995, the Court affirmed without decision an opinion of the Pennsylvania Supreme Court that the police violated the Fourth Amendment when they broke down the door of a residence only one or two seconds after they knocked, announced their presence, and said that they had a warrant. There were no exigent circumstances present.[31] Furthermore, in *Wilson v. Arkansas* (1995),[32] the Court found a search invalid when police in Arkansas, armed with a

COMPARATIVE CLOSEUP ▸▸ "The Unkindest Cut": Islam's Rule of Law

A Saudi police officer. *(Source: Newscom/Hassan Ammar)*

Shakespeare certainly did not have Saudi Arabia in mind when he had Mark Antony say, following the murder of Julius Caesar, that his stabbing by Brutus, Caesar's friend and a man whom Caesar trusted most of all, was "the unkindest cut of all." But certainly the law that provides for so-called chop-chops to be used against criminals in Islamic countries, governed by the Koran, constitutes the harshest criminal code in the world.

And in no Islamic country is the interpretation of Islamic law more strict than in Saudi Arabia. To describe Saudi law is to speak of the nation's religion, culture, and customs, all of which are bound closely together. Islam means complete submission to the will of God and to provide a well-ordered society. Alcohol is forbidden in Saudi Arabia, and possession of even small amounts of hashish or marijuana can carry a punishment of two years' imprisonment or deportation.[1]

The law of Islam (the Sharia) is the fundamental code in Saudi Arabia, and it contains three categories of crimes: *Hudud* (also known as *hadd*) crimes, or those against the divine or God's rights; *Quesas* (or *qasas*) and *Diyya* (*diyeh*) crimes, or those against the individual; and *Tazir* crimes, those left undetermined by religious law. For the crime of theft, even for the first offense, the penalty may be amputation of the left hand at the wrist. The penalty for slander is flogging, usually with eighty lashes, and the same penalty may be applied for consuming alcohol. The penalty for adultery and lesbianism is flogging of one hundred lashes. A woman who engages in adultery is subjected to flogging or burial to the waist in a pit; stoning may follow. Highway robbery is punishable by execution or crucifixion, the amputation of opposite hands and feet, or exile from the land. Transgression will be confronted by the Saudi armed forces until the foes of the imam (the prayer leader of a mosque) are defeated, and apostasy carries the death penalty.[2] Public executions are commonplace in Saudi Arabia. Hundreds of worshippers, including children and women, often gather at Justice Square in Riyadh and other cities on Fridays to observe these and other punishments. Believing that public beheadings and amputations deter other prospective offenders, people in the vicinity of Justice Square are encouraged by the police to witness these events. When a thief's right hand is cut off in public, a string is tied to the middle finger and the hand is hung from a hook high on a streetlight pole on Justice Square for all to see.[3]

[1]Women's Learning Partnership, "Islamic Republic of Iran: Penal Code Excerpts Relating to Women," www.learningpartnership.org/resources/legislation/nationallaw/iran (accessed July 30, 2010).

[2]Ibid.; also see Saudi Arabian International Schools, *An Introduction to the Kingdom of Saudi Arabia* (Riyadh, Saudi Arabia: Author, 1996), p. 17; Adel Mohammed el Fikey, "Crimes and Penalties in Islamic Criminal Legislation," *CJ International* 2 (July–August 1986), p. 13.

[3]Militant Islammonitor.org, "Amputations, Beheadings, Hangings, and Executions Continue in Muslim World—While Muhammed Cartoons Spark Outrage," February 13, 2006, www.militantislammonitor.org/article/id/1653 (accessed July 30, 2010).

search warrant after receiving an informant's tip that drugs were being sold at the defendant's home, identified themselves *as they entered* the residence, where they subsequently found drugs and paraphernalia.

Another decision relating to the area of police conduct at a private home during a search was rendered in March 2005. Following a drive-by shooting, police in Simi Valley, California, were searching a suspected gang member's house for *evidence* of a crime—weapons, ammunition, and gang paraphernalia, in the present case—rather than for contraband. Because of the high-risk nature of the case, a special weapons team entered the home, handcuffed the four occupants, and so detained them in a garage for two to three hours. The plaintiff alleged a violation of her Fourth Amendment rights. Supreme Court disagreed, finding that her detention was permissible, nor did the Court see a distinction between detention for a search for criminal evidence and detention for a search for contraband, because her detention was based on the existence of a warrant for a residence; furthermore, her being handcuffed was reasonable because of the officers' continuing safety interests.[33]

Furthermore, the Court upheld a search (with a warrant) of a third party's property when police had probable cause to believe it contained fruits or instrumentalities of a crime (e.g., a newspaper office containing photographs of a disturbance),[34] a search of a wrong apartment conducted with a warrant but with a mistaken belief that the address was correct,[35] and a warrantless search and seizure of garbage in bags outside the defendant's home.[36]

The Court has also attempted to define when a person is considered "seized"—an important issue because seizure involves Fourth Amendment protections. Is a person "seized" while police are pursuing him or her? Basically, there is no rule that determines the point of seizure in all situations—the standard is whether a suspect believes his or her liberty is restrained. This is ultimately a question for a judge or jury to decide.[37] In a recent roadblock case, the Court did provide some guidance, however. Where a police roadblock resulted in the death of a speeder, the Court said roadblocks involve a "governmental termination of freedom of movement," that the victim was therefore seized under the Fourth Amendment, and that the police were liable for damages.[38]

Two decisions in the 1990–1991 Supreme Court term expanded police practices. The Court looked at a police drug-fighting technique known as "working the buses." Police board a bus at a regular stopping place, approach seated passengers, and ask permission to search their luggage for drugs. Justice Sandra Day O'Connor, writing for the majority, said that such a situation should be evaluated in terms of whether a person in the passenger's position would have felt free to decline the officer's request or to otherwise terminate the encounter; it was held that such police conduct does not constitute a search.[39] In a companion decision in 2002, the justices held that the police—focusing on possible terrorists as well as drug couriers—may question passengers on buses and trains and may search for evidence without informing passengers that they can refuse. Police in Florida were on a Greyhound bus, asking questions of each passenger, when two men wearing heavy clothing on a warm day consented to a search of their luggage and bodies; police found bricks of cocaine strapped to their legs. The Court said the men were not coerced into consenting and that nothing about the fact that they were seated on a bus forced them to give their **consent**.[40]

The Court also decided that no "seizure" occurs when a police officer seeks to apprehend a person through a show of authority but applies no physical force (such as in a foot pursuit). In this case, a juvenile being chased by an officer threw down an object, later determined to be crack cocaine. The Supreme Court found no seizure or actual restraint in this situation.[41] Also, it should be noted that the Court held that no individualized suspicion of misconduct was required in either of these cases.

Supreme Court decisions have authorized a warrantless seizure of blood from a defendant to obtain evidence. (This was a case of driving under the influence, the drawing of blood was done by medical personnel in a hospital, and there were exigent circumstances—the evidence would have been lost by dissipation in the body.)[42]

However, when police compelled a robbery suspect to submit to surgery to remove a bullet, the Court held that such an intrusion to seize evidence was unreasonable; this case said there are limits to what police can do to solve a crime.[43]

mycrimekit

Review: *Warrantless Searches.*

Searches and Seizures with and without a Warrant

As is the case with making an arrest, the best means by which the police can search a person or premises is with a search warrant issued by a neutral magistrate. Such a magistrate has determined, after receiving information from a sworn affiant, that probable cause exists to believe that a person possesses the fruits or instrumentalities of a crime or that they are present at a particular location. Again, as with arrest, the "luxury" of searching and seizing with a warrant is usually confined to investigative personnel, who can interview victims and witnesses and gather other available evidence and then request the warrant. Street officers rarely have the opportunity to perform such a search, as the flow of events normally requires quick action to prevent escape and to prevent evidence from being destroyed or hidden.

Five types of searches may be conducted without a warrant: (1) searches incidental to lawful arrest, (2) searches during field interrogation (stop-and-frisk searches), (3) searches of automobiles that are carried out under special conditions, (4) seizures of evidence in "plain view," and (5) searches when consent is given.

Searches Incidental to Lawful Arrest. In *United States v. Robinson* (1973), the defendant was arrested and taken to the police station for driving without a permit—an offense for which a full-scale arrest could be made. Robinson was taken to jail and searched, and heroin was found. He tried to suppress the evidence on the grounds that the full-scale arrest and custodial search were unreasonable for a driver's license infraction. The Supreme Court disagreed, saying that the arrest was legal and that when police assumed custody of Robinson, they needed total control and therefore could perform a detailed inventory of his possessions: "It is the fact of the lawful arrest that establishes the authority to search and we hold that in the case of lawful custodial arrest a full search of the person is not only an exception to the warrant requirement of the Fourth Amendment, but is also a 'reasonable' search under that Amendment."[44]

The rationale for this decision was in part the possibility that the suspect might destroy evidence unless swift action was taken. But in *Chimel v. California* (1969), when officers without a warrant arrested an individual in one room of his house and then proceeded to search the entire three-bedroom house, including the garage, attic, and workshop, the Supreme Court said that searches incidental to lawful arrest are limited to the area within the arrestee's immediate control or that area from which he or she might obtain a weapon. Thus if the police are holding a person in one room of the house, they are not authorized to search and seize property in another part of the house, away from the arrestee's immediate physical presence.[45]

The Court approved the warrantless seizure of a lawfully arrested suspect's clothes even after a substantial time period had elapsed between the arrest and the search.[46] Another advantage given the police was the Court's allowing a warrantless in-home "protective sweep" of the area in which a suspect is arrested to reveal the presence of anyone else who might pose a danger. Such a search, if justified by the circumstances, is not a full search of the premises and may only include a cursory inspection of those spaces where a person could be hiding.[47]

Searches During Field Interrogation (Stop-and-Frisk Searches). In 1968, the U.S. Supreme Court heard a case challenging the constitutionality of on-the-spot searches and questioning by the police. The case, *Terry v. Ohio*, involved a suspect who was stopped and searched while apparently "casing" a store for robbery (see the Court Closeup: *Terry v. Ohio*).

The Court's dilemma in this case was whether to rule that in some circumstances the police do not need probable cause to stop and search people, and thus appear to invalidate *Mapp v. Ohio*, or to insist on such a high standard for action by the police that they could not function on the streets.[48] The Court held that a brief on-the-spot stop for questioning, accompanied by a superficial search (a pat-down search) of external clothing for weapons, was something less than a full-scale search and therefore could be performed with less than the traditional amount of probable cause. This case instantly became—and remains—a major tool for the police.

While *Terry* said the stop and frisk is legal under the Fourth Amendment in cases involving direct police observation, other cases have said that such a stop is legal when based on information provided by an informant[49] and when an individual is the subject of a "wanted" flier from another jurisdiction.[50] In summary, police officers are justified, both to provide for their own safety and to detect past or future crimes, in stopping and questioning people. A person may be frisked for a weapon if an officer fears for his or her life, and the officer may go through the individual's clothing if the frisk indicates the presence of a weapon. Regardless of the rationale for the stop and frisk, there will always be some argument about whether this type of search is being used frivolously or to harass individuals. However, in balancing the public's need for safety against individual rights, the Court was willing to tip the scales in favor of community protection, especially where the safety of the officer was concerned.[51]

An important expansion of the *Terry* doctrine was handed down in 1993 in *Minnesota v. Dickerson*,[52] in which a police officer observed a man leave a notorious crack house and then try to evade the officer. The man was eventually stopped and patted down, during which time the officer felt a small lump in the man's front pocket that was suspected to be drugs. After manipulating and squeezing the lump, the officer removed it from the man's pocket; the object was crack cocaine wrapped in a cellophane container. Although the defendant's arrest and conviction were later thrown out (the Supreme Court reasoned that the search was illegal because it went beyond the limited frisk for weapons, as permitted by *Terry*), the Court also allowed such seizures in the future when officers' probable cause is established by the sense of touch.

Another case extending *Terry*, *Illinois v. Wardlow*,[53] was decided in January 2000. The Court held that a citizen's running away from the police—under certain

COURT CLOSEUP ▸▸ *Terry v. Ohio*, 319 U.S. 1 (1968)

Cleveland Detective McFadden, a veteran of nineteen years of police service, first noticed Terry and another man at about 2:30 P.M. on the afternoon of the arrest in October 1963. McFadden testified that it appeared the men were "casing" a retail store. He observed the suspects making several trips down the street, stopping at a store window, walking about a half block, turning around, walking back, and pausing to look inside the same store window. At one point they were joined by a third party, who spoke with them and then moved on. McFadden claimed that he followed them because he believed it was his duty as a police officer to investigate the matter further.

Soon the two rejoined the third man; at that point McFadden decided the situation demanded direct action. The officer approached the subjects, identified himself, and then requested that the men identify themselves. When Terry said something inaudible, McFadden "spun him around so that they were facing the other two, with Terry between McFadden and the others, and patted down the outside of his clothing." In a breast pocket of Terry's overcoat, the officer felt a pistol. McFadden found another pistol on one of the other men. The two men were arrested and ultimately convicted of concealing deadly weapons. Terry appealed on the ground that the search was illegal and that the evidence should have been suppressed at trial.

The U.S. Supreme Court disagreed with Terry, holding that the police have the authority to detain a person briefly for questioning even without probable cause if they believe that the person has committed a crime or is about to commit a crime. Such detention does not constitute an arrest. If the officer reasonably suspects that he or she is in danger, the officer may also frisk a person.

conditions—supports reasonable suspicion to justify a search. Two Illinois police officers investigating drug transactions in an area of heavy drug activity observed Wardlow holding a bag. Upon seeing the two officers, Wardlow fled, but he was soon stopped. The officers conducted a protective pat down and then squeezed the bag; they felt a gun and arrested Wardlow. The Court reasoned that, taken together, several factors (the stop occurred in a high-crime area; the suspect acted in a nervous, evasive manner; and the suspect engaged in unprovoked flight upon noticing the police)[54] were sufficient to establish reasonable suspicion.

Another important Supreme Court decision in February 1997 took officer safety into account. In *Maryland v. Wilson*,[55] the Court held that police may order passengers out of vehicles they stop, regardless of any suspicion of wrongdoing or threat to the officers' safety. Chief Justice Rehnquist cited statistics showing officer assaults and murders during traffic stops and noted that the "weighty interest" in officer safety is present whether a vehicle occupant is a driver or a passenger. (Here, a Maryland state trooper initiated a traffic stop and ordered an apparently nervous passenger, Wilson, to exit the vehicle. While doing so, Wilson dropped a quantity of crack cocaine, for which he was arrested and convicted.)

Searches of Automobiles Carried Out Under Special Conditions. The third general circumstance allowing a warrantless search is when an officer has probable cause to believe that an automobile contains criminal evidence. The Supreme Court has traditionally distinguished searches of automobiles from searches of homes on the grounds that a car involved in a crime can be rapidly moved and its evidence irretrievably lost. The Court first established this doctrine in *Carroll v. United States* (1925). In this case, officers searched the vehicle of a known bootlegger without a warrant but with probable cause, finding sixty-eight bottles of illegal booze. On appeal, the Court ruled that the seizure was justified. However, *Carroll* established two rules: First, to invoke the *Carroll* doctrine, the police must have enough probable cause that if there had been enough time, a search warrant would have been issued; second, urgent circumstances must exist that require immediate action.[56]

Extending the creation of the *Carroll* doctrine, however, two new questions confronted the justices: whether impounded vehicles were subject to warrantless search and whether searches could be made of vehicles stopped in routine traffic inspections. In *Preston v. United States* (1964), the Court ruled that once the police had made a lawful arrest and then towed the suspect's car to a different location, they could not conduct an incidental search of the vehicle. The Court reasoned that because such a search was remote in time and place from the point of arrest, it was not incidental and therefore was unreasonable.[57]

Harris v. United States (1968) upheld the right of police to enter an impounded vehicle following a lawful arrest in order to inventory its contents.[58] Building on this decision, the Court later upheld a warrantless search of a vehicle in custody, saying that because the police had probable cause to believe it contained evidence of a crime and could be easily moved, it made little difference whether a warrant was sought or an immediate search conducted.[59]

In 1974, the expectation of citizens to privacy in their vehicles was further diminished when the Court said an automobile has "little capacity for escaping public scrutiny [as] it travels public thoroughfares where both its occupants and its contents are in plain view."[60] This position was reinforced in 1976 when the Court said that a validly impounded car may be searched without probable cause or warrant as it is reasonable for an inventory of its contents to be made as a protection against theft or charges of theft while the car is in police custody.[61]

An automobile may be searched following the lawful search of its driver or another occupant. Following the rationale of *Chimel*, the Court ruled that the entire interior of the car, including containers, may be examined even if the items are not within the driver's reach.[62] The Court went on to say that a warrantless search of an automobile incidental to a lawful arrest, including its trunk and any packages or luggage, is permissible if there is probable cause to believe that it contains evidence of a crime.[63] The Court also authorized a protective pat down of vehicle passenger compartments for weapons (similar to that of persons in *Terry v. Ohio*) after a valid stop and when officers have a reasonable belief that they may be in danger.[64] Finally, it was decided in 1987 that evidence seized by opening a closed container during a warrantless inventory search of a vehicle incidental to lawful arrest is admissible.[65]

During its 1990–1991 term, the Supreme Court extended the long arm of the law with respect to automobiles. In a May 1991 decision, the Court declared that a person's general consent to a search of the interior of an automobile justifies a search of any closed container found inside the car that might reasonably hold the object of the search; thus, an officer, after obtaining a general consent, does not need to ask permission to look inside each closed container.[66] One week later, the Court ruled that probable cause to believe that a container within a car holds contraband or evidence allows a warrantless search of that item under the automobile exception, even in the absence of probable cause extending to the entire vehicle.[67] This decision clarified the *Carroll* doctrine.

During its 1998–1999 term, the Court held that when an officer has probable cause to search a vehicle, the officer may search objects belonging to a passenger in the vehicle, provided the item the officer is looking for could reasonably be in the passenger's belongings.[68] (Here the officer was searching an automobile for contraband, searched a passenger's purse, and found drug paraphernalia there.)

In January 2005, the Supreme Court decided by a 6–2 vote that a motorist has no legitimate expectation of privacy during a traffic stop for contraband hidden in a vehicle and detected by a drug-sniffing dog. In *Illinois v. Caballes*,[69] the defendant had been stopped for speeding; while the state trooper was issuing a citation, another trooper walked a drug-sniffing dog around the car. The dog alerted at the trunk, and after a search the troopers found marijuana, for which Caballes was arrested and convicted. The Court noted that Caballes was stopped lawfully and that the entire episode lasted less than ten minutes; also, drug-sniffing dogs only detect illegal activity (as opposed to, say, thermal-imaging devices that police once used to seek out marijuana growing in a home, which the Court said in 2001 were illegal because such devices can also detect lawful activities, such as a person's taking a daily sauna or a bath).

More recently regarding vehicle searches, in April 2009 the Supreme Court overturned nearly three decades of a particular police practice by holding that, where an individual has been arrested and is in police custody away from his or her vehicle, unable to access the vehicle, officers may not then search the vehicle without a warrant. Here, the officers did so, and discovered a handgun and a plastic bag of cocaine; the Court said it is a violation of the Fourth Amendment's protection against unreasonable searches and seizures.[70] In essence, the Court is saying that police may search the passenger compartment of a vehicle incident to a recent occupant's arrest only if it is reasonable to believe that the arrestee might access the vehicle at the time of the search or that the vehicle contains evidence of the offense of arrest.

Seizures of Evidence in "Plain View." The police do not have to search for items that are in plain view. If such items are believed to be fruits or instrumentalities of a crime and the police are lawfully on the premises, they may seize them. For example, if an officer has been admitted into a home with an arrest or search warrant and sees drugs and paraphernalia on a living room table, he or she may arrest the occupants on drug charges as well as the other charges. If an officer performs a traffic stop for an offense and observes drugs in the backseat of the car, he may arrest for that as well. Provided that the officer was lawfully in a particular place and that the plain-view discovery was inadvertent, the law does not require the officer to ignore contraband or other evidence of a crime that is in plain view.

The Supreme Court has said that officers are not required to immediately recognize an object in plain view as contraband before it may be seized. (For instance, an officer may see a balloon in a glove box with a white powdery substance on its tip and

The U.S. Supreme Court, Washington, D.C.

later determine the powder to be heroin.)[71] Furthermore, fences and the posting of "No Trespassing" signs afford no expectation of privacy and do not prevent officers from viewing open fields without a search warrant,[72] nor are police prevented from making a naked-eye aerial observation of a suspect's backyard or other curtilage (the grounds around a house or building).[73]

Two decisions in the late 1980s have further defined the plain-view doctrine. In one case, an officer found a gun under a car seat while looking for the vehicle identification number; the Court upheld the search and the resulting arrest as being a plain-view discovery.[74] However, in another similar situation, the Court disallowed an arrest when an officer, during a legal search for weapons, moved a stereo system to locate its serial number, saying that this constituted an unreasonable search and seizure.[75]

Searches when Consent Is Given. Another permissible warrantless search involves citizens waiving their Fourth Amendment rights and consenting to a search of their persons or effects. It must be established at trial, however, that a defendant's consent was given voluntarily. In some circumstances, as with metal detectors at airports, an agent's right to search is implied.

In the leading case on consent searches, *Schneckloth v. Bustamonte* (1973), a police officer stopped a car for a burned-out headlight. Two other backup officers joined him. When asked if his car could be searched, the driver consented. The officers found several stolen checks in the trunk. The driver and passenger were arrested and convicted. On appeal, the defendants argued that the evidence should have been suppressed, as they did not know they had the right to refuse the officers' request to search the car. The Supreme Court upheld their convictions, reasoning that the individuals, although poor, uneducated, and alone with three officers, could reasonably be considered capable of knowing and exercising their right to deny officers permission to search their car.[76]

However, police cannot deceive people into believing they have a search warrant when they in fact do not. For example, the police, looking for a rape suspect, announced falsely to the suspect's grandmother that they had a search warrant for her home; the evidence they found was ruled to be inadmissible.[77] A hotel clerk cannot give a valid consent to a warrantless search of the room of one of the occupants; hotel guests have a reasonable expectation of privacy, and that right cannot be waived by hotel management.[78]

Finally, the right of police to search a home when one occupant consents and the other objects was the subject of a Supreme Court decision in March 2006. There, police responded to the home of a Georgia couple following a domestic disturbance. The wife told the officers that her husband was a drug user and had drugs in their home. An officer asked the husband for permission to search the residence and was denied. The wife granted consent, however, and led the officers to a bedroom where cocaine was kept. The defendant-husband appealed on the grounds that the drugs were the product of an unlawful search, and the Supreme Court agreed on the grounds that the Fourth Amendment should not ignore the privacy rights of an individual who is present and asserting his rights.[79] Note, however, that an occupant may still give police permission to search when the other resident is absent or does not protest.

Electronic Surveillance

It was the original view of the Supreme Court, in *Olmstead v. United States* (1928), that wiretaps were not searches and seizures and did not violate the Fourth Amendment; this represented the old rule on wiretaps.[80] However, that decision was overruled in 1967 in *Katz v. United States*, which held that any form of electronic surveillance, including wiretapping, is a search and violates a reasonable expectation of privacy.[81] The case involved a public telephone booth, deemed by the Court to be a constitutionally protected area where the user has a reasonable expectation of privacy. This decision expressed the view that the Constitution protects people, not places. Thus the Court has required that warrants for electronic surveillance be based on probable cause, describe the conversations to be overheard, be for a limited period of time, name subjects to be overheard, and be terminated when the desired information is obtained.[82]

However, the Supreme Court has held that while electronic eavesdropping (that is, an informant wearing a "bug," or hidden microphone) did not violate the Fourth Amendment (a person assumes the risk that whatever he or she says may be transmitted to the police),[83] the warrantless monitoring of an electronic beeper in a private residence violated the suspect's right to privacy. A federal drug agent had placed a beeper inside a can of ether, which was being used to extract cocaine from clothing imported into the United States, and had monitored its movements.[84]

Lineups

Review: *Identification of Suspects.*

A police **lineup**, as well as other face-to-face confrontations after the accused has been arrested, is considered a critical stage of criminal proceedings; therefore, the accused has a right to have an attorney present. If counsel is not present, the evidence obtained is inadmissible.[85] However, the suspect is not entitled to the presence and advice of a lawyer before being formally charged.[86]

Lineups that are so suggestive as to make the result inevitable violate the suspect's right to due process. (In one case, the suspect was much taller than the other two people in the lineup, and he was the only person wearing a leather jacket similar to that worn by the robber. In a second lineup, the suspect was the only person who had participated in the first lineup.[87]) In short, lineups must be fair to suspects; a fair lineup guarantees no bias against the suspect.

The Supreme Court has held that a suspect may be compelled to appear before a grand jury and give voice exemplars for comparison with an actual voice recording. Appearance before a grand jury is not a search, and the giving of a voice sample is not a seizure that is protected by the Fourth Amendment.[88]

Fifth Amendment

> No person shall be held to answer for a capital, or otherwise infamous crime, unless on a presentment or indictment of a Grand Jury, except in cases arising in the land or naval forces, or in the Militia, when in actual service in time of war or public danger; nor shall any person be subject for the same offense to be twice put in jeopardy of life or limb; nor shall be compelled in any criminal case to be a witness against himself, nor be deprived of life, liberty, or property, without due process of law; nor shall private property be taken for public use, without just compensation.

A major tool used in religious persecutions in England during the sixteenth century was the oath. Ministers were called before the Court of Star Chamber (which, during much of the sixteenth and seventeenth centuries, enforced unpopular political policies and meted out severe punishments, including whipping, branding, and mutilation, without a jury trial) and questioned about their beliefs. Being men of God, they were compelled to tell the truth and admitted to their nonconformist views; for this, they were often severely punished or even executed.[89] In the 1630s, the Star Chamber and similar bodies of cruelty were disbanded by Parliament. People had become repulsed by compulsory self-incrimination; the privilege against self-incrimination was recognized in all courts when claimed by defendants or witnesses. Today, the **Fifth Amendment** applies not only to criminal defendants but also to any witness testifying in a civil or criminal case and anyone testifying before an administrative body, a grand jury, or a congressional committee. However, the privilege does not

Review: *Interrogations and Confessions.*

extend to blood samples, handwriting exemplars, and other such items that are not considered to be testimony.[90]

The right against self-incrimination is one of the most significant provisions in the Bill of Rights. Basically it states that no criminal defendant shall be compelled to take the witness stand and give evidence against himself or herself. No one can be compelled to answer any question if his or her answer can later be used to implicate or convict him or her. Some people view the defendant's "taking the Fifth" as an indication of guilt; others view this as a basic right in a democracy, wherein a defendant does not have to contribute to his or her own conviction. In either case, the impact of this amendment is felt daily by the criminal justice system.

Decisions Supporting *Miranda*: Confessions

Traditionally, the U.S. Supreme Court has excluded physically coerced confessions on the grounds that such confessions might very well be untrustworthy or unreliable in view of the duress surrounding them. As the quality of police work has improved, police use of physical means to obtain confessions has diminished. Some cases that have come before the Supreme Court involved psychological rather than physical pressure on the defendant to confess. One such case involved an accused who was questioned for eight hours by six police officers in relays and was told falsely that the job and welfare of a friend who was a rookie cop depended on his confession. He was also refused contact with his lawyer. The Court reversed his conviction, not so much on the grounds that the confession was unreliable but on the grounds that it was obtained unfairly.[91]

In the 1960s, the Supreme Court ruled in *Escobedo v. Illinois* (1964)[92] (discussed later) and in *Miranda v. Arizona* (1966)[93] (see Court Closeup: *Miranda v. Arizona*) that confessions made by suspects who have not been notified of their constitutional rights cannot be admitted into evidence. In these cases, the Court emphasized the importance of a defendant having the "guiding hand of counsel" present during the interrogation process.

Once a suspect has been placed under arrest, the *Miranda* warning must be given before interrogation for any offense, be it a felony or a misdemeanor. An exception is the brief routine traffic stop; however, a custodial interrogation of a suspect for driving under the influence (DUI) requires the *Miranda* warning.[94] Moreover, after an accused has invoked the right to counsel, the police may not interrogate the same suspect about a different crime.[95] Once a "Mirandized" suspect invokes his or her right to silence, interrogation must cease. The police may not readminister *Miranda* and interrogate the suspect later unless the suspect's attorney is present. If, however, the suspect initiates further conversation, any confession he or she provides is admissible.[96] (This decision involved a suspect who was arrested on a state criminal charge and invoked his right to have counsel present at questioning; then, one day later, the police returned, re-Mirandized him, and during this period of questioning he said that he was willing to talk; he then confessed to child molestation.)

However, in a significant decision in February 2010, the U.S. Supreme Court modified this ruling in *Maryland v. Shatzer*.[97] There, a detective attempted to question a prison inmate concerning allegations of sexually abusing his son; Shatzer invoked his *Miranda* right to have counsel present during interrogation, so the questioning ceased, Shatzer was released back into the general prison population, and the investigation was closed. Three years later, Shatzer had been released from prison, rearrested, and returned to prison; the earlier investigation was reopened and another detective sought to question Shatzer in prison. This time Shatzer waived his *Miranda* rights and confessed. On appeal, the U.S. Supreme Court held that, because Shatzer had experienced a break in *Miranda* custody of *more than two weeks* between the first and second attempts at interrogation, his confession did not have to be suppressed. Justice Antonin Scalia wrote, "The Court concludes that the appropriate period is 14 days, which provides ample time for the suspect to get reacclimated to his normal life, consult with friends and counsel, and shake off any residual coercive effects of prior custody.[98]

Decisions Modifying *Miranda*: Interrogations

Miranda, Escobedo, and *Mapp* combined to represent the centerpiece of the "due process revolution" of the Court of Chief Justice Earl Warren in the 1960s. However, several decisions, including many by the Court of Chief Justice Warren Burger, have dealt severe blows to *Miranda*.

It has been held that a second interrogation session held after the suspect had initially refused to make a statement did not violate *Miranda*.[99] If a suspect waives his or her *Miranda* rights and makes voluntary statements while irrational (allegedly "following the advice of God"), those statements too are admissible.[100] The Court also decided that when a suspect waived his or her *Miranda* rights, believing the

COURT CLOSEUP ▸▸ *Miranda v. Arizona*, 384 U.S. 436 (1966)

While walking to a Phoenix, Arizona, bus stop on the night of March 2, 1963, eighteen-year-old Barbara Ann Johnson was accosted by a man who shoved her into his car, tied her hands and ankles, and drove her to the edge of the city, where he raped her. He then drove Johnson to a street near her home, letting her out of the car and asking that she pray for him.

The Phoenix police subsequently picked up Ernesto Miranda for investigation of Johnson's rape and included him in a lineup at the police station. Miranda was identified by several women; one identified him as the man who had robbed her at knifepoint a few months earlier, and Johnson thought he was the rapist.

Miranda was a twenty-three-year-old eighth-grade dropout with a police record dating back to age fourteen, and he had also served time in prison for driving a stolen car across a state line. During questioning, the police told Miranda that he had been identified by the women; Miranda then made a statement in writing that described the rape incident. He also noted that he was making the confession voluntarily and with full knowledge of his legal rights. He was soon charged with rape, kidnapping, and robbery.

At trial, Miranda's court-appointed attorney got the officers to admit that during the interrogation the defendant was not informed of his right to have counsel present and that no counsel was present. Nonetheless, Miranda's confession was admitted into evidence. He was convicted and sentenced to serve twenty to thirty years for kidnapping and rape.

On appeal, the U.S. Supreme Court ruled:

> [T]he current practice of incommunicado interrogation is at odds with one of our Nation's most cherished principles—that the individual may not be compelled to incriminate himself. Unless adequate protective devices are employed to dispel the compulsion inherent in custodial surroundings, no statement obtained from the defendant can truly be the product of free choice.

interrogation would focus on minor crimes, but the police shifted their questioning to a more serious crime, the confession was valid—there was no police deception or misrepresentation.[101] When a suspect invoked his or her right to assistance of counsel and refused to make written statements but then voluntarily gave oral statements to police, the statements were admissible (defendants have "the right to choose between speech and silence").[102] Finally, a suspect need not be given the *Miranda* warning in the exact form that it was outlined in *Miranda v. Arizona.* In one case, the waiver form said the suspect would have an attorney appointed "if and when you go to court." The Court held that as long as the warnings on the form reasonably convey the suspect's rights, they need not be given verbatim.[103]

In 1994, the Supreme Court ruled that after police officers obtain a valid *Miranda* waiver from a suspect, they may continue questioning him or her when he or she makes an ambiguous or equivocal request for counsel during questioning. In this case,[104] the defendant stated during an interview and after waiving his rights, "Maybe I should talk to a lawyer." The officers inquired about this statement, determined that he did not want a lawyer, and continued their questioning. When a suspect unequivocally requests counsel, all questioning must cease. However, here the Court held that when the suspect mentions an attorney, the officers need not interrupt the flow of the questioning to clarify the reference but may continue questioning until there is a clear assertion of the right to counsel, such as "I want a lawyer."

Finally, in June 2010, the Supreme Court held (5–4) that suspects' mere silence—when they do not expressly waive their *Miranda* rights and speak only after remaining silent through a period of interrogation—does not mean they intend to invoke *Miranda.* There, a Michigan murder suspect remained silent during almost three hours of interrogation and finally answered yes to the following question: "Do you pray to God to forgive you for shooting that boy down?" This affirmative response was later used against him at trial, and he was convicted of first-degree murder. The majority held that earlier decisions concerning *Miranda* have put a greater burden on suspects to invoke their rights, while the dissenting opinion argued that the decision created a kind of paradox: "A suspect who wishes to guard his right to remain silent must, counterintuitively, speak." The Criminal Justice Legal Foundation, explaining the decision, stated, "The Supreme Court recognized the practical realities that the police face in dealing with suspects. They don't always answer the waiver question clearly. When they do not, Miranda should not apply, and the statement should be admissible as long as it is not compelled."[105]

Entrapment

The due process clause of the Fifth Amendment requires "fundamental fairness"—government agents may not act in a way that is "shocking to the universal sense of justice." Thus the police may not induce or encourage a person to commit a crime that he or she would otherwise not have attempted, that is, **entrapment.**[106] This is the current test used by many courts to evaluate police behavior. Some states take a broader view than others as to what constitutes entrapment. For example, a police department in a western state had police officers impersonate homeless people. The decoys pretended to be asleep or passed out from intoxication on a public bench, and paper money visibly protruded from their pockets. Several passersby helped themselves to the money and were arrested on the spot. On appeal, the prosecution argued that a thief is a thief, the people had the intent to commit theft, and the decoy operation simply provided an opportunity for dishonest people to get caught. The state's Supreme Court disagreed, calling the operation entrapment, adding that the situation could cause even honest people to be overcome by temptation.

However, the U.S. Supreme Court approved an undercover drug agent's provision of an essential chemical for the manufacture of illegal drugs. (The defendant, the majority said, was an "unwary criminal" who was already "predisposed" to commit the offense.)[107] Nor is it entrapment when a drug agent sells drugs to a suspect, who then sells it to government agents. Government conduct in this case is shocking to civil libertarians, but the focus here is the conduct of the defendant, not the government. As long as government's conduct is not outrageous and the defendant was predisposed to crime, the arrest is valid.[108]

The Supreme Court has held that police officers "may not originate a criminal design, implant in an innocent person's mind the disposition to commit a criminal act, and then induce commission of the crime."[109]

Sixth Amendment

> In all criminal prosecutions the accused shall enjoy the right to a speedy and public trial, by an impartial jury of the State and district wherein the crime shall have been committed, which district shall have been previously ascertained by law, and to be informed of the nature and cause of the accusation; to be confronted with the witnesses against him; to have compulsory process for obtaining witnesses in his favor; and to have the assistance of counsel for his defense.

Right to Counsel

Many people believe that the **Sixth Amendment** right of the accused to have the assistance of counsel before and at trial is the greatest right we enjoy in a democracy. Indeed, a close reading of the cases mentioned here would reveal the negative outcomes that are possible when a person—rich or poor, illiterate or educated—has no legal representation.

Over seventy years ago, in *Powell v. Alabama* (1932), it was established that in a capital case, when the accused is poor and illiterate, he or she enjoys the right to assistance of counsel for his or her defense and due process.[110] In *Gideon v. Wainwright* (1963), the Supreme Court mandated that all indigent people charged with felonies in state courts be provided counsel.[111]

Note that *Gideon* applied only to felony defendants. In 1973, *Argersinger v. Hamlin* extended the right to counsel to indigent people charged with misdemeanor crimes if they face the possibility of incarceration (however short the incarceration may be).[112]

Another landmark decision concerning the right to counsel is *Escobedo v. Illinois* (1964).[113] Danny Escobedo's brother-in-law was fatally shot in 1960; Escobedo was arrested without a warrant and questioned, but he made no statement to the police. He was released after fourteen hours of interrogation. Following police questioning of another suspect, Escobedo was again arrested and questioned at police headquarters. Escobedo's request to confer with his lawyer was denied, even after the lawyer arrived and asked to see his client. The questioning of Escobedo lasted several hours, during which time he was handcuffed and forced to remain standing. Eventually, he admitted being an accomplice to murder. Under Illinois law, an accomplice was as guilty as the person firing the fatal bullet. At no point was Escobedo advised of his rights to remain silent or to confer with his attorney.

Escobedo's conviction was ultimately reversed by the Supreme Court, based on a violation of Escobedo's Sixth Amendment right to counsel. However, the real thrust of the decision was his Fifth Amendment right not to incriminate himself; when a defendant is scared, flustered, ignorant, alone, and bewildered, he or she is often unable to effectively make use of protections granted under the Fifth Amendment without the advice of an attorney.[114] The *Miranda* decision set down two years later simply established the guidelines for the police to inform suspects of all of these rights.

What Constitutes an Interrogation?

The Supreme Court has stated that an interrogation takes place not only when police officers ask direct questions of a defendant but also when the police make remarks designed to appeal to a defendant's sympathy, religious interest, and so forth. This has been deemed soliciting information through trickery and deceit. The "Christian Burial Speech" case (discussed previously) and *Escobedo* demonstrated that even before (and certainly after) a suspect has been formally charged, a suspect in police custody should not be interrogated without an attorney present unless he or she has waived the right to counsel.

However, the Supreme Court upheld a conviction when two police officers, in a suspect's presence, discussed the possible whereabouts of the shotgun used in a robbery and expressed concern that nearby schoolchildren might be endangered by it. Hearing this conversation, the suspect led officers to the shotgun, thereby implicating himself. On appeal, the Court said that interrogation includes words and actions intended to elicit an incriminating response from the defendant and that no such interrogation occurred here; this was a mere conversation between officers, and the evidence was admissible.[115]

In another case, the Court ruled that if the police were present at and recorded a conversation between a husband and wife (this tape was later used against the husband at trial, where he claimed insanity in the killing of his son), an interrogation did not occur. The Court believed that the police merely arranged a situation in which it was likely the suspect would make incriminating statements, so anything recorded could be used against him in court.[116]

Two cases on police interrogations were heard during the 1990–1991 Supreme Court term. First, the Court held that a defendant who is in custody and has been given the *Miranda* warning may be questioned later on a separate as-yet-uncharged offense. In this case, the defendant appeared with an attorney at a bail hearing on robbery charges. Later, while he was still in custody, the police, after reading him his rights, questioned him about a murder; the defendant agreed to discuss the murder without counsel and made incriminating statements that were used to convict him.[117] In the second case, representing a victory for the defense, the Court held that once a criminal suspect has asked for and consults with a lawyer, interrogators may not later question him without his lawyer being present.[118]

Two recent decisions have expanded defendants' rights under the Sixth Amendment. First, in mid-2009 the U.S. Supreme Court ruled that criminal defendants have a constitutional right to cross-examine forensic analysts who prepare laboratory reports on illegal drugs and other evidence used at trial. The defendant—convicted for distributing and trafficking cocaine—challenged on appeal the lab analysis that confirmed cocaine was in plastic bags found in the vehicle in which he was riding. He argued, successfully, that the Sixth Amendment allowed him to confront witnesses against him and that he should have been allowed to question the lab analyst about testing methods and how the evidence was preserved.[119] Then, in early 2010, the Supreme Court held that the Sixth Amendment requires that immigrants have a right to be told by their lawyers whether pleading guilty to a crime could lead to their deportation; Justice John Paul Stevens wrote for the majority that "Our longstanding Sixth Amendment precedents, the seriousness of deportation, and the concomitant impact of deportation on families living lawfully in this country demand no less."[120]

Juvenile Rights

The criminal justice system's philosophy toward juveniles is very different from its philosophy toward adults. Consequently, police officers, who are constantly dealing with juvenile offenders, must know and apply a different standard of treatment in these situations. The approach is generally that society, through poor parenting, poverty, and so forth, is primarily responsible for the criminal behavior of juvenile offenders.

The prevailing doctrine that guides our treatment of juveniles is **parens patriae**, meaning that "the state is the ultimate parent" of the child. In effect, as long as we adequately care for and provide at least the basic amenities for our children as required under the law, they are ours to keep, but when children are physically or emotionally neglected or abused by their parents or guardians, the juvenile court and police may intervene and remove the children from that environment. Then the doctrine of **in loco parentis** takes hold, meaning that the state will act in place of the parent. The author can state from experience that there is probably no more overwhelming or awe-inspiring duty for a police officer than having to testify in juvenile court that a woman is an unfit mother and that parental ties should be legally severed. However, when a person chooses to be a negligent or abusive parent, it is clearly in everyone's best interest for the state to assume care and custody of the child.

The juvenile justice system, working through and with the police, seeks to protect the child. It seeks to rehabilitate, not punish; its procedure is generally amiable, not adversarial. That is why the term *in re*, meaning "concerning" or "in the matter of," is commonly used in many juvenile case titles—for example, a case would be called *In Re Smith* rather than the adversarial and more formal *State v. Smith*. Juvenile court proceedings are generally shrouded in privacy—that is, heard before a judge only. However, when a juvenile commits an act that is so heinous that the protective and helpful juvenile court philosophy will not work, the child may be remanded to the custody of the adult court to be tried as an adult.

Juvenile delinquency (an ambiguous term that has no widespread agreed-on meaning but has a multitude of definitions under state statutes[121]) became recognized as a national problem in the 1950s. As a result, several important decisions by the Supreme Court between 1960 and 1970 addressed the rights of juveniles. *Kent v. United States* (1966)[122] involved a sixteen-year-old male who was arrested in the District of Columbia for robbery, rape, and burglary. The juvenile court, without holding a formal hearing, waived the matter to a criminal court, and Kent was tried and convicted as an adult. Kent appealed, arguing that the waiver without a hearing violated his right to due process. The Supreme Court agreed.

Another landmark case extending due process to juveniles was *In Re Gault* (1967).[123] Gerald Gault was a fifteen-year-old who resided in Arizona and allegedly made obscene telephone calls. When a neighbor complained to police, Gault was arrested and eventually sent to a youth home (a previous crime, stealing a wallet, was also taken into account), to remain there until he either turned twenty-one or was paroled. Before his hearing, Gault did not receive a timely notice of charges. At his hearing, Gault had no attorney present, nor was his accuser present; no transcript was made of the proceedings, and Gault was not read his rights or told he could remain silent. Gault appealed on the grounds that all of these due process rights should have been provided. The Supreme Court reversed his conviction, declaring that these Fourteenth Amendment protections applied to juveniles as well as adults. This case remains the most significant **juvenile rights** decision ever rendered.

In 1970, the Supreme Court decided *In Re Winship*, which involved a twelve-year-old boy convicted in New York of larceny.[124] At trial, the court relied on the "preponderance of the evidence" standard of proof against him rather than the more demanding "beyond a reasonable doubt" standard used in adult courts. At that time, juvenile courts could apply any of three standards of proof (the third was "clear and convincing evidence"). The Court reversed Winship's conviction on the grounds that the "beyond a reasonable doubt" standard had not been used.

EXHIBIT 2 ▸

Do Life Without Parole Sentences for Juveniles Violate the U.S. Constitution?

Having ruled in 2005 that it is unconstitutional to execute someone for a capital crime committed while younger than eighteen years of age, in November 2009 the U.S. Supreme Court heard arguments concerning whether or not it is also unconstitutional to sentence teens to life without possibility of parole (LWOP) for a noncapital crime. The case heard by the Court involved a Florida youth, Terrance Graham; at age sixteen, Graham and an accomplice robbed a restaurant and beat the manager with a steel bar. Graham received probation for that crime, but a year later he and accomplices committed a home invasion robbery. For that crime, as well as for violating the terms of his probation, he was given life without parole. In May 2010, the U.S. Supreme Court ruled that the Eighth Amendment's ban on cruel and unusual punishment prohibits juveniles who commit crimes in which no one is killed from being sentenced to LWOP. Although thirty-seven states, the District of Columbia, and the federal government had laws allowing LWOP sentences for juveniles convicted of non-homicide offenses, the justices stated that the sentences at issue had been "rejected the world over" and that only the United States and perhaps Israel had imposed the punishment even for homicides committed for juveniles.

Sources: Graham v. Florida, No. 08-7412 (May 17, 2010); also see Adam Liptak, "Justices Limit Life Sentences for Juveniles," *New York Times*, May 17, 2010, www.nytimes.com/2010/05/18/us/politics/18court.html?pagewanted=print (accessed July 30, 2010).

Other precedent-setting juvenile cases followed. In *McKeiver v. Pennsylvania* (1971), the Supreme Court said juveniles do not have an absolute right to trial by jury; whether or not a juvenile receives a trial by jury is left to the discretion of state and local authorities.[125] In *Breed v. Jones* (1975), the Court concluded that the Fifth Amendment protected juveniles from double jeopardy, or being tried twice for the same offense.[126] (Breed had been tried both in California Juvenile Court and later in Superior Court—the state's trial courts, which exist in each of the state's 58 counties—for the same offenses.)

In March 2005, the U.S. Supreme Court, in *Roper v. Simmons*, ruled that the Eighth and Fourteenth Amendments forbid the execution of offenders who were under the age of eighteen when their crimes were committed.[127]

Exhibit 2 describes another recent—and significant—U.S. Supreme Court decision: whether or not juveniles could be sentenced to serve **life without parole** for committing crimes not involving murder.

SUMMARY

U.S. society places great importance on individual freedom, and the power of government has traditionally been feared; therefore, the U.S. Constitution, courts, and legislatures have seen fit to rein in the power of government agents through what is commonly referred to as the rule of law. This necessary aspect associated with having police in a democracy carries with it a responsibility for police practitioners to understand the law and—more important, perhaps—to keep abreast of the legal changes society is constantly undergoing.

The law is dynamic—that is, it is constantly changed by the Supreme Court and other federal courts and by state courts and legislatures. It is imperative that police agencies have a formal mechanism for imparting these legal changes to their officers.

The number of successful criminal and civil lawsuits against police officers today demonstrates that the police have not always done their homework and simply do not apply the law in the manner in which the federal courts intended. Officers must understand and enforce the law properly. In this grave business of adult cops and robbers, the means are in many respects more important than the ends. The courts and the criminal justice system should expect and allow nothing less.

KEY TERMS

affidavit
consent
crime-control model
due process model
entrapment
exclusionary rule
exigent circumstances
Fifth Amendment
Fourth Amendment
in loco parentis
interrogation
juvenile rights
life without parole
lineup
parens patriae
probable cause
rule of law
search and seizure
Sixth Amendment

REVIEW QUESTIONS

1. What is meant by the rule of law?
2. What protections are afforded citizens by the Fourth, Fifth, and Sixth Amendments?
3. What is an example of probable cause?
4. From both the police and community perspectives, what are the ramifications of having and not having the exclusionary rule?
5. How would you distinguish between arrests and searches and seizures with and without a warrant, and which form is best? Provide examples of each.
6. In what significant ways has the original *Miranda* decision been modified, and what is its long-term outlook, given the shifting composition of judges on the Supreme Court?
7. What major legal rights exist for juveniles, and what are the major differences in philosophy and treatment between juvenile and adult offenders?

LEARN BY DOING

1. Your criminal justice professor has assigned a class project wherein class members are to determine which amendment to the Bill of Rights—the Fourth, Fifth, or Sixth—contains the most important rights that are protected by citizens under a democracy. You are to analyze the three and present your findings as to which one is the most important
2. You are assigned the task of debating which period was the most important—the so-called "due process revolution" of the Warren Court (particularly during the 1960s, when the U.S. Supreme Court granted many rights to the accused through such decisions as *Gideon, Miranda, Escobedo,* and so forth), or the more conservative era that followed under the Rehnquist Court, during which time many of the Warren Court decisions were eroded and more rights were given to the police. Choose a side, and make your defenses.
3. From the time of his confirmation in 1969, Chief Justice Warren Burger viewed the exclusionary rule as an unnecessary and unreasonable intrusion on law enforcement. Prepare a pro/con paper that examines why there should and should not be an exclusionary rule as a part of our system of justice.

mycrimekit™

Go to MyCrimeKit.com and discover additional study tools and resources related to this chapter.

- Key Terms
- Review Questions
  - Multiple Choice Questions
  - True/False
  - Fill in the Blank
  - Essay
- FLASHCARDS: to test your knowledge of this chapter.
- *NEW YORK TIMES:* where you can read the latest articles related to criminology and criminal law.
- THE CAREER CENTER: where you can explore career opportunities in criminal justice and criminology.
- THE ONLINE RESEARCH LIBRARY: where you can explore the Cybrary and Research Navigator.

NOTES

1. Albert Venn Dicey, *Introduction to the Study of the Law of the Constitution*, 10th ed. (London: Macmillan, 1959), p. 187.
2. David Neubauer, *America's Courts and the Criminal Justice System*, 9th ed. (Belmont, CA: Wadsworth, 2008), pp. 294–300.
3. *Draper v. U.S.*, 358 U.S. 307 (1959).
4. *Illinois v. Gates*, 462 U.S. 213 (1983).
5. *U.S. v. Sokolow*, 109 S.Ct. 1581 (1989).
6. *Hunter v. Bryant*, 112 S.Ct. 534 (1991).
7. *People v. Defore*, 242 N.Y. 214, 150 N.E. 585 (1926).
8. *Weeks v. U.S.*, 232 U.S. 383 (1914).
9. This doctrine was overruled by the Supreme Court in *Elkins v. U.S.*, 364 U.S. 206 (1960).
10. *People v. Defore*, 242 N.Y. 214, 150 N.E. 585 (1926).
11. *Olmstead v. U.S.*, 277 U.S. 438, 48 S.Ct. 564 (1928).
12. *Mapp v. Ohio*, 367 U.S. 643 (1961).
13. John Kaplan, Jerome H. Skolnick, and Malcolm M. Feeley, *Criminal Justice: Introductory Cases and Materials*, 5th ed. (Westbury, NY: Foundation Press, 1991), pp. 258–259, 269.
14. *Rochin v. California*, 342 U.S. 165 (1952).
15. In *New York v. Quarles*, 467 U.S. 649 (1984).
16. *Nix v. Williams*, 52 LW 4732 (1984). This case began as *Brewer v. Williams*, 430 U.S. 387 (1977).
17. *U.S. v. Leon*, 82 L.Ed.2d 677 (1984).
18. *Murray v. U.S.*, 487 U.S. 533 (1988).
19. Kaplan, Skolnick, and Feeley, *Criminal Justice*, p. 269.
20. *California v. Minjares*, 443 U.S. 916 (1979).
21. Alexander B. Smith and Harriet Pollack, *Criminal Justice: An Overview* (New York: Holt, Rinehart and Winston, 1980), pp. 154–155.
22. *Payton v. New York*, 445 U.S. 573 (1980).
23. *Dunaway v. New York*, 442 U.S. 200 (1979).
24. *Delaware v. Prouse*, 440 U.S. 648 (1979).
25. *Michigan Department of State Police v. Sitz*, 110 S.Ct. 2481, 110 L.Ed.2d 412 (1990).
26. *Pennsylvania v. Muniz*, 110 S.Ct. 2638, 110 L.Ed.2d 528 (1990).
27. *Maryland v. Pringle*, 124 S.Ct. 795 (2004).
28. *Illinois v. Lidster*, 124 S.Ct. 885 (2004).
29. *Riverside County, Calif. v. McLaughlin*, 59 LW 4413 (May 13, 1991).
30. *U.S. v. Banks*, 124 S.Ct. 521 (2003).
31. *Pennsylvania v. Bull*, 63 LW 3695 (1995).
32. *Wilson v. Arkansas*, 115 S.Ct. 1914 (1995).
33. *Muehler v. Mena*, 125 S.Ct. 1465 (2005).
34. *Zurcher v. Stanford Daily*, 436 U.S. 547 (1978).

35. *Maryland v. Garrison*, 480 U.S. 79 (1987).
36. *California v. Greenwood*, 486 U.S. 35 (1988).
37. Rolando V. Del Carmen and Jeffrey T. Walker, *Briefs of One Hundred Leading Cases in Law Enforcement* (Cincinnati, OH: Anderson, 1991), p. 49.
38. *Brower v. County of Inyo*, 109 U.S. 1378 (1989).
39. *Florida v. Bostick*, 59 LW 4708 (June 20, 1991).
40. *U.S. v. Drayton*, 536 U.S. 194, 231 F.3d 787 (2002).
41. *California v. Hodari D.*, 59 LW 4335 (April 23, 1991).
42. *Schmerber v. California*, 384 U.S. 757 (1966).
43. *Winston v. Lee*, 470 U.S. 753 (1985).
44. *U.S. v. Robinson*, 414 U.S. 218 (1973).
45. *Chimel v. California*, 395 U.S. 752 (1969).
46. *U.S. v. Edwards*, 415 U.S. 800 (1974).
47. *Maryland v. Buie*, 58 LW 4281 (1990).
48. Smith and Pollack, *Criminal Justice*, p. 161.
49. *Adams v. Williams*, 407 U.S. 143 (1972).
50. *U.S. v. Hensley*, 469 U.S. 221 (1985).
51. Smith and Pollack, *Criminal Justice*, p. 162.
52. *Minnesota v. Dickerson*, 113 S.Ct. 2130 (1993).
53. *Illinois v. Wardlow*, 120 S.Ct. 673 (2000).
54. Ibid., at 673.
55. *Maryland v. Wilson*, 117 S.Ct. 882 (1997).
56. *Carroll v. United States*, 267 U.S. 132 (1925).
57. *Preston v. United States*, 376 U.S. 364 (1964).
58. *Harris v. United States*, 390 U.S. 234 (1968).
59. *Chambers v. Maroney*, 399 U.S. 42 (1970).
60. *Cardwell v. Lewis*, 417 U.S. 583 (1974).
61. *South Dakota v. Opperman*, 428 U.S. 364 (1976).
62. *New York v. Belton*, 453 U.S. 454 (1981).
63. *U.S. v. Ross*, 456 U.S. 798 (1982).
64. *Michigan v. Long*, 463 U.S. 1032 (1983).
65. *Colorado v. Bertine*, 479 U.S. 367 (1987).
66. *Florida v. Jimeno*, 59 LW 4471 (May 23, 1991).
67. *California v. Acevedo*, 59 LW 4559 (May 30, 1991).
68. *Wyoming v. Houghton*, 119 S.Ct. 1297 (1999).
69. *Illinois v. Caballes*, 543 U.S. 405 (2005).
70. *Arizona* v. *Gant*, 07-542 (2009).
71. *Texas v. Brown*, 460 U.S. 730 (1983).
72. *Oliver v. U.S.*, 466 U.S. 170 (1984).
73. *California v. Ciraolo*, 476 U.S. 207 (1986).
74. *New York v. Class*, 54 LW 4178 (1986).
75. *Arizona v. Hicks*, 55 LW 4258 (1987).

76. *Schneckloth v. Bustamonte*, 412 U.S. 218 (1973).
77. *Bumper v. North Carolina*, 391 U.S. 543 (1968).
78. *Stoner v. California*, 376 U.S. 483 (1964).
79. *Georgia v. Randolph*, 126 S.Ct. 1515 (2006).
80. *Olmstead v. U.S.*, 277 U.S. 438 (1928).
81. *Katz v. U.S.*, 389 U.S. 347 (1967).
82. *Berger v. New York*, 388 U.S. 41 (1967).
83. *Lee v. U.S.*, 343 U.S. 747 (1952).
84. *U.S. v. Karo*, 468 U.S. 705 (1984).
85. *U.S. v. Wade*, 388 U.S. 218 (1967).
86. *Kirby v. Illinois*, 406 U.S. 682 (1972).
87. *Foster v. California*, 394 U.S. 440 (1969).
88. *U.S. v. Dionisio*, 410 U.S. 1 (1973).
89. Kaplan, Skolnick, and Feeley, *Criminal Justice*, pp. 219–20.
90. Ibid., pp. 220–21.
91. *Spano v. New York*, 360 U.S. 315 (1959).
92. *Escobedo v. Illinois*, 378 U.S. 478 (1964).
93. *Miranda v. Arizona*, 384 U.S. 436 (1966).
94. *Berkemer v. McCarty*, 468 U.S. 420 (1984).
95. *Arizona v. Roberson*, 486 U.S. 675 (1988).
96. *Edwards v. Arizona*, 451 U.S. 477 (1981).
97. *Maryland* v. *Shatzer*, No. 08-680 (February 24, 2010).
98. Ibid., at p. 13.
99. *Michigan v. Mosley*, 423 U.S. 93 (1975).
100. *Colorado v. Connelly*, 479 U.S. 157 (1986).
101. *Colorado v. Spring*, 479 U.S. 564 (1987).
102. *Connecticut v. Barrett*, 479 U.S. 523 (1987).
103. *Duckworth v. Eagan*, 109 S.Ct. 2875 (1989).
104. *Davis v. U.S.*, 114 S.Ct. 2350 (1994).
105. *Berghuis* v. *Thompkins*, No 08-1470 (June 2010); also see Adam Liptak, "Mere Silence Doesn't Invoke *Miranda*, Justices Say," *New York Times*, www.nytimes.com/2010/06/02/us/02scotus.html?ref=adam_liptak (accessed July 30, 2010).
106. *Sherman v. U.S.*, 356 U.S. 369 (1958).
107. *U.S. v. Russell*, 411 U.S. 423 (1973).
108. *Hampton v. U.S.*, 425 U.S. 484 (1976).
109. Ibid., at 1540.
110. *Powell v. Alabama*, 287 U.S. 45 (1932).
111. *Gideon v. Wainwright*, 372 U.S. 335 (1963).
112. *Argersinger v. Hamlin*, 407 U.S. 25 (1973).
113. *Escobedo v. Illinois*, 378 U.S. 478 (1964).
114. Smith and Pollack, *Criminal Justice*, p. 177.
115. *Rhode Island v. Innis*, 446 U.S. 291 (1980).
116. *Arizona v. Mauro*, 481 U.S. 520 (1987).

117. *McNeil v. Wisconsin*, 59 LW 4636 (June 13, 1991).
118. *Minnick v. Mississippi*, 59 LW 4037 (1990).
119. *Melendez-Diaz* v. *Mass.*, No. 07-591 (June 2009).
120. *Padilla* v. *Kentucky* (No. 08-651), 253 S. W. 3d 482 (March 2010).
121. Arnold Binder, Gilbert Geis, and Dickson Bruce, *Juvenile Delinquency: Historical, Cultural, Legal Perspectives* (New York: Macmillan, 1988), pp. 6–9.
122. *Kent v. U.S.*, 383 U.S. 541 (1966).
123. *In Re Gault*, 387 U.S. 9 (1967).
124. *In Re Winship*, 397 U.S. 358 (1970).
125. *McKeiver v. Pennsylvania*, 403 U.S. 528 (1971).
126. *Breed v. Jones*, 421 U.S. 519 (1975).
127. *Roper v. Simmons*, 543 U.S. 551 (2005).

Civil Liability

Civil Liability

FAILING THE PUBLIC TRUST

All men are liable to error; and most men are . . . under temptation to it.

—John Locke

Where laws end, tyranny begins.

—William Pitt

Getty Images Inc.—Stone Allstock

Learning Objectives

AS A RESULT OF READING THIS CHAPTER, THE STUDENT WILL:

- Be able to explain the incidence, expense, and benefits of lawsuits against the police
- Understand the legal definition of a frivolous lawsuit
- Know several fundamental terms and concepts relating to liability
- Understand the meaning and uses of U.S. Code Title 42, Section 1983, and types of police actions that are vulnerable to Section 1983 claims
- Be able to explain how police officers might be held criminally liable for their misconduct
- Know how police facilities may bring about police liability
- Understand the areas of police liability in vehicle pursuits
- Know how police supervisors may be held liable for their inaction or their officers' misconduct
- Understand some of the liability issues related to computer evidence

Introduction

A police sergeant once commented to the author, "The decision-making process is not directed by the question 'Is it right or wrong?' but rather 'How much will it cost us if we're sued?'" While that may be a bit overstated or in jest, the specter of lawsuits certainly looms large over police officers, their supervisors, and their unit of government; however, we will see that civil liability has arguably provided a number of benefits to policing. This chapter focuses on this omnipresent facet of contemporary police work, discussing civil liability from a number of perspectives, and it cannot be overstated how important it is for students of criminal justice and in-service police personnel to know and understand this indispensable aspect of policing. To assist in this endeavor, dozens of examples and actual court cases are provided.

Policing is a challenging occupation. The police must enforce the laws, perform welfare tasks, protect the innocent, and attempt to prevent crime. They see people at their worst and participate each year in tens of thousands of arrests, searches, seizures, major incidents (such as hostage situations), and high-speed pursuits. They make split-second decisions, and they function as custodians of offenders in local jails. Perhaps no other occupation, with the exception of medicine, is as vulnerable to legal attack for the actions of its practitioners. Some observers even believe that community-oriented policing and problem solving (COPPS) could lead to an increase in civil liability filings because of the greater degree of involvement of police in the lives of citizens.[1]

The chapter begins by discussing the incidence, expense, benefits, and sometimes frivolous nature of lawsuits against the police. Next, with an eye toward helping readers develop a better comprehension of liability, is an overview of a number of basic terms and concepts. We then analyze the legal history of the major tool that is used against the police by citizens who believe the police have violated their constitutional rights: U.S. Code Title 42, Section 1983; included here is a comprehensive discussion, with many examples, of the kinds of police actions that foster liability suits. The liability of supervisors who fail to control their personnel is then reviewed. Finally, other areas of potential liability are examined: duty of care, failure to protect, vehicle pursuits, and computer evidence. The chapter concludes with a summary, key terms, review questions, and several scenarios and activities that provide opportunities to learn by doing.

Incidence, Expense, Benefits, and Nature of Lawsuits

The police are not irrationally paranoid when it comes to their being sued—to some officers, it probably seems to be a contemporary rite of passage or a fact of life that one "isn't really a cop" unless he or she has been sued. There is some basis in fact for this belief: Between 1980 and 2005, federal court decisions involving lawsuits against the police nearly tripled, and according to one study, the police are currently faced with more than thirty thousand civil actions annually.[2] Yet this number might seem small given that the police have millions of interactions with citizens each day.

The cost of civil suits against police can be quite high. For example, according to one study, from 1990 to 1999 Los Angeles paid in excess of $67.8 million in judgments and settlements in eighty lawsuits targeting police use of excessive force as well as police officers involved in sexual assault, sexual abuse, molestation, and domestic violence. This amount does not include the millions of dollars the city spent defending itself against any civil suits or lawsuits stemming from the Rampart Division scandal of the late 1990s,[3] during which a former Los Angeles Police Department (LAPD) officer testified that he and other officers routinely lied in court, stole and resold drugs, beat handcuffed suspects in the police station, and killed unarmed people and then planted guns and drugs on them; dozens of lawsuits were filed.[4]

Facing potential judgments amounting to millions of dollars, municipalities are forced to secure liability insurance to protect against civil litigation—insurance that is very expensive. But such expenditures are necessary: The cost of an average jury award of liability against a municipality is reported to be about $2 million.[5] In an attempt to prevent such large judgments, many cities and their insurers have made it a routine practice to settle many claims of police misconduct out of court as opposed to having a jury give the plaintiff(s) a large award. A U.S. Justice Department study of Los Angeles County (not including the LAPD) found that county officials, in settling sixty-one police misconduct cases, paid plaintiffs between $20,000 and $1.75 million per case.[6]

Such litigation, although costly in terms of both money and police morale, does have beneficial effects. Proponents of civil liabilities argue that these lawsuits keep the police accountable, give real meaning to citizens' rights, foster better police training, and can force police agencies to correct any deficiencies and review all policies, practices, and customs.[7]

It would be understandable if some officers felt that most (if not all) such lawsuits are frivolous in nature, merely an attempt to gain revenue from the officer(s) or jurisdiction defending against the suit; however, their perception of what constitutes a **frivolous lawsuit** may be very different from the legal definition: that it lacks an arguable basis in law or fact.[8] In fact, frivolous lawsuits against the police are quite rare. A study of published cases by the federal district courts indicates that less than 0.5 percent of those cases resulted in a judicial sanction against plaintiffs for cases that clearly lacked merit.[9]

Basic Terms and Concepts

Laws are enacted in three ways: by legislation, by regulation, and by court decision. Statutes and ordinances are laws passed by legislative bodies, such as the U.S. Congress, state legislatures, county commissions, and city councils. These bodies sometimes create a general outline of the laws they enact, leaving to a particular governmental agency the authority to fill in the details of the law through rules and regulations. During the past two decades, administrative rules and regulations constituted one of the fastest-growing bodies of new law.

When the solution to a legal dispute cannot be found in the existing body of law—statutes, rules, or regulations—judges must rely on prior decisions that their own or other courts have made on similar issues. These judicial decisions are known as **stare decisis** (meaning "let the decision stand"), and the judges who follow them are said to be relying on precedent. Of course, prior court decisions can be overruled or modified by a higher court or by the passage of new legislation. Furthermore, judges sometimes create their own tests to fairly resolve an issue. Statutes, judicial decisions, and tests may differ greatly from state to state; therefore, it is important for lawyers and criminal justice practitioners to read and understand the laws as they apply in their own jurisdictions.

It is also important to have a basic understanding of **tort liability**, a tort being an injury inflicted on one person by another. Three categories of torts generally cover most of the lawsuits filed against criminal justice practitioners: negligence, intentional torts, and constitutional torts.

Negligence arises when a police officer's conduct creates a danger to others; in other words, the officer did not conduct his or her affairs in a manner so as to avoid subjecting others to a risk of harm. The officer will be held liable for the injuries caused to others through his or her negligent acts. The law recognizes various levels or degrees of negligence: simple, gross, and willful or criminal negligence. Simple negligence involves a reasonable act performed by a reasonable officer in the scope of employment but performed without due care; the result is usually a charge of mental pain and anguish, for which an employer or an insurance company will pay damages. Gross negligence involves an unreasonable act for which damages for mental pain and anguish will be paid by either the employer (if the officer's acts were within the scope of employment) or the officer. Willful or criminal negligence involves an intentional act rather than negligence; the plaintiff will receive actual damages, mental pain and anguish damages, and punitive damages. These damages will be paid by the officer involved; neither the employer nor the insurance company will be compelled to pay.[10]

Intentional torts occur when an officer engages in a voluntary act that had a substantial likelihood of resulting in injury to another; examples are assault and battery, false arrest and imprisonment, malicious prosecution, and abuse of process. **Constitutional torts** involve police officers' duty to recognize and uphold the constitutional rights, privileges, and immunities of others, and violations of these guarantees may subject officers to civil suits, most frequently brought in federal court under 42 U.S. Code Section 1983[11] (discussed later).

Allegations of false arrest, false imprisonment, criminal behavior (such as assault and battery), and police misconduct (invasion of privacy, negligence, defamation, and malicious prosecution) are examples of torts that are commonly brought against police officers.[12] False arrest is the arrest of a person without probable cause—an arrest that is made even though an ordinarily prudent person would not have concluded that a crime had been committed or that the person arrested had committed it. False imprisonment is the intentional illegal detention and confinement of a person in a specified area, including but not limited to jail. Most false arrest suits result in a false imprisonment charge as well, but a false imprisonment charge sometimes can follow a valid arrest. For example, the police might fail to release an arrested person after a proper bail or bond has been posted, they might delay the arraignment of an arrested person unreasonably, or they might fail to release a prisoner after they no longer have authority to hold him or her. "Brutality" is not a legal tort action per se; rather, charges must be made as a civil assault and/or battery.

A single act may also be a crime as well as a tort. For example, if Officer Smith, in an unprovoked attack, injures Citizen Jones, the state will attempt to punish Smith in a criminal action by sending him to prison or fining him or both. The state would have the burden of proof at a criminal trial, having to prove Smith guilty "beyond a reasonable doubt." Furthermore, Jones may sue Smith for money damages in a civil action for the personal injury he suffered. Jones would argue that Smith failed to carry out his duty to act reasonably and prudently and that this failure resulted in Jones's injury. This legal wrong, of course, is a tort; Jones would have the burden of proving Smith's acts were tortious by a "preponderance of the evidence"—a lower standard and thus easier to satisfy in civil court.

The U.S. system of government has both federal and state courts. Federal courts are intended to have somewhat limited jurisdiction and tend not to hear cases involving private (as opposed to public) controversies unless federal law is involved or both parties agree to have their dispute settled there. Thus most tort suits are filed in state courts. There are two means by which a federal court may acquire jurisdiction of police misconduct suits. The first is the predominant source of our later discussions, referred to as a "1983 suit," a name that is derived from the fact that the suits are brought under the provisions of Title 42, Section 1983, of the U.S. Code. The significant part of this statute and its legislative history follow.

The second means by which a federal court may assume jurisdiction over a police misconduct suit is to allege what some legal commentators call a ***Bivens* tort**, a name that derives from a 1971 case, *Bivens v. Six Unknown Named Agents of the Federal Bureau of Narcotics.*[13] The U.S. Supreme Court held that a civil suit based directly on the Fourth Amendment could be filed. In *Bivens*, federal narcotics agents conducted an illegal search, arrest, and interrogation, but a suit by the plaintiffs could not be filed under Section 1983 because that section covers only police agents acting under state law. Civil suits to recover damages for violations of constitutional rights by federal officers have thus become known as *Bivens* suits.

A suit may also be filed against an employer under the doctrine of **respondeat superior**, an old legal maxim meaning "let the master answer"; this doctrine is also termed **vicarious liability**. In sum, an employer is liable in certain instances for the wrongful acts of its employee. It is generally inapplicable if a jury determines that the employee's negligent or malicious acts were outside the legitimate scope of the employer's authority. Although U.S. courts have expanded the extent to which employers can be sued for the torts of their employees, the courts are still reluctant to extend this doctrine to police supervisors (sergeants and lieutenants) and administrators. The courts realize that, first of all, police supervisors have little discretion in hiring decisions. Second, the duties of police officers are largely established by the governmental authority that hired them rather than by their supervisors. However, if a supervisor has abused his or her authority, was present when the misconduct occurred and did nothing to stop it, or otherwise participated in the misconduct, he or she can be held liable for the tortious behavior of his or her officers.[14] (This issue is discussed at greater length later in this chapter.)

Another issue that involves the question of who may be sued involves immunity and whether police departments and the employing governmental unit can be sued for damages caused by police misconduct. Under common law, the government could not be sued because the king could do no wrong. This doctrine, known as **sovereign immunity**, was also adopted in 1795 in the Eleventh Amendment to the U.S. Constitution, which states, "The judicial power of the United States shall not be construed to extend to any suit in law or equity, commenced or prosecuted against one of the United States by citizens of another state, or by citizens or subjects of any foreign state." This amendment therefore bars suits against states, state agencies, and instrumentalities in federal courts; the Supreme Court has also said it bars suits by citizens of the same state.[15]

Municipal governments, however, do not enjoy the same protection since they are creations of state laws and, as such, are not truly "sovereigns." Thus, they do not enjoy blanket immunity and are only cloaked with immunity to the extent that the state sees fit to do so.[16]

Section 1983 Litigation

History and Escalation

Prior to discussing specific kinds and examples of civil litigation against the police and their supervisors, it is prudent to first gain an understanding of a major legal instrument that is used by citizens against the police when they feel the police have acted in such a manner as to violate their individual rights: U.S. Code Title 42, **Section 1983**.

In the years following the Civil War, Congress, in reaction to the states' inability to control the Ku Klux Klan's lawlessness, enacted the Ku Klux Klan Act of 1871. This was later codified as Title 42, Section 1983, of the U.S. Code. Its statutory language is as follows:

> Every person who, under color of any statute, ordinance, regulation, custom, or usage of any State or Territory, subjects, or causes to be subjected, any citizen of the United States or any other person within the jurisdiction thereof to the deprivation of any rights, privileges, or immunities secured by the Constitution and laws, shall be liable to the party injured in an action at law, suit in equity, or other proper proceeding for redress.

This legislation was intended to provide civil rights protection to all persons protected under the act when a defendant acted "under color of any statute" (misused power of office). It was also meant to provide an avenue to the federal courts for relief of alleged civil rights violations.

The original intent of the law did not include police misconduct litigation. In fact, the law was virtually ignored for ninety years until the U.S. Supreme Court's 1961 decision in *Monroe v. Pape*,[17] where thirteen members of the Chicago Police Department broke into a home without a warrant, forced the family out of bed at gunpoint, made them stand naked while the officers ransacked the house, and subjected the family to verbal and physical abuse. The plaintiffs (Monroe and his family) claimed that the officers acted "under color of law" as set forth in Section 1983, thus violating their constitutional rights. The U.S. Supreme Court agreed, holding the officers liable.

There was a virtual boom of Section 1983 suits from 1967 through 1976.[18] Several factors contributed to this surge in Section 1983 actions. First, some lawyers believe that clients receive more competent judges and juries in the federal forum than in state courts because federal judges, who are appointed for life, may be less concerned about the political ramifications of their decisions than locally elected judges often are. Also, federal prosecutors may be more aggressive in arguing to jurors from a multicounty area, whereas local prosecutors must argue to jurors who elected them and who may know the defendant-officer. Furthermore, federal rules of pleading and evidence are uniform, federal procedures of discovery are more liberal, and lawyers have easier access to published case law in assisting them to prepare a federal suit.[19] Just as important, Congress passed Section 1988 of the Civil Rights Act in 1976, which allows attorney's fees to the prevailing party over and above the award for compensatory and punitive damages, meaning that a plaintiff's verdict in a police shooting case can be quite profitable.

Also, in 1978, in *Monell v. Department of Social Services,*[20] the Supreme Court held that Congress, in the 1871 act, *did* intend that municipalities and other local governments be included as "persons" to whom Section 1983 applies. Local governing bodies and corporate "persons," therefore, can be sued for damages under Section 1983 if such deprivation was the direct result of an official policy or custom of a local unit of government.

Defenses and immunities against Section 1983 suits exist, however. The states themselves, for example, are granted absolute immunity from Section 1983 suits,[21] as are judges, prosecutors, legislators, and federal officials. Federal officials usually act under color of federal law, as opposed to state law, as specified in the act. Police officers are granted **qualified immunity**, meaning that as long as they acted in good faith and their conduct was reasonable, they have a defense. Over the years, the courts have struggled to develop a test for what is meant by "good faith." In 1975, the Supreme Court developed a test that considered both what the officer's state of mind was at the time of the act in question (the subjective element) and whether the officer's act violated clearly established legal rights (the objective element).[22] Overzealous conduct that is not undertaken in good faith and that occurs without regard for the rights of citizens can and will result in a finding of liability.

Police Actions Leading to Section 1983 Liability

Following are some cases based on Section 1983 liability:

- In 1991, Los Angeles motorist Rodney King was beaten following a pursuit by police officers, an incident that was captured on an eighty-one-second videotape that captured the nation's attention. He was awarded $3.8 million.[23]
- In 1995, federal law enforcement officers at Ruby Ridge, Idaho, used deadly force to seize two citizens, resulting in the federal government's agreement to pay survivors almost $4 million because of unconstitutional use of deadly force. That same year, a federal jury awarded Ramona Africa, the sole survivor of a bombing of her residence by Philadelphia police, $1.5 million (the police had dropped explosives into the home of a radical group trying to make members leave their home). The bombing destroyed sixty-one other homes and killed eleven people, and the total cost to the city exceeded $59 million.[24]
- A jury acquitted four New York police officers of criminal charges in the shooting death of Amadou Diallo. The officers had mistaken Diallo's wallet for a gun and opened fire, discharging forty-one rounds and striking him nineteen times. His parents were awarded $3 million in a settlement with the city.[25]
- Abner Louima was sexually assaulted with a toilet plunger by New York City police officers, a case that resulted in an $8.8 million settlement.[26]

The common thread in all these highly publicized cases (other than the fact that all involved an unconstitutional use of force by the police) was that they used U.S. Code Title 42, Section 1983.

As suggested, Section 1983 is an appropriate legal tool for citizens who believe they have been victims of police brutality. In *Jennings v. City of Detroit*,[27] a twenty-two-year-old single African-American man was permanently paralyzed following a beating at a police station; the jury award was $8 million (settled for $3.5 million). In *Gilliam v. Falbo*,[28] the U.S. District Court for Ohio awarded $72,000 to a young man beaten by two officers, and in *Haygood v. City of Detroit*,[29] a thirty-five-year-old plaintiff was awarded $2.5 million in punitive damages and $500,000 in compensatory damages after being subjected to racial slurs, beaten, and chained to a bed for twelve hours (charges against the officers were never filed).

Even off-duty activities may get police officers into serious difficulty for acting "under color of law." Part-time work as security guards often opens the door to legal problems. In *Carmelo v. Miller*,[30] two off-duty officers were working security at a baseball game. They received information that someone was displaying a gun and stopped a man who fit the description. The officers searched, arrested, beat, and kicked the suspect and his companion. No gun was found in the area, and one of the beaten men required medical treatment. The officers were found liable. In *Stengel v. Belcher*,[31] an off-duty officer entered a bar carrying a .32-caliber handgun (which he was required to carry off duty at all times) and a can of Mace. An altercation broke out, and without identifying himself the officer got involved, killing two men and seriously wounding another. The plaintiffs recovered $800,000 in compensatory damages.

Clearly, the use of off-duty weapons and policies requiring that they be carried pose a risk of liability. In *Bonsignore v. New York*,[32] a mentally unstable twenty-three-year veteran police officer shot his wife five times and then killed himself, using a .32-caliber pistol that departmental policy required him to carry when off duty. Evidence produced at trial demonstrated that Officer Bonsignore's unsuitability for police duties was well known by the department—it had even provided him a limited-duty assignment as station house janitor—yet the police code of silence protected him. The jury awarded Mrs. Bonsignore nearly a half million dollars.

Suits involving **wrongful death** are also becoming more frequent, and the following cases illustrate how the law applies in this regard. In *Prior v. Woods*,[33] a twenty-four-year-old man was killed outside his home by police officers who mistook him for a burglar; the jury awarded his estate $5.75 million. In *Burkholder v. City of Los Angeles*,[34] a Los Angeles police officer killed a man in his early twenties who, while naked and under the influence of drugs, was climbing a light pole (the man had seized the officer's club but had not struck the officer). The jury awarded $450,000 in damages and $150,000 in attorney's fees to his survivors.

Generally, police officers are not liable for damages under Section 1983 for merely arresting someone, but that protective shroud vanishes if the plaintiff proves the officer was negligent or violated an established law or right (as in cases of false arrest). As an illustration, in *Murray v. City of Chicago*,[35] Murray's purse and checkbook were stolen; she reported the theft to the police. Later, some of the stolen checks were cashed (by another party) and Murray was arrested; she appeared in court and cleared up the matter, explaining that she had been the victim, and all charges were dropped. Several months later, she was arrested again at her home by Chicago officers who used an invalid arrest warrant that was related to the earlier mix-up. Murray was taken to the police station, strip-searched by male officers, and detained for six hours before being released. The federal court ruled that the officers acted in good faith but that if the policy or custom of the city was shown to have encouraged such unwarranted arrests, the city could be held liable.

Search and seizure, an especially complicated area of criminal procedure, is ripe for Section 1983 suits, primarily because of the ambiguous nature of the probable cause doctrine. In *Duncan v. Barnes*,[36] police officers obtained a warrant to search a suspect's home for heroin and executed the warrant in early morning hours. With guns drawn, officers entered two bedrooms, forcing the two females and one male inside to stand nude, spread-eagled against a wall, while their rooms were searched. Soon the officers realized that they had entered the wrong apartment, and they left the apartment in total disarray. The occupants, students at a court-reporting school, were so upset that they missed classes for two weeks; as a result, their certification and employment as court reporters were delayed. The court had little difficulty finding that the officers had acted in an unreasonable manner.

Negligence by police officers is another cause of action under Section 1983. Negligence can be found in the supervision and training of personnel, among other things. In *Sager v. City of Woodland Park*,[37] an officer accidentally killed a person when the shotgun he was pointing at the head of the prisoner discharged while the officer was attempting to handcuff the prisoner with his other hand. At trial, the officer stated that he had seen the technique in a police training film. The training officer, however, testified that the film was intended to show how *not* to handcuff a prisoner; unfortunately, none of the trainers had made that important distinction to the class, so the court ruled that improper training resulted in the prisoner's death. In *Popow v. City of Margate*,[38] an innocent bystander was killed on his front porch at night by a police officer engaged in foot pursuit, and the court held the city negligent because the officer had had no training on night firing, shooting at moving targets, or using firearms in a residential area.

The accompanying Career Profile addresses the very weighty matter of police civil liability.

Criminal Prosecutions for Police Misconduct

Whereas Section 1983 is a civil statute, Title 18, **Section 242**, of the U.S. Code makes it a *criminal* offense for any person acting willfully "under color of law," statute, regulation, or custom to deprive any person of the rights and privileges guaranteed under the Constitution and laws of the United States. This law, like Section 1983, dates from the post–Civil War era and applies to all people regardless of race, color, or national origin. Section 242 applies not only to police officers but also to other public officials; prosecutions of judges, bail-bond agents, public defenders, and even prosecutors are possible under the statute.

CAREER PROFILE

Name: Samuel G. Chapman

Degrees: Bachelor's and master's, criminology, University of California, Berkeley

What CJ-related jobs have you held?

Consultant on police functions and use of police dogs; professor emeritus, University of Oklahoma; Assistant Director, President's Commission on Law Enforcement and the Administration of Justice, Washington, D.C.; Chief, Multnomah County Sheriff's Office, Portland, Oregon; police officer, Berkeley, California

As a long-time police practitioner, university professor, and expert witness, what advice do you have concerning police liability?

Police departments must take civil rights litigation seriously. Actually, civil rights lawsuits are seen by many as an occupational hazard in policing.

When a lawsuit has been filed, the allegations should be evaluated by the government's attorneys. Fact-finding may disclose that the allegations appear to have little merit. It could be that the lawsuit is of dubious substance, really seeking what is called a "convenience settlement"—a defendant's paying the plaintiff a dollar amount less than what the defendant's costs would be to prepare for trial. But if after fact-finding it appears that the department and its officers are culpable, the defense team should start settlement negotiations early. The defense should make a meaningful offer, keeping it in the range of settlements for cases of a similar sort elsewhere.

At the same time, the defense (both the government and the officer) must commence their discovery, with the goal of minimizing loss should the case eventually go to trial. Settlements that occur just before trial are invariably costly. The defense team should also evaluate the courtroom record of the plaintiff's law firm and opposing attorneys, since some firms are more competent than others.

Fact-finding will often indicate that a case is realistically defensible. If so, the defense team may decide to reject a convenience settlement and prepare for trial. This will cause the plaintiffs to evaluate whether to expend resources and time in pursuing a case that they are not likely to win. When the defense decides to stand up and fight, it establishes the jurisdiction as a "hard target" and sends a message that lawsuits with little merit are going to be forcefully defended.

Whoever is named to defend officers and police agencies must be skilled in handling civil rights cases. It is a grave mistake for the government to take a "bargain basement" approach by assigning staff attorneys who have little or no experience working with these highly technical types of litigation.

The police can fight back by suing those who sue them, but this means hiring counsel, which is expensive. And even if the lawsuit is successful and brings a dollar judgment against the defendant, such a defendant is usually poor and thus unable to meet any financial judgment levied against him or her.

The government's best defense against an adverse judgment in a civil rights lawsuit is to thoroughly train and regularly retrain its police personnel, and to supervise them well. Also, the police department's rules, regulations, policies, and procedures must be kept current. Then, if officers perform as trained and properly under departmental guidelines, a persuasive defense can be mounted against any allegations of misconduct.

An example of the use of Section 242 is the murder of a drug courier by two U.S. customs agents while the agents were assigned to the San Juan International Airport. The courier flew to Puerto Rico to deposit approximately $700,000 in cash and checks into his employer's account. He was last seen being interviewed by the two customs agents in the airport; ten days later, his body was discovered in a Puerto Rico rain forest. An investigation revealed that the agents had lured the victim away from the airport and had murdered him for his money, later disposing of the body. They were convicted under Section 242 and related federal statutes, and each agent was sentenced to a prison term of 120 years.[39]

Liability of Police Supervisors

Review: *Police Liability.*

Negligent supervision and direction of officers involve a breach of a duty to provide effective systems for the evaluation, control, and monitoring of police employees' performance. This breach of duty may come in the form of failure to provide written and verbal directives, to develop adequate policies and guidelines, or to articulate clearly to employees how duties are to be performed. It may also involve a supervisor's direction to an employee to engage in an illegal activity or the supervisor's approval of an illegal activity.[40] In such cases, Section 1983 allows for a finding of personal liability on the part of police supervisory personnel.

McClelland v. Facteau,[41] a Section 1983 suit against a state police agency chief as well as a local police chief, was such a case. McClelland was stopped by Officer Facteau (a state employee) for speeding. He was taken to the city jail; there he was not allowed to make any phone calls, he was questioned but not advised of his rights, and he was beaten and injured by Facteau in the presence of two city police officers. McClelland sued, claiming that the two police chiefs were directly responsible for his treatment and injuries due to their failure to properly train and supervise their subordinates. Evidence was produced of prior misbehavior by Facteau. The court ruled that the chiefs could be held liable if they knew of prior misbehavior yet did nothing about it.

Another related case was that of *Brandon v. Allen*.[42] In this case, two teenagers who were parked in a "lovers' lane" were approached by an off-duty police officer, Allen, who showed his police identification and demanded that the boy exit the car. Allen struck the boy with his fist and stabbed him with a knife; then he attempted to break into the car where the girl was seated. The boy was able to reenter the car and manage an escape. As the two teenagers sped off, Allen fired a shot at them with his revolver, and the shattered windshield glass severely injured the youths to the point that they required plastic surgery. Allen was convicted of criminal charges, and the police chief was also sued under Section 1983. The plaintiffs charged that the chief and others knew of Allen's reputation for being mentally unstable (none of the other police officers wanted to ride in a patrol car with him). At least two formal charges of misconduct had been filed previously, yet the chief had failed to take any remedial action or even to review the disciplinary records of officers. The court called this behavior "unjustified inaction," held the police department liable, and allowed the plaintiffs' damages. The U.S. Supreme Court upheld this judgment.[43]

Police supervisors have also been found liable for injuries arising out of an official policy or custom of their department. Injuries resulting from a chief's verbal or written support of heavy-handed behavior resulting in excessive force by officers have resulted in such liability.[44]

Today's police supervisors are definitely in a "need to know" position where the law is concerned. They are caught in the middle: Not only can they be sued for improper hiring, training, and supervision of their officers, but other civil rights laws can be used by officers who believe they were improperly disciplined or terminated. Indeed, Section 1983 can also be used by unsuccessful job applicants if they can show that the administrator's tests were not job related, included inherent bias, or were not properly administered or graded. The same holds true if it can be shown that proper testing methods were not used in the promotion or the discipline or firing of personnel. Police supervisors have lost in suits in which they disciplined male and female officers who were having a private relationship,[45] in which they disciplined African-American officers who removed the U.S. flag from their uniforms to protest perceived discriminatory acts by the city,[46] and in which they disciplined officers for "improper" political party membership.[47]

Other Areas of Potential Liability

Next we look at several interrelated areas in which liability on the part of the police may be found if they fail to perform their duties properly, perform them in a negligent manner, make poor decisions, or abuse their authority.

Duty of Care

While citizens often speak of the broad police duty to serve and protect their community, their lives, and their property, a legal duty is very specific and more limited. This doctrine of **duty of care** is derived from common law and holds that police have no duty to protect the general public from harm, absent a special kind of relationship (discussed below). The Supreme Court addressed this doctrine in 1856 in *South v. Maryland*,[48] a case in which a sheriff was sued for refusing to protect a citizen from injuries inflicted from a violent crowd. The court said that peace officers protect the general public, not specific individuals. Since *South,* the doctrine of duty of care has been adopted at the state and federal levels, with most courts ruling that the state is not required to provide police services.[49] This may come as a surprise to many people, but the legal view is that police can only act once a crime is or has already been committed and that they cannot be held liable for failure to arrive in time to save any particular individual from harm unless the victim has a special relationship with the police, such as a protected witness. There are neither sufficient resources nor enough police to act as personal bodyguards for every citizen, twenty-four hours a day. No duty of care exists unless it is established that the agency owed a special duty to the injured party.

Police legal duties can arise from many sources, including laws, customs, court decisions, and agency policies. As examples, a state statute prohibiting drunk driving might also order the police to arrest any persons operating motor vehicles while under the influence of intoxicants, and a police department policy in the same state may require officers who stop such suspected motor vehicle operators to perform field sobriety tests at the scene of the traffic stop.[50]

Special Relationships

Special relationships are those where the officer knows or has reason to know the likelihood of harm to someone if he or she fails to do his or her duty; they are thus defined by the circumstances surrounding an injury or damage. A special relationship can be based on the following three areas:

1. Whether the officer could have foreseen that he or she was expected to take action in a given situation to prevent injury is one consideration.[51] (For example,

a police officer failed to remove an intoxicated operator of a motor vehicle from a highway.)

2. Departmental policies or guidelines that prohibit a certain course of action are also examined.[52] (For example, when a drunk driver killed another driver, the court noted that the police department had a standard operating procedure manual that mandated that an intoxicated individual who would likely do physical injury to himself or others "*will* be taken into protective custody.")
3. Spatial and temporal proximity of the defendant-officer's behavior to the injury damage is another factor.[53] (For example, an individual was arrested for drunk driving, taken into custody, found to have a 0.166 blood alcohol level, and released three hours later, then had a fatal car accident.)

Proximate Cause

Related to the duty of care and liabilities of the police is the matter of **proximate cause**. Once a plaintiff has demonstrated the existence of a police duty of care and has shown the officer breached that duty, he or she must still prove that the officer's conduct was the proximate cause of the injury or damage. Proximate cause is established by asking "But for the officer's conduct, would the plaintiff have sustained the injury or damage?" If the answer to this question is no, then proximate cause is established, and the officer can be held liable for the damage or injury. This requirement of negligence limits liabilities, however, in situations where damage would have occurred regardless of the officer's behavior.[54] For example, an officer is involved in a high-speed chase, and the offending driver strikes an innocent third party. Generally, if the officer did not act in a negligent fashion and did not cause the injury, there would be no liability on the officer's part.[55]

Proximate cause may be found in such cases as when an officer leaves the scene of an accident aware of dangerous conditions (spilled oil, smoke, vehicle debris, stray animals) without proper warning to motorists.[56] In such a case, Louisiana state troopers responded to a one-car accident caused by an oil spill on a dangerous portion of the roadway. Initially, the troopers asked the state's department of transportation to cover the spill with sand and then ignited flares to warn oncoming motorists of the danger; the troopers then returned to other patrol duties. Soon the oil had absorbed the sand and the flares went out; then an unsuspecting motorcyclist slid on the oil, struck a tree, and died. The court held that the troopers breached their duty to provide warning to drivers of the danger and that this breach was the proximate cause of the motorcyclist's death.[57]

Persons in Custody

Courts generally recognize that police officers have a duty of care to persons in their custody.[58] This means that police officers have a legal responsibility to take reasonable precautions to ensure the health and safety of persons in their custody, keeping detainees free from harm, rendering medical assistance when necessary, and treating detainees humanely.[59] Custody is not restricted to those persons who are incarcerated, however; a duty of care is owed by the police, for example, to persons in their physical custody outside a jail setting, such as when arresting or transporting prisoners and mental patients or when holding persons in booking or interrogation areas regardless of whether they have been formally charged with a crime.[60]

This general duty of care to persons in police custody seldom results in liability for self-inflicted injury or suicide because these acts are normally considered to result from the detainee's own intentional conduct rather than from some form of police negligence.[61] There are exceptions to this rule, however.[62] Most courts, for example, have held that if a prisoner's suicide is "reasonably foreseeable," the jailer owes the prisoner a duty of care to help prevent that suicide. As the court stated in *Joseph v. State of Alaska* (where an intoxicated jail inmate hanged himself with a nylon cord not taken from his sweatpants at booking, and the jail's video camera lens had been obscured):

> While a prisoner's mental illness, intoxication, or other impairment may be the reasons why the jailer knows or should know that the prisoner is suicidal, other signs—such as declared intent to commit suicide—are also sufficient.[63]

If the suicidal tendencies of an inmate are known, the duty of care required of the custodian is elevated.[64] In such special cases, officers must ensure that measures are taken to prevent self-inflicted harm; included here are detainees who suffer from a disturbed state of mind and those who are impaired by drugs or alcohol. Duty of care to an impaired individual may include removing shoes, belts, clothing, and other articles from the detainee.[65]

Safe Facilities

Another area of police liability, one that involves both persons in custody and proximate cause, is the need to provide safe facilities. Courts have even considered the design of detention facilities as a source of negligence, such as in a Detroit case where the construction of a jail's holding cell did not allow officers to observe detainees' movements: The construction of the cell doors hampered detainee supervision, there were no electronic monitoring devices for observing detainees, and there was an absence of detoxification cells required under state department of corrections rules. Therefore, following a suicide in this facility, the court concluded that these conditions constituted building defects and were the proximate cause of the decedent's death.[66]

The need to provide a secure environment for detainees extends beyond the confines of the detention center. In a Delaware case, a constable used his private vehicle to transport mental patients and did not handcuff patients while in transport. One patient, who had declared his intention to kill himself, unfastened his seat belt, jumped out of the vehicle while it was in motion, and died. The court found that because the constable knew his vehicle was inadequate for such transports and did not restrain the patient or heed his intention to commit suicide, his misconduct constituted wantonness.[67]

Failure to Protect

A **failure to protect** may occur if a police officer neglects to protect a person from a known and foreseeable danger, a claim that most often involves battered women. However, other circumstances can create a duty to protect people from crime. Informants, witnesses, and other people dependent on the police can be a source of police liability if the police fail to take reasonable action to prevent victimization—officers' conduct cannot place a person in peril or demonstrate deliberate indifference for his or her safety.

For example, one morning Juan Penilla was on the porch of his home and became seriously ill. His neighbors called 911, and two police officers arrived first. They found him to be in grave need of medical care, cancelled the request for paramedics, broke the lock and door jam on the front door of Penilla's residence, moved him inside the house, locked the door, and left. The next day, family members found Penilla dead inside the house as a result of respiratory failure. His mother sued under Section 1983, and the court found that the officers' conduct clearly placed Penilla in a more dangerous position than the one in which they found him.[68] Another example is when the Green Bay, Wisconsin, Police Department released the tape of a phone call from an informant, which led to the informant's death.[69]

Vehicle Pursuits

You may be familiar with a 2007 decision by the U.S. Supreme Court regarding the proper level of deadly force that may be used by officers during vehicle pursuits. Still, the police must act reasonably in such instances or they may be found civilly liable. In this section, we discuss vehicle pursuits in more detail, including the kinds of actions by officers that may lead to their being civilly liable.

First, police officers are afforded no special privileges or immunities in the routine operation of their patrol vehicles.[70] Police officers driving in nonemergency situations do not have immunity for their negligence or recklessness and are held to the same standard of conduct as private citizens. When responding to emergency situations, however, officers are governed by statutes covering emergency vehicles.[71] In such circumstances, most jurisdictions afford the police limited immunity for violations of traffic laws; in other words, they are accorded some protections and privileges not given to private citizens and are permitted to take greater risks that would amount to negligence if undertaken by citizens.[72]

Few operational patrol issues are of greater concern to police leadership than police pursuits because of the tremendous potential for injury, property damage, and liability that accompanies them. As one police procedure manual describes it, "The decision by a police officer to pursue a citizen in a motor vehicle is among the most critical that can be made."[73] Civil litigation arising out of collisions involving police pursuits reveals such pursuits to be high-stakes undertakings with serious and sometimes tragic results.[74] Indeed, several hundred people are killed each year during police pursuits,[75] and many of them are innocent third parties.

Pursuits place the police in a delicate balancing act. On one hand is the need for police to show criminals that flight from the law is no way to freedom. If a police agency completely bans high-speed pursuits, its credibility with both law-abiding citizens and law violators may suffer; public knowledge that the agency has a no-pursuit policy may encourage people to flee, decreasing the probability of apprehension.[76] Still, according to one observer, because of safety and liability concerns, "a growing number of agencies have the position that if the bad guy puts the pedal to the metal, it's a 'freebie.' They will not pursue him."[77]

On the other hand, there is indeed the high-speed threat to everyone within range of the pursuit, including suspects, their passengers, other drivers, and bystanders. One police trainer asks a simple question to help officers determine whether to continue a pursuit: "Is this person a threat to the public safety other than the fact the police are chasing him?" If the officers cannot objectively answer yes, the pursuit should be terminated.[78]

In May 1990, two Sacramento County, California, deputies responded to a call about a fight. At the scene, they observed a motorcycle with two riders approaching their vehicle at high speed. Turning on their red lights, the deputies ordered the driver to stop. The motorcycle operator began to elude the officers, who initiated a pursuit that reached speeds of more than a hundred miles per hour over about 1.3 miles. The pursuit ended when the motorcycle crashed; the deputies' vehicle could not stop in time and struck the bike's passenger, killing him. The passenger's family brought suit, claiming that the pursuit violated the crash victim's due process rights under the Fourteenth Amendment.

In *County of Sacramento v. Lewis*,[79] decided in May 1998, the U.S. Supreme Court held that the proper standard to be employed in these cases is whether the officer's conduct during the pursuit "shocks the conscience." (Was the conduct offensive to a reasonable person's sense of moral goodness?) The Court further determined that high-speed chases with no intent to harm suspects do not give rise to liability under the Fourteenth Amendment and therefore closed the door on liability for officers involved in pursuits that do not "shock the conscience." But the Court left unanswered many important questions, such as whether it will allow an innocent third party to file a claim against the police for damages and whether a municipality can be held liable for its failure to train officers in pursuit issues.

In sum, a pursuit is justified only when the necessity of apprehension outweighs the degree of danger created by the pursuit. Agencies generally require field supervisors (sergeants) to discontinue the pursuit when it is unjustified or becomes too dangerous.[80]

Computer Evidence

It is almost impossible to investigate a fraud, embezzlement, or child pornography case today without dealing with some sort of computer evidence. Even evidence in a homicide or narcotics case may be buried deep within a computer's hard drive. As a result, many police agencies have recruited self-taught "experts" to fill the role of computer evidence specialists. These specialists are usually highly motivated and have some knowledge of the rules of evidence and some experience in testifying in court. Other police agencies have enlisted the support of personnel at local universities or computer repair shops to help them with computer evidence.[81]

The increased exposure to computer evidence by people both inside and outside policing brings an increase in potential legal liabilities. For example, if a police agency seizes the computerized records of an ongoing business, there may be negative financial consequences for the business. If it can be shown that the police accidentally destroyed business records through negligence, a criminal investigation might well become the civil suit of the decade. Furthermore, if a seized computer contains a newsletter, a draft of a book, or any computer bulletin board system, there may be liability under the Privacy Protection Act.[82]

The risk of liability in such cases may be reduced substantially if police investigators follow generally accepted forensic computer evidence procedures. Guidelines approved by the Department of Justice's Computer Crime and Intellectual Property Section dictate how the police are to search, seize, and analyze computers. It is crucial that the police be trained in the proper procedures for handling computers as well as in the rules of evidence. The federal government has made computer evidence training a priority for federal, state, and local law enforcement officers.[83]

SUMMARY

This chapter examined the incidence, expense, benefits, and sometimes frivolous nature of lawsuits against the police; a number of basic terms and concepts that are ingrained in the area of civil liability; Section 1983, a major litigation tool that is used against the police by citizens who believe the police have violated their constitutional rights; the liability of supervisors who fail to control their personnel; and other areas of potential liability such as duty of care, failure to protect, vehicle pursuits, and computer evidence. Included were many examples of the kinds of police actions that foster liability lawsuits, police actions leading to liability, and new areas of potential police liability such as vehicle pursuits and computer evidence.

The weight and breadth of the chapter's litigated cases and decisions against police officers—and their organizations and cities or counties—speak for themselves. Perhaps what has been shown most unequivocally is that the consequences of failing to properly hire, train, and supervise police personnel can be quite costly, in both human and financial terms. The need is clear and present for officers to know and understand the law regarding liability, to always project themselves in the best possible light, and to conduct themselves in a manner that demonstrates that their behavior was a good-faith effort to do their job properly.

Americans know the police have a difficult job to do and are likely willing to accept less than perfect behavior from them, but the kinds of improper and illegal actions shown in this chapter simply cannot and will not be tolerated.

KEY TERMS

Bivens tort
constitutional torts
duty of care
failure to protect
frivolous lawsuit
intentional torts
negligence
negligent supervision
proximate cause
qualified immunity
respondeat superior
Section 242
Section 1983
sovereign immunity
special relationship
stare decisis
tort liability
vicarious liability
wrongful death

REVIEW QUESTIONS

1. What are the incidence and benefits of lawsuits against the police?
2. What is the legal definition of a frivolous lawsuit?
3. What is meant by negligence and Title 42, Section 1983, of the U.S. Code?
4. What caused an increase in Section 1983 lawsuits?
5. What are some types of police actions that are vulnerable to Section 1983 actions?
6. What is meant by duty of care and failure to protect?
7. How might police facilities and vehicles be involved in police liability?
8. What are the areas of civil liability in the area of police vehicle pursuits?
9. What are some examples of how police supervisors may be held criminally liable for their officers' misconduct?
10. What are some of the liability issues related to computer evidence?

LEARN BY DOING

1. Sergeant Tom Gresham is newly promoted and assigned to patrol on the graveyard shift; he knows each officer on his shift, and several of them are his close friends; you are his patrol lieutenant. Gresham was an excellent patrol officer and prides himself on his reputation and ability to get along with his peers. He believes that doing so will result in greater productivity from his officers, and he makes efforts to socialize with them after work. Gresham also believes that a supervisor should not "get in the way of good police work," and his officers say he is "a cop's cop." In his view, his duty shift officers perform very well, generating the highest number of arrests and citations in the entire department. Unfortunately, his shift is also generating the highest number of citizen complaints for abusive language and improper use of force. Gresham believes that such complaints are "the price of doing business." One Monday morning, Gresham is surprised at being summoned to your office. You show Gresham a substantial number of use-of-force

complaints lodged against his officers during the past two weeks while he was away on vacation. Despite your efforts to explain the gravity of the situation, Gresham fails to grasp the seriousness of the complaints and how his supervisory style may have contributed to them.

a. What do you believe are some of Sergeant Gresham's problems as a new supervisor? Could anything have been done *before* he assumed his new position to help him understand his role better?

b. As Gresham's superior officer, what advice would you give to him? Are there any other supervisory or command officers who you should ask to be involved in dealing with the situation?

c. What corrective action must Sergeant Gresham take immediately with his team of officers?

2. Independently employ a number of methods in order to get a good understanding of police liability, such as the following:
   - Interview a district attorney, judge, or private attorney who is experienced in matters involving police misconduct, or research the literature and news articles to determine the nature of civil suits and amounts of awards against the police, as well as what the police and citizens can do to avoid civil litigation.
   - Interview some police executives to determine what they are doing in terms of training and policies to minimize the chances of successful lawsuits against their officers.
   - Discuss with police practitioners the technical areas of their work in which they must be constantly be retrained and certified because of possible litigation and to avoid causing unnecessary harm to citizens (focusing on the weapons and tools they use).
   - Determine how local police attempt to protect themselves against lawsuits, such as with false arrest insurance, keeping abreast of court decisions involving police negligence, and so on.

mycrimekit™

Go to MyCrimeKit.com and discover additional study tools and resources related to this chapter.

- Key Terms
- Review Questions
  - Multiple Choice Questions
  - True/False
  - Fill in the Blank
  - Essay
- MEDIA REVIEW: where you can review the topic of *police liability.*
- FLASHCARDS: to test your knowledge of this chapter.

- NEW YORK TIMES: where you can read the latest articles related to criminology and criminal law.
- THE CAREER CENTER: where you can explore career opportunities in criminal justice and criminology.
- THE ONLINE RESEARCH LIBRARY: where you can explore the Cybrary and Research Navigator.

NOTES

1. See, for example, John L. Worrall and Otwin Marenin, "Emerging Liability Issues in the Implementation and Adoption of Community Oriented Policing," *Policing: An International Journal of Police Strategies and Management* 22 (1998): 121–136.
2. Isidore Silver, *Police Civil Liability* (New York: Matthew Bender, 2005), p. 4.
3. The Feminist Majority Foundation and the National Center for Women & Policing, "Gender Differences in the Cost of Police Brutality and Misconduct: A Content Analysis of LAPD Civil Liability Cases: 1990–1999," www.womenandpolicing.org/Excessive Force.asp?id=4516 (accessed August 2, 2010).
4. "LAPD Officers Take Stand in Rampart Scandal Trial," archives.cnn.com/2000/LAW/10/16/lapd.corruption.tria (accessed August 2, 2010).
5. Victor E. Kappeler, *Critical Issues in Police Civil Liability*, 4th ed. (Long Grove, IL: Waveland Press, 2005), p. 4.
6. Ibid., p. 11.
7. G. P. Alpert, R. G. Dunham, and M. S. Stroshine, *Policing: Continuity and Change* (Long Grove, IL: Waveland Press, 2006).
8. *Harper v. Showers*, 174 F.3d 716, 718 (5th Cir. 1999).
9. S. F. Kappeler and V. E. Kappeler, "A Research Note on Section 1983 Claims Against the Police: Cases Before the Federal District Courts in 1990," *American Journal of Police* 11 (1): 65–73.
10. H. E. Barrineau III, *Civil Liability in Criminal Justice* (Cincinnati, OH: Pilgrimage, 1987), p. 58.
11. Ibid., p. 5.
12. Charles R. Swanson, Leonard Territo, and Robert W. Taylor, *Police Administration: Structures, Processes, and Behavior*, 6th ed. (Upper Saddle River, NJ: Prentice Hall, 2005), p. 549.
13. *Bivens v. Six Unknown Named Agents of the Federal Bureau of Narcotics*, 403 U.S. 388, 29 L.Ed.2d 619, 91 S.Ct. 1999 (1971).
14. Swanson, Territo, and Taylor, *Police Administration*, pp. 438–439.
15. *Hans v. Louisiana*, 134 U.S. 1 (1890); also see "Sovereign Immunity," www.lectlaw.com/def2/s103.htm (accessed August 3, 2010).
16. Ibid.
17. *Monroe v. Pape*, 365 U.S. 167, 81 S.Ct. 473 (1961).

18. Wayne W. Schmidt, "Section 1983 and the Changing Face of Police Management," in *Police Leadership in America*, ed. William A. Geller (Chicago: American Bar Foundation, 1985), p. 228.
19. Ibid., p. 227.
20. *Monell v. Department of Social Services*, 436 U.S. 6587 (1978).
21. *Alabama v. Pugh*, 438 U.S. 781 (1978).
22. Swanson, Territo, and Taylor, *Police Administration*, p. 558.
23. Kappeler, *Critical Issues in Police Civil Liability*, p. 2.
24. J. R. Daughen, "Potential Cost of Philadelphia House-Bombing Incident Up to $59 Million," *Philadelphia Daily News*, April 14, 2005, p. B8.
25. Ibid.
26. T. Mauro, *The Legal Intelligencer*, *230*(5) (2000): 4.
27. *Jennings v. City of Detroit*, Wayne County Circuit Court, Michigan (August 1979).
28. *Gilliam v. Falbo*, U.S. District Court, Southern District of Ohio (April 1982).
29. *Haygood v. City of Detroit*, Wayne County Circuit Court, Michigan, No. 77-728013 (December 29, 1980).
30. *Carmelo v. Miller*, 569 S.W. 365 (1978).
31. *Stengel v. Belcher*, 522 F.2d 438 (6th Cir. 1975).
32. *Bonsignore v. New York*, 521 F. Supp. 394, aff'd., 683 F.2d 635 (2d Cir. 1982).
33. *Prior v. Woods*, U.S. District Court, (E.D. Michigan) (October 1981).
34. *Burkholder v. City of Los Angeles*, L.A. County Superior Court, California (October 1982).
35. *Murray v. City of Chicago*, 634 F.2d 365 (1980).
36. *Duncan v. Barnes*, 592 F.2d 1336 (1979).
37. *Sager v. City of Woodland Park*, 543 F. Supp. 282 (D. Colo. 1982).
38. *Popow v. City of Margate*, 476 F. Supp. 1237 (1979).
39. On appeal, the Section 242 convictions were vacated, as the victim was not an inhabitant of Puerto Rico; therefore, he enjoyed no protection under the U.S. Constitution. On resentencing in January 1991, the agents each received fifty years in prison for convictions of several other federal crimes under Title 18.
40. Kappeler, *Critical Issues in Police Civil Liability*, p. 29.
41. *McClelland v. Facteau*, 610 F.2d 693 (10th Cir. 1979).
42. *Brandon v. Allen*, 516 F. Supp. 1355 (W.D. Tenn. 1981).
43. *Brandon v. Holt*, 469 U.S. 464, 105 S.Ct. 873 (1985).
44. See, for example, *Black v. Stephens*, 662 F.2d 181 (1991).
45. See, for example, *Swope v. Bratton*, 541 F. Supp. 99 (W.D. Ark. 1982).
46. See, for example, *Leonard v. City of Columbus*, 705 F.2d 1299 (11th Cir. 1983).
47. See, for example, *Elrod v. Burns*, 427 U.S. 347 (1975).
48. *South v. Maryland*, 59 U.S. (18 How.) 396 (1856).
49. *Reiff v. City of Philadelphia*, 477 F. Supp. 1262 (E.D. Pa. 1979).
50. Kappeler, *Critical Issues in Police Civil Liability*, pp. 25–26.
51. *Irwin v. Ware*, 467 N.E.2d 1292 (1984).
52. *Fudge v. City of Kansas City*, 239 Kan. 369, 720 P.2d 1093 (1986), at 373.
53. *Kendrick v. City of Lake Charles*, 500 So.2d 866 (La. App. 1 Cir.1986).

54. Kappeler, *Critical Issues in Police Civil Liability*, p. 27.
55. *Fielder v. Jenkins*, 833 A.2d 906 (N.J. Super. A.D. 1993).
56. Silver, *Police Civil Liability*, p. 4; also see *Coco v. State*, 474 N.Y.S.2d 397 (Ct.Cl. 1984); and *Duvernay v. State*, 433 So.2d 254 (La. App. 1983).
57. *Naylor v. Louisiana Dept. of Public Highways*, 423 So.2d 674 (La. App. 1982).
58. *Joseph v. State of Alaska*, 26 P.3d 459 (2001).
59. *Thomas v. Williams*, 124 S.E.2d 409 (Ga. App. 1962).
60. *Morris v. Blake*, 552 A.2d 844 (Del. Super. 1988).
61. *Guice v. Enfinger*, 389 So.2d 270 (Fla. App. 1980).
62. *Manuel v. City of Jeanerette*, 702 So.2d 709 (La. App. 3 Cir. 1997).
63. *Joseph v. State of Alaska*, 26 P.3d 459 (2001), at 474.
64. *Saunders v. County of Steuben*, 693 N.E.2d 16 (Ind. 1998).
65. *Manuel v. City of Jeanerette*, 702 So.2d 709 (La. App. 3 Cir. 1997).
66. *Davis v. City of Detroit*, 386 N.W.2d 169 (Mich. App. 1986).
67. *Morris v. Blake*, 552 A.2d 844 (De. Super. 1988).
68. *Penilla v. City of Huntington Park*, 115 F.3d 707 (9th Cir., 1997).
69. *Monfils v. Taylor*, 165 F.3d 511 (7th Cir. 1998), cert. den., 528 U.S. 810 (1999).
70. *Seide v. State of Rhode Island*, 875 A.2d 1259 (2005).
71. Silver, *Police Civil Liability*, p. 8.
72. *Seide v. State of Rhode Island*, 875 A.2d 1259 (2005).
73. Tulsa, Oklahoma, Police Department, *Procedure Manual* (Ronald Palmer, chief of police), June 10, 1998, p. 1.
74. John Hill, "High-Speed Police Pursuits: Dangers, Dynamics, and Risk Reduction," *FBI Law Enforcement Bulletin* (July 2002): 14–18.
75. Voices Insisting on Pursuit Safety, "Facts and Statistics," www.pursuitsafety.org/mediakit/statistics.html (accessed August 3, 2010).
76. C. B. Eisenberg, "Pursuit Management," *Law and Order* (March 1999): 73–77.
77. A. Belotto, "Supervisors Govern Pursuits," *Law and Order* (January 1999): 86.
78. G. T. Williams, "When Do We Keep Pursuing? Justifying High-Speed Pursuits," *Police Chief* (March 1997): 24–27.
79. *County of Sacramento v. Lewis*, 118 S.Ct. 1708 (1998).
80. Oklahoma County Sheriff John Whetsel, quoted in Nicole Marshall, "Hot Pursuit," *Tulsa World*, June 15, 1998, p. A11.
81. Michael R. Anderson, "Reducing Computer Evidence Liability," *Government Technology* (February 1997): 24, 36.
82. Ibid.
83. Ibid.

Accountability

Accountability

ETHICS, USE OF FORCE, CORRUPTION, AND DISCIPLINE

The rain, it raineth on the just
And also on the unjust fella
But mainly on the just because
The unjust steals the just's umbrella.

—*Lord Charles Bowen's adaptation of a quote in the Book of Matthew*

But justice is inverted when those engines of the law,
Instead of pinching vicious men, keep honest ones in awe.

—*Daniel Defoe*

Superstock Royalty Free

Learning Objectives

As a result of reading this chapter, the student will:

- Understand what is meant by police accountability
- Be able to define ethics, including the principles of double effect, noble cause corruption, and the "Dirty Harry problem"
- Be able to delineate some of the unique ethical problems that community policing can pose
- Know how Packer's crime-control model and due process model are implicated in the matter of ethics
- Understand the uses and limits of police force and how a force continuum can help officers to gauge the appropriate use of force for different situations
- Know the types of police brutality
- Understand some factors that contribute to police violence
- Know what constitutes inappropriate use of force by the police
- Be able to define bias-based policing, and know how it can be addressed
- Be able to explain how and why police corruption began and what factors within both the community and policing seem to foster and maintain it
- Understand the constitutional limitations that federal courts have placed on officers' rights and behaviors
- Know the general process that police agencies use to deal with citizen complaints
- Know some of the factors used for determining sanctions for officers who are to be disciplined

Introduction

"Character," it might be said, "is who we are when no one is watching." Unfortunately, character cannot be trained at the police academy nor given to someone in a pill or intravenously. Character and ethical conduct, for police officers, means they would never betray their oath of office, their public trust, or their badge. Character and ethics are sine qua non for the police—without those attributes, nothing else matters. These qualities constitute the foundation of their occupation and will certainly affect the officers' philosophy concerning when to use force and whether or not to engage in corruption or report other officers who do. Therefore, perhaps no general area of policing carries more controversy, concerns, problems, and questions than the aspects of policing that are discussed in this chapter concerning police accountability: ethics, use of force, corruption, and discipline.

First the subject of police ethics—its definitions, types, and problems—is examined. Incorporated in this discussion are ethical ideals, including differing views of how much latitude the police should be permitted in doing their work, as well as some ethical issues that are posed in this era of community policing and problem solving. Next we consider the equally controversial area of police use of force, and we discuss the use-of-force continuum, police shootings, and legal restrictions. In a related vein, we then look at police brutality; also discussed is the "hot button" issue of bias-based policing and other field tactics. We then consider police corruption: types and causes, problems posed by the police code of silence, and some possible solutions for dealing with it. Next is an overview of areas in which the federal courts have placed limitations on behaviors of the police by virtue of their unique role. Included here are freedom of speech, search and seizure, self-incrimination, freedom of religion, sexual misconduct, residency requirements, moonlighting, misuse of firearms, and alcohol and drug abuse. The chapter concludes with an examination of disciplinary policies and practices, including handling citizens' complaints and doling out sanctions. A summary, key terms, review questions, and several scenarios and activities that provide opportunities to learn by doing conclude the chapter.

Review: *Ethics and Corruption.*

Police Ethics

In a broad sense, for the police, being ethical should include holding themselves and others accountable for their actions. **Accountability**, like character and ethics, is also a significant watchword for today's police, and certainly all citizens expect their public servants to be accountable. What does accountability mean for the police? Beyond the obvious, such as having character and ethics and being good stewards of the public's trust, the term can also include the following: Police officers will treat all persons with dignity and respect and in a lawful manner; they will not use more force than necessary; they will not demonstrate bias for or against any particular group of persons; they will make every effort to ensure that all officers are well trained to meet the highest standards of professionalism; and they will maintain adequate policies, procedures, rules, regulations, general orders, and so forth for ensuring the public's trust, which includes procedures for investigating alleged incidents of bias and unprofessional behavior. Consider the following scenario.

A Scenario

Assume that the police have strong suspicions that Jones is a serial rapist, but they have not secured enough probable cause to obtain a search warrant for Jones's car and home, where evidence might be found. Officer Brown feels frustrated and, early one morning, uses a razor blade to remove the current registration decal from the license plate on Jones's car. The next day he stops Jones for operating his vehicle with an expired registration; he impounds and inventories the vehicle and finds evidence of several sexual assaults, which ultimately leads to Jones's conviction on ten counts of forcible rape and possession of burglary tools and stolen property. Brown receives

The police have long been criticized for a variety of reasons, as shown in this 1874 caricature of police as pigs. *(Courtesy The Granger Collection, New York)*

accolades for the apprehension. Was Officer Brown's removal of the registration decal legal? Should Brown's actions, even if improper or illegal, be condoned for "serving the greater public good"? Did Brown use the law properly?

This hypothetical sequence of events and the accompanying questions should be kept in mind as we consider the definitions and problems of police **ethics**. Exhibit 1 describes some means by which a police agency's culture of integrity can be measured.

Definitions and Types of Problems

Proper ethical behavior has always been the cornerstone of policing (based on the Law Enforcement Code of Ethics, discussed in Exhibit 2) and is what the public expects of its public servants. Ethics usually involves standards of moral conduct and what we call "conscience"—the ability to recognize right from wrong and to act in ways that are good and proper; it concerns choices of good and bad actions as well as moral duties and obligations.

There are both absolute and relative ethics. **Absolute ethics** is a concept wherein an issue only has two sides: Something is either good or bad, black or white.

EXHIBIT 1

Measuring a Police Department's "Culture of Integrity"

Researchers believe they have found a quantitative method that allows police executives to assess their agency's level of resistance to corruption. A national survey of 3,235 officers in thirty police departments asked them to examine eleven common scenarios of police misconduct. The study was based on the premise that organizational and occupational culture can create an atmosphere in which corruption is not tolerated. Survey questions were designed to indicate whether officers knew the rules governing misconduct and how strongly they supported those guidelines, whether they knew the disciplinary penalties for breaking those rules and believed them to be fair, and whether they were willing to report misconduct. Respondents found some types of transgressions to be significantly less serious than others. The more serious the transgression was perceived to be, the more willing officers were to report a colleague and to believe that severe discipline was appropriate. Four scenarios that were not considered major transgressions by officers included operating a private security business while off duty, receiving free meals, accepting free holiday gifts, and covering up a police drunk-driving accident. Indeed, a majority of respondents said they would not report a fellow officer for accepting free gifts, meals, or discounts or for having a minor traffic accident while under the influence of alcohol.

The intermediate levels of misconduct included using excessive force on a car thief following a foot pursuit, a supervisor's offering time off during holidays in exchange for a tune-up on his personal vehicle, and accepting free drinks in return for ignoring a late bar closing. Very serious forms of misconduct, as perceived by the respondents, included accepting a cash bribe, stealing money from a found wallet, and stealing a watch from a crime scene.

Source: Adapted from "How Do You Rate? The Secret to Measuring a Department's 'Culture of Integrity,'" *Law Enforcement News*, October 15, 2000, pp. 1, 6. John Jay College of Criminal Justice, CUNY, 555 W. 57th St., New York, NY 10019.

The original interest in police ethics focused on such unethical behaviors as bribery, extortion, excessive force, and perjury. Few communities can tolerate the absolute unethical behavior of rogue officers; for instance, anyone would have a hard time trying to rationally defend a police officer's stealing.

Relative ethics, as demonstrated in the preceding scenario, can be much more complicated and can have varying shades of gray. The problem here is this: What is considered ethical behavior by one person may be deemed highly unethical by someone else. Not all police ethical issues are clear-cut. For example, communities seem willing at times to tolerate extralegal behavior by the police if there is a greater public good, especially in dealing with such problems as gangs and the homeless or with offenders like the serial rapist in our scenario.

A community's acceptance of relative ethics may send the wrong message: that there are few boundaries placed on police behaviors and that, at times, "anything goes" in the fight against crime. Giving false testimony to ensure that a public menace is "put away" or using illegal wiretapping to get evidence from an organized crime figure's telephone conversations might sometimes be viewed as "necessary" and "justified," though illegal. This viewpoint—the principle of **double effect**—holds that if one commits an act to achieve a good end, even though an inevitable but intended effect is negative, then the act might be justified. Other related catchwords for this phenomenon are **noble cause corruption** and the "**Dirty Harry problem**."[1] (The latter is based on the 1971 Warner Brothers film of the same title in which Detective Harry Callahan [Clint Eastwood] uses extralegal methods to accomplish legitimate police goals. For example, Callahan tortures a vicious kidnapper until he learns where he has hidden the victim. Such treatment might be condoned by many people because the heinous treatment of the offender is viewed as less shocking than what the offender did to his victim.)

The discussion of noble cause corruption and double effect is closely entwined with Herbert Packer's two classic models of law enforcement: crime control and due process.[2] The crime-control model holds that repression of criminal conduct is the most important function of the police; police efficiency, with an emphasis on speed and finality, is a top priority; the due process model, conversely, operates under the principle that efficiency is less important than eliminating errors and that the protection of the process of law is more important than any end result of conviction. Under the due process model, there is a recognition that the coercive power of the state (including all the tools and resources at the disposal of the police and prosecutors) is sometimes subject to abuse and must be guarded against by due process.

Noble cause corruption is a type of wrongdoing that stems from a crime-control orientation. It is a type of means-end thinking in that the end of crime control justifies the means, even if the means are otherwise unethical or illegal. Therefore, in this view police officers may feel compelled to lie ("testilying") under oath, use physical coercion during an interrogation, ignore exculpatory evidence if they feel they have the right offender in custody, overlook criminal acts of an informant, plan or manufacture evidence, and so on. What sets apart these acts from other ethical issues is that they are done for arguably good motives.[3]

The accompanying Career Profile provides some insight from one who has worked in an internal affairs unit—and therefore dealt with citizens' complaints and investigated officers' actions that were called into question.

Ethics and Community Policing

With the shift to community-oriented policing and problem solving, some concerns have been raised about the increased number of ethical dilemmas that COPPS officers confront because they have greater discretion and more public interaction than other officers. Gratuities—free gifts that are supposedly given to the police without obligation—are an example of an ethical problem that can arise with more frequency under COPPS. Whether the police should receive such minor gratuities as free coffee and meals is a long-standing and controversial issue, one for which there will probably never be widespread consensus. Proponents argue that police deserve such perks and that minor gratuities are the building blocks of positive social relationships. Harmless gratuities, it is maintained, may create good feelings in the community toward police officers, and vice versa. Opponents believe, however, that the receipt of gratuities can lead to future deviance. This is the **slippery slope perspective**, which holds that the acceptance of minor gratuities begins a process wherein the recipient's integrity is gradually subverted, which eventually leads to more serious unethical conduct.[4] Given that judges, educators, and other professionals neither expect nor receive such gifts, some people (and police agencies) conclude that

CAREER PROFILE

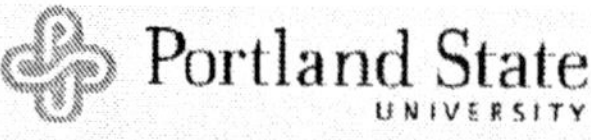

Name: Darrel Schenck

Position: Adjunct Instructor of Criminology and Criminal Justice, Portland State University

College attended: University of Oregon and University of Portland

Degrees: B.S. in Sociology and M.S. in Criminal Justice

Current teaching position: Portland State University

What CJ-related jobs have you held and when?

As a deputy sheriff (1977–1985), I patrolled in a one-person car and responded to police calls for service in an urban and rural setting.

As a sergeant of the Portland Police Bureau (1985–1995), I worked in an administrative function to help the Bureau use a strategic planning process to make a transition to a more community-oriented approach to handling crime and safety problems. We, as police officers, still responded to emergency calls for service, but realized that to have a real impact on public safety problems we couldn't do it alone. We needed to share that responsibility with other public agencies and community members.

As a lieutenant (1995–1999), I managed personnel activities, including allocation of resources, major crime or safety incidents, and special investigations. I led the development of various community policing partnership models, such as precinct citizens advisory council, high school youth council, and various apartment tenant councils.

As a captain (1999–2001), I directed a community-policing training center in Oregon for the Department of Justice, COPS Office. We provided training to police and community members in a six-state region on building police–community problem-solving partnerships.

My final assignment in law enforcement was to manage the Police Bureau's Internal Affairs Division. I led investigations of citizen complaints and officer misconduct problems. Our division also investigated major incidents such as officer-involved shootings to identify conduct, procedural, or training implications. I led a partnership effort to help build an independent police oversight office to receive all citizen complaints for the police and refer valid complaints to the Police Bureau for review and investigation as necessary. We worked as partners to address appeals of the Police Bureau's findings regarding complaints that were investigated.

What positions did you like most?

My role in the Internal Affairs Division was my favorite assignment. I realized very soon how important this job is in a police department. Handling conduct complaints is instrumental in identifying better training methods, clarifying and strengthening policies, improving performance, and—most importantly (contrary to what most think)—the role of Internal Affairs protects officers' reputations against fallacious complaints. Police get a lot of citizen complaints due to the nature of the job, and often these complaints describe behavior that needs improving or disciplining. But most complaints are generally invalid for numerous important reasons and can be harmful to an officer's reputation.

What qualities/characteristics most helped you succeed in the field?

Use of authority in a judicious manner and keeping an open mind—two things not always easy to do. It is easy to generalize about people and make assumptions that can impact your actions as a police officer. Police judge others continuously; it is an important part of the job, sometimes solves crime problems, and often helps to keep an officer or others safe. But at the same time it is a pitfall. Judgments can be harmful, unfair, and illegal. It is a lesson learned that is vital to police work.

What is the typical salary students can expect entering this field?

Salaries range from about $40,000 starting in patrol to over $100,000 for top command positions. Overtime is plentiful and often accounts for an additional $5,000 or more a year.

What advice would you give students early in their college career to help them find a rewarding job in criminal justice?

You need not have a criminal justice major to be successful in law enforcement. Some of my most successful police friends majored in history, political science, and biology in college. It is the journey through college that helps to prepare (in part) for a career in law enforcement.

gratuities are unethical. As an example, after firing an officer for stealing cigars, sandwiches, magazines, and other goods from merchants, the Bradenton, Florida, Police Department established a policy prohibiting sworn personnel from accepting discounted meals from restaurant owners.[5]

The following scenario involves COPPS and gratuities:

> The sheriff's department has a long-standing policy concerning the solicitation and acceptance of gifts. A deputy has been working a problem-solving project in a strip mall area that has experienced juvenile loitering, drug use, prostitution, and vandalism after hours in the parking lot. The mall manager, Mr. Chang, believes it is his moral duty to show his appreciation to the deputy and has made arrangements for the deputy and his family to receive a 15 percent discount at every store in the mall. Knowing that the department policy requires that such offers be declined, the deputy is also aware that Chang will feel very hurt if the proffered gift is refused.[6]

A particularly strong consideration in this scenario is that the mall manager is Asian American and might be extremely hurt if his gift were rejected. Some policy issues are also presented in this scenario. For example, in developing rapport with a mall restaurant manager, is an officer who was formerly prohibited from accepting a free meal now free to do so? Assume that other deputies learn of Chang's new discount arrangement and go to the mall expecting to be treated similarly, resulting in complaints to the sheriff by several business owners. Certainly some people would hold this action to be unethical, given the officers' motivation (personal gain) and their exploitation of the situation.

In sum, the subject of police ethics is not simplistic in nature. We all know that officers should do right, not wrong, but the existence and use of relative ethics make this a complicated issue at best. What can be said is that police officers must be recruited and trained with ethics in mind because they will be given much freedom to become more involved in their community and given wider discretion to make important decisions when addressing neighborhood disorder.

Exhibit 2 shows the very important Law Enforcement Code of Ethics, which police officers are sworn to uphold; the code not only contributes to the professional image of law enforcement, but it also brings about self-respect among officers and affords feelings of mutual respect among police personnel.

Use of Force

A Tradition of Problems

Throughout U.S. history, police agencies have faced allegations of brutality and corruption. In the late nineteenth century, New York Police (NYPD) Sergeant Alexander "Clubber" Williams epitomized police brutality; he spoke openly of using his nightstick to knock a man unconscious, batter him to pieces, or even kill him. Williams supposedly coined the term *tenderloin* when he commented, "I've had nothing but chuck steaks for a long time, and now I'm going to have me a little tenderloin."[7] Williams was referring to opportunities for graft in an area in New York City that was the heart of vice and nightlife, often termed Satan's Circus. This was Williams's beat, where his reputation for brutality and corruption became legendary.[8]

EXHIBIT 2

Law Enforcement Code of Ethics and Law Enforcement Oath of Honor

The Law Enforcement Code of Ethics (LECE) was first adopted by the International Association of Chiefs of Police in 1957 and has been revised several times since then. It is a powerful proclamation, and tens of thousands of police officers across the United States have sworn to uphold this code upon graduating their academies. Unfortunately, however, the LECE is also quite lengthy, covering rather broadly the following topics as they relate to police officers: primary responsibilities, performance of one's duties, discretion, use of force, confidentiality, integrity, cooperation with other officers and agencies, personal/professional capabilities, and private life.

Recently the IACP adopted a separate, shorter code that would be mutually supportive of the LECE—but also easier for officers to remember and call to mind when they come face-to-face with an ethical dilemma. It is the Law Enforcement Oath of Honor, and the IACP is hoping this oath will be implemented in all police agencies and by all individual officers. It may be used at swearing-in ceremonies, graduation ceremonies, promotion ceremonies, beginnings of training sessions, police meetings and conferences, and so forth.

The Law Enforcement Oath of Honor is as follows:

On my honor,
I will never betray my badge[1],
my integrity, my character,
or the public trust.
I will always have
the courage to hold myself
and others accountable for our actions.
I will always uphold the constitution[2],
my community[3] and the agency I serve.

The Law Enforcement Oath of Honor is also flexible, and can be adjusted as appropriate for nations, countries, or governments by inserting the appropriate terms. For example:

At the [1], insert the appropriate term, such as badge; profession; country.

At the [2], insert the appropriate term, such as constitution; laws; monarch.

At the [3], insert the appropriate term, such as community; country; land; nation.

Source: Based on International Association of Chiefs of Police, "What Is the Law Enforcement Oath of Honor," www.theiacp.org/PoliceServices/ExecutiveServices/ProfessionalAssistance/Ethics/WhatistheLawEnforcementOathofHonor/tabid/150/Default.aspx (accessed July 30, 2010).

"Clubber" Williams. *(Courtesy NYPD Photo Unit)*

Although police brutality and corruption are no longer openly tolerated, a number of events have demonstrated that the problem still exists and requires the attention of police officials, such as the so-called police riot in 1968 during the Democratic National Convention.

Legitimate Uses of Force

American society recognizes three legitimate and responsive forms of force: the right of self-defense, including the valid taking of another person's life in order to protect oneself from harm; the power to control those for whom one is responsible (such as a prisoner or a patient in a mental hospital); and the relatively unrestricted authority of police to use force as required. Police work is dangerous—a routine arrest may result in a violent confrontation, sometimes triggered by drugs, alcohol, or mental illness. To cope, police officers are given the unique right to use force, even deadly force, against others. There are, of course, limitations on when an officer may exercise deadly force (they will be discussed later in this chapter).

Egon Bittner defined **police use of force** as the "distribution of non-negotiably coercive remedies."[9] He asserted that the duty of police intervention in matters of societal disorder "means above all making use of the authority to overpower resistance. This feature of police work is uppermost in the minds of people who solicit police aid. Every conceivable police intervention projects the message that force may . . . have to be used to achieve a desired objective."[10] The exercise of force by police can take several forms, ranging from a simple verbal command to the use of lethal force. These forms of force are discussed next as continuums.

Review: *Types of Force.*

Use-of-Force Continuums

Use of force continuums have been evolving for over three decades and have been explained and depicted in very simple (e.g., as a staircase, wheel, or ladder) to more elaborate illustrations. A basic force continuum (and one that existed for a long while) instructed officers to move up the "ladder" or "staircase" and employ increasing levels or types of force as an aggressor became more physical or violent; it typically contained the following five escalating steps: officer presence/verbal direction, touch control, empty-hand tactics and chemical agents, hand-held impact weapons, and lethal force.[11]

Today, however, more and more police executives and force experts believe this simplistic, sequential depiction of the force continuum is ill-suited for today's police and that police use of force cannot always be employed in such a sequential, stair-step fashion. Even with policies and procedures accompanying such a continuum, confusion remained among many officers: "Where am I now on the ladder?" or "Is it now time to climb up to the next rung of the ladder?" Such a simple continuum also fails to properly represent the dynamic encounter between the officer and a resistant suspect and to take into account the wide array of tools that are available to today's officers. How can a department dictate by a continuum in what situations, say, a baton or pepper spray or Taser or other less-lethal weapons should be used?

As a result of this confusion, many agencies now have policies requiring their officers to be "objectively reasonable" in their use of force; in essence, "objectively reasonable" means that in determining the necessity for force and the appropriate level of force, officers shall evaluate each situation in light of the known circumstances; such an assessment includes the seriousness of the crime, the level of threat or resistance presented by the subject, and the danger to the community.

A new approach to determining proper use of force has recently been developed by two special agents of the Federal Bureau of Investigation and attempts to "more accurately reflect the intent of the law and the changing expectations of society" and provide officers with "simple, clear, unambiguous, and consistent guidelines in the use of force."[12] Known as the **dynamic resistance response model (DRRM)**, this approach combines a use of force continuum with an application of four broad categories of suspects. *Dynamic* indicates that the model is fluid, and *resistance* demonstrates that the suspect controls the interaction. In this view, a major failing of past continuums has been that the emphasis is on the officer and the amount of force used. DRRM instead emphasizes that the suspect's level of resistance determines the officer's response. The model also delineates suspects into one of four categories (see Figure 1).

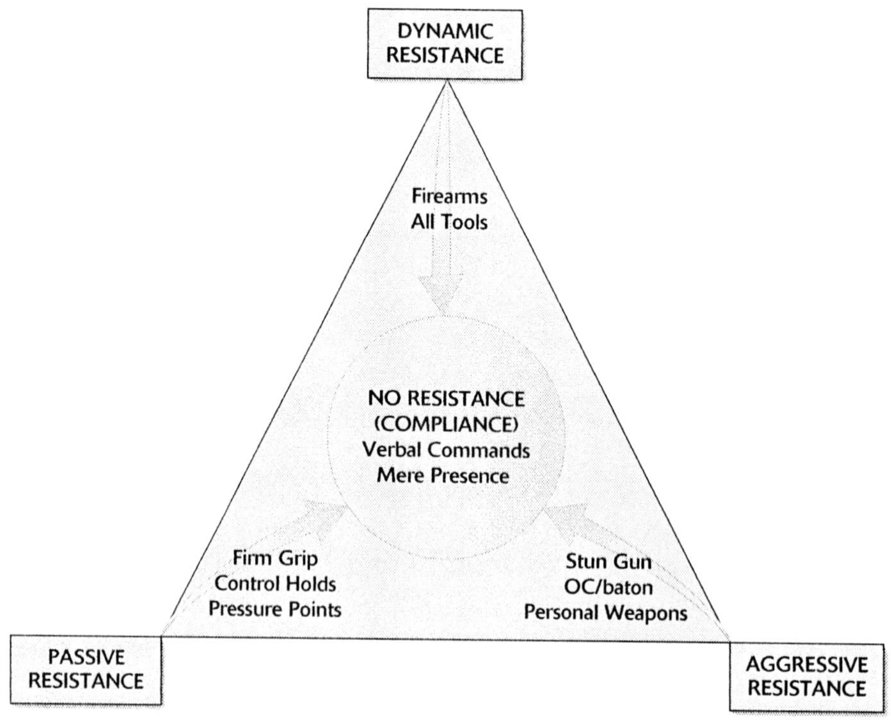

Figure 1
Dynamic Resistance Response Model
Source: FBI Law Enforcement Bulletin, September 2007.

As shown in Figure 1, if a passively resistant suspect fails to follow commands and perhaps attempts to move away from the officer or escape, appropriate responses include using a firm grip, control holds, and pressure points to gain compliance. On the other hand, an aggressively resistant suspect—one who is taking offensive action by attempting to push, throw, strike, tackle, or physically harm the officer—would call for such responses as the use of personal weapons (hands, fists, feet), batons, pepper spray, and a stun gun. Finally, because a deadly resistant suspect can seriously injure or kill the officer or another person, the officer is justified in using force, including deadly force, as is *objectively reasonable* to overcome the offender.

In the DRRM, a suspect's lack of resistance (compliance) is in the center of the triangle, which is emphasized as the goal of every encounter. If a suspect's resistance level places him or her on one of the three corners of the triangle, the officer's response is intended to move the suspect's behavior to the center of the triangle and compliance. The sole purpose of the application of force is to gain compliance.

Police Shootings: Conundrum and Controversy

Clearly, nothing can inflame a community and raise tensions like **police shootings**, and there has been no dearth of high-profile police shooting incidents during the early part of this millennium:

- In July 2005, more than thirty Los Angeles officers, including its SWAT team, responded to a hostage situation and were caught in a crossfire from the front and back of an auto sales lot; the nineteen-month-old daughter of the suspect was killed. The Police Commission found that there was poor communication and a breakdown in command and control during the incident and that seventeen officers needed additional training. The probe involved microscopic analysis of about 130 bullets and more than 100 casings involving thirteen firearms.[13]
- In April 2007, three NYPD officers were indicted for manslaughter and reckless endangerment for a shooting incident where they fired fifty rounds at a car of unarmed men leaving a bachelor party at a strip club; the groom died on his wedding day (the three officers were later acquitted).[14] The incident heightened racial tensions and, for many people, brought to mind the 1999 NYPD killing of an unarmed West African, Amadou Diallo, whom officers shot as he was reaching for his wallet, firing 41 shots and striking him 19 times.

These are what are known in police parlance as **contagious shootings**—gunfire that spreads among officers who believe that they or their colleagues are facing a threat. It spreads like wildfire and often leads to an outcry from community leaders or family members. The phenomenon appears to have also happened in 2005 when eight officers fired 43 shots at an armed man in Queens, New York, killing him. In July 2005, three officers fired 26 shots at a pit bull that had bitten a chunk out of an officer's leg in a Bronx apartment building; in 1995, in the Bronx, officers fired 125 bullets during a botched robbery, with one officer firing 45 rounds.[15]

These incidents that also involve minority group members will often heighten the tension and lead to charges of racism against the entire police agency. One *Washington Post* columnist offered that "it is the police culture, more than race, that is at the crux of the problem . . . a mentality of brutality."[16] Such kinds of police uses of force even caused one organization, Human Rights Watch, to state the following in a report titled *Shielded from Justice: Police Brutality and Accountability in the United States:*

> Police abuse remains one of the most serious and divisive human rights violations in the United States. The excessive use of force by police officers, including unjustified shootings, severe beatings, fatal chokings, and rough treatment, persists because overwhelming barriers to accountability make it possible for officers who commit human rights violations to escape due punishment and often to repeat their offenses.[17]

Human Rights Watch also noted in the report that officers who repeatedly commit human rights violations tend to be a small minority but that "they are protected, routinely, by the silence of their fellow officers and by flawed systems of reporting, oversight, and accountability; by the scarcity of meaningful information about trends in abuse; data lacking regarding the police departments' response to those incidents; and their plans or actions to prevent brutality."[18]

Paradoxically, for all their severity and inflammatory nature, the extent of police shootings is largely unknown. As the *New York Times* stated:

> We like to think we live in the information age. For all the careful accounting, however, there are two figures Americans don't have: the precise number of people killed by the police, and the number of times police use excessive force. Despite widespread public interest and a provision in the 1994 Crime Control Act requiring the Attorney General to collect the data, statistics on police shootings and use of non-deadly force continue to be piecemeal products of spotty collection and are dependent on the cooperation of local police departments. No comprehensive accounting for the nation's 17,000 police departments exists.[19]

The *New York Times* suggests that this lack of accurate statistics makes it impossible to draw meaningful conclusions about deadly encounters between the police and the civilian population and that the major reason for the vacuum is the failure of the police in many cities to keep and report accurate figures that distinguish between what the police see as "justifiable" shootings—those in which the suspect posed a serious threat—and incidents where an officer may have unlawfully fired at an unarmed civilian.[20]

Notwithstanding this lack of data collection for such incidents, the U.S. Department of Justice has relatively new legal means to investigate allegations of racial bias in police departments. The law authorizing such investigations, passed in 1994 after the Rodney King beating in Los Angeles, compels police agencies to initiate safeguards against excessive force and racial bias (for instance, computer systems to track complaints and disciplinary actions) to determine whether the police engaged in "a pattern and practice" of racial discrimination or brutality.[21]

Legal Restrictions

When the colonists came to this country from England, they brought with them a principle of common law that authorized the use of deadly force to apprehend any and all fleeing felony suspects. As American laws and society evolved, however, it became possible for police to use deadly force against people who were at great distances from them, including people suspected of nonviolent property crimes. The justification and necessity for the fleeing-felon rule came into question.[22] Then the U.S. Supreme Court's 1985 decision in ***Tennessee v. Garner***[23] greatly curtailed the use of deadly force. The Court held that the use of deadly force to prevent the escape of all felony suspects was constitutionally unreasonable. It is not better, the Court reasoned, that all felony suspects die than that they escape. Where the suspect poses no immediate threat to the officer or to others, the harm resulting from failing to apprehend him or her does not justify the use of deadly force to do so. (The misuse of firearms will be discussed more fully later in this chapter.)

Police Brutality

Many people contend that there are actually three means by which the police can be "brutal." There is the literal sense of the term, which involves the physical abuse of others. There is the verbal abuse of citizens, exemplified by slurs or epithets. And, for many who feel downtrodden, the police symbolize brutality because the officers represent the Establishment's law, which serves to keep minority groups in their place. It is perhaps the last form of **police brutality** that is of greatest concern for anyone who is interested in improving community relations. Because it is a philosophy or frame of mind, it is probably the most difficult to overcome.

Citizens' use of the term *police brutality* encompasses a wide range of practices, from profane and abusive language to actual physical force or violence.[24] Some would claim that there is little (if any) police brutality in today's enlightened police agencies. Others acknowledge that police brutality exists today but add that *"brutality is the prerogative of the police state. To tolerate any of it is to differ from the police state only in degree"* (emphasis in original).[25]

While no one can deny that some police officers use brutal practices, it is impossible to know with any degree of accuracy how often and to what extent these incidents occur. They are low-visibility acts, and many victims decline to report them. Although it is widely believed that brutality is a racial matter primarily involving white police and black victims, Albert Reiss found that lower-class white men were as likely to be brutalized by the police as lower-class black men.[26] What is most disturbing is that 37 percent of the instances of excessive force occurred in settings controlled by the police—station houses and patrol cars. In half the situations, a police officer

Scenes from the *Walker Report* of the 1968 Chicago Democratic National Convention.

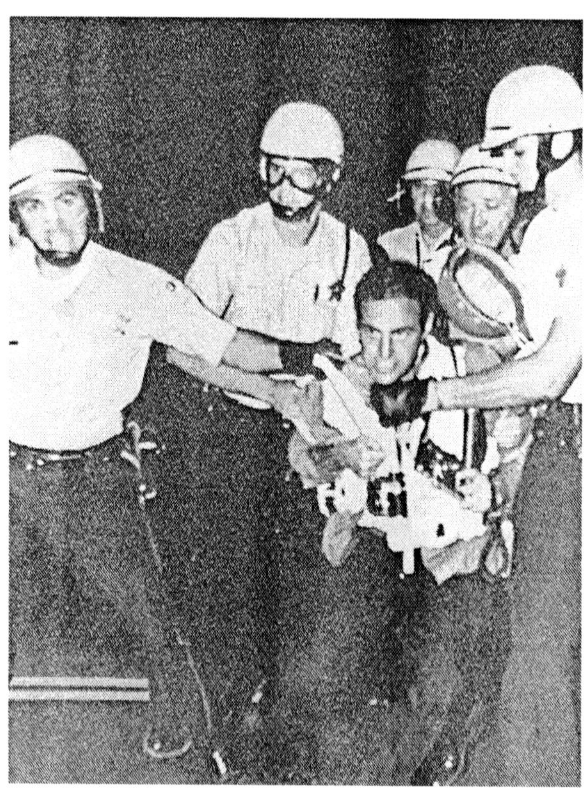

did not participate but did not restrain his or her colleague, indicating that the informal police culture did not disapprove of the behavior.[27]

It is doubtful that police brutality will ever disappear forever. There are always going to be, in the words of A. C. Germann, Frank Day, and Robert Gallati, "Neanderthals" who enjoy their absolute control over others and become tyrannical in their arbitrary application of power.[28] Therefore, many people support the use of formal citizen complaint review procedures for investigating allegations of brutality and excessive use of force.

Vehicle Pursuits

In 2007 the U.S. Supreme Court issued a major decision concerning the proper amount of force the police may use during high-speed vehicle pursuits. The fundamental question was whether or not the serious danger created by the fleeing motorist justifies the use of deadly force to eliminate the threat. In other words, was the level of force used proportionate to the threat of reckless and dangerous driving? The incident involved Harris, a nineteen-year-old Georgia youth, driving at speeds up to ninety miles per hour and covering nine miles in six minutes, with a deputy sheriff in pursuit; the chase ended in a violent crash that left Harris a quadriplegic. His lawyers argued that the Fourth Amendment protects against the use of excessive force, such as high-speed drivers having their cars rammed by police (by intentionally stopping a fleeing vehicle in such a manner, a "seizure" occurs for Fourth Amendment purposes). Conversely, the deputy's lawyers argued that such drivers pose an escalating danger to the public and must be stopped to defuse the danger (the deputy's supervisor had authorized the use of the precision immobilization technique, or PIT, where the officer uses his patrol vehicle to cause the speeder's to spin out; PIT was not used in the Harris chase, however). The Court's 8–1 opinion, authored by Justice Antonin Scalia, stated, "A police officer's attempt to terminate a dangerous high-speed car chase that threatens the lives of innocent bystanders does not violate the Fourth Amendment, even when it places the fleeing motorist at risk of serious injury or death."[29]

Bias-Based Policing and Other Field Tactics

Bias-based policing—also known as "driving while black or brown" (DWBB)—involves unequal treatment of any person on the basis of race, ethnicity, religion, gender, sexual orientation, or socioeconomic status. A 2007 study released by the Bureau of Justice Statistics found that while black, Hispanic, and white drivers are equally likely to be pulled over by the police, blacks and Hispanics are much more likely to be searched and arrested, and police are much more likely to threaten or use force against blacks and Hispanics than against whites in any encounter, whether at a traffic stop or elsewhere. The report warned that the findings do not prove that police treat people differently along racial lines and that the differences could be explained by driver conduct or other circumstances.[30] Nonetheless, traffic stops are a politically volatile issue, and such studies underscore minority groups' complaints that many stops and searches are based on race rather than on legitimate suspicions. This dynamic was certainly at the root of the controversy over a law enacted in Arizona in mid-2010, authorizing police to stop and determine someone's immigration status if they suspected that he or she was an illegal immigrant (a federal judge quickly issued a preliminary injunction against that and other highly controversial provisions of the law).

Some police executives defend officers' selective stopping of citizens as effective crime fighting, based not on prejudice but on probabilities: the statistical reality that certain people are disproportionately likely to commit crimes. Bernard Parks, former African American police chief of Los Angeles, explained:

> We have an issue of violent crime against jewelry salespeople. The predominant suspects are Colombians. We don't find Mexican-Americans, or blacks, or other immigrants. It's a collection of several hundred Colombians who commit this crime. If you see six in a car in front of the Jewelry Mart, and they're waiting and watching people with briefcases, should we play the percentages and follow them? It's common sense.[31]

Still, bias-based policing has become a despised police practice in the new millennium. Profiling on the basis of race is given no public support. The best defense for the police may be summarized in two words: *collect data.* Collecting traffic-stop data helps chiefs and commanders to determine whether officers are stopping or searching a disproportionate number of minorities and enables them to act on this information right away. Technology—including mobile data computers and wireless handheld devices—can be used for this purpose.

Exhibit 3 shows what the Sacramento, California, Police Department has done to study and address biased policing, although no such complaints had been reported in the city.

Other police field practices, such as the following, also can be sources of tension between minorities and police:

- *Delay in responding to calls for service.* Studies of police work have found that patrol officers sometimes delay responding to calls for service, especially in cases of family disturbances.[32] Although this delay may be justified on grounds of officer safety (that is, an officer must await backup), and while these studies did not demonstrate any pattern of racial bias, delays do not improve public perceptions of the police.
- *Verbal abuse, epithets, and other forms of disrespect.* Offensive labels for people are a regular aspect of the working language of some police officers. One study found that 75 percent of all officers used some racially offensive words, most of which were not uttered in the presence of citizens; however, police openly ridicule and belittle citizens in 5 percent of all encounters.[33] In some situations, the police use the terms as a control technique in an attempt to establish their authority.[34] Nonetheless, verbal abuse should be avoided at all times.

EXHIBIT 3

Sacramento Searches for Biased Policing

In the late 1990s, the Sacramento, California, Police Department (SPD) began a study on racially biased policing. The goal was to determine the degree of intrusiveness of traffic stops and whether or not such stops were indicative of racially biased policing. Even though there were no reported complaints of such policing, the SPD recognized the importance of responding to national concern about the problem. The researchers began by collecting reports, editorials, and anecdotal information for insight into approaches taken by other agencies. Meetings were held with the community, civil rights organizations, the police union, and agency staff. Officers were invited to provide input on how to conduct the study. The SPD also invited the American Civil Liberties Union, the Mexican American Legal Defense and Education Fund, and neighborhood associations to participate.

Once the study began, officers filled out data-collection forms for each traffic stop, which included the officer's badge number, age, race, and unit assignment. The study examined data on traffic patterns and type of crimes throughout the city.

In the end, the SPD came to the conclusion that rarely could an officer identify the race of the drivers or occupants of cars before they were actually stopped. The study did find that traffic stops involving African Americans occurred at a disproportionately higher rate than the overall African American population, so the study was extended for two years to examine whether systems existed that encouraged bias-based policing. Now, as part of its community policing program, "Police as Problem Solvers/Peacemakers Initiative," the SPD is providing technical assistance to other local police agencies interested in collecting data on biased policing.

Source: Adapted from Tammy Jones, "Sacramento Searches for Biased Policing," in *Community Links* (Washington, DC: Community Policing Consortium, February 2003), pp. 1–2.

- *Excessive questioning and frisking of minority citizens.* Allegations of harassment by police are often raised by racial minorities who believe they have been unnecessarily subjected to field interrogations. Many officers, because they are trained to be suspicious and must often confront individuals in questionable circumstances, regard such activities as legitimate and effective crime-fighting tactics.
- *Discriminatory patterns of arrest and traffic citations.* African Americans are arrested more often than whites relative to their numbers in the population.[35] African American complainants request arrests more often than whites. Since most incidents are intraracial, this can result in more arrests of African Americans.[36] Police have been found more likely to arrest both white and African American suspects in low-income areas. Insofar as African Americans are disproportionately represented among the poor, however, this factor is likely to result in a disproportionately high arrest rate for African Americans.[37]
- *Excessive use of physical force.* Police have been found to use force in about 5 percent of all encounters involving offenders. In about two-thirds of the incidents involving force, its application was judged to be reasonable. White and African American officers used excessive force at nearly the same rate. It is known that "a sizable minority of citizens experience police misconduct at one time or another."[38] The result, of course, is that many racial minorities perceive that their race is being unduly brutalized. And, to them, perception is reality.

A Related Issue: Domestic Violence

A 1996 federal law, titled the **Domestic Violence Offender Gun Ban** (popularly known as the **Lautenberg Amendment**), bars anyone—including police and military personnel—from carrying firearms if they have a conviction for domestic violence. Although no figures are available regarding loss of jobs, that has been the case for hundreds of police officers across the United States. In many cases, officers found to have past misdemeanor convictions have lost their jobs.[39]

No one denies that a police officer who beats a spouse or child should be fired. The ban's supporters maintain that the police must also be held accountable when they commit any type of domestic violence and that their easy access to firearms can cause a domestic argument to escalate to homicide.[40] However, critics of the law, including many politicians, police associations, and unions, argue that the law is too broad.

Assume, for example, that a police officer tells her fifteen-year-old son that he cannot leave the house and hang out with some kids she knows to be using drugs. He attempts to leave and calls her some names, so she grabs him by the arm and sits him down. Except for a bruise on his arm, he is not injured, but he calls the police, a report is filed, and she is convicted of misdemeanor assault in a trial by judge with no right to trial by jury. Because of the domestic-violence law, she loses her right to carry a gun and, thus, her career is ended.[41] Because police agencies typically have no unarmed positions, the law in effect ends the careers of officers who are affected by it.

The issue is not whether abusive police officers should be fired but whether the law as it is written is effective and legal. Several state lawsuits, including lawsuits by the National Association of Police Officers (which argues that officers are being "sacrificed on the altar of political correctness"[42]), have challenged the constitutionality of the law. In August 1998, the U.S. Court of Appeals for the District of Columbia Circuit exempted police and federal law enforcement agents within its jurisdiction from the law.

Police Corruption

History: Long-Standing "Plague"

"For as long as there have been police, there has been **police corruption**," observed Lawrence Sherman concerning the oldest and most persistent problem in American policing.[43] To make the point, corruption has long plagued the NYPD, as determined by the Knapp Commission, which investigated police corruption there in the early 1970s.[44] Knapp's 1973 report stated that there are two primary types of corrupt police officers: the "meat-eaters" and the "grass-eaters." Meat-eaters, who probably constitute a small percentage of police officers, spend a good deal of their working hours aggressively seeking out situations that they can exploit for financial gain, including gambling, narcotics, and other lucrative enterprises. No change in attitude is likely to affect meat-eaters; their income is so large that the only way to deal with them is to get them off the force and prosecute them. Grass-eaters constitute the overwhelming majority of those officers who accept payoffs; they are not aggressive but will accept gratuities from contractors, tow-truck operators, gamblers, and the like.

The Knapp Commission also identified several factors that influence how much graft police officers receive, the most important of these being the character of the individual officer. The branch of the department and the type of assignment also affect opportunities for corruption. Typically, plainclothes officers have more varied opportunities than uniformed patrol officers, and uniformed officers located in beats with, say, several vice dens will have more opportunities for payoffs. Another factor is rank: the amount of the payoff received generally ascends proportionally with rank.

Police corruption can be defined broadly, from major forms of police wrongdoing to the pettiest forms of improper behavior. Another definition is "the misuse of authority by a police officer in a manner designed to produce personal gain for the officer or for others."[45] Police corruption is not limited to monetary gain, however. Gains may be made through the acceptance of services received, status, influence, prestige, or future support for the officer or someone else.[46]

Events like those described in Los Angeles and other cities have focused attention on the broader issue of rogue cops in police departments across the country, especially in minority neighborhoods.[47] The brazenness and viciousness of today's corrupt police officers trouble even their staunchest defenders.

Types and Causes

Several factors contribute to police corruption, among them the rapid hiring of personnel, civil service, and union protections that make it difficult to fire officers,[48] and temptations from money and sex.

Two theories—the "rotten apple" theory and the "environmental" theory—have been suggested to explain police corruption. The rotten apple theory holds that corruption is the result of having a few bad apples in the barrel who probably had character defects prior to employment. The environmental theory suggests that corruption is more the result of a widespread politically corrupt environment; politically corrupt cities create an environment in which police misconduct flourishes.[49]

Police corruption takes two basic forms: external and internal. External corruption includes those activities (such as gratuities and payoffs) that occur from and through police contacts with the public. Internal corruption involves the relationships among police officers within the workings of the police department; this includes payments to join the police force, to get better shifts or assignments, to receive promotions, and the like.[50]

Ellwyn Stoddard, who coined the term *blue-coat crime,* described several different forms of deviant practices among both police and citizens. In the following list, those coming first would probably elicit the least fear of prosecution, and those at the end would probably invoke major legal ramifications:[51]

- *Mooching.* Receiving free coffee, meals, liquor, groceries, laundry services, and so forth.

- *Chiseling.* Demanding free admission to entertainment or price discounts on goods and services.
- *Favoritism.* Using license tabs, window stickers, or courtesy cards to gain immunity from traffic arrest.
- *Prejudice.* Behaving less than impartially toward minority group members or others who are less likely to have influence in city hall.
- *Bribery.* Receiving payments of cash or gifts for past or future assistance in avoiding prosecution, including political payoffs for favoritism in promotions. Police officers who accept payoffs or protection money are said to be "on the pad."
- *Shakedown.* Stealing expensive items for personal use and attributing the loss to criminal activity when investigating a burglary or unlocked door.
- *Perjury.* Following the "code" that demands that officers lie to provide an alibi for fellow officers apprehended in unlawful activity.
- *Premeditated theft.* Being involved in planned burglaries that involve the use of tools or keys to gain entry; also any prearranged act of unlawful acquisition of property that cannot be explained as a spur-of-the-moment theft.

The most common and extensive form of corruption involves the receipt by police officers of small gratuities or tips. Officers may regard discounts and free services as relatively unimportant, while the payment of cash—bribery—is a very different matter.[52] Former New York City Police Commissioner Patrick V. Murphy was one of those who "drew the short line," telling his officers that "except for your paycheck, there is no such thing as a clean buck."[53] Such police officials would argue that even the smallest gratuities can create an expectation of some patronage or favor in return. Retail establishments do not offer gratuities to other persons in professional positions (doctors, lawyers, educators) for performing their duties, and the argument can certainly be made that the police should be similarly viewed and treated.

Withrow and Dailey offered a uniquely different viewpoint toward gratuities.[54] They propose a "**model of circumstantial corruptibility**," stating that the exchange of a gift is influenced by two elements: the role of the giver and the role of the receiver. The role of the *giver* determines the level of corruptibility, in this model; the giver is either taking a position as a:

- *presenter,* who offers a gift voluntarily without any expectation of a return from the receiver;
- *contributor,* who furnishes something toward a result and expects something in return; or a
- *capitulator,* who involuntarily responds to the demands of the receiver.

The role of the receiver of the gift is obviously very important as well; the receiver can act as an:

- *acceptor,* who receives the gift humbly and without any residual feelings of reciprocity;

- *expector,* who looks forward to the gift and regards it as likely to happen, and will be annoyed by the absence of the gift; or
- *conqueror,* who assumes total control over the exchange and influence over the giver.

The function of the model is centered on the intersection of the giver and the receiver. For example, when the giver assumes the role of the presenter and the receiver is the acceptor, the result is a giving exchange, and corruption does not occur. However, if giver and receiver occupy other roles, corruptibility can progress to higher levels of social harm, which Withrow and Dailey termed a "hierarchy of wickedness." Bribery results when something of value is given and the giver expects something in return, while the receiver agrees to conform his or her behavior to the desires of the giver. It is therefore of great importance that the police consider the role of the giver as well as their own intentions when deciding whether or not to accept a gratuity. In certain circumstances, the exchange of *any* gratuity is ethical or unethical regardless of its value.

Another serious form of police corruption is related to drugs. Until the 1960s, most police corruption was associated with the protection of gambling operations, illegal liquor establishments, prostitution, and similar "victimless" activities. More recently, however, drug-related police corruption has probably surpassed those earlier forms of deviance. A typology of drug-related corruption has been developed by David Carter, who believes that the numbers of such cases "have notably increased":[55]

> *Type I drug corruption* occurs when an officer seeks to use his or her position simply for personal gain. This type of drug corruption includes giving information to drug dealers about investigations, names of informants, planned raids, and so forth; accepting bribes from drug dealers in exchange for nonarrest, evidence tampering, or perjury; stealing drugs from the police property room for personal consumption; "seizing" drugs for personal use without arresting the person possessing the drugs; taking either the profits of drug dealers' sales or the drugs themselves for resale; and extorting money or property from drug traffickers in exchange for nonarrest or nonseizure of drugs.
>
> *Type II drug corruption* involves the officer's search for legitimate goals and may not even be universally perceived as being corrupt. Officer gain may involve organizational benefit, perhaps a form of "winning" or "revenge." Included are such actions as giving false statements to obtain arrest or search warrants against suspected or known drug dealers, committing perjury during hearings and trials of drug dealers, planting or creating evidence against known drug dealers, using entrapment, and falsely spreading rumors that a dealer is a police informant in order to endanger that person.

See the "Comparative Closeup: Corruption in Mexico" for a discussion of where police corruption is possibly at its worst: Mexico.

CLOSEUP ▸▸ Corruption in Mexico

Mexican police on the beat during the Cervantino Festival, Guanajuato, Mexico.
(*Courtesy Fotosearch. Used with permission.*)

It is almost unimaginable that the word *corrupt* best describes a nation's police force, but such is the long-standing case in Mexico. It is no secret that law enforcement in Mexico is a "for-profit" business. Following is a typical account: Bernard Masow, chief economist at The Globalist Research Center, was traveling with his wife near the Mexico City airport when one of the many traffic officers there ordered them to the curb. Masow was told he had violated the speed limit (a physically impossible act, given the bumper-to-bumper traffic), and the officer said he would confiscate Masow's driver's license—and as proof he produced a stack of confiscated driver's licenses. Finally, Masow gave the officer five $20 bills, which he pocketed while walking away, waving them on.[1] However, this incident pales in comparison to the real corruption occurring among Mexico's police who are lured into the drug business. Indeed, in late 2009 federal police raided several local police stations in the northern part of Nuevo León state as part of a sweep to try to clean up local forces allegedly corrupted by drug-trafficking gangs. That occurred one day after several dozen heavily armed federal police squared off against scores of local police in Monterrey, aiming at each other with semi-automatic assault weapons and threatening to kill one another. Federal police also raided local police stations there, amid a crackdown on corrupt local police. In one nine-day period, seventy-eight police officers, including a local police chief, were detained on suspicion of being in the pay of Mexico's powerful drug-trafficking groups.[2] Across the country, forty police "group chiefs" have been dismissed for failure to pass security and trustworthiness background checks.[3] The police have also been implicated in kidnappings and killings related to the drug traffic. Furthermore, the problem of police corruption has resulted in many standoffs between corrupt police and the nation's military; in 2009, nearly seventy confrontations took place between police and soldiers, ranging from police spying for drug cartels to exchanges of gunfire with police guarding drug lords.[4]

[1]Adapted from Bernard Masow, "Greasing Palms: Corruption in Mexico," *The Globalist*, June 27, 2005, www.theglobalist.com/storyid.aspx?Storyid=4640 (accessed July 31, 2010).

[2]Adapted from David Luhnow, "Mexico Cracks Down on Local Police Corruption," June 10, 2009, online.wsj.com/article/SB124459457211800501.html (accessed July 31, 2010).

[3]M3 Report, "Mexico: Police Corruption Rampant," January 28, 2009, m3report.wordpress.com/2009/01/29/mexico-police-corruption-rampant.

[4]Olga R. Rodriguez and Julie Watson, "Soldiers Wary of Often-Corrupt Mexican Police," Associated Press, www.newstimes.com/news/article/Soldiers-wary-of-often-corrupt-Mexican-police-211046.php (accessed August 1, 2010).

Code of Silence

Patrick V. Murphy wrote that "the most difficult element to overcome in the fight against corruption in the department was the **code of silence**."[56] This keeping quiet in the face of misconduct by other officers has been well documented. Evidence of the fraternal bond that exists in policing was first reported by William Westley as early as 1970, when more than 75 percent of the officers surveyed said that they would not report another officer for taking money from a prisoner, nor would they testify against an officer accused by a prisoner.[57] (In a related vein, see Exhibit 1.)

For example, Officer Jack Smith finds himself in a moral dilemma. He knows of another officer's misconduct; he witnessed the officer putting expensive ink pens in his pocket while securing an unlocked office supply store on the graveyard shift. If reported, the misconduct will ruin the officer, but if not reported, the behavior could eventually cause enormous harm. To outsiders, this is not a dilemma at all; the only proper path is for Smith to report the misconduct. To philosophers, the doctrines of utilitarianism (the ethic of good consequences) and deontology (the ethic of rights and duties) require that Officer Smith work to eliminate corruption. But the outsiders and the philosophers are not members of the close fraternity of police, nor do they have to depend on other officers for their own safety.

There are several arguments for and against Officer Smith's informing on his partner. Reasons for informing include the fact that the harm caused by a scandal would be outweighed by the public's knowledge that the police department is free of corruption; also, individual episodes of corruption would be brought to a halt. The officer, moreover, has a sworn duty to uphold the law. Any employee has a right to be allowed to do his or her duty, including blowing the whistle on employers or colleagues. Reasons against Officer Smith's informing include the fact that a skilled police officer is a valuable asset whose social value far outweighs the damage done by moderate corruption. Also, discretion and secrecy are obligations assumed by joining and remaining within the police fraternity; dissenters should resign rather than inform. Furthermore, it would be unjust to inflict punishment of dismissal and disgrace on an otherwise decent officer.[58]

How does one reconcile these two varying points of view? Probably the first thing to do is to realize that each view is morally defensible. A person who is in charge of investigating police corruption would no doubt be warmer toward the punitive view, while at the other extreme would be the person who would overlook such behaviors at all times. The ideal position might be in the middle—to maintain a commitment to professionalism and ethics without overreacting (e.g., without insisting that officers report on their fellows every time they see someone napping or conducting personal business while on duty).

The good news is that a recent survey by the National Institute of Justice found that about 83 percent of all officers in the United States do not accept the code of silence as an essential part of the mutual trust necessary to good policing.[59]

Investigation and Prosecution

Federal powers and jurisdiction for investigating and prosecuting police corruption were significantly expanded through the Hobbs Act in 1970.[60] Two important elements of this federal statute that allow the investigation of police corruption are extortion and commerce. Whenever a police officer solicits a payoff from a legitimate business owner to overlook law violations (e.g., a tavern owner who was selling alcohol to minors), extortion (involving fear) occurs, and that extortion affects legitimate commerce. The Hobbs Act may be employed by the prosecutor when these two elements are present. The meaning of extortion has been expanded so that it now covers most payoff arrangements that involve public officials.[61] The only areas of police corruption that may be beyond the reach of the Hobbs Act are internal corruption and the acceptance of isolated gratuities.

The federal perjury statute (18 U.S.C. 1621) and the federal false sworn declaration statute (18 U.S.C. 1623), both enacted in 1970, have also become powerful weapons for prosecutors in investigating public corruption. Both statutes deal with false testimony under oath, and in an investigation of corruption they are pertinent at the grand jury stage.[62]

Possible Solutions

Several other measures are possible for overcoming the pernicious effects of police corruption. In addition to the obvious need for an honest and effective police administration, it is also necessary to train recruits on the need for a corruption-free department. The creation and maintenance of an internal affairs unit and the vigorous prosecution of law-breaking police officers are also critical to maintaining the integrity of officers. In addition, there should be some mechanism for rewarding the honest police officers that should minimally include protection from retaliation when they inform on crooked cops. All police officers should be given formal written guidelines on the departmental policy on soliciting and accepting gifts and gratuities. This apprises officers of the administration's view of such behavior and assists the chief executive in maintaining integrity and disciplining wayward officers. Figure 2 is an example of a good policy concerning gratuities.

Also, computers can assist with investigations of police corruption. Indeed, information that was uncovered about corruption within the Chicago Police Department was obtained through an $850 software program known as Brainmaker, an early-warning program intended to flag at-risk officers before they commit acts that could get them arrested or fired. With this type of approach, at-risk officers can be provided with counseling before serious problems occur.[63]

Exhibit 4 shows what one city has done, and the kind of software that it used, to create an early-warning system.

1. Without the express permission of the Sheriff, members shall not solicit or accept any gift, gratuity, loan, present, or fee where there is any direct or indirect connection between this solicitation or acceptance of such gift and their employment by this office.
2. Members shall not accept, either directly or indirectly, any gift, gratuity, loan, fee, or thing of value, the acceptance of which might tend to improperly influence their actions, or that of any other member, in any matter of police business, or which might tend to cast an adverse reflection on the Sheriff's Office.
3. Any unauthorized gift, gratuity, loan, fee, reward, or other thing falling into any of these categories coming into the possession of any member shall be forwarded to the member's commander, together with a written report explaining the circumstances connected therewith. The commander will decide the disposition of the gift.

Figure 2

A Sample Gratuity Policy (Washoe County, Nevada)

EXHIBIT 4

A Means of Policing the Police

A lawsuit filed recently by dozens of plaintiffs, alleging that they were roughed up by a band of Oakland, California, officers calling themselves "the Riders," was settled for $11 million and resulted in a new Personnel Information Management System (PIMS) being implemented in 2005. PIMS will document use-of-force incidents, citizen complaints, attendance, shootings, and accidents, as well as commendations, awards, and letters of appreciation. Its main purpose is to help supervisors identify trends that might indicate [when] an officer needs an intervention. Based on a Phoenix, Arizona, model, the system holds the supervisor all the way up the chain accountable for doing something and is a tremendous risk management tool; it emphasizes guiding employees, not merely disciplining them. At the extreme, it allows for getting to people before they "crash and burn, and kill somebody in a police pursuit, traffic accident, or whatever." The system refreshes itself nightly by collecting new information added that day. An Oakland police captain emphasized that a lot of use-of-force problems, incidents, or attendance issues do not make one a bad officer; an officer working in a busy area abundant with shootings will be involved in more car chases and fights and have more use-of-force incidents than one working in a less active downtown area.

Source: Jim McKay, "Policing the Police: Oakland, Calif., Tackles Police Misconduct Issues with Database," *Government Technology,* October 2004, p. 48.

Limitations on Officers' Constitutional Rights

Police officers are generally afforded the same rights, privileges, and immunities outlined in the U.S. Constitution for all citizens. However, by virtue of their position, they may be compelled to give up certain rights in connection with an investigation of on-duty misbehavior or illegal acts. These rights are the basis for legislation such as the Peace Officers' Bill of Rights, labor agreements, and civil service and departmental rules and regulations that guide an agency's disciplinary process.

Following is a brief overview of some areas in which the federal courts have placed **limitations on officers' constitutional rights** and have held sworn officers more accountable by virtue of the higher standard required by their occupation.

Free Speech

Although the right of freedom of speech is one of the most fundamental and cherished of all American rights, the Supreme Court has indicated that "the State has interests as an employer in regulating the speech of its employees that differ significantly from those it possesses in connection with regulation of the speech of the citizenry in general."[64] Thus the state may impose restrictions on its police employees that it would not be able to impose on civilians; however, these restrictions must be reasonable. For example, a department may not prohibit "any activity, conversation, deliberation, or discussion which is derogatory to the Department," as such a rule obviously prohibits all criticism of the agency by its officers, even in private conversation.[65]

Another First Amendment–related area is that of personal appearance. The Supreme Court has upheld several grooming standards for officers (regarding length of hair, sideburns, and mustaches) to make officers readily recognizable to the public and to maintain the esprit de corps within the department.[66]

Searches and Seizures

The Fourth Amendment to the U.S. Constitution protects "the right of the people to be secure in their persons, houses, papers, and effects, against unreasonable searches and seizures." The Fourth Amendment usually applies to police officers when they are at home or off duty in the same manner as it applies to all citizens. However, because of the nature of their work, police officers can be compelled to cooperate with investigations of their behavior when ordinary citizens would not. For example, regarding equipment and lockers provided by the department to the officers, the officers have no expectation of privacy that affords or merits protection.[67]

However, lower courts have established limitations on searches of employees themselves. The question of whether prison authorities have the right to search their employees arose in a 1985 Iowa case in which employees were forced to sign a consent form as a condition of hire. The court disagreed with such a broad policy, ruling that the consent form did not constitute a blanket waiver of all Fourth Amendment rights.[68] Police officers may also be forced to appear in a lineup, a clear "seizure" of their person.

Self-Incrimination

The Supreme Court has addressed questions concerning the Fifth Amendment as it applies to police officers who are under investigation. In ***Garrity v. New Jersey***,[69] a police officer was ordered by the attorney general to answer questions or be discharged. The officer testified that information obtained as a result of his answers was later used to convict him of criminal charges. The Supreme Court held that the information obtained from the officer could not be used against him at his criminal trial because the Fifth Amendment forbids the use of coerced confessions. However, it is proper to fire a police officer who refuses to answer questions that are related directly to the performance of his or her duties, provided that the officer has been informed that any answers may not be used later in a criminal proceeding.[70]

Religious Practices

Police work requires that personnel be available and on duty twenty-four hours a day, seven days a week. Although it is not always convenient or pleasant, shift configurations require that many officers work weekends, nights, and holidays. It is generally assumed that an officer who takes such a position agrees to work such hours and abide by other such conditions; it is usually the personnel with the least seniority on the job who must work the most undesirable shifts. However, there are occasions when the requirements of the job interfere with an officer's ability to attend religious services or observe religious holidays. The carrying of firearms may even conflict with an officer's beliefs. In these situations, the employee may be forced to choose between his or her job and religion.

Title VII of the Civil Rights Act of 1964 prohibits religious discrimination in employment. It requires reasonable accommodation of religious beliefs but not to the extent that the employee has complete freedom of religious expression.[71]

Sexual Misconduct

To be blunt, there is ample opportunity for police officers to become involved in adulterous or extramarital affairs. Few other occupations or professions offer the opportunities for sexual misconduct that police work does. Police officers frequently work alone, usually without direct supervision, in activities that involve frequent contact with citizens, usually in relative isolation. The problem seems to be pervasive in police departments of all sizes. Unfortunately, it is also an area of police behavior that is not easily quantified or understood.[72]

Allen D. Sapp suggested several possible categories of sexually motivated behaviors by police officers (again, the extent to which each occurs is unknown):[73]

- *Sexually motivated nonsexual contacts.* Officers initiate contacts with female citizens, without probable cause or any legal basis, for the purpose of obtaining names and addresses for possible later contact.
- *Voyeuristic contacts.* Officers seek opportunities to view unsuspecting women partially clad or nude, such as in parked cars on "lovers' lanes."
- *Contacts with crime victims.* A wide variety of behavior can occur, including unnecessary callbacks to homes of female victims, bodily contact with accident victims, and sexual harassment by officers.
- *Contacts with offenders.* Officers may also harass female offenders by conducting body searches and pat downs or frisks.
- *Sexual shakedowns.* Officers may demand sexual services from prostitutes or other citizens.
- *Citizen-initiated sexual contacts.* "Police groupies"—often young women who are sexually attracted to the uniform, weapons, or power of the police officer—may seek to participate in sexual activities with officers. This category may also include offers of sexual favors in return for preferential treatment or calls to officers from lonely or mentally disturbed women seeking officers' attention.
- *Sex crimes by officers.* Officers may sexually assault jail inmates and citizens.

In a related vein, several federal courts have recently considered whether police agencies have a legitimate interest in the sexual activities of their officers when such activities affect job performance. In one such case, the court held that the dismissal of a married police officer for living with another man's wife was a violation of the officer's privacy and associational rights.[74]

Other courts, however, have found that off-duty sexual activity can affect job performance. When a married city police officer was found to be having consensual sexual relations with unmarried women other than his wife, the department contended that the officer's conduct—which became public—severely damaged public confidence in the department. A Utah court held that adultery was not a fundamental right and refused to strike down a statute criminalizing adultery.[75] In a Texas case, when a male officer's extramarital affair led to his being passed over for promotion, the city civil service commission, the Texas Supreme Court, and the U.S. Supreme Court upheld the denial; they concurred with the city police chief's argument that such a promotion would adversely affect the efficiency and morale of the department and would be disruptive.[76]

Residency Requirements

Many government agencies specify that all or certain members in their employ must live within the geographic limits of their jurisdiction—that is, employees must reside within the county or city of employment. Such residency requirements have been justified on the grounds that officers should become familiar with and be visible in the jurisdiction of employment or that they should reside where they are paid by the taxpayers to work.[77] Perhaps the strongest rationale given by employing agencies is that criminal justice employees must live near their work so they can respond quickly in the event of an emergency.

Moonlighting

The term *moonlight* means to hold a second job in addition to one's normal full-time occupation. The courts have traditionally supported the limitations police agencies have placed on the amount and kind of outside work their employees can perform.[78] For example, police restrictions on moonlighting range from a complete ban on outside employment to permission to engage in certain forms of work, such as investigations, private security, and criminal justice education. The rationale for agency limitations is that "outside employment seriously interferes with keeping the [police and fire] departments fit and ready for action at all times."[79]

Misuse of Firearms

As noted above, the use of firearms by police, whether justified or not, can have drastic consequences on both the officer(s) involved and the community. Police agencies typically attempt to restrain the use of firearms through written policies and frequent training of a "shoot/don't shoot" nature. Still, a broad range of potential and actual problems remains with respect to the use and possible misuse of firearms. Police agencies generally have policies regulating the use of handguns and other firearms by their officers, both on and off duty. The courts have held that such regulations need only be reasonable and that the burden rests with the disciplined police officer to show that the regulation was arbitrary and unreasonable.[80]

Police firearms regulations may address several basic topics: shooting in defense of life, shooting to stop fleeing felons, identifying juveniles, shooting at or from vehicles, firing warning shots, shooting animals, carrying secondary weapons, carrying weapons off duty, and registering weapons.[81] Next we briefly discuss each of these topics.

Following the 1985 *Tennessee v. Garner* decision (discussed previously), firearms policies are likely to be written from the "defense of life" perspective, which permits shooting only to defeat an imminent threat to an officer's life or to another person's life (as opposed to previous policies, which included and allowed for the killing of fleeing felons).[82] Regarding juveniles, agencies generally do not instruct their officers to make a distinction between adults and juveniles when using deadly force, based on the pragmatic view that an armed juvenile can kill as well as an adult and that it is often impossible to tell if an offender is a juvenile or an adult.[83]

Shooting at or from moving vehicles has been severely limited in recent years. Some of the reasons include difficulty in hitting the target, ricochets striking innocent bystanders, difficulty in penetrating the automobile body and tires, and injuries and damages that might result should the vehicle go out of control.[84] A general consensus among police administrators is that warning shots should be prohibited as they might strike an innocent person. From a safety standpoint, "what goes up must come down," so firing a warning shot into the ground or into a tree, if allowed at all, is restricted to only a few kinds of situations.

Police agencies generally allow their officers to kill animals in self-defense, either for prevention of substantial harm to others or for relief from suffering when the animal is injured so badly that humaneness requires its killing.[85] Secondary, or backup, weapons are generally permitted so that officers who are disarmed during a confrontation have a second weapon and so that they can less conspicuously be prepared to protect themselves during routine citizen stops. A concern is that backup weapons may be used as "throwaways" in the event that an officer shoots an unarmed suspect, but the practice is generally accepted as long as the weapons are registered.[86] Similarly, carrying weapons off duty has also been controversial; however, given that while in their jurisdictions they are viewed as being on duty twenty-four hours a day, officers are generally allowed to carry such weapons, provided the weapons are registered and officers qualify on the pistol range regularly with them.[87]

Most agencies require their officers to use only department-approved weapons on and off duty and may require that the weapons be inspected, fired, and certified by the department's armorer. In addition, some agencies require that the firearms be registered by make, model, serial number, and even ballistics sample.[88]

Courts and juries are increasingly becoming harsher in dealing with police officers who misuse their firearms. The current tendency is to investigate police shootings to determine whether the officer acted negligently or whether the employing agency was negligent in training and supervising the officer.

Alcohol and Drug Abuse

Alcoholism and drug abuse problems are much more acute when they involve police employees. It is obvious, given the law of most jurisdictions and the nature of their work, that police officers must not be walking time bombs; they must be able to perform their work with a clear head that is unbefuddled by alcohol or drugs.[89] Police departments typically specify in their policy manual that no alcoholic beverages may be consumed within a specified period prior to reporting for duty. Such regulations have uniformly been upheld as rational because of the hazards of police work.

Enforcing such regulations occasionally means that police employees are ordered to submit to drug or alcohol tests. In 1989, the U.S. Supreme Court issued a major decision on drug testing: *National Treasury Employees Union v. Von Raab,*[90] which dealt with drug-testing plans for U.S. customs workers. This decision addressed all three of the most controversial drug-testing issues: whether testing should be permitted when there is no indication of a drug problem in the workplace, whether the testing methods are reliable, and whether a positive test proves there was on-the-job impairment.[91]

The Supreme Court held that although only a few customs employees tested positive, drug use is such a serious problem that the program was warranted. Second, the Court found nothing wrong with the testing protocol. In addition, while tests may punish and stigmatize a worker for extracurricular drug usage that may have no effect on his or her on-the-job performance, the Court indicated that this dilemma is still no impediment to testing.

Disciplinary Policies and Practices

Maintenance of Public Trust

Clearly, the public's trust and respect are precious commodities, quickly lost through improper behavior by police employees and the improper handling of an allegation of misconduct. Serving communities with professionalism and integrity should be the goal of every police agency and its employees in order to ensure that trust and respect are maintained. The public expects that police agencies will make every effort to identify and correct problems and respond to citizens' complaints in a judicious, consistent, fair, and equitable manner.

Employee misconduct and violations of departmental policy are the two principal areas in which discipline is applied.[92] Employee misconduct includes acts that harm the public, such as corruption, harassment, brutality, and violations of civil rights. Violations of policy may involve a broad range of issues, from substance abuse and insubordination to tardiness or minor violations of dress.

Due Process Requirements

There are well-established minimum due process requirements for discharging public employees:

They must be afforded a public hearing.

They must be present during the presentation of evidence against them and have an opportunity to cross-examine their superiors.

They must have an opportunity to present their own witnesses and other evidence concerning their side of the controversy.

They may be represented by counsel if they so choose.

They must have an impartial referee or hearing officer presiding.

There must be an eventual decision for or against them based on the weight of the evidence introduced during the hearing.

Such protections apply to any disciplinary action that can significantly affect a police employee's reputation or future chances for special assignment or promotion.[93]

At times, police administrators determine that an employee must be disciplined or terminated. Grounds for discipline or discharge can vary widely from agency to agency, and the agency's formal policies and procedures should specify what constitutes proper and improper behavior.

Complaints

Origins

A personnel **complaint** is an allegation of misconduct or illegal behavior against an employee by anyone inside or outside the organization. Internal complaints—those made from within the organization—may involve supervisors who observe officer misconduct, officers who complain about supervisors, civilian personnel who complain about officers, and so on. External complaints originate from outside the organization and usually involve the public.

Every complaint, regardless of the source, must be accepted and investigated in accordance with established policies and procedures. Anonymous complaints are the most difficult to investigate because there is no opportunity to obtain further information or to question the complainant about the allegation. Such complaints can have a negative impact on employee morale, as officers may view them as unjust and frivolous.

Types and Causes

Complaints may be handled informally or formally, depending on the seriousness of the allegation and the preference of the complainant. A formal complaint occurs when a written and signed or tape-recorded statement of the allegation is made and the complainant asks to be informed of the investigation's disposition. Figure 3 provides an example of a complaint form used to initiate a personnel investigation.

An informal complaint is an allegation of minor misconduct, made for informational purposes, that can usually be resolved without the need for more formal processes. The supervisor may simply discuss the incident with the employee and resolve it through informal counseling as long as more serious problems are not discovered and there is no history of similar complaints.

The majority of complaints against officers fall under the general categories of verbal abuse, discourtesy, harassment, improper attitude, and ethnic slurs.[94] It is clear that the verbal behavior of officers generates a significant number of complaints.

In addition, minority citizens and those with less power and fewer resources are more likely to file complaints of misconduct and to allege more serious forms of misconduct than citizens with greater power and more resources.

Figure 3
Formal Complaint Form

Control Number ________

Date & Time Reported ________ Location of Interview ________ Interview ____ Verbal ____ Written ____ Taped

Type of complaint: ____ Force ____ Procedural ____ Conduct ____ Other (Specify)

Source of complaint: ____ In Person ____ Mail ____ Telephone ____ Other (Specify)

Complaint originally received by: ____ Supervisor ____ On Duty Watch Commander ____ Chief ____ IAU ____ Other (Specify)

Notifications made: received by: ____ Division Commander ____ Chief of Police ____ On-Call Command Personnel ____ Watch Commander ____ Other (Sepcify)

Copy of formal personnel complaint given to complainant? ____ Yes ____ No

Complainant's Name: ________ Address: ________ Zip ____

Residence Phone: ________ Business Phone: ________

DOB: ____ Race: ____ Sex: ____ Occupation: ____

Location of Occurrence: ________ Date & Time of Occurrence: ________

Member(s) Involved:
(1) ________ (2) ________
(3) ________ (4) ________

Witness(es) Involved:
(1) ________ (2) ________
(3) ________ (4) ________

(1) ____ Complainant wishes to make a formal statement and has requested an investigation into the matter with a report back to him/her on the findings and actions.

(2) ____ Complainant wishes to advise the Police Department of a problem, understands that some type of action will be taken, but does not request a report back to him/her on the findings and actions.

CITIZEN ADVISEMENTS

(1) If you have not yet provided the department with a signed written statement or a tape-recorded statement, one may be required in order to pursue the investigation of this matter.

(2) The complainant(s) and/or witness(es) may be required to take a polygraph examination in order to determine the credibility concerning the allegations made.

(3) Should the allegations prove to be false, the complainant(s) and/or witness(es) may be liable for criminal and/or civil prosecution.

________ Signature of Complainant ________ Date & Time

________ Signature of Member Receiving Complaint

Receipt and Referral

Administrators must have a process for receiving complaints that is clearly delineated by departmental policy and procedures. Generally, a complaint is made at a police facility and is referred to a senior officer in charge to determine what its seriousness is and whether immediate intervention is needed.

In most cases, the senior officer will determine the nature of the complaint and will identify the employee involved; he or she then refers the matter to the employee's supervisor to conduct an initial investigation. The supervisor completes the investigation, recommends any discipline, and sends the matter to the internal affairs unit (IAU) and the agency head to finalize the disciplinary process. This method of review ensures that consistent and fair standards of discipline are applied.

Investigative Process

Generally, the employee's supervisor will conduct a preliminary inquiry of the complaint, commonly known as fact-finding. If it is determined that further investigation is necessary, the supervisor may question employees and witnesses, obtain written statements from those who were involved in the incident, and gather any necessary evidence, including photographs. Care must be exercised that the accused employee's rights are not violated. The initial investigation is sent to the appropriate division commander and forwarded to the IAU for review.

Determination and Disposition

Once an investigation has been completed, the supervisor or IAU officer must make a determination about the culpability of the accused employee and report that determination to the administrator. The following categories of dispositions are commonly used:

- *Unfounded.* The alleged act did not occur.
- *Exonerated.* The act occurred but was lawful, proper, justified, or in accordance with departmental policies, procedures, rules, and regulations.
- *Not sustained.* There was insufficient evidence to prove or disprove the allegation made.
- *Misconduct not based on the complaint.* Sustainable misconduct was determined but was not a part of the original complaint. For example, a supervisor investigating an allegation of excessive force may find that the force used was within departmental policy but that the officer made an unlawful arrest.
- *Closed.* An investigation may be halted if the complainant fails to cooperate or if it is determined that the action does not fall within the administrative jurisdiction of the police agency.
- *Sustained.* The act did occur and was a violation of departmental rules and procedures. Sustained allegations include misconduct that falls within the broad outlines of the original allegation.

Once a determination of culpability has been made, the complainant should be notified of the department's findings. Details of the investigation or recommended punishment should not be included in the correspondence. As shown in Figure 4, the complainant will normally receive only information concerning the outcome of the complaint.

POLICE DEPARTMENT
3300 Main Street
Downtown Plaza
Anywhere, U.S.A. 99999

June 20, 2007

Mr. John Doe
2200 Main Avenue
Anywhere, U.S.A.

Re: Internal Affairs #000666-98
Case Closure

Dear Mr. Doe,

Our investigation into your allegations against Officer Smith has been completed. It has been determined that your complaint is SUSTAINED, and the appropriate disciplinary action has been taken.

Our department appreciates your bringing this matter to our attention. It is our position that when a problem is identified, it should be corrected as soon as possible. It is our goal to be responsive to the concerns expressed by citizens so as to provide more efficient and effective services.

Your information regarding this incident was helpful and of value in our efforts to attain that goal. Should you have any further questions about this matter, please contact Sergeant Jane Alexander, Internal Affairs, at 555-9999.

Sincerely,

I.M. Boss
Lieutenant
Internal Affairs Unit

Figure 4
Citizen's Notification of Discipline Letter

Appeal of Disciplinary Measures

If an officer disagrees with a supervisor's recommendation for discipline, the first step of an appeal may involve a hearing before the division commander, who usually holds the rank of captain or deputy chief. The accused employee may be allowed labor representation or an attorney to assist in asking questions of the investigating supervisor, clarifying issues, and presenting new or mitigating evidence. If the employee is still not satisfied, an appeal hearing before the chief executive, which is usually the final step in appeals within the agency, is granted. The chief or sheriff communicates a decision to the employee in writing. Depending on labor agreements and civil service rules and regulations, some agencies extend their appeals of discipline beyond the department. For example, employees may bring their issue before the civil service commission or city or county manager for a final review. Employees may also have the right to an independent arbiter's review.

Level of Discipline and Type of Sanction

When an investigation against an employee is sustained, the level of discipline and type of sanction must be decided. Management must be very careful when recommending and imposing discipline because of its impact on the overall morale of the agency's employees. If employees view the recommended discipline as too lenient, it may send the wrong message that the misconduct was insignificant; on the other hand, discipline that is viewed as too harsh may have a demoralizing effect on the officer involved and on other agency employees and may result in allegations that the leadership is unfair.

Listed here, in order of severity from least to most, are the seven types of sanctions that police agencies commonly use:[95]

1. *Counseling.* This counseling is usually a conversation between the supervisor and the employee about a specific aspect of the employee's performance or conduct. It is warranted when an employee has committed a relatively minor infraction or when the nature of the offense is such that oral counseling is all that is required. No documentation or report is placed in the employee's personnel file.
2. *Documented oral counseling.* Usually the first step in a progressive disciplinary process, documented oral counseling is intended to address relatively minor infractions. It takes place when the employee has had no previous reprimands or more severe disciplinary action of the same or similar nature.
3. *Letters of reprimand.* These letters are formal written notices regarding significant misconduct, more serious performance violations, or repeated offenses. It is usually the second step in the disciplinary process and is intended to provide the employee and the agency with a written record of the violation of behavior. It identifies what specific corrective action must be taken to avoid subsequent and more serious disciplinary action.
4. *Suspension.* The step of suspension is a severe disciplinary action that results in an employee being relieved of duty, often without pay. It is usually administered when an employee commits a serious violation of established rules or after written reprimands have been given and no change in behavior or performance has resulted.
5. *Demotion.* In a demotion, an employee is placed in a position of lower responsibility and pay. It is normally used when an otherwise good employee is unable to meet the standards required for the higher position or when the employee has committed a serious act requiring that he or she be removed from a position of management or supervision.
6. *Termination.* The most severe disciplinary action that can be taken is termination. It usually occurs when previous serious discipline has been imposed and there has been inadequate or no improvement in behavior or performance, but it may also occur when an employee commits an offense so serious that continued employment would be inappropriate.

7. *Transfer.* Many agencies use the disciplinary transfer to deal with problem officers. Officers can be transferred to a different location or assignment, and this action is often seen as an effective disciplinary tool.

SUMMARY

This chapter has examined ethics as well as several topics that might well be termed the *underbelly* of the field: police use of force, police brutality, bias-based policing, police corruption, and the code of silence. We also considered a number of areas in which federal courts have placed limitations on police behaviors by virtue of the unique role of the police and the necessary higher standard of behavior: freedom of speech, search and seizure, self-incrimination, freedom of religion, sexual misconduct, residency requirements, moonlighting, misuse of firearms, and alcohol and drug abuse. The chapter also examined disciplinary policies and practices.

Clearly, it would be a much better profession—and society—if these unsavory topics could be omitted, but ours is not a perfect world, nor are the police perfect. This chapter underscored the serious nature of police misbehavior and society's attempts to hold officers accountable. Police behavior is being closely scrutinized today, and the police are held to a much higher standard of behavior than ever before, especially since incidents involving violations of public trust often harm innocent or undeserving people and receive national attention.

KEY TERMS

absolute ethics
accountability
bias-based policing
code of silence
complaint
contagious shootings
"Dirty Harry problem"
Domestic Violence Offender Gun Ban
double effect
dynamic resistance response model (DRRM)
ethics
Garrity v. New Jersey
Lautenberg Amendment
limitations on officers' constitutional rights
model of circumstantial corruptibility
noble cause corruption
police brutality
police corruption
police firearms regulations
police shootings
police use of force
relative ethics
slippery slope perspective
Tennessee v. Garner
use-of-force continuums

REVIEW QUESTIONS

1. What is meant by police ethics, and what are some of the unique ethical problems that community policing can pose?
2. What is meant by noble cause corruption and the "Dirty Harry problem," and how do they each relate to Packer's crime-control and due process models of law enforcement?
3. What is meant by use of force continuum, how can it be problematic, and what is the general structure and function of the dynamic resistance response model (DRRM)?
4. What are the types of police brutality and use-of-force incidents?
5. What did the Supreme Court relatively recently decide with regard to police use of deadly force in stopping speeding vehicles in high-speed pursuits?
6. What are some organizations recommending be done in terms of tracking and dealing with incidents of police use of force?
7. What is meant by bias-based policing, what do recent studies say about police stops and searches of minorities, and what is the result in relations between minorities and police?
8. What are the purposes of the Lautenberg Amendment and the Domestic Violence Offender Gun Ban, and how can they affect the police?
9. How and why does police corruption occur, and what factors within both the community and policing seem to foster and maintain it?
10. Which constitutional limitations have federal courts placed on officers' rights and personal behavior?
11. What is the general process that police agencies use to deal with citizen complaints?
12. What are some factors used to determine the level of discipline and type of sanction for officers who are to be disciplined?

LEARN BY DOING

1. As the head of your professional standards unit in your sheriff's office, you are assigned to address the following letter, received by your sheriff. What will be your actions in response to the matter?

   Last night my seventeen-year old daughter, Jamie, was stopped by one of your deputies for speeding. I do not know the deputy's name, but his badge number is 336. I don't know what kind of people you have in your agency, but this one got very sarcastic with my daughter and said some things that weren't very nice. He even told her that if she would go out with him on a date, he wouldn't give her a ticket. When she told him that she would not go out with him, he gave her a ticket.

   I know a dispatcher there, and if I don't hear that this deputy is disciplined for his behavior, I will send a letter to the County Commission as well.

   Signed: A Concerned, Irate Taxpayer

2. Officer King has been a member of your agency for six years and one of your subordinates for two years. Her productivity, both in terms of quality and quantity, as well as her interactions with the public, have generally been at or above standard, and her performance evaluations have been satisfactory or above. In recent weeks, however, all aspects of her work have shown a significant decline; furthermore, there have been complaints from other officers about her not responding to calls for service in a timely manner (resulting in their having to cover for her) as well as inadequate investigations of traffic collisions and other matters. In addition, King's reports are often late or submitted only after you have sent her several reminders. Today a citizen contacts you to complain about her rudeness while taking a burglary report yesterday. You decide it is time to call her into your office to discuss these matters. How will you address this situation?
3. Your police agency has a policy concerning the solicitation and acceptance of gifts; essentially, it states that no personnel shall accept any gift, gratuity, loan, fee, or thing of value which might tend to improperly influence their actions in any manner. Your subordinate, Officer Fisher, recently addressed a problem at a municipal country club that involved a lot of after-hours juvenile loitering and vandalism problems in the club's parking lot. The club manager, Mr. Chang, wishes to show appreciation to the officer and has made arrangements for the officer and family to receive a 15 percent discount when eating or golfing there. Fisher approaches you for guidance: accept the offer or not? What would be your response and accompanying explanation?

mycrimekit™

Go to MyCrimeKit.com and discover additional study tools and resources related to this chapter.

- Key Terms
- Review Questions
  - Multiple Choice Questions
  - True/False
  - Fill in the Blank
  - Essay
- MEDIA REVIEW: where you can review the *types of force* and *ethics and corruption.*
- MEDIA VIDEO: *Police Excessive Force in African-American Communities*
- FLASHCARDS: to test your knowledge of this chapter.
- *NEW YORK TIMES:* where you can read the latest articles related to criminology and criminal law.
- THE CAREER CENTER: where you can explore career opportunities in criminal justice and criminology.
- THE ONLINE RESEARCH LIBRARY: where you can explore the Cybrary and Research Navigator.

NOTES

1. See Carl Klockars, "The Dirty Harry Problem," in *Police and Society: Touchstone Readings*, 2nd ed., ed. Victor E. Kappeler (Prospect Heights, IL: Waveland Press, 1999), pp. 329–346.
2. Herbert Packer, *The Limits of the Criminal Sanction* (Stanford, CA: Stanford University Press, 1968).
3. Jocelyn M. Pollack, "Ethics and Law Enforcement," in *Critical Issues in Policing: Contemporary Readings,* 5th ed., ed. Roger G. Dunham and Geoffrey P. Alpert (Long Grove, IL: Waveland Press, 2005), pp. 280–303.
4. Brian Withrow and Jeffrey D. Dailey, "When Strings Are Attached: Understanding the Role of Gratuities in Police Corruptibility," in *Contemporary Policing Controversies, Challenges, and Solutions: An Anthology,* ed. Quint Thurman and Jihong Zhao (Los Angeles: Roxbury, 2004), pp. 319–326.
5. "No Free (or Discounted) Lunch for Bradenton Cops," *Law Enforcement News,* October 15, 2000, p. 6.
6. Kenneth J. Peak, B. Grant Stitt, and Ronald W. Glensor, "Ethics in Community Policing and Problem Solving," *Police Quarterly* 1 (1998): 30–31.
7. L. Morris, *Incredible New York* (New York: Bonanza, 1951).
8. James A. Inciardi, *Criminal Justice,* 5th ed. (Orlando, FL: Harcourt Brace, 1996).
9. Egon Bittner, "The Functions of the Police in Modern Society," in *Policing: A View from the Street,* ed. Peter K. Manning and John Van Maanen (Santa Monica, CA: Goodyear, 1978), pp. 32–50.
10. Ibid., p. 36.
11. Adapted from Lorie A. Fridell, "Improving Use-of-Force Policy: Policy Enforcement and Training," in ed. Joshua A. Ederheimer and Lorie A. Fridell *Chief Concerns: Exploring the Challenges of Police Use of Force,* (Washington, DC: Police Executive Research Form, April 2005), p. 48.
12. Charles Joyner and Chad Basile, "The Dynamic Resistance Response Model," *FBI Law Enforcement Bulletin* (September 2007), p. 17.
13. Patrick McGreevy and Richard Winton, "LAPD Shooting Blamed on Poor Supervision," *Los Angeles Times,* December 6, 2006, www.theppsc.org/forums/showthread.php?t=1620 (accessed July 30, 2010).
14. Associated Press, "3 NYPD detectives acquitted in groom slaying," April 25, 2008, www.msnbc.msn.com/id/24305660 (accessed August 1, 2010).
15. Michael Wilson, "50 Shots Fired, and the Experts Offer a Theory," www.nytimes.com/2006/11/27/nyregion/27fire.html?ei=5088&en=357cf73362b1de61&ex=1322283600&partner=rs&pagewanted=print (accessed July 30, 2010).
16. "L.A. Police Corruption Case Continues to Grow," *Washington Post,* February 13, 2000, p. 1A.
17. Human Rights Watch, *Shielded from Justice: Police Brutality and Accountability in the United States* (New York: Author, 1998).

18. Ibid.
19. Fox Butterfield, "When the Police Shoot, Who's Counting? *New York Times,* April 29, 2001, p. A1.
20. Ibid.
21. Kit R. Roane, "Policing the Police Is a Dicey Business: But the Feds Have a Plan to Root Out Racial Bias;" *U.S. News and World Report,* April 30, 2001, p. 28.
22. James J. Fyfe, Jack R. Greene, William F. Walsh, et al., *Police Administration,* 5th ed. (New York: McGraw-Hill, 1997), 197–198.
23. *Tennessee v. Garner,* 471 U.S. 1, 105 S.Ct. 1694, 85 L.Ed.2d 1 (1985).
24. George F. Cole and Christopher E. Smith, *The American System of Criminal Justice,* 12th ed. (Florence, KY: Cengage, 2010), p. 228.
25. A. C. Germann, Frank D. Day, and Robert R. J. Gallati, *Introduction to Law Enforcement and Criminal Justice* (Springfield, IL: Charles C Thomas, 1976), p. 225.
26. Albert J. Reiss Jr., "Police Brutality: Answers to Key Questions," *Transaction* (July–August 1968): 10–19.
27. Ibid.
28. Germann, Day, and Gallati, *Introduction to Law Enforcement and Criminal Justice,* p. 225.
29. *Scott v. Harris,* 550 U.S. 372 (2007), at p. 13.
30. Office of Justice Programs, Department of Justice, "Police Stop White, Black, and Hispanic Drivers at Similar Rates According to Department of Justice Report," www.ojp.usdoj.gov/newsroom/pressreleases/2007/BJS07020.htm (accessed July 31, 2010).
31. Randall Kennedy, "Suspect Policy," *New Republic,* September 13, 1999, pp. 30–35.
32. Donald Black, *Manners and Customs of the Police* (New York: Academic Press, 1980), p. 117; Richard J. Lundman, "Domestic Police-Citizen Encounters," *Journal of Police Science and Administration* 2 (March 1974): 25.
33. Jerome Skolnick, *The Police and the Urban Ghetto* (Chicago: American Bar Foundation, 1968).
34. Samuel Walker, *The Police in America: An Introduction* (New York: McGraw-Hill, 1983), p. 234.
35. Ibid., p. 235.
36. Robert Friedrich, "Racial Prejudice and Police Treatment of Blacks," in *Evaluating Alternative Law Enforcement Policies,* ed. Ralph Baker and Fred A. Meyers (Lexington, MA: Lexington Books, 1979), pp. 160–161.
37. Douglas A. Smith and Christy A. Visher, "Street-Level Justice: Situational Determinants of Police Arrest Decisions," *Social Problems* 29 (December 1981): 167–187.
38. Albert J. Reiss, *The Police and the Public* (New Haven, CT: Yale University Press, 1971), p. 151.
39. "Beat Your Spouse, Lose Your Job," *Law Enforcement News,* December 31, 1997, p. 9.
40. Ibid.
41. Adapted from Jerry Hoover, "Brady Bill Unfair in Broad Approach to Police Officers," *Reno Gazette Journal,* September 25, 1998, p. 11A.
42. "Denver Cop's Case Galvanizes Opponents of Lautenberg Gun Ban," *Law Enforcement News,* February 14, 1999, p. 1.

43. Lawrence W. Sherman, ed., *Police Corruption: A Sociological Perspective* (Garden City, NY: Anchor, 1974), p. 1.
44. See Peter Maas, *Serpico* (New York: Viking, 1973); *The Knapp Commission Report on Police Corruption* (New York: George Braziller, 1973).
45. Herman Goldstein, *Policing a Free Society* (Cambridge, MA: Ballinger, 1977), p. 188.
46. Ibid.
47. Gordon Witkin, "When the Bad Guys Are Cops," *Newsweek,* September 11, 1995, p. 20.
48. Ibid., p. 22.
49. Lawrence W. Sherman, "Becoming Bent," in *Moral Issues in Police Work,* ed. F. A. Elliston and M. Feldberg (Totowa, NJ: Rowan and Allanheld, 1985), pp. 253–265.
50. Christian P. Potholm and Richard E. Morgan, eds., *Focus on Police: Police in American Society* (New York: Schenkman, 1976), p. 140.
51. Ellwyn R. Stoddard, "Blue Coat Crime," in *Thinking about Police: Contemporary Readings,* ed. Carl B. Klockars (New York: McGraw-Hill, 1983), pp. 338–350.
52. Walker, *The Police in America,* p. 175.
53. David Burnham, "Police Aides Told to Rid Commands of All Dishonesty," *New York Times,* October 29, 1970, p. 1.
54. Brian L. Withrow and Jeffrey D. Dailey, "When Strings Are Attached," in *Contemporary Policing: Controversies, Challenges, and Solutions,* ed. Quint C. Thurman and Jihong Zhao (Los Angeles: Roxbury, 2004), pp. 319–326.
55. David L. Carter, "Drug Use and Drug-Related Corruption of Police Officers," in *Policing Perspectives: An Anthology,* ed. Larry K. Gaines and Gary W. Cordner (Los Angeles: Roxbury, 1999), pp. 311–323.
56. Patrick V. Murphy and Thomas Plate, *Commissioner: A View from the Top of American Law Enforcement* (New York: Simon and Schuster, 1977), p. 226.
57. William A. Westley, *Violence and the Police* (Cambridge, MA: MIT Press, 1970), pp. 113–114.
58. Thomas E. Wren, "Whistle-Blowing and Loyalty to One's Friends," in *Police Ethics: Hard Choices in Law Enforcement,* ed. William C. Heffernan (New York: John Jay Press, 1985), pp. 25–43.
59. David Weisburd and Rosanne Greenspan, *Police Attitudes Toward Abuse of Authority: Findings from a National Study* (Washington, DC: U.S. Department of Justice, National Institute of Justice, Research in Brief, May 2000), p. 5.
60. See 18 U.S.C., Section 1955.
61. See, for example, *United States v. Hyde,* 448 F.2d 815 (5th Cir. 1971), cert. den., 404 U.S. 1058 (1972); *United States v. Addonizia,* 451 F.2d 49 (3d Cir.), cert. den., 405 U.S. 936 (1972); and *United States v. Kenney,* 462 F.2d 1205 (3d Cir.), as amended, 462 F.2d 1230 (3d Cir.), cert. den., 409 U.S. 914 (1972).
62. Herbert Beigel, "The Investigation and Prosecution of Police Corruption," in *Focus on Police,* ed. Christian P. Potholm and Richard E. Morgan (New York: Schenkman, 1976), pp. 139–166.
63. "Artificial Intelligence Tackles a Very Real Problem—Police Misconduct Control," *Law Enforcement News,* September 30, 1994, p. 1.

64. *Pickering v. Board of Education*, 391 U.S. 563 (1968), p. 568.
65. *Muller v. Conlisk*, 429 F.2d 901 (7th Cir. 1970).
66. *Kelley v. Johnston*, 425 U.S. 238 (1976).
67. See *People v. Tidwell*, 266 N.E.2d 787 (Ill. 1971).
68. *McDonell v. Hunter*, 611 F. Supp. 1122 (SD Iowa 1985), aff'd. as mod., 809 F.2d 1302 (8th Cir. 1987).
69. *Garrity v. New Jersey*, 385 U.S. 483 (1967).
70. See *Gabrilowitz v. Newman*, 582 F.2d 100 (1st Cir. 1978).
71. *United States v. City of Albuquerque*, 12 EPD 11, 244 (10th Cir.); also see *Trans World Airlines v. Hardison*, 97 S.Ct. 2264 (1977).
72. Allen D. Sapp, "Police Officer Sexual Misconduct: A Field Research Study," in *Crime and Justice in America: Present Realities and Future Prospects*, ed. Paul F. Cromwell and Roger G. Dunham (Upper Saddle River, NJ: Prentice Hall, 1997), pp. 139–151.
73. Ibid.
74. See *Briggs v. North Muskegon Police Department*, 563 F. Supp. 585 (W.D. Mich. 1983), aff'd. 746 F.2d 1475 (6th Cir. 1984).
75. *Oliverson v. West Valley City*, 875 F. Supp. 1465 (D. Utah 1995).
76. *Henery v. City of Sherman*, 928 S.W.2d 464 (Sup. Ct. Texas), cert. den., 17 S.Ct. 1098 (1997).
77. See, for example, *Cox v. McNamara*, 493 P.2d 54 (Ore. 1972); *Brenckle v. Township of Shaler*, 281 A.2d 920 (Pa. 1972); *Flood v. Kennedy*, 239 N.Y.S.2d 665 (1963); and *Hopwood v. City of Paducah*, 424 S.W.2d 134 (Ky. 1968).
78. Richard N. Williams, *Legal Aspects of Discipline by Police Administrators*, Traffic Institute Publication 2705 (Evanston, IL: Northwestern University, 1975), p. 4.
79. See *Lally v. Department of Police*, 306 So.2d 65 (La. 1974).
80. Charles R. Swanson, Leonard Territo, and Robert W. Taylor, *Police Administration*, 5th ed. (Upper Saddle River, NJ: Prentice Hall, 2005), p. 586.
81. Ibid.
82. Ibid.
83. Kenneth James Matulia, *A Balance of Forces: Model Deadly Force Policy and Procedure* (Alexandria, VA: International Association of Chiefs of Police, 1985), pp. 23–24.
84. Catherine H. Milton, Jeanne Wahl Halleck, James Larndew, et al., *Police Use of Deadly Force* (Washington, DC: Police Foundation, 1977), p. 52.
85. Matulia, *A Balance of Forces*, p. 52.
86. Ibid., p. 177.
87. Ibid.
88. Ibid., p. 78.
89. See *Krolick v. Lowery*, 302 N.Y.S.2d 109 (1969), p. 115; and *Hester v. Milledgeville*, 598 F. Supp. 1456, 1457 (M.D. Ga. 1984).
90. *National Treasury Employees Union v. Von Raab*, 489 U.S. 656 (1989).
91. Robert J. Alberts and Harvey W. Rubin, "Court's Rulings on Testing Crack Down on Drug Abuse," *Risk Management* 38 (March 1991): 36–41.

92. V. McLaughlin and R. Bing, "Law Enforcement Personnel Selection," *Journal of Police Science and Administration* 15 (1987): 271–276.

93. Ibid.

94. Allen E. Wagner and Scott H. Decker, "Evaluating Citizen Complaints Against the Police," in *Critical Issues in Policing: Contemporary Readings,* 3rd ed., ed. Roger G. Dunham and Geoffrey P. Alpert (Prospect Heights, IL: Waveland Press, 1989), pp. 302–318.

95. Kenneth J. Peak, Larry K. Gaines, and Ronald W. Glensor, *Police Supervision and Management: In an Era of Community Policing,* 3rd ed. (Upper Saddle River, NJ: Prentice Hall, 2010), p. 260.

Technology Review

Technology Review

TOOLS FOR THE TASKS

We've arranged a civilization in which most crucial elements profoundly depend on science and technology.

—Carl Sagan

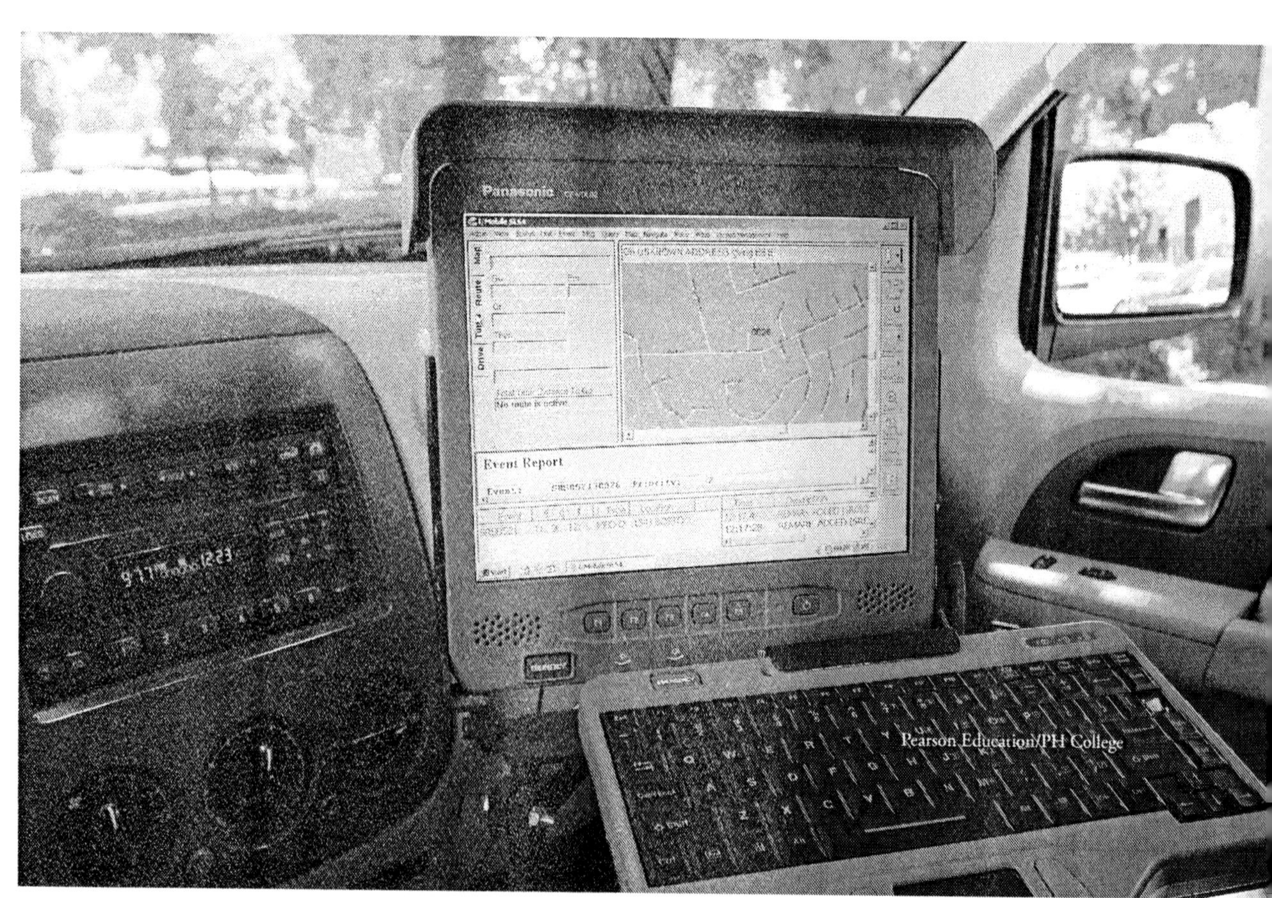

Pearson Education/PH College

Learning Objectives

As a result of reading this chapter, the student will:

- See how new uses for software are being applied to old problems of crime and national security
- Understand some of the major discoveries in less-lethal weapons
- Be aware of how wireless technology, mapping, and profiling systems have benefited the police
- Understand how technology assists the police in their traffic- and gang-suppression functions
- Know some of the recent developments in firearms training and investigation
- Be able to explain how police training and communications functions are enhanced by technology
- Have an understanding of the purposes for which robots are being used in policing
- Be aware of how augmented reality, unmanned aerial vehicles, and nanotechnology might benefit law enforcement in the future

Introduction

As will be seen, technology has had tremendous impact in policing, rapidly expanding and changing the work of criminal investigators in the forensics arena, while also providing many more capabilities for those whose work is at the street level. As will also be shown, even more exciting technologies are on the horizon. Indeed, one might say that our only limitations are our imagination and the amount of money that we are willing and able to devote to research and development.

This chapter begins by showcasing twelve new uses of technologies for addressing old crime and security problems. Then we consider some fundamental problems that exist in the area of policing and technology, particularly the need for better-trained personnel who understand computer hardware and software. Next we discuss technologies that are being developed to combat terrorism; then we look at the development and status of less-lethal weapons, followed by a consideration of wireless technology for use in databases, in crime mapping, and in analyses of serial offenders and gunshots. Then we examine how electronic capabilities are being applied to several traffic functions. Following a review of developments with fingerprints and mug shots, new uses of technologies in the area of crime-scene investigations are presented, and we then consider how computers are assisting with regard to firearms, particularly in training officers and in solving cases involving guns. Following short commentaries on police use of intelligence systems to address gang activity and expanding uses of robots in policing, we review three exciting technologies that loom on the horizon in terms of research and development: nanotechnology, augmented reality, and unmanned aerial vehicles. The four exhibits in the chapter explain some new uses for technologies. The chapter concludes with a summary, key terms, review questions, and several scenarios and activities that provide opportunities for you to learn by doing.

Selected Examples: New Technologies for Old Problems

Following are a dozen examples of new uses of software now being deployed by criminal justice agencies to combat problems of crime and to enhance security throughout the United States. Note that some are in the early stages of development, are still controversial and as yet unproven for scientific accuracy, and may be quite expensive to obtain. Nonetheless, these vignettes demonstrate the unlimited potential for applying computer technologies for policing:

1. A fast-food worker in Chicago was robbed at knifepoint, and responding officers had the restaurant's surveillance video enhanced by a Regional Computer Forensics Laboratory (RCFL); a clearer picture of the suspect was compared against the Illinois driver's license database, resulting in a match and arrest of the suspect.[1]
2. Smartphones are rapidly catching up with mobile phones in police application. Officers can run queries from motor vehicle and criminal databases, send and receive information from other officers or dispatchers, and obtain information about speeders or drunk drivers; the greatest advantage is e-mail capability, with officers on patrol no longer needing to go to a laptop and log on.[2]
3. Sending the police a crime tip via text message might seem "old hat" at this point, but in reality it is a relatively new practice now spreading across the United States. And sending crime information will not compromise citizens' anonymity because the messages are relayed through third-party companies' servers that encrypt the cell phone numbers before the messages reach the police department.[3]
4. Community policing has expanded its horizons with the police use of Twitter, by which officers can send out "tweets" to a large segment of the population that might not read the news or watch it on television. This method of engaging the community is a positive complement to police agencies' use of other Web tools and social media sites such as Facebook and MySpace.[4]

5. Although not as yet in use by the police, the U.S. military has developed a new rifle that makes the firing of a bullet more intelligent. The shooter aims at the target with the laser sight and gets a distance reading; the bullet then explodes as it reaches that point, or the shooter can adjust that distance by up to 3 meters earlier or later. Inside the bullet is a chip that receives radio signals from the gun, telling it the distance to the target. If the bullets can be fitted with a stun system, a blinding light, or even a gas that knocks out targets, then they become very useful not only for the military but also in police hostage situations and when interacting with dangerous subjects and others who are in a position where they cannot be seen or interacted with easily—and they may reduce the number of fatal casualties on both the police and civilian sides.[5]
6. Handheld voice-translation devices are being tested by several police agencies. The units contain interchangeable computer chips loaded with more than one thousand phrases from different languages, including Spanish, Arabic, Vietnamese, Cantonese, and Mandarin. The translators offer a menu from which users select a phrase and language with a stylus, and the device then speaks in the chosen language.[6]
7. With a wireless video networking system, officers in several states can literally watch each other's back from anywhere in their area and receive real-time video either in the field or in the office. In Oklahoma City, with nearly 500 cameras covering 555 square miles, the system streams video to laptops in the city's 700 patrol cars; when an event occurs, commanding officers take control of the cameras in the area and provide the video to officers at the scene.[7]
8. With more than 500,000 registered sex offenders in the United States, 100,000 of whom are "lost" by disappearing into society without properly notifying authorities, keeping track of them has proven difficult for the police. To help the police keep tabs on the offenders, a Web-based application has been developed that includes a database of registered sex offenders accessible to local police agencies. A Massachusetts-based firm purchases data from sources around the country and strings a range of information together in the database. For example, a previously known address of a wanted felon may yield the names of others who have lived at that address; the police can then know the names of people who have been in contact with the offender and contact them about the missing offender's whereabouts.[8]
9. An academic researcher at Columbia University has applied a geographic information system (GIS) to protect citizens against domestic violence. GIS has been adapted to study patterns of domestic violence throughout New York City, analyze the effectiveness of domestic violence outreach programs, and offer presentations to city agencies and nonprofit organizations. The number and time of occurrence of domestic violence reports filed and geographic information—data on streets, boundaries, congressional districts—are obtained and help the mayor's domestic violence office plan its activities.[9]

10. A tool for **voice-stress analysis** is gaining popularity among police agencies for use with suspects and in prisons for use with inmates. At least 1,500 such agencies are using voice-stress analysis software when questioning subjects. The software (which costs about $10,000) is typically loaded onto a laptop. During an interrogation, the subject talks into a microphone, and the words are translated on screen into graphs that measure speech with algorithms and formulas, showing patterns indicative of confusion and cognitive dissonance. Critics, however, say no studies show the system works. They point to several anecdotal accounts where persons being questioned made false confessions and argue that such people confess because they are afraid of the analyzer. Clearly, more studies are needed to determine whether voice-stress analysis is, as one writer stated, "good science, or just bunk."[10]
11. Under recent legislation, Arizona law enforcement officials can investigate profits from alleged immigrant smuggling across the 389-mile Arizona–Mexico border. People who smuggle immigrants across the border—and who collect an average of $1,000 for each person they assist—prefer Western Union transfers because they are not easily traced. Special software is now used to analyze data documenting Western Union financial transfers of amounts greater than $750, looking for evidence of smuggling. Investigators, armed with a court subpoena, request data relating to persons sending and receiving wire transactions of $750 or more during a certain time period. Computers sift through the data looking for suspicious patterns. If a person can prove no illegal activity is involved, the money is released. Money found to be associated with trafficking is seized and deposited into a revolving account that helps fund the operation.[11]
12. The Department of Homeland Security has completed installation of next-generation **biometrics**, which are technologies that scan human body characteristics, such as facial and voice patterns, fingerprints, eye irises and retinas, and hand measurements, to verify someone's identity. Mandated by Congress and used at 104 land border ports, biometric and biographical information can be compared against watch lists of terrorists, criminals, and immigration violators. Federal penitentiary escapees, convicted rapists, drug traffickers, and others have also been nabbed at the borders using biometrics.[12]

The accompanying Career Profile includes the views of a police officer who has had considerable experience working with police technologies.

Exhibit 1 describes several new applications for use in identifying an old and simple piece of Americana: the vehicle license plate.

Police and Technology of the Future: Problems and Prospects

First the good news: It is anticipated that police officers of the future will function in very different ways and on very different terms than officers of the past. There will be few time and space constraints because all officers will be equipped with a pager, a cell

CAREER PROFILE

Name: Grant Humerickhouse

Position: Police officer

City, State: Madison, Wisconsin

College attended: Michigan State University

Major: Criminal justice

Year hired: 2006

Please give a brief description of your job.

My department is very progressive in its diversity and with problem-oriented policing. During my second year in patrol, I had an opportunity to be part of a community policing team, working with property managers and owners who wanted their property to be safe—and with college students who wanted to have parties and stay out late. Finding the balance was not only good for me as a young officer but challenging and exciting from a problem-oriented policing standpoint.

What appealed to you most about the occupation?

While I was in college, an Introduction to Criminal Justice course instructor told many tales about high-speed pursuits, gory homicide scenes, and arrests during his career. This fueled my dreams of driving fast, catching bad guys, and experiencing something new each day. I wanted to talk to all types of people, learn their problems and help them, assist victims, be the voice for the oppressed, and work for justice.

How would you describe the interview process?

The application process was grueling. I was asked to admit things very few people in my life knew about and to discuss every person I had ever lived with, every place I had worked, every boss, every co-worker, every phone number, and the list was endless.

What is a typical day like?

There is nothing predictable and nothing ordinary about policing. Although rewarding, fulfilling, and challenging, it is extremely difficult on a person emotionally, mentally, and physically. I have learned that I am not omniscient, omnipotent, or able to solve every problem. I remember my first suicide investigation, my first child abuse case, my first car crash, the first time a bad guy got away—including the colors, sounds, and feelings.

What qualities and characteristics are most helpful for this position?

Policing should not be a choice but a calling. The unpredictable hours, missed holidays, graveyard shifts, and tears are offset by the rewards. Know your limitations, and always tell the truth; integrity is your professional life. Also, be comfortable with technology: I am expected to master computer-aided dispatching, mobile data computers, and mobile audio and video recordings, to name a few applications.

What career advice would you give someone in college beginning their criminal justice studies?

Talk to people about the job, go on a ride-along, explore the myriad different paths that law enforcement has to offer. Talk to your family about your career choice; you are going to have to lean on them after a bad day. Be honest and forthright about your drug use, traffic tickets, and every other dirty little secret the department asks you to admit.

License plate recognition devices mounted on a patrol car. *(Courtesy Orange County, Florida, Sheriff's Office and FBI Law Enforcement Bulletin)*

EXHIBIT 1

License Plate Recognition Systems: Boon or Bane?

License plate recognition systems have long been in use for traffic enforcement; cameras, either mounted on a mobile tripod or permanently fixed on a pole, trigger a flash camera when a vehicle is exceeding the speed limit. Today, however, cameras are being mounted on police patrol cars or in fixed locations and used for many more purposes, such as searching for stolen cars. In the event of a "hit" on a license plate in a stolen vehicle database, an alarm alerts the officer of the match. The officer can then contact dispatch to see if the information is correct. The cameras can also help in more serious investigations, such as where a partial license plate number is obtained from a witness to a hit-and-run. Furthermore, if a bank robbery occurs during the noon hour, the personnel operating the plate reader can pass along the plates that were read at that location at that time as possible suspects. Or, if a serious crime is committed in an area, detectives can search the system to see if they have data on the cars that were parked there.[1] In late 2009, Tiburon, California, perhaps became the first U.S. city to permanently install six cameras that recognize license plate characters at two roads that basically line its borders, essentially to accomplish the above objectives.[2] Such applications have, of course, drawn criticism from privacy rights advocates as well as from citizens concerned with how the cameras are used to track people's movements, and what is done with the data they produce. Others, however, believe the cameras reduce the need for agencies to hire more officers and are the "future of law enforcement."[3]

[1]Adapted from Jim McKay, "License Plate Recognition Systems Extend the Reach of Patrol Officers," *Government Technology,* April 9, 2008, www.govtech.com/gt/articles/282014 (accessed August 7, 2010).

[2]Demian Bulwa, "Tiburon to Record Every Car Coming and Going," *San Francisco Chronicle,* November 20, 2009, www.sfgate.com/cgi-bin/article.cgi?f=/c/a/2009/11/19/BAP71ANBF4.DTL&tsp=1 (accessed August 6, 2010).

[3]McKay, "License Plate Recognition Systems Extend the Reach of Patrol Officers."

phone, and a laptop computer with software that includes encryption programs and sophisticated databases and search engines. Officers will have software that allows them to have real-time chats with officers from other agencies, in other states, or even in other countries. Before going on the streets, every rookie will be an expert at using computers and will be able to use crime-analysis software.[13]

As the saying goes, however, "The fleas come with the dog." The alliance between police and technologies can also pose new challenges. For example, from

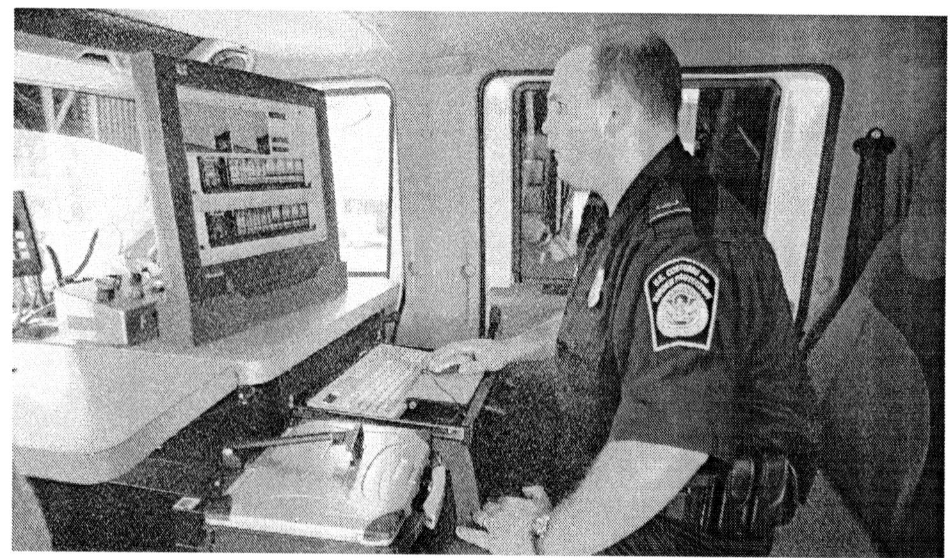

A CBP officer looks at an X-ray of an entire truck for potential contraband. *(Courtesy U.S. Customs and Border Protection)*

1995 to 1998 (the last year of the program), the federal Office of Community Oriented Policing Services poured hundreds of millions of dollars into police agencies for new equipment.[14] However, many departments lacked the in-house computer expertise to install or run the software and equipment—even today, many police executives believe that they hire people to be police officers, not computer programmers or database experts. But the nature of the policing business is changing, and today many police agencies employ civilian information technology staff who understand how that capability supports the operational needs of the police officer on the street. For the future, however, the challenge remains for the police to be able to address such criminal schemes as digital compression, remote storage, audit disabling, anonymous remailers, digital cash, computer penetration and looping, and cloning of cellular phones and phone cards.[15]

Technology Versus Terrorists

The terrorist attacks on September 11, 2001, not only changed the way federal, state, and local law enforcement agencies approach their mission (in essence, they now also protect citizens against attack from the outside rather than only from within the United States) but also set in motion research and development of new technologies for protecting against terrorist acts. And Americans seem accepting of more surveillance and screening technologies even if it means giving up some of their privacy: Polls conducted immediately after the September 11 attacks revealed that an overwhelming majority of Americans—about 75 percent—thought it necessary to give up some personal freedoms for the sake of security.[16] Following are some technologies that have been or are being developed to supplement luggage scanners and metal detectors to assist in detecting and foiling terrorists.

A low-dose X-ray imager can see through garments to detect stashed weapons, drugs, or other contraband. (The September 11 terrorists slipped through checkpoints with box cutters.) Surveillance cameras can scan faces and feed the images to a computer that scours a database of digital mug shots for a match. These devices were used during the 2001 Super Bowl in Tampa, Florida, and identified several petty criminals in the crowd. Soon after that, however, many Floridians and the state's civil liberties union protested their use.[17] Better bomb-detecting technology is also being developed, including machines that perform a cross-sectional X-ray scan of checked baggage, and ion-detecting swabs can find bomb residue on hand luggage. Also being considered for limited use are "smart cards"—IDs equipped with memory chips that store personal data and that can track movements and transactions.[18]

Development and Status of Less-Lethal Weapons

Recorded history is full of accounts of the need to protect ourselves from a hostile environment.[19] Certainly, international police forces have attempted to employ many means to protect themselves and the public at large. Next we briefly consider **less-lethal**

weapons developed since professional policing first appeared with London bobbies. Some of these weapons seem a bit archaic and even humorous, but it will be shown that the police and those who are engaged in research and development have long sought—and are still seeking—the perfect tool that can be deployed safely and efficiently.

Note that although the term *nonlethal weapon* is often used to describe these tools, this term is inappropriate because any tool or weapon can be lethal if it is used in an improper or unintended manner. For this reason, the term *less-lethal weapon* is more properly used to designate a weapon designed to produce only a temporary effect and minimal medical consequences for healthy people.[20]

1829: The Unveiling

When London's new bobbies began patrolling the streets in September 1829, they were armed with a baton, or truncheon, that still is a standard-issue weapon. Traditionally, it was made of hardwood, and it was two to four centimeters in diameter and thirty to sixty-five centimeters in length.[21]

In similar fashion, when policing came to New York City in 1844, officers were armed with thirty-three-inch clubs, which officers were not reluctant to use. Charges of police brutality were common in the mid-nineteenth century, when officers allegedly clubbed "respectable" citizens with frequency.[22] Until the end of the nineteenth century, the baton remained a staple tool among American police. As late as 1900, when the Chicago Police Department numbered 3,225 officers, the only tools given the new patrolmen were "a brief speech from a high-ranking officer, a hickory stick, whistle, and a key to the call box."[23] Charges of police brutality continued.

1860s–1950s: Chemical Weapons

From 1860 to 1959, only one major category was added to the small array of less-lethal police tools: **chemical weapons**. CN gas (chloroacetophenone) was synthesized by German chemists in 1869 and was the first tear gas; it produced a burning sensation in the throat, eyes, and nose. It became available for use in aerosol cans in 1965; Chemical Mace was the most well-known brand. By 1912, chemical weapons were increasingly used for quelling riots and subduing criminals.[24]

CS gas (2-chlorobenzalmalononitrile) was first synthesized in 1928 as a white powder that stored well. It was adopted by many police forces because it had a greater effect than CN, causing a very strong burning sensation in the eyes that often caused them to close involuntarily. Severe pain in the nose, throat, and chest; vomiting; and nausea are also associated with its use.[25]

1960s: A Technological Explosion

The 1960s witnessed major technological advances in less-lethal weaponry. Aerosol chemical agents, developed to provide alternatives to police batons and firearms, became the most popular less-lethal weapons for police use. Mace seemed like "manna from heaven."[26] CR gas (dibenzoxazepine) appeared in 1962; six times more potent than CS and twenty times more potent than CN, it caused extreme eye pressure and occasionally hysteria. CS gas cartridges, which were fired by shotguns at a range of 125 meters, were used in the United States and Britain as early as 1968.

In 1967, alternatives to lethal lead bullets were first used in Hong Kong. Wooden rounds, fired from a signal pistol with a range of twenty to thirty meters, were designed to be ricocheted off the ground, striking the victim in the legs. The wooden rounds proved to be fatal, however, and direct fire broke legs at forty-six meters. Rubber bullets were developed and issued to British troops and police officers in 1967, only a few months after the wooden rounds appeared. Intended to deliver a force equivalent to a hard punch at twenty-five meters, the rubber bullets caused severe bruising and shock. Also intended to be ricocheted off the ground, the rubber bullet was designed so that riot police could outrange stone throwers.[27] Rubber bullets were employed by Seattle police officers in December 1999 during protests against the World Trade Organization meeting.[28]

During the 1960s, British riot police began employing water cannons, which were designed to fire large jets of water at demonstrators. Resembling armored fire engines, water cannons were also used in Belgium, France, Germany, and the United States. Nontoxic blue dye was added to the water for marking the offenders. For a time, the firing of a CR solution was contemplated.[29]

In 1968, another unique riot-oriented weapon was unveiled in America: the Sound Curdler, which consisted of amplified speakers that produced loud shrieking noises at irregular intervals. Attached to vehicles or helicopters, the device was first used at campus disturbances.

1970s: Beanbag Guns, Strobe Lights, and "New Age" Batons

Another unique tool was introduced in 1970: a gun that shot beanbags rather than bullets. The apparatus fired a pellet-loaded bag that unfurled into a spinning pancake and was capable of knocking down a two-hundred-pound person at a range of three hundred feet. Although its manufacturer warned that it had potentially lethal capabilities, it quickly became popular in several countries, including Saudi Arabia and South Africa.[30]

Several other inventions were added to the less-lethal arsenal in the 1970s. The Photic Driver, first used by police in South Africa, produced a strobe effect; its light caused giddiness, fainting, and nausea. A British firm developed a strobe gun that operated at five flickers per second. Another apparatus, known as the Squawk Box, had two high-energy ultrasound generators operating at slightly different frequencies that produced sounds and caused nausea and giddiness.[31]

Other inventions of the early 1970s included an electrified water jet; a baton that carried a six-thousand-volt shock; shotgun shells filled with plastic pellets; plastic bubbles that immobilized rioters; a chemical that created slippery street surfaces for combating rioters; and an instant "cocoon," an adhesive substance that, when sprayed over crowds, made people stick together.[32]

Two new types of projectiles were developed in 1974: the plastic bullet and the TASER Electronic Control Device (ECD). The "softer" plastic bullets could be fired from a variety of riot weapons at a speed of 160 miles per hour and a range of thirty to seventy meters, making them attractive to riot police. Like wooden bullets, however, these new plastic bullets could be fatal, and several people died in Northern Ireland during the early 1980s after being struck in the head by them.[33]

The **TASER ECD** resembled a flashlight and shot two tiny darts into its victim. Attached to the darts were fine wires through which a transformer delivered a fifty-thousand-volt electrical shock, which would incapacitate a person at a distance of fifteen feet. Police officers in every state except Hawaii, Massachusetts, Michigan, and New Jersey had tried the device by 1985, but its use was not widespread because it had range limitations and because it was not always effective on people under the influence of drugs; heavy clothing could also render it ineffective.[34] The stun gun, also introduced in the mid-1970s, initially competed with the TASER ECD as the police tool of choice. Slightly larger than an electric razor, it also delivered a fifty-thousand-volt shock when its two electrodes were pressed directly against the body. Like the TASER ECD, its amperage was so small that it did not provide a lethal electrical jolt. It would apply a localized electrical application to cause pain compliance but not incapacitation.[35]

You may be familiar with a federal survey that indicated that about one-fourth (23 percent) of all municipal police agencies and 30 percent of sheriff's offices authorize their personnel to use a TASER ECD or stun gun.[36] These percentages will likely increase rapidly—or, quite possibly, have already increased tremendously—because the units have become easier to carry (now as small as six inches by three inches in size and seven ounces in weight) and more effective to use (including a range of up to thirty-five feet; data port storage of date, time, and duration of deployment; a red-dot laser light; and enhanced accountability (units can be upgraded to include audio and video recordings of usage). Indeed, it is now estimated that nearly 14,500 law enforcement and military agencies now deploy TASER ECD technology in more than forty countries, and more than 5,580 agencies deploy them to all of their patrol officers.[37]

Although the TASER X26 is the standard less-lethal TASER ECD device that is so popular and typically carried by patrol officers, research and development are ongoing at TASER International, Inc., and several new developments have been announced recently. First, the new TASER CAM was introduced, which offers increased protection for officers because the suspect's behavior prior to the TASER ECD's deployment can be recorded with full audio and video, even in zero light conditions. Also new is the TASER X3, a multi-shot ECD that can engage multiple targets and display Warning Arcs while loaded.

The TASER X12 Less Lethal Shotgun (LLS) by Mossberg utilizes a reengineered pump-action shotgun that fires a less-lethal, self-contained, wireless ECD (termed the XREP) that delivers a neuromuscular effect similar to that of the handheld X26 ECD; the LLS effect can also be delivered to a maximum effective range of 100 feet with blunt impact force. (See photographs of each TASER; although not apparent in the photograph, the TASER X12 is bright yellow in color—a warning to users only that it is less lethal; it will not accept standard shotgun rounds.)[38]

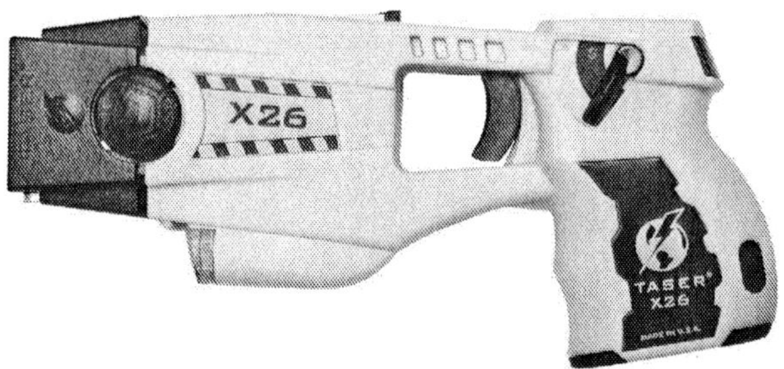

Pictured are the TASER ECD X26—the standard model that is typically carried by patrol officers; the TASER X3 (multi-shot ECD); and the TASER X12 (shotgun). *(Courtesy TASER International, Inc.)*

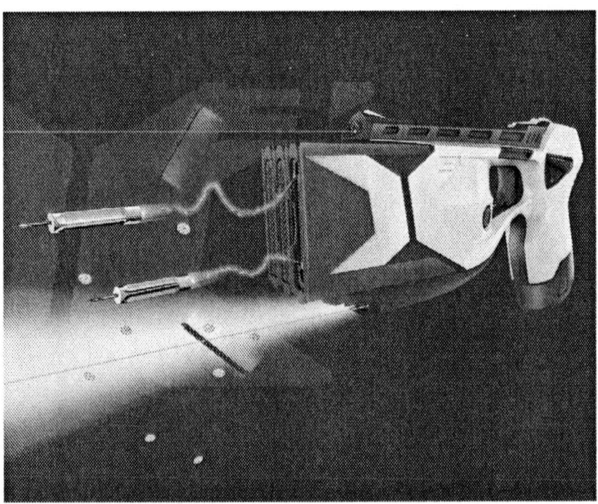

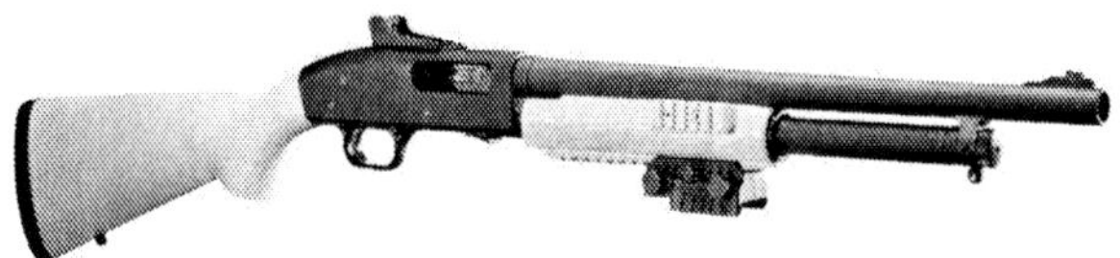

A study announced in late 2007 by the Wake Forest University School of Medicine, however—touted as "the first large, independent study to review every TASER deployment and to reliably assess the overall risk and severity of injuries in real world conditions"—reported that 99.7 percent of nearly a thousand cases of TASER use resulted in only mild injuries, such as scrapes and bruises, or no injuries at all; only three subjects (0.3 percent) suffered injuries severe enough to need hospitalization.[39]

In October 2009, TASER International, Inc., issued a training bulletin advising law enforcement officers to aim the TASER at the abdomen, back, and leg areas, rather than the chest area. Although the TASER poses an "extremely rare" risk of inducing a heart attack, TASER observed that "arrest scenarios often involve individuals who are in crisis and are at a heightened risk of serious injury or death, regardless of actions taken by law enforcement"; also, sudden cardiac arrest is "a leading cause of death in the United States, and often occurs in an arrest scenario," and "plaintiff attorneys will likely file an excessive use of force claim against the law enforcement agency and officer, and try to allege that the TASER ECD played a role in the arrest related death." In addition, aiming the TASER away from the chest "lessens the risk of shot placement into areas that are undesirable such as the head, face, neck, and female breast."[40]

The Continuing Quest

Today the quest continues for a noncontroversial and effective alternative to lethal force. The TASER ECD has probably developed more rapidly than any other tool and arguably carries the most promise for close-in applications. Still, police nationwide—some in cities that have witnessed loud public outcries in the aftermath of fatal police shootings—continue to seek a weapon that offers a less-lethal alternative, one that stops short of the deadly firearm. One has to wonder if there can ever be a less-lethal weapon developed that can truly and completely replace the firearm.

Pepper spray (oleoresin capsicum) is also a popular less-lethal tool—although it is useful only when the officer is positioned in close proximity to the suspect—and it is now in use by 97 percent of municipal police and sheriff's departments.[41] This spray inflames the mucous membranes of the eyes, nose, and mouth, causing a severe burning sensation for twenty minutes or less.[42] The spray is highly effective in subduing suspects without causing undue harm or long-term aftereffects.[43]

mycrimekit™
Review: *Wireless Technology and Policing.*

Use of Wireless Technology

Instant Access to Information

Mobile data systems have been available since the 1970s, but the first-generation systems were based on large proprietary computers that were very costly and were often beyond the reach of many small- and medium-size police agencies. The first digital data were not transmitted from police headquarters to a cruiser until the

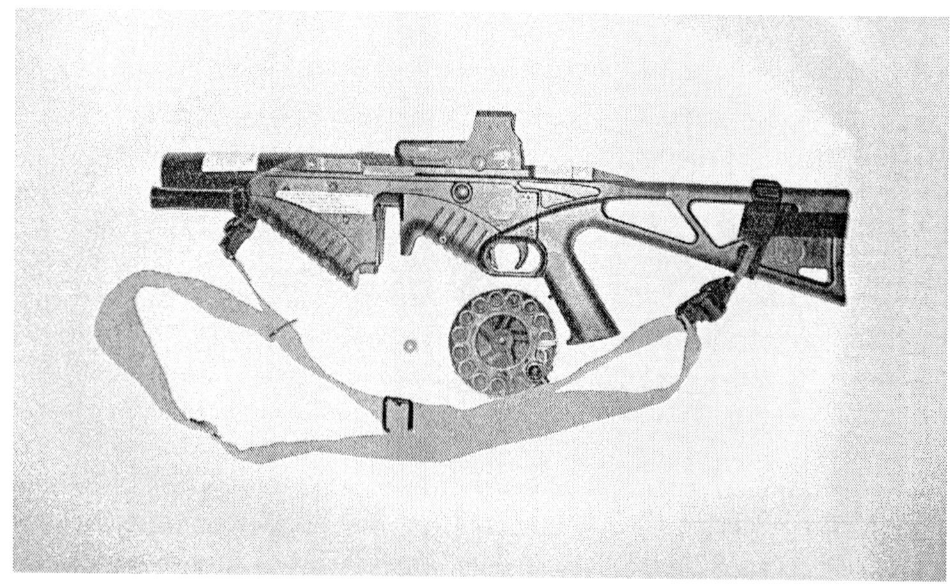

A relatively new less-lethal tool is a compressed-air gun that fires small pellets filled with oleocapsicum or other gases. *(Courtesy Sparks, Nevada, Police Department)*

mid-1980s. Today, armed with a notebook computer and a radio modem, police officers can have almost instant access to information in numerous federal, state, and local databases. Even small agencies can now afford a network and mobile data terminals (MDTs).[44]

A growing number of U.S. police departments, including small agencies, are using laptop computers with wireless connections to crime and motor vehicle databases. These systems are believed to pay for themselves in increased fines and officer safety. Officers can access court documents, in-house police department records, and a system of **computer-aided dispatching (CAD)** and can enter license numbers into their computers. Through a national network of motor vehicle and criminal history databases, they can locate drivers with outstanding warrants, expired or suspended licenses, and so on. Furthermore, rather than using open radio communications, police officers use their computers to communicate with one another via e-mail.[45]

Also relatively new on the scene are handheld personal data assistants—PDAs—which double as cell phones and allow officers on foot, motorcycle, and horseback to send and receive still images (including mug shots and driver's license photos) and listen to radio calls. The San Diego, California, police department recently obtained a $1 million contribution from Qualcomm Inc., that was used in part to purchase 400 such PDAs for officers.[46]

Integrated Databases

In 1999, a "railway killer" (who rode on trains and was suspected of as many as twenty-three murders) was engaged in a rampage across the U.S. Southwest. U.S. Border Patrol agents in Texas unknowingly picked up the killer near the Mexican

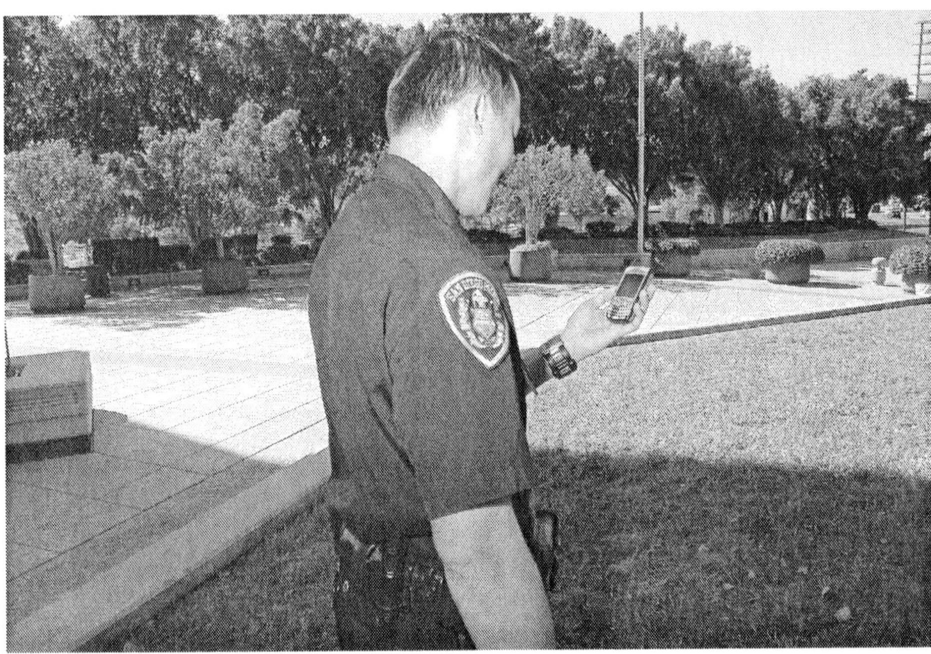

Officers without access to in-car computers can now use PDAs—handheld computers, which double as cell phones and are used by officers on foot, motorcycle, and horseback. Officers can send and receive still images (including mug shots and driver's license photos) and listen to radio calls. *(Courtesy Qualcomm and San Diego Police Department)*

border and dutifully checked the agency's database for any outstanding warrants. Finding none, they released him, and within a few days he struck again, killing two women. Several federal and local law enforcement agencies wanted the suspect for questioning, but the Border Patrol had no way of searching those agencies' databases; had it been able to do so, the killing spree might have ended sooner.[47]

Agencies will be able to cross-search databases when the U.S. Department of Justice builds its proposed Global Justice Information Network to link crime networks—including police, courts, and corrections agencies—at the local, state, national, and international levels. This is being termed a new course for the criminal justice community, which is at a historic turning point with these integration efforts. Such systems will improve the quality of information and decisions made by criminal justice officials.[48]

Evidence: *Crime Mapping.*

Crime Mapping

Conclusive evidence from clay tablets found in Iraq proves that maps have been around for several thousand years—perhaps tens of millennia.[49] A relatively recent development in policing is computerized crime mapping, which has become increasingly popular among law enforcement agencies.[50] In fact, a federal study found that departments with 100 or more officers used computer crime mapping 35 percent of the time.[51] **Computerized crime mapping** combines geographic information from global positioning satellites with crime statistics gathered by a department's CAD system and demographic data provided by private companies or the U.S. Census Bureau. (Some agencies acquire information from the Census Bureau's Internet site.) The result is a picture that combines disparate sets of data for a whole new perspective on crime. For example, maps of crimes can be overlaid with maps or layers of causative data: unemployment rates in the areas of high crime, locations of abandoned houses, population density, reports of drug activity, or geographic features (such as alleys, canals, or open fields) that might be contributing factors.[52] Furthermore, the hardware and software are now available to nearly all police agencies for a few thousand dollars.

The importance of crime mapping is evidenced by the fact that in 1997 the National Institute of Justice (NIJ) established the Crime Mapping Research Center (CMRC) to promote research, evaluation, development, and dissemination of geographic information systems technology for criminal justice research and practice. The CMRC holds annual conferences on crime mapping to give researchers and practitioners an opportunity to gain both practical and state-of-the-art information on the use and utility of computerized crime mapping.[53]

Exhibit 2 describes what has become a powerful Web-based crime-fighting tool that provides mountains of information to the police and the public: the Automated Regional Justice Information System, or **ARJIS**, based in San Diego County, California. The system affords tactical, investigative, statistical, and crime analysis information to police and a wealth of information to the public, including crime mapping.

EXHIBIT 2

ARJIS: Power of the Web

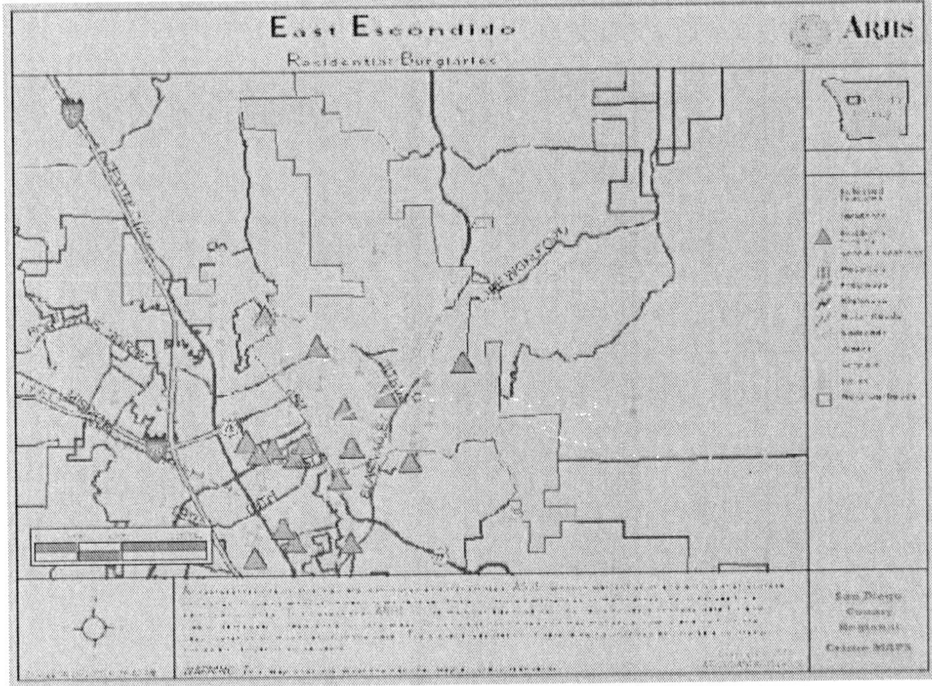

The ARJIS system of San Diego County affords tactical, investigative, statistical, and crime analysis information to police and a wealth of information to the public. Here, a map shows East Escondido citizens the locations of residential burglaries during a recent one-month time frame. *(Courtesy ARJIS.)*

The Automated Regional Justice Information System (ARJIS) was the first multiagency, interactive, publicly accessible crime-mapping Web site in the nation, serving only San Diego County. ARJIS has now evolved into a complex criminal justice enterprise network used by seventy-one local, state, and federal agencies in the two California counties that border Mexico; it integrates more than 6,000 workstations, with more than 11,000 authorized users generating more than 35,000 transactions daily.

ARJIS is used for much more than crime mapping, including tactical analysis, investigations, statistical information, and crime analysis. ARJIS is responsible for major public safety initiatives, including wireless access to photos, warrants, and other critical data in the field, crime and sex offender mapping, crime analysis tools evaluation, and an enterprise system of applications that help users solve crimes and identify offenders. ARJIS also serves as the region's information hub for officer notification, information sharing, and the exchange, validation, and real-time uploading of many types of public safety data.

Source: Automated Regional Criminal Justice Information System, "What Is ARJIS?" www.arjis.org/WhatisARJIS/tabid/54/Default.aspx (accessed August 7, 2010).

Another excellent example of mapping success is the New York Police Department's CompStat program, which provides up-to-the-minute statistics, maps, and patterns and establishes causal relationships among crime categories. CompStat also puts supervisors in constant communication with the department's administration, provides updates to headquarters every week, and makes supervisors responsible for responding to crime in their assigned areas.[54]

Locating Serial Offenders

Most offenders operate close to home and tend to operate in target-rich environments to "hunt" for their prey. **Geographic profiling**—a relatively new development in the field of environmental criminology—analyzes the geography of such locations and the sites of the victim encounter, the attack, the murder, and the body dump and maps the most probable location of the suspect's home.[55]

Geographic profiling is most effective when used in conjunction with linkage analysis. For example, the Washington State Attorney General's office uses a **homicide investigation and tracking system (HITS)** that includes crime-related databases and links to vice and gang files, sex offender registries, corrections and parole records, and department of motor vehicle databases. HITS can scan these databases simultaneously. When an agency in the state has a major crime in its jurisdiction, the case is loaded into a central system, which scans every database and linking file for connections by comparing eyewitness descriptions of a suspect and vehicle. It then builds a data set containing profiles of the offender, the victims, and the incidents. The data set then goes into a geographic information system (GIS), where the program selects and maps the names and addresses of those suspects whose method of operation fits the crimes being investigated.[56]

Gunshot Locator System

A primary difficulty for the police is determining the location of gunshots. Technology is now being tested that is similar to that used to determine the strength and epicenter of earthquakes. Known as a **gunshot locator system**, it uses microphone-like sensors placed on rooftops and telephone poles to record and transmit the sound of gunshots by radio waves or telephone lines. Software is then used to alert a dispatcher and to pinpoint the origin of gunshots via a flashing icon on a computerized map. Ideally, the system, which triangulates based on how long it takes the sound to reach the sensors, would greatly reduce police response time to crime scenes, meaning quicker aid for victims and a greater likelihood of arrests.[57]

In Chicago, technology is being tested that recognizes the sound of a gunshot within a two-block radius, pinpoints the location of the shot with a surveillance camera, focuses on the location, and places a 911 call in less than one second. A microphone surveillance system, located twenty feet above the ground, contains an acoustic sensor that recognizes a sound as a gunshot and sends range and bearing data to a camera, which starts out with a wide angle, tilts, and zooms in on the area; it then sends a 911 message to a call center.[58]

A related use of geographic technology—used extensively with military tanks and in the private sector (such as in taxicab firms, car rental franchises, and express delivery companies)—is the Global Positioning System, which plots locations of vehicles and even people with remarkable accuracy. The police, for example, have adapted GPS for the problem of knowing exactly where search-and-rescue dogs are and how effective they have been in their search efforts. A small specially designed backpack containing software is attached to the dog; after a search for lost persons, data from the backpack are downloaded to show where the dog has searched as well as areas that may need to be searched further.[59]

Electronics in Traffic Functions

Collision Investigations

A multicar traffic collision (also termed a traffic crash) can turn a street or highway into a parking lot for many hours, sometimes even days. The police must collect evidence relating to the collision, including measurements and sketches of the scene, vehicle and body positions, skid marks, street or highway elevations, intersections, and curves. These tasks typically involve a measuring wheel, steel tape, pad, and pencil. The cost of traffic delays—especially for commercial truck operators—is substantial.

Some police agencies have begun using GPS to determine such details as vehicle location and damage, elevation, grade, radii of curves, and critical speed. A transmitter takes a series of "shots" to find the exact locations and measurements of collision details like skid marks, area of impact, and debris. That information is then downloaded into the system, and the coordinates are plotted on an aerial shot of the intersection or roadway. Using computer technology, the details are then superimposed on the aerial shot, thus re-creating the collision scene to scale. Digital photos of the collision are incorporated into the final product, resulting in a highly accurate depiction of the collision. Furthermore, with a fatal collision or one with major injuries, what once required up to eighteen hours for several officers is reduced to mere minutes.[60]

Similarly, other agencies use a version of a surveyor's "total station," electronically measuring and recording distances, angles, and elevations as well as the names and features of objects. Data from the system can be downloaded into a computer

Some agencies use Global Positioning Systems to accurately draw traffic diagrams. Here, police and technical personnel employ the system at a fatal traffic collision location.
(Courtesy Sparks, Nevada, Police Department)

for display or printed out on a plotter. The system consists of four components: a base station, a data collector, a tripod, and a prism (which reflects an infrared laser beam back to the tripod-mounted base station). With this device, officers can get measurements in an hour or so at major traffic collision scenes, push a button, and have lines drawn for them to scale; this process enables officers to get 40 percent more measurements in about 40 percent less time, allowing the traffic flow to resume much more quickly. This system is also being used at major crime scenes, such as murders.[61]

Arrests of Impaired Drivers

During a vehicle stop for driving under the influence (DUI), officers might spend a long time questioning the driver and conducting a barrage of screening tests. Then, if an arrest is made, the officer necessarily devotes a lot of time transporting and processing the arrestee at the jail before beginning formal testing of urine or blood. This delay in formal testing can skew test results because the alcohol has had time to metabolize.

New instruments now help automate the DUI arrest process. One tool used routinely during a drunk-driving stop is a breath-screening device—a small portable machine that resembles a video game cartridge. The DUI suspect blows into the device, and the officer gets a reading of the amount of alcohol in the suspect's system. It is hoped that this device can be adapted in such a way that the test can be used in court. Fewer hours would then be spent transporting DUI suspects and testing them, only to find that they were below the legal limit and thus cannot be prosecuted for DUI.

The revamped instrument would be attached to a notebook or a laptop computer that officers would use to help speed them through the process; an officer would simply run a magnetic-strip driver's license through a reader on the computer to bring up all of the driver's information. The computer would prompt the officer to start the test and would supply a readout of the results on the screen. The officer would then transmit the test results over telecommunications lines to a central location for recording.[62]

Prevention of High-Speed Pursuits

There are controversies over the tremendous potential for injury, property damage, and liability that accompanies high-speed pursuits by police—this is such a concern that some agency policies completely prohibit such pursuits by officers. Such techniques as bumping, crowding, employing the three-cruiser rolling roadblock, and using tire spikes can all result in personal injuries and significant damage to vehicles.

Tire spikes can be deployed when a fleeing vehicle is approaching and then retracted so that other vehicles and police cars can pass safely. However, tire spikes often do not work effectively, or they result in the suspect losing control of the vehicle (although some spike devices are designed to prevent loss of control by breaking off in the tires and thus deflating them slowly).[63] Furthermore, use of the spikes is limited to times and places where other traffic can be diverted.

One device can stop a stolen vehicle with a short pulse of electric current that disrupts the vehicle's ignition system. When a subscriber reports his or her vehicle stolen to authorities and requests stolen vehicle assistance, the police then provide confirmation to the automotive company that the vehicle is in fact stolen; the company's employees then pinpoint the vehicle's exact GPS location and send a remote signal to prevent the stolen vehicle from starting the next time someone attempts to start it. This capability not only can help authorities recover stolen vehicles but also can prevent dangerous high-speed pursuits from starting.[64] Other similar devices are being refined, miniaturized, and demonstrated for federal, state, and local law enforcement agencies and transportation officials across the United States.

Databases for Fingerprints and Mug Shots

Though perhaps not as exotic as DNA identification, fingerprints are still a reliable means of positively identifying someone, and advances continue to be made in the field (see Exhibit 3). Throughout the country, filing cabinets are filled with ink-smeared cards that hold the keys to countless unsolved crimes if only the data could be located. An **automated fingerprint identification system (AFIS)** allows this legacy of data to be rapidly shared. One such system is the Western Identification Network (www.winid.org), established by nine states as a way to share their 17 million fingerprint records. These states were later joined by local agencies and the Federal Bureau of Investigation, the Internal Revenue Service, the Secret Service, and the Drug Enforcement Administration. The system can generally provide a match within a few hours and has helped solve more than five thousand crimes. A digital photo exchange facility known as WINPHO is now being added to supplement fingerprint data.[65]

The Boston Police Department, like most others in the United States, was devoting tremendous resources to identifying prisoners with mug shots and fingerprints. Then the department replaced all of its mug shots and inked fingerprints with a citywide integrated electronic imaging identification system—the first system of its kind in North America. The Boston Police Department is also the first city to receive the FBI's certification for electronic fingerprint submission.

Instead of transporting prisoners to a central booking facility in downtown Boston—a task that took forty thousand hours of officers' time per year—officers at the eleven district police stations can electronically scan a prisoner's fingerprints, take digital photographs, and then route the images to a central server for easy storage and access. This network gives investigators timely access to information and mug shot lineups and is saving the police department $1 million per year in labor and transportation costs while freeing officers from prisoner transportation duties.[66]

EXHIBIT 3

New Developments with Fingerprints

The following are two new developments reported in late 2009 with respect to fingerprinting:

- The Sarasota County, Florida, Sheriff's Office has deployed handheld devices that scan fingerprints to aid officers working in the field. The sheriff's office purchased fourteen of the handheld scanners that connect to federal, state, and local databases to identify individuals. The devices allow police officers to positively identify people in the field, instead of returning to the jail to process the information; they have also allowed officers to identify numerous individuals who gave false names and who entered the U.S. illegally.[1]
- Technology developed by Britain's University of Warwick can identify partial, distorted, scratched, smudged, or otherwise warped fingerprints in just a few seconds. Many other fingerprint techniques have tried to identify a few key features on a fingerprint and match them against a database of templates, but University of Warwick researchers consider the entire detailed pattern of each print and transform the topological pattern into a standard coordinate system, allowing them to "unwarp" any fingerprint that has been distorted by smudging, uneven pressure, or other distortion, that can then be mapped onto an "image space" of all other fingerprints in a database. This unwarping is so effective that it also, for the first time, allows comparison of the position of individual sweat pores on fingerprints.[2]

[1]Elaine Rundle, "Handheld Fingerprint Scanners Let Florida Police Identify Individuals in the Field," *Government Technology*, October 27, 2009, www.govtech.com/gt/articles/732179?elq=302656ff52-f541aea04863fb3cce6692 (accessed August 7, 2010).

[2]Peter Dunn, "New Technology Revolutionizes Fingerprint Identification," *Government Technology*, October 26, 2009, www.govtech.com/dc/articles/732107?elq=302656ff52f541aea04863fb3cce6692 (accessed August 7, 2010).

Technology involving mug shots and imaging systems can be useful in a variety of situations. For example, as a police officer responds to a domestic violence call, the CAD system searches the address and finds a restraining order against the ex-husband or boyfriend; moments later, a street map and digital mug shot of the suspect appear on the officer's laptop computer monitor. The officer is thus aided with an image of the suspect and his or her criminal history before arriving at the scene.[67]

New Technologies for Crime Scenes

Several technologies exist or are being developed that are relevant to crime-scene investigations. Three-dimensional CAD or "computer-aided design" software is now available and can be purchased for a few hundred dollars. Known as 3-D CAD, users create scenes that can be viewed from any angle, so nontechnical people can visualize very technical evidence. Juries can "view" crime scenes and see the location of evidence; they can view just what the witness says he or she saw. Police give the CAD system the exact dimensions and get a scaled drawing. A five-day, forty-hour course teaches 3-D CAD to police investigators, traffic collision reconstructionists, and evidence technicians.[68]

Often, crime-scene evidence is too sketchy to yield an obvious explanation of what happened. A new software program named Maya has been developed for the field of forensic animation; this software helps experts determine what probably occurred. Maya is so packed with scientific calculations that it can create a virtual house from old police photos and can replicate the effects of several types of forces, including gravity, indicating how a fall could or could not have produced massive injuries; how flames would spread in a house fire; or how smoke might have cut a pilot's visibility in a plane crash.[69]

The federal Department of Energy is testing a prototype laptop computer equipped with digital video and still cameras, laser range finders, and GPS. A detective using it can "beam" information from a crime scene back to a laboratory to get input from experts. Researchers are also working on a so-called lab-on-a-chip that would give police the ability to process more evidence—including DNA samples—at the crime scene, eliminating the risk of contamination en route to the lab.[70]

Developments with Firearms

Handguns are, and nearly always have been, the weapon of choice for violent criminals, especially murderers. Handguns are also used with greatest frequency—in about seven of every ten incidents—when police officers are murdered.[71] It is therefore important that everything that is technologically possible be done to train the police to use lethal force against citizens, to identify those who would use lethal force against others, and to keep out of harm's way.

Computer-Assisted Training

A device known as **FATS** (for firearms training system) is said to be "as close to real life as you can get."[72] Recruits and in-service officers alike use the system. They are given a high-tech lesson in firearms and can be shown a wide variety of computer-generated scenarios on a movie screen, with an instructor at a console controlling the scene. Using laser-firing replicas of their actual weapons, they learn not only sharpshooting but also judgment—when to shoot and when not to shoot. The system, consisting of a container about the size of a large baby buggy with a computer, a laser disc player, a projector, and a hit-detect camera, can be transported to sites throughout the state. Some sites combine FATS with a driving simulator and have recruits drive to the scene of a bank robbery and then bail out of their car into a FATS scenario.[73]

Recent developments have made firearms simulators even more realistic than the basic FATS system just described. One new version has a synchronized "shootback cannon." If an individual on a projection screen pulls a gun and fires toward the trainee, a cannon, which hangs above the screen, pelts the trainee with pain-inducing .68-caliber nylon balls. This newest generation of FATS—which are getting more realistic and better at breaking down how the trainee reacted under stress—now cost between $25,000 for a small system and $200,000 for a trailer that police departments can haul from station to station.[74]

Using Gun "Fingerprints" to Solve Cases

Every gun leaves a unique pattern of minute markings on ammunition. If gun makers test-fire their weapons before the guns leave their factories, the police can use spent ammunition recovered from crime scenes to trace a gun, even when the gun itself is not recovered. This technology could even be taken to the next level: creating an automated database of the fingerprints of new guns. A $45 million multiyear contract was recently awarded to a Montreal, Canada, firm by the U.S. Bureau of Alcohol, Tobacco, Firearms, and Explosives to help fund the development of such technology.[75]

Several problems need to be resolved, however: (1) Criminals can easily use a nail file to scratch a new gun's firing pin; (2) even if the system worked and turned up a serial number, the number could be used to trace the gun to its initial owner and not necessarily to the criminal; (3) the database would not include the estimated 200 million weapons already in circulation; and (4) gun lobbies would undoubtedly oppose the system as being "suspiciously like a national gun registry."[76]

Gang Intelligence Systems

Often a witness to gang violence has only a brief view of the incident—a glimpse of the offenders and their distinguishing characteristics and their vehicles and license plate numbers. Police are now armed with laptop computers and cellular phones to assist in solving gang-related crimes. Recently, for example, the California Department of Justice began installing CALGANG (known as GangNet outside California), an intranet software package linked to nine other sites throughout the state. It is essentially a clearinghouse for information about individual gang members, the places they frequent or live, and the cars they drive. Within a few minutes, a police officer in the field can link to CALGANG through a laptop and cellular phone, type in information, and wait for matches. Other officers can be moving to make the arrest even before the crime laboratory technicians have dusted the scene for fingerprints.[77]

Robotics

Recent advances in **robotics** ("bots" in tech-speak) have allowed policing (and soldiering) to become safer. Robots are now fitted with video capability, including night vision; a camera (also useful for photographing crime scenes); a TASER ECD; and even the ability to engage in two-way communications.[78] Robotics researchers at Carnegie-Mellon University recently developed a small remote-controlled prototype robot with a top speed of twenty miles per hour designed for surveillance in urban settings; it can see around corners and deliver information from locations where human access is dangerous.[79] Other new applications of robots for policing are discussed in Exhibit 4.

Although bomb-handling robots have been in use for several years, recently the military employed a robot that can sniff explosive devices. Such robots—with seven-foot arms (that scan the inside and undercarriage of vehicles for bombs), lights, video cameras (that zoom and swivel), obstacle-hurling flippers, and jointed arms (that have handlike grippers to disable or destroy bombs)—were sent to Iraq in early 2007 to give soldiers the ability to better detect and deal with roadside bombs.[80] The government will spend about $1.7 billion on ground-based military robots between fiscal 2006 and 2012.[81] Their use in policing cannot be far behind; for example, they would be very helpful if programmed to sniff for methamphetamine ingredients.

EXHIBIT 4

Using "Robotic Ferrets" to Ferret Out Crime and Contraband

The U.S. maritime system consists of more than three hundred sea and river ports, with more than 3,700 cargo and passenger terminals. Cargo containers—more than six million of them entering U.S. seaports annually, with each container ship having the capacity to carry in excess of three thousand containers—afford key targets for potential terrorists. In addition, drugs and even illegal immigrants are also smuggled in containers. However, a new type of robot may soon make it easier to detect drugs, weapons, explosives, and illegal immigrants concealed in cargo containers. Dubbed the "cargo-screening ferret," the device will be the world's first cargo-screening device able to pinpoint illicit substances and people inside standard steel freight containers. When placed inside a container, the ferret will attach itself magnetically to the top, then automatically move around and examine its contents, sending a steady stream of information back to its controller. Recent advances in both laser and fiber-optic technologies allow sensors carried on the small robot to detect the specific "fingerprint" of illegal substances at much lower concentrations than is now possible. The ferret could also replace current cargo-screening methods, such as the use of sniffer dogs and external scanners for detecting explosives and drugs, and offer major advantages in combating human trafficking: Sensors on board the ferret will be able to detect tiny traces of carbon dioxide that indicate the presence of humans concealed in the containers.

Source: Adapted from Blake Harris, "Robotic Ferret Will Detect Hidden Drugs, Weapons and Humans in Containers," *Government Technology* (June 12, 2009), www.govtech.com/dc/articles/695248?utm_source=newsletter&utm_medium=email&utm_campaign=Justice%20and%20Public%20Safety%20Authority_2009_6_22 (accessed August 7, 2010).

More Technologies for Tomorrow: Augmented Reality, UAVs, Nanotechnology

The following three technologies are still far removed from day-to-day use but promise to greatly alter police methods in the future.

Augmented Reality

One of the most powerful emerging technologies, **augmented reality (AR)**, uses wearable components to overlay virtual (computer-generated) information onto a real-world view in a way that improves and enhances the ability to accomplish a variety of missions and tasks. Still in the early stages of research and development, AR combines the real and the virtual, displaying information in real time.[82] AR is already here: If you watch televised sports, you may have noticed the yellow first-down lines superimposed on a football field or the driver and speed information tagged to race cars speeding around a track. At a more advanced level, today's military fighter pilots can observe critical information superimposed on the cockpit canopy.[83]

Fundamentally, an AR system consists of a wearable computer, a head-mounted display, and tracking and sensing devices along with advanced software and virtual three-dimensional (3-D) applications. It is a mobile technology designed to improve situational awareness and to speed human decision making. Among the many possible uses in the future of policing are the following (some of which have already been developed but need to be refined for street use and, oftentimes, made more affordable for purchase):[84]

- Real-time language translation, along with data on cultural customs and traditions
- Real-time intelligence about crimes and criminals in the patrol area
- Facial, voiceprint, and other biometric recognition data of known criminals

- Integration of chemical, biological, and explosives sensors that denote local contamination
- Accessibility of scalable 3-D maps (with building floor plans, utilities systems, and so forth)

Similarly, special weapons and tactics (SWAT) officers could be provided with advanced optics that provide zoom, thermal, and infrared imaging for locating fleeing criminals, as well as a friend-or-foe indicator that could reduce or eliminate friendly-fire casualties. Investigative personnel could use speaker-recognition technology for accurately matching voices against known criminals and for lip reading from a distance; thermal imaging might improve interrogations by indicating the truthfulness of suspects' statements. Supervisors could use video feed from their personnel on the street to determine what their officers are seeing in real time and to monitor their physical status during critical incidents.[85] Certainly a number of issues would accompany the planned adoption of AR. Acceptance by officers themselves may prove problematic, given the bulk and mobility issues associated with additional equipment, and the public (including the courts) may be uncomfortable with the constitutional issues and legal ramifications that AR abilities might raise.

Would AR bring us dangerously close to a real-life "Robo-Cop" scenario? The answer to that question is in the eye of the beholder. It cannot be questioned, however, that AR technology and the uses described above will soon be available and could provide the police with a new degree of efficiency and effectiveness never seen before. The question is whether or not the public—and the police—will be willing to accept this "virtual intrusion" in their daily lives.

In a similar vein, technology will also be available soon to allow realistic simulated humans to be used as a tool for training in decision making. Law enforcement personnel need experience making decisions in which other people—whether suspects, bystanders, or team members—are involved. A 3-D computer graphic would represent a variety of settings; the trainee would have the ability to move about, look around, and direct actions toward a variety of computer representations of human figures that move naturally, display appropriate gestures and expressions, and exhibit realistic patterns of speech. Such simulation technology, which should be available and affordable within the next five to ten years, will have a very positive impact on police training.[86]

Unmanned Aerial Vehicles

Another technology that warrants close attention is that of the **unmanned aerial vehicle (UAV).** UAVs are powered aerial vehicles that do not carry human operators and are designed to carry nonlethal payloads for missions such as reconnaissance, command and control, and deception. UAVs, which are directed by a ground or airborne controller, come in a variety of designs, from one that fits into a backpack to one with a longer wingspan than a Boeing 747. More than two dozen companies in the United States are currently involved in production of prototype UAV products.[87]

While UAV research and development are almost totally focused on military applications at present, the potential uses for law enforcement should not be ignored. For example, a low-flying UAV could patrol a given stretch of road, on vigil for speeders; images could be piped to a monitor in a patrol car along with rate of speed, direction of travel, and Global Positioning System (GPS) coordinates, which can be overlaid on a map for the officer on the ground.[88] UAVs could also provide real-time reconnaissance, surveillance, and target spotting in a variety of situations.[89]

Boyd and colleagues argue that, overall, government and law enforcement seem to lag behind the private sector in both the use of new technologies and the development of expertise in such applications.[90] A common theme among members of the Society of Police Futurists International is the fear that the law enforcement profession will never catch up with the necessary computer-based investigative skills to keep pace with criminals who use computer technology. But technology involves much more than using computers to hack into systems or to commit identity theft. Whether through nanotechnology, AR, or biometrics, criminals will always attempt to steal, misuse, or exploit others. If law enforcement does not anticipate such illicit uses, the victims of these crimes will eventually rely on private sources for relief.

Nanotechnology

The term **nanotechnology** is based on the root *nanos*, meaning "one billionth." It is the engineering of components that have at least one physical dimension the size of one hundred nanometers or less. (For perspective, a human hair is gigantic in the realm of nanotechnology.) This technology allows for "getting small," which means making objects smarter, more powerful, and more economical (e.g., the computers of the 1940s were the size of a room, compared to those of today). Nanotechnology allows for revolutionary new products using new materials and substances that are not accessible with other technologies. Such products, ranging from knives that never need sharpening to better spaceships and computers, will be stronger, lighter, and even interactive—and may possibly mean the end of disease as we know it.[91]

With regard to policing, a Dutch company has already developed a handheld device that uses nanotechnology to detect marijuana, cocaine, and other drugs in saliva within two minutes.[92] Surely many more nanotechnology applications for the police cannot be too far off—in fact, it is already being tested for the next generation of body armor.[93]

SUMMARY

mycrimekit

Investigate: *Crime Mapping and Crime Analysis.*

This chapter examined the exciting high-technology developments in policing (and some with applications in corrections as well), including those in the areas of less-lethal weapons, wireless technology, electronics, imaging systems, firearms, and communications. This is an exciting time for the police—more new technologies than ever are being made available to aid them in their efforts to analyze and address crimes. This chapter has shown the breadth of research and development that is underway.

The rapid expansion in computer technology, while certainly a strong advantage for society overall, bodes ill as well. The first problem lies in adapting the computer technologies to the needs of policing. While the U.S. Air Force can drop a smart bomb down a smokestack and the U.S. Army is rapidly moving toward the electronic battlefield, modern-day crooks and hackers engage in a variety of cybercrimes and (even though the technology exists) the police are still unable to halt all high-speed chases that threaten the lives of officers and citizens.[94]

Obviously, many challenges remain. For example, we must continue to seek a weapon with less-lethal stopping power that can effectively and safely be employed. We must also strive to enhance police effectiveness and efficiency through electronic means. As has been noted, "It is not enough to shovel faster. Criminal justice must enter the Information Age by incorporating technology as a tool to make the system run efficiently and effectively."[95]

KEY TERMS

ARJIS
augmented reality (AR)
automated fingerprint identification system (AFIS)
biometrics
chemical weapons
computer-aided dispatching (CAD)
computerized crime mapping
FATS
geographic profiling
gunshot locator system
homicide investigation and tracking system (HITS)
less-lethal weapons
mobile data systems
nanotechnology
robotics
TASER ECD
unmanned aerial vehicle (UAV)
voice-stress analysis

REVIEW QUESTIONS

1. What are some of the major discoveries in less-lethal weapons for use by the police?
2. What are four new uses of software that are being applied to old problems of crime and national security?
3. How has the development of wireless technology benefited the police?
4. How can mapping and profiling systems aid the police, and what do these systems specifically provide?
5. How does technology assist the police traffic function? How has it affected gang intelligence?
6. What are some recent developments in the area of firearms training and investigation?
7. How are the police training and communications functions enhanced by technology?
8. What new developments have recently occurred in the use of robots by the police?
9. What are augmented reality, unmanned aerial vehicles, and nanotechnology, and how might these technologies benefit law enforcement?

LEARN BY DOING

1. Assume you are in the research, planning, and development unit of your police organization. Your chief executive officer has tasked you to "bring the agency into the new decade" by making recommendations concerning technologies that the department should acquire. Using information and descriptions of the technologies presented in this chapter, select and prioritize ten new technologies (either extant or in development) that you believe your agency should obtain, and write a justification for each in terms of its crime-fighting capabilities.
2. You are preparing a guest lecture at the regional police academy on the subject of less-lethal weapons. One of the academy instructors calls you and says the class seems to be very interested in the potential applications in policing for both unmanned aerial vehicles and robots. Prepare a response.
3. You are a federal law enforcement agent guest lecturing in an area criminal justice class. Eventually the topic of discussion concerns terrorism, and a student poses the following question: "If funding—and peoples' imaginations—were not a limitation, which technologies do you believe should be developed and put into use to thwart any and all terrorist attacks, including those that are chemical or biological in nature?" What is your response?

mycrimekit

Go to MyCrimeKit.com and discover additional study tools and resources related to this chapter.

- Key Terms
- Review Questions
  - Multiple Choice Questions
  - True/False
  - Fill in the Blank
  - Essay
- MEDIA REVIEW: where you can review the topics of *crime mapping, crime analysis,* and *wireless technology and policing.*
- FLASHCARDS: to test your knowledge of this chapter.
- *NEW YORK TIMES:* where you can read the latest articles related to criminology and criminal law.
- THE CAREER CENTER: where you can explore career opportunities in criminal justice and criminology.
- THE ONLINE RESEARCH LIBRARY: where you can explore the Cybrary and Research Navigator.

NOTES

1. See Regional Computer Forensics Laboratory, National Program Office, "About RCFLs," www.rcfl.gov/index.cfm?fuseAction=Public.P_about, and "RCFL Locations," www.rcfl.gov/index.cfm?fuseAction=Public.P_locations (accessed August 6, 2010).
2. Hilton Collins, "Smartphones Boost Government Efficiency, Bring Security Risks," *Government Technology*, March 3, 2009, www.govtech.com/gt/624307 (accessed August 7, 2010).
3. Elaine Rundle, "New Tools for Fighting Crime: Police Encourage Citizens to Text Their Crime Tips," *Government Technology*, November 10, 2008, www.govtech.com/gt/424044 (accessed August 7, 2010); also see Mitch Stacy, "Police wnt u to fight crime w/text msgs," Associated Press (July 3, 2008), www.msnbc.msn.com/id/25498622 (accessed August 6, 2010).
4. Jim McKay, "Cops on the Tweet to Solve Crimes and Educate the Public," *Government Technology* (August 31, 2009), www.govtech.com/gt/717300 (accessed August 6, 2010).
5. Christopher Lehne, "Army Testing XM-25 'Smart' High-Explosive Weapon for Soldiers," Militaryspot.com, www.militaryspot.com/news/item/army_testing_xm-25_smart_high-explosive_weapon_for_soldiers (accessed August 6, 2010).
6. Jim McKay, "Lost in Translation," *Government Technology* (July 2005): 56.
7. Jim McKay, "Getting the Picture," *Government Technology* (January 2009), pp. 22–24.
8. Jim McKay, "Keeping Tabs," *Government Technology* (August 2005): 58.
9. Merrill Douglas, "Putting Violence on the Map," *Government Technology* (June 2006): 50.
10. Jim McKay, "Good Science or Just Bunk," *Government Technology* (June 2006): 46–48.
11. Leslie Friesen "On the Wire," *Government Technology* (September 2005): 62.
12. "DHS Completes Foundation of Biometric Entry System," *Government Technology* (January 2, 2006), www.govtech.net/magazine/channel_story.php/97728 (accessed August 6, 2010); also see SearchSecurity.com Definitions, "Biometrics," searchsecurity.techtarget.com/sDefinition/0,,sid14_gci211666,00.html (accessed August 7, 2010).
13. See, generally, Jennifer Gavigan, "The State-of-the-Art Police Agency: Software," *Law and Order*, November 2008, www.hendonpub.com/resources/articlearchive/details.aspx?ID=207106 (accessed August 7, 2010).
14. Jennifer Nislow, "Big Benefits, Huge Headaches," *Law Enforcement News*, May 15/31, 2000, p. 1.
15. "Cybergame for the Millennium: Cops 'n' Robbers Playin' Hide 'n' Seek on the Net," *Police Futurist* 8(1) (Spring 2000): 4.
16. "Polls: Trade Some Freedom for Security," *Law Enforcement News*, September 15, 2001, p. 1.
17. "Surveillance Cameras Stir Up Static," *Law Enforcement News*, July–August 2001, p. 13.
18. Dana Hawkins and David LaGesse, "Tech Versus Terrorists," *U.S. News and World Report*, October 8, 2001, pp. 16–17.
19. Kenneth J. Peak, "The Quest for Alternatives to Lethal Force: A Heuristic View," *Journal of Contemporary Criminal Justice* 6(1) (1990): 8–22.
20. S. Sweetman, *Report on the Attorney General's Conference on Less Than Lethal Weapons* (Washington, DC: U.S. Department of Justice, National Institute of Justice, 1987).

21. Peak, "The Quest for Alternatives to Lethal Force," p. 10.
22. Ibid.
23. Ibid.
24. T. S. Crockett, "Riot Control Agents," *Police Chief* (November 1968): 8–18.
25. M. H. Haller, "Historical Roots of Police Behavior: Chicago, 1890–1925," *Law and Society Review* 13(2) (1976): 303–323.
26. T. F. Coon, "A Maze of Confusion over Amazing Mace," *Police* (November–December 1968): 46.
27. Sarah Manwaring-White, *The Policing Revolution: Police Technology, Democracy, and Liberty in Britain* (Brighton, Sussex: Harvester Press, 1983).
28. Neil deMause, "Pepper Spray Gets in Their Eyes: Media Missed Militarization of Police Work in Seattle," *FAIR*, March/April 2000, www.fair.org/index.php?page=1029 (accessed August 7, 2010).
29. Manwaring-White, *The Policing Revolution*, pp. 141–142.
30. Peak, "The Quest for Alternatives to Lethal Force," pp. 15–16.
31. Ibid., p. 16.
32. Manwaring-White, *The Policing Revolution*, pp. 145–146.
33. Ibid., pp. 142–143.
34. Sweetman, *Report on the Attorney General's Conference on Less Than Lethal Weapons*, pp. 4–5.
35. M. S. Serrill, "ZAP! Stun Guns: Hot But Getting Heat," *Time*, May 1985, p. 59.
36. U.S. Department of Justice, Bureau of Justice Statistics, *Local Police Departments, 2003* (Washington, DC: Author, 2006), p. iii; U.S. Department of Justice, Bureau of Justice Statistics, *Sheriff's Offices, 2003* (Washington, DC: Author, 2006), p. iii.
37. Personal communication, Hilary Gibeaut, TASER International, Inc., September 14, 2009.
38. Ibid.
39. Medical News Today, "Study Suggests TASER Use by U.S. Police Is Safe," October 9, 2007, www.medicalnewstoday.com/articles/84955.php (accessed August 7, 2010).
40. TASER Protect Life, "TASER Training Bulletin 15.0 Regarding Medical Research Update and Revised Warnings," bloximages.chicago2.vip.townnews.com/nctimes.com/content/tncms/assets/editorial/4/f9/358/4f935852-be9c-11de-835f-001cc4c002e0.pdf.pdf?_dc=1256168943 (accessed August 7, 2010).
41. U.S. Department of Justice, Bureau of Justice Statistics, *Local Police Departments, 2003*, p. iii; U.S. Department of Justice, Bureau of Justice Statistics, *Sheriff's Offices, 2003*, p. iii.
42. "Effectiveness Times Three," *Law Enforcement News*, May 15, 1993, p. 1.
43. Ibid., p. 6.
44. Blake Harris, "Goin' Mobile," *Government Technology* 10 (August 1997): 1.
45. Kaveh Ghaemian, "Small-Town Cops Wield Big-City Data," *Government Technology* 9 (September 1996): 38.
46. *San Diego Union-Tribune*, "San Diego Police Get New Technology" (November 14, 2008), www.policegrantshelp.com/news/1756993-San-Diego-police-get-new-technology (accessed August 7, 2010).
47. CNN.com, "'Railway Killer' suspect surrenders in Texas," July 13, 1999, www.cnn.com/US/9907/13/railway.killings.03 (accessed August 7, 2010).

48. Tod Newcombe, "Combined Forces," *Government Technology* (April 2001): 15.
49. U.S. Department of Justice, National Institute of Justice, *Crime Mapping and Analysis by Community Organizations in Hartford, Connecticut* (Washington, DC: Author, March 2001), p. 1.
50. Donna Rogers, "Getting Crime Analysis on the Map," *Law Enforcement Technology* (November 1999): 76–79.
51. U.S. Department of Justice, National Institute of Justice, *Crime Mapping Research Center* (Washington, DC: Author, 2000), pp. 1–3.
52. Lois Pilant, "Computerized Crime Mapping," *Police Chief* (December 1997): 58.
53. U.S. Department of Justice, *Crime Mapping Research Center*, pp. 1–3; the CMRC Web site address is www.ojp.usdoj.gov/nij/maps/welcome.htm.
54. Pilant, "Computerized Crime Mapping," pp. 64–65.
55. Bill McGarigle, "Crime Profilers Gain New Weapons," *Government Technology* (December 1997): 28–29.
56. Ibid.
57. Justine Kavanaugh, "Locator System Targets Shooters," *Government Technology* (June 1996): 14–15.
58. Jim McKay, "Triggered Response," *Government Technology* (December 2005): 62.
59. "GPS-Loaded Dogs to the Rescue," *Government Technology* (April 1997): 24.
60. Alison Bath, "Accident Scene Investigation Is High Tech," *Reno Gazette-Journal* (Sparks Today section), November 18, 2003, p. 4.
61. Bill McGarigle, "Electronic Mapping Speeds Crime and Traffic Investigations," *Government Technology* (February 1996): 20–21.
62. Justine Kavanaugh, "Drunk Drivers Get a Shot of Technology," *Government Technology* (March 1996): 26.
63. Ibid.
64. Christen da Costa, "GM Adds Remote Kill Switch to OnStar Vehicles," *Gadget Review*, July 22, 2009, www.gadgetreview.com/2009/07/gm-adds-remote-kill-switch-to-onstar-vehicles.html#ixzz0vyaGMzgy (accessed August 7, 2010).
65. Ibid., p. 46.
66. Tod Newcombe, "Imaged Prints Go Online, Cops Return to Streets," *Government Technology* (April 1996): 1, 31.
67. Corey Grice, "Technologies, Agencies Converge," *Government Technology* (April 1998): 24, 61.
68. Tod Newcombe, "Adding a New Dimension to Crime Reconstruction," *Government Technology* (August 1996): 32.
69. John McCormick, "Scene of the Crime," *Newsweek*, February 28, 2000, p. 60.
70. Joan Raymond, "Forget the Pipe, Sherlock: Gear for Tomorrow's Detectives," *Newsweek*, June 22, 1998, p. 12.
71. Samuel G. Chapman, *Murdered on Duty: The Killing of Police Officers in America*, 2nd ed. (Springfield, IL: Charles C Thomas, 1998), p. 33.
72. Patrick Joyce, "Firearms Training: As Close to Real as It Gets," *Government Technology* (July 1995): 14–15.

73. Ibid.
74. John McCormick, "On a High-Tech Firing Line," *Newsweek*, December 6, 1999, p. 64.
75. Vanessa O'Connell, "The Next Big Idea: Using 'Fingerprints' of Guns to Solve Cases," *Wall Street Journal*, February 10, 2000, p. A1.
76. Ibid.
77. Ray Dussault, "GangNet: A New Tool in the War on Gangs," *Government Technology* (January 1998): 34–35.
78. Brian Huber, "Wis. Police Get Robo-Cop's Help," PoliceOne.com, November 14, 2006, www.policeone.com/police-technology/robots/articles/1190983 (accessed August 7, 2010).
79. "Remote-Controlled, Throwable Robots Developed at Carnegie Mellon in Conjunction with U.S. Marine Corps Are Being Sent to Iraq for Testing," *ScienceDaily*, July 29, 2004, www.sciencedaily.com/releases/2004/06/040629013646.htm (accessed August 7, 2010).
80. James Hannah, "Bomb-Sniffing Robots Put to Test in Iraq," MSN.com, March 30, 2007, www.msnbc.msn.com/id/17874529 (accessed August 7, 2010).
81. Ibid.
82. Thomas Cowper, "Improving the View of the World: Law Enforcement and Augmented Reality Technology," *FBI Law Enforcement Bulletin* (January 2004): 13.
83. Ibid.
84. Ibid., p. 15.
85. Ibid., p. 16.
86. Chris Forsythe, "The Future of Simulation Technology for Law Enforcement: Diverse Experience with Realistic Simulated Humans," *FBI Law Enforcement Bulletin* (January 2004): 19–21.
87. Brian P. Tice, "Unmanned Aerial Vehicles: The Force Multiplier of the 1990s," www.airpower.maxwell.af.mil/airchronicles/apj/apj91/spr91/4spr91.htm (accessed August 7, 2010).
88. Anna Broache, "Police Agencies Push for Drone Sky Patrols," August 9, 2007, CNET News, news.cnet.com/Police-agencies-push-for-drone-sky-patrols/2100-11397_3-6201789.html (accessed August 7, 2010).
89. Tice, "Unmanned Aerial Vehicles."
90. Sandy Boyd, Alberto Melis, and Richard Myers, "Preparing for the Challenges Ahead: Practical Applications of Futures Research," *FBI Law Enforcement Bulletin*, January 2004, p. 5.
91. National Nanotechnology Initiative, "FAQs: Nanotechnology," www.nano.gov/html/facts/faqs.html (accessed August 7, 2010).
92. Nanowerk, "Handheld Nanotechnology Device Detects Cocaine, Marijuana in saliva," www.nanowerk.com/news/newsid=8328.php (accessed August 7, 2010).
93. Doug Wyllies, "Nanotechnology Being Tested for Next-Gen Body Armor," Policeone.com, www.policeone.com/police-products/body-armor/articles/1888039-Nanotechnology-being-tested-for-next-gen-body-armor (accessed August 7, 2010).
94. George Nicholson and Jeffrey Hogge, "Retooling Criminal Justice: Interbranch Cooperation Needed," *Government Technology* 9 (February 1996): 32.
95. James Q. Wilson, "Six Things Police Leaders Can Do About Juvenile Crime," *Subject to Debate* (Newsletter of the Police Executive Research Forum), September/October 1997, p. 1.

Index

Page references followed by "f" indicate illustrated figures or photographs; followed by "t" indicates a table.

Q

R